Pass the 7

A Training Guide for the NASD Series 7 Exam

by

Robert Walker

For help, please email series7questions@firstbooks.com

FIRST BOOKS ®

PORTLAND • OREGON
FIRSTBOOKS.COM

From the Author

Most people are interested in test-taking tips for passing the Series 7. Our advice is to answer at least 70% of the questions right, although many customers prefer to answer no more than 30% of the questions wrong. Either way, they give you the license, and—remember—you do not have to show your work for the Series 7. If you manage to choose the right answer, you get it right, even when you have no clue what you're doing. Remember that you have a 25% chance of getting each question right with your eyes closed, which is partly why we recommend keeping them open. In other words, my cat could get a 25% on the Series 7, maybe a 29% if he didn't sleep so darned much. It's a multiple choice test, and good test takers know that you're not looking for the right answer to the question; you're trying to determine the three wrong answers. So, make sure you read the lesson on test taking strategy, since good test taking is probably the single most important determinant to success on these NASD exams.

That, and getting at least 70% of the questions right.

We're not sure why no one ever saw the humor involved with this material and this process, but we think the Series 7 is pretty darned funny most of the time. What, you didn't think convertible debentures or debit put spreads could be amusing?

Hmm. Maybe it's just us.

In any case, while this book attempts to cover the important concepts for the Series 7, we do not pretend that we have listed every word and every phrase you will encounter on your exam. If we tried to do that, the book would come in a 15-volume set, each one about 1,000 pages long. And, even that wouldn't completely cover it. See, there is really no end to the scope of the Series 7. To see what we mean, visit www.nasd.com or www.nyse.com and check out the reading list they give for the Series 7 in the exam outline. One of those books is the classic *Security Analysis* by Benjamin Graham, Warren Buffett's former professor. Great book, but it also happens to be 725 pages long, and if you read it cover to cover you'd maybe end up getting one more question right on the exam. In fact, even if you read every word of every book on that list, you still wouldn't have covered every factoid that might be thrown at you on your exam. So, what are you supposed to do?

Our approach is to cover all the fundamental concepts likely to be tested on your Series 7 exam, cover them thoroughly, and cover them in a way you'll both understand and remember. The concepts that need explanation are explained in a highly detailed, engaging fashion. The concepts that can be covered with bullet points are covered with bullet points. And the concepts that have only a remote chance of showing up at the testing center are usually just introduced into a practice question and explained quickly.

So, we're not going to pretend you won't see a *few* questions on your Series 7 that are unfamiliar. That's the nature of the beast. What we try to do is make sure you are familiar with *most* of the questions that are all but guaranteed to pop up. For example, we aren't going to sweat the variable rate demand note too much, but we also aren't going to rest until you've had a chance to understand bond yields or why an option is "in-the-money."

Ever noticed how the large vendors call their materials "license exam manuals"? That's possibly because they're not intended to be read but only referenced occasionally and attacked with a yellow highlighter in a vain attempt to make *sense* of the material. We call "Pass the 7" what it is—a book. There are stories here that help connect the dots. There is a flow of ideas that allows you to read 100 pages in an afternoon and actually understand what you're reading. If Warren Buffett, one of the most sophisticated minds in the investing world, can write clear, concise, humorous shareholder letters explaining how billions of dollars have been invested, why can't somebody explain the Series 7 material in a clear, concise, humorous book?

Turns out, somebody can—we decided we should do the hard work for you and lay it all out in Plain English, using stories and examples that you'll remember and understand. We aren't trying to impress you with our vast and rather trivial knowledge of the securities industry—we're only trying to help you pass the test.

We're not a bunch of bitter, burned-out brokers who couldn't cut it in the sales profession. We don't talk to you as if you should already know what bid-asked means, the difference between NYSE and NASDAQ, and countless other important details. We assume it's all new to you and that it all requires some very clear, concise explanations.

For more information on the test itself, visit www.nasd.com, click on the "brokers" link, then "exam requirements and study guides." You can get the exam outline, find out the cost to register, etc. But we'll let the regulators tell you why you have to take the exam and what you can do with the license. Our job is simply to help you pass the test.

Ready?

Let's get started anyway.

Table of Contents

The following section headings indicate how our chapters relate to the "7 Critical Functions Performed by a Registered Representative" structure of the NYSE exam outline.

Section 3 – Provides customers and prospective customers with information on investments and makes suitable recommendations.

Section 5 – Explains the organization, participants, and functions of various securities markets and the principal factors that affect them.

Section 2 – Evaluates customers in terms of available investment capital, current holdings, and financial needs, and helps them identify their investment objectives.

Section 7 – Monitors the customer's portfolio and makes recommendations consistent with changes in economic and financial conditions as well as the customer's needs and objectives.

Section 4 – Opens, transfers, and closes customer accounts and maintains appropriate account records.

Section 6 – Obtains and verifies the customer's purchase and sale instructions, enters orders, and follows up on completion of transactions.

Section 1 – Seeks business for the broker-dealer through customers and potential customers.

The Big Picture

Just down the street a company has been making and selling fruit pies for over 50 years. Frank & Emma's Fruit Pies the company is called. It's been a good business, but now that Frank & Emma have passed on, their three children have decided that the market for their fruit pies is much bigger than either Frank or Emma ever imagined. After talking to several advisers, Jeremy, Jason, and Jennifer decide it's time to raise some serious cash and invest it back into the business.

The local banks, however, aren't interested in lending the company the $100 million it needs to build a new factory, hire 100 more employees and set up distribution centers throughout the Midwest. Luckily, there are investors who might be willing to provide the capital in exchange for owning a little slice of Frank & Emma's Fruit Pies. Actually, the investors will provide the company with m-o-n-e-y, but we prefer to use words like "capital" because it makes us sound much smarter than we really are. Basically, if a company wants your money for one year or less, we go ahead and call that the "money market." But if a company wants your money for more than a year—usually *much* more—then maybe you get a little nervous so we dignify the whole thing by calling it the "capital market." In the "capital market" investors provide capital (m-o-n-e-y) to corporations in exchange for ownership positions, called "equity securities." Just as homeowners have equity/ownership in their homes, stockholders have equity/ownership in the corporations whose stock they hold.

Frank & Emma's Fruit Pies would use the stockholders' money to make the business a whole lot sweeter. The money (capital) that investors provide to Frank & Emma's Fruit Pies would allow the business to pay for equipment, wages, computers, and all the basic ingredients businesses need in order to grow from small companies to bigger, sweeter corporations. What do the shareholders get in return?

Basically, slices of the big earnings pie. If the company has earnings (profits), the shareholders are entitled to their share of the pie. An ever-growing earnings or "profit pie" means that the shares get bigger and taste better all the time. Eventually, not only will the shares get bigger and sweeter, but Frank & Emma's might start cutting checks to the shareholders every quarter and calling them "dividends," which are perhaps the most fun checks they'll ever cash.

Or not. Maybe the business won't spend the money wisely and will end up running the whole thing into the ground. See, there's always a risk when you buy a company's equity securities. But, if things work out the way we think, your slice of the pie could end up feeding you and your grandchildren's grandchildren, the way Microsoft, IBM, and Coca-Cola (to name just a few companies) have enriched their early investors beyond their wildest dreams.

So Jeremy, Jason, and Jennifer decide to offer 30% of the company for sale to public investors. They don't plan to do the offering themselves, though. The process of issuing stock to public investors is very complex, with little room for error. So, they hire a firm called an underwriting or investment-banking firm. Like a bank, the firm could raise money for Frank & Emma's Fruit Pies, but this wasn't a loan. The underwriting firm would promise to buy all the stock the company was issuing and immediately re-sell it to investors, keeping a piece of the proceeds for their efforts. It was a firm commitment of capital on the part of the underwriters, but if everything went according to plan, they would walk away with a nice profit, and Frank & Emma's Fruit Pies would have the $100 million it needed to expand the business. Since the brothers and sister owned the majority of the company, their own wealth would most likely grow, too, right along with the company's increased profits. And if everything went as planned, the investors who bought the slices of the big pie would also see their equity/ownership stakes in the company grow, too.

The underwriters registered the stock with the Securities and Exchange Commission, which under the Securities Act of 1933 requires companies issuing securities to provide disclosure to investors in the form of a prospectus. The registration statement with the SEC and the prospectus delivered to investors must reveal not just the promises of success but all the chances for failure, as well. Only if an investor has been provided with essential or "material" facts can he/she make an informed decision about buying or not buying a particular security.

So the company and the underwriters performed due diligence in providing information on the company's story to investors: its history, plans for the future, purpose for raising the money, as well as information on the management and board of directors. Also, a section on the risks involved in buying stock in this particular company was prepared and placed toward the front of the document. Some of the risks included were:

- The fluctuating price of oil can unpredictably raise delivery costs and compromise profit margins
- Unionized laborers can unpredictably raise labor costs and force slowdowns in production and delivery
- Product liability risks, should contaminated ingredients ever make their way

into the production line, would have a material negative effect on the price of the stock

It took a long time to get the SEC to finally give the green light, but, eventually, the underwriters were permitted to sell the shares to pension funds, mutual funds, and individual investors, who all liked Frank & Emma's Fruit Pies' chances for future success, weighed carefully against their possibility for failure.

The underwriting was over in a few days, and after keeping the "spread" or profit margin from the proceeds, the underwriters gave the company $100 million, which was quickly invested in new equipment, employee salaries, computer systems, and an aggressive TV and radio marketing campaign. Frank & Emma's Fruit Pies was looking a whole lot sweeter with the fresh infusion of capital.

Now that it is a public company, Frank & Emma's has to file quarterly and annual reports with the SEC, which is actually kind of a pain in the neck. So, they hired an in-house attorney and accountant primarily to work on the 10-Q (quarterly) and 10-K (annual) reports. In the reports, the company discloses financial information to investors, as required by the Securities Exchange Act of 1934. This Act, sometimes called the "People Act," requires issuers of securities to file reports so public investors have enough information to decide whether to invest or stay invested in the company.

Public investors apparently like what they read in the reports because the shares keep trading among investors at higher and higher prices. Sold at a public offering price of $10, the stock is now trading over NASDAQ as high as $25. NASDAQ, the main stocks traded "over the counter," and the NYSE are part of the secondary market. When the stock was first issued, it was issued in the primary market, where the issuer received the proceeds. When those shares trade back and forth among investors, we call that process the secondary market, where the issuer does not get the proceeds. Underwriters work in the primary market. Broker-dealers work in the secondary market, facilitating trades between investors and making commissions or markups for their services. Some broker-dealers maintain an inventory of over-the-counter stock, acting as market makers. A market maker allows investors to sell their securities when the time comes to sell and, hopefully, receive a decent price from an interested buyer. The market maker buys stock from one party at the lower "bid" price and sells the stock to another at the higher "ask" price. Maybe the bid for 10,000 shares of Frank & Emma's common stock is $25.00 and the ask is $25.25. If the market maker can buy 10,000 shares at the bid and immediately re-sell them at the ask, they will keep the 25-cent "spread" per share, which is a quick $2,500 profit. What if they buy the 10,000 shares and then no buyers show up to take them off their hands?

That's the risk they take by making a market in the stock. Market makers act as principals, which means they have money at risk. When a firm sells a customer a stock from its inventory, it is said to be acting as a "dealer" or "principal." When it simply arranges the trade for a customer, it is said to be acting as a "broker." That's why the firm is called a "broker-dealer," since it can act either as a broker, earning a commission, or as a dealer, earning a profit or markup on a particular trade. They can't do both on the same trade; they either act as a broker or a dealer on any particular trade.

And, they also get involved in the primary market taking companies public. When they do that, they call themselves underwriters/investment bankers. When they help investors unload and purchase securities in the secondary market, they call themselves broker-dealers.

You will be working for one of these broker-dealer firms, helping investors choose investments in stocks, bonds, options, mutual funds, and other products. Some investors will need the income provided by bonds. Others will need the growth offered by stocks. Still others will choose to risk their money on options. So, when a new customer decides to establish an investment account with you, you will fill out a customer account form that provides basic information on the customer's financial situation and investment goals. The younger the investor, the more likely you will recommend stocks, such as the stock in Frank & Emma's Fruit Pies. Or, maybe some day Frank & Emma will decide to offer bonds to investors, whereby the company simply borrows money from the public investors and pays a rate of interest on the loan/bonds until the loan is paid off in full. Instead of offering equity, then, the company would be offering debt securities. And that would make the bondholders creditors, who have to be paid on time. If not, the company goes into bankruptcy, and all the pie makers and other equipment could be sold at auction, the proceeds returned to the bondholders.

But bankruptcy seems like a remote possibility since Frank & Emma's is now a better-established company, with manufacturing facilities in Chicago, Cleveland, Milwaukee, and Indianapolis. Their fleet of delivery vans now stocks the shelves of regional grocers like Jewel and Dominick's, as well as serving up pies to school, hospital, and large corporate cafeterias. Their cash flow is strong, their sales are growing 20% a year, but the company could still benefit from a fresh infusion of capital.

Rather than cut the big earnings pie into more slices by selling equity/stock, Jeremy and his siblings have decided to heed the advice of their investment bankers by offering bonds to investors. Not just any bonds, though. Convertible bonds. When the underwriters offer the bonds to investors, they will point out the slightly lower rate of return paid by the convertibles. Bonds offered by corporations with the same A+ rating by Standard & Poor's would pay approximately 6% interest, while Frank & Emma's convertible debentures will offer only 5.15%. However, investors holding out for the higher 6% will get exactly that—six percent—and nothing more. What happens if the stocks of those companies go up? Nothing. The bondholders keep making their same old 6%. However, in exchange for taking a lower coupon/interest rate, the owners of Frank & Emma's convertible debentures can use their par value of $1,000 to buy Frank & Emma's common stock at a set price of $50 per share. In other words, they can convert the bonds into 20 shares of stock, whenever they feel like it ($1,000 / $50 = 20 shares).

What if the stock is really worth $65 at the time?

Excellent. Then they could buy 20 shares worth $65 each, making their convertible bond worth at least $1,300. Which doesn't happen for other bonds unless interest rates drop sharply, and that would make the Frank & Emma bonds more valuable, too.

So, this way the investors are creditors of the corporation who have to be paid 5.15% interest every year. But, unlike creditors who hold non-convertible bonds, Frank & Emma's bondholders will enjoy a big price increase if the common stock goes up. If the bonds are convertible into common at $50 a share, each bond will "buy" 20 shares of stock, regardless of its price. So, the bonds should trade for whatever 20 shares of stock trade for. If the stock goes to $60, 20 shares would be worth $1,200. That would be the bond's "parity" price, where the number of shares the bondholder could buy is worth exactly what the bond is trading for. If the share price goes to $70, the parity price of the bonds would be $1,400, since 20 shares would now be worth $1,400.

And so on.

So, the underwriters sell $50 million worth of the bonds, Frank & Emma's employs the new capital to grow the business, and the big equity pie is not cut into more slices.

Yet.

If the convertible bondholders decide to convert, the same earnings pie will be cut into more (thinner) slices, which is called "dilution of equity." And that nasty side effect is why the current shareholders got to vote on this issuance before it happened. But, a majority did agree to approve it, and many of the existing investors snatched up some of the convertibles to boot. Why not? They already believe in the stock of the company—why not receive a 5.15% interest payment on a piece of paper worth whatever 20 shares of common stock are worth? If the stock stays flat, they collect $51.50 every year. And if the stock goes up, they collect $51.50 every year...as the market price of the bond skyrockets.

Such a deal!

While the market price for FREM common stock and FREM convertible bonds is important to Jeremy, Jason, and Jennifer, the three have more important day-to-day concerns. So, let's let Frank & Emma's run their business a while, while we talk about serving your own customers, the investors kind enough to supply growing companies like FREM with capital.

Tomorrow morning you get a phone call from a Ms. Michelle Montoya. Michelle has been referred to you through a friend, who spoke highly of your recommendations and attention to detail. First thing you do is pull out a new account form for Ms. Montoya, filling it in with her contact information, employment situation, financial information, and investment goals. Once this is completed, you will sign it and get the signature of your supervisor. Michelle does not have to sign the new account form—she'll sign other documents—but this is just a profile you can use to make recommendations.

If Michelle is showing a high net worth and high tax bracket, you might interest her in tax-free municipal bonds issued by cities and states to fund roads, schools, and other necessary infrastructure improvements. Since the IRS generally does not tax the interest, these bonds offer lower nominal interest rates (coupon rates), but high tax-bracket people still come out ahead. If you're in the 30% bracket and receive a 10% nominal yield on a corporate bond, you only keep 70% of that, since the other 30% goes to the IRS. Therefore a 10% corporate bond would be equivalent to a 7% municipal bond, since either way the investor keeps $70 a year. They might receive $100 on the corporate bond, but $30 is "shared" with Uncle Sam. The municipal bond pays $70 and the investor keeps all of it.

Equivalent.

Michelle likes the idea of some tax-free income, so you and she agree to put 25% of her money into general obligation municipal securities issued by Chicago, Cleveland, and New York City. To get a slightly higher yield, you also use some of that 25% to purchase revenue bonds, backed only by the revenues on sports stadiums and toll roads, issued by the same municipalities. See, the general obligation bonds are a legal obligation of the issuer to pay bondholders with tax money. Revenue bonds are backed by the revenues generated from the facility built with the proceeds of the bonds. If the revenue bond builds a toll road, the bonds are backed by the tolls, for example. The state or city doesn't have to step in to pay back the bondholders, so revenue bonds are riskier than general obligation (GO) bonds. Therefore, they have a higher yield.

So 25% of Michelle's money is now invested in tax-free municipals.

Michelle is 41 years old and plans to work at least another 20 years. With such a long time horizon, you suggest she invest 50% of her capital in common stock like FREM. Michelle has never considered investing in FREM, but she has seen the pies at the supermarket and was quite taken by a recent French Silk with Pecan creation that she picked up on a whim at Wal-Mart.

You and Michelle decide to invest in common stock for the growth she'll need between here and retirement. Some of the companies have relatively few shares outstanding, making them "small cap" stocks, like FREM. These "small cap stocks" have less established histories but also potentially brighter futures than "large cap" stocks, in general. Their P/E ratios are high, since much of the perceived value is built on speculation of future profits. But, if the future is as bright as investors hope, millionaires are created, just as they were when investors took a chance on companies such as Microsoft®, IBM®, Oracle®, and Starbucks®.

So, Michelle now has 25% in tax-free municipals and 50% in common stocks of companies as small as Frank & Emma's and as large as General Electric. That's diversification, or the "don't put all your eggs in one basket" principle of equity investment.

What about the other 25%?

Michelle puts 20% in the money market, which is a very boring holding place for cash. Money market securities are short-term debt obligations that will be paid back within 1 year (usually 270 days maximum) by high-quality issuers. Commercial paper, banker's acceptances, and jumbo CD's are the most common of these safe, short-term debt securities that will end up paying Michelle some interest without subjecting her principal to any significant risk.

And the final 5% Michelle decides to use speculating in equity options. Calls and puts, in other words. Although not your strong suit, you decide that 5% is not a lot to risk on these high-risk securities that derive their value from an underlying stock. Which is why options are called "derivatives."

Ever heard that you shouldn't try to time the market?

Well, options are all about trying to time the market.

If you think a stock is going up in a hurry, buy a call. If the stock goes up in a hurry, the value of the call skyrockets.

What if the stock drops in a hurry, instead?

The call expires worthless and you lose.

Magically, you can make just as much money when stocks do belly flops by buying puts. If you have a WorldCom August 70 put when WorldCom drops to $10 a share, your put would be worth at least that $60 difference. And you might have bought the thing for just $5.

Or not.

It's all speculation, this world of options, but since Michelle has plenty of financial means and is only risking 5% of her capital on options, you decide not to talk her out of it. Instead, you send her the OCC disclosure document that lays out all the risks and characteristics of options trading and get her to sign an options agreement. As soon as your firm's ROP (registered options principal) approves the account, Michelle can start trading.

Now that you have met your suitability requirements with Michelle by carefully recommending securities that make sense given her time horizon, risk tolerance, and financial means, you must continue to deal fairly and equitably with her. The NASD's Member Conduct Rules try to ensure that customers get a fair deal from their agents and broker-dealers, and if you violate these rules the NASD has a whole system in place to handle infractions, called Code of Procedure (COP). Just like on the street, somebody breaks the rules, call a COP. Under Code of Procedure, you could be fined, sanctioned, suspended, expelled, or even barred from doing business with any other firm.

Which is bad.

You can appeal these decisions, but who wants to end up there?

No one. So, to avoid going through this Code of Procedure, make sure you take the time to evaluate your customer's needs and make suitable recommendations. Don't "borrow" money from customer accounts, even when you fully intend to replace it after hitting it big at the racetrack. Don't use inside information to make recommendations, and always forward written complaints to your supervisor/principal at the firm. Above all, never deceive a client for financial gain. That's called fraud, and it can not only get you suspended, but also get you thrown in jail.

So, here's the big picture: in order for a company to expand, it needs capital. It accesses this capital in the "primary market," where investment bankers sell the company's securities to investors, keeping a "spread" for their trouble. The issuing corporation takes the capital and buys equipment, technology, or whatever it needs for expansion. Investors can now trade their stocks and bonds with other investors on the secondary market. Securities firms like yours might work both the primary market as underwriters, and the secondary market as broker-dealers or market makers. Whether offering new stock to a customer in the primary market or helping her trade in the secondary market, your firm's actions are regulated by their self-regulatory organization (SRO)—the NASD or NYSE—as well as the government body called the SEC. Regulators like truthfulness and full disclosure. That's why companies who access the public markets have to disclose all kinds of stuff before issuing their securities and then have to disclose all kinds of stuff through quarterly and annual reports filed with the SEC. This way investors have a fair shot at discerning a good investment opportunity from a poor one. There is always risk, but through full disclosure, truthfulness, and fair dealings, investors can manage this risk, using a highly regulated professional such as yourself to help choose suitable investments.

Now that you have a grasp of the big picture, let's start looking at all the details your exam will expect you to know. But, no matter how detailed the material may get, please remember one thing:

This is not rocket science.

It isn't even close.

Just keep in mind the big ideas, and the little ones should fall in place.

Ready?

Sure you are.

CHAPTER 1

Equity Securities

Let's say you own a small, growing business. You're convinced you could turn it into a much bigger company if you only had $100,000. Trouble is, you don't seem to have an extra hundred grand lying around.

However, you do have a friend who could provide some financing. You ask if you can borrow the money, but your friend has a better idea. Rather than borrow money from him, why not let him buy into your company as an equity investor? This way you print up a certificate and sell this piece of paper to him for $100,000, which you will use to grow your business. He'll use the paper as evidence of his status as a proportional owner of your company. If the company does well, so do you and so does he. His piece of paper or "equity stake in the company" is worth more money, and maybe you feel so gosh-darned generous you start cutting him a check every three months and call it a "dividend," which is sort of a thank-you note you can actually cash at the bank. And everybody's happy.

That's basically the deal with equity securities. It's all about corporations selling paper to raise money. The folks who buy the paper don't get interest payments, because they aren't lenders. They're investors who think the company's chances for success are reasonably good. So good, in fact, that they choose to become part-owners of the company, owning exactly as much of the enterprise as their equity stake entitles them to. If they want a bigger stake, guess what they have to do—buy more equity.

COMMON STOCK

The most basic form of this "equity" or "ownership" is known as common stock. Common stock is easily transferable, which means it can be sold without breaking a sweat. If investors get tired of looking at the stock certificates, they can sell them to other investors. That's how common stock works. You get tired of it, you sell it. You start to miss it, you buy it back.

A corporation hires a firm (usually a bank) to keep track of all of those <u>transfers</u>

of ownership, by the way, and guess what we call them? The <u>transfer</u> agent. The transfer agent keeps the ownership records of the company's stock. Equate the word "certificates" with "transfer agent." The transfer agent deals with issuing and validating certificates, recording all the name changes when investors sell their certificates, that sort of thing. Lost, stolen, mutilated…if there's a problem with the certificates, contact the transfer agent. They can validate them or re-issue them, as the case may be. And, usually for a fee. They're a business. They like fees.

Just to make sure the transfer agent does a good job, the corporation also hires another outside firm—typically a bank—and we refer to this bank as the registrar. The registrar audits/oversees the transfer agent, just to make sure there aren't more shares outstanding than the company is authorized to sell.

AUTHORIZED, ISSUED, TREASURY, OUTSTANDING

Which brings us to four very important terms: <u>authorized</u>, <u>issued</u>, <u>treasury</u>, and <u>outstanding</u>. To answer most test questions successfully, all you really have to do is take the number of "issued" shares and subtract the number of "treasury" shares to get the number of shares "outstanding." But, if you want to grasp the concept of the four terms, you'll need to read the next few paragraphs.

Sorry about that.

Authorized shares represent the number of shares a company has authorized itself to issue to the public, a number disclosed in the corporate charter. Let's say a company is authorized to issue 1,000,000 shares of common stock, according to the charter. When they first sell shares to the public during their IPO, they probably won't issue all of them the first time out. The number they actually issue would be known, surprisingly enough, as issued shares. This corporation could issue 1 million, but they only issue 500,000. Therefore, there are 500,000 issued.

For various reasons, the corporation might decide to buy back some of those shares that are out in the secondary market. Why? Well, their stock has value. It could be used to acquire other companies. Or, they could send it to shareholders as a stock dividend. Whatever their reasons for repurchasing it, the important point is that corporations can buy stock and hold it in the treasury. We call this treasury stock. Since it's sort of locked up in a vault, it has no voting rights and pays no dividends. But, it can be used in many ways by the issuing corporation. For the test, you just have to take the number of shares actually issued and subtract the number repurchased and held in the treasury. If this corporation had issued 500,000 shares and then purchased 100,000 for the treasury, they would have how many shares left outstanding?

Exactly. 400,000 shares outstanding.

So, just take "issued" and subtract "treasury" to get the number of shares "outstanding."

500,000 Issued

-100,000 Treasury =

400,000 Outstanding

No big deal, really. When we talk about a company's "earnings per share" or "EPS," we're only talking about the outstanding shares, which are also the only shares that get to vote.

RIGHTS, PRIVILEGES OF COMMON STOCK OWNERSHIP

Owners of common stock enjoy several important rights the exam wants you to know about. The first right is the right of common stockholders to vote for any major issue that could affect their status as a proportional owner of the corporation. Things like stock splits, mergers, acquisitions, board elections, and changes of business objectives all require shareholder approval. But one thing shareholders never get to vote on is whether a dividend is paid and, if so, how much it should be. We have a pretty good idea what the shareholders of, for example, Anheuser-Busch would say about dividends, right? "Yeah, give me 100 bucks a share and a free pony keg, please."

Sorry, not at this time.

Shareholders vote their shares. If you own 100 shares of common stock, you have 100 votes to cast. Let's say there are three seats up for election on the Board of Directors. There are two ways that your votes could be cast for the election. Under statutory voting, you can only cast the number of shares you own for any one seat. So, you could cast up to 100 votes for any one seat, representing a total of 300 votes for three seats. Under cumulative voting, you could take those 300 votes and split them up any way you wanted among the three candidates. You could even cast all 300 votes for one candidate and give nothing to the others. That's why the exam might want you to say that cumulative voting gives a benefit to the small/minority shareholders. In other words, if we can manage to get a candidate on the slate who will look out for us small shareholders, we can all cast all of our votes for her. The big guys will still get their way with the other candidates, but this gives us a fighting chance every once in a while.

Beyond voting, common stockholders also have the right to inspect the corporation's financials through quarterly (10Q) and annual (10K) reports, just to see how the corporation is spending the shareholders' money and running the show up there at headquarters.

Should a corporation go belly-up and have to be liquidated, common stockholders get in line for their piece of the proceeds. Unfortunately, they are last in line. They are behind all the creditors, including bondholders, and also behind preferred stock holders.

But, at least they are in line, and if there are any residuals left, they get to make their claim on those assets. That's known as a "residual claim on assets," by the way, because they like to get real creative with the language in this industry. The test could also refer to common stock as the most "junior" security, since all other securities represent senior claims.

The exam might also point out that shareholders, who are owners of the corporation, have "limited liability," which means they are shielded from the debts of the company and lawsuits filed against it. I'm not sure why they bring this up—it's not like the bondholders *are* liable, just something the exam might mention. Limited liability is a good news–bad news thing. The bad news is when you buy common stock, you can lose all your money. The good news is that when you buy common stock, you can only lose all your money.

Finally, the exam might say that common stock owners have a "claim on earnings and dividends." That's true—as owners, they have a share of the profits. Some of the profits/earnings are reinvested into the business, which tends to make the share price rise. Some of the profits might be paid out as dividends, so let's take a look at that.

DIVIDENDS

Did you know that a dividend is only paid if the Board of Directors decides to pay it?

That's right, if a corporation doesn't declare a dividend, the dividend doesn't get paid. End of story.

But, if they do declare a dividend, the board gets to decide three dates. The NASD/NYSE (depending on where the stock trades) decides the fourth one. Here's how it works. The day that the Board declares the dividend is known as the declaration date. The board decides when they'll pay the dividend, too, and we call that the payable date. Notice how creative the language is there—we call the day the dividend is d-e-c-l-a-r-e-d the *declaration date*, and the day the dividend is p-a-y-a-b-l-e the *payable date*. Remember, if you get yourself in a jam on the exam, break down the words and ask yourself what they probably mean, because most terms probably mean exactly what their names imply. The party in charge of transfers is the "transfer agent." The company that issues securities is called the "issuer," and so on.

Anyway, the board of directors wonders who should receive this dividend—how about investors who actually own the stock as of a certain date? We call that the record date because an investor has to be the "owner of record" as of that date if she wants to receive the dividend. Now, since an investor has to be the owner of record as of the Record Date to receive the dividend, there will come a day when it's too late for investors to buy the stock and also get the dividend.

Why?

Regular Way Settlement

Because stock transactions don't settle until the third business day following the trade date. To "settle" means that the buyer has become the new official owner of the stock, on the books with the transfer agent. If a stock is sold on a Tuesday, the trade doesn't actually settle (ownership doesn't officially change) until Friday, the third business day after the trade. This is known as regular way settlement, or "T + 3," where the "T" stands for Trade Date.

By the way, guess why they call it "regular way settlement." Yep—because it's the regular way of settling trades. We'll worry about the funky "cash settlement" later, and I know you can't wait for that.

So, if an investor has to be the owner of record on the record date, and it takes three business days for the buyer to become the new owner, wouldn't she have to buy the stock at least three business days prior to the record date?

Yep.

So, if she buys it just two business days before the record date, her trade won't settle in time. We call that day the ex-date or "ex-dividend" date, because starting on that day investors who buy the stock will not receive the dividend. On the ex-date, it's too late. Why? Because the trades won't settle in time, and the purchasers won't be the owners of record (with the transfer agent) as of the record date. The answer to your exam question might be that "if the trade takes place on or after the ex-date, the seller is entitled to the dividend." Of course, if the trade takes place before the ex-date, the buyer will get the dividend.

The NASD sets the ex-date, as a function of "regular way" or "T +3" settlement. The ex-date is two business days before the record date.

So, remember DERP. Declaration, Ex-Date, Record Date, Payable Date. The board sets all of them except the Ex-Date, which is set by the NASD/NYSE.

If investors don't qualify for the dividend starting with the ex-date, guess what? The amount of the dividend is taken right out of the stock price when trading begins on the ex-date. If the dividend to be paid is 70 cents, and the stock closed at $20 the day before, it would open at 19.30 (the dividend comes out) on the ex-date.

One of the problems people have while studying for the Series 7 is that too much information seems to be "test world" and not "real world." I know from teaching live classes that candidates get tired of just memorizing chunks of information that seem completely divorced from reality. All this "XYZ" and "ABC" stuff gets a little tiring, so let's take a look at how the DERP thing would play out in the so-called "real world." The following is a news release from Equity Office Properties announcing a dividend paid way back in 2005:

Equity Office declares first quarter common dividend

Mar 16, 2005-- Equity Office Properties Trust (EOP), a publicly held office building owner and manager, has announced that its Board of Trustees has declared a first quarter cash dividend in the amount of $.50 per common share. The dividend will be paid on Friday 15 April 2005, to common shareholders of record at the close of business on Thursday 31 March 2005.

So, March 16 is the Declaration Date. The Payable Date is April 15. The Record Date is Thursday, March 31st. The article doesn't mention the Ex-Date (because that's not established by the company), but we can figure that it must be…right, Tuesday, March 29th. If you bought the stock on Tuesday, your trade wouldn't settle until Friday, April 1st, which means the seller's name would be on the list of shareholders at the close of business on Thursday, March 31st.

Quick note: EOP is a REIT, and the "T" in "REIT" stands for "trust." That's why the press release refers to the board as the "Board of Trustees." EOP is a Real Estate Investment Trust, but the stock works like any other stock. It simply pays a nice dividend. As we'll see later, REITs are just shares of stock that tend to pay nice dividend yields. If you owned 1,000 shares of EOP as of the record date, what would you receive?

A check for $500. So, if the dividend stays the same or increases in Q2, Q3, and Q4, you'll collect at least $2,000 just for sitting on your shares of EOP this year. Ever heard that the rich get richer? This is partly why.

It also brings up a testable point as to how a dividend can be paid. A dividend can be paid in the following ways:

- Cash (which means they cut you a check)
- Stock (more shares of stock)
- Shares of a subsidiary
- Product (extremely rare, all stories about Procter & Gamble apocryphal)

Cash dividends are taxable (usually at a maximum of 15%). Stock dividends are not taxable.

PRACTICE:

1. **An investor purchases common stock on a Thursday. Under regular way settlement, the transaction will settle**
   A. Friday
   B. Monday
   C. Tuesday
   D. Wednesday

2. **The Board of Directors declared a dividend on Monday, March 1st. If the record date is Tuesday, March 16th, the ex-dividend date is**
   A. Monday, March 15th
   B. Friday, March 12th
   C. Thursday, March 18th
   D. Tuesday, March 23rd

3. **Which of the following is/are true concerning Treasury stock?**
   A. has been issued and repurchased by the company
   B. reduces the number of outstanding shares
   C. tends to raise EPS
   D. all of the above

ANSWERS:

1. C – Thursday is the trade date or the "T" in "T + 3." T + 1 is Friday, T + 2 is Monday, and T + 3 is Tuesday.

2. B – go back two business days

3. D – they buy it back to leave fewer shares outstanding; therefore, the same total earnings/profits of the company are divided among fewer shares for a higher EPS.

STOCK SPLITS, STOCK DIVIDENDS

The big idea behind stock splits and stock dividends is that when the investor ends up with more shares, the total value of his investment is unchanged. If he had 100 shares at $10 before, that was worth $1,000. No matter how many shares he has after the split or the stock dividend, the total value is still just $1,000. So, when a corporation does a 2:1 stock split, the investor would have twice as many shares. What would the price per share be?

Half as much.

Yep. The investor has $1,000 worth of stock both before and after the split. He used to have 100 shares worth $10 each. Now he has 200 shares worth $5 each. A thousand bucks, either way.

The test might want you to work with an uneven split, like a 5:4 ratio. This is where the company gives investors five shares for every four that they own.

A possible exam question might read:

Joe Tidewater owns 100 shares of XYZ Corp. common stock currently trading at $50. XYZ Corp. declares a 5:4 stock split. What will Mr. Tidewater's stock position be after the 5:4 split?

I.   500 shares

II.   125 shares

III. @$50 each

IV.   @ $40 each

A.   I, III

B.   I, IV

C.   II, III

D.   II, IV

Okay, if Joe Tidewater had 100 shares worth $50, what was the total value? $5,000. Well, that's what his investment will be worth after the split, too, so let's see how the numbers work out.

Just multiply Joe's 100 shares by the first number, and divide that by the second number.

$$100 \text{ X } 5 \text{ divided by } 4 = 125 \text{ shares.}$$

Joe will have 125 shares.

What will each share be worth?

Well, he still has $5,000 worth of XYZ Corp. stock; he just has to divide that total amount over more shares. $5,000 divided by 125 shares gives us a share price of $40.

The answer, then, is "D".

A stock dividend would work the same way in terms of more shares/lower price. If an investor receives a 20% stock dividend, that's 20% more shares of stock, but the total value of the investment is the same. It's just divided among more shares. So an investor with 200 shares of XYZ common stock @40 would have $8,000 of XYZ stock. If XYZ sent her a 20% stock dividend, she would then have 240 shares. Her $8,000 would then be divided among 240 shares, yielding a per-share price of $33.33.

Why do companies do this? For one reason: to push the share price *down*. Companies have concluded that when their stock price goes up "too high," many investors, especially the Average Joe and JoAnne, get scared off. Since stock prices are determined purely through supply and demand, if we scare off the little guy, there won't be as much demand for our stock, and the stock price will drop. So, if our share price goes up to $100, let's knock it back to $50 with a 2:1 split. Doesn't the investor own the same percentage of the company's bottom line either way?

Sure, which is why Warren Buffett has never gotten into this mess. As I write this, his company's common stock now trades for about $110,000...*per share*. No, that's not a typo. Berkshire-Hathaway is too busy to waste their time manipulating the share price. If the price is too high for you, don't buy it. And, good luck trying to daytrade this sucker. Traders buy stock in "round lots" of 100 shares. So, one round lot would cost you a cool $11 million.

Point is, nothing really changes after a stock dividend or a forward stock split. The investor simply has more shares at a lower price, which means her cost basis in the stock changes. Long 100 shares @50 might become Long 125 shares @40. Just keep track of your cost basis so that when you sell someday you can tell the IRS how much of a capital gain or loss you realized on the stock. But whether you have 100 shares @50 or 125 shares @40, you've paid $5,000 for a certain percentage of ownership.

It's like this. Let's say you and a friend are on a diet. You decide to splurge and order pizza for lunch, but since you're on this diet you're not going to cut the thing in half and eat half a pizza, for crying out loud. Since you're on a diet, you can only have small pieces, so you decide to cut the pie into 20 slices, and you each eat only 10 small pieces. Or, maybe your friend is overzealous and talks you into cutting the pie into 50 slices, whereby you each consume only 25 teeny, tiny, little pieces.

Umm, you're eating half the pie either way, right?

Same thing for a stock dividend or a forward stock split. No matter how they slice the earnings pie, you own the same percentage before and after this non-event. They've made the shares smaller and "cheaper," but you have more of them. A "forward split," by the way, just means you end up with more shares. A 2:1, 3:2, or 5:4 split would be a forward split that pushes the share price down.

Well, sometimes companies have the opposite problem—their share price is so low that the big, institutional investors (pension funds, mutual funds, insurance companies) won't touch it. These entities usually won't touch a stock trading below $5, so if our company's stock is trading for $1, we might need to increase that price. One way to do it would be to become a more competitive, profitable company and let the increased profits take the share price up.

Nahhhhh, too much work. Let's do a reverse stock split instead.

If the test question says that Joann is long 100 shares of LMNO @$1, we might find LMNO doing a reverse split of 1:10. That means for every 10 shares she owns now, she'll end up with only one really big share. She'll have 10 shares when it's all over, in other words. If the shares were trading for $1 before the split and everybody now has shares that are 10 times bigger, the share price magically becomes…yes, $10 a share. Joann is now long 10 LMNO @$10.

Awesome—LMNO is a $10 stock, just like that!

Just remember that whether the exam is talking about a stock dividend, a forward split, or a reverse split, the investor's cost basis changes because the share price changes. But no change in *value* actually occurs. See, there's a big difference between a change in *price* and a change in *value*. It's not how many dollars you paid for the stock. It's, "How much did you pay for the *earnings*?" Remember, a share of stock represents a slice of the earnings pie, so how much are you paying for these earnings? A $100 stock with $10 of earnings associated with it is much *cheaper* than a $1 stock with 1 penny of earnings. The first one trades at a "multiple" or P/E of only 10, while the second one will cost you 100 times the earnings, or a P/E of 100. Looks cheaper, but the $1 stock is really 10 times more expensive than the $100 stock. P/E just means "Price to Earnings."

Finally, remember that shareholders vote on stock splits, whether forward (5:4, 2;1, 3:2) or reverse (1:7, 1:10, etc.). Shareholders do not vote on dividends, period.

WHAT IS A SHARE OF COMMON STOCK?

Before we move on, let's make sure we understand exactly what a share of stock is. When you buy a company's common stock, you simply own a percentage of the company. What are all owners interested in? Profits, called *earnings*. The bottom line, baby. You start your own business for one main reason—to earn a profit. You buy a <u>share</u> of somebody else's business for the same reason—to <u>share</u> in the profits. So, you only buy a share of common stock if you think the company will earn a profit, increase that profit, and, eventually, pay some of that profit out to you as a dividend, just as you paid your buddy who invested $100,000 into your growing business a dividend once you were up and running. That's all there is to it—you want to <u>share</u> in the earnings/profits of the company? Buy some *shares* of common stock.

What if there aren't any earnings?

Then you hope you can make use of the "greater fool" theory and sell the stock in the unprofitable company to someone who is still convinced it's going to go up forever. Remember, during the tech bubble, people were willing to pay 1,000 times earnings for YHOO. Unfortunately, the drugs did eventually wear off.

This Certificate Represents Ownership of

1,000 fully paid shares of common stock in the

FRANK & EMMA'S FRUIT PIES CORPORATION

RIGHTS, WARRANTS

One of the rights common stockholders enjoy is the right to maintain their proportionate ownership in the corporation. We call this a "preemptive right" because the existing shareholders get to say yes or no to their proportion of the new shares before (pre-) the new shareholders get a chance to buy any. Otherwise, if you owned 5% of the company, you'd end up owning less than 5% of it after they sold the new shares to everyone *but* you, which could be called "dilution of equity" to make us sound smarter than we really are. Sort of a "first dibs for current investors" thing happening here, but the exam will probably call it "preemptive rights." For every share owned, an investor receives what's known as a right. It's an equity security with a very short life span. It works like a coupon, allowing the current shareholders the chance to purchase the stock below the market price over the course of a few weeks. If a stock is trading at $20, maybe the existing shareholders can take two rights plus $18 to buy a new share. Those rights act as coupons that give the current shareholders two dollars off the market price. So, the investors can use the rights, sell them, or let them expire in a drawer somewhere, like most coupons. The exam might mention the phrase "standby underwriting." That means that when the company does the rights offering, there is an underwriter standing by, willing to use any of the rights that nobody else wants. That would make it a "firm commitment," and would only pertain to a "rights offering."

A warrant is a long-term equity security. There are no dividends attached to a warrant. If you own a warrant, all you own is the opportunity to purchase a company's stock at a pre-determined price. If you have a warrant that lets you buy XYZ for $30 per share, then you can buy a certain number of shares at that price whenever you feel it makes sense to do so, like when XYZ is trading for at lot more than $30 per share. When issued, the price stated on the warrant is above the current market price of the stock. It usually takes a long time for a stock's price to go above the price stated on the warrant. But, they're good for a long time, typically somewhere between two and ten years.

Warrants are often attached to a bond offering. Corporations pay interest to borrow money through bonds. If they attach warrants, they can "sweeten" the deal a little and maybe offer investors a lower interest payment. Why would you take 4% when your buddy gets 6% on his bond? Doesn't he make $60 a year, while you only make $40? Yes. But if the company's common stock rises, he'll still be making $60 a year, while you could make a huge profit on the common stock. If you have a warrant to buy 1,000 shares @30 and those shares rise to $50, are you going to cry about that $20 a year your buddy made? Not when you just made about $20,000, right? In fact, why not give your buddy a call right after you cash in your profits and offer to buy him lunch, especially if he was ever talking trash about your decision to take 4% when he got 6%.

PREFERRED STOCK

Another equity security tested on the Series 7 is preferred stock. This stock gets preferential treatment during liquidation, and its owners always receive dividends before owners of common stock. The preferred dividend is printed right on the stock certificate. The par value for a preferred stock is always $100. The stated dividend is a percentage of that par value. Six-percent preferred stock would pay 6% of $100 per share, or $6 per share per year.

We hope.

See, dividends still have to be declared by the Board of Directors. Preferred stockholders aren't creditors. They're just proportional owners who like to receive dividends. If the board doesn't declare a dividend, do you know how much an owner of a 6% preferred stock would receive?

Nothing.

However, if the investor owned cumulative preferred, that might be different. They wouldn't necessarily get the dividend now, but the company would have to make up the missed dividend in future years before it could pay dividends to any other preferred or common stockholders. If the company missed the six bucks this year and wanted to pay the full six bucks next year, cumulative preferred stockholders would have to get their $12 before anybody else saw a dime.

This 6% works more like a maximum than a minimum. If an investor wants the chance to earn more than the stated 6%, he'd have to buy participating preferred, which would allow him to share in dividends above that rate, if the company has the money and feels like distributing it.

Another type of preferred has a rate of return that is tied to another rate, typically the T-bill rate. If T-bill rates are up, so is the rate on the adjustable preferred, and vice versa. Because the rate adjusts, the price remains stable.

CONVERTIBLE PREFERRED

A highly testable type of preferred stock is convertible preferred. This type lets an investor exchange one share of preferred for a certain number of common shares whenever the investor wants to make the switch. Say the convertible preferred is convertible into 10 shares of common stock. Therefore, the convertible is usually worth whatever 10 shares of common stock are worth. If so, they trade at "parity," which means "equal." Just multiply the price of the common stock by the number of shares the investor could convert the preferred into. That gives you the preferred's parity price.

So, if the convertible preferred were convertible into 10 shares of common and the common stock went up to $15 a share, how much would the convertible preferred be worth at parity?

10 X $15, or $150.

The test question will either tell you how many shares the investor can convert into, or it will make you take the par value and divide it by the conversion price given. If the question says the convertible is convertible at $10, just take $100 of par divided by that $10, and you'll see that the investor can convert to 10 shares of common. Convertible at $20 would be $100 divided by $20 = 5 shares. Either way, if it's convertible at 10, you have a 10:1 relationship. If it's convertible at $20, you have a 5:1 relationship. Use those 10:1 and 5:1 relationships as your tool. If they give you the common stock price, multiply by the first number to get the parity price of the preferred. If they give you the preferred's market price, divide by the first number to get the parity price of the common.

It's basically a gift certificate. If you have a gift certificate worth $100, how many blue jeans can you buy if they're priced at $20?

5.

What if you want T-shirts priced at $10?

You can get 10.

So, when they say the preferred is "convertible at $20," or "convertible at $10," just ask how far your "gift certificate" would go. Preferred stock is a gift certificate worth $100 toward the purchase of/conversion to common stock at a set price.

Let's make sure you have it by looking at a practice question:

XYZ 4% preferred stock is convertible @25. Currently, XYZ common trades at $28 per share; therefore, the parity of XYZ preferred is:
A. $100
B. $112
C. $33
D. $53

The answer is "B," $112. How did we get that? How far does the gift certificate of $100 (par value) go if the stock costs $25 upon conversion?

4 shares.

What are 4 shares now worth? Four times $28 = $112.

If a security has a fixed payment, the market compares that fixed payment to current interest rates. Current interest rates represent what investors could receive if they bought low-risk debt securities. If low-risk debt securities are paying 4%, and your preferred stock pays you a fixed 6%, how do you feel about your preferred? Pretty good, right, since it's paying a higher rate than current interest rates. If somebody wanted to buy it, they'd have to pay a higher price. But, if interest rates shoot up to 10%, suddenly your 6% preferred doesn't look so good, right? In that case the market price would go down. Not the par value—par value is etched in stone. It's the market price that fluctuates.

Market prices adjust for interest rates: rates up/prices down, rates down/prices up. Well, as we mentioned, if the rate adjusts along with the T-bill rate, the price doesn't need to move. But for other types of preferred, the price moves in the opposite direction of interest rates, just like bond prices. That's because the value is really determined by a comparison of the fixed rate of return to current interest rates.

But, if we add another variable, now the security's price isn't so sensitive to interest rates. Convertible preferred has a value tied to interest rates, like other preferred stock, but its value is also tied to the value of the common stock into which it can be exchanged or converted. If rates are up, preferred prices drop. But if you're holding a convertible preferred while the common stock is skyrocketing, the price of the preferred would skyrocket right along with it. Remember, it's worth a fixed number of common shares. If the value of the common goes up, so does the value of the convertible preferred. So, the exam might want you to know that convertible preferred stock is less sensitive to interest rates than other types of preferred.

The exam might want to know all kinds of stuff.

Finally, remember that preferred stock generally does not have a maturity date, and usually does not give the owner voting rights. Two specific cases where preferred stock *does* get to vote are: 1) the corporation defaults on the dividend payment a certain number of times or 2) the corporation wants to issue preferred stock of equal or senior status.

ADR'S

Then you've got your ADR's. That stands for American Depository Receipt, and like many of the acronyms you'll need to know for the exam, this one means exactly what it says. It's a <u>receipt</u> issued to somebody in <u>America</u> against shares of foreign stock held on <u>deposit</u> in a foreign branch of an American Bank. Look for an answer like "a foreign stock in a domestic market" or something that "facilitates U.S. investors in purchasing foreign stock." The investor buys shares of a Japanese corporation's stock, only the shares are held in a bank in Japan, which issues a receipt to the investor in America. The receipt is what is traded in America. It pays dividends, maybe, but they are paid in the foreign currency and then have to be converted into U.S. dollars, which is why ADR owners are subject to currency risk. Also, if the stock is worth a certain number of Yen on the Japanese markets, that won't work out to as many U.S. dollars when our dollar is strong, although it would work out to more American dollars if our dollar is weak.

In the real world people often don't even realize they own ADR's. If somebody tells you he owns stock in Toyota or Nokia, he really owns their ADR's. I'm certainly not going to buy a stock quoted at 1,174.567 Yen, right? Heck no. I'll buy the Toyota ADR in American dollars, thank you.

The exam might point out the holders of ADR's have receipts that represent 1 to 10 shares of the foreign stock and have the right to exchange the ADR for the actual shares of foreign stock. If the corporation sponsors the creation of the ADR, the industry cleverly calls them "sponsored ADR's," and, when feeling especially punchy, might refer to them as ADS's or "American Depository Shares" to make sure they have at least four names.

Generally, a sponsored ADR would give voting rights to the owner, while an unsponsored ADR would not.

REITS

Investing in real estate has many advantages and disadvantages. The advantages are that property values usually go up and that real estate provides nice diversification to a securities portfolio. The disadvantages include the fact that real estate costs a lot of money, and it isn't liquid. It often takes months to get a house sold, or sold for a decent price, so the lack of liquidity keeps many investors from buying real estate, especially commercial real estate (shopping malls, skyscrapers, factories, etc.).

Which is where REITs come in. A Real Estate Investment Trust (REIT) is a company that owns a portfolio of properties and sells shares to investors. You could buy into REITs that own apartment buildings, office buildings, shopping centers, hotels, convention centers, self-storage units, timber, you name it. Now, if there were no REITs, it's safe to say that I would probably never be investing in shopping centers or office buildings. But through REITs, I can participate in big, commercial (or residential) real estate without having to be rich or putting up with the traditional liquidity problems. I can liquidate my REITs as fast as I can sell any other stock. If you've ever heard of the Chicago Mercantile Exchange, you may know that they use a ton of prime commercial real estate located right along the Chicago River for their wild and woolly operations. That building they're in is owned by the same Equity Office Properties mentioned earlier in the press release for the upcoming dividend. EOP earns vast amounts of money leasing that space out to the CME, plus all the other outstanding office space on the 30 floors above it. I own a few shares of that REIT called Equity Office Properties, so when I'm walking around the Loop, I do enjoy knowing I actually own a teeny, tiny little piece of that huge building at 30 S. Wacker generating all those millions of dollars. How much of the building do I own? I believe I own the fake bonsai in the really cool concrete planter out front. Hey, it's a start. Plus, Sam Zell informed me over lunch the other day that if I sell a few more Pass the 7™ books, I may end up owning all the up and down buttons on the middle bank of elevators.

Someday.

So, REITs are just equity securities that give the investor an ownership stake in a trust that owns a bunch of real estate. They do not pass through losses (only real estate *partnerships* do that), they pay out nice dividend yields, but the dividend is taxed at your ordinary income rate, not the kinder, gentler 15% maximum rate on "qualified dividends."

Now, actually, you might have seen Equity Office Properties in the news, so for the sake of accuracy, let's point out that they were actually purchased in early 2007 for cash. In other words, a public company with nosy shareholders like me is now a private company that gets to keep its business, you know, private. And this development demonstrates how "real-world" the Series 7 material actually is. I just told you about shareholder voting, and I happened to pick EOP to use for an actual dividend example. Now, I'm telling you that a few weeks ago, the shareholders of EOP voted to approve the acquisition offer of $55.50 per share from a large private buyer. Don't let anyone tell you that the Series 7 is all about "useless stuff." You won't use all of it, of course, but you might be shocked how much this information does relate to the so-called "real world."

YIELD, TOTAL RETURN

There are only two ways that I know of to make money on stocks. One, the stock price goes up, and/or, two, the stock pays me a dividend. If I'm looking only for the share price to go up, I'm a "growth investor." If I'm solely interested in the dividends, I'm an "income investor." If I want both growth and income, guess what kind of investor I am?

Would you believe "growth and income"?

But, really, that's the only way to make money on stocks. You either sell the stock for more than you bought it someday, or the stock paid you some nice dividends. Otherwise, you wasted your money.

So, measuring the return on equity securities really comes down to two concerns: capital appreciation (growth) and dividends (income). If you buy a stock at $10, and a year later it's worth $20, that's a capital appreciation of 100%. If the stock pays $2 in annual dividends and costs $20 on the open market, that's a yield of 10%. Yield just asks how much an investor has to pay to receive how much in dividends.

Annual Dividend Divided By Market Price = Dividend Yield

Substitute the word "get" for "yield," because yield simply shows how much you get every year compared to what you put down to get it. The test may give you a "quarterly dividend" in the question. If so, multiply it by four—there are four financial quarters per year, which is sort of why they call them "quarters."

Another concept is "total return." Here, just add the dividend received plus the capital growth/appreciation. In other words, if you buy a stock for $10 and the market price rises to $12, you have $2 of capital appreciation (sometimes called a "paper gain" or an "unrealized gain" just to make sure it has three separate names). If the stock pays $1 in dividends, you're basically "up $3" on a $10 investment.

That's a total return of "3 outa' 10" or 30%.

Mutual funds publish their 1-, 5-, and 10-year total returns. These simply measure the growth in the share price plus the dividend and capital gains distribution paid per share every year.

Total return. Exactly what it sounds like.

PRACTICE:

4. **Which of the following represents the most expensive common stock?**
   A.   market price – $10, P/E 25
   B.   market price – $15, P/E 20
   C.   market price – $95, P/E 19
   D.   market price – $100, P/E 21

5. **An issuer's transfer agent would perform all the following tasks except**
   A.   canceling old certificates
   B.   recording transfers of ownership
   C.   transferring funds among client accounts
   D.   validating torn, mutilated certificates

6. **The registrar is responsible for which of the following?**
   A.   recording changes of ownership
   B.   filing the corporate charter
   C.   overseeing/auditing the transfer agent
   D.   selling mutual fund shares to large institutional buyers

7. **An investor is long 100 shares of XXR @50. After XXR declares a 5:4 split, the investor will be long how many shares at what price?**
   I.   100 shares
   II.   125 shares
   III. $50
   IV. $40

   A.   I, III
   B.   I, IV
   C.   II, III
   D.   II, IV

8. **Robin Danestegg owns 300 shares of QRZ @40. After QRZ pays a 20% stock dividend, Robin will be long how many shares at what price?**

I.   300 shares

II. 360 shares

III. $40

IV. $33.33

A. I, III

B. I, IV

C. II, III

D. II, IV

9. **An investor who owns which of the following securities might receive more than the stated rate of return?**

A. common stock

B. cumulative preferred

C. participating preferred

D. all of the above

10. **MTG Corporation has the following dividend payment record on its 5% cumulative preferred stock. In 2005 the company paid a $3 dividend. In 2006 the company missed the dividend payment. If the company wants to pay dividends to other preferred and common stockholders in 2007, how much must owners of MTG cumulative preferred stock be paid first?**

A. $5

B. $10

C. $12

D. the difference between par value and fair market value divided by CPI

11. **XXX convertible preferred stock can be converted into XXX common stock at $10. If XXX common is currently trading at $14.50, what is the parity price for XXX convertible preferred stock?**

A. $104.50

B. $145.00

C. $1,450

D. not enough information provided in the question

12. **All of the following statements are true of rights and warrants except**
    A. Warrants are better.
    B. Warrants are sometimes attached to bond offerings.
    C. Rights are short-term instruments with an exercise price below CMV.
    D. Warrants are long-term instruments with an exercise price above CMV.

13. **Which TWO of the following statements are true concerning cumulative voting?**
    I.   Said to benefit the majority over the minority investor.
    II. Said to benefit the minority over the majority investor.
    III. Allows investors to cast only the number of shares owned as votes.
    IV. Allows investors to split total votes in any way they choose.

    A. I, IV
    B. I, III
    C. II, IV
    D. II, III

14. **A company may pay dividends in which of the following ways?**
    A. cash
    B. stock
    C. shares of a subsidiary
    D. all of the above

ANSWERS:

4. A – the highest P/E ratio is the most expensive stock, ignore the market price

5. C – the transfer agent deals with certificates and the names of those who own them

6. C – the corporation files its own charter—the registrar oversees the transfer agent

7. D – more shares at a lower price

8. D – more shares at a lower price

9. D – cumulative preferred might be making up for arrearages; participating preferred often raises the dividend. The stated return on common stock is zero, so

any dividend paid would be more than the stated rate. A smart-aleck question, but if you like two choices, you must go with "all the above."

10. C – $2 in arrears plus $5 in arrears plus the current $5 = $12

11. B – 10 shares times the CMV of $14.50 = $145

12. A – nothing is "better" than anything else on this exam

13. C – minority shareholders could nominate a "pro-minority" candidate and cast all their votes for that one candidate

14. D – some things just need to be memorized

WRAP UP

Before we wrap up this discussion of equity securities, let's take a look at things from the perspective of your client, Michelle Montoya. If Michelle owns 300 shares of Frank & Emma's Fruit Pies, what does that actually mean?

Well, since FREM is still a growing company, we call it a "growth stock," which means Michelle won't be receiving any dividend checks any time soon. But that's okay. Michelle is in her early 40's—she can cash dividend checks in retirement, at which point Frank & Emma's should be paying dividends. What will she get in the meantime? With any luck, she'll watch the value of her shares grow right along with the growth in profits at Frank & Emma's. If the Frank & Emma's earnings pie grows, her slices of the pie—called "shares of stock"—will grow right along with it, right? What if Frank & Emma's really drops the ball and goes bankrupt?

Hate it when that happens. That "non-systematic" risk, which is the risk of one stock dropping, can be taken care of by not putting all your eggs in one basket. Michelle's FREM holdings only represent a small percentage of the equity securities she has invested in, and the equity securities only represent a percentage of the portfolio, which is also diversified into municipal securities, corporate bonds, money market securities, and a few options here and there just to keep things interesting. So, even if the worst-case scenario played out and the company went belly-up, it wouldn't take Michelle's entire portfolio with it. In fact, it's even possible that the day that unlikely event occurred, she could see a gain in another stock that outweighed the loss on FREM. Diversification—that's what it's all about.

As an owner of FREM common stock, Michelle has the right to vote for the board members. Well, she has the right, but she's been sorta' too busy to open the proxy statements they keep sending her. However, if the company wanted to acquire a competitor or merge with a larger food service company, she'd get to vote on the merger or acquisition. If Frank & Emma's offers additional common stock to a new batch of investors, they'd have to do a "rights offering" where Michelle gets a certain number of rights allowing her to maintain her percentage of ownership, if she chooses to exercise her rights. Frank & Emma's files quarterly and annual reports that Michelle can easily access online if she wants to check out their sales, their balance sheet, their profit margin, management's discussion of all the risks the company faces, etc.

If Michelle starts to really jones for dividends, maybe she'll buy some Frank & Emma's preferred shares and know with reasonable certainty that her dividend check is, truly, in the mail. What kind of returns will she get? It depends on how solid Frank & Emma's finances appear to be and where current interest rates are when the preferred shares are issued. If rates are high, Michelle might buy preferred stock with a fat dividend attached. What if rates go higher? Then, she bought too soon, and the market price of her preferred shares would drop.

As Michelle gets older her taste for the wild ups and downs of the stock market will probably fade, and she'll become less of a "growth" and more of an "income" investor. If so, she'll want to buy some Frank & Emma's debt securities, which are called bonds. The bonds will not give Michelle any voting rights and won't offer a huge amount of growth potential, but they will do something common stock never does—they will state the rate of return she will get every year.

So, as you can probably guess, it's time to look at bonds now.

But first…

WHAT NOW?

- Review this chapter, taking notes on key terms, possibly making flash cards. *Approximately 1 hour – 1.5 hours.*
- If you have the Pass the 7 QuizSet, take the Chapter 1 Quiz on Equity Securities. *Approximately 30 minutes.*
- If you have the Audio CD Set, listen to tracks 1 and 2 on Disc 1. *Approximately 40 minutes.*

CHAPTER 2

Debt Securities

As we mentioned, a few years down the road Frank & Emma's Fruit Pies may decide they could sure use another big, sweet batch of capital from investors. However, maybe they already have enough owners. After all, you can only cut the earnings pie into so many slices before everybody goes hungry. So, instead of rounding up equity investors, the investment bankers will round up lenders interested in fronting Frank & Emma's some money in exchange for interest payments. Rather than selling pieces of paper called equity securities, the underwriters would be offering pieces of paper known as "debt securities," which we always call "bonds," except when we call them something else. Corporate bonds represent loans *from* investors *to* the corporation. Investors buy the bonds, and the corporation then pays them interest on the loan and promises to return the principal amount of $1,000 at the end of the term.

It's like a mortgage. Your family wants to expand, so you decide to acquire a house. Trouble is, you don't seem to have enough cash on hand to buy the thing outright. So, you borrow the money by issuing a piece of paper known as a mortgage. You carry the loan for 15–30 years, returning the principal amount plus interest until the debt is paid in full. In this case, you are just like a corporation selling bonds. Only difference is you pay back the principal little by little, while a corporation returns the principal all at once, at the end when the bond matures. Or, if you're doing an "interest only" loan, you're actually doing the same thing. Only difference is, the corporation is using *other people's* money.

How much did you put down on your house—the full purchase price? Wouldn't that have been fun, to just "buy the house," literally? Since it's pretty tough to buy a house by just cutting a check, we usually use "leverage." To use "leverage" means to use a lot of borrowed money. On the exam, when you see the word "leverage" just insert the phrase "borrowed money." A "highly leveraged" company has simply financed operations by issuing a lot of debt/borrowing a lot of money. And when we get to a chapter on margin accounts, we'll see that investors often use leverage by borrowing half the purchase price of a stock from their friendly broker-dealer.

Anyway, a bond has a specific value known as either "par" or the "principal" amount printed right on the face of the certificate. Since it's printed on the face of the certificate, the exam could also call it the "face amount," since every concept needs at least three different names in this industry. In Series Sevenland, bonds have a par value of $1,000 and, occasionally, $5,000. This is the amount an investor will receive with the very last interest payment from the issuer. You might think of this as the investor "getting his original money back." Up to that point, the investor has only been receiving interest payments against the money he loaned to the corporation by purchasing their bond certificates. So the bond certificate has "$1,000" printed on the face, along with the interest rate the issuer will pay the investor every year. This interest rate could be referred to as the coupon rate or "nominal yield."

Don't let the word "nominal" intimidate you. It means "name." The nominal yield is named right there on the certificate. It can also be referred to as the "coupon rate" because bonds used to come with coupons that investors would present when it came time to claim their interest checks. They would present these interest coupons twice a year, because that's how often most bonds pay interest—twice a year, also called "semi-annually." So, the interest rate a bondholder receives is a stated, known thing. That's a big difference from common stock, where you simply own a percentage of a company and hope that company becomes more valuable.

If you buy a 5% bond, you get 5% of $1,000 every year, which is $50 per year. Nominal yield is a known, stated thing. But when interest rates start changing, as interest rates will do, the value of your bond will change, as we'll now look at in more detail than you probably ever wanted.

RATES, YIELDS, PRICES

Interest rates represent what new bonds have to pay in order to attract new investors. But, bonds are issued with a fixed interest rate (like a fixed mortgage). If the bond is an 8% bond, it will always be an 8% bond, and it will always pay 8% of the par value every year no matter who owns it at the time.

For some reason, that concept seems to be tough for many candidates to accept, and I'm not sure why. What do we call bonds in general—fixed income securities, right? Why do we call them fixed-income securities? Because the income these securities pay is *fixed*. It's fixed or named on the bond. If it's a 5% bond, it pays $50 a year. If it's a 13% bond, it pays $130 a year and I hope somebody checked the credit rating on *that* one.

So, please, remember that if a bond pays a nominal yield/coupon rate of 8%, it will ALWAYS pay 8% of par or $80 per year. So, whenever interest rates change, they will change the bond's price. When rates on new bonds go up above 8%, the existing bond's price will go down, since new bonds would be issued with coupon rates higher than 8%. When rates go down below 8%, the bond's price will go up, since new bonds would be issued with coupon rates lower than 8%.

And the yields will move right along with interest rates, like this:

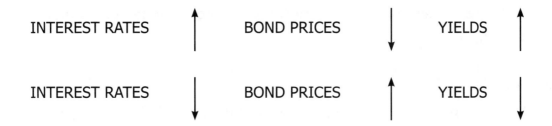

DISCOUNT BONDS

Remember, even though a bond has a par value of $1,000, we don't necessarily expect the bond to trade at $1,000 in the open market. As with a stock, a bond's price fluctuates. Why?

Interest rates.

If a bondholder has a bond that pays a nominal yield of 8%, what is the bond worth when interest rates in general climb to 10%?

Not as much, right? If you had something that paid you 8%, when you knew you could be receiving more like 10%, how would you feel about the bond?

Not too good.

But, when interest rates fall to 6%, suddenly that 8% bond looks pretty good, right?

Current Yield

When we take a bond's price into consideration, we're looking at a concept known as current yield. Current yield just takes the annual interest paid by the bond to an investor and divides it by what an investor would have to pay for the bond.

Current Yield = Annual Interest divided by the Market Price

It's just how much you get compared to what you put down to get it.

$80/$800 gives us a current yield of 10%.

It's the same formula used for Dividend Yield. It's just that bonds pay interest, rather than dividends. But "yield" just asks how much do I get every year compared to what I pay to get it? So, if interest rates go up to 10%, suddenly, this bond that pays only 8% isn't worth as much, right? The only motivation for buying this 8% bond sitting out on the open market would be if an investor could get it at a discount. And, if she can get the $80 that the bond pays in annual interest for just $800, isn't she really getting 10% on her money? That's why we say her current yield is equal to 10%, higher than the nominal yield that never, ever changes.

Rates up, price down. But the yields are going up, right along with rates.

Of course rates and yields go up together, right? Rates are what new bonds pay; yields are what existing bonds offer, after we factor in their market price.

As soon as you see a current yield higher than the coupon rate, you know you're looking at a discount bond. An 8% bond with a 10% current yield, for example, has to be a discount bond. But, there are two more yields the test wants you to be comfortable with.

Yield to Maturity

The first one is easy. It's the yield to maturity, the theoretical return an investor gets if she holds the bond all the way to maturity. At maturity, an investor receives the par value, which is $1,000. If the investor puts down only $800 to buy the bond and receives $1,000 when the bond matures, doesn't she receive more at maturity than she paid?

Yep. That's why her yield to maturity is higher still. She gets all the coupon payments, plus an extra $200 when the bond matures. If you see a YTM that is higher than the coupon rate, you're looking at a discount bond. For example, a 4% nominal yield trading at a 5.50 YTM is a discount bond. The YTM would also be higher than the current yield: nominal, current, yield to maturity, in that order.

Yield to Call

Like homeowners, sometimes issuers get tired of making interest payments that seem too high. That's why some bonds are issued as "callable," meaning that after a certain time period the issuer can buy the bonds back from investors at a stated price. A bond that matures in 10 or 20 years is often callable in just 5 years. Since the investor who bought a bond for less than par is going to make money when the principal of $1,000 is returned, do you suppose he'd rather make his profit sooner or later?

Sooner, right? When you're making money, you want to make it as fast as possible. That's why yield to call is the highest of all for a discount bond.

PREMIUM BONDS

Of course, whatever can go up can also go down. What happens when interest rates fall?

Bond prices RISE.

Here's why.

If you owned this 8% bond and saw that interest rates have just fallen to 6%, how would you feel about your bond?

Pretty good, right? After all, it pays 2% more than new debt is paying.

Do you want to sell it?

Not really. But you might sell it to me if I paid you a...that's right, a premium. If I paid you $1,200, you might be willing to sell it.

From my perspective, I see that new debt is only going to pay 6%, which is too low for my needs. Even though I have to pay more than par for your 8% bond, it will all work out if I can get all those interest payments at a higher-than-prevailing rate.

Current Yield

So, we've just pushed the price of the bond up as interest rates went down. Dividing our $80 of annual interest by the $1,200 we put down for the bond gives us a current yield of 6.7%. That's lower than the coupon rate, which is why the CY is below our coupon rate/nominal yield. Whenever you see a coupon of 8% and current yield of 6.7% (or anything lower than that 8% printed on the bond), you know you're looking at a premium bond. Remember, the coupon rate/nominal yield doesn't change. Therefore, the only way to get the yield lower than the coupon is to pay more than par for the bond. Just like the only way to get the yield higher than the coupon is to pay less than par for the bond.

YTM

Now, when this investor's bond matures, how much does she get back from the issuer? Only $1,000. So, she put down $1,200 and will only get back $1,000 at maturity. Pretty easy to see why her Yield to Maturity (YTM) goes down.

YTC

Remember when we decided that a person who buys a bond at a discount wants the bond to return the principal amount sooner rather than later? Well, if you pay more than the par value for a bond, you're going to lose some money when the bond returns your principal, right? So, if you're going to lose money, do you want to do it quickly, or spread it out over time, collecting the higher-than-prevailing-rate interest payments in the meantime?

Pretty clear that we're pushing for the latter, right?

That's why a person who purchases a bond at a premium will have a lower yield to call than maturity. He's going to lose money in either case, so he'd rather lose it over 10 or 20 years (maturity) rather than 5 years (call).

So, yield to call is the lowest yield for a bond purchased at a premium.

Disclosing Yield on Customer Confirmations

When a customer purchases a bond from you, the registered representative, your firm will send her a trade confirmation no later than the T + 3 settlement date. And, on this trade confirmation your firm has to disclose either the YTM or the YTC. Should you disclose the best possible yield or the worst possible yield?

Always prepare your customer for the worst or most conservative yield, so there are no bad surprises, right?

Well, for a discount bond, which yield is lower, YTM or YTC? YTM. That's what you would disclose to a customer who purchases a bond at a discount.

For a premium bond, which yield is lower? YTC. That's what you would disclose to a customer who purchases a bond at a premium.

Please go back through this section and complete the following seesaw. Rates are on the right, price is on the left. So, place the words "premium," "par," and "discount" where they go on the left, and fill in CY, YTM, and YTC where they go on the right:

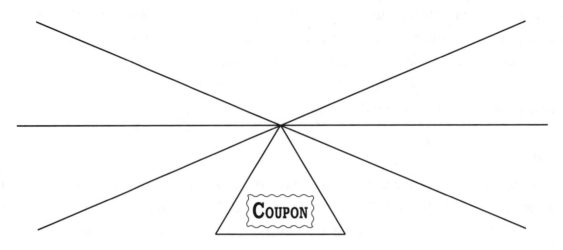

RETIRING THE DEBT

A bond has a maturity date that represents the date when the issuer will pay the last interest check and the principal. At that point, it's all over—the debt has been paid in full, just like when you pay off your car, student loan, house, etc. This can be referred to as "maturity" or "redemption."

As we saw with "yield to call," many bonds are repurchased by the issuer at a set price if interest rates drop. So, a bond might not mature/be redeemed. It might be called.

Also, sometimes the issuer will simply make an offer to repurchase your bonds at a certain price. You can accept or reject the offer, known as a "tender offer." You would "tender your bonds" to the issuer for payment, and that would retire the debt. Or, you could just hang onto them, unlike with a call. When a bond is called, remember, it's all over.

When we look at municipal securities in the next chapter, we'll see that many city, county, and state governments will issue a new batch of bonds before the first call date and then park the proceeds in an escrow account as they impatiently await the first call date stipulated in the indenture. That's known as "advance" or "pre-refunding," but we'll save that for the next chapter.

BOND CERTIFICATES

There are four different forms that a bond can take in terms of the certificate itself. In the olden days, bonds were issued as "bearer bonds," which meant that whoever "bore" or had possession of the bond was assumed to be the owner. No owner name at all on the certificate; it just said "pay to the bearer," so whoever bore the bond received the principal at maturity. In order to receive the interest investors holding bearer bonds used to clip coupons attached to the bond certificate every six months. There was no name on the interest coupon, either, so the IRS had no way of tracking the principal or the interest income. And you know how much that irritates the IRS. So, bonds haven't been issued in bearer form since the early 80's—that doesn't mean they don't exist. A few are still floating out there on the market, so you have to know about them for the test. Just remember: no name on certificate, no name on payment coupons.

Bonds also used to be registered as to principal only. That meant that we had a name on the bond certificate—the person who would receive the principal amount at maturity. But, again, with the silly little unnamed interest coupons. Therefore, only the principal was registered, thus the name "registered as to principal only."

Anyway, the bond market got smart in the early 1980's and started registering both pieces of the debt service. Now, the issuer has the name of the owner [principal] and automatically cuts a check every six months for the interest. Therefore, the IRS—who is here to help—can also help themselves to a bit of the proceeds for the interest and principal income. We call these bonds fully registered, because both pieces of the debt service (interest, principal) are registered. And you know how that pleases your friends and mine at the Internal Revenue Service.

Book entry/journal entry bonds are still fully registered. It's just that it's done on computer, rather than on paper. The investor keeps the trade confirmation as proof of ownership, but we still have an owner name on computer, and we automatically cut interest checks to the registered owner.

QUOTES

Bonds are quoted either in terms of their price, or their yield. Since the coupon rate or nominal yield doesn't change, if you give me the price, I can figure the yield. And, if you give me the yield, I can figure the price. This process is known as "interpolation," by the way, which is just a fancy word for converting bond yields into bond prices, and vice versa. If we're talking about a bond's price, we're talking about bond points. A bond point is worth $10. You'll need to memorize that for the test. So, if a bond is selling at "98," that means it's selling for 98 bond points. With each point worth $10, a bond selling for 98 bond points is trading for $980. A bond trading at 102 would be selling for $1,020. Although fractions have been eliminated from stock and options pricing, they are still very much alive in the world of bond pricing. If a bond point is worth $10, how much is 1/2 a bond point worth? Five dollars, right? A quarter-point would be worth $2.50, right? An eighth is $1.25, and so on. Therefore, if you see a bond priced at 102 3/8, how much does the bond cost in dollars and cents? Well, "102" puts the price at $1,020, and 3/8 of $10 is $3.75. So, a bond trading at 102 3/8 costs $1,023.75.

$$102 \ [\$1,020] + 3/8 \ [\$3.75] = \$1,023.75$$

If we're talking about basis points, we're talking about a bond's yield. Yield to maturity, to be exact. If I say that a bond with an 8% coupon just traded on a 7.92 basis, I'm telling you that the price went up above par, pushing the yield to maturity down to 7.92%. "Trading at a basis of…" just means that the price pushed the yield to maturity to a particular percentage, or number of "basis points." A basis point is the smallest increment of change in a bond's yield. When the media talks about the Fed easing interest rates by fifty basis points, they're talking about 1/2 of 1 percent. We would write 1% as .01, right? Well, basis points use a 4-digit display system, so .01 is written as:

.0 1 0 0.

Then, we read that figure as "100 basis points." Two percent would be 200 basis points. One-half of one percent would be written as .0050 or "50 basis points." So, a bond trading at a 7.92 basis means that the YTM is 7.92% or 792 basis points. An easy way to work with basis points is to remember that all the single-digit percentages are expressed in hundreds. 400 basis points just means 4%. Anything less than 100 basis points is less than 1%. So 30 basis points is only .3 of 1%

NOTATION

The exam might want to see the look on your face when they make you read the following:

10M XYZ 8s debentures of '13, callable @103 in '08

Huh?

Well "10M" means $10,000 par value or 10 bonds. XYZ is the issuing corporation, and they pay "8s" or 8% in interest each year. The little "s" means you get the $80 in two **semi-annual** payments of $40 each. Remember that—a test question might ask how much the investor receives at maturity on this bond. The answer is $1,040. Remember that interest is always paid retroactively, meaning for the previous 6 months. So, when the bond matures, you get your final interest payment (for the previous 6 months) plus the principal/par value of $1,000. This investor owns 10 bonds, so she would receive $10,400 at maturity.

Assuming we make it that far—remember, if interest rates drop in 2008, the company can buy back the bonds for $1,030, end of story. That's what "callable at 103 in '08" means.

ACCRUED INTEREST

First, we need a handle on the concept. We have been discussing the annual interest of a bond. Well, if we can express the interest per year, we can also express what the interest per day is, right? Heck, we could even do the interest-per-minute, but, luckily, the exam doesn't go quite that far.

And let's not give it any ideas, okay?

The tricky part is that different issuers use different days in their months and years. For a corporate or municipal issuer, we consider every month to have 30 days, and every year to have 360 days. Yes, even February has 30 days for corporate and municipal bonds. Don't ask about Leap Year. The exam has plenty it can use against you without going there.

The following table might help:

TYPE	SETTLES	MONTHS	YEARS
Corporate/Municipal bond	T + 3	30 days	360 days
Treasuries	T + 1	Actual	Actual

So, if a corporate bond pays $80 in annual interest, how much is that per day?

Just divide $80 by 360 days to get about 22.2 cents per day. That's what the owner of the bond earns in interest every day.

How often does the owner receive a check for her interest?

In Series Sevenland, twice a year, or semi-annually. But, they don't always like to name the months. Like most things in the securities industry, the payment months are abbreviated. You'll only see one letter as an abbreviation, too. If you see a "J & J" bond, you'll have to think about which two "J" months would be six months apart.

January and July, right?

Here's how the chart works out for interest payment months:

J	J
F	A
M	S
A	O
M	N
J	D

Reading left to right, we pair January with July, February with August, March with September, April with October, May with November, and June with December. So if

you buy an "A & O" bond, you'll receive your two interest checks on the first of April and the first of October. If it's the 8% bond we've been discussing, how much will you receive each time?

That's right, $40. $80 per year divided into two semi-annual payments.

If they don't add a number to the "A & O," that means the checks are received on the first of each month. If they add a "15" to the abbreviation, that means the checks are received on the 15th of each month, as in an "A & O 15" bond.

Now, the check might be received on the first day of April. That doesn't cover that day's interest, though. A bondholder earns interest every day she owns the bond, including weekends and holidays. Doesn't matter when the check arrives. The check covers the previous six months' worth of interest, nothing more.

Did we mention this stuff is complicated?

Anyway, the concept behind accrued interest is that a bond is usually traded somewhere between the two interest payment dates. If the bond owner got her last interest check on the first of April, then sells the bond on July 16, what happens?

Well, who is going to receive the next interest check?

The buyer of the bond, who is about to become the new owner. Should we trust the buyer to deliver the seller's portion of that check when the buyer receives it?

Not a chance.

So, the buyer is going to pay the seller her portion of the interest right up front.

That's what the whole accrued interest concept comes down to. The buyer has to pay the seller the price of the bond, plus the interest that belongs to the seller, who hasn't gotten a check since the last payment date.

You can answer these questions step-by-step.

Let's try one now for practice:

Dale Dawson sells Jim Jacobs an XYZ Corp. 8% A&O bond on Wednesday, June 19. How much in accrued interest must be paid, and who pays the interest?

I.   Dale pays the interest.
II. Jim pays the interest.
III. Accrued interest is $18.44 per bond.
IV. Accrued interest is $1.84 per bond.

A. I, III
B. I, IV
C. II, III
D. II, IV

Well, we know who pays the interest. Jim—the buyer—pays Dale—the seller.

How much does Jim have to pay Dale in accrued interest?

Step one, find the settlement date. Corporate and municipal bonds settle "T + 3," or three business days after the trade date. That's why the test likes to make the trade date Wednesday or Thursday, so the weekends can confuse you a little.

Don't let them. Just remember that weekends don't count as business days. So "T" is Wednesday. We count Thursday as one, Friday as two, and…Monday as the third business day after the Trade date. Monday will be June 24th.

Step two, count the days.

On the settlement date, the buyer starts earning interest. So, the seller is entitled to every day up to—but not including—the settlement date. The settlement date's interest belongs to the buyer. So, if the trade settles on the 24th of June, the seller is entitled to 23 days of interest.

This A&O bond last paid interest on the 1st of April. How many days in April is the seller entitled to?

Thirty.

So, 30 days for April plus 30 days for May plus 23 days for June = 83 days of accrued interest.

Step three, find the interest-per-day that the bond pays. The bond pays $80 per year divided by 360 days, or 22.2 cents a day.

Step four, multiply the daily interest by the number of days that have accrued. Twenty-two cents a day times 83 days equals $18.44 per bond that Jim Jacobs must pay Dale Dawson, on top of the price of each bond.

The answer to that seemingly hard question, then, is "C."

Now, we already know the exam likes to challenge you as much as possible. So, once you get used to doing accrued interest questions concerning corporates and muni's, you might find yourself staring at a question concerning Treasuries, also referred to as "government securities."

Don't panic. Govies work the same way, with two major differences. First, Treasuries settle the next business day or "T + 1." And, Treasuries use actual or calendar days. Now July has 31 days, and February 28.

Other than that, it's the same process. Step 1—find the settlement date. Step 2—count the days up to, but not including, the settlement date. Step 3—find the interest paid per day. Step 4—multiply the daily interest by the number of days. Step 5—move on with your life.

So, you could probably answer the following question right now:

A J & D 5% government bond trades on Wednesday, August 14th. How much accrued interest will the buyer pay the seller?
A.   13.7 cents
B.   28 cents
C. $1.65 per bond
D. $10.27 per bond

Step one—when does the trade settle? Thursday, August 15th. Govies settle on the next business day. T + 1.

Step two—count the days. This bond last made an interest payment on the first of June, so how many days have accrued?

June	30	
July	31	
Aug	14	(up to, not including, the settlement date of the 15th)

Looks like 75 days total, right?

Step three—find the interest per day. $50 per year divided by 365 (actual) days = 13.7 cents per day.

Step four—multiply the days by the daily interest. 75 days times 13.7 cents = $10.27 per bond.

The answer is "D."

Next question, please?

Oh yeah, something that is related to yet different from accrued interest is called the "long coupon." If a bond has a payment schedule of, say, January and July, it might be issued in, say, March but not make the first payment until January. If so, that would be a coupon payment bigger than the usual six months' worth. So, they call that a "long coupon," in case you don't already have enough to memorize.

PRACTICE:

15. **Debbie Benture sells her XXY 6% J & J bond on Thursday, March 14. How many days of accrued interest will she pay for this transaction?**
    A. 60
    B. 78
    C. 0
    D. 73

16. **Debbie Benture buys an XXY 6% J & J bond on Thursday, March 14. How many days of accrued interest will she pay for this transaction?**
    A. 60
    B. 78
    C. 0
    D. 73

17. **What is true about a bond with an 8% coupon trading at a 10% Yield to Maturity?**
    A. It is trading at a discount.
    B. The price of the bond went up.
    C. Interest rates have fallen.
    D. The bond is trading at a premium.

18. **Which of the following bonds is trading at a premium?**
    A. 8% coupon, 9.10 basis
    B. 8% coupon, 9.50 basis
    C. 8% coupon, 7.70 basis
    D. 8% coupon, 8.00 basis.

ANSWERS:

15. C – why would the seller pay accrued interest? It's the buyer who pays the seller.

16. B – step one: find settlement. If the "T" or Trade date is Thursday, March 14th, the trade will settle in three business days, or Tuesday, March 19th. Debbie has to pay the seller for every day up to (not including) the settlement date, because up to the settlement date the seller is the owner of the bond. So, Debbie pays her for 18 days in March, plus 30 days each for January (that's the first "J" in a J & J bond) and February. 18 + 30 + 30 = 78 days. How were you supposed to know it was a corporate bond? XXY looks like a corporation, right? Sure isn't the federal government.

17. A – if the yield is higher, it's because somebody bought it at a lower price. The coupon doesn't change, so if the yield is higher, the price is lower. If the yield had been lower than the coupon/nominal rate, the price would have been higher. So, when you see a yield higher than the coupon, you know the bond was traded at a discount, and vice versa for a premium bond.

18. C – if the basis (YTM) is lower than the coupon, the bond was traded at a premium.

YIELD CURVES

Municipal bonds are usually issued under a "serial maturity," which means that a little bit of the principal will be returned every year, until the whole issue is paid off. Investors who buy bonds maturing in 2015 will generally demand a higher yield than those getting their principal back in 2007. The longer your money is at risk, the more of a reward you demand, right? If a friend wanted to borrow $1,000 for one month, you'd probably do it interest-free. What if they wanted to take three years to pay you back? You could get some interest on a thousand dollars by buying a bank CD, which carries no risk, right? So, if somebody's going to put your money at risk for an extended period of time, you demand a reward in the form of an interest payment.

Same with bonds. If your bond matures in 2015 when mine matures in 2007, isn't your money at risk for 8 more years? That's why your bond would be offered at a higher yield than mine. If I buy a bond yielding 5.65%, yours would probably be offered at more like 5.89%. The extra 34 basis points is your extra reward for taking on extra risk.

This is how it works under a normal yield curve, where long-term bonds yield more than short-term bonds. Guess what, sometimes that yield curve gets inverted. Suddenly, the rule flies out the window, and folks are getting higher yields on short-term bonds than on long-term bonds. The cause of this is generally a peak in interest rates. When bond investors feel that interest rates have gone as high as they're going to go, they all clamor to lock in the high interest rates for the longest period of time. In a rush of activity, they sell off their short-term bonds in order to hurry up and buy long-term bonds at the best interest rate they're likely to see for a long time. Well, if everybody's selling off short-term bonds, the price drops [and the yield increases]. And if they're all buying up long-term bonds, the price increases [and the yield drops]. That causes the yield curve to invert, a situation that usually corrects itself very quickly.

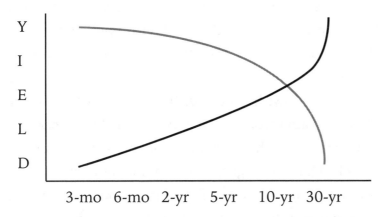

NOTE: the curve sloping upward is a "normal yield curve," where as the term to maturity increases, so does the yield. The curve sloping downward is an "inverted yield curve," a fairly rare situation where short-term debt securities yield more than long-term.

YIELD SPREAD

Another yield concept the test might throw at you considers the difference in yields between high-rated and low-rated bonds. If folks are demanding a much greater yield on low-rated bonds than on high-rated bonds, that's a negative indicator for the economy. Basically, it means folks are nervous about issuers' ability to repay. If investors don't demand a much higher yield on the low-rated bonds, that means in general they are confident about issuers' ability to repay, which is a positive indicator. So, when the "yield spread narrows," there is much reason to rejoice, although, personally, I hope I have better things to celebrate.

RISKS TO BONDHOLDERS

Credit risk is the risk of default, which is what Moody's and Standard & Poor's measure when they rate bonds. Treasury debt has no real default risk, while many corporate bonds carry major default risk. Remember that "high-yield" is just a polite way of saying "junk," which means "serious default risk." Event risk for a bondholder entails the chance that the corporation whose bonds they own is acquired by another company that is highly leveraged. What if S&P and Moody's decide to downgrade the bond ratings once they become the obligation of the highly leveraged acquiring company?

Hate it when that happens.

Interest rate risk is the risk that rates will suddenly shoot up, sending the market price of your bond down. The longer the term on the bond, the more volatile its price. When rates go up, all bond prices fall, but the long-term bonds suffer the most. And, when rates go down, all bond prices rise, but the long-term bonds go up the most. So, a 30-year government bond has no default risk, but carries more interest rate risk than a 10-year corporate bond.

Purchasing power risk has to do with inflation. If inflation erodes the value of money, an investor's return simply ain't worth what it used to be. Fixed-income investments carry purchasing power risk, which is why investors often try to beat inflation by investing in common stock. The ride might be a wild one, but the reward is that we should be able to grow faster than the rate of inflation, whereas a fixed-income payment is, well, fixed, even when inflation rises. Note that high inflation does not help stocks. It's just that in a period of high inflation, stock will probably perform better than fixed-income securities. So, during an expansion, where inflation tends to rise, you're better off in equities/stock. During a period of decline/contraction, bonds are the place to be, since their price will rise as interest rates fall due to the cooling demand for money/expansion.

Call risk is the risk that interest rates will drop and bondholders will have their bonds called. If this happens, they reinvest at lower rates and lose the full appreciation in price that would have resulted as interest rates kept falling. If rates were likely to fall, I'd want a non-callable bond, myself. Even though non-callable bonds offer lower yields than callable bonds, that's okay. I'd like to hang on to this one as rates go down, pushing the market price up, and the issuer has no way of forcing it out of my hands.

Reinvestment risk is somewhat related to call risk. When you receive the principal, you go ahead and reinvest it into new bonds—what kind of rates/yields are bonds offering now?

Low ones.

Another way to look at reinvestment risk is to remember that bonds paying regular interest checks force investors to reinvest into new bonds every few months or so. What kind of rates/yields will debt securities be offering when they go to reinvest the coupon payments?

Nobody knows, which is why it's a risk.

To avoid reinvestment risk buy a debt security that gives you nothing to reinvest along the way—zero coupons, e.g., Treasury STRIPS.

Notice how bondholders can get hit comin' or goin'. If it's a corporate bond—and even some municipal securities—you could end up getting stiffed (default risk). If rates go up, the price of your bond gets knocked down (interest rate risk). If rates go down, callable bonds are called (call risk), and the party's over, plus you have to reinvest the proceeds at a lower rate than you were getting (reinvestment risk). And, even if none of the above calamities strikes, inflation could inch its way up, making those coupon payments less and less valuable (purchasing power risk).

Oh well. If you want fixed-income, you take on these risks to varying degrees, depending on which bond you buy and when you buy it.

So, nobody ever wins by purchasing bonds, right?

Right.

Except when they do.

Can you think of a situation where buying bonds could turn out extremely profitable? What if you purchased a bunch of 30-year, non-callable bonds right when interest rates were sky-high and getting ready to plummet? Wouldn't that make your purchase price extremely cheap (rates high/price low) and, then, suddenly the market price would shoot sky-high as interest rates started to fall, the faster the better?

How often is that going to happen, and how are you going to know when rates have peaked?

Beats me. But if you figure it out, please contact me at your earliest convenience.

DEFAULT RISK

To protect bondholders, Congress passed the Trust Indenture Act of 1939. If a corporation wants to sell $5,000,000 or more worth of bonds that mature outside of one year, they have to do it under a contract or "indenture" with a trustee, who will enforce the terms of the indenture to the benefit of the bondholders. In other words, if the issuer stiffs the bondholders, the trustee/trust company can get a bankruptcy court to forcibly sell off the assets of the company so that bondholders can recover some of their hard-earned money.

TYPES OF CORPORATE BONDS

Remember that a corporate bond pays a fixed rate of interest to the investor, and that bond interest has to be paid, unlike a dividend on stock that is paid only if the board of directors declares it. We'll see that a bondholder usually doesn't suffer as much price volatility as a stock investor. But, unlike the owner of common stock, bond holders don't get to vote on the things we looked it in the preceding chapter. The only time bondholders get to vote is if the corporation goes into bankruptcy. Creditors will be offered various little scenarios by the corporation who can't actually pay them, and the bondholders will get to vote on these terms.

Since bankruptcy is always a concern, corporations often secure the bonds by pledging specific assets like airplanes, government securities, or real estate. Would you believe we call these "secured bonds"? For a secured bond the issuer pledges title of the assets to the trustee, who just might end up selling them off if the issuer gets behind on its interest payments. Investors who buy bonds attached to specific collateral are secured creditors, the first to get paid should the company go belly up. If the collateral used is real estate, we call it a mortgage bond. If the collateral is securities, we call it a collateral trust certificate. And if the collateral is equipment, such as airplanes or railroad cars, we call it an equipment trust certificate. Since these bonds are the most secure, they offer the lowest coupon payment, too. Remember, if you take a small risk, you usually only get a small reward.

Most corporate bonds are backed by a promise known as the "full faith and credit" of the issuer. That's why we might want to see what S&P and Moody's have to say about a particular issuer's full faith and credit. If the credit is AAA, we probably won't be offered a huge coupon payment. But if the issuer is rated right at the cut-off point of BBB (Baa for Moody's), then we might demand a bigger pay-off in exchange for buying bonds from an issuer just one notch above junk status. Regardless of the rating, if we buy a bond backed simply by the full faith and credit of an issuer, we are buying a debenture. Debenture holders are general creditors and get paid after secured bondholders. Therefore, debentures pay a higher coupon than secured bonds, since they carry more risk.

"Sub" means "below," as in "submarine" for "below the water," or "subterranean" for "below the ground." Subordinated debentures are below debentures when it comes to liquidating a company and paying out money to the bondholders. Since these bonds are riskier, they pay a higher coupon than debentures.

If all the bondholders have been paid and there's still money left over (it could happen, right?), then we start talking about paying out some money to stockholders. Preferred gets preference, so we pay them first, and common stock is always last in line.

Liquidation Priority

So, if a company goes belly up, interested parties get paid off in the following order of priority:

1. Employees/wages
2. IRS/taxes
3. Secured creditors
4. Debentures/general creditors
5. Subordinated debentures
6. Preferred stock
7. Common stock

Yes, the IRS, an inherently benevolent society, makes sure that employees get paid first…that way they can tax the wages as they come for all the other taxes the corporation has failed to pay.

Warms your heart, doesn't it?

Remember that an "income bond" only pays income if the company has income. It's usually issued by a company coming out of bankruptcy and usually offers a high coupon, just in case it ever gets around to making a payment.

Moody's, S&P & Fitch

There's nothing worse than lending some corporation $1,000 and then finding out they're, like, not going to pay you back. What? But, dude, you *owe* me.

This is known as a "default" because even when somebody stiffs you we have to dress up the language to make it sound more dignified. I'd like to see somebody explain to Tony Soprano that they have "elected to default on their debt obligations at this time," but in the world of corporate finance sometimes you front your hard-earned money to a corporation, and they, like, stiff you. And you can't send two thugs to their door with a pair of pliers and a blow torch, unfortunately. You have to send a much more expensive set of thugs known as "bankruptcy attorneys" to the courthouse door and hope they can knock some sense into the judge before he lets the deadbeats walk away without paying you back at least *something*.

So, how likely is it that a bond will go into default? Isn't going to happen on a Treasury. It might happen on some municipal securities. But when you get into the category of corporate bonds, you see that it happens much more than you'd like. Luckily, Moody's, S&P and Fitch all give bond ratings designed to help you gauge the likelihood of default. Remember that this is *all* that the bond rating agencies are talking about—the risk of default. They aren't making any recommendations with these ratings. The highest quality issuers have AAA/Aaa (S&P/Moody's) ratings. The "investment grade" issues go from AAA/Aaa down to BBB/Baa. And below that, dude, watch out!

STANDARD & POOR'S (& FITCH)	MOODY'S
AAA	Aaa
AA	Aa
A	A
BBB	Baa
BELOW THIS IS JUNK, NON-INVESTMENT GRADE, HIGH-YIELD, SPECULATIVE	
BB	Ba
B	B

So, credit quality is the highest on the AAA/Aaa-rated bonds. As credit quality drops, you take on more default risk, right? So, you expect to be compensated for the added risk through a higher yield. High yield and low quality go hand in hand, just as low yield and high quality do. How does a bond become "high yield" or "junk"? That just means that a brand new issue of low-rated bonds would have to offer fat coupons to get you interested in lending the money, and existing bonds would simply trade at lower and lower prices as people get more and more nervous about a possible default. As the price drops, the yield…*increases*.

Remember that—it's not just interest rates that can knock down a bond's market price. When S&P, Moody's, or Fitch downgrades an issuer's credit rating, the market price of those bonds will drop, increasing their yield. In fact, when the first headline comes out that the ratings agencies are sort of keeping a real close watch on a particular company, that doesn't usually do a lot for the market price of that company's bonds. Although it, by definition, sure does boost the yield, right? Price down, yield UP.

Not sure how detailed the exam will get, but please note that an S&P rating such as "BBB" actually has three levels: BBB+, BBB, BBB-. Just like in school, S&P can add pluses and minuses to the A's and B's. Moody's uses 1, 2, and 3. After "Aaa," Moody's then subdivides the next three ratings into: Aa1, Aa2, Aa3, then A1, A2, and A3, and, for those unafraid to teeter on the cut-off, they have Baa1, Baa2, and Baa3. So, what's the lowest investment-grade rating from S&P? BBB-. For Moody's, it would be Baa3. In the *Wall Street Journal*, the story would probably read, "XYZ has recently been downgraded by S&P (or Moody's) to one notch above junk status." That means their bonds are now rated BBB- (Baa3), and one more notch below that puts them in the exciting world of junk bonds. Of course, you're a good salesperson. You aren't going to call me up and try to sell me some junk bonds, are you? Heck no. But you might try to interest me in some "high-yield" bonds, instead.

Oh, high-yield? Sure, I'm into that—just don't try and sell me none of that junk.

As you can see above, it's just a different name for the same darned thing.

Some investors will go for the higher yield offered on the lower quality bonds. But they better not come crying to us if the corporation goes into default. Risk versus reward—you want a big reward, you take on a big risk. You want low-risk bonds, you get lower returns.

Most customers would really like you to sell them a no-risk, high-yield bond.

They'd probably also like a good-tasting beer with no calories and a 30-year mortgage fixed at 2%.

Sinking Fund

Since the issuing corporation has to return the principal value of the bond at some point, they usually establish what's known as a sinking fund. If you actually held your interest-only mortgage 30 years, maybe your spouse would have to gently remind you, "Remember to add the $300,000 to this month's interest check, honey. Gotta pay the principal back." Since that's how corporations pay back the principal (all at once), they set some money aside in escrow, which means they park it in safe, dependable U.S. Treasury securities. With this sinking fund established, the company would be able to return the principal, make a "tender offer" where they offer to buy back the investors' bonds, or complete a "call." Having this money set aside sure can't hurt the old rating with S&P and Moody's either, right?

Callable and Convertible

The "callable" concept is easy. Just means that after a certain period of time, the issuer might be able to call up the bondholders and announce that they're buying back the bonds at a certain price already agreed upon. A bond might be callable starting in the year 2009 at 104, meaning that in the year 2009 the issuer can retire the debt by giving each bondholder a check for $1,040 plus any accrued interest.

When might they want to call a bond? Probably when interest rates have fallen, right? Isn't that when homeowners refinance their homes? Works the same way for bond issuers. When rates go down, they start to think maybe the outstanding debt could be replaced with brand-new, much cheaper debt. If interest rates fall to 6%, they reason, let's issue new debt at 6% and use the proceeds to retire the outstanding debt we're currently paying 8% on.

Pretty simple.

Replacing one bond issue with another is called "refunding." It tends to happen when interest rates fall. It allows the issuer to issue less-expensive debt and retire more-expensive debt.

It's not such a great deal for the bondholders, though. What can they do with the proceeds of the call? Reinvest them. At what rate? A lower rate. This is called reinvestment risk. Upon reinvestment, the bondholders will get a lower rate of return, since interest rates have now fallen. And, what happens to bond prices as rates decline?

Right, they go up.

Only they stop going up when the bonds are called away, meaning the bondholder doesn't get the full appreciation in price he would have otherwise gotten. So, since the bondholder takes on this risk, callable bonds yield more than non-callable. As always, if you want something good from the corporation, they take something away. Just like we saw in the equity chapter—if the preferred stock is convertible, you get a lower dividend. If the bond comes with a warrant, you get a lower yield on the bond.

Then, there are convertible bonds, which can be converted into a certain number of shares of the issuer's common stock. Bonds have a par value of $1,000, so the investor applies the $1,000 of par value toward purchasing the company's stock at a pre-set price. When a convertible bond is issued, it is given a conversion price. If the conversion price is $40, that means that the bond is convertible into common stock at $40. In other words, the investor can use the par value of her bond towards the purchase of the company's common stock at a set price of $40. Bonds have a par value of $1,000, so if she applies that $1,000 toward the purchase of stock at $40 per share, how many shares would she be able to buy? 25 shares, right? $1,000 of par value divided by $40 per share of stock tells us that each bond can be converted into 25 shares of common stock. In other words, the two securities trade at a 25:1 relationship, since the big one (bond) can be turned into 25 of the little ones (stock). The company sets the conversion price; they have no control over where their common stock trades on the open market, right? If the price goes up, the value of the convertible bonds goes up. Just like if the price goes down, that drags down the market value of the bonds.

So how much is this particular bond worth at any given moment?

Whatever 25 shares of the common stock are worth.

Just take Par and divide it by the conversion price to find out how many shares of common stock the bond could be converted into.

In this case it's 25 shares, since $1,000 would go exactly that far when purchasing stock priced at $40 a share.

Par/Conversion price = # common shares
1,000/40 = 25 shares

So how much is the bond worth?

Depends. How much are 25 shares of the common stock worth?

Since the bond could always be converted into 25 shares, it generally has to be worth whatever 25 shares of the common stock are worth. When the bond trades for exactly what the 25 shares are worth, we call this relationship "parity," which is just a fancy word for "same" or "equal." Since one's price depends on the other, the two should have a price that is at "parity."

So, if a bond is convertible into 25 shares of IXR common stock, and IXR is trading @50, what is the bond's price at parity?

25 X $50 = $1,250.

And, if the common stock went up to $60 a share, the bond would be worth 25 times that number, right?

25 X $60 = $1,500.

Sometimes the test gets tricky and gives you the bond's market price, asking for the stock's parity price.

Don't sweat it.

It's a 25:1 relationship, so instead of multiplying the stock price by 25, just divide the bond's price by 25. If the bond trades at $1,250, just divide that by 25 to get to the common stock's parity price of $50.

See, once you get that 25:1 relationship determined, you're good to go. If the relationship is 25:1, either multiply the stock's price or divide the bond's price by 25. Just depends on what the question gives you. So, when you see a question on convertibles, look for the conversion price. Divide par by that conversion price, and now you have the relationship. If the bond is convertible at $40, it trades at a 25:1 relationship to the stock. What if the bond were convertible at $50?

20:1.

Convertible at $25?

40:1.

And so on.

Sometimes the question will come right out and say that the bond is convertible into a certain number of shares.

Great, now they've already done the work for you. If it's convertible into 50 shares, it trades at a 50:1 relationship. Usually you have to divide par by the conversion price to get that number. Sometimes the test just gives you that relationship straight up. Either way, just work through the problem step by step. It isn't that difficult really. Just ask yourself how far the par value would go if divided by the conversion price of the stock. Whatever you come up with will allow you to answer the question.

So, all you have to do is find the ratio. $1,000 of par value divided by $40 per share gives us a ratio of 25:1. If the question gives you the stock price, multiply by 25 to find the bond's parity price. If it gives you the bond price, divide by 25 to find the common stock's parity price.

PRACTICE:

19. MMY Corporation has convertible debentures that can be exchanged for shares of MMY common stock at a set price of $40. If MMY common is currently trading at $57 dollars, what is the parity price of the MMY convertible debentures?

A. $1,017

B. $1,425

C. $1,000

D. $1,765

20. Which TWO of the following statements are true of callable bonds?

I.   Bonds are typically called when interest rates are rising.

II. Bonds are typically called when interest rates are falling.

III. Bonds trading at a discount are more likely to be called.

IV. Bonds trading at a premium are more likely to be called.

A.   I, III

B.   I, IV

C.   II, III

D   II, IV

21. Which TWO of the following are associated with falling interest rates?

    I.   bond prices rising

    II. bond prices falling

    III. coupon rates rising

    IV. coupon rates falling

    A. I, III

    B. I, IV

    C. II, III

    D. II, IV

22. Which of the following bonds is most susceptible to a call?

    A. 6% nominal, matures in 2010, callable @103

    B. 6% nominal, matures in 2015, callable @par

    C. 9% nominal, matures in 2020, callable @par

    D. 9% nominal, matures in 2020, callable @103

23. If a company is liquidated, the following parties will be paid in which order?

    I.   preferred stockholders

    II. secured bondholders

    III. subordinated debenture owners

    IV. common stockholders

    A. I, II, III, IV

    B. II, I, III, IV

    C. II, III, I, IV

    D. I, II, IV, III

24. Which of the following represents a true statement concerning bearer bonds?

    A. They no longer exist.

    B. The government called all bearer bonds in 1983.

    C. They no longer exist on the primary market.

    D. They yield more than book-entry bonds.

25. 50 basis points is equal to

    A.   50%

    B.   5%

    C.   .5%

    D.   .05%

26. Which of the following bond ratings implies the highest yield?

    A.   Aa

    B.   Baa

    C.   BBB

    D.   Ba

27. If the yield curve inverts, which of the following would carry the lowest price?

    A.   T-bond

    B.   T-bill

    C.   T-note

    D.   10-year debenture

28. All of the following represent secured bonds except

    A.   collateral trust certificate

    B.   debenture

    C.   mortgage bond

    D.   equipment trust certificate

29. All of the following would increase the market price of an outstanding bond except

    A.   Interest rates fall.

    B.   S&P upgrades the credit rating.

    C.   Moody's upgrades the credit rating.

    D.   The company undergoes a reverse stock split.

ANSWERS:

19. B – "convertible at 40" means 1 bond can be exchanged for 25 shares. If each share is now worth $57, 25 of them are worth $1,425. Parity.

20. D – bonds are called when rates fall. Issuers of bonds are borrowers, so, just like people with mortgages, when rates fall, they refinance their debt at a lower rate. Why would a bond be trading at a premium? Because rates have fallen.

21. B – bond prices refer to bonds trading on the secondary market. As rates on new bonds fall, the market prices of existing bonds rise. Rates down, price up—commit that to memory. Coupon rates ARE interest rates, so if the exam says that rates are falling, it is also saying that coupon rates on new bonds are falling. Which, again, makes the bonds already out there on the secondary market look more attractive.

22. C – if you held these four mortgages, which one would you refinance first? The one with the highest interest rate—9%. Which 9% mortgage should you refinance first, the one you can pay off at par, or the one you can pay off with a $30 per bond penalty? Right? If you don't see it, send an email to walker@passthe7.com

23. C – memorize it, but it also makes sense. Pay the secured creditors, then the general creditors (debentures), then the SUB-ordinated creditors. If there's still money left—and I'm not sure why there would be—give PREFERENCE to preferred. Common is last—that's why it's called "common."

24. C – they don't get issued this way on the primary market, but there are still some bearer bonds in investors' safe deposit boxes.

25. C – anything less than 100 basis points is less than 1%

26. D – the lowest credit rating scares buyers the most—as they pay less and less for the bond, what happens to the yield?

27. B – an evil question. The inverted yield curve makes the T-bill yield the most—so what does that say about its price?

28. B – debentures are backed by the issuer's promise to pay, nothing more.

29. D – stock splits don't really achieve much of anything.

U.S. GOVERNMENT DEBT

U.S. Government Debt is very safe stuff. If you buy a bill, note, or bond from the United States Treasury, you do not have to worry about default risk. You're going to get your money back. You just aren't going to get rich in the process. In fact, you usually need to be rich already to get excited about U.S. Government debt, but that's another matter. For the test, just remember that U.S. Government/Treasury debt is just about the safest debt known to humankind. Safe and boring. Also remember that the interest income is exempt from state and local taxes. I mean, usually, it's the tax rate you pay the federal government that bothers you, but it is nice to avoid paying state and local taxes on interest earned on your U.S. Treasuries. If you live in a high-tax state such as Maryland, you have to enjoy earning lots of interest on T-bills, T-notes, T-bonds, etc., knowing that your state can't touch any of it.

T-BILLS

T-bills pay back the face amount, and investors try to buy them for the steepest discount possible. If the T-bill pays out $1,000, you'd rather get it for $950 than $965, right? In the first case you make $50 interest; in the second case you make only $35. That's why the BID *looks* higher than the ASK for T-bills trading on the secondary market. The bid is the discount that buyers are trying to get; the ask is the discount the sellers are willing to give up.

So, the quote might look like this:

BID   ASK
5.0%   4.75%

In other words, the buyers want a 5% discount; the sellers are only willing to give up a 4.75% discount from the par value.

These bills mature in one year or less (4 weeks, 13 weeks, 26 weeks, 52 weeks), so there are no coupon payments. These work like short-term "zero coupon" bonds, where the difference between the discounted purchase price and the face amount IS the investor's return. T-bills are offered in minimum denominations of $1,000. Like all Treasuries, T-bills are issued in book entry/journal entry form. I mean, if the U.S. Government had to pay for all the paper, ink, and printing services on all their T-bills, T-notes, and T-bonds, they could end up running, like, a *deficit*. The maturities available change from time to time. Currently (as you can see at www.treasurydirect.gov) the available maturities are 4 weeks, 3 months, 6 months, and something I don't expect the test to mention: extremely short-term "cash management bills." That website, by the way, offers a great primer on bills, notes, bonds, etc. As you'll see, T-bills are auctioned every Monday by the Federal Reserve Board. The big institutions put in "competitive tenders," trying to buy the bills for the lowest possible price. A pipsqueak like me puts in a "non-competitive" tender that will be filled, since I'm not trying to lowball Uncle Sam. Yes, Morgan Stanley will probably get a better price on T-bills today, but they also might not get their bid filled at all. I'm going to let that website mentioned above take us home on T-bills:

Key Facts

- Bills are sold at a discount. The discount rate is determined at auction.
- Bills pay interest only at maturity. The interest is equal to the face value minus the purchase price.
- Bills are sold in increments of $1,000. The minimum purchase is $1,000.
- All bills are auctioned every week.
- Bills are issued in electronic form.
- You can hold a bill until it matures or sell it before it matures.
- In a single auction, an investor can buy up to $5 million in bills by non-competitive bidding or up to 35% of the initial offering amount by competitive bidding.

T-NOTES, T-BONDS

T-notes are offered with 2–10-year maturities. T-bonds go from 10 to 30 years. These both make semi-annual interest payments, and are both quoted in 32nds. A quote of 98.16 means $980 plus 16/32nds or 1/2. So a T-bond priced at 98.16 costs $985. A price of 98.24 would be $987.50. In other words "24/32nds" is the same thing as "3/4s." If they hit you with a tough question here, one that doesn't reduce nice and easy to 1/2s or 1/4s, just multiply the number of 32nds by ".3125," and move on with your life.

Also note that 30-year T-bonds are callable in the last five years. For example, the T-bonds issued in 1980 were finally called in 2005.

STRIPS

The Treasury Department can also take T-notes and T-bonds and "strip" them into their various interest and principal components. Once they strip the securities into components, they can sell interest-only or principal-only zero coupon bonds to investors. We call these STRIPS, an acronym which stands for the "separate trading of registered interest and principal of securities." Of course, if you can tell someone what a STRIP is and the fact that it stands for the "separate trading of registered interest and principal of securities," chances are you're going to impress them enough to buy whatever the heck you're pitching. Either that, or they'll think you're an egghead with no social life, but go ahead and memorize it, anyway. As long as you're already going to be memorizing more information than you ever wanted to or ever thought possible, why not also know that STRIPS stands for…well, you know what it stands for. Enough already.

For the test, if an investor needs to send kids to college and needs to have an exact amount of money available on a future date, put him into STRIPS. This way, he'll pay a known amount and receive a known amount on a future date. He won't get rich, necessarily, but he won't lose the kid's college fund daytrading debit call spreads, either.

TREASURY RECEIPTS

Broker-dealers sell the same basic product, only they call them treasury receipts. For both receipts and STRIPS, just remember that they are purchased at a discount and mature at the face value. And remember that the STRIP is guaranteed by Uncle Sam, while a Treasury Receipt is not.

TIPS

As if government securities weren't safe enough, the Treasury department recently decided to protect investors from inflation. The Treasury Inflation-Protected Securities adjust for inflation, meaning that if inflation rises, you receive more money, and when it falls, you receive less. If you can find a safer security than a TIP, please buy it.

Just don't expect to get much yield for your money.

I-BONDS

An I-bond is a savings bond issued by the U.S. Treasury, which means it's absolutely safe and also exempt from state and local income taxes. An I-bond pays a guaranteed rate that is fixed but also pays more interest income when inflation rises. The semi-annual inflation rate announced in May is the change between the CPI (inflation) figures from the preceding September and March; the inflation rate announced in November is the change between the CPI figures from the preceding March and September. So, since they adjust the interest income to levels of inflation, there's no default risk and no real purchasing power risk, either. There are also tax advantages. First, the interest isn't paid out; it's added to the value of the bond. You can, therefore, defer the taxes until you cash in the bond. And, if you use the proceeds for qualified education costs in the same calendar year that you redeem the bonds, the interest is tax-free. The investor does not even have to declare that the I-bonds will be used for educational purposes when she buys them. As long as she uses the proceeds in the same year she redeems the bonds—and meets the other requirements of the Education Savings Bond Program—the interest is tax-free.

GOVERNMENT AGENCIES

The U.S. Government also has agencies that issue debt securities. Ginnie Mae, or GNMA, is the most testable. Rather than trying to understand Ginnie, Fannie, and Freddie, let's just remember some key points. They all issue mortgage-backed securities and all carry "prepayment" risk. That's just the risk that interest rates will drop, folks will pay off their mortgages, and investors will get their money back sooner than they wanted it, reinvesting it at a lower rate. Note that these are residential, not commercial, mortgages. Ginnie is the only one backed by the full faith and credit of the U.S. Government, who insures all the mortgages in the pool. Fannie (FNMA) and Freddie (FHLMC) are public companies, so you can buy stock in them. No stock in Ginnie. Ginnie Mae requires a $25,000 minimum investment. She pays out a check monthly, since she's just passing through home owners' mortgage payments [which are made monthly] to the holder of her pass-through certificates.

I would expect the exam to stick to the Ginnie, Fannie, Freddie side of things, but if it is feeling especially ornery on the day you take it, it might mention a few others. With that in mind, please note that other government <u>agencies</u>—not direct obligations of the U.S. Government—are part of the Federal Farm Credit System, which is composed of the Banks for Cooperatives ($ for feed and grain), Intermediate Credit Banks ($ for equipment), and Federal Land Banks ($ for mortgages/land). The FFCS is a group of privately owned lenders that provide different types of financing for farmers. The FFCS sells debt securities in order to raise the funds lent out to farmers. Again, the securities are not guaranteed by the U.S. Treasury. Rather, they are the obligation of the lenders in the system. The securities pay interest semi-annually and are only available in book (journal entry) form.

CMO'S

CMO's are sold by companies, who buy up mortgage-backed securities and create a fancy product called a collaterized mortgage obligation, or CMO. Investors get their principal back one "tranche" or "slice" at a time in a CMO. They are usually rated AAA, so default risk is not a major concern. You just never know if you'll get your money back sooner [rates fall] or later [rates rise]. The risk of receiving your principal sooner than expected is called "prepayment risk," which is associated with falling interest rates. The risk of receiving your principal later than expected is called "extension risk," and is associated with rising interest rates.

CMO's often do not have an active secondary market, so an investor who is very concerned with liquidity would not purchase a CMO. Two specific types of CMO's are called PAC's and TAC's. A "PAC" is a "planned amortization class," while a "TAC" is a "targeted amortization class." Since there is a "plan" with the PAC, the exam might say that it protects the investor more against prepayment and extension risk. A TAC does offer some protection against prepayment risk but not extension risk. In either case, there is a "support class" created to protect against prepayments—if the principal is repaid more quickly than expected, it goes into a support class. For the PAC, if interest rates rise and principal is being repaid more slowly, money will be transferred from the support class to protect that PAC owner against extension risk. This would not happen for the owner of a TAC.

CMO's are not extremely liquid and often too complex to be suitable for many investors. Registered representatives should get the customer's signature on a suitability statement when selling these products.

MONEY MARKET

The money market just refers to debt securities (no stock) set to mature in one year or less. A 30-year bond becomes a money market security once it's about to mature in one year or less. Safe, liquid instruments. They're very liquid and resistant to default risk, but they pay low rates of interest and do not provide inflation protection. The issuers tend to be solid, which is why the loans don't have to pay huge rates of interest. See, when you combine a high credit rating and a very short term, loans can be made at some pretty low interest rates. The exam may refer to money market securities as "cash equivalents," which would be found on the top line of a company's balance sheet. And that's generally how I view money market securities: as good as cash. Better, actually, because this stuff that's as good as cash is earning some interest. Not much sometimes, but usually much better than you could make on a bank deposit.

But bank deposits are insured up to 100K by the FDIC.

Good point. But, if you want that level of safety, you make almost nothing. You don't make a ton on money market securities, either, but at least you're putting your cash to work and you're not risking it in the stock market where anything can happen, or the bond market, where interest rates could skyrocket and knock down the value of your holdings.

The following word associations should help here:

- Money market   Matures in 1 year or less, highly liquid, little default risk
- TAN's, BAN's, RAN's   Short-term Municipal Notes, TAN's most likely to be used
- Negotiable CD's   "Jumbo's." $100,000 min., excess uninsured by FDIC
- Repurchase Agrmt   We'll buy it right back for more money, agreed?
- Banker's Acceptance   Facilitates Foreign Trade, Matures 270 days Max.
- Commercial Paper   Unsecured Note, issued by Corps, 270 days Max Maturity

Also, not every testable term warrants a detailed discussion, so we will now expose you to other testable terms in bullet-point fashion. You'll see some of these again in practice questions and, perhaps, on the actual exam:

- Eurodollar deposit: U.S. dollar–denominated deposits at foreign banks or foreign branches of American banks.

- Eurodollar bond: A U.S. dollar–denominated bond issued by an overseas company and held in a foreign institution outside both the U.S. and the issuer's home nation. Eurodollar bonds are subject to fewer regulatory restrictions. They are not registered with the SEC and can be sold at lower interest rates than in the U.S.

- Eurobond: A bond issued in a currency other than the currency of the country or market in which it is issued.

- Yankee bond: A bond denominated in U.S. dollars and issued in the United States by foreign banks and corporations. Would not subject an American to currency exchange risk, since he's being paid in the U.S. currency.

- Disintermediation: investors pulling money out of bank deposits and investing them into higher returning debt securities.

- LIBOR: international rate that banks borrow from other banks at; stands for "London Inter-Bank Offered Rate."

- Demand note: a loan with no fixed term that is payable upon demand if the lender says, "pay up."

- Put bond/variable rate demand obligation: allows the investor to force the issuer to repurchase the bond, usually at par. Most valuable when rates are likely to rise.

PRACTICE:

30. All of the following pay interest subject to state taxes except
   A. GNMA
   B. FNMA
   C. Municipal securities
   D. T-Bills

31. The quote on your customer's T-bond is BID 101.12 - ASK 101.16. Therefore, she can sell her T-bond for

A. $1,013.75

B. $1,015.00

C. $1,011.20

D. $1,011.60

32. A quote for a T-bill is BID 5% - ASK 4.5%. What is true in this case?

A. the bid represents a higher price

B. the bid represents a lower price

C. the ask represents a lower price

D. the ask represents the suggested price by the FRB

33. BID 98 3/4 - ASK 99 1/2 would be a quote for a

A. T-bill

B. municipal serial bond

C. T-bond

D. corporate bond

34. All of the following are true of corporate zero coupon bonds except

A. interest is received at maturity

B. interest is taxed annually

C. the return to the investor is zero

D. the bonds pay no interest

35. Which of the following CMO's leaves the investor with the most prepayment risk?

A. PAC

B. TAC

C. ZAC

D. MAC

ANSWERS:

30. D – the states can't tax the interest on Treasury securities. The Feds don't tax most municipal securities, but the states can do what they want with muni's. GNMA, FNMA, and FHLMC are subject to tax at all levels.

31. A – 101 means $1,010. The "and 12" means "and 12/32nds." Multiply each 32nd by .3125 and move on with your life.

32. B – the steeper the discount, the lower the price. Wouldn't you rather buy something at a 5% discount than a 4.5% discount? So would the market maker.

33. D – has to be a corporate bond. T-bills are quoted as a % discount from par. T-bonds have the weird "spot + 32nd" thingie. And a "serial" issue is quoted in terms of yield.

34. C – be a good test taker. A good test taker would never believe choice "C," which is why choice C is the answer.

35. B – a TAC has a "target," while a PAC has a "plan." The other two are fictitious.

SUITABILITY

Let's not forget Michelle Montoya, our loyal client who seems to be bringing home more and more money every paycheck, most of which she wants to invest. Her risk tolerance only allows her to buy so much stock (equity); therefore, much of the new money she puts into her investment account goes into bonds and bond mutual funds. In fact, that's a pretty typical pattern—the older somebody gets, the more money they put in bonds as opposed to stock. No big surprise there. The older people get the more conservative their politics become, so why wouldn't their investments become more conservative as well?

Even most younger and middle-aged investors get the bejeezus scared out of them by the stock market's volatility, so they usually put a percentage of their investment capital into debt securities: bonds, certificates, notes, whatever the heck you want to call them. What type of bonds should Michelle be buying? Well, she isn't such a wimp that she requires the absolute umbilical safety provided by Treasuries. She is in a high tax bracket, and as we'll see in the chapter on municipal securities, municipal securities are for folks in high tax brackets. So, we originally allocated 25% of her money toward general obligation and revenue bonds issued by Cleveland, Chicago, and New York City, and we'll keep that as-is.

As she gets closer to retirement, let's stop putting new money into equities and put it, instead, into corporate bonds. Michelle enjoys receiving interest checks every six months, and who can blame her? She can either go shopping for clothes, or go shopping for more bonds that pay more interest, allowing her to buy more bonds that pay more interest. After running a risk profile, we conclude that Michelle is not a junk bond investor. The thought of default would keep her up at night, and as the great JP Morgan once told a panicked investor, "Sell down to the sleeping point."

Still, we don't want to insist on AAA (Aaa) ratings for *all* of the corporate bonds. That would put too much emphasis on safety and end up giving Michelle crummy yields. So, let's diversify her corporate bond holdings by allocating 20% to AAA, 20% to AA, 20% to A, and 40% to BBB. Those are all investment grade bonds, and while she takes on more default risk on the BBB-rated bonds, she balances that by putting 60% into bonds rated in the top three credit tiers.

That's how we deal with default risk—what about interest rates? As we saw at the beginning of this chapter, interest rates jump all over the place, sending bond prices all over the place, as well. Should we be wimps and buy bonds with short maturities? We could protect against interest rate risk that way, but what kind of yield do we get on short-term bonds? Really low rates, which is why corporations often borrow money short-term through commercial paper and why municipalities often borrow money short-term through anticipation notes (TAN's, BAN's, etc.). When you borrow short-term, you pay lower rates. So when you lend money short-term (buying short-term bonds) you *receive* low interest rates. Okay, so let's go as far out on the yield curve as possible to get the maximum yield possible. Sure, and as long as rates don't go up suddenly, we won't get crushed.

Hmm, too risky.

Here's an idea, let's buy some short-term, some intermediate-term, and some long-term bonds. Maybe you've heard a financial planner talk about building a "bond ladder" before. There are different ways to do it, but here's one way:

Let's buy an equal number of bonds that mature in one year, two years, three years, and so on up to a ten-year maturity. The bond that matures in one year will pay out the principal of $1,000 next year, and we'll simply use it to buy a 10-year bond. At that point, we'll again have bonds maturing in one year, two years, three years…up to 10 years. Every time the one-year bond matures, use the proceeds and buy a 10-year bond. This way, no matter where interest rates go, she'll have some short-term bonds that don't get hurt so much, and only so much of her money will be in the 10-year notes/bonds, whose market price will suffer the most.

So, we've now dealt with both default risk and interest rate risk by staggering the credit ratings and staggering the terms to maturity.

What happens if inflation rises? Well, that basically means that interest rates rise, and we just dealt with that by building our bond ladder, which puts only some of the bonds at high risk. The fact that her coupon payments will be less valuable…well, that's why we put money into equities, which are the most resilient in terms of fighting the ravages of inflation. What do we do about call risk, which is the risk that rates will go down? Well, we could give up some yield by purchasing non-callable bonds, or we could just live with the fact that some bonds will be called when rates fall. We'll take the proceeds and keep climbing the bond ladder all the way to retirement.

Also notice that within her municipal bond allocation we didn't buy bonds issued by just one municipality. While it's pretty rare that a city or state goes bankrupt, it can happen. And, if it did, wouldn't we look silly trying to explain to Michelle (and possibly her attorneys) why absolutely *every* last bond we bought was issued by the state that just did the unthinkable—default on its bonds. Or economic conditions in the Rust Belt could deteriorate, so we don't want all of our bonds issued in Indiana, Ohio, and Pennsylvania. Or the Southwestern U.S. could go into a tailspin, which is why we wouldn't want all the bonds issued by or within New Mexico, Texas, and Arizona. Or, Hurricane Katrina could hit and wipe out entire cities in three or four different states, making it really tough for the issuers to pay bond interest and principal.

Of course, we could theoretically make higher returns by buying the riskiest securities, but Michelle Montoya is a human being who has to sleep at night. Let's help her manage her risk and maintain her sanity. Remember that a customer's psychological profile is just as important as her financial needs when it comes to recommending an investment portfolio. Yes, Warren Buffett will make much higher returns than Michelle Montoya will with his big, well-researched-but-still-risky-as-heck bets. Then again, if Warren Buffett loses $10 million buying junk bonds, something tells me the lights will still be on at his house. And, I don't know about you, but if Michelle's $500,000 portfolio suddenly plummets to $100,000, I don't want to take her next phone call and try to explain the value of p-a-t-i-e-n-c-e, especially when her attorneys get on the line and start explaining the value of a-r-b-i-t-r-a-t-i-o-n.

Whenever Michelle has a short-term need for liquidity, we'll put some of her money into the money market. She started out with 5% there, and I don't see why we'd need to allocate more than that, unless she's planning on buying a house or investment property in the near future.

So, Michelle is invested in corporate stock and corporate bonds. She has a small percentage in "cash," which is like a hip way of saying "money market." And the rest of her portfolio is devoted to municipal bonds, which just happens to be the LARGEST section on your exam. And, coincidentally, the very next chapter in the book.

But first…

WHAT NOW?

- Review this chapter, taking notes on key concepts and possibly making flash cards. *Approximately 1.5 hours.*
- If you have the Pass the 7 QuizSet, take the Chapter 2 Quiz on Debt Securities. *Approximately 1 hour.*
- If you have the Audio CD set, listen to tracks 3 and 4 on Disc 1. *Approximately 35 minutes.*

CHAPTER 3

Municipal Securities

OVERVIEW

Benton Falls is a growing suburb of a large Midwestern city. Nestled between rolling hills to the east and a lazy, meandering river to the west, the town is often listed as one of the best places to live in America. The residents of Benton Falls enjoy an excellent public school system, thousands of acres of forest preserve and public parks, three museums, a world-class zoo, and several large, well-used public libraries.

How do they pay for all of it?

By taxing the heck out of property owners. See, the excellent schools, parks, and cultural venues the community boasts help to raise the property values in Benton Falls far above the national median. But, as property values rise, the residents become more affluent. And, the more affluent they become, the more they increase their demands for excellent schools, parks, and cultural venues.

Since the Benton Falls village budget is usually strained to the limit, whenever the good people of Benton Falls require an improvement in the public schools, libraries, or forest preserves, the village government has to sell bonds in order to raise the money required to make the improvement. For example, if the residents want to build a soccer complex within the park district, they first have to approve the issue by a vote authorizing the local government to borrow money through a bond sale. Why do they have to vote?

Because, ultimately, it's the voters who pay back the bond investors through property tax dollars.

This describes a general obligation bond, which is a legal obligation of a local government to pay back the bondholders out of the "general fund." The general fund includes property taxes, generally. So, it's property owners, generally, who end up paying for the improvements to schools, parks, roads and other essential services.

Therefore, property owners (and all registered voters) get to vote before the local government borrows money for a new school or park.

Of course, the nicer the schools and parks, the more valuable the properties are too, so many of these bonds actually do end up getting approved. But usually not without a fight.

On the other hand, a revenue bond doesn't have to be approved by the voters. See, sometimes a local government will come up with a public improvement project that "pays for itself." For example, governments have discovered, much to their delight and amazement, that drivers will actually pay money to drive on toll roads, even when there are plenty of free alternate routes available. So, if the project itself will end up generating revenue, the whole thing can be built with the proceeds of a revenue bond. Projects such as toll roads, airports, sports stadiums, and convention centers are often funded with revenue bonds, because those amenities can all generate plenty of revenue. Or maybe you've never paid $25 to park your car at a big-city sports stadium, plus $50 for mediocre seats, and $5 for a lukewarm, watered-down beer?

Anyway, since revenue bondholders aren't paid from general taxes, these revenue bonds can be issued without voter approval. The general obligation bonds, which are paid back from general taxes, have to be approved by the voters, who are generally taxed more and more all the time.

So, let's say that the good people of Benton Falls decide it's time to build a new high school. First, the school board hires a consulting company to draw up an estimate of all the costs involved with purchasing the land, building the school, et cetera. The

consulting firm performs the analysis and charges the school district half a million dollars to tell them the new high school will cost $20 million.

Sounds about right, the school board says. The school board then hires a local law firm to serve as the bond counsel. The bond counsel helps the school board draw up legal documents and renders a legal opinion that assures the school board that they do have the legal authority to issue the bonds; the bond interest will be federally tax exempt; and the bonds are not subject to the arduous filing requirements of the Securities Act of 1933. Since the bond counsel has no reservations, they issue what's known as an unqualified legal opinion.

While the school board and the bond counsel work out the legal details of the bond issue, a concerned parents group distributes flyers and holds town hall meetings to generate enthusiasm for the bond issue among the registered voters. The school board gets the referendum placed on the next ballot. In March, as residents vote in the presidential and senatorial primaries, they also vote to approve the school district's plan to borrow the $20 million through the issuance of general obligation bonds, all backed up by property taxes.

With the voter approval secured, the school district then starts looking for underwriters to sell the bonds to the public and, thereby, raise the needed $20 million. So, the school district publishes an official notice of sale in the Bond Buyer calling for competitive bids from potential underwriters. Underwriters are financial firms that make a living selling new issues of municipal bonds to investors. They buy the bonds from the issuer and re-sell them to the public for a profit, known as the "spread." An underwriter would pay close attention to the Bond Buyer in order to scout out business opportunities.

So, one morning a seasoned underwriter named Dale Crawford is sipping his morning coffee and spreading cream cheese over a cinnamon-raisin bagel as he peruses the daily Bond Buyer. On page 17, he sees that Benton School District 207-U is soliciting competitive, sealed bids for a new $20 million issue of general obligation bonds. Interested, he goes to the Bond Buyer's website and downloads a detailed official notice of sale. The official notice of sale states that the principal is to be repaid $1 million each year for 20 consecutive years. The coupon rates are left blank, since this is what potential underwriters must determine when they submit their bid. The issuer would like to see low coupon rates, since that represents the cost of borrowing the money. Investors, on the other hand, would like to see high coupon rates, since those same coupon rates represent the investors' return. So, experts like Dale have to use their skill and experience to find the perfect balance between giving the issuer the lowest cost of borrowing and giving investors incentive to buy the bonds.

Dale calls the principals at four other municipal underwriting firms, and the five firms form an underwriting group known as a syndicate.

Don't worry, this syndicate is perfectly legal. To "syndicate" something means to put it into general circulation, the way a local newspaper columnist can become a "syndicated columnist" appearing in 100 newspapers throughout the country, or the way Rush Limbaugh can be syndicated to virtually every radio market in America.

So, Dale's firm acts as the syndicate manager and holds a meeting the following Tuesday at their offices. The syndicate members carefully determine the coupon rates for each of the 20 maturities in the serial issue, giving higher yields to the later-maturing bonds, as investors generally expect to be compensated more when their money is tied up for a longer period of time. That phenomenon, by the way, is called a normal yield curve. In a normal yield curve bonds with, say, 20-year maturities will yield more than bonds that mature in 2 or 5 years. A quick glance at the financial section of your morning newspaper will show that rates/yields increase as you move from low-yielding T-bills (1 year), to higher-yielding T-notes (up to 10 years) and up to the highest-yielding of the three, T-bonds (up to 30 years). If not, you're looking at a rare situation known as an inverted yield curve, but let's get back to Dale and his syndicate before we get mired in a maze of minutiae.

When all the coupon rates are determined, the syndicate calculates the Net Interest Cost (NIC), which represents the School District's total cost of borrowing. Sometimes the True Interest Cost (TIC) is used instead. Think of the phrase tick-tock when you see the word TIC. Like a clock (tick-tock), TIC includes the TIME value of money. Whether we use NIC or TIC, we're looking at the issuer's cost of borrowing the money, so if this turns out to be the lowest of all the competitive bids, Dale's syndicate will win the underwriting business. Like any borrower, all the School District wants is to get the money at the lowest possible interest rate. That's all you care about when you get a mortgage, right? What's it going to cost you to borrow the money?

In order to have their bid considered, the syndicate has to put down a good faith deposit equal to 1% of the total par value or $200,000. The bids must be submitted to the School Board President by Friday, April 13th, twelve o'clock noon. Dale's syndicate submits the bid, with the good faith deposit attached, and nervously awaits the opening of the sealed bids.

When the bids are opened at noon on April 13th, Dale's syndicate does, in fact, win the bid, because if they didn't we'd have to start talking about a completely different made-up syndicate, which would make this whole thing even less interesting.

Assuming that's possible.

Anyway, since this is a firm commitment underwriting, Dale's syndicate signs a contract with the school board putting the syndicate on the hook for all the bonds. That means that the syndicate will either sell bonds to investors or buy them for their own account. One way or another, the School District will get their twenty million.

So, the pressure is on.

As manager, Dale draws up a syndicate letter that details all the terms for operation and sends a copy to each syndicate member. The spread is to be $10, meaning that the issuer will receive $1,000 per bond, but the investors will actually pay $1,010. The $10 spread is split into three pieces:

Manager's fee	1/8th point
Additional takedown	3/8ths point
Selling concession	1/2 point

In "bond points," which are each worth $10, that works out to $1.25 to the manager for every bond sold, $3.75 per bond to each syndicate member for their allotment of bonds, and $5.00 per bond to whoever sells the bonds. See, if the syndicate members can't sell their bonds, they let members of the selling group make the sale, and give them $5.00 per bond. It would be nice to make the full $8.75 (known as "total takedown"), but when you have to get the bonds sold, it's better to concede the $5 to a selling group member than end up eating the bonds for your own account.

Dale has to keep track of which sales are credited to which syndicate members, and that's part of the reason his firm gets $1.25 or 1/8th of a bond point per bond. The fact that his sister-in-law sits on the Benton Falls School Board, of course, has nothing to do with it.

The syndicate letter states that orders for the bonds will be received during the week of April 22nd. On Friday, April 26th at 4 o'clock the offering period ends, which means that the syndicate members had better get their bonds sold by that time, no exceptions.

Monday morning, April 22nd, the syndicate members start calling mutual funds, pension funds, and various high-net-worth individual investors. Luckily, Moody's has already attached their Aa1 rating to the bonds, and that makes the selling process a little easier. In fact, the issue is fully subscribed several hours before the deadline. There are actually more subscribers than bonds, so Dale imposes the order priority whereby all Pre-Sale orders are filled first, followed by Group Net orders, Designated orders, and, lastly, Member orders. An easy way to remember that priority is:

Please	Pre-Sale
Sell	Syndicate
Da'	Designated
Muni's	Member

That simply means that the pre-sale orders taken before Monday April 22nd get first priority. Yes, the big mutual funds usually put their orders in before anyone else, even before the bonds have been priced. In exchange for doing that, they're first in line to get their orders filled. After that, however, it's not first come–first served. The orders are filled according to their type. Syndicate or "group net" orders are credited to the whole syndicate. They take a higher priority than those Designated to a particular syndicate member. And the Member orders from syndicate members buying for their firm's own account are, naturally, the last to be filled.

Once Dale has sorted out which orders get filled, preliminary confirmations—sometimes called when-issued confirmations—are sent to the buyers. These confirmations tell each buyer how many bonds they will receive once the bonds are officially issued.

The following week the bonds are printed. Official statements disclosing the school district's financial condition and all the terms of the bond issue accompany all the final confirmations that are sent to the buyers. The buyers submit payment for the bonds, and Dale takes the proceeds and divvies up the spoils among the syndicate and selling group members. A check for the $20,000,000 (minus the 200K good faith deposit) is cut to Benton School District 207-U.

And everybody's happy.

Believe it or not, ground has already been broken for the new school, as the school board raised $1 million dollars ahead of the bond sale through what's called a Bond Anticipation Note or BAN. In anticipation of receiving the $20 million, in other words, the school district was able to talk a short-term tax-exempt money market mutual fund into fronting them a million bucks, just enough to get the general contractor and construction manager to show up and start putting up a new school. Or at least wear their hard hats for the awkward ribbon-cutting photo on the front page of the local paper.

At this point, then, everybody's happy. The parents are happy to drive by the construction site and dream of the new school their children will someday attend. The school board is happy that the district is expanding and operating in the black. The syndicate is happy to walk away with their spread or profit from underwriting and selling the bonds. And the investors are happily looking forward to their first tax-free interest payments.

What happens to the bonds now?

Many individuals simply lock them up in their safe-deposit boxes and keep them there until maturity, smiling all the way to the bank each time they receive their semi-annual, federally tax-exempt interest checks.

The mutual funds and pension funds might hold the bonds, or they might decide to trade them. There is, after all, a secondary market for municipal bonds. It is, however, not as liquid or active as the secondary market for, say, Treasury bonds, or corporate stock. A market maker for, say, MSFT common stock would be publishing Bid and Ask prices all day long, because there are plenty of shares to buy at one price (Bid) and sell at another price (Ask/offer) all throughout the day. But, since the secondary market for municipal bonds is much thinner, a municipal securities dealer usually only responds with either a Bid or an Offer. If somebody wants to sell a bond to the dealer, the dealer responds with a Bid, which represents what the dealer will pay for the bond (what the seller will receive). If somebody wants to buy a bond that the dealer has in inventory, the dealer responds with an Offer, which is what the dealer will sell the bond for (what the buyer will pay). In other words, if a mutual fund wants to sell a municipal bond to a dealer, the dealer might say, "Bid-98 1/2." That means the dealer will buy the bond for $985 if the seller wants to let go of the bond at that price. If a mutual fund wants to buy a bond from a dealer, the dealer might say, "Offered at 99 1/8," which means the dealer will sell the bond for $991.25, if the buyer is interested. Bonds are often sold in terms of their yield, so a dealer could say, "Bid-4.10," which means he will buy the bond from a seller at a price that represents a yield of 4.10%. Or, if a buyer wants to purchase a bond, the dealer could respond, "Offered at 3.85," which means the buyer can purchase the bond at a price representing a yield to maturity of 3.85%. Remember that yields and prices are inversely related, so the higher the yield, the lower the price, and vice versa.

That's enough background for now. Remember that the questions on municipal securities comprise the biggest section on your Series 7 exam, with the questions on Options a close second. If you can do well on those two sections, that will take the pressure off of everything else.

But before jumping into the exciting world of standardized options, let's first make sure you understand the many, many testable points on municipal securities.

Ready?

THE DETAILS OF MUNICIPAL SECURITIES

There are two main types of municipal bonds: general obligation and revenue. A good way to study is to take a piece of paper and write "GO" as one column heading and "Revenue" as the other. See if you can list everything associated with GO's and Revenue bonds in their proper category. And, do that on the scratch paper they give you at the testing center—it will help you get many, many municipal bond questions right. And getting many, many municipal bond questions right is the key to this exam. That, plus getting all the other questions right.

GENERAL OBLIGATION BONDS

The word "obligation" means that the municipality is legally obligated to pay the debt service (interest and principal) on the bonds issued. GO's are backed by the full faith and credit of the municipality, which is a key phrase to write under your "GO" heading. Where does a municipality get the money they'll need to pay off the bonds? Well, if necessary, they'll dip into all the sources of revenue available to a city or state, like parking fees, property taxes, fishing licenses, marriage licenses, whatever. And, if they have to, they'll even raise taxes in order to pay the debt service on a general obligation bond.

Whoah! Raise taxes?

You bet they will. That's why "GO's" require voter approval. So we can put "voter approval" under our "GO" heading.

Since municipalities get a major chunk of their revenue from property taxes, a "GO" bond will also be associated with property taxes. The test wants you to know a fancy phrase for property taxes, which is ad valorem, so let's write it down now under "GO."

Just need to memorize it. It means property taxes.

A municipality might assess property at 50% of its market value. So, a home with a market value of $500,000 would have an assessed value of only half that, or $250,000. As a homeowner, you take the assessed value of your home and multiply it by a rate known as the millage rate to find your tax bill. If the millage rate is "7 mills," that just means you multiply the assessed value of $250,000 by .007 to get a tax bill of $1,750.

If you see the term "millage," you're looking at a GO bond. If the test makes you figure somebody's tax bill, first of all remind it that you're not a qualified tax professional, and, second, remember that "mill" means "thousand." Seven "mills" means there is a 7 in the thousandth place (.007). Multiply the assessed value by that many thousandths and move on with your life.

Some municipalities limit the number of mills that can be levied against property. If so, they might end up issuing limited tax bonds, which means property tax rates can only go so high to pay the debt service on a particular GO. When certain limits have been placed on the types of taxes or tax rates used to back the bonds, the bonds are referred to as "limited tax bonds." In order to keep the voters happy, maybe the city council or state legislature insisted that the bonds could only be issued if the taxes used to finance them were limited. So, they're still general obligation bonds, but analysts would be mindful that the taxes used to support them are limited in some way. Also, most issuers keep their borrowing in check by imposing a debt limit. Tell the exam that the debt limit is the maximum amount of general obligation debt that an issuer can have outstanding at any one time. By keeping their general obligation debt within a certain limit, the municipality can protect residents from excessive taxes.

REVENUE BONDS

Revenue bonds are still municipal securities. The difference is that the issuer doesn't put the "full faith and credit" behind the debt service payments. A revenue bond identifies a specific source of revenue, and only that revenue can be used to pay the interest and principal on the bond. User fee is the first phrase you should associate with "revenue bond." Have you ever driven on a tollway? What did you drop in the basket? A user fee, right? Well, that money you put in the toll basket helped to pay the debt service on the revenue bond issued to build the tollway. If money problems arise, we won't raise property taxes. We'll raise the tolls, the user fees. You don't like the higher tolls? Use the freeway. But, homeowners aren't affected one way or another since their property taxes cannot be used to finance the toll road—only your generous quarters can be used for that.

Since we don't have property tax on the table, we don't need any type of voter approval. So you never want to associate "voter approval" with a revenue bond. That belongs under the "GO" heading. You might even put "no voter approval" under your Revenue Bond heading, just to help keep that highly testable point straight.

There are other ways that a municipality could identify specific sources of revenue for a bond issue. For example, if the residents of a county wanted their roads paved, the county could levy a special tax on gasoline throughout the county and let motorists pay for the new roads each time they fill up their tanks. This "special tax" will be used to pay the debt service on the revenue bonds, which are issued to raise the money required to pave the roads. That's an example of a special tax bond, a type of revenue bond. Any tax that is not a property or sales tax is considered a special tax, including taxes on business licenses, excise taxes, and taxes on gasoline, tobacco, hotel/motel, and alcohol. The exam might even refer to these as "sin taxes" if it's feeling especially judgmental on testing day.

There are also special assessment bonds. Say that a wealthy subdivision experiences problems with their sidewalks. The concrete is chipped, threatening the property values of the homes in the exclusive subdivision. The residents want the municipality to fix the sidewalks. The municipality says, okay, as long as you pay a special assessment on your property, since you're the only ones who'll benefit from this improvement. That special assessment will be the revenue used to pay the debt service on a special assessment bond, which is issued to raise the money to fix the sidewalks.

Isn't it a neat process? We identify a future source of revenue, like tolls, park entrance fees, or special taxes on gasoline. Then, we issue some debt securities against this new source of revenue we're creating. We take the proceeds from selling the debt securities and get the project built. Then those revenues we identified come in, and we use them to pay the interest and, eventually, the principal due to investors who bought the bonds.

In fact, you might find it interesting that right after the state attorneys general settled with the big tobacco companies for billions of dollars, those states immediately borrowed money by issuing revenue bonds backed by the payments that big tobacco companies would be making in the future. So these states who act as if they want to stamp out Big Tobacco actually cannot afford to let Phillip Morris go out of business since they've already borrowed against the money that Phillip Morris, RJR Reynolds, etc. will be paying the states for years to come.

And you were afraid that municipal securities would turn out to be a dull subject—not on my watch. In any case, cities like Chicago and New York have public housing projects, which are under HUD, a unit of the federal government. Municipalities issue PHA (Public Housing Authority) or NHA (New Housing Authority) bonds to raise money for housing projects. The debt service is backed by the rental payments, which are in turn backed by contributions from Uncle Sam. PHA's and NHA's are considered the safest revenue bond because of this guaranteed contribution from the federal government. Sometimes they are referred to as "Section 8" bonds because everything needs at least three names.

Industrial Development Revenue Bonds carry the same credit rating as the corporation occupying the facility. The issuing municipality does not back the debt service in any way. The debt service will be paid from lease payments made by a corporation, and it's the corporation that backs the debt service. As you know, corporations (can you say pets-dot-com?) have been known to go belly-up occasionally. If they're the ones backing up the debt service, you can imagine what happens when they themselves no longer have any assets behind them.

Ouch.

And if it happens the issuer won't be there to bail out the bondholders. Here's how it works. A municipality tells a software company they'd like to build them a new corporate campus. All the corporation has to do is sign a long-term lease with the city. Those lease payments will cover the debt service.

We hope.

And if not, oh well.

Like we said, Industrial Development Revenue Bonds are only backed by the occupying corporation's full faith and credit.

Whatever that's worth.

Revenue bonds will be issued under what's known as an indenture, sometimes called the bond resolution. That's just a contract in which the issuer makes promises known as protective covenants.

- If you were thinking of buying one of these revenue bonds backed only by the revenue generated at the facility, you would probably be pleased to know that the **rate covenant** allows the facility to charge higher and higher rates if that's what it takes to pay you your interest and principal.

- A **maintenance covenant** is a promise to keep the tollroad or sports stadium properly maintained—if not, no one would be willing to pay to use the thing, right?

- The **insurance covenant** means that the facility is insured against, say, a tornado or a lawsuit filed by the widow of a rowdy football fan who tumbles down a flight of concrete steps after being over-served.

- The **books and audit covenant** means that you don't have to just take the issuer's word for it when they say that all the expenses are being covered and there will be no problem paying you your interest and principal—the books are subject to an outside audit by an accounting firm.

- The **nondiscrimination covenant** promises that political heavy hitters and their families will also have to pay to use the stadium, tollroad, convention center, etc.

The bond indenture would contain the flow of funds statement. This tells us whether debt service is to be paid right off the top (gross revenue pledge) or after operating expenses have been paid (net revenue pledge). The indenture tells the bondholders whether future bonds can be issued giving those bondholders equal status with the original bondholders should the whole thing go belly up. The exam might say that if your bond issue were a "closed-end issue" future bonds would have a "junior lien" or subordinate status to yours if the project goes belly up. If you are buying an "open-end issue," future bonds would have equal status with yours, as long as the issuer passes the "additional bonds test." The additional bonds test is just a document showing that the project will generate plenty of revenue to pay the original bondholders as well as the future bondholders.

So, we have two main types of municipal bonds: GO's and Revenue Bonds. There are many different types of revenue bonds, but they all have one thing in common: they identify a specific source of revenue that can be used to pay debt service, while GO's can dip their hands into many different piles to pay the debt service.

Double Barrel

A hospital is something that benefits the whole community, which is why the issuer might put its "full faith and credit" behind the bond issue used to build or expand the hospital. However, hospitals also generate revenues, which can also be used to pay debt service. In this case, the issuer has two sources of revenue to pay debt service, which is why we call it a double-barreled bond. Anything backed by full faith and credit *and* revenues is called a "double-barreled bond." Since the full faith and credit of the issuer backs the issue, we consider this to be a GO.

Moral Obligation

A special type of revenue bond is known as a moral obligation bond. While revenue bonds are only serviced by specific sources of revenue, a moral obligation bond provides for the possibility of the issuer going to the legislature and convincing them to honor the "moral obligation" to pay off the debt service. This is a moral obligation, not a legal one.

TAN, RAN, BAN, TRAN

Remember how corporations will borrow money short-term at low interest rates by issuing commercial paper?

Sure you do, we just talked about it in the debt securities chapter. Anyway, municipalities can borrow money more cheaply by borrowing short-term (just like you get a lower interest rate on a 15-year than a 30-year mortgage). Municipalities issue "anticipation notes," meaning the notes will be paid off by some money they anticipate receiving very soon. If property taxes won't be collected for another three months, why wait? Why not borrow the money now from a pension fund or a tax-exempt money market mutual fund? We call that a TAN for "tax anticipation note." Maybe the revenues from the tollway system will be collected in a few weeks, but, again, why wait? Why not borrow the money from an institution by selling them a RAN or "revenue anticipation note"? Maybe we want to back up the note with both taxes *and* revenues—if so, let's get real creative and call it a TRAN for "tax & revenue anticipation note."

But my personal favorite has to be the BAN or "bond anticipation note." The school district has a big bond issue coming out that will supply hordes of cash, but, again, why wait? Why not borrow the money now by issuing a bond anticipation note. In other words, the school district goes to the money market mutual fund and says, "Hey, we'd like to borrow some money because we're about to borrow some money."

Whatever, dude. As long as you pay us back and it's tax-free, why not?

How do you know if these notes are good credit risks? Moody's and S&P both rate them. If the note receives a "MIG" rating, that means it is high enough to be a "Moody's Investment Grade" obligation. S&P uses "SP1, SP2, and SP3" to indicate how solid the note is.

So, when they need to borrow money for a new school, municipalities borrow long term by issuing bonds. When they just need a few million until next payday, they'll issue notes and pay lower interest rates. No different from how the federal government borrows long-term through T-bonds and short-term through T-bills. Different needs, different rates of interest paid.

REFUNDING/ADVANCE REFUNDING

When do homeowners refinance their mortgages? When interest rates are falling, right? Homeowners paying 8% might get tired of servicing their debt at that rate when prevailing interest rates are falling well below 8%, right?

Well, municipalities feel the same way. If a municipality is paying 8% on a bond issue when interest rates are falling to 6%, they might want to issue a new batch of bonds paying just 6% and use the proceeds to pay off the creditors currently costing them 8%. If the bond issue has passed its legal call protection period, the municipality could borrow new money at the lower interest rate and use some of it to pay off the current loan, just like a homeowner refinancing a mortgage long before he's even started paying the sucker off. This is known as refunding. Just means replacing expensive debt with cheaper debt.

If the bond issue had not reached the first call date, the municipality could still issue cheaper debt at 6% and put the proceeds in escrow. The proceeds earn interest on treasury securities, and as soon as the first call date is reached, the municipality uses the proceeds to call or "buy back" the outstanding bonds. Here, they've refunded the outstanding debt in advance of the first call date, which is why we call this advance refunding or "pre-refunding."

The exam might expect you to know that once a bond has been advance refunded, its credit rating becomes triple-A, since the money needed to pay off the debt is already parked in an escrow account. Or, to mess with you, they might say that "its liquidity increases," which is another way of saying the same thing. A safe secure bond is easy to sell/liquidate, which is why the price is high and the yield is low. A shaky bond is tough to sell/liquidate, which is why the price is low and the yield is high.

Again, this is all a far cry from rocket science.

ISSUING MUNI'S

Issuing municipal bonds involves a very detailed legal process, so the issuer hires a bond counsel to guide them through the legalities.

Bond Counsel

A bond counsel is simply a law firm specializing in public finance and the complexities of guiding a bond issue through the city council, the voters, the state legislature, etc. The bond counsel provides a "legal opinion" in which they attest to the following:

- Issuer's Authority to Borrow
- Tax-Exempt Status of the interest

There are two types of testable opinions that the bond counsel could render: qualified and unqualified. While we always want our attorneys to be qualified, we don't necessarily want their opinions to be qualified. A "qualified" opinion means that something is in doubt. The attorneys have attached "qualifiers" to their opinion.

What the issuer hopes for is an "unqualified" opinion from the bond counsel. That means everything looks fine to the bond counsel.

Finding the Underwriters

So, municipalities are forever borrowing money. They raise money by selling bonds, and those bonds are taken to the capital markets by underwriters, who keep part of the proceeds for their trouble. We call the part of the proceeds kept by the underwriters "the spread." So, underwriters are the municipal securities firms who raise money for municipalities by lining up interested investors. How do municipalities find underwriters interested in making the spread? By advertising in the daily Bond Buyer. Through an official notice of sale, the issuer announces to prospective underwriters that they would like to raise a certain amount of money. They tell the underwriters what type of bond—GO or revenue—what they need the money for, how soon they want to pay it back, when the bids will be accepted, where to send the bid, how much of a "good faith deposit" is required, etc.

Actually, what's published in the Bond Buyer is a summary official notice of sale. Interested municipal underwriters would then download the full official notice of sale and the bid form they'll need to complete. These underwriters join a group called a "syndicate." First thing the syndicate does is figure out the coupon rates that the bonds will have to pay, with each maturity year paying a slightly higher yield. Then, they figure out how much they'll have to pay the issuer for the bonds, and how high they can re-sell them to the investors. Again, the difference between those two prices is the "spread" that the underwriting syndicate makes.

Municipalities want the lowest debt service they can possibly get, which is why they always award their business to the group of underwriters who can sell bonds to the public at the lowest cost to the municipality. We call that cost the Net Interest Cost, or NIC. That's all the municipality cares about—the lowest net interest cost, which is their cost of borrowing money from the public. Net interest cost is basically the total cost of all the interest payments the issuer will make until the bonds are retired. If bonds are purchased from the issuer at a discount, that amount is *added* to the net interest cost, and if bonds are purchased at a premium, that amount is *subtracted*. In other words, if the issuer pays back more than they received, that has to be added to their cost of borrowing, and when they receive more than they pay out at maturity, that's subtracted. TIC stands for "true interest cost." TIC factors in the time value of money. Whether the issuer is using NIC or TIC, they're looking at the cost of borrowing the money, which is all they care about.

If it's a GO, the municipality will take competitive, sealed bids from potential underwriters. If it's a revenue bond, they'll just select a group of underwriters and hammer out the terms in a negotiated underwriting. What the issuer is looking for in either case is the lowest cost of borrowing available, whether measured as NIC or TIC. So, if it's a competitive underwriting, maybe the Director of Public Finance or the School Board President will open the sealed bids at noon on such-and-such a date, awarding the underwriting to the syndicate who turned in the lowest NIC or TIC.

The bidding syndicates have already made a good faith deposit. The ones who lost get the deposit back. The winning syndicate has simply made their deposit on a big batch of bonds that need to be unloaded in the near future. Most municipal underwritings are done on a "firm commitment basis," which means the winning syndicate is going to buy all the bonds from the issuer, whether they end up selling them to investors or not.

Da' Syndicate

Again, da' syndicate makes da' "spread," which is just the difference between what they pay the municipality for the bonds and the price at which they sell the bonds to the public. Say the issuer gets $990 per bond, and the syndicate sells the bonds to the public for $1,000 each. That's a spread of $10 per bond. How does that $10 get split?

Into four pieces. One of the underwriters will act as the manager. They'll take some money right offa' the top. Then, the underwriting expenses get deducted. The syndicate members will get the next piece of the spread, known as the "additional takedown," split according to each member's share of the bonds. Whoever sells a bond gets the last and biggest piece, the concession. A syndicate member who sells a bond from their allotment would get the additional takedown plus the concession. Those two pieces are known together as the "total takedown." If you want the "total takedown," you have to sell a bond; if somebody else sells one of your bonds, you give up or "concede" the concession, keeping only the "additional takedown," which is the piece that syndicate members get, one way or the other.

See, in order to make sure the bonds get sold, the syndicate might let other broker-dealers help sell them. If another broker-dealer sells a bond for the syndicate, the syndicate gives the B/D the concession. They "concede" that portion of the spread, in other words. These broker-dealers outside the syndicate make up a group of sellers, so the industry creatively dubbed them the "selling group."

Okay. A bond point is worth $10. How much is a half-point worth?

$5.

Quarter-point?

$2.50.

Eighth of a point?

$1.25.

And so on.

So let's say the spread is $10. That means that the bond is sold for $10 more than the issuer receives—how does that $10 get split up?

Let's say the manager gets 1/4 point or $2.50. That's the Manager's Fee.

The underwriting expenses equal 1/8 point or $1.25.

The syndicate members get 1/4 point or $2.50. That's the additional takedown.

Whoever sells the bond gets the 3/8 point concession, or $3.75.

So, if the manager sells a bond, they cover the expenses of $1.25 and keep the rest of the spread—$8.75. If a syndicate member sells one of their bonds, they keep what's called the "total takedown" or $6.25. In other words, the manager gets their piece, or $2.50, and $1.25 goes to cover expenses. The rest of the $10 goes to the syndicate member who sold their bond. If somebody outside the syndicate sells bonds, that dealer keeps the selling concession. In that case the member of the "selling group" keeps $3.75. The syndicate member who let them sell their bond gets $2.50. $1.25

covers underwriting expenses, and the manager—as always—gets their manager's fee of $2.50.

As Al Capone would attest, it's good to be the manager of the syndicate.

Since the syndicate is at risk for these bonds, the big question is, "What happens say we don't sell all a' these bonds?" Answers to these and other questions are agreed to among the underwriters in a document called, ironically, the "agreement among underwriters." To make sure it has at least two names, the exam might also call this the "syndicate letter," where the terms of the underwriting are laid out for all syndicate members to see.

Two types of syndicate accounts: Western and Eastern. Under a Western/divided account, a syndicate member only has to worry about selling their share of the bonds. If they sell their allotment, they walk.

Western walks.

Under an Eastern/undivided account, all syndicate members are responsible for selling their bonds, as well as their share of any unsold bonds. If a syndicate member gets 10% of the bonds and sells their entire allotment, that's great. But if the other clowns don't do so good, leaving the syndicate with 1,000 unsold bonds, the member is going to be responsible for 10% of those, too. So even though the member sold their allotment, they're going to have to sell 100 more bonds, worth about $100,000. If they can't sell them, they eat them.

Eastern eats.

Remember:

> Western walks.   Eastern eats.

Sometimes the darned muni's sell like hotcakes, though, and we don't worry about unsold bonds. Now we have the opposite problem as a syndicate, which is that there are more buyers than bonds. What happens if the issue is "oversold" or "oversubscribed"? Well, we could do several paragraphs on this process, or we could just remember the following mnemonic:

> Please
> Sell
> Da'
> Muni's

Which is designed to help you remember the order for allocating oversold municipal securities:

> Pre-Sale
> Syndicate (or "Group Net Order")
> Designated
> Member

Official Statement

The most detailed information about an issuer's financial condition is found in the Official Statement. This is what is delivered with final confirmation of the purchase to the investor. If the official statement isn't quite ready, the issuer can prepare a preliminary official statement. Either way, municipal underwriters have to make sure that if an official statement is prepared it is delivered to all buyers of the bonds. As the MSRB explains:

> Official statements typically include information regarding the purposes of the issue, how the securities will be repaid, and the financial and economic characteristics of the issuer with respect to the offered securities. Investors may use this information to evaluate the credit quality of the securities. Although functionally equivalent to the prospectus used in connection with registered securities, an official statement for municipal securities is exempt from the prospectus requirements of the Securities Act of 1933.

There you have it.

Wrap-up

So, what just happened? The issuer needed to raise some money. They hired the bond counsel to guide them through all the legalities. They found underwriters through the official notice of sale in the Bond Buyer and ended up getting the lowest cost of borrowing possible through a competitive bidding process. The winning underwriting syndicate sold the bonds to investors for the highest price possible and kept the difference between that price and the price they paid to the issuer for the bonds. The issuer ended up with the money they needed to raise. The underwriters ended up with their piece of the profits or "spread." And, the investors ended up with municipal bonds that will pay interest checks twice a year that will usually be tax-exempt at the federal level.

BOND BUYER

The daily Bond Buyer is the information source for the primary market, meaning the new-issue market where municipalities raise money through their underwriting syndicate. If your firm is a municipal securities underwriter, you're receiving this newspaper and reading it every day. The exam might want you to say that the Bond Buyer provides information on the primary market, even though there is actually some secondary (trading) market info in there as well. Underwriters could see the total par value of municipal securities that are about to be offered in the next 30 days. This is called the "visible supply." If we're about to do a primary offering of municipal securities, we might want to know how many other bonds are trying to be absorbed by the market, right? We also might want to see how well the market absorbed the bonds offered last week, called the "placement ratio." The placement ratio tells us the dollar amount sold out of the dollar amount offered the previous week. If the market tried to absorb $100 million par value of muni's last week but only ended up absorbing $90 million, that's a placement ratio of 90%, meaning some of the underwriters are sitting on some bonds they would have rather sold.

The Bond Buyer is where underwriters find Official Notices of Sale announcing the issuer's need to raise X amount of money by a certain date in order to build a school, road, hospital, etc. Actually, what we see in the Bond Buyer is a summary official notice of sale, which gives us info on how to get the full official notice of sale, complete with a bid form that we can use to try to come up with the lowest NIC/TIC required to win the underwriting business through a competitive bid. Or, maybe we prefer to contact the issuer willing to do a negotiated underwriting in order to, you know, negotiate.

There are also various indices published in the Bond Buyer, which I'll simply list as bullet points:

- REVDEX 25: yield-based index tracking the revenue bond market. A weekly index of 25 revenue bonds with 30 years to maturity rated A or higher. Remember, rising yields equals falling prices.
- 40 Bond Index: a daily price-based index comprised of 40 GO and revenue bonds. This one's based on price, remember, which is inversely related to yield, as we may have mentioned about 1,000 times at this point.
- 20 Bond Index: weekly index comprised of 20 GO bonds with 20 years to maturity rated A or higher.
- 11 Bond Index: weekly index comprised of 11 of the 20 bonds from the 20-bond index, rated AA or higher. These yields will be lower than yields on the 20 Bond Index because the average quality of these 11 bonds is higher.

SECONDARY MARKET

Municipal bonds do trade in the secondary market, but not as actively as corporate stocks and bonds or Treasury bonds. If a school district raises $2,000,000 by issuing bonds, how many bonds are there to trade?

2,000 if the denominations are $1,000, and just 400 if the denominations are

$5,000. In other words, there's very little liquidity in some of these issues. That's why a municipal bond dealer will usually only provide *either* a bid or an offer price. If you want to buy a municipal bond, the dealer will quote you an offer price; if you want to unload a municipal bond, the dealer will give you a bid. If you like the dealer's price, you have a deal. If not, storm out of the showroom and wait for the inevitable phone call explaining the amazing discount that was just approved four seconds ago by the sales manager.

Sometimes a broker-dealer will have a customer come in trying to liquidate some municipal bond no one at the office has ever heard of. The broker-dealer will submit a "bids wanted" to see what various municipal bond dealers will pay for the customer's funky municipal bond. If the customer wanted to buy a funky municipal bond no one's ever heard of, the firm could send out an "offers wanted" to see how much the various dealers would charge for the bonds.

Since most municipal securities are issued under a serial maturity with different yields for different maturity years, quotes are usually given in terms of yield to maturity. If the municipal bond dealer says "it's offered at 5.60," that means he'll sell the bond at a price that makes the yield to maturity 5.6%. That was a firm quote, by the way, meaning the dealer will do the deal at that price. Had he said, "looks like the offer is around 5.60," that would have been a nominal quote. He's just sharing information there, but if he gives a firm quote, he has to honor it. Muni dealers who publish quotes can only publish firm quotes. The nominal quotes are between the dealer and an interested party. Sometimes we'll call these "workable indications." The nice, little old lady sitting in the broker-dealer's office wants to liquidate 1,000 bonds issued 20 years ago by a small school district in rural South Dakota. The broker-dealer calls a municipal bond dealer asking for a workable indication or a "likely bid" the dealer would pay for the bonds. The language used by the municipal securities dealer would be vague, with phrases such as the following attached to his nominal quote:

- It looks like
- Subject
- Last I saw
- It's around

When we get down to doing the deal, the dealer will then give a firm quote, but right now they're just feeling the situation out.

Since most municipal securities usually don't trade actively, time isn't as critical as it is when trading stocks. Therefore, dealers sometimes give "out firm with recall" quotes. Maybe the dealer will give you a firm quote that's good for the next hour.

However, if somebody else calls, he'll call you back and give you 5 minutes to make up your mind.

Municipal securities dealers publish quotes on particular bonds and report the trades taking place to a service called Munifacts. Remember that Munifacts provides secondary market quotes for municipal securities. So does Bloomberg.

CREDIT RISK ANALYSIS

How would an investor know a strong municipal bond issuer from a weak one? Same way he'd do it for a corporate bond—Moody's, S&P, and Fitch, known as "statistical ratings agencies."

Just as we did at the beginning of the detailed look at municipal securities, a municipal bond analyst at Moody's, S&P or Fitch would also keep GO's and Revenue Bonds in separate categories. He would analyze a GO with much different criteria than he would use to analyze a revenue bond.

GO Analysis

A GO is backed by the full faith and credit of a municipality. Where does a municipality get the money needed to back up this sweeping promise to pay debt service?

That's right, mostly from taxpayers. So, what is the general attitude toward taxes and debt in the municipality? A GO analyst wants to know that for sure. How close is the municipality to any self-imposed debt limit? If it's already close to the limit, an analyst might not like to see another bond issue going out at this point. Are residents moving in and bringing their tax dollars with them, or are they moving away and taking their tax dollars with them? Are jobs coming in or fleeing the municipality? What's the economic health? Are the residents affluent? Less so? What about the city's, county's or state's budget—are there any big underfunded pension liabilities that they are *also* legally obligated to pay? The exam may bring up the "underfunded pension liability," since so many states and other issuers have big, fat, pension fund obligations that no one seems to know how they'll be able to pay. If an analyst is judging the issuer's ability to repay the bondholders, seeing that the issuer has also promised to pay out about $2 billion more than they apparently have to state workers is not going to help the credit rating.

In short, the issuer is the borrower. Do they have enough money from tax revenues versus their obligations to assure that bond holders will not get stiffed? If so, they get a good credit rating. If they're in way over their heads, their bonds get a lower rating, which means they have to offer higher yields to investors, just as someone with a low credit score has to pay a higher rate on his mortgage.

The Debt Statement

A municipality has two types of debt: direct debt and overlapping debt. For example, Chicago has debt for which it is directly responsible, but since Chicago also comprises part of Cook County, the city is responsible for some of Cook County's debt, too. In other words, the debt is coterminous or overlapping. If a city made up, say, 10% of the county, the city would be responsible for 10% of the county's debt. A city or county could also have coterminous/overlapping debt with school districts, water and sewer districts, park districts, etc. We just take the geographical area that the city comprises of the other taxing body and hold the city responsible for that percentage of the overlapping taxing body's debt. To find a municipality's "net overall debt" or "total direct and overlapping debt," we just add the municipality's direct debt to the overlapping debt.

Revenue Bond Analysis

Now, a project built by a revenue bond functions more like a small business and is analyzed accordingly. Here, we don't really care about taxes and debt and other boring concerns like that. We just want to know if the proposed enterprise is going to fly, baby, so we order a feasibility study. Just like a new business. Is there a legitimate need for the project? If it's a ski lodge, it's not feasible to build it just east of Orlando, Florida, is it? Is there existing competition? If it's a ski lodge just west of Aspen or Vale, Colorado, do we really think it can compete? And, most important, on paper does there appear to be more money coming in the front door than blowing out the back door? Analysts want to see available revenues that are twice as large as the debt service they'll be used to pay. That would be a debt service coverage ratio of 2:1. Just means there's twice as much coverage as debt, and that's a good thing.

Revenue bonds fund projects that generate revenues, and those revenues are what the municipality uses to pay the debt service. The order in which debt service will be paid is stated in the bond indenture and is called the flow of funds statement. Under a gross pledge, debt service is paid first, out of gross income. Under a net pledge, operations and maintenance (expenses) are paid first, followed by debt service, which is paid out of net revenue. So it's just a question of whether debt service is paid off the top (gross pledge) or after something else (net pledge).

Once the facility has been built by a revenue bond issue, the facility might need to be expanded or improved. In order to raise the necessary funds, the municipality could issue additional bonds backed up by the revenues generated by the facility. In order to do that, they have to pass the additional bonds test. Just means that on paper they can show that debt service on the outstanding bonds plus debt service on the new bonds can be covered sufficiently by the revenues generated by the facility. If the outstanding bonds had been issued under an open-end indenture, that's all the issuer has to do. If the bonds had been issued under a closed-end indenture, the issuer would have to make the new bondholders junior/subordinate creditors to the original bondholders.

Aren't you glad you know that?

TAXATION

If the bond is issued for "public purpose" and is providing an essential service, the federal government will not tax the interest on the bond. That's the interest.

Capital Gains

Capital gains are a different story. If you buy a muni bond from somebody at $900 and sell it later for $980, you have a capital gain to deal with. Figuring your gain or loss involves many steps, unfortunately. In fact, you might feel as if you've mistakenly signed up for the CPA exam, but this is actually much easier than it seems.

No, really.

First of all, if a municipal bond is purchased at a premium, that premium has to be amortized or "stepped down" over the holding period. If you buy a bond for $1,100, you've paid $100 above the par value. If you hold that bond until maturity, you'll lose $100 when the thing pays out only $1,000. Well, the IRS doesn't want you to wait until maturity to take a big loss all in one year. The IRS wants you to take a little bit of that loss every year that you hold the bond. If the bond matures in 10 years, the IRS wants you to take 1/10th of your loss every year, or $10. So, if you buy a bond that matures in ten years for $1,100, you will take a $10 loss each year on your tax returns.

The template that you'll use for the test question looks like this:

Price

- Par

= Premium

Divided by Term =

Amortize/year

X

Holding period =

Adjustment

Say the test question looked like this:

Some dude buys some muni bond at, like, 120. The bond will, like, mature in 10 years. So, like, what is the dude's capital gain or loss at, like, maturity?

No problem.

The price paid was $1,200, so we put that on top and see that we have a $200 premium. Like this:

Price	$1,200
- Par	$1,000
= Premium	$200

The bond will mature in 10 years, so we divide the $200 over 10 years, like this:

Price	$1,200
- Par	$1,000
= Premium	$200
Divided by term =	10 years
Amortize/year	$20/year

How long did the investor hold the bond?

The full term. So, we multiply the $20/year by the full 10 years to get a total adjustment of $200. Like this:

Price	$1,200
- Par	$1,000
= Premium	$200
Divided by term =	10 years
Amortize/year	$20/year
X	X
Holding Period =	10 years
Adjustment	$200

Now, we go to the master template for capital gains/losses, which just takes Proceeds minus Adjusted Cost. The proceeds when the bond matures would be $1,000. The investor originally paid $1,200, but we adjust that cost DOWN by the $200 adjustment to get an adjusted cost of $1,000, too. So, the investor has no gain/loss at maturity:

Proceeds	$1,000
- Adjusted Cost	$1,000 ($1,200 paid less $200 adjustment)
= Gain/Loss	ZERO

For a premium bond, remember to subtract the amount of the adjustment from the original price paid by the investor. Amortize = subtract.

Whenever an investor holds the bond for the full term there is no gain or loss at maturity…simply because it was dealt with year by year. Let's say in that question we just examined the investor had held the bond only six years before selling it @110. We would use the same template, but some of the numbers would change:

Price	$1,200
- Par	$1,000
= Premium	$200
Divided by term =	10 years
Amortize/year	$20/year
X	X
Holding Period	6 years
Adjustment	$120

So now the investor's proceeds are $1,100 (sold @110) and the adjusted cost is the original $1,200 minus the $120 adjustment, or $1,080.

Proceeds	$1,100
- Adj Cost	$1,080 (original $1,200 minus the $120 adjustment)
= Gain	$20

In this case the investor has a gain, then, of $20. And he'll pay capital gains taxes on that money to your friends and mine at the IRS.

So, if the investor holds the bond the full term, there will be no gain or loss at maturity. If the investor sells the bond after a few years, he could have a gain or a loss, depending on the numbers you plug into the template.

All premium bonds are amortized on the test, so it doesn't matter whether the investor bought it from the issuer at a premium or from some investor for a premium. Discount bonds are a different story. If Max Gaines buys a bond from Joe Kuhl @98, you don't do anything special. If Max holds the bond until maturity, he'll make $20 on it (buy at $980, matures at $1,000). That twenty bucks will be taxed as interest income by the IRS, who likes to keep everything nice and simple.

If the bond is purchased at a discount, the investor has to do something special called accretion, which is a fancy word that means "add to." Amortization means subtract from; accretion means add to. Accountants would probably call it stepping down (amortize) or stepping up (accrete) the investor's cost basis, but everybody's really saying the same thing. Whatever we call it, the concept is that only original issue discount (OID) bonds are accreted tax-free. If the investor buys a bond on the secondary market at a discount, the amount she receives later above her purchase price will be taxable, in order to keep the tax code nice and simple just like Congress and the IRS like it.

This is where the concept of zero coupon bonds intersects with the concept of tax-free interest on a municipal bond. Remember how zero coupon bonds work—the investor's interest income received is the difference between the price paid and the amount received at the end. So, that's not a buy and a sell; it's just a funky way of receiving interest all at the end. A municipal bond could be sold as a zero coupon bond at $500 (originally issued at a discount), maturing in 10 years at par, or $1,000. That means the investor would make the $500 difference as interest income. Interest income is tax-free on municipal securities, so we aren't going to tax the poor guy on the difference between $500 (paid) and $1,000 (received). He's not realizing a capital gain—this is just how a zero coupon bond pays interest. So, we let him step up/accrete/add to his cost basis a little bit for every year he holds the bond. The template we use here looks a lot like the one we used for premium bonds, actually:

> Price
> Vs. Par =
> Discount
> Divided by term
> Accrete/year
> X
> Holding Period
> Adjustment

Notice how only two words were changed: discount, accrete. Instead of paying more for the bond, this investor pays less (a discount). Instead of subtracting from his cost basis (amortize), we'll be adding to it (accrete).

Let's say an investor buys a zero coupon/OID bond @500, and the bond matures at par in 10 years. If so, our numbers would look like this:

> Price $500
> Vs. Par = $1,000
> Discount $500
> Divided by term = 10 years
> Accrete/year $50/year
> X   X
> Holding Period = 10 years
> Adjustment $500

So, if the investor holds the bond the full 10 years, he'll receive the $1,000 proceeds (par). His original cost base was $500, but he gets to add another $500 (accrete) to his cost base, stepping it up to $1,000. The difference between his proceeds and adjusted cost, then, is zero, which is why he has no gain or loss at maturity. Remember, that $500 is interest income, so this is how we prevent him from being taxed on a tax-free municipal bond. We just step-up or add to his cost basis so everything "zeroes out" in the end.

Now, if he held the bond only 6 years and sold it @88, things would be different. Now he would only adjust his cost by $300, right? $50 per year times a six-year holding period = $300 adjustment. So, his adjusted cost would be $800. His proceeds are $880 (@88), so he would realize a capital gain of $80 here. If he had sold it for anything less than $800, he would have realized a capital loss. As before, when the investor holds the bond the full term, there is no gain/loss at maturity. If the investor holds the bond a few years and then sells it, you never know what will happen until you run the numbers.

We've explained the OID as if it's always issued at a deep discount; it might not be on the test. If the test question says the bond is originally issued at 93, then you're working with a discount of $70 divided over the term to maturity. Why would an issuer sell a bond @93? Well, it really doesn't matter, does it? If it's in the test question, you just take it and run with it. But if you're an inquiring mind that has to know, think of it this way. Perhaps this is one of the bonds that mature at the very end of a serial maturity, and this is how we offer a higher yield to the buyers of these longer-term bonds, by issuing them at a discount. In this case, the coupon rate on the bond issue will be the same for all bonds, but the early maturing bonds will be sold at a premium, while the later maturing bonds will be sold at a discount. That way the yields are higher for the later maturing bonds.

Whatever.

Again, all premium bonds are amortized. For discount bonds, only OID's are accreted. Secondary market discounts are NOT accreted—the difference is taxed as ordinary income.

Interest Income

So that's the capital gains part. The interest part is nowhere near as simple as we've led you to believe up to now. So, I guess it's time to tell you the truth—can you handle the truth?

Here goes. The interest on general obligation bonds is going to be tax-exempt at the federal level, but your state could tax the interest if you buy a bond from an out-of-state issuer. If you live in Georgia and buy a bond issued by the State of Alabama, Georgia can tax that interest. Plus if you live in Atlanta, Georgia, and Atlanta has a tax on bond interest, your city could tax you as well.

How could you avoid being taxed by Georgia and the city of Atlanta?

Buy a bond issued by Atlanta, Georgia. The State will give you a break, and so will Atlanta.

Finally, if you live in Atlanta and buy a bond issued by Valdosta, Georgia, the federal government will give you the tax break, and so will the State of Georgia, since both

Valdosta and Atlanta are in that state. But, what about Atlanta—did you help them out? Not at all—so they can tax you. How do you get Atlanta off your back? Buy one of *their* municipal securities—hey, now you're catchin' on, boy. You help us finance our schools, we'll help you deal with your little tax problem.

Nice and simple, the way the tax code always works.

SITUATION	**FEDERAL**	**STATE**	**LOCAL**
Resident of Topeka, KS, buys a Toledo, OH, municipal bond	EXEMPT	TAXABLE	TAXABLE
Resident of Topeka, KS, buys a Wichita, KS, municipal bond	EXEMPT	EXEMPT	TAXABLE
Resident of Topeka, KS, buys a Topeka, KS, municipal bond	EXEMPT	EXEMPT	EXEMPT

And if you thought that was confusing, check this out—not *all* municipal securities pay tax-free interest. The ones used for public purpose/essential services do, but if the IRS determines that the bond is for "private purpose," it's either subject to AMT or fully taxable. Those Industrial Development Revenue bonds (IDR's) are often fully taxable, and a bond used to build yet another parking garage in New York City would probably either subject the investor to AMT taxes or be fully taxable. So, who decides how the bond will be taxed? Well, hopefully the bond counsel knew what the heck she was doing when she rendered her opinion, right? Because, if she disagrees with the IRS on this issue, guess who generally wins?

If the exam says your customer wants a municipal bond but is concerned about AMT, put her into a general obligation bond, such as a school bond. Or look for the concept of "essential, public purpose."

TAX-FREE AND TAX-EQUIVALENT YIELD

The exam might ask you to determine whether a particular GO bond pays a higher or lower "equivalent yield" compared to a particular corporate bond.

For example, the exam could ask you something like this:

Jeremiah Jones is in the 30% tax bracket. Jeremiah is trying to determine whether he should purchase a 7% New Haven general obligation bond or a 9.5% XYZ Corp. debenture. As his registered rep, you should recommend that Jeremiah:

A. buy the XYZ debenture

B. buy the New Haven GO

C. stop pestering you about municipal securities

Well, we can probably weed out choice "C." But, we still have to figure out whether the GO or the corporate gives Jeremiah Jones a better yield. Sure, 9.5% is a bigger number than 7%, but the GO provides interest that is not taxed. What happens to the interest Jeremiah earns on a corporate bond?

30% goes to Uncle Sam.

So, which bond would put more money in Jeremiah's pocket?

A couple of easy math formulas will provide you with the right answer every time. If you know the yield for the GO or "tax-free" bond, you take that percent and divide it by 100% minus the customer's tax bracket. In other words, divide .07 by .70, because Jeremiah is in the .30 tax bracket. 100 - .30 = .70.

So, .07 divided by .70 = 10%

That would be the tax-equivalent yield. Means the corporate debenture would have to be offering Jeremiah that much for him to get an equivalent yield.

And it isn't. It's only offering 9.5%, right?

So, we'd have to recommend that Jeremiah buy the New Haven GO.

If we knew the taxable yield on the corporate, we could find the tax-free equivalent yield by multiplying the 9.5% by .70. That would tell us that Jeremiah's "tax-free equivalent yield" is 6.65% on this bond that says 9.5% on the bond certificate. If the GO (municipal bond) offers anything higher than 6.65%, let's buy that muni.

The GO, in fact, offers 7%, which is higher than the 6.65% that the corporate bond yields after taxes are taken out.

Again confirming that the GO offers a higher yield.

So, if you have the tax-free yield, divide it by (100% - tax bracket 1%).

If you have the taxable yield, multiply it by (100% - tax bracket 1%).

And, if the question gives you both the coupon rate and the YTM, use the YTM.

Did we mention this stuff is hard?

Good.

THE MSRB

The SEC is the ultimate securities regulator and is part of the federal government. National securities exchanges and associations such as the NASD, NYSE, CBOE, etc., are "self-regulatory organizations" or "SRO's." The SRO that regulates municipal securities firms is the MSRB, which stands for the "Municipal Securities Rulemaking Board." This organization has lots to say about how municipal securities dealers do business. They have nothing to say about the issuers. They have no power over an issuer like California or New York City. They have all kinds of power over the folks who do municipal securities business with them.

But they don't actually enforce anything.

Ever heard the phrase, "We don't make the rules; we just enforce them?"

Well, at the MSRB the motto is, "We don't enforce the rules, we just make them."

If you can remember that just about everybody can enforce an MSRB rule except the MSRB, you'll probably get another test question right there. Specifically, you need to know that the following bodies can enforce MSRB rules: for bank dealers we have the FDIC, FRB, and the Comptroller of the Currency; for broker-dealers we have the NASD and the SEC. But not the MSRB itself.

All right, so that's who the MSRB is. Unfortunately for you, they have 41 "General" rules, and they are all highly testable. Since they are the "General" rules, they all start with the letter "G." We'll list them in order, but we're not telling you to memorize each rule by rule number, unless you happen to be a savant. You'll need to know what the rules mean and how they're applied.

MSRB Rules

> **Rule G-1.** A separately identifiable department or division of a bank...is that unit of the bank which conducts all of the activities of the bank relating to the conduct of business as a municipal securities dealer.

Comment: some banks have departments/divisions that conduct municipal securities business. The exam might refer to them as "bank dealers" or "dealer-banks."

> **Rule G-2.** No municipal securities dealer shall effect any transaction in, or induce or attempt to induce the purchase or sale of, any municipal security unless such municipal securities dealer and every natural person associated with such municipal securities dealer is qualified in accordance with the rules of the Board.

Comment: nothing terribly surprising here. The MSRB is just saying that the firm, the principals, and the representatives have to meet the qualifications and registration requirements of the MSRB. They then clarify that with the next rule.

> **Rule G-3.** No municipal securities dealer or person who is a municipal securities representative, municipal securities principal, municipal securities sales principal or financial and operations principal (as hereafter defined) shall be qualified for purposes of rule G-2 unless such municipal securities dealer or person meets the requirements of this rule. The term "municipal securities representative" means a natural person associated with a municipal securities dealer, other than a person whose

functions are solely clerical or ministerial, whose activities include one or more of the following:

(A) underwriting, trading or sales of municipal securities;

(B) financial advisory or consultant services for issuers in connection with the issuance of municipal securities;

(C) research or investment advice with respect to municipal securities; or

(D) any other activities which involve communication, directly or indirectly, with public investors in municipal securities; provided...

Comment: the words "clerical or ministerial" are often used in regulations to distinguish between those who are actively involved in the investment business of the firm and those who are maybe just working as the receptionist or performing filing, word processing, or other general office work. As we can see, if the individual (natural person) is involved with underwriting, trading, or selling municipal securities, he is a "municipal securities representative" and must register. Also, if he is involved with financial advisory/consulting activities for issuers, providing research/advice on municipal securities, or communicating with public investors, he is a "municipal securities representative" and subject to registration requirements. This rule goes on to state that municipal securities representatives brand new to the securities business must go through a 90-day apprenticeship period. During this period, they can be paid a salary (no commissions) and can only deal with other dealers or institutional investors, not with public investors. A public investor is the "retail investor," the average Joe and JoAnne, and we protect them much more than we protect other dealers or big institutions. In fact, the basic idea is that an institutional investor will know if the apprentice screws up and will generally be quite happy to inform him of same in a very pleasant, professional tone of voice. The apprentice also must pass the appropriate exam within 180 days or stop all sales activities immediately. Of course, if you had already worked in the business with a Series 6 or Series 7 for at least 90 days, you would have already completed your apprenticeship period.

The term "municipal securities principal" refers to the individuals who are "directly engaged in the management, direction or supervision of" all the activities mentioned for representatives, plus:

- maintenance of records with respect to the activities enumerated
- training of municipal securities principals or municipal securities representatives.

The rule then goes into extreme details concerning the fact that the qualification exams (52, 53, etc.) are confidential and that people who fail must wait 30 days to retest the first time, 30 days to retest the second time, and then 6 months every time after that. Of course, that's the way all of these exams work, so there's nothing surprising there. Continuing Education requirements are also discussed, but we'll leave the rest of the details alone for now to avoid overexciting you.

> **Rule G-4.** No municipal securities dealer or natural person shall be qualified for purposes of rule G-2 if, by action of a national securities exchange or registered securities association, such municipal securities dealer has been and is expelled or suspended from membership or participation in such exchange or association, or such natural person has been and is barred or suspended from being associated with a member of such exchange or association for violation of any rules of such exchange or association which prohibit any act or transaction constituting conduct inconsistent with just and equitable principles of trade, or which requires any act the omission of which constitutes conduct inconsistent with such just and equitable principles of trade.

Comment: in English, the above might be translated to, "Look, if you've already been in trouble with other regulators, your chances of getting registered aren't lookin' real good." Notice the phrase "conduct inconsistent with just and equitable principles of trade." That phrase is used by the NASD, the NYSE, and the MSRB. If the conduct of a firm, a principal, or a representative is not consistent with being fair to customers, and being fair *among* all customers, then we've got ourselves a problem. For example, there are plenty of reps out there who have told customers to cut checks for investments in *their* name. The rep then either puts the money in his own bank account or maybe establishes a little joint account at an online broker. You know, two grand of his own money and fifty grand of the customer's money, split right down the middle. In order to conceal the fact that he's investing or simply spending the client's money, he sends monthly account statements to the client that are totally bogus, making it appear that the investment is doing just fine. This would be conduct that is sort of "inconsistent with just and equitable principles of trade." And, this happens much more frequently than you might believe.

The SEC, called "the Commission," under the Securities Exchange Act of 1934 has the power to allow or disallow somebody from registration with the MSRB. But, if you accidentally spent all of your client's money while lying to her with bogus account statements, I would not anticipate the SEC going out of its way for you.

Rule G-5. This rule makes it clear that it is a violation of MSRB rules to violate any SEC rules or rules of the other SRO's that the firm belongs to. As usual, the regulators are pretty much on the same page when it comes to what constitutes "conduct inconsistent with just and equitable principles of trade."

Rule G-6. This rule states that since firms are members of the NASD, they have to meet the fidelity bond requirement of NASD Rule 3020. Let's see how the NASD defines the "fidelity bond" issue:

> Each member required to join the Securities Investor Protection Corporation who has employees and who is not a member in good standing of the American Stock Exchange, Inc.; the Boston Stock Exchange; the Midwest Stock Exchange, Inc.; the New York Stock Exchange, Inc.; the Pacific Stock Exchange, Inc.; the Philadelphia Stock Exchange, Inc.; or the Chicago Board Options Exchange shall:

> (1) Maintain a blanket fidelity bond, in a form substantially similar to the standard form of Brokers Blanket Bond promulgated by the Surety Association of America, covering officers and employees which provides against loss and has agreements covering at least the following:

> -Fidelity

> -On Premises

> -In Transit

> -Misplacement

> -Forgery and Alteration (including check forgery)

> -Securities Loss (including securities forgery)

> -Fraudulent Trading

Comment: so, certain firms that have employees need to meet fidelity bonding requirements just in case anyone accidentally loses securities or tries to steal them.

Rule G-7. This rule stipulates that municipal securities firms have to get all kinds of information about their principals and representatives. The firm needs to check the individual's employment history over at least the past 10 years, a record of all residences over the past five years, a record of any disciplinary history involving the SEC, state regulators, banking regulators, SRO's, etc., and—of course—any felonies or any misdemeanors related to forgery, fraud, burglary, perjury, bribery, etc. In other words, submit a U-4, which is the standard form used whenever an agent or principal associates with a firm.

Rule G-8. This rule illustrates what a pain in the neck it is to keep all the required records. Member firms have to keep "account records for each customer account and account of such municipal securities dealer. Such records shall reflect all purchases and sales of municipal securities, all receipts and deliveries of municipal securities, all receipts and disbursements of cash, and all other debits and credits relating to such account." Firms also need to keep a daily itemized record of everything mentioned above in something called a "blotter" or "other records of original entry." There needs to be a record of each security carried by the member for its own account or the accounts of its customers. The firm needs to obtain customer account information, just as NASD firms are required to do. In fact, if you're a broker-dealer involved in municipal securities, you're a member of the NASD. You follow both sets of rules, which are usually on the same page, more or less. The firm needs:

- customer's name and address
- whether customer is of legal age
- tax identification or social security number
- occupation
- name and address of employer
- information about the customer used for suitability/recommendations
- signature of municipal securities representative and signature of a municipal securities principal indicating acceptance of the account
- with respect to discretionary accounts, customer's written authorization to exercise discretionary power or authority with respect to the account, written approval of municipal securities principal who supervises the account, and written approval of municipal securities principal with respect to each transaction in the account, indicating the time and date of approval
- whether customer is employed by another broker, dealer or municipal securities dealer

As we'll see when we look at NASD rules, firms like to get their customers to sign a pre-dispute arbitration agreement. Once that's signed, the customer cannot sue the firm in civil court. Instead, all claims are taken to arbitration, as they are in Major League Baseball. In arbitration, there is one decision and no appeals. The arbitrators don't have to explain their decision, and some of them come from the securities industry. Therefore, the rules state that firms need to make it very clear what arbitration is and what the heck the customer is being asked to sign.

The firm needs to keep records of all customer written complaints, including the action taken to resolve the complaints. Records of political contributions made to issuers must also be kept, as we'll see in one of the rules up ahead.

Rule G-9. This rule simply explains that some records must be maintained for three years, and some for six years. Customer complaints, for example, are kept for six years, possibly because after six years it's too late to file an arbitration claim. Written and electronic communications, written agreements, customer account information, powers of attorney, transaction records, etc., are kept for three years.

Rule G-10. When the firm receives a written customer complaint, the firm must send an "investor brochure" that explains the customer's remedies, such as the arbitration we mentioned above.

Rule G-11. This rule provides mind-numbing detail for syndicate procedures. It's actually a good one to review, as it brings up concepts we've mentioned in this chapter. But to prevent this book from weighing in at 30 pounds, let's keep moving.

Rule G-12. This is the "uniform practice" rule, so it's extremely detailed. It defines the terms "settlement date" and the specific types of settlement: cash, regular way, when/as/and if issued. Cash settlements occur on the day of the trade. Regular way settlement is "T + 3 business days." A "when, as, and if issued" settlement is what the buyer of a new issue receives. In other words, the bonds have been sold but not actually created and delivered yet. Dealers must confirm transactions with one another, and this rule provides an amazing level of detail on that process.

When firms deliver securities to the buyer's broker-dealer, there are all kinds of rules about the denominations they have to come in and all the special ways they might have to be marked. The test could ask about a "mutilated certificate," which is not good delivery unless it is validated by the "trustee, registrar, transfer agent, paying agent or issuer of the securities or by an authorized agent or official of the issuer." If there's no legal opinion, the bond must be marked "ex-legal," or else delivery can be rejected by the other dealer. If the bonds have those funky, old-fashioned coupons, those coupons must be attached. If you get some weird question about a coupon bond that is in default, tell the test that all coupons would need to be attached for purposes of good delivery: past due coupons, currently due coupons, coupons due in the future.

Rule G-13. This rule covers quotations. The phrase "bona fide" means that a quotation that is published has to be legitimate. So, don't be publishing BID prices unless you're prepared to actually buy some of those municipal securities at that price, for example. Also, make sure that your Bid and Offer prices represent your best judgment of the fair market value for those securities, rather than, say, gouging the heck out of your loyal customers. And, if a member is participating in a joint account, meaning that several firms control the same securities, the members cannot put out different quotes on these bonds to different parties. The exam might say that they cannot "indicate more than one market for the same securities."

Rule G-14. Municipal securities firms have to report transactions to "RTRS," which is the MSRB's "Real-Time Transaction Reporting System." As this rule explains, reporting transactions is important for the purpose of regulatory enforcement and also provides transparency to the public, meaning it allows investors to quickly know the market price and volume for a particular security. Trades must generally be reported within 15 minutes to RTRS.

Rule G-15. When a firm executes a trade with or for a customer, they must provide a written trade confirmation no later than settlement. Confirmations must include information such as:

- Name, address, telephone # of the dealer
- Customer name
- Purchase from or sale to the customer
- Capacity in which firm acted (agent for customer, principal for own account)
- Trade date and time of execution
- Par value
- CUSIP #
- Yield and dollar price
- Accrued interest
- Extended principal (total amount paid for the bonds, before commissions or accrued interest)
- Total dollar amount of the transaction

The trade confirmation must always disclose the most conservative or lowest yield to customers. For discount bonds, they must disclose the YTM. For premium bonds, they must disclose YTC. Only exception is if a bond has been advance refunded. In this case, we know for sure when the bond will be called, so yield-to-call is the only yield that matters at this point. The bonds aren't going to make it to maturity, so yield to maturity is now meaningless.

If the bond is insured against default, as many revenue bonds are, the customer must receive evidence of that insurance, either on the face of the certificate or in a document attached to the certificate.

Rule G-16. At least once each two calendar years, each municipal securities dealer shall be examined to determine, at a minimum, whether such municipal securities dealer and its associated persons are in compliance with all applicable rules of the Board (MSRB) and all applicable provisions of the Act (Securities Exchange Act of 1934) and rules and regulations of the Commission (SEC) thereunder.

Comment: that one's very clear as is—I just added the parenthetical clarifications.

This next one is real shocker, though.

Rule G-17. In the conduct of its municipal securities activities, each broker, dealer, and municipal securities dealer shall deal fairly with all persons and shall not engage in any deceptive, dishonest, or unfair practice.

Rule G-18. Each broker, dealer and municipal securities dealer, when executing a transaction in municipal securities for or on behalf of a customer as agent, shall make a reasonable effort to obtain a price for the customer that is fair and reasonable in relation to prevailing market conditions.

Comment: notice how it doesn't say "the best possible price." Just says that if you're acting for a customer who wants to buy or sell a municipal security, try to make a reasonable effort to get them a good price. Is that too much to ask?

Rule G-19. This rule is sort of a re-statement of G-8. It tells the dealer which account information it must obtain before executing transactions with or for customers in municipal securities. For a non-institutional investor (regular Joe and JoAnne), the firm must obtain the following:

- the customer's financial status;
- the customer's tax status;
- the customer's investment objectives; and
- such other information used or considered to be reasonable and necessary by such broker, dealer or municipal securities dealer in making recommendations to the customer.

The rule states that all recommendations to customers must be suitable and if granted discretion, the firm needs to be sure that what they're purchasing for their clients (without even talking to them first) is suitable. And, as always, churning is considered impolite. Churning is defined as "executing transactions that are excessive in size or frequency in view of information known to such municipal securities dealer concerning the customer's financial background, tax status, and investment objectives."

Rule G-20. It's okay for a principal or a member firm to give gifts to their employees. But, in general, this rule forbids members from giving to anyone other than an employee or partner of the firm anything worth more than $100 per year. You can probably imagine how many exceptions I'm going to have to lay on you now. First, the rule states that an occasional ticket to a sporting, theatrical, or other entertainment event that is sponsored by the firm is okay, as long as it doesn't happen so often and so extensively that it raises questions of propriety. Second, the firm can sponsor legitimate business functions recognized as deductible expenses by the IRS. Third, gifts of reminder advertising (pens, coffee mugs, golf balls, etc.) are usually okay. A municipal firm could contract somebody for services, as long as there is a written agreement that spells out exactly what the heck this person is going to be doing for the firm and how much they'll be compensated, and the agreement is approved by the employer of the person whose services are being contracted. This rule also states that in connection with primary offerings, it is not okay to make or accept payment of non-cash compensation. Non-cash compensation would be, for example, merchandise, gifts and prizes, travel expenses, meals and lodging. But, of course, there are exceptions. Gifts that aren't preconditioned on somebody meeting a sales target can be given if they don't exceed $100. The occasional ticket to an entertainment venue is okay, as long as it's not excessive or preconditioned on meeting a sales target. And, if it's legitimate and by-the-book, an education seminar can be paid for by the "offeror" to a representative or principal, as long as the attendance is not preconditioned on the meeting of a sales target, only the associated person's expenses (not the guests') are reimbursed, the firm approves the attendance ahead of time, and the location is appropriate to the purpose of the meeting. In other words, if the offeror's headquarters are in LaCrosse, Wisconsin and the associated person works in Appleton, why again does the "seminar" always have to be held in Maui?

Hmm. Again, try not to raise any question of propriety.

Finally, the member can provide non-cash compensation to its reps for doing a great job. But the rule states that the compensation has to be "based on the total production of associated persons with respect to all municipal securities within respective product types distributed by the firm. And, the credits are equally weighted for each product type."

> **Rule G-21.** (a) Definition of "Advertisement." For purposes of this rule, the term "advertisement" means any material (other than listings of offerings) published or designed for use in the public, including electronic, media, or any promotional literature designed for dissemination to the public, including any notice, circular, report, market letter, form letter, telemarketing script or reprint or excerpt of the foregoing. The term does not apply to preliminary official statements or official statements, but does apply to abstracts or summaries of official statements, offering circulars and other such similar documents prepared by brokers, dealers or municipal securities dealers.

Comment: okay, I see several potential test questions here. The exam will ask you which of the following must be approved by a principal. Advertising must be approved, but as we see above, listings of offerings are not included in this definition, and neither are preliminary or official statements. Official and preliminary official statements are prepared by the issuer. The MSRB has nothing to say about issuers. Then again, if a firm creates a summary or abstract of either document, the MSRB considers that advertising, which must be approved by a principal. A listing of offerings would just be a statement of fact—the firm has these bonds for sale at this price. Advertising is something that presents a message that could, perhaps, be misconstrued. Rather than a straight-up statement of fact, maybe the piece exclaims, "Our firm can make you rich!" Unfortunately, that's not going to make it past compliance. How about, "Wealth management and tax-relief strategies for the discerning investor." Perfect. See, the regulators get quite upset when important facts are left out of a presentation, or when an advertisement implies more safety than an investment actually provides, or higher returns than anyone is likely to see.

Rule G-22. What if somebody just happens to be a principal at an underwriting firm while also serving as mayor of the city issuing the bonds? He would be in a position to control both parties; therefore, a control relationship exists. In this case, the firm would have to disclose the control relationship to customers before executing transactions in that issuer's securities. If the disclosure is made verbally, a written disclosure has to be sent no later than settlement. If it's a discretionary account, this is one time when the customer would have to be notified before the trade is executed. As we'll see in a later section, a discretionary account allows the firm to execute trades without first contacting the customer. If it's a transaction in a security where a control relationship exists between the issuer and the firm, however, the customer would have to be notified in order to authorize the transaction.

Rule G-23. This rule regulates financial advisory activities. Issuers usually pay a financial firm to advise them "with respect to the structure, timing, terms and other similar matters concerning such issue or issues." These advisors charge handsome fees for their expertise. Rule G-23 states that if the firm acts as a financial advisor to an issuer, there must be a written agreement that "sets forth the basis of compensation for the financial advisory services to be rendered." Now, believe it or not, some of these municipal securities firms are pretty darned interested in making as much money as possible. So, they sure appreciate the advisory fees, but now maybe they would like to help underwrite this new issue of bonds they just advised the issuer on. For a competitive, sealed bid (GO), the underwriter would need the written permission of their client, the issuer, in order to participate in the syndicate. For a negotiated bid (revenue bond) the financial advisory relationship has to be terminated in writing, the issuer has to consent to the advisor getting involved with the underwriting process, and the firm must disclose the underwriting compensation and the potential conflict of interest to the issuer and get a written acknowledgment from the issuer that the disclosure was received. See, if the firm changes roles from that of a disinterested adviser with no stake in the bond issue to a very interested buyer of those bonds, that's a different relationship. Now the firm isn't necessarily thinking about the issuer's needs anymore. In fact, the cheaper that the firm can buy those bonds from the issuer, the more money they make, which might not be best for the issuer who was just paying an advisory fee to the firm. You will likely take either the Series 66 or 63 next, and either way you'll learn that the advisory relationship is a fiduciary relationship in which the client's needs must always be placed first. Whenever that becomes difficult to do, the advisor must disclose the potential conflict of interest. For a sealed, competitive bid, there is no reason to terminate the financial advisory relationship, since the issuer has to award the business to the lowest bid, end of story. For a negotiated underwriting, the firm who was just giving disinterested advice for a fee is now negotiating the price they'll pay for the issuer's bonds.

Rule G-24. Municipal securities firms sometimes perform services for an issuer and may, thereby, find out information that could be used to their advantage. For example, maybe they act as the paying agent, which means they cut the interest and principal checks to the bondholders. How much creativity would it take for this "paying agent" to send a slick, colorful marketing piece that says, "Has your bond matured? Why not buy a new one from us?" with the final principal and interest checks? Not much, of course. So, this rules states that no firm acting in a "fiduciary or agency capacity" for an issuer "shall use information discovered through performing those services for the purpose of soliciting purchases, sales, or exchanges of municipal securities or otherwise make use of such information for financial gain except with the consent of such issuer or such broker, dealer, or municipal securities dealer or the person on whose behalf the information was given."

Rule G-25. This rule is called "Improper Use of Assets." It tells firms not to offer guarantees against loss to customers. Investing in securities involves risk, and that's just the nature of the beast. Your firm cannot shield the investor from risk, acting as an insurance company. Now, the exception here is that the dealer can sell the investor a put option giving him the right to sell the bond back prior to redemption, usually for par. Or, the dealer can enter into one of those repurchase agreements that we glossed over in the Debt Securities chapter. In those two cases, there would be a written agreement with all of the terms spelled out, not some empty promise that the investor "can't possibly lose when investing at this firm." A representative or principal might want to "share" in the profits and losses of a customer account, which makes the regulators rightfully nervous. If an associated person wants to share in the account of a client, he'll need to establish a joint account with the customer, and the exam might say he needs "the client's written consent, the consent of the employing firm, and must share in proportion to his investment in the account." In other words, even if you could get a joint account going with one of your customers, you can't put in $50 to his $50,000 and split everything "right down the middle."

Rule G-26 has to do with the process of transferring a customer account to another firm. We will save that excitement for a later chapter called "Customers and Brokerage Procedures." In other words, the NASD and MSRB rules, as usual, are on the same page.

> **Rule G-27.** Supervision. (a) Obligation to supervise. Each municipal securities dealer shall supervise the conduct of the municipal securities activities of the dealer and its associated persons to ensure compliance with Board rules and the applicable provisions of the Act and rules thereunder. Each dealer shall specifically designate one or more associated persons qualified as municipal securities principals, municipal securities sales principals, financial and operations principals in accordance with Board rules, or as general securities principals to be responsible for the supervision of the municipal securities activities of the dealer and its associated persons as required by this rule. A written record of each supervisory designation and of the designated principal's responsibilities under this rule shall be maintained and updated as required under rule G-9.

Comment: This rule is pretty clear, actually, once you get used to the fancy legalese. It just means that the firm is supervised by certain types of principals, who need to pass some rather difficult exams and get themselves registered as municipal securities principals. The Series 53, for example, might be required, or the Series 24. This rule also stipulates that the firm must have written supervisory procedures that "codify the dealer's supervisory system for ensuring compliance." What are the principals responsible for?

- Customer complaints
- Supervision of municipal securities representatives
- Monitor correspondence between representatives and customers
- Approve new accounts
- Approve all transactions on a daily basis
- Required maintenance and retention of required books and records
- Review at least annually the written supervisory procedures of the firm
- Update the written supervisory procedures in response to rule changes by the MSRB and other regulators

Rule G-28. Transactions with Employees and Partners of Other Municipal

Securities Professionals. No municipal securities dealer shall open or maintain an account in which transactions in municipal securities may be effected for a customer who such municipal securities dealer knows is employed by, or the partner of, another municipal securities dealer, or for or on behalf of the spouse or minor child of such person unless such municipal securities dealer first gives written notice with respect to the opening and maintenance of such account to the municipal securities dealer by whom such person is employed or of whom such person is a partner.

Comment: in English that just means that before opening an account for somebody who works at a municipal securities firm, or for the spouse or minor child of somebody who works at a municipal securities firm, the municipal securities dealer has to notify the employer in writing. And, after every transaction for this person, the municipal securities dealer has to send a duplicate trade confirmation to the employing dealer and has to act in accordance with any instructions that the employing broker-dealer has provided for the handling of this account. Also, this rule doesn't cover transactions in municipal fund securities, just municipal securities purchased "a la carte."

Rule G-29. Each broker, dealer and municipal securities dealer shall keep in each office a copy of all rules of the Board (MSRB) and shall make such rules available for examination by customers promptly upon request.

Comment: so the MSRB rules contain a rule about MSRB rules. Keep a few copies on hand and make sure you provide them to customers upon request. Why is a customer requesting a copy of the MSRB Rulebook? A, she's ticked off at something your firm did, and, B, she doesn't realize the rules are available online at www.msrb.org.

Rule G-30.

(a) Principal Transactions. No municipal securities dealer shall purchase municipal securities for its own account from a customer or sell municipal securities for its own account to a customer except at an aggregate price (including any mark-down or mark-up) that is fair and reasonable, taking into consideration all relevant factors, including the best judgment of the municipal securities dealer as to the fair market value of the securities at the time of the transaction, the expense involved in effecting the transaction, the fact that the municipal securities dealer is entitled to a profit, and the total dollar amount of the transaction.

(b) Agency Transactions. No municipal securities dealer shall purchase or sell municipal securities as agent for a customer for a commission or service charge in excess of a fair and reasonable amount, taking into consideration all relevant factors, including the availability of the securities involved in the transaction, the expense of executing or filling the customer's order, the value of the services rendered by the municipal securities dealer, and the amount of any other compensation received or to be received by the municipal securities dealer in connection with the transaction.

Comment: so, there's quite a bit of leeway for a firm in deciding if the markup/markdown or commission was fair and reasonable. Perhaps this explains why firms generally love executing transactions in municipal securities, especially on a principal basis.

Rule G-31. No municipal securities dealer shall solicit transactions in municipal securities with or for the account of an investment company as defined in the Investment Company Act of 1940, as compensation or in return for sales by such municipal securities dealer of participations, shares, or units in such investment company.

Comment: the NASD prohibits the same "shelf space programs" in its "anti-reciprocity rules" codified in NASD Rule 2830. What they're saying is that the firm cannot approach a municipal bond mutual fund with a pitch like this, "So, if you were willing to execute all of your trades through our firm, we would be willing to sell your fund to our investors ahead of all other funds." I know, many of you just can't see what the heck is wrong with this one-hand-washes-the-other approach, especially if you ever worked in city government. But, the point is that the mutual fund uses their investors' money to pay for everything, including trading commissions. It would be sort of nice if the fund would, then, obtain "best execution" on all of their trades, since they are using the customers' money to buy and sell portfolio securities. If they're cutting sleazy little deals with broker-dealers in which they pay fat commissions in exchange for the broker-dealer pushing the fund to new investors, the mutual fund investors are getting screwed. See, when the fund gathers new investors, that doesn't help the existing investors at all. It does give the fund more assets against which to charge management and 12b-1 fees, and it also gives them more assets to park in the money market in order to generate enough interest to pay ever higher board of director salaries. But, that's not helping the investors. Plus, the broker-dealer making this pitch should probably take the radical approach of recommending mutual funds to their customers based on suitability, rather than pushing whatever less-than-stellar fund pays them the most in commissions.

Rule G-32 stipulates the information that must be disclosed to investors who purchase new issues of municipal securities. In a new offering, the dealer has to deliver the official statement no later than the due date for confirmation. If the issuer is not putting an official statement together, that has to be disclosed to investors in writing. If the dealer is involved in a negotiated underwriting, they must disclose the following to investors:

- The underwriting spread
- The amount of any fee received by the municipal securities dealer as agent for the issuer in the distribution of the securities
- The initial offering price for each maturity in the issue that is offered or to be offered in whole or in part by the underwriters

Rule G-33. This rule standardizes how accrued interest must be calculated. If you take a quick look at this one, you'll see something rather scary: even though the Series 7 information seems difficult, it is really just an entry-level view of the industry. Imagine if one of *those* formulae were actually on the exam. ☺

Rule G-34. This rule is about CUSIP numbers and is probably too detailed to make a good test question.

Rule G-35. This rule simply makes bank dealers subject to the NASD Code of Arbitration procedure. We'll look at NASD Arbitration in more detail in the final chapter of this book.

Rule G-36. This rule has to do with the underwriter's responsibility to deliver official statements, advance refunding documents, and special forms associated with both. Underwriters have to send a copy of the final official statement to the MSRB and fill out Form G-36(OS). Also, if the official statement is later amended, an amended official statement and form must be filed. If the issue is for the purpose of advance refunding, underwriters submit a copy of the advance refunding document and a completed Form G-36(ARD). If underwriters have filed the above paperwork but the issue is then cancelled, they must notify the MSRB of that unfortunate fact. Of course, it is the managing underwriter/syndicate manager who is responsible for dealing with this paperwork.

Rule G-37. Political Contributions and Prohibitions on Municipal Securities Business. As a resident of Chicago, I find this rule especially interesting. See, a municipal underwriting firm in Chicago wouldn't take too long to figure out that the best way to get invited to the table for a bunch of lucrative, no-bid "negotiated" underwritings of municipal bonds would be to contribute, say, half of whatever they make to the mayor's political campaign. Not to mention that the governor and certain members of the state legislature might turn out to be really helpful allies in their quest to underwrite lucrative municipal bonds issued by the State of Illinois.

Hint: the state recently did a $10 *billion* pension bond underwriting, so what's a few percentage points of $10 billion work out to be?

So, the MSRB takes the radical view that municipal securities dealers should not buy their way into the underwriting process. Let's see how the MSRB explains the rule:

> (a) Purpose. The purpose and intent of this rule are to ensure that the high standards and integrity of the municipal securities industry are maintained, to prevent fraudulent and manipulative acts and practices, to promote just and equitable principles of trade, to perfect a free and open market and to protect investors and the public interest by: (i) prohibiting brokers, dealers and municipal securities dealers from engaging in municipal securities business with issuers if certain political contributions have been made to officials of such issuers; and (ii) requiring brokers, dealers and municipal securities dealers to disclose certain political contributions, as well as other information, to allow public scrutiny of political contributions and the municipal securities business of a broker, dealer or municipal securities dealer.

Okay, so if the dealer has made political contributions to an official of the issuer in the past two years, they may not underwrite any of that issuer's municipal bonds. If the contribution were made by the firm, a municipal finance professional associated with the firm, or any political action committee (PAC) controlled by the firm or any municipal finance professional with the firm, the above prohibition would apply.

Except when it wouldn't. As the MSRB explains in its page-turning prose, "this section shall not prohibit the municipal securities dealer from engaging in municipal securities business with an issuer if the only contributions made by the persons and entities noted above to officials of such issuer within the previous two years were made by municipal finance professionals to officials of such issuer for whom the municipal finance professionals were entitled to vote and which contributions, in total, were not in excess of $250 by any municipal finance professional to each official of such issuer, per election."

So, notice there are two requirements there—first, the municipal finance professional has to be eligible to vote for the official they're contributing to, and the contribution cannot exceed $250.

To make sure everything's on the up and up, member firms have to submit quarterly statements to the MSRB concerning political contributions on Form G-37. For anything other than the little $250 contribution by a municipal finance professional eligible to vote for the official, the MSRB wants the name and title of each official and/or PAC receiving contributions, listed by state, amount of the contribution, and whether it was made by the firm, a municipal finance professional, a non-municipal finance executive, or a PAC controlled by any of those folks. The form also lists which issuers the firm has done underwriting business with in the preceding quarter, listed by state.

Rule G-38. Speaking of Chicago, I remember reading an interesting story in the *Sun-Times* a while back that pointed out how the mayor's brother was paid something like $180,000 a year as a "consultant" for a large Wall Street firm that happened to be the largest underwriter of Chicago municipal bonds. When the press asked the firm exactly what sort of "consulting" the mayor's brother might do for them, they got no answers. Well, that was then—this is now. In fact, if you diligently peruse these MSRB rules, you'll see how they often mention "former rule G-38." In the old days, a firm could use a so-called "consultant" as long as they followed some rather lax rules requiring a written agreement and a little bit of disclosure. Now, check out what the current Rule G-38 thinks about the use of so-called "consultants" . . .

> Prohibited Payments. No municipal securities dealer may provide or agree to provide, directly or indirectly, payment to any person who is not an affiliated person of the municipal securities dealer for a solicitation of municipal securities business on behalf of such municipal securities dealer.

Okay, so what is an "affiliated person of the municipal securities dealer"? Here we go:

> The term "affiliated person of the municipal securities dealer" means any person who is a partner, director, officer, employee or registered person of the municipal securities dealer (or, in the case of a bank dealer, any person occupying a similar status or performing similar functions for the bank dealer) or of an affiliated company of the municipal securities dealer.

Hmm. So, I didn't notice an exemption for the mayor's brother in there. Why would the MSRB have a rule such as this? Think how easy it would be for an underwriting firm to "hire" the immediate family of mayors, governors, and other key politicians to act as so-called "consultants" when, in fact, it's just a glorified bribe. If we give the governor's sister-in-law $125,000, she can get us the negotiated underwriting deal on about $25 million of upcoming revenue bonds. To make it look legitimate, we'll hire her as a consultant and let her work from home. As long as she sends in a few emails, maybe even a spreadsheet or two, we got ourselves a "consulting engagement" at about $40,000 an hour to a person who's never had a finance class and can't even balance her own checkbook.

And, it's not just the underwriting firms who might abuse the system. This rule actually protects firms from being basically shaken down by seedy family members of key political figures. "Hey, I hear you'd like to get in on that next big bond issue. Turns out, as the Governor's baby brother, I'm looking for a little, uh, you know, *consulting* work, myself, so maybe we should, you know, talk." At least now they can say that they are precluded from pursuing such a consulting arrangement due to MSRB Rule G-38. Which they would be happy to explain in a darkened parking garage, say, around 2 AM down by the canal?

Rule G-39. Everybody hates telemarketing these days it seems. We'll see the NASD Rule in the final chapter, which is going to mirror this one very closely. Basically, the SRO's are stipulating that firms need to be very careful about their telemarketing practices. Callers have to identify the firm they represent and the fact that they are calling about securities investment opportunities. If someone says she isn't interested and asks to be put on the do-not-call list, put her on the do-not-call list and do-not-call her. There is a firm-specific list and a national list, so you have to make sure that your next victim—I mean, prospect—is not on either list. Prospects are not to be called before 8 AM or after 9 PM in their time zone.

Rule G-40. This rule just stipulates that firms need to establish an Internet electronic mail account to allow for electronic communications with the MSRB. A Primary Electronic Mail Contact has to be established to serve as the official contact person for purposes of electronic mail communication between the municipal securities dealer and the MSRB. The firm may also establish an Optional Electronic Mail Contact. The firm needs to file a Form G-40 electronically informing the MSRB who these electronic mail contacts are. And the testing committee really needs to find better things to talk about on the Series 7.

> **Rule G-41.** Every municipal securities dealer shall establish and implement an anti-money laundering compliance program reasonably designed to achieve and monitor ongoing compliance with the requirements of the Bank Secrecy Act ("BSA"), and the regulations thereunder.

Comment: this rule then states that if the firm complies with the anti-money laundering compliance program of the NASD (Rule 3011), then they comply with MSRB Rule G-41. We will discuss the NASD rule in the final chapter, which means we're finally done talking about MSRB rules at this point.

You, however, are just getting started. Please become an expert on MSRB rules for this exam. That will provide a major edge at the exam center.

WHAT NOW?

- Review this chapter, taking notes on key concepts and possibly making flash cards. *Approximately 1.5 – 2 hours.*

- If you have the Pass the 7 QuizSet, take all three quizzes on Municipal Securities. *Approximately 5 hours.*

- If you have the Audio CD set, listen to tracks 1 and 2 on Disc 2. *Approximately 55 minutes.*

- Sign up for a two-week subscription to the daily Bond Buyer at www. bondbuyer.com.

- Visit www.msrb.org and go through their glossary as well as skimming all the "General" Rules (G-1 through G-41).

CHAPTER 4

Options

Guy steps into a tavern. After a hard day at the office, he's full of attitude. He plops down at the last open stool and slaps a stack of twenties on the bar, just loud enough to get the bartender's attention. The bartender, an attractive redhead in a pressed, white oxford shirt and lime green tie, looks up from the pitcher of ale she's pouring.

"Just a sec'," she says, afraid to take her eyes off the thick head of foam gathering at the top.

"No hurry," the guy says, although it's clear he's not in the mood to wait.

Bartender finally comes up and takes his order. Bourbon and Pepsi. Not Coke—Coke's for losers. He wants *Pepsi* with his Bourbon.

The waitress shrugs and mixes him his drink.

Three guys sitting to his right heard the crack about Coca-Cola and decide to take the bait.

"You don't like Coke, huh, buddy?" says the dark-haired guy in the denim shirt.

"Nope," the guy says. "Don't like the drink, don't like the stock."

"What, you're a trader?" the blond dude with the big shoulders says, wiping foam from his blond mustache.

"Just a guy who says Coke is headed where it belongs—down the toilet."

The three friends all raise their chins to the same level.

"That's a bold statement," the dark-haired guy says. "My dad drove a route for Coke twenty years."

"Good for him," the guy says. "Used to be a decent company—that's history, though. I say Coke is a dog, and I'll bet anybody at this bar it won't go above twenty-five bucks a share the rest of the year."

He says the last part loud enough to get everyone's attention. Even the jukebox seems to quiet down at this point.

"Oh yeah?" somebody shouts from a corner booth. "I'll take that bet."

"Me, too!" somebody cries from over by the pool tables.

Pretty soon the guy has over a dozen loud-talking, well-lubed happy hour customers standing in line to bet the cocky newcomer that Coca-Cola common stock will, without a doubt, rise above $25 a share at some point between today (March 1) and the rest of the year.

How do they make this bet?

The guy breaks out a stack of cocktail napkins and on each one he writes the following:

BUY 100 SHARES
COCA-COLA
@25
THRU 3rd Friday December

Anybody who thinks Coca-Cola stock will rise above $25 a share has to pay the guy $300. Guy ends up collecting $300 from 15 different customers, walking out with $4,500 in premiums.

What's his risk as he steps onto the rainy sidewalk outside?

Unlimited.

See, no matter how high Coca-Cola common stock goes between today and the 3rd Friday of December, this guy would have to sell it to any holder of the cocktail napkin for $25 a share. Theoretically, his risk is unlimited, since there's no limit to how much he'd have to pay to get the stock.

What if the stock never makes it above $25 in the next 9 months?

That's what he's hoping! If it never makes it above $25, nobody will ever call him up and ask to buy the stock for $25. In short, he'll walk away with the $4,500 in premiums, laughing at all the suckers at the bar who bet the wrong way.

What the guy sold everybody at the bar was a Coca-Cola Dec 25 call @3. As the writer of that option, he granted any buyer willing to pay $300 the right to buy Coca-Cola stock for $25 per share any time between today and the end of the contract. When would the person holding that option want to use or exercise it?

Only if Coca-Cola were actually worth more than $25 a share. In fact, since they each paid $3 a share for this right, Coca-Cola will have to rise above $28—their break-even point—before it ever becomes worth the trouble of exercising the call.

Either way, the guy who sold/wrote the calls gets the $4,500 in premiums. If Coke never makes it above $25, he'll never have to lift a finger. Just smile as the calls expire on the third Friday of December.

Think of a call option as a bet between a buyer and a seller. The buyer says the price of a particular stock is going up. The seller disagrees. Rather than argue about it all day, they put their money where their mouths are by buying and selling call options.

The buyer pays the seller a premium. Because he pays some money, he gets the right to buy 100 shares of a particular stock for a particular price within a particular time frame. If the buyer has the right to buy the stock, the seller has the obligation to sell the stock to the buyer, if the buyer chooses to exercise his right.

Buyers have rights. Sellers have obligations.

The buyer pays a premium, and he receives the right to buy a particular stock at a particular price. That particular price is known as the strike price.

CALLS

A "MSFT Aug70" call gives the call buyer the right to buy MSFT for $70 at any time up through the expiration date in August. If the stock goes up to $90 before expiration, the call owner could still buy the stock for $70. If MSFT went up to $190, the call owner could still buy it at the strike price of $70. So you can probably see why call buyers make money when the underlying stock goes up in value.

That's right. Call buyers are betting that the stock's market price will go up above the strike price. That's why they're called "bulls." Bull = up. If you hold an Aug 70 call, that means you're "bullish" on the stock and would like to see the underlying stock go UP above 70. How far above?

As far as possible. The higher it goes, the more valuable your call becomes. Wouldn't you love to buy a stock priced at $190 for only $70?

That's what call buyers are hoping to do.

So for a call, just compare the strike price to the stock's market price. Whenever the underlying stock trades above the strike price of the call, the call is said to be "in the money." A MSFT Aug 70 call would be in the money as soon as MSFT began to trade above $70 a share. If MSFT were trading at $80 a share, the Aug 70 call would be in the money by exactly $10.

PRACTICE:

36. A MSFT Jun 50 call is in the money when MSFT trades at which of the following prices?
   A. $49.00
   B. $50.00
   C. $51.00
   D. $49.05

37. How far is a MSFT Jan 90 call in the money with MSFT trading at $85?
   A. $5
   B. $90
   C. $87.50
   D.   none of the above

38. How far are the IBM Aug 70 calls in the money if IBM trades at $77?
   A. $77
   B. $7
   C. $0
   D.   none of the above

ANSWERS:

36. C, there is really no way to miss that question. Only one price is above $50.

37. D, would you pay $90 for an $85 stock? If so, please give me a call ASAP so we can set up some trading opportunities for you.

38. B, take the market price minus the strike price.

THE PREMIUM

The money you pay for your life or auto insurance policy is called a "premium." That's also what we call the money paid for an option; in fact, as you'll see with hedging, options can be used as insurance policies to protect against the risk of owning securities.

How much does an investor have to pay in premiums for an option?

Depends.

Option premiums really just represent the probability that a buyer could win a particular bet. If the premium is cheap, it's a long-shot bet. If the premium is expensive, the bet is probably already working in favor of the buyer with time left for things to get even better. As with everything else, you get what you pay for when trading options.

Time and Intrinsic Value

There are only two types of value that an option can possess: intrinsic value and time value. For calls, intrinsic value is another way of stating how much higher the stock price is compared to the strike price of the call. If the underlying stock is trading at $75, the MSFT Aug 70 call is how far in the money? Five dollars. The stock price is above the call's strike price by $5; therefore, the call has intrinsic value of five dollars. That just means that an investor could save $5 by owning that call and using it to buy the underlying stock.

But, if the stock is trading below the strike price, the option is out of the money. With MSFT trading at $65, the Aug 70 call would have absolutely no intrinsic value. So, if there is a premium to be paid for this "out-of-the-money" call, it's only because there's plenty of time for things to improve. In other words, if the option doesn't expire for another three months, speculators might decide that the stock could easily climb more than 5 points in that time period. If so, the market will attach time value to the call. Time value simply means that the option could become more valuable given the amount of time still left before expiration.

Whenever a call is at or out of the money, the premium represents time value. Whenever a call is in the money, you can find the time value attached to it by subtracting intrinsic value from the premium. Let's say MSFT is trading at $72, and the Aug 70 calls are selling for a premium of $5. That means the call is in the money by $2 ($72 market vs. 70 strike price), yet an investor has to pay a premium of $5. So, where is that extra three dollars coming from?

Time value. If there is still plenty of time on the option, speculators might gladly pay an extra $3, even if the stock is only above the strike price by $2 at this point.

Premium of $5 minus intrinsic value of $2 = time value of $3.

PREMIUM	5
- INTRINSIC VALUE	-2
TIME VALUE	3

So for calls, intrinsic value is a way of stating how much higher the stock price is than the strike price. Time value equals whatever is left in the premium above that number.

What if MSFT were trading at $69 with the MSFT Aug 70 calls @5—how much time value would that represent?

PREMIUM	5
- INTRINSIC VALUE	-0
TIME VALUE	5

All time value. In other words, with the stock trading at only $69, the right to buy it at $70 has NO intrinsic value. (If you disagree, please call us at your earliest convenience; we have some options we'd like to sell you here in friendly Chicago, IL). In fact, if the stock were trading right at the strike price of 70, there would still be no intrinsic value to the MSFT Aug 70 call, right? If you want to buy a $70 stock for $70, do you need to buy an option?

No.

You only buy the call because you want to end up buying the stock for LESS than it's currently trading, which will happen if the stock moves above the strike price.

So, if you pay $5 for a MSFT Aug 70 call with the stock trading at $70 (at the money) or below (out of the money), you're paying purely for the time value on the option.

BREAK-EVEN, MAX GAIN, MAX LOSS

So far we've been talking about the option itself. If we're looking at the options investor, we have to remember that he won't begin to profit until the stock starts trading above the strike price by an amount greater than what he paid for the call. If an investor paid $5 for an Aug 70 call, he will only start making money when the stock goes above $75. So, he breaks even (BE) at $75 and begins to profit above $75.

$$\text{Strike Price} + \text{Premium} = \text{Break Even}$$
$$70 \quad + \quad 5 \quad = \quad 75$$

Another way to remember the break-even on a call is to "Call UP from the Strike Price." If you see a test question about the break-even for an investor who buys a MSFT Aug 70 call @5, just add the $5 premium to the strike price of 70 to get a BE of $75. Or "call up" from 70 by the premium of five.

What about the guy who sells the MSFT Aug 70 call @5. Where does that investor break even?

Same place:

Strike price plus premium.

That might be tough to accept at first. To be honest, it would be much easier if you did just accept it, but perhaps you're an inquiring mind who just has to know.

So here goes. See, if the stock goes up five bucks to $75, the buyer's 70 call is worth $5 (intrinsic value). He could then sell it for exactly what he paid and be "even." The seller, however, sold the option for $5 and could now (to avoid being exercised) buy it back for its intrinsic value of $5, leaving him even. In other words, the break-even point is where the buyer and seller "tie." Nobody's made anything, but nobody's lost anything.

And, if you don't quite understand that, just remember that the break-even on a call is the same for the buyer and the seller: strike price + premium.

The Series 7 will ask you to figure the break-even point, the maximum gain, and the maximum loss for either the buyer or the seller of the call. Those are all hypothetical situations. See, sometimes you calculate what actually happened for an options investor; sometimes you figure out what *could* happen. If the test is talking about break-even, maximum gain, or maximum loss, it is asking you to look at what could happen. This is how it works for calls:

Buyers

The maximum loss is the premium they pay. Why? Because buyers can only lose whatever they pay for the option, end of story. There are no "loser fees," in other words.

To find the break-even point add the premium to the strike price. A MSFT Aug 70 call @5 would have a break-even point of $75. Strike price of 70 + premium of 5 = 75.

There is no limit to the call buyer's maximum gain. How high can the price of the underlying stock go before expiration?

Nobody knows. That's why the buyer's maximum gain is unlimited. His purchase price is fixed as the "strike price." The sell price is unlimited; it's wherever the market takes the stock, with no limit on the upside.

Sellers

What's the most that the seller can win on this call option?

Sellers can only make the premium. Always. So, the seller's maximum gain is the premium.

The break-even point is the same for buyers and sellers: strike price + premium, end of story.

The call seller's maximum loss is unlimited. If the buyer has an unlimited maximum gain, what do you suppose the seller's maximum loss is?

That's right, unlimited. His sale price is fixed at the "strike price." His purchase price is wherever the market takes the stock, which could be as high as infinity.

More, even.

We're not saying it will happen; we're saying it could happen.

Remember that whatever the buyer can win, that's what the seller can lose.

Whatever the buyer can lose, that's all the seller can win. Buyers and sellers break even at the same place.

Call BUYER	Call SELLER
Max Loss = Premium	Max Gain = Premium
Max Gain = Unlimited	Max Loss = Unlimited
Break-even = Strike Price + Premium	Break-even = Strike Price + Premium

GAINS AND LOSSES

Before we move forward, let's remember that options go in-the-money or out-of-the money. People don't do that. People have gains and losses, based on how much they paid for an option versus how much they received for the option. So, terms such as time value, intrinsic value, in-the-money, out-of-the-money, and at-the-money refer only to options. Terms such as gains, losses, and break-even refer to the options investor. Like this:

THE OPTION	THE INVESTOR
Time value	Gains
Intrinsic value	Losses
In-the-money, out-, at-the-money	Break-even

The T-chart

When the exam wants you to tell it whether an investor ends up with a gain or a loss, and exactly how much he or she gained or lost, approach the problem step-by-step. These are essentially bookkeeping questions, where you track everything the investor paid and everything he/she received. This might seem complicated, but luckily you have a friend who is here to help.

Your friend's name is Mr. T-chart. Mr. T-chart wants to help you pass your exam. Say, "Hello, Mr. T-chart."

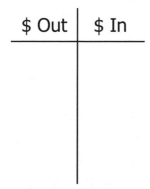

$ Out | $ In

Mr. T-chart's job is to help you track debits and credits. Whenever you buy or go long, you have a debit (Dr). Whenever you sell or go short, you have a credit (Cr). So debits are for the money going out of the account; credits are for money that comes into the account. If you end up with more money coming in than going out, you have a gain. If you end up with more money out than in, you have a loss. The rest simply involves running the numbers.

So let's start running.

Here's a possible Series 7 question:

> **An investor with no other positions buys an XYZ Jun 50 call @4 when the underlying instrument upon which the derivative is based is trading at 52. If the stock is trading at $52 at expiration and the investor closes his position for the intrinsic value, what is the investor's gain or loss?**
>
> A. $1,000 loss
>
> B. $100 loss
>
> C. $200 gain
>
> D. $200 loss

Whoa! They actually expect people to know that kind of stuff for the Series 7?

You betcha. And this is one of the easiest questions they could ask you about options, so let's get on top of this one right now.

First of all, draw your T-chart and use whichever labels you prefer: - and +, "$ out" and "$ in", "Dr" and "Cr," whatever works for you:

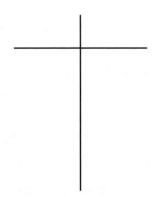

Okay. When the investor buys the call for $4, that's money out, so let's place "4" in the debit column.

The next part looks tricky but really isn't. The phrase "at expiration" means the last day of trading. At this point, all time value has evaporated. Since the option will soon expire, it is only worth the in-the-money amount. The intrinsic value. At expiration, an option either has intrinsic value, or it is worthless. So, what is the intrinsic value of the Jun 50 call when the stock is trading at $52? Two dollars. So, at expiration, the Jun 50 call would be worth exactly $2. In this question the investor is closing his position for the intrinsic value. If he bought to open the contract, he sells it to close. When he sells the call for its intrinsic value of $2, that represents a credit, right? When you buy something, money comes out of your wallet. When you sell something, money comes into your wallet. Same for an options investor.

All right. So, if $4 went OUT of his account, and only $2 came back INTO his account, he ends up with a loss of how much? Two dollars. An option covers 100 shares, so just multiply $2 by 100 to get a total loss of $200.

The answer to the question is "D," a $200 loss.

See? It's really not that hard. You just have to do it step by step. Many students get into trouble by trying to arrive at the answer all at once. Doesn't work that way for options. You have to weed through all the information thrown at you and break the problem down into steps. These options questions might look like math questions, but really they're just testing your ability to organize information. If you need two numbers, they'll be sure and give you five or six. They're testing your ability to separate relevant information from irrelevant, and then sort all the information into neat, usable steps. Just remember the basics, watch out for traps, and let Mr. T-chart sort everything out for you.

Would you like another question?

Let's do one, anyway.

On June 12 June Jorgenson bought an XYZ Jun 50 call @ 3 when XYZ Corporation's common stock was trading at $47. On June 15, June exercises her Jun 50 call when the underlying stock is trading at $55 and immediately sells the stock on the open market. What is June's gain or loss on the Jun 50 call that she purchased on June 12?

A. $300 gain

B. $300 loss

C. $200 gain

D. none of the above

This is a good way for the exam to challenge your ability to separate relevant from irrelevant information. In the above question most of the information is unnecessary and, at best, distracting. It's mostly weeds, so let's grab the only information we need and forget all the rest. The question is just asking you whether June Jorgenson made any money on her Jun 50 call and if so, how much?

So, break out the best weapon in your arsenal, the all-powerful Mr. T-chart. On a separate piece of paper, draw your chart and fill it in with the following numbers.

June Jorgenson paid how much for the call? Three dollars. Place "3" in your debit column. When she exercises the call, what happens? That's right, she buys the stock at the strike price of $50. So, let's write "50" in the debit column. If she immediately sells the stock on the open market, where the stock is trading at $55, she'll have "55" coming in, right? So, we'll place "55" in the credit column.

What are we left with? $53 went out, $55 came in. Looks like a gain of $2 per share times 100. The answer must be "C" then, a gain of $200.

EXERCISE, TRADE, EXPIRE

Notice how in the first question, the investor bought an option and sold it. That's called trading options, where you'll see terms such as "opening" and "closing." No stock is involved in that case. In the question we just did with June Jorgenson an option was exercised. Now stock <u>was</u> involved, which is why the strike price and market price ended up in our T-chart. Sometimes options are exercised; sometimes they are opened and closed; and sometimes they expire worthless. So, when figuring gains and losses for questions like the ones above, remember that only three things can happen once an option contract has been opened:

- Exercise
- Close Position
- Expire

If the call goes in the money, the investor could choose to exercise it. That means he buys stock at the strike price and sells it immediately at the current market price. If so, you'll be entering both the strike price (Dr) and the market price (Cr) into your T-chart—just make sure you place the numbers in the right columns. The investor could also close his position for the intrinsic value. For intrinsic value just compare the market price to the strike price and place the difference in your T-chart. To close the position, remember that if he bought to open, he sells the option to close. If he sold to open, he buys the option back to close. And, finally, the option could expire worthless—put a zero in the T-chart to signify expiration. The exam questions will give clues as to which of the three events has occurred. Just make sure you read the question carefully so you'll know what the exam expects. In terms of expiration, know that ordinary options expire in 9 months or sooner. There are also long-term options called "LEAPS," and these have much longer shelf lives—12 to 39 months. So, if you think it's hard to predict where Google common stock will close a week from next Friday, you can also buy a LEAPS contract that allows you to predict where it will close 38 months from next Friday.

Sounds like a bit of a leap, doesn't it?

PRACTICE:

39. Joe Schmoe is long an XYZ Dec 50 call @2.50. On the third Friday of December, XYZ is trading @56 and Joe closes the contract for its intrinsic value. What is the result?
   A.   gain of $250
   B.   loss of $250
   C.   gain of $350
   D.   loss of $350

40. Joe Schmoe buys an ABC Apr 85 call @3.25. With ABC trading @89.50, Joe exercises the call and immediately sells the stock for a
   A.   loss of $125
   B.   gain of $125
   C.   loss of $50
   D.   gain of $450

41. Joe Schmoe shorts an XYZ Jun 50 call @3.75. With XYZ @51, Joe closes the contract for its intrinsic value, realizing a
   A.   loss of $375
   B.   gain of $375
   C.   gain of $275
   D.   loss of $1,000

ANSWERS:

39.   C – use the T-chart. He pays the premium of $250, so put that in the debit column. When he closes the contract, he sells it, so he takes in the intrinsic value of $6 per share or $600 total. $250 out - $600 in. That's a gain of $350.

40.   B – use the T-chart again. Step one, he pays $3.25, so put that in the debit column. When he exercises the call he has the "right to buy stock at the Strike Price," so

put the strike price in the buy/debit column, too. Now you have $3.25 per share and $85 per share in the debit column. He sells the stock for $89.50, so put that in the credit column. With $88.25 in the debit column and $89.50 in the credit column, he gains the difference of $1.25 or $125 total.

41. C – anything "short" goes in the credit column, so put $3.75 per share in the credit column. He buys it back to close, and it's worth exactly $1 per share when he does. He makes the difference between $3.75 and $1 per share, or $275 total.

THE LANGUAGE MAKES IT FUN

It would be a lot easier if we could just refer to the two parties in the options contract as the buyer and the seller. Unfortunately, we have other ways of referring to each. The exam might talk about the buyer of an option, or it might refer to him as being "long the option." Or, maybe he is referred to as the owner or the "holder" of the option.

It's all the same thing.

To sell an option is to write an option. If you sell an option, you are said to be "short" the option.

All means the same thing. Why would they use the word "hold" instead of "buy" or "own"? Think back to our guy in the tavern. When he sold the little cocktail napkins, the buyers were now holding the option in their hands. And, we call the seller the "writer," because, as you remember, our guy in the tavern literally wrote the terms of the contract on each cocktail napkin.

Buyer-holder-owner.

Seller-writer.

Why would we call the buyer "long" and the seller "short"?

Because it blows people's minds and, therefore, makes them confused and us the experts.

Long = buy. Short = sell.

Just because.

BUYER	SELLER
Long	Short
Holder	Writer
Owner	

So far, we've been talking about calls, which give investors the right to buy stock. Let's take a look at puts now, which give investors the right to sell stock at the strike price before expiration.

PUTS

If we clipped the following coupon from the newspaper, what would it allow us to do?

```
┌ ─ ─ ─ ─ ─ ─ ─ ─ ─ ─ ─ ─ ─ ─ ─ ─ ┐
│                                  │
│              SELL                │
│          100 SHARES              │
│            IXR @40               │
│    THRU 3ᴿᴰ FRIDAY OCTOBER       │
│                                  │
└ ─ ─ ─ ─ ─ ─ ─ ─ ─ ─ ─ ─ ─ ─ ─ ─ ┘
```

That coupon represents an IXR Oct 40 put. As the holder/owner/buyer of this put we have the right to sell IXR stock for $40.

What if IXR is only worth $2?

Awesome! We get to sell the stock for $40 at any time before the end of trading on Friday, October 20, even if it's worth only two bucks on the open market. In fact, even if it's worth zero, we can still sell it for the $40 strike price.

That's how a put works. A put buyer gets the right to sell IXR at the strike price before the contract expires. No matter how low IXR goes, the holder of an Oct 40 put has the right to sell 100 shares of IXR for $40 each before the end of trading on the third Friday of October.

Who buys puts? Investors who think a stock is about to drop in price. Bears. Bear = down. (Bulls point UP, like the horns on a Bull. Bears point DOWN, like the claws on a Bear, or just remember "bear down.")

Strange as it seems, as the stock price drops below the strike price, the value of the put goes up.

Think of it like this—if a stock is now at $20, wouldn't you like to sell it to somebody for $40? If you were ready to exercise the put, you could just buy the stock for $20, then immediately sell it to the put writer for $40. That would involve exercising the put. As we saw with calls, though, options investors don't always exercise their options, but, rather, close the positions for their intrinsic value. If they take in more than they spend, they end up with a profit. And if they spend more than they take in, they don't.

For puts, intrinsic value is the amount of money that a put's strike price is above the market price, which is another way of saying that the market price has fallen below the strike price. An October 40 put has how much intrinsic value when the underlying stock trades at $20?

$20. Wouldn't you love to sell something worth only $20 for $40?

Talk about putting it to somebody, huh? The owner of a put profits when he can sell higher than the market price. He needs the stock price to go down, below the strike price. That's when he profits, when the stock is losing value. Sounds illegal, perhaps, but it's not. In fact, it's a beautiful opportunity to make money as a stock loses money.

So puts go in the money when the market price of the stock drops below the strike price. And, if you've already noticed that buying puts is very similar to selling stock short, I really like your chances of passing this exam the first time. Not that I'm particularly worried about those who didn't see that. In any case, let's take a second and look at how the two strategies are the same, and how they're different:

BUYING A PUT	SELLING STOCK SHORT
Bearish (profits when stock goes down)	Bearish (profits when stock goes down)
Limited loss (just the premium paid)	UN-limited loss
Less of a capital commitment	More capital, plus margin interest
No uptick rule	Short sale must conform to uptick rule
Loses time value quickly	Stock can drop slowly, still profitable

TIME AND INTRINSIC VALUE

IXR OCT 40 PUT @5 WITH IXR TRADING AT $38

PREMIUM	5
- INTRINSIC VALUE	-2
TIME VALUE	3

IXR OCT 40 PUT @5 WITH IXR TRADING AT $40

PREMIUM	5
- INTRINSIC VALUE	-0
TIME VALUE	5

So, in the first case, the put has $2 dollars of intrinsic value, since it would allow the buyer to sell the stock for $2 more than it's worth. The premium costs $5, so the additional $3 is time value. In the second case, the put has zero intrinsic value, since nobody needs the right to sell at $40 when the stock is at $40. So, the $5 premium is ALL time value.

PRACTICE:

42. A MSFT Jun 65 put @3 has how much intrinsic value with MSFT @65?

   A. $3

   B. $2

   C. $65

   D. 0

43. An IBM Mar 75 put @3 has how much time value with IBM @74?

   A. $1

   B. $3

   C. $2

   D. none of the above

ANSWERS:

42. D

43. C

Easier Than They Look

There are exactly two things you can do with stock: buy it, or sell it. How do you make money? By buying low and selling high. When you buy an option, you're hoping to buy low and sell high, which you can do with either a call or a put. If you buy a call, you're picking your buy price—hopefully, the market price will go above that, so you can buy low (strike price) and sell high (market price). If you buy a put, you're picking your sell price—hopefully, the market price will go below that, so you can buy low (market price) and sell high (strike price).

Okay. So you can see why a bearish investor might buy puts.

Why would anyone sell them?

Max Gain, Max Loss, Break-even

Back to our tavern. It's Monday after that third Friday in December, and our hero is back at the bar buying all the call buyers cheap beer just so they'll stick around long enough for him to rub it in.

Yes, unfortunately, for everyone but the seller/writer of the calls, Coca-Cola only made it to $22, and the calls all expired worthless. So, with the $4,500 still in his pocket, the guy is in a pretty good mood. He's in such a good mood that he can't keep himself from not only dissing Coca-Cola but talking up his favored Pepsi. Pepsi is such an awesome stock, he swears, stirring his Bourbon and Pepsi, that it couldn't possibly fall below $70 a share in the next nine months. He's so confident his favorite stock won't fall below $70 that he'll take a bet with anyone who says the stock is a loser. You have to pay him three hundred dollars to make the bet, but it gives you the right to sell him 100 shares of Pepsi for $70, no matter how low it goes in the next nine months. Even if the stock drops to ZERO dollars, you can make him pay you $70 a share.

The 15 losers look at each other and decide the temptation is just too great. They imagine how much fun it will be to see the dude's face when they all make him give them $70 a share for a worthless stock. What if they're wrong? Then, just like before, they lose part or all of their premium. But that's all they can lose, too.

How much can our Pepsi-loving dude make? Same as before—just the premium. That's all the seller of an option can ever make. In fact, if you can remember that any time somebody starts with a credit in their T-chart, that's ALL they can ever make (maximum gain), you will save yourself lots of frustration and probably snag a few more test questions.

How much can he lose on this Pepsi put?

The good news for him as the writer/seller/short dude of a put (as opposed to a call) is that his maximum loss is NOT unlimited. In fact, you won't see the word "unlimited" associated with puts. A stock can only go down to zero, which caps the maximum loss for the seller and the maximum gain for the buyer. If this guy collects $3 a share ($300 total) from these argumentative happy hour drinkers for the right to sell him stock at $70 per share, the worst that could happen is that he'd pay $70 for a stock worth zero and would have only collected $3 per share. A maximum loss of $67 per share, and it could only happen if PepsiCo, like, went out of business in the next nine months. Which could never happen, unless it did.

So, like before, the guy lines up the same 15 buyers and takes $300 from each one. He takes out a cocktail napkin for each buyer and writes:

So, after finishing his drink and buying the house another round, the guy walks out with $4,500 and the obligation to buy Pepsi for $70 a share, no matter what it's actually worth at the time. Oh well. He's confident that the stock will remain at $70 or above. If so, those Pepsi puts will end up just as worthless as the Coke calls did.

So, the buyer and seller of a put have the following maximum gain, maximum loss, and break-even:

BUYER
Max Loss = Premium
BE = SP - Premium
Max Gain = BE down to zero

SELLER
Max Gain = Premium
BE = SP - Premium
Max Loss = BE down to zero

PRACTICE:

44. IBM is trading at $93. Which of the following options would, therefore, command the highest premium?

A. IBM Aug 90 call

B. IBM Oct 90 call

C. IBM Aug 95 put

D. IBM Nov 100 put

45. Which position exposes the investor to the greatest risk?

A. Long XYZ Mar 80 call @3

B. Long XYZ Mar 85 put @4

C. Short XYZ Mar 80 put @2

D. Short XYZ Mar 20 put @2

46. Paula Padilla purchases a put for $300. Three hundred dollars represents

A. the price per share

B. Paula's maximum gain

C. Paula's maximum loss

D. Paula's break-even

47. An investor buys an ABC Apr 45 put @2.50. With ABC trading @41, he exercises his put for a

A. loss of $250

B. gain of $250

C. gain of $150

D. loss of $4,500

48. An investor shorts an ABC Apr 45 put @2.50. Which of the following stock prices would prove the most profitable for the put writer?

A. $44

B. $43

C. $42

D. $45

ANSWERS:

44. D – the option with the most intrinsic value ($7) AND the most time would have to be the most expensive, right?

45. C – the most risk is always on the short/sell/write side of the contract. Which put has a bigger maximum loss? The first one has a max loss of $78, which is much more than the max loss of $18 in choice D.

46. C – Paula, like any put buyer, or ANY buyer of anything, can only lose what she pays.

47. C – he pays $2.50 per share for the put and pays $41 for the stock. $43.50 in the debit column. He has the "right to sell stock at Strike Price," so put the $45 in the credit column. The difference of $1.50 per share or $150 total is his gain.

48. D – when you sell/write/short an option, you want it to expire worthless. Only the price of $45 would cause the option to expire worthless. The other three prices would leave intrinsic value on the contract, which the seller never wants to see at expiration. If you sell something, you want to walk away and never pay another dime. That happens if the thing expires at-the-money or out-of-the money. At which point it's worthless.

So far we've discussed the lion's share of what the exam will focus on concerning options, so please make sure you're comfortable with everything we've looked at so far in this chapter before worrying about everything that comes next. What comes next can be a bit mind boggling, but, still, I'm confident that most of your exam questions will focus on the concepts we've discussed. We've discussed single options so far, and now we're going to have even more fun discussing multiple options. Multiple options include straddles and spreads, where the investor is dealing with two options at the same time. If the investor is dealing with two options that don't quite make a straddle or spread, we simply call it a combination. For combinations, break out Mr. T and pity the fool who wrote the question.

THE STRADDLE

A straddle means that an investor has either bought a call and a put with the same strike price, or sold a call and a put with the same strike price. Both with the same expiration months, as well.

Why the heck would somebody want to do that?

Say an investor sees that XYZ Corporation is trading at $50 a share. He hears that due out the next day is a major news release that could either cause the stock to shoot up significantly or down significantly. In other words, the investor expects volatility; he's just not sure in which direction the stock will move.

So, he buys or "goes long" a straddle, buying a Jun 50 call and a Jun 50 put. In other words he is "straddling the market" at $50, with one foot on the call side, and one foot on the put side.

Calls go in the money when the stock price goes above the strike price, and puts go in the money when the stock price goes below the strike price. One way or the other, this investor is convinced he'll make some money. One option will expire; the other one will go in the money.

He hopes.

Of course, he has to buy two options, which is why he has a "total premium." If he buys a Jun 50 call @3 and a Jun 50 put @2, he has a total premium of $5. Like any other options buyer, if he starts with a debit (money out), he has to recover that amount to break even. In other words, if the call goes in the money by $5, he breaks even; if the put goes in the money by $5, he breaks even there. If you ever see two break-even points in a test question, they must be talking about a straddle. In this case the break-even points for the buyer and seller are $45 and $55.

SP + Both Premiums and SP - Both Premiums

Let's find the maximum gain and loss for the buyer and seller of this straddle.

The buyer's maximum loss is the seller's maximum gain. The buyer can lose the total premium of five, which is the maximum the seller can make.

We've already established the two break-even points—45 and 55. And, since the buyer holds a call, his maximum gain is unlimited, which means the seller (who has written a naked call) has an unlimited maximum loss.

Easy stuff.

Let's try a tougher question then:

An investor anticipating volatility goes long an XRQ Oct 60 call @4 and an XRQ Oct 60 put @3. If XRQ is trading @54 at expiration and the investor closes both positions for their intrinsic value, what will be his gain or loss?

A. $700 loss

B. $700 gain

C. $100 loss

D. not enough information provided in the question

Okay, let's break out the T-chart and attack this question.

Ready?

The investor bought two options, so he has two premiums in the debit column. On a separate piece of paper let's place "4" and "3" in debit, then. Now we need to find the intrinsic value for each position. If XRQ is trading at $54, what's the right to buy it at $60 worth?

Zero. So the call he bought at $4 could be sold back for zero. Write "0" under credit.

If XRQ is trading at $54, what's the right to sell it at $60 worth?

Right, six dollars.

So we put "6" under credit.

Run the numbers, and we see that $700 went out, and $600 came back in. The answer is "C, a $100 loss."

Now let's try a question for the seller of a straddle:

An investor who anticipates stability shorts a Jun 90 call @4 and a Jun 90 put @3.5. He closes both positions for their intrinsic value at expiration, when the underlying stock is trading at $111. What is the investor's gain or loss?

A. $5 loss

B. $13.5 loss

C. $13.5 gain

D. $1 loss on the put, not too sure about the call

No need to panic. The above question is no harder than the question before it, especially when we use the awesome power of our T-chart.

The investor places the "4" and the "3.5" under credit, right, since he sold both options?

Okay. Now we have to find the intrinsic values because that's what he pays when he buys back both positions to close out the straddle. So, if the stock is at $111, what's the right to sell it at $90 worth at expiration?

Nothing. Place "0" under debit, then, since that's what he'd pay to buy back the put.

If the stock is at $111, what's the right to purchase it at $90 worth?

Right, $21. That's a debit, because he'd have to buy back the call to close the position.

Add it all up, and we see that $7.5 came in, with $21 going out. Looks like a loss of about $13.5, doesn't it? The answer, then, is "B, $13.5 loss." As you can see, straddles are pretty easy.

PRACTICE:

49. If an investor expects the price of a stock to remain unchanged over the next three months, which of the following would be most suitable?
A. long straddle
B. short call
C. short put
D. short straddle

50. What are the break-even points for the following position? :
Long XYZ Oct 50 call @1.50
Long XYZ Oct 50 put @1.50
I. $53
II. $51.50
III. $47
IV. $48.50

A. I, IV
B. I, III
C. II, III
D. II, IV

51. **An investor is long an Oct 40 call and short an Oct 35 put. This position is best described as a(n)**

    A.   long straddle

    B.   debit spread

    C.   combination

    D.   iron butterfly

52. **An investor buys an ABC Apr 45 call @1 and writes an ABC Apr 45 put @2. At expiration, ABC trades at $46. Therefore the investor realizes a**

    A.   loss of $300

    B.   gain of $300

    C.   gain of $200

    D.   loss of $500

53. **If an investor anticipates volatility but does not have an opinion on market direction, he would most likely**

    A.   sell a straddle

    B.   buy a call

    C.   buy a straddle

    D.   buy a put

ANSWERS:

49. D – never buy an option if you think the market will remain unchanged. If you buy an option, you need the market to change in a hurry. Otherwise, the time value comes off your option and you sell it for less than you paid, if it doesn't expire on you. If you think the market will be flat, sell an option. Why sell just one, though, when you can sell both a call and a put with the same strike price? Short straddle.

50. B – for a straddle, enter the premiums in the T-chart. Add and subtract their total from the strike price. $50 plus $3 and $50 minus $3. It's really nothing new from single calls and single puts. Just that we're doing both at the same time.

51. C – if it's not quite a straddle and not quite a spread, just call it a combination.

52. C – he breaks even on the call, and the put expires, letting him pocket the premium.

53. C – volatility assumed, direction unknown. Buy/long a straddle.

SPREADS

A "spread" is another type of multiple options position the exam will expect you to work with. With a straddle, we saw that the investor bought two options or sold two options. The two options were different types. One was a call, the other a put.

For spreads, the type of option is the same. We're either talking about two calls for a call spread, or two puts for a put spread. To open a call spread, an investor buys a call and sells a call. To open a put spread, an investor buys a put and sells a put. Usually the expiration months are the same. For example, the investor buys a Jan 50 call and sells a Jan 60 call.

That would be a call spread. A debit call spread to be exact.

DEBIT SPREAD

Why is it a "debit" spread?

Well, which call is worth more, the Jan 50 or the Jan 60? In other words, would somebody rather buy a stock at $50 or at $60?

Fifty dollars. Calls with lower strike prices are always worth more money. So even before we attach premiums, do you suppose this investor has more money coming in or going out of his T-chart?

Well, the Jan 50 call is worth more—did he buy or sell it?

He bought it. So he paid more for the Jan 50 call than he received for selling the Jan 60 call. We call this a debit call spread because the investor starts out with a debit. And, like any options investor who starts with a debit, the debit represents the investor's maximum loss.

Okay, let's say the investor went long the Jan 50 call @5 and shorted the Jan 60 call @3. Go ahead and enter that in a T-chart. We place "5" in the debit column, since that's what he paid for the Jan 50 call. We place "3" in the credit column, since that's what he received for selling the Jan 60 call. He starts with a net debit of $2, so his maximum loss is $2.

What's his maximum gain?

This part is easy. What's the difference between the two strike prices?

Jan   60 call

Jan   50 call

Ten.

So just take ten and subtract the loss of two.

10 minus 2 = 8.

So, his maximum gain is $8. That's one of the great things about spreads: the max gain and max loss will always add up to the difference between the two strike prices.

Max gain + Max loss = Strike Price difference

So, if the max loss is 2, the max gain is 8 when the difference between strike prices is 10. If the max gain is 7, the max loss is 3, and so on. You'll never see the word "unlimited" associated with spreads, because the max gain and max loss are always going to be known numbers that add up to the difference between the two strike prices.

Break-evens for spreads are even easier. For call spreads, just add the net premium of $2 to the lower strike price. The lower strike price is $50. Add two to get $52. That's where the investor would break even.

So, how does the investor who establishes a debit call spread make money?

When both options go in the money, becoming much more valuable.

If the stock goes up to $70 a share, how much is the right to buy it at $60 worth?

$10.

Long Jun 50 call
Short Jun 60 call @3 (now worth) $10

What's the right to buy it at $50 worth?

$20.

Long Jun 50 call @5 (now worth) $20
Short Jun 60 call @3 (now worth) $10

So the option he bought for $5 he could sell back for $20. And the option he sold for $3, he could buy back for $10. If he did that, he'd have a total of $15 going out, and $23 coming in. Looks like he just made his maximum gain of $8, right? 23 in vs. 15 out = a gain of $8. Great. And where did he make his maximum gain? When both options went in the money, meaning they were "exercisable." When we started, the difference between the two premiums was $2. When the options went in the money, the difference widened to $10. For a debit spread, the investor wants the difference in premiums to WIDEN and/or wants both options to be EXERCISED. Just like so many Americans have allowed themselves to widen and are in dire need of exercise.

Debit = widen and exercise.

You have to know that for the test.

It might help to remember that "d-e-b-i-t" has five letters, as does the word "w-i-d-e-n."

Also, if you look at the investor's position, you can see why he'd love to see both options exercised:

Long Jun 50 call

Short Jun 60 call

Looking at the position, we see that he's obligated to sell stock at $60, but if so, that means he has the right to buy it for $50. Buy for $50, sell for $60. Not a bad thing. So, he can make a maximum of that $10 difference, minus what his initial debit is.

CREDIT SPREAD

To make the debit spread a credit spread, all we'd have to do is switch the words "buy" and "sell" so that our investor sells the Jan 50 call @5 and buys the Jan 60 call @3. If he did that, he'd start out with a net credit of $2. As always, if the investor starts with a credit, that credit represents his maximum gain. So, his maximum gain is two. Gee, the difference in strike prices is still 10, right? 10 - 2 = 8, right?

So the investor's maximum loss is $8.

Buyers and sellers break even at the same place, so the credit spread also breaks even at the lower strike price plus the net premium. Call UP from the lower strike price by the net premium to get $52 as the break-even point.

Now, if the underlying stock were at $40 at expiration, how would the investor fare?

Well, if the stock is trading at $40, what's the right to buy it at $50 worth?

Zero.

What's the right to buy it at $60 worth?

Zero.

As Billy Preston sang years ago, "nothing from nothing leaves nothing." A premium of zero means the options have expired worthless, and the difference between zero and zero is zero. When we started, the premiums were $3 and $5, exactly two dollars apart. Now how far apart are they?

Not at all.

Their difference has narrowed, and they have expired. Credit spread investors want the difference between premiums to narrow, and the options to expire worthless.

Narrow and expire. Might help to remember that "n-a-r-r-o-w" has six letters, just like the word "c-r-e-d-i-t."

And, if you look at his position, you see that he is obligated to sell at $50 and has the right to buy at $60. Buying at $60 to sell at $50 is the worst that can happen, which is why he can lose that $10 difference, minus what he starts with as a credit.

BULL AND BEAR SPREADS

What if the exam asked you to identify the two spreads as either "Bull" or "Bear?"

Easy. Just use the following acronym:

B
U
L
L
S

Which stands for "Because U are Long the Lower Strike." If you are long the lower strike, then you are a bull. If not, you're a bear.

So, the following spreads are all BULL spreads, because "u" are long the lower strike:

Long MSFT Oct 50 call @4
Short MSFT Oct 60 call @1

Long IBM Mar 45 put @4
Short IBM Mar 50 put @7

Notice this "BULL" thing works for both call and put spreads. If you're long the lower strike price number (50 vs. 60, 45 vs. 50), you're a BULL. Which is why the following would be BEAR spreads:

Short MSFT Oct 50 call @4
Long MSFT Oct 60 call @1

Short IBM Mar 45 put @4
Long IBM Mar 50 put @7

PUT SPREADS

Put spreads work exactly like call spreads, only different. An investor buys a put and sells a put. If he spends more than he takes in, he has a debit put spread. If he takes in more than he spends, he has a credit put spread. For example:

An investor buys an Apr 50 put and sells an Apr 40 put. The investor will profit if which of the following events occur:

I.   difference in premiums narrows

II.   difference in premiums widens

III. the puts expire worthless

IV. the puts go in the money

A.   I, III

B.   I, IV

C.   II, III

D.   II, IV

Okay, this almost looks like a difficult problem. You might even think the test forgot to include some necessary information.

It didn't. Although we don't see any premiums attached to the puts, we still know which one is worth more money. Would you rather sell your computer for $300 or $100? Three hundred, right? So the right to sell something at a higher price is always worth more than the right to sell it at a lower price. Puts with higher strike prices are worth more money.

So the Apr 50 put is worth more than the Apr 40 put. Which one did the investor buy? The more expensive put. So, he starts with a debit.

We can now answer the question. Debit = widen and exercise. You don't see the word "exercise" in choice "IV"?

That's okay. Only options that are in the money can be exercised. So the correct choices are "II" and "IV." The answer is "D."

His position gives him the obligation to buy at $40, but if that occurs, he can sell the stock for $50. Which is why his maximum gain would be that $10 difference minus the debit he starts with.

One way the exam likes to make test-takers sweat is by asking options questions that do not even provide the premiums. That's okay. We don't always need the premiums in order to answer the questions. Let's say the exam asked you the following:

An investor with no other positions is long a Jun 50 call and short a Jun 60 call. This investor will profit if:

I.   difference in premiums narrows

II. difference in premiums widens

III. both options expire worthless

IV. both options are exercised

A.   I, III

B.   I, IV

C.   II, IV

D.   II, III

Step one, which option has more value?

Long 1 Jun 50 Call

Short 1 Jun 60 Call

Look at the right side to complete step one. A "call" is the "right to buy," so would you rather buy a stock at $50 or at $60?

$50, right? So let's put a plus-sign by the more valuable option, like this:

Long 1 Jun 50 Call+

Short 1 Jun 60 Call

Step two, did the investor buy or sell the more valuable option?

The investor went "long," which means he bought the more expensive option. So, he starts with a DEBIT.

Step three, what do debit spreads want?

Debit spreads want two things: widen, exercise. So the answer to this seemingly tough question is "C," widen-exercise.

PRACTICE:

54. All of the following positions represent spreads except

    A.   Long 10 XYZ Oct 50 calls, short 10 XYZ Oct 60 calls

    B.   Long XYZ Oct 50 call, short XYZ Oct 40 put

    C.   Long XYZ Nov 30 call, short XYZ Nov 40 call

    D.   Long XYZ Nov 70 put, short XYZ Nov 60 put

55. Which of the following positions is BULLish?

    A.   Short XYZ Dec 20 put, long XYZ Dec 30 put

    B.   Short XYZ Jan 40 call, long XYZ Jan 30 call

    C.   Buy DFZ Sep 90 put, write DFZ Sep 80 put

    D.   Hold XYZ Oct 30 call, write XYZ Oct 20 call

56. What does an investor with the following position need in order to profit?

Long XYZ Oct 40 call

Short XYZ Oct 50 call

    I.   difference in strike prices narrows

    II.   difference in premiums widens

    III. both options expire

    IV. both options go in the money/are exercised

    A.   I, III

    B.   I, IV

    C.   II, III

    D.   II, IV

57. What does an investor with the following position need in order to profit?

Long XYZ Oct 40 put

Short XYZ Oct 50 put

I. difference in premiums narrows

II. difference in premiums widens

III. both options expire

IV. both options go in the money/are exercised

A. I, III

B. I, IV

C. II, III

D. II, IV

58. What does an investor with the following position need in order to profit?

Short XYZ Oct 40 call

Long XYZ Oct 50 call

I. difference in premiums narrows

II. difference in premiums widens

III. both options expire

IV. both options go in the money/are exercised

A. I, III

B. I, IV

C. II, III

D. II, IV

59. What does an investor with the following position need in order to profit?

Long XYZ Oct 60 put

Short XYZ Oct 50 put

I. difference in premiums narrows

II. difference in premiums widens

III. both options expire

IV. both options go in the money/are exercised

A. I, III

B. I, IV

C. II, III

D. II, IV

ANSWERS:

54. B – a spread is two calls or two puts. One is long, the other short.

55. B – go to the lower strike price. If they're long, they're a bull. If not, they're a bear

56. D – it's a debit spread, since he bought the more valuable call

57. A – it's a credit spread, since she sold the more valuable put

58. A – it's a credit spread, since she sold the more valuable call

59. D – it's a debit spread, since he bought the more valuable put

MORE JARGON

There are still other ways to refer to spreads. Rather than explain them in detail, I'm going to opt for the handy-dandy table format:

EXAMPLE	DESCRIPTION	NAME(S)
Long Jun 50 call Short Jun 60 call	Same expiration, different strike PRICE	Price spread, vertical spread
Long Jun 50 call Short Aug 50 call	Same strike price, different expiration	Time spread, calendar spread, horizontal spread
Long Jun 50 call Short Aug 40 call	Different strike price, different expiration	Diagonal spread

If the exam really wanted to make you sweat, it could use several different terms at once. For example, the following position can be referred to as a bear call spread, a credit call spread, a price spread, and/or a vertical spread:

Long XYZ Jun 50 call
Short XYZ Jun 40 call

HEDGING

To hedge a stock position means to "bet the other way, too." If you bet your buddy that the Atlanta Falcons will win the Super Bowl this year, you can also bet another buddy that they won't. To "hedge your bets" you could bet $100 that the Falcons would win and $45 that they won't. This way, you can't have a total loss. Unfortunately, you also can't win as much, right? If the Falcons win, you coulda'/shoulda' made $100, but you'll have to give the other buddy $45 of it now. But, this way if the Falcons do not win the Super Bowl, at least you get $45 from the second buddy, losing only $55 total, while you could have lost $100 with just one bet in one direction.

The word "hedge" is based on the way people grow hedges to establish the boundaries on their property. Your property is your stock—with a hedge, you can establish the boundaries in terms of what you're willing to lose.

HEDGING LONG POSITIONS

Let's say one of your favorite stocks looks like it's about to do a belly flop. What should you do about it?

Sell the stock?

Yes. You could sell the stock, but that's a drastic measure, especially when it's also possible that the stock will rally, and you'd sure hate to miss out if it did. If you've ever taken a 50% profit on a stock, only to watch it go up 300% from there, you know exactly what I'm talking about.

So, instead of taking a drastic measure, maybe you could buy an option that names a selling price for your stock.

Let's see, which option gives an investor the right to sell stock at a particular price?

That's right, a PUT.

So, if you thought one of your stocks might drop sharply, you could buy a put, giving you the right to sell your stock at the put's strike price, regardless of how low it actually goes.

Protection

It's like a homeowner's insurance policy. If you own a home, you buy insurance against fire. Doesn't mean you're hoping your house burns down, but, if it does, aren't you glad you paid your premium? Buying puts against stock you own is a form of insurance. Insuring your downside, you might say. In Series Sevenland we call it "protection."

A question might look like this:

Vito Marcello purchases 100 shares of QSTX for $50 a share. Mr. Marcello is bullish on QSTX for the long-term but is nervous about a possible downturn. To hedge his risk and get the best protection, which of the following strategies would you recommend?

A. Sell a Call

B. Buy a Call

C. Sell a Put

D. Buy a Put

Okay, first of all, when we say "hedge," all we mean is "bet the other way." If an investor buys stock, he is bullish, or betting the price will go up. To hedge, he'd have to take a bearish position, betting that the stock might go down. There are two "bearish" positions he can take in order to bet the other way or "hedge." He could sell a call, but if the test wanted you to recommend that strategy, the question would have said something about "increasing income" or "increasing yield."

And this one doesn't. This one gives you the key phrase:

and get the best protection

Whenever you see the word "protection," remember that the investor has to BUY an option. If an investor is long stock, he would buy (or go "long") a put for protection.

Max Gain, Loss, Break-even

Let's see how the protection might work for Mr. Marcello. Let's say he bought that stock for $50 and paid $3 for an Oct 45 put. That Oct 45 put gives him the right to sell the stock for $45, regardless of how low the stock actually drops. Downside insurance for a premium of $3. With a "deductible" of how much? $5 per share (buy stock at $50; right to sell for a loss of only $5). It really is a $500 deductible insurance policy good through the third Friday of October. Just like a car owner, who can handle the first $500, after that, damaged or destroyed property is passed off to the other side of the contract, who probably isn't too happy about having to cut a check but that's life.

When the test asks you about the investor's break-even point, be careful. Just like the homeowner who pays a premium to insure his house, this investor would rather not have to use the insurance. Right? If you have to use your insurance, something bad just happened. It's a lot better because of the insurance, but your car or house are now totaled, just as your stock could be wiped out in the stock market equivalent of a tropical storm or hurricane. The insurance just gives somebody the ability to sleep at night, knowing that he can replace his property for a fair price should calamity strike.

So, what he wants is for his stock to go UP. And, since he paid $3 to protect his $50 stock, how much ground does the stock have to gain before he breaks even?

Exactly. It has to go up to $53. Remember, he doesn't want to use this put; he's just hedging his risk. Insuring his downside. He paid three for the put; the stock has to make three bucks before he breaks even.

So, the investor breaks even at the stock cost plus the price of the premium.

Long 100 shares QSTX @50
Long 1 QSTX Oct 45 put @3

Might be easier to just use a T-chart. Put the price of the stock and the price of the put in the T-chart, and you'll see why the break-even becomes 53. Wouldn't the stock have to rise to $53, so we could put that number in the credit column and make the T-chart "even"? You can always find the break-even on a hedged position just by entering the stock price and the premium on the correct side of the T-chart. If it's a buy or a "long" position, place that number on the Debit side. If it's a sell or a "short" position, place that number on the Credit side. Then just ask yourself what number would make both sides equal.

What's the maximum gain for this investor, who owns stock and a put to protect his downside?

Well, how high could his stock rise? It's unlimited, right? So his maximum gain is still unlimited.

What about his maximum loss?

Easy. When he bought the stock at $50, what was the most he could have lost?

All of it—fifty bucks. If the stock went to zero, he would have had no protection. But, in the question he has purchased a sale price of $45 by purchasing the Oct 45 put. If that stock collapses to zero now, he can sell it for $45. Looking at his T-chart, we would place "45" in the credit column, since that's the amount of money he would get for selling his stock at the strike price.

So, what's his maximum loss? Well, under the worst scenario $53 went out, $45 came back in. The most this investor could lose is $8 per share, or a total of $800.

He's not happy about losing $800, but he's probably giddy over not losing $5000.

That's what we mean by "protection."

Increasing Overall Return

But, the question might have looked like this:

Barbara Bullbear purchases 100 shares of QSTX for $50 a share. Ms. Bullbear is bullish on QSTX for the long-term but is nervous about a possible downturn. To hedge her risk and increase income, which of the following strategies would you recommend?

A. Sell a Call
B. Buy a Call
C. Sell a Put
D. Buy a Put

Well, as we saw, you don't increase your income by buying a put. When you buy something, money comes out of your wallet. In this case, Barbara Bullbear has to sell an option. What's the only bearish option she could sell?

A call. Call sellers are bearish. Since Barbara already owns the stock, this would be a <u>covered call</u>. Let's say she bought the stock at $50, then writes a Sep 60 call at $3. If the stock shoots up to the moon, what would happen? Ms. Bullbear would be forced to honor her obligation to sell the stock at the strike price of $60. Well, she only paid $50 for the stock, so she just made ten bucks there. And, she took in $3 for writing the call. So, she made $13, which represents her maximum gain.

Max gain = (stock cost vs. strike price) + premium

Her maximum loss is much larger than the investor who bought the put in the preceding question. In this case Ms. Bullbear has not purchased a sale price for her stock. All she did was take in a premium of $3. That is the extent of her downside insurance. She paid $50 for the stock and took in $3 for the call. So, when the stock falls to $47 she has "broken even." And, if you prefer to use the T-chart, place the 50 that she paid for the stock in the Debit column and the 3 that she received for selling the call in the Credit column. What number would balance both sides? 47.

Now that Ms. Bullbear has broken even at $47, what's to prevent her from losing everything from that point down to zero?

Right, nothing at all. So $47 is her maximum loss. Break-even down to zero.

Notice the difference between Long Stock–Long Put and Long Stock–Short Call. When an investor goes long stock–long a put, she leaves her upside totally unimpeded. Her maximum gain remains "unlimited." And, her maximum loss is usually much smaller than the writer of the covered call. Only problem is she has to pay some money. Long Stock–Short a Call investors get limited downside protection and also cap their upside. But, they also get to take in some money.

Just depends on what they want to do, which is why the exam will give you the clue.

Okay, so that's half of it. In both cases so far the investor started out long the stock. The exam could also ask you what an investor who is short stock should do in order to hedge his risk.

HEDGING SHORT POSITIONS

The trouble with short sellers is they turn everything upside down. Since they sell something they'll eventually have to buy back, they're hoping the stock's price goes down. Short sellers have heard all about "buy low–sell high." They just prefer to do it the other way around: Sell High. Buy Low. Another way to put it is that a short seller's upside is down, and his downside is up. So if an investor sells a stock short for $50, what's his risk?

Right, that the stock could go above $50. Remember, he still has to buy this stock back, and he definitely doesn't want to buy it back for more than he first sold it for. Which option gives an investor the right to buy stock at the strike price?

Calls.

Protection

If this investor wants protection, he'll have to buy a call.

The test question could look like this:

An investor shorts 100 shares of ABC at $50. In order to get the best protection against a possible increase in price, which of the following strategies would you recommend?

A. Buy a put

B. Sell a put

C. Sell a call

D. Buy a call

The answer is "D," buy a call. Again the word "protection" means the investor has to buy an option. If he is concerned about his purchase price, he buys a call, which gives him the right to purchase stock at a strike price. Maybe he's willing to risk having to repurchase the stock at $55 but not a penny higher. Therefore, he buys a Sep 55 call for $2. Using our T-chart, where would we plug in the numbers?

Max Gain, Loss, Break-even

Well, if he shorts (sells) the stock at $50, that's a credit, right? So, let's place $50 in the credit column. He paid $2 for the call, so that's "2" in the debit column.

Okay, where does this investor break even, then? $48, right? 50 in the credit column, 2 in the debit column, so 48 would make things even.

And if you prefer to analyze the position, start with step one—look at the stock position. He shorted the stock at $50, which means he wants it to go down. If he paid $2 for the option, doesn't the stock have to work his way by exactly $2 before he breaks even?

You bet it does. So when the stock goes down to $48, this investor breaks even.

Is there anything to prevent him from making everything from that point down to zero?

Nope. So $48 is his maximum gain, too. Break-even down to zero.

What about his maximum loss? Well, let's say disaster strikes. The stock skyrockets to $120 a share. Does he have to buy it back at that price in order to "cover his short?"

Nope. At what price could he buy back the stock?

The strike price of $55. That was the protection he bought. And, if he exercised his call, his T-chart would show that $50 came in when he sold short, while $57 came out (when he bought the stock at $55 after buying the call at $2). That's a loss, but it's only a loss of $7, which ain't too bad considering how risky it is to sell a security short.

So if a short seller needs protection, he buys a call. It's the same thing as long stock–long a put, only upside down.

Increasing Overall Return

Now, let's look at the mirror image of the covered call. Say this same short seller wanted to hedge his bet while also increasing income. If he starts out bearish, he hedges with a bullish position. To increase income, he'll have to sell a position. Only bullish position he can sell is a put. So, he goes short stock–short a put.

If he shorts the stock at $50 and sells a Jun 40 put @ 3, where would he break even? Well, short sellers want to see the stock go down. However, since he took in $3, he can let his stock position work against him by $3. This investor breaks even at $53.

Right? That's what selling an option does for a hedger; it offsets the potential loss by the amount of premium collected. And, your T-chart tells you that $50 came in when he sold the stock short, plus $3 that came in for selling the put. So 53 is the break-even point.

What's the most he can lose?

Well, how high could the stock jump? Unlimited. Does he have the right to buy the stock back at a particular price?

Nope. So, his maximum loss is unlimited.

Like the covered call writer, he has also capped his "upside." His upside is down, remember. When the stock goes down to zero, does he get to buy it back at zero?

Nope. The investor who bought the Jun 40 put is going to make him buy the stock for $40. Now the investor realizes his maximum gain. Shorted at $50, bought it back at $40. That's a gain of $10. He also took in $3 for writing the put. So, his maximum gain is $13. Stock price vs. Strike price + premium.

PRACTICE:

60. An investor long stock would receive best protection if she

    A.   Bought calls

    B.   Sold puts

    C.   Sold calls

    D.   Bought puts

61. An investor long stock wants to hedge and increase income. What should he do?

    A.   Buy puts

    B.   Sell puts

    C.   Sell calls

    D.   Buy calls

62. An investor short stock would get best protection by

    A.   Buying puts

    B.   Selling calls

    C.   Selling puts

    D.   Buying calls

63. An investor short stock wants to hedge and increase yield. She should

  A. buy calls

  B. buy puts

  C. sell puts

  D. sell calls

64. What is the maximum loss for the following position?
Long 100 shares XYZ @60
Long 1 XYZ Apr 60 put at 3.35

Answer: _____

65. What is the maximum loss for the following position?
Long 100 shares XYZ @60
Short 1 XYZ Apr 75 call at 3.85

Answer: _____

66. What is the maximum loss for the following position?
Short 100 shares XYZ @60
Long 1 XYZ Apr 60 call at 3.75

Answer: _____

67. What is the maximum loss for the following position?
Short 100 shares XYZ @60
Short 1 XYZ Apr 40 put at 3.20

Answer: _____

ANSWERS:

60. D – to "protect," you buy an option. If you're long stock, you hedge by betting the other way—buy a put.

61. C – to increase income/yield, you have to sell an option. Its "arrow" has to be pointed the other way. Long stock–sell a call.

62. D – to "protect," you buy an option. If you're short stock, you hedge by betting the other way—buy a call.

63. C – to increase income/yield, you have to sell an option. Its "arrow" has to be pointed the other way. Short stock–short a put.

64. $335 – if you buy at 60 and can sell at 60, you can't lose on the stock. You can only lose the premium in this case. It's like a "zero deductible" insurance policy.

65. $5,615 – if that stock goes to zero, the only thing working in the investor's favor is the premium. If you lose $6,000 on a stock but took in $385, you lost your maximum of $5,615.

66. $375 – if you sell and buy stock at the same price, you lose zero. You can only lose the premium in this case.

67. Infinity – you're short stock. If it goes up, you have no "right to buy." You would only be forced to buy if the stock went your way—down. If it goes up, it just keeps a' goin' up to infinity. More even.

NON-EQUITY OPTIONS

The bad news is, there's still more that the exam wants you to know about options.

The good news is it's all based on the stuff we've discussed so far. It's just that these options cover things other than stock. These options cover stock indexes, T-bond prices, T-bond yields, and foreign currencies. The numbers will look a little different, but they still come down to calls and puts, which can be bought or sold.

Simple. Just like the other options we've discussed.

Sort of.

Those other options are called "equity options," by the way, because the underlying instrument is an equity security, common stock. The options we'll cover now are not based on common stock. That's why they're called non-equity options.

INDEX OPTIONS

The first type, the index option, derives its value from various stock indexes. You're probably familiar with the S&P 500 index. Did you know you could buy puts or calls on the value of that index? Sure. The symbol for that option, by the way, is SPX.

Here's how it works. The S&P 500 index is a big basket of stocks hand-picked by the experts at Standard & Poor. These 500 stocks represent, according to the folks at S&P, the most important in the overall market. By grouping these 500 stocks, we can track the overall movement of the market. So, when investors buy or write calls on the SPX, they're betting on the point value of the S&P 500, which gets figured every trading day.

So the buyer of an SPX call says the point value of the S&P 500 is going up in the short-term, while the writer says the point value of the index is not. Exercise involves the delivery of cash rather than stock. That's right, if the buyer exercises the call, the seller would pay the buyer cash. How much cash? The intrinsic value or "in the money" amount.

Let's say the call has a strike price of 500. If the holder exercises the call when the index is at 520, the call would be in the money 20 points, so the seller would have to send the buyer 20 points' worth of cash. How much is a point worth?

$100. Twenty points times $100 each equals a total of $2,000 that the seller would deliver to the buyer. And he would deliver it by the next business day. No need for a T + 3 thing, since no stock is changing hands, only money.

All you have to do with index options is multiply everything by 100. The real point value of a "500" call is "50,000." 520 is really 52,000, which is why the seller pays the buyer $2,000 in cash upon exercise.

The premium is also multiplied by $100.

Here's an example:

Long 1 SPX Jun 500 call @ 8

In this case, the investor has a strike price of 500 (or 50,000), for which he pays 8 X $100, or $800. In order to break even, the SPX option would have to go in the money by 8 points. That would be 508.

Here's your practice question:

An investor buys 1 SPX Mar 600 call when the index is @590 for a premium of 9. What is the investor's gain or loss if he exercises the option when the SPX closes at 612?

A. $100 loss

B. $300 loss

C. $300 gain

D. $100 gain

As always, let's get serious and break out Mr. T-chart.

The investor buys the call for $9, so let's place "9" in the debit column.

How much money comes in upon exercise? Well, how much is the call in-the-money? That's right, by 12 points, so let's place "12" under credit. That's what the writer would pay the buyer upon exercise.

Total it up, and we see that $9 went out, while $12 came in, for a net gain of $3. Multiply $3 by 100 to get our answer, which is "C, $300 gain."

Remember that the index is valued as of the end of the trading day, so it would be real dangerous to exercise your index option in the morning. If your call went deep in the money at 11 o'clock in the morning, you still need to wait and see where the index closes. The S&P and other indexes often go up for part of the day before finishing in negative territory. I highly doubt the test would go there, but the OCC Disclosure Document does indicate that if you exercise an option before the index has been officially totaled up for the day, and that option ends up going *out of the money*, you would have to pay the *seller* the amount that your option is out of the money.

And then drop and give everybody at the exchange 200 pushups.

So, here are some key things to remember about index options:

- exercise involves delivery of cash, not stock
- index is valued at the end of the trading day
- multiplier is $100

Capped Index Options

Hypothetically, there is no limit to how high an index can rise, and that's what makes selling calls on an index mighty dangerous. Therefore, capped index options may be available. If we set the cap interval at 30 points, as soon as the buyer's option goes up that high, it's automatically exercised. That way the seller knows what his maximum loss is and, therefore, the buyer knows his maximum gain. If it's an SPX Aug 400 call, it would be automatically exercised as soon as the S&P 500 hit 430 or higher, assuming the cap interval is 30. If it's an OEX (S&P 100) Aug 400 put, it would be automatically exercised if the S&P 100 hit 370 or lower.

Very similar to the way commodities will stop trading once they "hit the limit" for the day. To prevent the price of cocoa or corn from spiraling out of control, once the price moves a certain amount, the contract stops trading. The movement is "capped."

Now, if you're a former CBOE trader, you may be wondering what the heck I'm smoking with these "capped index options" that don't even exist. If they don't "exist," why are they still explained in the OCC Disclosure Document called "Characteristics and Risks of Standardized Options" that all new options customers must receive?

Hmm.

INTEREST RATE OPTIONS

My opinion is that the Series 7 is likely to ask several questions on interest rate options, because it gives the exam yet another excuse to talk about the relationship of bond prices and interest rates/yields. Since they can throw in that sometimes confusing concept along with some funky options few people have ever worked with, they can make you sweat.

And, like any elite fraternity, the Nu Alpha Sigma Delta house is looking forward to making all of you pledges sweat.

Don't sweat it. You're going to be ready for their little attitudes.

Price-based Bond Options

Okay, remember the "bond see-saw" from Debt Securities? It might have seemed a bit overwhelming, but all it does is provide a model of what happens when interest rates go up or down. Remember that on a bond the borrower/issuer prints a stated interest rate. Since that rate is fixed, whenever prevailing interest rates change, they change in relation to that fixed rate on the bond. So, the price or value of the bond changes accordingly, as does its yield. You don't have to do a lot of calculations for the exam, and the exam doesn't ask that you become an expert on debt securities. You just have to master the relationships of interest rates, bond prices, and bond yields.

If interest rates go up, bond prices go down. If interest rates go down, bond prices go up.

And yields move with interest rates.

So, who might be looking at a price-based option? Well, the manager of a bond portfolio would be concerned about the price of bonds. What would cause the price to go down? Right, rising interest rates. So, her risk is that interest rates will go up and push down the value of the bonds in her portfolio.

How could she hedge her risk?

Well, with options, there are always two ways to hedge. If you want protection, you buy an option. If you want to increase income, you sell an option. If the portfolio manager is bullish on bond prices, she'd have to take an appropriate bearish position to hedge. Bears buy puts and sell calls; therefore, the portfolio manager could hedge against rising interest rates by selling calls to increase income or by buying puts for protection.

That's the concept behind it.

Let's look at an example.

First of all, the bond prices we're talking about are U.S. Government T-bonds. The amount of T-bonds covered in one option contract is $100,000. In other words, a lot of money. The strike price of a T-bond call is the percent of par at which a call buyer could purchase $100,000 worth of T-bonds. So, you might see something like this on your exam:

Aug '21 T-bond Sep 101 call @1.16

The "Aug '21" means that this series of T-bonds matures in August of 2021. Upon exercise, the buyer of this call could purchase $100,000 of T-bonds for 101% (the 101 strike price) of par, or $101,000, before it expires in September. Obviously, this investor would be bullish on the price of T-bonds. Must believe that interest rates are going which way?

That's right, down.

How much does he pay for this option?

Well, the "1" stands for 1% of par. 1% of $100,000 is $1,000, so the investor would pay $1,000 and some change. Remember, these are govies, so the point-16 isn't a decimal. It's the number of 32nds. 16/32 times $1,000 gives us $500, so the premium is $1,500. If the price of T-bonds shoots up, this call goes in the money, just like any other call.

Back to our portfolio manager. Would she buy the above call?

No. She's only worried about the price of bonds falling. She might sell this call, to profit from her risk side. Or, she could buy a T-bond put if she wanted "protection" from her risk side. Her only hedge would be a bearish position on the price of T-bonds. If she wants to "increase income," she sells a call. If she wants "protection," she buys a put.

Guess what?

Yield-based Options

She could also use yield-based options. The portfolio manager is only concerned that interest rates might go up and push down the price of her bonds, right? Well, if interest rates go up, what else goes up?

That's right, yields. Yields go the same way interest rates go.

It's prices that move the other way.

The portfolio's enemy is higher yields. So, if she can't beat them, why not join them?

That's the concept behind hedging. If the other side is about to win, you bet on the other side a while. You profit from a temporary situation that otherwise would have left you with a loss.

So if the portfolio manager is bearish on prices, she's bullish on yields. Therefore, if she wants protection, she can either buy a price-based put, or buy a yield-based call. Right? If bond prices are going down, bond yields are going up. To increase income, she could sell price-based calls, or sell yield-based puts. Both options would work for her if she's right about interest rates rising.

Remember, it's all based on simple math. You just have to break things down and organize them properly. Never forget the premise:

> **If rates are up, prices are down, and yields are up.**
> **If rates are down, prices are up, and yields are down.**

Let's say our portfolio manager wanted protection. Her hedge is a bearish position on bond prices, which is the same thing as a bullish position on bond yields. So, she might protect against a drop in price by betting on the corresponding increase in yields. Maybe she goes long the following position:

> **Long 1 Mar 75 call @1**

That "75" is notation for a yield of "7.5%." In basis points, it would be expressed as 750 basis points. The premium of $1 needs to be multiplied by $100, which is what the investor would pay to buy this yield-based call.

So if she pays $100 for the call, she has to make $100 to break even. She needs to make 10 basis points. Each basis point is worth $10, so she needs to make ten of them to break even. That would happen if yields go to 7.6%, or 760 basis points. Upon exercise, she would receive 10 basis points times $10 each, or $100, and break even because 760 basis points is 10 points above her strike price of 750 basis points.

Simple, right?

Finally, yield-based options are "European style," meaning they can be traded at any time but only exercised on the expiration date. Of course, if you get that question, your odds of making it through the rest of the day alive are statistically zero.

FOREIGN CURRENCY OPTIONS

When you're talking about currency exchange rates, this is what it all comes down to:

If one goes up, the other goes down.

That's what you have to remember about foreign currencies. If the U.S. dollar's value goes up, the other currency you're measuring it against goes down, and vice versa.

The easy way to attack these questions is to remember the following mnemonic:

E

P

I

C

American Exporters buy Puts. American Importers buy Calls. And, of course they sell the opposite positions.

Let's say we make computers in Madison, Wisconsin. We import hard drives from a company in Canada that insists on being paid in Canadian dollars within 60 days of issuing the purchasing order.

Okay, so we have to pay a certain number of Canadian dollars for those hard drives 60 days from now.

What's our risk?

That the value of the Canadian dollar could skyrocket, forcing us to use more of our hard-earned American dollars to buy enough Canadian dollars to satisfy the contract terms. Let's say the contract price is 1 million Canadian dollars. How much is that in U.S. dollars?

Depends on the exchange rate, which is why importers and exporters constantly have to hedge their foreign currency risks. If the exchange rate between the U.S. dollar and the Canadian dollar is as follows:

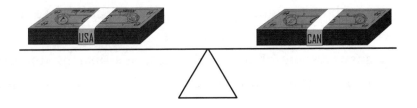

Then, we will be paying $1 million American for those hard drives. That's because we'll take one of our dollars and turn it into one of their C$, one million times.

But if the exchange rate should tip, and suddenly their C$ has shot up in value against our weak dollar, it's going to take more of our dollars to buy their C$.

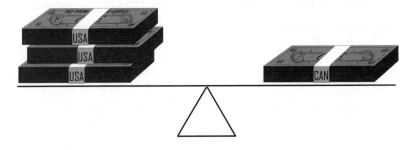

If our dollar weakens against a strengthened Canadian dollar, it might take three of our dollars to convert to just one C$. We have to pay 1 million C$, regardless of the exchange rate. If it takes three of ours to get one of theirs, how much are we really going to pay for those hard drives?

That's right. Three million dollars.

Hope you bought a call on the Canadian dollar, right? A call gives you the right to buy C$ at a strike price, even if the underlying C$ goes up in value.

That's why "Importers buy Calls."

Now, let's say that we're going to <u>export</u> our assembled personal computers to a retailer in Japan, who is going to pay us in Yen in 60 days. We agree that they'll pay us 100 million Yen for a certain number of our computers. What's that amount going to be worth to us in 60 days?

That's our risk.

If the exchange rate right now is 100 Yen = 1 U.S. dollar, then we actually receive $1,000,000 dollars U.S., when we take their 100 million yen and divide them into 1 million piles of a hundred. Not too bad.

But what if our dollar strengthens against their suddenly weakened yen? Suddenly, their currency is so weak that it takes not 100, but 1 million of theirs to equal one of ours? Yikes!

Sixty days later they send us that box of 100 million Yen, and we put 1 million Yen in each pile, ending up with 100 piles, each one worth exactly a dollar.

In other words, we get $100 when we were expecting $1,000,000!

Ooops. Hope somebody bought a put on the Yen. Or at least sold a call to offset the major loss we just took on the exchange rate.

You can now answer some of the exam questions, just by understanding the risks, and remembering that American Exporters buy Puts, American Importers buy Calls.

E

P

I

C

The exam will also want you to know what the contract terms mean. The size of each foreign currency option varies by currency, so the exam will give you the amount in the question.

If you see something like:

Canadian dollar (50,000) Oct 75 call at .60

This is what it breaks down to. The "50,000" refers to the number of Canadian dollars covered by this one contract. The "75" is the strike price. Remember that these options are quoted in terms of American cents. So, the "75" means that each Canadian dollar can be purchased at the strike price of 75 American cents, regardless of how high the Canadian dollar goes relative to the American dollar. The ".60" means "six-tenths of one penny," so it just has to be multiplied by the penny (.01) to get .006. This contract covers 50,000 Canadian dollars, so multiply that by .006 to get $300.

$300 is what an investor would pay for this call.

If this investor were concerned that the Canadian dollar might skyrocket, chances are he's an importer who has to pay for a product in Canadian dollars. This call would tell him the maximum cost of the contract, and could also be used to profit, should his risk materialize.

One more pain-in-the-neck: Japanese Yen are quoted in hundredths of American cents. So, if you're given a premium of ".52," you'll have to put two zeroes in front of it (.0052) before multiplying by the penny (.01).

OPTIONS ACCOUNTS

Now that we've sufficiently analyzed how options work, let's talk about further testable points. If you're a little worn out from all the hedging, straddling, and spreading that's been going on in the previous pages, you may find this stuff refreshingly simple.

First, there is nothing stopping you from obtaining the "OCC Disclosure Document" yourself. In fact, you can get one by visiting www.cboe.com or www.optionsclearing.com and poking around a bit. It's called "Characteristics and Risks of Standardized Options," and it's basically the prospectus used by the OCC (who *issues* the options) to comply with the Securities Act of 1933. When a customer opens an options account, he/she must receive this disclosure brochure, which explains how options work and discloses all the many risks involved. At what point must the customer receive this document? No later than when the account is approved for trading by the ROP.

OPENING THE ACCOUNT

Here are the steps for opening an options account:

1. Registered rep discusses suitability issues with the customer: net worth, experience with options, types of options trades anticipated.

2. Registered rep sends OCC Disclosure Brochure either now or *at the time the* Registered Options Principal (ROP) approves the account. Registered rep also indicates when the OCC Disclosure Brochure called "Characteristics and Risks of Standardized Options" was sent/delivered to customer.

3. As soon as ROP approves account, first options trade may occur.

4.   Customer has 15 days to return a signed options *agreement*. If not, only closing transactions would be allowed—no new positions.

POSITION LIMITS

The customer's signature on the options agreement means that he/she understands the devastating risks associated with options but chooses to trade anyway, and that he/she will abide by the rules of the options exchange. For example, they won't take the electronic quotes they get and re-sell them on a website. They won't write calls and then flee the country whenever they go deep in the money. And, they'll abide by any position limits that may be in place. A position limit means that a customer, or a group of customers "acting in concert," will not try to corner the market, so to speak. If a standardized option has a position limit of 25,000, that means that an investor can have no more than 25,000 bull or bear positions in that option. If he buys 20,000 calls, there are 5,000 bull positions left. He could, therefore, buy 20,000 calls and write 5,000 puts. I'm talking about "per class" here, meaning all MSFT calls or puts, not all MSFT Oct 30 calls, which would be a series. He could also establish 25,000 bear positions (buy puts, sell calls) on a particular underlying security. The OCC provides a list of options and their position limits, and I hope to sell enough Pass the 7 books someday to have to check myself before establishing 25,000 contracts, but that's another issue. I don't think the exam would ask for some hard-and-fast number for the maximum number of contracts. That number is subject to constant revision; a better test question would have you remember which two positions are bullish, and which two are bearish. Also know that the same numbers used for position limits are used for exercise limits. That means that if the option is subject to a limit of 25,000, that number represents the maximum number of open bull or bear positions you can have at one time and also the maximum number of contracts you can exercise over five consecutive business days. As I write these fascinating words, the maximum number for position/exercise limits is 250,000, so if you ever find yourself hampered by that constraint, chances are, it's time for a new hobby.

As I read through the exciting rules of the CBOE this afternoon, I see that if a customer has 200 or more positions on the same side of the market, the firm has to notify the exchange of that fact. That seems a bit too arcane even for a Series 7 question, but you never know considering how infrequently the test writers have been getting out lately.

REGISTRATION OF REPRESENTATIVES, PRINCIPALS

As CBOE Rule 9.2 declares:

No member organization shall be approved to transact options business with the public until those persons associated with it who are designated as Options Principals have been approved by and registered with the Exchange. Persons engaged in the management of the member organization's business pertaining to option contracts shall be designated as Options Principals.

There are Registered Options Principals (ROPs), Compliance Registered Options Principals (CROPs) and even Senior Registered Options Principals (SROPs). A ROP or "registered options principal" approves the new accounts and approves all the orders executed at the firm to ensure suitability. We just mentioned the ROP when we said that the customer must receive the OCC disclosure document either at or before the time that the ROP approves the account. The CBOE says that the CROP "shall be responsible to review and to propose appropriate action to secure the member organization's compliance with securities laws and regulations and Exchange rules in respect of its options business." The CROP or "compliance registered options principal" can have no sales functions unless it's a small firm (under $1 million in gross commissions, or fewer than 10 registered representatives). Instead, he/she is in charge of compliance, which often involves approving communications at the firm. As CBOE Rule 9.21 states:

> All advertisements, sales literature (except completed worksheets), and educational material issued by a member pertaining to options shall be approved in advance by the Compliance Registered Options Principal or designee. Copies thereof, together with the names of the persons who prepared the material, the names of the persons who approved the material and, in the case of sales literature, the source of any recommendations contained therein, shall be retained by the member or member organization and be kept at an easily accessible place for examination by the Exchange for a period of three years.

So, as with NYSE, NASD, and MSRB firms, options firms who belong to the CBOE keep their communications on file three years, two years readily accessible, and they approve communications before they go out. Of course, it isn't feasible to pre-approve all correspondence between the firm and customers, so correspondence has to be regularly monitored. But, when the communications are called advertising, sales literature, and—in the case of options—educational material, the stuff needs to be both pre-approved and filed internally.

This next rule says it quite clearly, so let's just copy and paste:

Exchange Approval Required for Options Advertisements and

Educational Material. In addition to the approval required by paragraph (b) of this Rule, every advertisement and all educational material of a member pertaining to options shall be submitted to the Department of Compliance of the Exchange at least ten days prior to use (or such shorter period as the Department may allow in particular instances) for approval and, if changed or expressly disapproved by the Exchange, shall be withheld from circulation until any changes specified by the Exchange have been made or, in the event of disapproval, until the advertisement or educational material has been resubmitted for, and has received, Exchange approval.

So, advertising and educational material on options is subject to some pretty uptight scrutiny. I mean, NASD firms usually just file communications internally. Even when they have to file sales literature/advertising pertaining to investment companies with the NASD, it's within 10 days *after* first use in most cases. Oh well. If you thought people could lose money in mutual funds, you wouldn't believe how fast they can piss it away on puts and calls. So, the regulators figure let's go ahead and see what you intend to tell your customers *before* they start shorting spreads and straddling things they have no business straddling, shall we?

Also, the rule states that "no written materials respecting options may be disseminated to any person who has not previously or contemporaneously received one or more current options disclosure documents."

In English that means that you really shouldn't send somebody some slick sales literature enticing them to start writing call spreads on foreign currency options unless they have already received the OCC Disclosure Document, or are receiving it with the little packet that contains the slick sales literature. What about advertising? Advertising is not something you *send* to someone—advertising involves using the mass media (newspaper, magazine, radio, TV, billboard, etc.). That stuff doesn't accompany an OCC Disclosure Document, although it probably warns you to read that thing before doing something crazy like opening an options account. Sales literature is written communication that is delivered directly to the prospect, including the text of a live seminar or even a cold-calling *script*. And educational material is defined as "explanatory material limited to information describing the general nature of the standardized options markets or one or more strategies." And, of course, there's no way to get through a rule without at least one exception. Lucky for you, there are two. The following do not need to be approved by the exchange:

- advertisements or educational material submitted to another self-regulatory organization having comparable standards pertaining to such advertisements or educational material and

- advertisements in which the only reference to options is contained in a listing of the services of a member organization.

Since we're having such a good time with this, let me make just one more point about all this stuff straight from the mouth of the CBOE:

> Any statement referring to the potential opportunities or advantages presented by options shall be balanced by a statement of the corresponding risks. The risk statement shall reflect the same degree of specificity as the statement of opportunities, and broad generalities should be avoided. Thus, a statement such as "with options, an investor has an opportunity to earn profits while limiting his risk of loss," should be balanced by a statement such as "of course, an options investor may lose the entire amount committed to options in a relatively short period of time."

Just so we're clear—that's copied and pasted text from the CBOE. Didn't want you to think I had inserted a little humor into that with the "of course, an options investor may lose the entire amount committed to options in a relatively short period of time." Of course, I would have rewritten it to say something like, "With options, an investor always earns fantastic profits while limiting his risk except in those situations where he loses all his money really fast."

Good to see the CBOE has a sense of humor, though. Must be a Chicago thing.

Anyway, I lied when I said "one more point." I really wanted to make *three* more points but was afraid you'd stop reading if I gave it to you straight. The CBOE also offers the following comments about communications for options firms:

- It shall not be suggested that options are suitable for all investors.
- Statements suggesting the certain availability of a secondary market for options shall not be made.

That last bullet point means that sometimes you go to close out 10,000 contracts and, guess what, nobody wants to buy your stupid little 10,000 contracts. Unless you'd be interested in reducing your asking price by, say, 75%?

Now, here's another case where we have to keep the terms "sales literature," "advertising," and "educational material" separate. Advertising and educational material may not "use recommendations or past or projected performance figures, including annualized rates of return." What's the big deal? Well, I, myself once got lucky and bought some PCLN calls for $35 which I quickly sold for $285. What kind of profit percentage is that? There were three contracts since I'm such a big-time player, which means my little T-chart had $855 in the money-in column versus $105 in the money-out column. That's a profit of over 700%. Since it took just one week to do it, let's annualize that by multiplying by 52—your firm can now put out a TV ad that says, "One of our customers recently made an annualized return of 36,400% without even knowing what the heck he was doing!"

No, the truth is, I only made about $100 when all the transactions were totaled out for the year, which is just a little bit contradictory of the "36,400% annualized return" the advertisement is using to sucker people into trading options.

Then there's sales literature, and this stuff can use projected performance figures, as long as a whole bunch of disclosure is provided including the fact that the quoted rate of return is not a certainty, all related costs of commissions, margin, etc., are disclosed, and all risks are disclosed. Also, the sales literature must state that supporting documentation for the impressive claims and scenarios being laid out will be provided upon request. And, as with the advertisements of an investment adviser, if the firm is touting the performance of their awesome recommendations/trades, the period quoted should cover at least the most recent 12-month period.

A test question may expect you to know that the CROP must review the following:

- Advertising, sales literature, educational material
- General prospecting letters
- Seminar transcripts
- Allocation of exercise notices

Wait, I didn't tell you about the SROP! The Senior Registered Options Principal is in charge of "supervision of customers' accounts and orders." If he/she delegates supervisory duties, he/she has to be able to supervise and control the folks to whom they're delegating. Basically, the SROP is like the executive producer in Hollywood—you might see other people on the set flailing about, but, ultimately, the responsibility for *everything* stops at his or her desk.

TAXATION

As we said earlier, three things can happen once an option contract is opened:
- Expire
- Close
- Exercise

Let's see about the tax implications for each event.

EXPIRE

Ordinary options expire within 9 months, so all gains and losses will be short-term. A short-term gain, as discussed in the Taxation chapter, is taxed at the investor's ordinary income rate. If you buy an option this November, and it expires next April, you lose all the money you paid. It will be a short-term loss that you claim for April's tax year, which is when you "realize" the loss. Back in November you were just putting down some money. Only in April of next year will you actually realize your loss. If you sell an option in November that expires the following April, you'll realize a short-term capital gain in April.

CLOSE

Options can be closed for either a gain or a loss. The investor/trader doesn't realize the gain or loss until both sides of the T-chart have been completed, so to speak. If she buys an option in November for $300 and sells it to close next April for $400, she realizes a $100 short-term capital gain in April. Obviously, if she only sells it for $200, she would realize a $100 short-term capital *loss* in April.

Same thing for the seller of the option. When they close with a "closing purchase," they either realize a short-term capital gain or loss when they do so.

EXERCISE

It gets trickier when an option is exercised. The options premium will affect either the cost basis or the proceeds on the stock transaction. For example, when a call owner exercises her call, maybe she gets to buy the stock for $50 a share. If she paid $2 for the right to buy at $50, her cost basis on the stock acquired through exercise is really $52. Her proceeds will only come into play if and when she sells the stock.

The seller of that call took in her $2 a share. Upon assignment of the contract, the seller also sells the stock for $50, meaning he's taken in a total of $52 for selling that stock. Proceeds are what you take in when you sell.

So, the premium was added to the call buyer's cost basis on the stock. The premium was added to the call seller's proceeds on the stock.

Nice and simple, as always.

If you buy a put, you get the right to sell stock, so the premium will affect your proceeds. If you buy a Jun 50 put @2, you pay $2 for the right to sell stock at $50. If you exercise the put and actually sell the stock at $50, did you take in $50 per share? No, you only took in $48 per share, so $48 is your proceeds. Your cost basis is whatever you bought the stock for before putting it in somebody's reluctant face.

The reluctant face who sold you that put has the obligation to buy the stock at $50. So, the cost basis on the stock will be $50 per share, right?

No, since he took in your $2 first, the IRS—who is here to help—says he really only has a cost basis of $48.

POSITION	UPON EXERCISE	PREMIUM	EFFECTS
Long Call	Buys stock	Add to strike price	Raises cost base
Short Call	Sells stock	Add to strike price	Raises proceeds
Long Put	Sells stock	Subtract from strike price	Lowers proceeds
Short Put	Buys stock	Subtract from strike price	Lowers cost base

FUNDAMENTALS OF OPTIONS

The Series 7 will have plenty of questions concerning which options are in the money or out of the money; plenty of questions on max gain, max loss, and break-even for both buyers and sellers of calls and puts; and plenty of questions where you calculate a pretend options trader's gain or loss on a position. I would much rather discuss this material, but, luckily for you, many options questions are based simply on a set of facts that can be memorized. Whenever we get to an area that is mostly memorization, I try to shift to bullet-point mode, saving the witty, side-splitting prose for other sections of this fascinating book.

So, let's load up the bullets:

- Each equity options contract covers 100 shares
- Contracts are adjusted for stock splits, stock dividends
- Equity options expire at 11:59 PM Eastern on the Saturday immediately following the 3rd Friday of the expiration month
- Last opportunity to close/trade an option is 4:02 PM Eastern on the 3rd Friday
- Last opportunity to exercise an option is 5:30 PM Eastern on the 3rd Friday
- Options contracts are issued by the OCC (Options Clearing Corporation)
- OCC guarantees performance of the contract, even if the seller disappears
- Buyers open with an "opening purchase" and can close with a "closing sale"
- Sellers open with an "opening sale" and can close with a "closing purchase"
- Ordinary options are offered 9 months into the future

- LEAPS are long-term options that can last from 12 to 39 months
- Options are called "derivatives"
- American style exercise means the contract can be exercised anytime up to expiration
- European exercise means the contract can be exercised on the expiration day only
- Options allow for leverage—less money down, but a higher % gain potentially
- Buying puts is safer than selling short—less money can be lost, and no uptick rule
- Bulls buy calls or sell puts
- Bears buy puts or sell calls
- Buyers have more upside potential
- Sellers have more risk
- Buyers have rights
- Sellers have obligations (to the buyer of the contract)
- Options transactions settle T + 1
- When exercised, the stock purchased or sold through the contract settles T + 3
- Options are paid in full—not bought on margin
- Options are bought inside margin accounts, but they're paid in full
- Advertisements must be submitted to the exchange 10 days prior to initial use
- All advertisements must be maintained on file by the member firm for three years
- Foreign currency options expire on the Friday before the third Wednesday of the month (seriously)

ADJUSTING CONTRACTS FOR STOCK SPLITS, DIVIDENDS

If you own a MSFT Oct 50 call, you own the right to buy 100 shares of MSFT for $50, meaning you get to buy $5,000 of Microsoft common stock if you want to between now and late October. Well, what if you had attended the annual meeting in Redmond, Washington, last year after a few shots of Jack Daniels and started giving Steve Ballmer a hard time, calling him an "incompetent, bald-headed bureaucrat" and calling the board of directors a "den of do-nothing dunces." They might then find out you're holding calls on the stock and decide to make them go suddenly out of the money. They get wind that you own 100 Oct 50 calls that have just gone in the money. So, they effect a 2:1 stock split. Suddenly, the stock drops from $52 a share to $26 a share, sending your calls from in-the-money to worthless.

Well, they could try that, except it wouldn't work. If they do a 2:1 stock split, each MSFT Oct 50 call you own would become 2 MSFT Oct 25 calls. Remember, with each contract you have the right to buy $5,000 worth of MSFT stock, no matter how they decide to slice $5,000 worth of stock.

If it's a 5:4 or 3:2 split, just treat the test question like a question on 100 shares of stock. If you have 100 shares of stock @50, it becomes 125 shares of stock @40 after a 5:4 split. Actually, it becomes the same thing after a 25% stock dividend, too. Either way, an Oct 50 call would become an Oct (125 shares) 40 call. So, rather than creating some handy-dandy table, just know the concept. If it's a 2:1 split, you get twice as many contracts at half the strike price. If it's an uneven split or a stock dividend, just treat the question as if it were asking what happens when somebody is long 100 shares at that particular strike price.

Oh heck, maybe I should just give you the table:

POSITION	EVENT	BECOMES
Jul 50 call	2:1 split	2 Jul 25 calls
Jul 50 call	5:4 split, 25% stock dividend	Jul (125 shares) 40 call
Jul 50 call	3:2 split	Jul (150 shares) 33.33 call

EXERCISING A CONTRACT

Let's say Mr. Long is holding a MSFT Oct 50 call with MSFT trading at $57. Since Mr. Long only paid $2 a share for the contract, he's in a pretty good mood today. He could just sell the contracts and walk away with a profit of about $5 a share, or he could exercise his *right to buy* 100 shares of Microsoft for $50 a share.

Today, Mr. Long decides to exercise the contract, just to be difficult. So, your firm sends notice to the OCC. The OCC (in the middle of all trades) passes the contract off to any firm who has at least one customer short that series of option. See, the folks who end up getting hurt with Mr. Long's call didn't necessarily sell one to Mr. Long. But, if it's a MSFT Oct 50 call, it can be assigned to anybody who wrote a MSFT Oct 50 call to anybody. Options, like dollar bills, are "fungible." That means that if 50 people put dollar bills in a box, shook up the box and let everybody pull out a dollar bill, nobody would end up getting cheated, right? A dollar bill is a dollar bill. A MSFT Oct 50 call is a MSFT Oct 50 call.

So, the OCC assigns the contract to a broker-dealer at random.

Now, the broker dealer who receives the assignment notice didn't write the call. One of their customers did. Which one should they pass it off to? How about the guy who makes all the pesky phone calls and writes all those nasty letters? Why not?

Because the firm can use only the following methods to decide who gets hit with this hot potato known as an assignment notice:

• Random
• FIFO
• Any other fair method

Of course, if it isn't "random" or "FIFO," what, exactly, *would* be "another fair method"? Rock-paper-scissors?

Also random.

Oh well—they can't use LIFO, which might be a false answer choice. It's "first-in-first-out," not "last-in-first-out," in other words.

Nobody wants the assignment notice, so the firm has to be fair in how they assign it. Unless that letter-writing guy takes it too far. Then, they can start sticking it to 'em. For real.

Anyway, when Mr. Long bought that call way back when, the transaction settled T + 1. In other words, Mr. Long bought the call, and the OCC issued it next business day. Now that he's exercising the call, he's buying stock, though. This transaction is a stock transaction that will settle regular way T + 3. If Mr. Long were exercising a put, his stock would end up being sent to the seller's broker-dealer, and the sell side would deliver cash T + 3, just like any other stock transaction.

OPTIONS — BIG IDEAS

1. Whenever somebody starts with a Debit, that's all he/she can lose. If an investor is long an option, the premium is the maximum loss. If someone buys a straddle, the two premiums he paid represent the maximum loss. And the debit that a debit spread investor starts out with represents the maximum loss. In other words, if you start with a debit, that's all you can ever lose.

2. Whenever somebody starts with a Credit, that's all he/she can gain. If somebody is short an option, short a straddle, or doing a credit spread, the credit they begin with is their maximum gain.

3. People do not go in-the-money or out-of-the-money, only options do that. If XYZ stock trades at $83, the XYZ 80 calls are in-the-money by $3. An investor can easily have an option go in-the-money and still lose money himself. If you buy an XYZ Mar 80 call for $5 back in January and the stock only rises to $83 by expiration in March, your option will only be worth $3 at expiration,

meaning that you paid $2 too much for it. So, in that case your option went in the money, while you had a $2 loss.

4. Break-even, max gain, and max loss. Investors have break-even points. For a call, just add the premium to the strike price. For a put, just subtract the premium from the strike price. Doesn't matter if the investor bought or sold. If they bought, the option needs to make back the amount they spent. If they sold, the option can move in favor of the buyer by the same amount that they received. Max gain and max loss tell an investor the most he/she can make and lose on the deal. If you buy a call, you have an unlimited max gain, since a stock could theoretically run forever. You can only lose your premium paid. If you sell a naked call, you could lose everything that the buyer could win, which is unlimited. You can only make the premium received. A put buyer can only lose the premium paid. Their max gain is just strike price minus premium. A 50 put at 2 means the buyer could make 48. The seller can only make the $2 premium and could lose 48.

5. Buyers pay money and won't break even until the stock moves by the amount of the premium paid. If you buy a 50 call at 2, the stock needs to move up $2 so that even if it never goes beyond there by expiration, it will still have an intrinsic value of $2, meaning you could sell it for the exact amount you paid for it. Even-steven.

6. Sellers receive money and won't break even until they lose the bet by the amount of the premium. If you sell a 50 call at 2, the stock can move up $2 and you're okay. If it never goes beyond there by expiration, it will have an intrinsic value of $2, meaning you could buy it back for the exact amount you sold it. Even-steven.

7. Buyers are gamblers; Sellers are bookies. Buyers make bets. They can only lose the amount they put down and can usually win a whole lot more, just like gamblers at a casino. Sellers are the bookies, the house. They can only make the money that gamblers put down and could (theoretically) lose a whole lot more. Call buyers and Put sellers are both bullish, but call buyers can make a whole lot more, theoretically. If you're bullish on MSFT, you could buy an MSFT Oct 70 call @5. Or you could sell an MSFT Oct 70 put @5. If the stock goes to 85, who makes more money? The put seller makes the $5 as the put expires worthless. But the call buyer makes $10, since he paid $5 and can now sell the call for $15 (difference between strike price of 70 and the market price of 85, right?). Plus, the stock could have gone even higher, at which point the buyer keeps making money, but the put seller maxed out long ago at the premium of $5. Buyers have bigger upsides. Sellers can

make the premium and nothing more; they can also lose much more than the premium.

8. Buy low. Sell high. Calls with lower strike prices are worth more. Always. A Mar 50 call is always worth more than a Mar 60 call. One gives you the right to buy at 50, one at 60. Which one is more valuable? The right to BUY at 50. Puts with higher strike prices are worth more. Always. A Mar 60 put is always worth more than a Mar 50 put. One gives you the right to sell at 60, one at 50. Which is more valuable? The right to sell at 60. So, when determining whether an investor wants a spread to widen or narrow with no premiums given, determine which option is worth more. If he bought the more valuable one, it's a debit spread. If he sold the more valuable one, it's a credit spread. Debit = widen, Credit = narrow. Long the 50 call/Short the 60 call—widen or narrow? He bought the more expensive option, the option to buy a stock cheaper, so it's a debit spread. Long the 50 put/Short the 60 put—widen or narrow? He bought the cheaper option and sold the more expensive option, the right to sell higher, so it's a credit spread. Debit = widen, Credit = narrow.

9. If a debit spread widens, the investor makes the amount that it widened. If an investor buys one option at $4 and sells one at $1, that's a spread of $3. If the options premiums are $10 apart at expiration, the investor makes the difference between where the spread started (3) and finished (10). He makes $7, in other words.

10. If a credit spread narrows, the seller makes the amount that it narrowed. If an investor sells one option at $4 and buys one at $1, that's a spread of $3. If the options premiums are $0 apart at expiration (both expire worthless), the investor makes the difference between where the spread started (3) and finished (0). He makes $3, exactly what he started with.

11. For hedging, identify the risk and bet that way. If you are long stock, you want the stock to rise. What's your risk, though? That the stock could fall. So, your risk is pointing down. Who bets that something might go down? Long puts, short calls. If you are short stock, you want the stock to fall. Your risk is that it could rise. Who bets that stock might rise? Long calls, short puts.

12. Buy protection, Sell to increase income/yield. For the "best" hedge or protection, buy an option. Best-Buy. To increase income or yield, sell an option. If you're long stock, you buy a put for protection or sell a call to increase income. If you're short stock, you buy a call for protection or sell a put to increase income.

13. If the stock goes beyond the break-even point, the buyer makes the difference.

If it's an XYZ Oct 50 call at 3, both the buyer and the seller have a break-even point of $53. If the stock finishes at $57, the buyer makes the difference of $4.

14. If the stock fails to hit the break-even point, the seller makes the difference. If it's an XYZ Oct 50 call at 3, and the stock finishes at $48, the option expires worthless, so the seller makes the difference between $3 (what he received) and $0 (what he paid).

WHAT NOW?

- Review this chapter. *Approximately 2.5 hours.*
- If you have the Pass the 7 QuizSet, take the Options Quizzes. *Approximately 4 hours.*
- If you have the Audio CD set, listen to all tracks on Disc 3. *Approximately 80 minutes.*
- Obtain the OCC Disclosure Document and spend ½ hour reading it. Approximately ½ hour like you'll actually do it.

CHAPTER 5

Investment Companies

(Mutual Funds, etc.)

Imagine what it's like to allow a perfect stranger into your home and let them ask a bunch of awkward personal questions about finances, health problems, you name it, and then ask you to trust them with your life savings. As if trusting this person weren't hard enough, this "financial services representative" is also asking you to understand all the different investment options available and all of their implications. How do you decide how much risk to take? How do you do an accurate comparison of all the sales charges and operating expenses, knowing that the sales representative helping you with your decision will only get paid if you invest through him?

That's pretty much what it's like to be your client, so let's take a look at mutual funds from your clients' perspective. They meet with you, maybe at the kitchen table, and you all share a cup of coffee or maybe a cold drink depending on the time of year and their willingness to be nice to a salesperson. You ask them to bare their soul concerning how much money they make, how much credit card debt they've been silly enough to amass at this point, how far they've stretched the equity in their home trying to cover that credit card debt, and how miserably they've failed to save any money over the years. Then, you pull out a slick, colorful catalog of various mutual funds they can choose from.

MUTUAL FUND CATEGORIES

First, they don't know a mutual fund from a hole in the ground. Second, they're even less curious about mutual funds than the average Series 7 candidate, which is scary. And, third, they don't understand half of what you're saying about 12b1 fees, expense ratios, Morningstar ratings, and contingent deferred sales charges. Even before they settle on a particular fund from a particular family, they have to decide on the following *categories* of mutual funds:

Domestic Equity Funds
- Small Cap Growth
- Small Cap Value
- Small Cap Blend
- Mid-Cap Growth
- Mid-Cap Value
- Mid-Cap Blend
- Large Cap Growth
- Large Cap Value
- Large Cap Blend
- Specialty—natural resources
- Specialty—real estate
- Specialty—communications
- Specialty—technology
- Specialty—financial services
- Specialty—utilities
- Specialty—healthcare

Balanced Funds
- Target-Date 2030+
- World Allocation
- Target-Date 2015–2029
- Convertibles
- Moderate Allocation
- Target-Date 2000–2014
- Conservative Allocation

International Stock Funds
- Specialty—precious metals
- Latin America Stock
- Diversified Emerging Markets
- Foreign Small/Mid Growth
- Foreign Small/Mid Value
- Foreign Small/Mid Blend
- Foreign Large Cap Growth
- Foreign Large Cap Value
- Foreign Large Cap Blend

Fixed-Income Funds
- High-Yield Bond
- Emerging Markets Bond
- Short-Term Bond
- Short-Term Government
- Intermediate-Term Bond
- Intermediate-Term Government
- Long-Term Bond
- Long-Term Government
- Inflation-Protected Bond

Municipal Bond Funds
- High-Yield Muni
- Short-Term Muni
- Intermediate-Term Muni
- Long-Term Muni

Money Market
- Taxable
- Tax-Exempt

We haven't even begun to show the investor all the different names of funds from different fund families—the above represent just *categories* under which most funds could be placed. Do they want the Fidelity Intermediate-Term Municipal Bond Fund or the Intermediate Tax-Exempt Bond Fund from T. Rowe Price? Which of the 29 domestic stock funds that you sell would they like to choose this evening? The one that returned 10% over five years but was negative last year, or the one that returned 8.5% over five years but was up 2.7% last year?

Since mutual fund investing can be extremely baffling and overwhelming to an investor, the NASD insists that you can help your clients sort it all out without stepping all over yourself.

WHAT IS A MUTUAL FUND?

First of all, what the heck *is* a mutual fund?

Think of a mutual fund as a big portfolio pie that can serve up as many slices as investors care to buy. Investors send in money to buy slices of the big pie; the fund uses the money to buy ingredients, like IBM, MSFT, and GM. When an investor sends in, say, $10,000, the pie gets bigger, but it also gets cut up into more slices—however many she is buying with her $10,000. That way each slice stays the same size. The only way for the slices to get bigger is for the pie to get sweeter, which happens when securities in the fund go up in value.

Su-weet!

Now, couldn't an investor bypass the mutual fund and just buy stocks and bonds in whatever companies or governments he chooses?

Sure, but most people refuse to change the oil in their car—why would they suddenly become do-it-yourselfers with six- and seven-figure retirement nest eggs? Takes a lot of work to decide which stocks or bonds to purchase. If you only have $400 to invest, you can't take a meaningful position in any company's stock, and even if you tried, you'd end up owning just *one* company's stock. Remember that "non-systematic risk" we discussed, the risk of owning just a few stocks? We said that diversification would protect against that risk, and mutual funds own stocks and bonds from many different issuers, and the portfolio is run by professionals who know when it's time to rebalance the portfolio as sure as the crew at Jiffy Lube knows when it's time to rotate my tires.

ADVANTAGES OF MUTUAL FUND INVESTING

The exam may bring up the many advantages of mutual fund investing over picking stocks and bonds individually, so let's take a look:

- Investment decisions made by a professional portfolio manager
- Ease of diversification
- Ability to liquidate a portion of the investment without losing diversification
- Simplified tax information (1099's make tax prep easier)
- Simplified record keeping (rather than getting 50 annual reports from 50 companies, you get two reports per year from one mutual fund)
- Ease of purchase and redemption of securities
- Automatic reinvestments of capital gains and income distributions at NAV
- Safekeeping of portfolio securities
- Ease of account inquiry

Most of the above bullet points are self-explanatory, but let's add some clarification since you were nice enough to buy the materials from us. The first point is probably the main reason people buy mutual funds—no way are they willing to try this stuff at home. They have no knowledge of stocks, bonds, taxation, etc., and they have even less interest in learning. Let a professional portfolio manager—often an entire *team* of portfolio managers—decide what to buy and when to buy or sell it. As we mentioned, it's tough to have your own diversified portfolio in individual stocks and bonds because a few hundred or thousand dollars will only buy a few shares of stock or a few bonds issued by just a few companies. Any one company could turn out as profitable as Enron, WorldCom, and eToys, and with their luck, many investors would end up purchasing two out of the three. On the other hand, a mutual fund would usually hold stock in, say, 50 or more companies, and their bond portfolios are also diversified. Therefore, even with the smallest amount of money accepted by the fund, the investor is immediately diversified. The exam calls this the "undivided interest concept." That just means that your $50 owns a piece of all the ingredients in the portfolio, just as the rich guy's $1 million does. Yes, you own a much smaller piece, but you're also just as diversified as the rich guy is—you both own your percentage of everything inside the portfolio. Notice that another bullet point said, "Ability to liquidate a portion of the investment without losing diversification." See, if you own 100 shares of IBM, MSFT, and GM, what are you going to do when you need $5,000 to cover an emergency? If you sell a few shares of each, you'll pay three separate commissions. If you sell 100 shares of any one stock, your diversification is seriously reduced. With a mutual fund, you redeem a certain number of shares and remain just as diversified as you were before the sale. And, you can usually redeem/sell your shares without getting hit up for any fees.

What exactly do we mean by "diversification"? As the NASD exam outline indicates, mutual funds can diversify their holdings by:

- Industries
- Types of investment instruments
- Variety of securities issuers
- Geographic areas

If it's a stock fund, it is basically a growth fund, a value fund, an income fund, or some combination thereof. No matter what the objective, the fund will usually purchase stocks from issuers across many different industries. In a mutual fund prospectus you'll often find a pie chart that shows what percentage of assets is tied up in a particular industry. Maybe it's 3% in telecommunications, 10% retail, 1.7% healthcare, etc. That way if it's a lousy year for telecommunications or retail, the fund won't get crushed the way a small investor who owns only one telecomm company's stock or bonds would. A bond fund can be diversified among investment interests. That means they buy some debentures, some secured bonds, some convertible bonds, some zero coupons, some mortgage-backed securities, and even a few money market instruments to be on the safe side. Even if the fund did not spread their investments across many different industries (telecomm, pharmaceutical, retail, etc.) and chose, instead, to focus on just a few industries, they would still purchase securities from a variety of issuers. So, if they like retail, they can still buy stock in a variety of companies—Wal-Mart, Target, Sears, Nordstrom's, Home Depot, etc. And, since any geographic area could be hit by an economic slump, a tsunami, or both, most funds will spread their holdings among different geographic areas. I mean, the Pacific Rim countries sure look promising, but I don't want all my holdings in companies from Japan, Taiwan, and Singapore.

The exam might require you to know the definition of a "diversified fund." Let's go to the most important document on mutual funds, the Investment Company Act of 1940, which defines a diversified fund like so:

"Diversified company" means a management company which meets the following requirements: At least 75 per centum of the value of its total assets is represented by cash and cash items (including receivables), Government securities, securities of other investment companies, and other securities for the purposes of this calculation limited in respect of any one issuer to an amount not greater in value than 5 per centum of the value of the total assets of such management company and to not more than 10 per centum of the outstanding voting securities of such issuer.

So, how does the "Act of 1940" then define a "non-diversified company"?

"Non-diversified company" means any management company other than a diversified company.

Oh. Thanks.

That just means that if the fund wants to promote itself as being "diversified," it has to meet the definition—no more than 5% of its assets are in any one company, and they don't own more than 10% of any company's outstanding shares. If it doesn't feel like meeting the definition, it will have to refer to itself as a "non-diversified fund."

TYPES OF MUTUAL FUNDS

We already took a look at the overwhelming array of mutual funds available. Now, let's get into the nitty-gritty.

EQUITY FUNDS

The primary focus of equity funds is to invest in equity securities. Might have been easier to just call them "stock funds," but the investment world likes to use fancy language whenever possible.

Within equity funds, we find different objectives. Growth funds invest in companies that appear likely to grow their profits faster than competitors and/or the overall stock market. These stocks usually cost a lot compared to the profits that they might or might not have at this point. For example, Amazon and Starbucks are "growth stocks," but you have to pay dearly for this perceived growth. As I write this sentence, Amazon trades at 45 times the earnings/profits of the company, while Starbucks trades at 57 times the earnings. In other words the market price compared to the earnings is very high. What should we call the comparison between price to earnings?

How about the "price to earnings" ratio? The "p/e ratio" just compares how high the stock price is to the earnings per share. A share of stock is just a slice of the company's profit pie—how much of the profits belong to each slice of the pie? That's the earnings per share. The question is, how many times the earnings per share are you willing to pay for the stock? If you're willing to pay high "p/e ratios," you're a growth investor. Also note that dividend income, if any, would be incidental (not important) to the fund's goal of finding growth opportunities. In other words, if your investor is seeking income, by definition, they don't want growth funds.

What if you prefer to buy stocks trading at low price-to-earnings ratios? You're looking for *value*, so the industry decided to call you a "value investor." Value funds simply seek out companies trading for much less than the portfolio management team decides they're actually worth. GM is in a world of hurtin' as I write this witty monologue. But, if a value fund thinks the stock is worth a lot more than folks realize, they'll snap it up now at a low price-to-earnings multiple and wait for the turnaround that inconveniently hasn't happened yet. The exam might say that value funds buy stocks in established companies that are currently out of favor. Or, the test might want you to declare that value funds "seek to purchase stocks trading below their estimated intrinsic value." Right—they like stocks trading cheaper than they should be. Since the share price is depressed while the dividend keeps getting paid, value stocks tend to have high dividend yields. Therefore, they are considered more conservative than growth funds.

What if you just can't make up your mind between a growth fund and a value fund? Luckily, there are funds that blend both styles of investing, and the industry cleverly calls these "blend funds."

If your investor's objective is to receive income from equities, the industry would be happy to sell her an "equity income fund." Believe it or not, what these funds do is buy equities that provide fairly dependable income. Receiving dividends tends to reduce the volatility of an investment, so equity income funds are lower risk than equity growth funds.

What if you can't decide between a mutual fund family's growth funds and its income funds? Chances are, they'll get real creative and sell you a "growth and income fund."

A growth and income fund buys stocks in companies expected to grow their profits and also pay dependable, respectable dividend income. Since we've added the income component, growth & income funds would have lower volatility than growth funds. So, from highest to lowest volatility, we would find growth, then growth & income, and then equity income funds. I have a catalog from one of the largest mutual fund families in the world which puts them in exactly that order, and even uses the color red for the highest volatility—growth—as in, "Warning! This stuff can jump up and down in a hurry."

That same catalog places balanced funds in a lower volatility category than growth, growth & income, and equity income funds. Why? Because a balanced fund keeps a large percentage of its assets in both the stock and the bond markets. The bond market is not as volatile as the stock market, so if the fund devotes, say, 40% or more to the bond market, that will reduce the price fluctuation/volatility of the fund. What percentage is devoted to the stock and to the bond markets? Read the prospectus, and don't expect the fund to maintain an exact mix, either. One of the prospectuses on my desk says, basically, that the balanced fund will always maintain a mix of 80% stocks–20% bonds, except when it maintains a mix of 80% bonds–20% stocks.

And you wonder why I talk from both sides of my mouth.

In any case, stock is not for everybody. Even if an investor wants to own some stock/equity, chances are you'll still put a percentage of her hard-earned money into bond funds. A rule-of-thumb is that whatever your age is, that's the percentage that you should put into fixed-income. So, which type of fixed-income (bond) funds should the investor purchase? If the investor is not in a high tax bracket or is investing in an IRA, 401(k), etc., we'll be recommending taxable bond funds—corporate and U.S. Government bonds, in other words. The investor's time horizon will determine if we should purchase short-term, intermediate-term, or long-term bond funds. Her risk tolerance will tell us if she needs the absolute umbilical safety of U.S. Treasury funds or is willing to party with high-yield corporate bond funds. If the investor is in a taxable account and wants to earn interest exempt from federal income tax, we put her into—get this—a tax-exempt bond fund, which purchases municipal bonds. If the investor is in a tax-addicted state such as Maryland, Virginia, or California, we can sell her the "Tax-Exempt Fund of Maryland," Virginia, or California. Now, the dividends she receives will generally be exempt from both federal and state income taxes. Whether she ends up getting ahead or not, at least she'll know that Uncle Sam and her state governments will get squat from her dividend distributions (notice how we said nothing about capital gains except in this cheap little parenthetical). But, we're not done just because we put her into a tax-exempt bond fund—how much of a yield does she want and how much risk can she withstand? If she's willing to roll the dice, we can put her into the "High-Yield Tax-Exempt Fund" and pray that not too many of the states or water and sewer districts actually stiff us on the interest and principal they're supposed to pay. If her risk tolerance is lower, we'll buy funds that stick primarily to investment-grade municipal bonds.

We've also seen that an investor's need for liquidity tells us how much to park in the safe, boring money market. There are both taxable and tax-exempt money market mutual funds. The tax-exempt money market funds buy short-term obligations of states, counties, cities, school districts, etc. They pay *really* low rates of interest, but since it's tax-free, rich folks still come out ahead. We're talking about TAN's, RAN's, BAN's, etc.

As we saw at the beginning of the chapter, there are categories such as "specialty—healthcare." You may be shocked to learn that this mutual fund actually specializes in purchasing stocks in healthcare companies. That means that during a slump in that industry, we can't expect the fund to do particularly well. What about when the industry is on a tear? Everything's great. So, the trick is to buy when the industry is in a slump and sell on the day that the industry hits a peak. And, if you can do that, stop studying for this silly exam and start doing exactly that at your earliest convenience. Some funds specialize on a particular industry, some on geographic regions. As we said, you can buy the Latin America, the Europe, or the Pacific Rim fund. You would then hope that those regions don't go into a major economic slump or suffer a natural disaster. See, when the fund concentrates heavily in a particular industry or geographic region, it generally takes on more volatility. There are asset allocation funds, and—believe it or not—what they do is allocate their assets. The percentage for equity, fixed-income, and money market is fairly rigid, so if you're too lazy to buy your own equity, fixed-income, and money market mutual fund, you can buy an asset allocation fund and let them subdivide things for you. I've seen definitions that say that asset allocation funds are another name for balanced funds, and I'm not sure how I could argue with that. I mean, if a balanced fund invests a percentage in equity and a percentage in debt, how is that different from an asset allocation fund, which invests a percentage in equity and a percentage in debt securities?

Both international and global funds appeal to investors who want to participate in markets not confined to the U.S. The difference between the two is that an international fund invests in companies located anywhere but the U.S. A global fund would invest in companies located and doing business anywhere in the world, including the U.S. Remember that when you move away from the U.S. you take on more political/social risk as well as currency exchange risk.

Could you take a guess as to what a precious metals fund would invest in? I thought so.

What if you don't believe that portfolio managers are likely to beat an index such as the S&P 500 over the long-term? First of all, you're in good company with plenty of evidence to support your notion. Secondly, if you can't beat the S&P 500 index, join it. Just buy an index fund that contains the same 500 stocks and only trades a stock if Standard & Poor's kicks it out of the index, forcing you to sell that one and buy the one that S&P is welcoming into the club. Passive management, in other words, as opposed to active management. An index is just an artificially grouped basket of stocks. Why are there 30 stocks in the Dow Jones Industrial Average, and why are the 30 particular stocks that are in there in there?

Because the Dow Jones publishing company says so.

Same for the S&P 500. S&P decided that these 500 stocks make up an index, so there you have it. Investors buy index funds because there are no sales charges and very low expenses. Since there's virtually no trading going on, the "management fees" should be—and typically are—very low. So, for a no-brainer, low-cost option, you can put your money into an index and expect to do about as well as that index, no better, no worse.

Since the NASD decided to add a few new items to this exciting list of fund types, we will now devote a disproportionate amount of verbiage to "funds of funds" and "principal protected funds."

FUNDS OF FUNDS

Mutual funds are open to the average investor, not just to the big, sophisticated individuals and institutional investors that include pension funds, insurance companies, university endowments, etc. Since the mutual fund is open to the average Joe and JoAnne, they can't focus on extremely risky investment strategies. It would be sort of rude to take the average Joe and JoAnne's retirement nest egg and lose it all on a couple of ill-placed foreign currency bets or ill-timed short sales. But, when the investors are all rich folks and institutions, the regulators can relax a little bit.

This is where hedge funds come in. In general, hedge funds are only open to institutions and to individuals called "accredited investors." We'll look at these "accredited investors" when we discuss another fascinating topic called "Reg D private placements under the Securities Act of 1933." There, too, the well-moneyed accredited investor can do things the average Joe and JoAnne can not, but we'll save that excitement for another section. An accredited investor has over $1 million in net worth and makes > $200,000 per year. If it's a married couple, the assets held jointly count toward that $1 million figure, and the annual income needs to be > $300,000, just to make sure you have even more numbers to learn for your exam.

Why does the investor need to be rich? Because these hedge funds use some very high-risk strategies including short selling, currency bets, risky options plays, etc. If you're an average Joe and JoAnne, it wouldn't be cool to let you risk all of your investment capital on such high-risk investing. On the other hand, if you're a rich individual or a big institution, chances are your hedge fund investment is just a percentage of the capital you invest. So, if you lose $1 million, chances are you have several more million where that came from.

A typical arrangement for a hedge fund is to have a limited number of investors form a private investment partnership. The fund typically charges 2% of assets as a management fee and extracts the first 20% of all capital gains. Then, they start thinking about their investors (we hope). Once you buy, there's a good chance you will not be able to sell your investment for at least one year, even if it stinks. Rather than trying to beat an index such as the DJIA, hedge funds generally go for "absolute positive investment performance"—usually 8% or so—regardless of what the overall market is doing.

Now, just to keep everything nice and simple, although a non-accredited investor cannot invest directly in a hedge fund, there are mutual funds called "funds of hedge funds," which she can invest in. As the name implies, these mutual funds would have investments in several different hedge funds. In most cases, the investor would not be able to redeem her investment, since hedge funds are illiquid (they don't trade among investors). Also, these investments would involve high expenses, since there would be the usual expenses of the mutual fund, on top of the high expenses of the hedge funds the mutual fund invests in.

So, other than the fact that they're really expensive, very risky, and make it really tough for the investor to liquidate her position, they're a great investment. The main testable points on hedge funds would seem to be:

- Open to sophisticated, accredited investors with high net worth
- Illiquid—usually can't be sold for at least 1 year
- Employ riskier, more diverse strategies
- Charge high management fees and usually 20% of all gains
- Non-accredited investors can buy mutual funds that invest in hedge funds

PRINCIPAL-PROTECTED FUNDS

Would you believe that principal-protected funds focus on protecting investors' principal? Why these people can't just buy Treasuries, I do not know. Perhaps they prefer paying expenses to getting the principal guarantee for free. These funds take a lot of steps to keep the principal invested stable, but those steps usually cost something—buying puts on indexes or individual stocks, for example, carries a cost. So, these funds can be rather expensive. In exchange for the guaranteed principal, the fund also might limit the upside that the investor can make. Reminds me of an "indexed annuity," but let's not get into that right now. Principal-protected funds would be suitable for a very conservative investor who needs a lump sum at a fixed point in the future. These are not for income investors, as there will be no income for a long while. Generally, the investor has to deal with a lock-up period of 5 to 10 years, during which no redemptions can be taken and all dividends/capital gains must be reinvested. The guaranteed principal begins after this lock-up period.

Now, this should be way ahead of the curve, but the mutual fund industry has recently added a new spin to this notion of promising a certain value to investors. There are actually funds now that will guarantee that when you sell, you will receive the *highest NAV* that the fund ever achieved during your holding period. No, that is not a typo. The fund does a bunch of sophisticated hedging strategies (just like a hedge fund does) in order to make money comin' or goin', and that adds to the already high expense ratio. But some people like knowing that they'll be able to sell at the highest price the fund reached over a certain holding period and are willing to pay higher expenses for that feature, god love 'em.

COMPARISONS OF MUTUAL FUNDS

Once we decide that the investor wants to invest in a growth fund or a value fund, how do we go about comparing one growth or value fund to another? The mutual fund prospectus would be a darned good place to go. In this handy piece of sales literature we will find the fund's investment objectives and style. Do they focus on companies valued at $5 billion and above? $1 billion and below? Do they use fundamental analysis, poring over income statements and balance sheets, possibly meeting with senior management of the companies whose stock they hold? Or, do they rely more on technical analysis—charts, patterns, trends, etc.? Is a company's dividend payout important when selecting investments for the portfolio, or is the fund really only looking at the growth potential? Is this a small cap, mid-cap, or large cap fund, and how is the fund defining "small, mid-, and large cap," anyway? There are also investment policies disclosed in the prospectus and the statement of additional information. Maybe the fund is telling you that it may invest up to 10% of its assets in securities of issuers outside the United States and Canada and not included in the S&P 500. Or, that they allow themselves to invest 10% of their assets in lower-quality debt securities rated below BB/Ba by S&P and Moody's, or even in debt securities no one has *ever* actually rated. If that stuff all sounds too risky for the investor, well, that's why we're disclosing it here in the prospectus before we ever think about taking his or her money.

The prospectus provides information on the party managing the portfolio. We call that party the investment adviser or the portfolio manager. Often, it's a team approach, so we can see the names of the individual portfolio counselors and how much experience they have doing this sort of thing. The prospectus I happen to be looking at now has a team of eight advisers, and their experience in the industry ranges from 18 to 40 years.

One of the most misunderstood aspects of mutual fund investing has to do with the fees and expenses. You'll often hear people say, "No, there's no expenses on any of my mutual funds—they're all no-*load*." As we'll see in more detail later, whether the fund is "no load" or not, all funds charge operating expenses. You might not get a bill for your share of the expenses, but the fund takes out enough money from the portfolio to cover their expenses, whether this happens to be a "no load" fund or one that charges either front- or back-end sales charges. Sales charges are one thing; expenses are another. Not all funds have sales charges, but all funds have expenses.

In the prospectus the investor can see how much of her check is going toward the sales charge, and how much of the dollars she then invests will be eaten up by ongoing operating expenses. The section that details the fees and expenses of the fund has been entitled "Fees and expenses of the fund" in the prospectus sitting on my desk at the moment. If two growth funds have similar 10-year track records but one has expenses of 1.5% while the other charges just .90%, that could certainly be the tiebreaker the investor is looking for. Expense ratios, in other words, are important factors when determining your investment into a particular fund. A large fund family that starts with "V" has been playing up the significance of expense ratios on long-term returns quite successfully lately. Perhaps you've seen the print ads or heard the radio commercials.

How well does the fund perform? The prospectus will show you "total return," usually as a bar chart and a table of numbers. Since I'm looking at a growth fund prospectus, the red bars are often very long and pointing in both upward and downward directions. Over the past 10 years, the fund has gone up as high as 45% and down as much as 22%. As we said, investing in growth stocks requires a higher risk tolerance and a longer time horizon. There was a 3-year period here where the fund averaged returns of *negative* 9%. Gee, sure hope you didn't need any of this money for a while or anything.

What is "total return"? As usual, it's much simpler than you might assume. The point of buying a mutual fund share is that it might go, you know, up. We call that "capital appreciation" since "going up" doesn't sound nearly as sophisticated. The mutual fund will usually also pay out dividends from all those stocks and bonds they're sitting on. And, at the end of the year, if they took more profits than losses while trading their stocks and bonds, they will distribute a capital gains check to share-holders. Total return takes all three of those things and compares it to where the fund started. If the fund started out with a "net asset value" or "NAV" of $10 and finished the year at $11 per share, that's $1 of "capital appreciation." If the fund also paid a dividend of 50 cents per share and a $1 capital gains distribution, we would add that $1.50 to the capital appreciation of $1 for a total of $2.50 of good stuff. Comparing that $2.50 to where we started—$10—gives us a total return of 25%. How likely is it that a fund could have a total return of 25%? The prospectus I happen to be looking at did 26%, 31%, and 45% during 1997, 1998, and 1999. So, naturally, it had a similar return the next three years, right? No, after that, it was anybody's guess: 7% in 2000, negative 12% in 2001, negative 22% in 2002. Which means the following year was probably even worse, right? No. In 2003 the fund had a total return of nearly 33% in a positive direction. Now we see why the prospectus says that "past results are not predictive of future results." Yeah. I guess not.

See, mutual funds are not short-term investments, especially not equity funds. You need a long time horizon, as this prospectus tells you on the very first page. Nobody knows what will happen this year or next. We can show you the returns over 1, 5, and 10 years and let you be the judge. If we've only been in existence four years, we'll show you the figures for one year and also "life of fund" or "since inception." But no one can tell you which funds will go up this year, let alone which funds will go up the most. If they could do that, why the heck wouldn't they just buy the funds that will go up the most each year and quit their day job?

As we've seen, taxation always plays a part on an investor's returns, so the prospectus will also show results after taxes have been figured in. Of course, this is a little tricky, as we see from the caveat in the prospectus on my desk:

> Your actual after-tax returns depend on your individual tax situation and likely will differ from the results shown below. In addition, after-tax returns may not be relevant if you hold your fund shares through a tax-deferred arrangement, such as a 401(k) plan, IRA, or 529 Savings Plan.

SALES CHARGES AND EXPENSES

If you and your friends wanted to launch a new mutual fund, how would you go about doing that? Forget the nightmare of SEC registration, I mean just from a business standpoint—how would you go about launching this mutual fund? You would need investors, right? Okay, how do you find investors? You have to advertise the fund and give people a number to call or a website to visit for more information. You'd have to print up a bunch of colorful prospectuses and mail them out whenever somebody requests one. And, most of these customers are going through a sales representative, and—believe it or not—sales representatives like you do not generally work for free. So those distribution costs are going to have to be covered somehow. You can cover them with a sales charge. If the net asset value (NAV) of our aggressive growth fund is $9.50, we might actually charge people $10.00 for a stock worth $9.50 and call the difference of 50 cents a sales charge. What's more, we will get away with it. Yes, mutual fund investing is somewhat unique in this way. It's a little bit like going into Nordstrom's and hearing the sales clerk say, "That will be $250 for the cashmere sweater, plus $13.50 to cover the cost of all those postcards we had to mail out to bring you into the store."

What? They're charging the customer an additional fee to cover advertising/distribution expenses?

Absolutely.

If the mutual fund is sponsored/underwritten/distributed by a member firm, there will be a sales charge on purchases or redemptions of the fund. This sales charge covers the distribution expenses of printing, selling, mailing, and advertising the fund, and also leaves a really nice profit for the underwriter/sponsor/distributor of the fund. How much of a sales charge will the investor pay?

Depends on the fund. 5.5% is not uncommon for small investments. The maximum allowed sales charge is 8.5%, but anything over 5.75% is generally considered impolite. So, if a mutual fund charges a maximum sales charge of 5.5%, that means that when the investor cuts her check, 5.5% of it goes to the distributors. Only the other 94.5% goes into the mutual fund for investment purposes.

So, if the NAV is $9.45 but the "public offering price" or "POP" is $10.00, the difference of 55 cents is the sales charge. How big is that sales charge? It is exactly 5.5% of the investor's $10 check. There are few calculations on the Series 7 exam, but you could be expected to know that the sales charge as a percentage equals:

(POP minus NAV) divided by the POP

If we plug our numbers into that quasi-formula, we see that $10 minus $9.45 is 55 cents. 55 cents divided by the POP of $10 equals 5.5%.

A-, B-, AND C-SHARES

A mutual fund that levies sales charges can get the sales charge from investors either when they buy or when they sell. "A"-shares charge a front-end load when the investor acquires them. A = "acquire." "B"-shares charge a back-end load when the investor sells them. B = "back end." For a "B"-share, the investor pays the NAV, but she will leave a percentage behind when she sells. The percentage usually starts to decline in the second year, and after several years (6 to 8), the back-end load goes away completely—effectively, the "B"-shares are converted to "A"-shares. "B"-shares are associated with "contingent deferred sales charges." Break down those words. The sales charge is deferred until the investor sells, and the amount of the load is contingent upon when the investor sells. For a test question on the proceeds of a B-share redemption, just take the NAV and deduct the appropriate percentage from the investor's proceeds. If the NAV is $10, the investor receives the $10, minus the percentage the fund keeps on the back end. So, if she sells 100 shares and there is a 2% back-end sales charge, she gets $1,000 minus $20, or $980 out the door.

So, since the back-end or deferred sales charge eventually goes away, as long as the investor isn't going to sell her shares for, say, seven years, she should purchase B-shares, right?

Wouldn't it be great if things were *ever* that simple in the world of investing? See, we've been acting as if distribution expenses are covered only by sales charges, either on the front-end (A-shares) or back-end (B-shares). Turns out, distribution expenses are covered only by the sales charge, unless the fund has a 12b1 fee.

What?

Yes, a "12b1" fee *also* covers distribution costs, and if you're annoyed at these things right now, you'll eventually learn to love them, as they will put money in your pocket once you begin to sell. 12b1 fees, like sales charges, go to salespersons like yourself. No doubt you've heard about so-called "no-load funds." Well, you may not have gotten the whole story. A no-load fund can still charge a 12b1 fee, as long as it doesn't exceed .25% of the fund's assets. Every quarter, when they take money out to cover expenses, these so-called "no load funds" can also take an amount not to exceed 25 basis points. Money market mutual funds have to be "no load," but that also means they can charge 12b1 fees up to .25%.

Hmm. So, again, should the investor buy the A-share or the B-share? The choice has to do with this 12b1 fee I'm currently babbling about. See, the A-shares for our aggressive growth fund might be as high as 5.5%, but the 12b1 fee we tack on will often be .25%, while the B-shares will pay a 12b1 fee of, say, 1.00%. That complicates things, doesn't it? While the person who bought the B-shares is waiting for that contingent deferred sales charge schedule to hit zero, he's paying an extra .75% every year in expenses. .75% times seven years is an extra 5.25%. Yeah, but still, the A-shares start out with a maximum of 5.5% upfront sales charge, so the B-shares are still better.

Oh, if things were only that simple. See, this 12b1 fee is a percentage. As your assets are growing over time, that .75% is also taking more *money* from you, even if it's a flat percentage—almost like the reverse of compounded interest. We're probably going beyond the depth of the exam, but I just can't stop myself. See, if you invest

$10,000 into a fund, the first year's 12b1 fee would be $75.00. If your investment grew to be $11,000 (as it should, since it's sort of the whole "growth" part of the so-called "growth fund"), the 12b1 fee is going to be $82.50. If the assets are eventually $13,000, the extra .75% in 12b1 fees equals $97.50.

And, as we'll soon see, 5.5% would probably be the *maximum* sales charge on the A-shares. If the investor puts in more money, she can maybe knock down the sales charge to 3 or even 2%, which is why long-term investors with a decent amount of money should almost always buy the A-shares.

Just to make the decision harder, there are also C-shares, which usually don't charge an upfront load but do carry a 1% 12b1 fee. The level 1% 12b1 fee (which is so much higher than the .25% allowed for a "no load" fund) is where we got the clever "level load" nickname, by the way. Some C-shares also charge a contingent deferred sales charge if the investor sells in less than 1 year or 1½ years, just to keep things nice and simple.

So, which type of share should an investor buy? Although I think this concept is a little too subjective (like what makes something "small cap" versus "mid-cap"), I'd recommend the following answers.

- Long-term investor with $50,000+ to invest: A-shares
- Intermediate term investor with small amount to invest: B-shares
- Short-term investor: C-shares

The only significant difference in expenses between A-shares on one hand, and B- and C-shares on the other has to do with the 12b1 fee. The fund also charges a management fee to cover the cost of hiring a portfolio manager. That would be the same for everybody and would have to be a separate line item—remember that. A mutual fund can't bury their management fees under the 12b1 fees or sales charges. Sales charges and 12b1 fees cover distribution costs. The management fee covers portfolio management—the fund has to keep the two separate. The next item in the expenses table of the prospectus would be "other expenses." When you add the management fee, the 12b1 fee and the "other expenses" fee, you have the expense ratio for the fund. For the A-shares, maybe the expense ratio is .70%. But, the expense ratio for the B- and C-shares could be 1.45%, due to that extra .75% 12b-1 fee. Please don't assume that the difference would always be .75%, though. I'm just using that as a typical, credible number. The fact that I'm too lazy to get up and look at a different prospectus has nothing to do with it.

If the investor purchases a B-share, she pays the NAV or "net asset value." Only if/when she sells would the fund take a sales charge from her. If the investor purchases the A-shares, she pays more than the NAV. That extra that she pays is the sales charge, as we said. When you add the sales charge to the NAV, you get the public offering price (POP). So, another little formula the exam could throw at you is:

NAV *plus the* Sales Charge *equals the* POP

It looks so much more intimidating as a formula. All we're saying is that if the NAV is $9.45 and the Sales Charge is 55 cents, the POP is $10.00. Or, they could really mess with you and ask you to *determine* the amount of the sales charge. That formula would be:

POP *minus the* NAV *equals the* Sales Charge

Which, again, looks much more intimidating as a formula. All we're saying is that if the POP is $10 and the NAV is $9.45, the Sales Charge must be 55 cents. As we saw earlier, that sales charge would be 5.5%, since the public offering price of $10 has a sales charge built into it representing exactly 5.5%. That's the percentage that goes to the distributors of the fund, leaving the other 94.5% for the investor to, you know, invest.

So, how and when is this net asset value (NAV) figured? The exam wants you to know that mutual funds use "forward pricing." That means that if you take my check for $10,000 at 11 AM, you won't know how many shares I'll end up buying. The fund will re-figure the NAV when trading closes that day, and then put my $10,000 into the fund at the NAV they come up with then. Same thing for a seller. A seller "redeems" her shares to the fund. When she turns in a redemption order at 1 PM she won't know the exact dollar amount of her check because the NAV won't be determined until after the markets close at 4 PM Eastern. The "net asset value" or NAV is nothing more than the value of one slice of the portfolio pie. The assets of the portfolio would be the value of the securities plus any cash they've generated minus any liabilities. Where did the liabilities come from? The fund might borrow money from time to time to handle redemptions—they don't always want to sell off stocks and bonds to pay investors ready to sell their shares, so they borrow some money. If the fund has $10,000,000 in assets and $550,000 in liabilities, the net assets of the fund would be $9,450,000. If there are 1 million shares, the NAV per share is $9.45. Sellers will receive $9.45 per share when they redeem their A-shares today, but they'll pay a POP higher than that if they're buying. Buyers of the B-shares will pay $9.45, but those redeeming/selling their shares will receive $9.45 per share minus whatever percentage they leave behind to the contingent deferred sales charge.

Just to keep everything nice and simple.

As we just said, the value of a mutual fund share is just the net assets of the fund divided by the shares. If a fund takes some of that cash and pays it out as a dividend or capital gains distribution, they reduce the net assets of the fund *without* reducing the number of shares. Hmm—so they're depleting the size of the pie but still cutting it into the same number of shares.

You betcha. And that's why whenever a mutual fund distributes a dividend or capital gain to the shareholder, the NAV per share is reduced by the amount of the dividend. So, tell the exam that on the "ex-dividend date" for a mutual fund, the NAV drops by the amount of the dividend or capital gain distributed to the shareholders.

Also remember that the NAV is sometimes referred to as the "bid" price, because that is the price the investor receives when selling. So, the answer to an exam question could be, "redemptions are executed at the next calculated bid price," or they could substitute "NAV" for "bid price," just to keep everything nice and simple.

REDUCING THE SALES CHARGE

Although A-shares do charge the front-end sales charge, you can also reduce that sales charge by employing various methods laid out in the prospectus.

Breakpoints

Perhaps you've noticed that in general the more you want to buy of something, the better the deal. Doesn't a small box of Lucky Charms™ at the convenience store cost a lot more per ounce than a shrink-wrapped pack of 10 boxes from Sam's Club? Same with mutual funds. If you want to invest $1,000, you're going to pay a higher sales charge than if you want to invest, say, $100,000. For mutual funds, investors are rewarded with breakpoints. Let's say that the L & H Fund had the following sales charge schedule:

INVESTMENT	SALES CHARGE
<$25,000	5.5%
$25,000 – $49,999	5.0%
$50,000 – $99,999	4.0%
$100,000 – $199,999	3.0%

That means that an investor who buys $100,000 worth of the fund will pay a much lower sales charge than an investor who invests $20,000. In other words, less money will be deducted from her check when she invests. A breakpoint means that at this <u>point</u> the fund will give you this <u>break</u>. A lower sales charge means that an investor's money ends up buying more shares. For mutual funds, we don't pick the number of shares we want; we send in a certain amount of money and see how many shares our money buys us. With a lower sales charge, our money will buy us more shares. Keep in mind that fractional shares are common. For example, $1,000 would buy 12.5 shares if the POP were $80.

Letter of Intent

So, what if we didn't have the $100,000 needed to qualify for that breakpoint? We could write a letter of intent explaining to the mutual fund our intention to invest $100,000 in the fund over the next 13 months. Now, as we send in our money, say, $5,000 at a time, the fund applies the lower 3% sales charge, as if we'd already invested the full amount. The lower sales charge means we end up buying more shares, right? So, guess what the fund does? It holds those extra shares in a safe place, just in case we fail to invest that $100,000 we intended to. If we don't live up to our letter of intention, no big deal. We just don't get those extra shares. In other words, the higher sales charge applies to the money actually invested.

Also, that letter of intent could be backdated up to 90 calendar days in order to cover a previous purchase. If an investor bought $3,000 of the L & H fund on March 10, he might decide in early June that he should write a letter of intent to invest $50,000 over 13 months. He could backdate the letter to March 10 to include the previous investment and would then have 13 months from that date to invest the remaining $47,000.

Breakpoints are available to individuals, husbands & wives, parents & minor child in a custodial account, corporations, partnerships, etc. So, if the mom puts in $30,000 and also puts in $20,000 for her minor child's UGMA account, that's a $50,000 investment in terms of achieving a breakpoint. The child cannot be an adult; he must be a minor. Corporations and other businesses qualify for breakpoints. About the only folks who don't qualify for breakpoints are investment clubs.

Another important consideration for breakpoints is that a sales rep can never encourage an investor to invest a lower amount of money in order to keep him from obtaining a lower sales charge offered at the next breakpoint. That's called breakpoint selling and is a violation punishable by death or dismemberment. Likewise, if a rep fails to point out to an investor that a few more dollars invested would qualify for a breakpoint, that's just as bad as actively encouraging him to stay below the next breakpoint. Remember, sales reps (broker-dealers) get part of the sales charge. It would definitely be to their advantage to get the higher sales charge. Unfortunately, they have to keep their clients' interests in mind, too.

Yes, unfortunately, they take all the fun out of this business.

Rights of Accumulation

If an investor's fund shares appreciate up to a breakpoint, the investor will receive a lower sales charge on additional purchases. In other words, when an investor is trying to reach a breakpoint, new money and account accumulation are counted the same way. So, if an investor's shares have appreciated to, say, $42,000 and the investor wanted to invest another $9,000, the entire purchase would qualify for the breakpoint that starts at $50,000. In other words, the $42,000 of value plus an additional $9,000 would take the investor past the $50,000 needed to qualify for the 4% sales charge.

This is known as rights of accumulation.

Please note that this has *nothing* to do with a letter of intent. If you write a letter of intent to invest $100,000, you'll need to invest $100,000 of new dollars into the fund to get the breakpoint you're intending to get. Rights of accumulation means that you could save money on future purchases, based on the value of your account.

Combination Privilege

Most "funds" are part of a "family" of funds. Many of these fund families will let you combine your purchase in their Income Fund with, say, their Index or Growth Fund in order to figure a breakpoint. They call this, very cleverly, a combination privilege. So, if the individual invests $20,000 in the Income Fund and $30,000 in the Growth Fund, that's considered a $50,000 investment in the family of funds, and that's the number they'd use to figure the breakpoint.

Just trying to keep everybody in our happy family.

Conversion/exchange Privilege

The fund might also offer a conversion/exchange privilege. This privilege allows investors to sell shares of, say, the L & H Growth Fund, in order to buy shares of the L & H Income Fund at the NAV, rather than the higher POP. If we didn't do that, the investor might get mad enough to leave our happy family, since there would be no immediate benefit to his staying with us. I mean, if he's going to be charged the POP, why not look for a new family with a growth fund that might actually, you know, grow?

But remember that buying the new shares at the NAV is nice for the investor, but the IRS still considers the sale a taxable event. So if you get a test question on the tax treatment, tell the exam that all gains or losses are recognized on the date of the sale.

BUYING AND SELLING YOUR MUTUAL FUND SHARES

We already looked at the detailed and slightly perplexing options for purchasing mutual fund shares. A "no load" fund is purchased at the NAV, but every quarter 12b1 fees are deducted from the fund's assets to cover the cost of distribution. If the fund has a "load," you can pay it upfront by buying an A-share and then save money on expenses going forward. You can also knock down your front-end sales charge by purchasing in quantity either all at once or through a Letter of Intent (LOI). If you buy the B-shares, you avoid the front-end sales charge, but you have two other concerns to keep in mind: 1) you'll leave a percentage on the table if you sell for the first several years; and 2) the fund will take a much higher 12b1 fee on your behalf every quarter, driving up your expenses. If you were only going to hold a fund for, say, two or three years, the C-shares would probably make sense. You would pay no front-end or back-end sales charge, and even though the 12b1 fee of 1% is a bit annoying, it's only being charged for two or three years.

PURCHASING SHARES

Who do you buy your mutual fund shares from? Or, for you English majors, from whom do you buy your mutual fund shares? Usually, through a well-dressed, overly caffeinated financial sales representative such as yourself. However, an investor could also just set up an account with the fund company and buy shares directly from them. Usually, the fund company will strongly encourage you to go through a financial adviser/registered representative, though, who is licensed to discuss investments with clients and maybe even get paid for it. If you go directly through the fund, the folks on the phone are just taking whatever order you'd like to place—don't ask 'em nothin' about suitability. Would you save money by bypassing the registered representative? No. The distributor of the fund would just keep all of the sales charge, rather than sharing it with the registered rep's broker-dealer and the registered rep. Believe it or not, most people do not wake up thinking, "Gee, I think I need to buy some shares of a well-diversified growth & income mutual fund today," so a registered representative such as yourself will be the one getting the ball rolling 99% of the time. Even if somebody calls the fund company, the person on the other end will probably recommend that he/she consult with a financial representative such as yourself (once you pass your exams and get licensed). Once you've set up an account through the registered representative, you can purchase additional shares in any of the following ways:

- Contacting your registered representative
- Mailing in your payment to the fund's customer service department (transfer agent)
- Telephoning the fund company
- Purchasing online
- Wiring the money from your bank account

Many people choose to set up an automatic investment program whereby, say,

$300 per month is drawn from their bank account and sent to the fund company. This puts them on a disciplined schedule of investing and also makes sure they don't purchase all their shares at just one price. With their luck, some investors will put in $50,000 at the absolute highest price of all time. The automatic plan uses "dollar cost averaging," which will be explored later in exciting detail.

When the investor opens her account, the fund needs to know if she wants to receive dividends and capital gains in the form of a check, or in the form of more shares. If she decides to automatically reinvest, there will be no tax advantages, but there is a big advantage to her in that she gets to reinvest at the net asset value, avoiding sales charges. Her money will grow faster this way, since every dollar she reinvests goes back into the fund and not a dime to the distributors. If she's in a retirement plan, she will automatically reinvest, since there are penalties for early withdrawals from retirement plans.

Mutual funds have minimum initial investments that are usually lower for IRA accounts than taxable accounts. Some funds will let you in the door for as little as $25 or $50. Others are upscale clubs who won't talk to you for less than $3,000. The minimum initial investment would be found in the prospectus, along with all the other vital information.

SELLING SHARES

Open-end mutual fund shares are not traded with other investors. When you want to sell your L&H Aggressive Growth Fund, you don't sell it to me; you sell it back to the L&H Aggressive Growth Fund. This is called a "redemption" or "redeeming your shares." When you redeem your shares, you receive the NAV per share if it's an A-share and the NAV minus the back-end sales charge if it's a B-share.

How do you go about putting in your redemption order?

- By contacting your registered representative
- By writing to the fund company
- By telephoning or faxing the fund company
- By going through the fund company's website

The fund company reserves the right to require what's known as a "signature guarantee" on any redemptions. A signature guarantee is an official stamp that officers of a bank can put on the required paperwork. When I inherited shares from a family member a few years back, I had to go to my bank for a signature guarantee in order to transfer ownership from the individual to the individual's estate, of which I am the executor. A "signature guarantee" is just a very common requirement when stock is being transferred or sold. They are usually obtained from a bank officer, or a member of a stock exchange.

The prospectus I've been using to write most of this fascinating chapter tells me that the fund reserves the right to require the pain-in-the-neck signature guarantee on any redemptions. The fund *will* require a signature guarantee if the redemption is:

- Over $75,000
- Made payable to someone other than the registered shareholder(s); or
- Sent to an address other than the address of record, or an address of record that has been changed within the last 10 days

Of course, if the Series 7 expects you to memorize even that bullet point list, God help us all. Also note that some mutual fund shares are actually issued (or were) as paper certificates. If that's the case, the investor will have to send in the certificates after signing them and also getting the signature guarantee.

Mutual funds are not exactly in love with redemptions. In fact, many will charge a redemption fee during the first year or so just to encourage you to sit tight. If you sell too soon, you might leave 1% of your investment behind. Note that this is not a back-end sales charge going to the distributors. This is just a little penalty that compensates the fund for the hassle of having to pay out redemptions.

But, whether mutual funds enjoy redeeming shares or not, the fact is that they have to redeem your shares promptly. The answer to the test question is "within 7 days." That requirement could only be suspended if an emergency shut down the exchanges and there was no way to value the fund's portfolio. So, be very skeptical of any answer that's trying to convince you that the fund can "halt redemptions." They'd *like* to do that, the same way you'd like to start selling mutual funds without having to sit for your Series 7.

SYSTEMATIC WITHDRAWAL PLANS

Many investors choose to invest into the fund systematically through an automatic deduction from their bank account. This way they actually invest rather than procrastinating, and they also use "dollar cost averaging," which avoids buying all the shares at an inconveniently high price. Well, when you go to sell/redeem your shares, it sure would stink to sell them all at the *lowest* price of all-time, right?

Therefore, some investors set up systematic withdrawal plans. You might think of this as "dollar-cost-average on the way in, dollar-cost-average on the way out," in case you don't have enough to think about at this point. In order to set up a systematic withdrawal plan the investor must have a minimum account value, often $5,000 or so. Payments are made first from dividends and then capital gains. If the dividends and capital gains don't cover the amount the investor wants to withdraw, the fund then starts redeeming shares. It's also a good idea to stop putting money into the fund once you begin the withdrawal plan. If you recall our wash sale rule, buying shares of a fund that were just sold a few days ago is going to make tax season even more annoying than it already is.

There are several payout or withdrawal options that might pop up on the exam.

Fixed-dollar Periodic Payments

As the name implies, if the investor wants to receive a fixed dollar payment periodically, we can offer her the cleverly named "fixed-dollar periodic payment." If she wants $300 per month, the fund will send her $300 a month. How long will her investment last? Until it's all gone. She's not fixing the time period—she's fixing the monthly payment, which will keep coming until all the funds have been withdrawn.

Fixed-percentage Periodic Payments

The investor might prefer to receive 2% of her account value each month, or maybe 5% each quarter. How much will the investor receive with each withdrawal? Who knows? Whatever 2% or 5% of the current account value happens to be.

Fixed-shares Periodic Payments

The investor can also have the fund redeem/liquidate, say, 10 shares per month and send a check. How large will that check be? Whatever 10 shares are worth that month. As we'll soon see, that's pretty much how a variable annuity works during the annuitization phase.

Fixed Time

Finally, if the investor wants her account liquidated/withdrawn over, say, three years, she'll give the fund an exact date, and they'll figure out how much to redeem each month (or other period) in order to exhaust the account by that date.

STRUCTURE AND OPERATION OF THE MUTUAL FUND COMPANY

So far we've been looking at a mutual fund in terms of what they are, who buys which ones, and how investors go about buying and selling them. Now, let's take a look at a mutual fund as a company—who performs which functions at, say, Fidelity, American Funds, AIG, etc.?

BOARD OF DIRECTORS

A mutual fund has a board of directors that oversees operations of the fund or family of funds. The board's responsibilities include:

- establish investment policy
- select and oversee the investment adviser, transfer agent, custodian
- establish dividends and capital gains policy
- approve 12b-1 plans

Remember, the board of directors does not manage the portfolio; it manages the company. The shareholders of the fund elect and re-elect the board members. Shareholders also vote their shares to approve the investment adviser's contract and 12b1 fees. Those with enough moxie to open the proxy do, anyway.

INVESTMENT ADVISER

Each fund has an investment adviser whose job is to manage the fund's investments according to its stated objectives. Shareholders and the board vote to hire/retain investment advisers, who are paid a percentage of the fund's net assets. That's why they try so hard. The more valuable the fund, the more they get paid. Their fee is typically the largest expense to a mutual fund. Investment advisers have to advise the fund (select the investments) in keeping with federal securities and tax law. They must also base their investment decisions on careful research of economic/financial trends rather than on hot stock tips from their bartender. Since everything needs at least two names, the investment adviser is also called the "portfolio manager."

CUSTODIAN

The fund also keeps its assets in a safe place at the custodian bank. Under very strict rules, some funds do this themselves, but most still let a bank take custody, since banks have vaults and security guards and stuff. The custodian receives the dividends and interest payments made by the stocks and bonds in the fund's portfolio. The custodian is also responsible for the payable/receivable functions involved when the portfolio buys and sells securities.

TRANSFER AGENT

The transfer agent is incredibly busy. This is the party that issues new shares to buyers and cancels the shares that sellers redeem. Most of these "shares" are simply electronic files (book entry), but it still takes a lot of work to "issue" and "redeem" them. While the custodian receives dividends and interest payments from the portfolio securities, it is the transfer agent that distributes income to the investors. The transfer agent acts as a customer service rep for the fund and often sends out those semi-annual and annual reports that investors have to receive. As we just saw, investors can purchase and redeem shares directly with the transfer agent, should their registered representative develop an attitude or an unhealthy love of golf.

UNDERWRITERS/DISTRIBUTORS/WHOLESALERS

Some funds are sponsored by underwriters, who bear the costs of distributing the fund up front and then get compensated by the sales charge that they either earn themselves or split with the broker-dealers who make the sales. Underwriters (AKA "wholesalers," "distributors," or "sponsors") also prepare sales literature for the fund, since they're the ones who will be selling the shares, either directly to the public or through a network of broker-dealers. If a fund distributes itself, it usually covers the distribution costs through a 12b1 fee, as we mentioned. The fund can call itself "no load" as long as the 12b1 fee does not exceed .25% of net assets. There is also a very famous mutual fund family that sells "100% no load funds." That means there is no sales charge and no 12b1 fee. How are they able to stay in business?

Through the management fees—the "100% no load" label helps them pull in more assets. The management fee is simply a % of those assets, so .50% of $1 million is nice, but .50% of $1 *billion* is even nicer.

Don't worry—mutual funds have figured out how to make a profit.

These are the methods of distribution for mutual fund shares:

- Fund/to underwriter/to dealer/to investor (assume sales charge here, a nice big one, probably)
- Fund/to underwriter/to investor (underwriter cuts out the other middleman but still gets a sales charge)
- Fund/to investor (no-load funds, which can charge 12b-1 fees no larger than .25% of assets, deducted quarterly)

SHAREHOLDER VOTING

In class, I usually see some very confused faces when I tell students that mutual fund shareholders get to vote. Perhaps my students have been too busy to notice. Or perhaps they file all their proxy materials with the junk mail. In any case, mutual fund shareholders are, obviously, shareholders, so they get to vote their shares in matters of major importance. If you get a test question about voting rights, tell the test that mutual fund shareholders vote on:

- Changes in investment policies and objectives
- Approval of investment adviser contract
- Approval of changes in fees
- Election of board members
- Ratification of independent auditors

CLOSED-END FUNDS

The third type of investment company defined by the Investment Company Act of 1940 is the "management company." Within this category, we find both open-end funds and closed-end funds. So far, we've been talking about the open-end funds. Let's say a few words on the closed-end variety. The main difference between the two is that open-end fund companies continually issue and redeem shares. When you find an investor for the L&H Aggressive Growth Fund, the fund will issue brand new shares to the investor, which is why you had to sell them with a prospectus. Open-end funds don't do an IPO and then force shareholders to trade the fixed number of shares back and forth. Rather, they issue new shares every time somebody wants to buy them, and they let the shareholders sell back/redeem the shares when they get tired of looking at them.

On the other hand, closed-end funds do an IPO, at which point there is a fixed number of shares. What if you want to sell your closed-end fund? You trade it the same way you trade any other share of stock. How much will you receive? Whatever a buyer is willing to pay. These things can trade at a discount to their NAV, or at a premium. It just depends on the supply and demand for these shares. So, if the test question says that the NAV is $9.45 with the POP at $9.00, something's up, right? You can't buy an open-end fund at a discount. As we saw, the cheapest you can buy them is at the NAV. B-shares are sold at the NAV and so are "no load" funds. But, no way can a public investor buy open-end shares at a discount. So, if the fund shares are selling below NAV, they have to be closed-end fund shares. Doesn't mean they *always* trade at a discount. If people really want your shares, they might pay a premium. In fact, some folks simply try to buy closed-end funds when they're trading at a discount and then sell them later if /when they begin trading at a premium. To be honest, the test question isn't entirely fair. I mean, if they say "NAV" and "POP," they're really talking about an open-end fund. A closed-end fund, like any other share of stock, would have a BID and an ASK price. But, the exam wants you to equate NAV with BID and POP with ASK. NAV or BID represent what the investor receives when selling. POP or ASK represent what the investor pays when purchasing. So, we're not saying that closed-end funds always trade at a discount to their NAV; we're saying that *only* the closed-end fund could do that. Since closed-end shares trade the same way that GE or MSFT shares trade, investors can both purchase them on margin and sell them short. To "sell short" involves borrowing shares from a broker-dealer and selling them, with the obligation to buy them back and replace them later. If the price falls, you buy low after you already sold high. If the price pulls a Google on you, you're screwed.

Another difference between open- and closed-end funds is that you would purchase, say, 100 shares of the closed-end fund and pay whatever that costs. For an open-end fund, you would just cut a check for, say, $1,000, and see how many shares you end up with. $100 would turn into 12.5 shares if the POP were $8.00. That little "point-5" of a share is the "fractional share." For a closed-end fund, you would either buy 12 shares or 13 shares, not 12.5. In fact, if the investor is not a total nancy-boy, he would buy at least a "round lot" of 100 shares.

The exam might also bring up the fact that open-end funds only issue common stock to investors. That's right—even if it's a bond fund, the investor isn't buying bonds in the mutual fund company. The investor is buying a percentage of the bond portfolio. How do you evidence ownership? Common stock. A closed-end fund can use leverage by issuing bonds to investors—I mean, borrowing their money and paying them back a rate of interest. They can also issue preferred stock and even common stock with greater/lesser voting rights, should the exam care to be that difficult the day you sit down to take it.

The investment objectives between an open-end and a closed-end fund could be exactly the same—there are closed-end corporate bond funds, tax-exempt bond funds, aggressive growth funds, etc. Here in Chicago, in fact, Nuveen Investments is the largest issuer of closed-end municipal bond funds (www.nuveen.com offers a darned nice primer on open-end and closed-end funds, by the way). Why would you want those versus the open-end variety? Well, what happens to your yield when the price of the bond drops—it goes up, right? So, if you can buy somebody's closed-end bond fund at a discount, you just goosed your yield a little bit. What about when you want to sell your shares? Well, let's hope they're trading at a premium by then. If not, welcome to the NFL.

ETF'S

Perhaps you have heard of "ETF's" or seen advertisements for the well-known varieties called "Spiders," "Diamonds" and "QQQ." An "ETF" is an exchange-traded fund. Why did they name it that? Because it is a fund that trades on an exchange and this is not an industry brimming with creative types.

Trade Like Shares of Stock

An ETF is just a closed-end fund, typically an index fund. That means that if an investor wants to do as well as a particular index, she can track that index with an exchange-traded fund (ETF). To track the S&P 500, she can buy the "Spider," which is so named because it is an "SPDR" or "Standard & Poor's Depository Receipt." Of course, she could already have been doing that with Vanguard's S&P 500 open-end index fund. But, that is a boring old open-end fund, and how does an investor buy or sell those shares? Directly from the open-end fund. No matter what time of day, if we put in a redemption order, we all receive the same NAV at the next calculated price—forward pricing. So, if the S&P 500 drops 80 points in the morning and rises 150 points by mid-afternoon, there is no way for us to buy low and then sell high.

But with the ETF version investors can buy and sell their shares as often as they want to. They can try to buy when the index drops and sell when it rises. Unlike the open-end versions, these ETF's can be bought on margin and can be sold short for those who enjoy high-risk investment strategies. The test might say that ETF's facilitate "intra-day trading," which just means that you can buy and sell these things as many times as you want throughout the day.

Cost Comparisons

So, are the closed-end ETF's cheaper than the open-end index fund versions?

Depends how you do it. If you were only going to invest $500, the open-end fund by Vanguard would be cheaper. By the way, I don't work for Vanguard. I'm just using them because they have a low expense ratio, and their S&P 500 index fund is the biggest fund in America. Anyway, you wouldn't pay a sales charge and the expenses are only .18% (18 basis points) at the time of this writing. The ETF has an expense ratio of only .11% (11 basis points). But, since the ETF version (Spider) is a stock, you would pay a commission to buy it, just as you would pay to buy shares of GE, Wal-Mart, etc. So, if you invested $500 into the ETF and paid a $10 commission, that commission would work out to be 2% (200 basis points), which is much higher, and that's before we factor in the expenses. On the other hand, if you're investing a larger amount, such as $100,000, the same $10 commission is now 1 basis point (.0001) versus the 18 basis points (.0018) for the open-end index fund's operating expenses. So, I think it's safe to say that for a small amount of money—as usual—the open-end mutual fund is a great option. For larger amounts of money, though, the ETF might be cheaper, assuming the investor is paying low commissions.

Diversification

As with the open-end index funds, ETF's offer diversification. For a rather small amount of money, an investor can own a little piece of, say, 500 different stocks with the SPDR, or 100 stocks with the QQQ. It is also easy to implement asset allocation strategies with ETF's. An investor can find ETF's that track all kinds of different indexes (small cap, value, growth, blue chip, long-term bonds, etc.). If an investor wanted to be 80% long-term bonds and 20% small-cap stock, that goal could be achieved with just two low-cost ETF's. This point is not necessarily a comparison to the open-end index funds, which would offer the same advantage. Rather, it is a comparison to purchasing individual bonds or small cap stocks. In order to spread the risk among many bonds and small cap stocks, an investor would have to spend large sums of money. With an ETF (as with the open-end index funds) diversification can be achieved immediately with a much smaller investment.

Taxation

The exam may point out that there are some tax advantages with ETF's. That is because an investor can turn her ETF into what's known as "creation units," rather than actually selling anything. See, even though ETF's aren't redeemable for cash, the investor can basically exchange them for the underlying security, which is called a "creation unit." Another tax advantage would be the same as the open-end index fund variety—there is virtually no selling of shares within the portfolio, so there are few capital gains distributions.

Summary

The main testable points concerning ETF's would seem to be:
- Closed-end index funds
- Trade like shares of stock, intra-day
- Investors pay a commission rather than a sales charge
- Shares can be bought on margin, sold short
- ETF's have low expense ratios
- ETF's are convenient for investors seeking diversification/asset allocation
- ETF's are very low-cost when purchased in larger quantities
- Indexes include small-cap, mid-cap, large-cap, growth, value, S&P 500, Dow Jones, NASDAQ, even fixed income
- Offer certain tax advantages

WHAT NOW?

- Review this chapter. *Approximately 45 min – 1 hour.*
- If you have the Pass the 7 QuizSet, take the Chapter 5 Quiz on Investment Companies. *Approximately 35 min.*
- If you have the Audio CD set, listen to Disc 4, Tracks 1 and 2. *Approximately 30 min.*
- Obtain several mutual fund prospectuses, especially those with A-, B-, and C-shares. Read through the documents carefully. *Approximately 1.5 hours.*

CHAPTER 6

Retirement Planning

(Including Annuities, Insurance)

NOTE: In this chapter we do not always provide maximum annual contribution limits for retirement plans. Although these maximum contributions could surface on your exam, we do not think that books are the best place to publish information that is ever-changing. Please visit our website or use another trusted source for maximum contribution limits.

OVERVIEW

Chances are you already know something about IRA's, 401(k)'s, Keoghs, and pension plans. Let's take a look at what the exam wants you to know about this stuff.

The two big categories for retirement accounts are "qualified" and "non-qualified." If a retirement plan is "qualified," that means it qualifies for special tax treatment by your friends and mine at the IRS and, therefore, has to comply with certain rules. It's covered by "ERISA," which means it has to include all eligible employees and various other stuff we'll look at later. It also involves pre-tax contributions, for the most part.

NON-QUALIFIED BUSINESS PLANS

If a plan is "non-qualified," it is an informal plan that does not have to comply with ERISA and does not need formal IRS approval. All employees do not have to be covered by a non-qualified plan. In fact, that's what makes a plan "non-qualified." If any type of employee can be excluded from the plan, the plan is "non-qualified." Common examples include deferred compensation and the workplace savings plan or payroll deduction. In either case, the employer runs the plan and basically just puts some of the employee's money in a safe place, where it will be held until retirement. Deferred compensation means, "We'll hold back some of your salary now, let you invest it, and give it to you when you retire, at which point you'll be in a lower tax bracket." These are usually for executives.

SMALL BUSINESSES

A small business can establish a SEP-IRA, which stands for "Simplified Employee Pension" IRA. This allows the business owner to make *pre-tax* contributions for herself and any eligible employees. 25% of compensation can be contributed to a SEP, up to the current maximum (which was $44,000 for 2006 and $45,000 for 2007). SEP contributions are not mandatory on the part of the business owner. It's just that if the business makes *any* contributions, they have to be made to all eligible employees as stipulated in the plan agreement. To establish a SEP, the employer uses a model agreement put out by the IRS (download it at www.irs.gov) that they and the employee sign. It does not have to be filed with the IRS, who does not issue an opinion or approval. That's another sign of a non-qualified plan—more informal, no IRS sign-off required.

Another type of plan for small businesses is called the SIMPLE IRA plan. This is for businesses with no more than 100 employees. The SIMPLE IRA may allow participants to put more money away than the SEP. Of course, that depends on how much they earn. If they earn a lot, a SEP might be better. But, if the participant made only, say, $15,000 and wanted to sock a bunch of cash away for retirement, the SIMPLE would allow her to put up to $10,000 for 2006 and $10,500 for 2007. In a SEP, her allowed % of $15,000 would have been much less than either $10,000 or $10,500. So, SEP's allow high earners to save more than they could save in a SIMPLE IRA, while SIMPLE IRA's allow lower-earning employees to save more than they would be able to put away in a SEP, should the exam really feel like harassing you. Both provide for *pre-tax contributions*, meaning all the money will be taxable when it's distributed during the golden years.

In a SIMPLE plan business owners must match the employee's contributions up to 3% of compensation or contribute 2% of the employee's compensation, whether he contributes or not. There is also a funky thing about SIMPLE IRAs in the first two years. During that time, the participant could only roll the money into another SIMPLE IRA to avoid tax. During this phase, if she tried to roll it into a Traditional IRA, she'd get dinged with a 25% penalty (not 10%), plus ordinary income tax on all of it, plus it could be treated as an excess IRA contribution (6% penalty), so, all in all, not a real good idea. Once the two years have passed, everything's fine. Go ahead and transfer it to a 401(k), traditional IRA, 403(b), etc.

In a "money purchase plan" the employer has to make a contribution as a percentage of an employee's salary, regardless of profitability. The exam might indicate that money purchase plans do not offer much flexibility. The current maximum contribution is the same as it is for SEP and other plans discussed below—$44,000 for 2006 and $45,000 for 2007.

QUALIFIED BUSINESS PLANS

DEFINED CONTRIBUTION

401(k) plans are considered defined contribution plans, because an employer defines how much they will contribute on behalf of the employee. Employers generally match all or part of an employee's contributions up to a certain level, as stipulated in their plan literature. Since this plan is qualified, it has to follow all the guidelines of ERISA, covering all eligible employees, whether the company wants to or not. Even though most 401(k) plans offer a matching contribution up to a certain percentage of the worker's salary, not all of them do. Some folks would participate, anyway, because the 401(k) has much higher contribution limits than a Traditional IRA or Roth IRA, for example. Although 401(k) plans offer pre-tax contributions, as of January 1, 2006, employees can designate some or even all of their contributions as being after-tax "Roth" contributions. That means they'll get no tax break now, but when the money comes out later, it will be tax-free if they do it right. The maximum contribution limit is the same whether you do pre-tax contributions, after-tax (Roth) contributions, or a combination of both—$15,000 for 2006 with an extra $5,000 for folks 50 years and older who want to make a "catch-up" contribution. As with a Roth IRA, all the individual needs to do is wait five years and reach at least age 59½, and the money comes out tax-free. If they don't meet the qualifications, though, the money could be taxed. Unlike the Roth IRA, it doesn't matter how much income the individual earns. Finally, designated Roth 401(k) contributions cannot be rolled into a Roth IRA, just to make sure you have more details to remember.

Profit-sharing is also a "defined contribution" plan, but the contributions can be very flexible. It's based on corporate profits, so in a year of no profits, guess what?

No sharing.

Contributions to employee accounts are limited to 25% of compensation, as they are for the SEP-IRA. Some profit sharing plans make higher contributions to employees closer to retirement, and are therefore called "age-weighted profit sharing plans."

DEFINED BENEFIT

Defined benefit plans are the opposite of defined contribution. For a defined contribution plan, the employer says something like, "We'll match your contributions up to 10% of your salary." For a defined benefit plan, the employer has to get sufficient returns on their investments to pay a defined benefit, such as 70% of your average salary over the last three years of service. These plans are great for folks who have put in many years at the company—usually the plan bases the payout on the final years of service, where the salary is the highest for the employee. So, they either define how much they'll put in on your behalf (contribution) or how much you'll receive (benefit) when you retire. If they define the benefit, they bear the investment risk. If they only define the contribution, you bear the investment risk, which I'm sure they mentioned in the little brochure.

SOLE PROPRIETORS

Keogh Plans, sometimes referred to as HR-10's, are for the self-employed. Not for S-corps, C-corps or other entities, only sole proprietors. If the individual in the test question has side income or is self-employed, he or she can have a Keogh. They can contribute a certain percentage of their self-employment income into the Keogh.

How much?

A lot. For 2006, a self-employed individual can put in 20% of compensation up to $44,000, a number that will continue to change every year except when it doesn't. The employer can contribute up to 25% of the employee's compensation. If you have a book talking about "100% of compensation," first that's because they don't like to bother themselves with facts and, secondly, that means that the workers could actually put in more money than what the sole proprietor contributes, taking it up to an amount equal to 100% of compensation. A sole proprietor doesn't actually pay him or herself a "salary," so the 100% thing is not available. I am convinced that the 20/25% thing is as far as you need to go on Keoghs, which are dying off anyway. Remember that only sole proprietors have them.

NON-PROFITS

TSA's are "tax-sheltered annuities." They are for school and other non-profit organization employees. Non-profit organizations are tax-exempt and called either "403b" or "501c3" organizations, so the exam can refer to these plans by those labels, too. In one class a student said, "Aren't these kind of like 401(k)'s for non-profits?"

Basically. Only the investments are more limited and are usually annuities, thus the name tax-deferred or tax-sheltered annuity. On the exam, assume that these plans are funded with a pre-tax contribution, and the employees will pay ordinary income tax on all the money when they pull it out at retirement. But, as with the 401(k), individuals can now designate some or all of their contributions as after-tax "Roth" contributions.

Students don't qualify; janitors at the school do. Gotta be an employee. The 403b/TSA is also a qualified plan because the school may not exclude, say, janitors, while covering teachers or cover administrators while leaving teachers out in the cold.

Section 457 plans are for state and municipal government workers. The current maximum contribution is the same as it is for 401(k) plans offered by businesses in the private sector. The contributions are made pre-tax, so all money coming out is taxed as ordinary income.

ERISA

Qualified plans offered by businesses are covered by ERISA, which stands for Employee Retirement Income Security Act. It governs retirement plans in the private sector. It spells out things like vesting, funding, disclosure, etc. Vesting means that at some point even the employer's contributions belong to the employee. Or, at least some percent of those contributions. If you're in a 401(k) and your employer has put in $10,000 in matching contributions, you'd walk away with only $3,000 if you were only 30% vested. If you were 70% vested, you'd probably forego the temptation to accidentally key your supervisor's car in the parking garage as you walk out with $7,000. And, if you were 100% vested, you might even go back to meet a former colleague for lunch once in a while. The vesting schedule has to be laid out. And it can't take longer than 6 years for an employee to become fully or "100% vested." There has to be money in the plan and the contributions are governed by the section on "funding." The section on "reporting" makes sure that employees are provided regular updates on the account. The employee also gets to choose a beneficiary.

Who is eligible for these qualified plans? Gotta be 21 years old and work at least 1,000 hours a year.

That's ERISA in a nutshell, a really small nutshell.

INDIVIDUAL PLANS

TRADITIONAL IRA

The first thing you need to remember is: The I stands for INDIVIDUAL.

An IRA is an Individual Retirement Account, so don't let the exam trick you into saying a husband and wife should open a "joint IRA." There is no such thing. If a spouse is non-working, an individual can contribute the current maximum on his or her behalf in the spouse's INDIVIDUAL Retirement Account. They can do this if they file jointly for income taxes. But under no circumstances can two people jointly own an IRA.

Who can have a Traditional IRA? Anyone with earned income. How much can they contribute? 100% of earned income up to the current maximum of $4,000 for 2005 and 2006. But, there are also "catch-up provisions" that allow people 50 and older to put in an extra $500 for 2005 and $1,000 for 2006. Remember on the exam—they might not get to *deduct* their contributions, but if they have earned income, they can have and contribute to an IRA. So, don't let the exam trick you into saying a wealthy executive with a 401(k) is somehow prohibited from having an IRA. He can contribute to his IRA; if he's covered by an employer plan or makes too darned much money, he might not get to deduct the contribution, but the contribution can still be made.

There are two types of IRA's, Traditional and Roth. Traditional IRA's can be funded with pre-tax dollars. That means if you make $25,000 a year and contribute $4,000 to your traditional IRA, you're only taxed on the remaining or "post-contribution" amount of $21,000. Of course, when you pull the money out at retirement, you'll pay ordinary income tax on all of it. See, with retirement plans, you either pay tax before it goes in, or when it comes out. Luckily, you don't have to pay tax on both ends. You shouldn't take any money out until you're 59½ years old unless you want to pay a 10% penalty on the money taken out. Luckily, there are a few ways to avoid the penalty (but not the ordinary income tax):

- Become disabled
- Die
- Buy a first home for residential purposes (up to $10K)
- Use $ for certain medical and educational expenses
- 72(t) series of substantially equal payments

An individual should wait until he's 59½ to take distributions; he also has to start taking it out by the time he's 70½ . If not, the IRS will slap a 50% insufficient distribution penalty on him, which seems a little harsh but is unfortunately how it is. To keep things nice and simple, it's not the year in which the individual turns 70½ (like anybody actually celebrates or notices their 70½ th birthday). It's April 1st (not the 15th, which would have made too darned much sense) of the year following the year in which the individual turns 70½ .

This is called the "required minimum distribution" that the IRS is requiring him to distribute to himself at a minimum.

ROTH IRA

The Roth IRA is funded with after-tax dollars. Therefore, the money comes out tax-free as long as the individual is 59½ years old and has had the account for at least 5 years. For the Roth there is no requirement to start taking the money out at 70½. Since the IRS isn't going to tax that money, they couldn't care less when it starts coming out. In fact, no matter how old she is, if she still has earned income, she can still contribute to her Roth (not her Traditional) IRA.

The contribution limits for both the traditional and the Roth are 100% of earned income up to the current maximum. For 2006, an extra $1,000 may be contributed for people 50 and older. If an individual has both a Traditional and a Roth IRA, the contribution limit would be the total allocated among the two accounts. If the maximum is $4,000, maybe $2,700 for the Traditional and $1,300 for the Roth.

INCOME LIMITS

In the "real world" there are income limits for Roth IRA's, but I would not expect the exam to hit you with those. Do remember, though, that there are no income limits for the Traditional IRA. Don't worry about how much money somebody makes in the test question, or if she's covered by an employer plan. All that would change is the amount she can deduct from her contribution. See, nothing is simple. We'd like to say that all contributions to a Traditional IRA are pre-tax, but, if the individual is covered by an employer plan or makes what the IRS deems a high salary, she might only get to deduct some of her contribution, or even none of it.

So what?

Either way, she can make her maximum contribution. She'd just have to keep track of how much went in after-tax or her "cost basis," so she doesn't get taxed twice on that money when it comes out with everything else. So, it's a hassle, but if she has earned income, she can contribute to her Traditional IRA. She might not deduct 100% or even any percent of it, but it can still go in there.

Whether you deduct or not, the real beauty of these plans is that the earnings grow tax-deferred. Since you don't have to remove cash or sell stocks to pay the current tax bill, your principal is larger, which means that more money can make more money, which can make more money all the time…compounded returns is what we call that. In other words, if you can get a 5% return on your investments, it's better to make 5% of a bigger and bigger number, as opposed to shrinking the size of your principal each year by paying the tax collectors.

So tax-deferred earnings provide a major benefit to the individual.

INVESTMENT RESTRICTIONS

IRA's are not really for high-risk speculation. Toward that end, there are to be no short sales, margin trading, or naked options in these accounts. Also no tangibles or life insurance. And municipal bonds make no sense for a Traditional IRA. Municipal bonds pay tax-exempt interest, which is why their coupon payments are so low. All money coming out of the IRA is taxed, so the municipal bond's tax advantage is destroyed and all the individual is left with is a lower coupon payment. That and a good arbitration case.

ROLLOVERS AND TRANSFERS

If you want to move your IRA from one custodian to another, your best bet is to do a transfer. Just have the custodian cut a check to the new custodian, nice and simple. You can do as many of these direct transfers as you want. If, however, you do a *rollover*, things get tricky. First, you can only do one per year, and, second, it must be completed within 60 days. Plus, the custodian withholds 20% of the money, and that will become a huge hassle, so, if at all possible, do the transfer. In a rollover, the custodian cuts a check in your name. You cash it and then send the money to the new custodian, but you have to make up the 20% that was withheld. Otherwise, what they withheld is treated as an early distribution, and now the 10% penalty thing plus ordinary income, plus much heartburn and lost sleep, etc. Imagine rolling over a $100,000 IRA, where you receive a check for only $80,000 and then have to come up with an additional $20,000 within 60 days or get penalized and taxed.

No thanks. Also note that what the "real world" calls a "direct rollover" is considered a "transfer" on the exam. A "rollover" on the test means the individual has the check cut in *her* name.

EDUCATION SAVINGS PLANS

529 PLANS

These are not retirement plans, but we usually talk about them when discussing retirement plans because of the tax deferral.

529 Savings Plan

The 529 Savings plan allows investors to save/invest for education. Usually, it would be a family member socking away money for a nephew's or grandchild's education, but, actually, the donor and the beneficiary do not need to be related. The beneficiary also does not have to be a child. The person who opens the account is the owner; the beneficiary is the person who will use the money for education. Lots of flexibility in these plans. The donor can contribute up to the gift tax exclusion ($12,000 for 2006) without incurring gift taxes and can even do a lump sum contribution for the first five years ($60,000 in 2006) without incurring gift tax hassles. A married couple—grandpa and grandma, for example—could double that amount and contribute $120,000 currently. Note that if somebody uses the five-year-up-front method, they can't make any more gifts to the beneficiary for the next five years without dealing with gift taxes. We're talking about avoiding gift taxes—the states would actually set the maximum that may be contributed on behalf of a beneficiary.

Contributions are made after-tax, and the withdrawals used for qualified education expenses are tax-free at the federal level. A qualified withdrawal would be taken to cover tuition, room & board, books and no more than seven pitchers of beer per week. Kidding with the last item—the expenses do need to be directly related to education; otherwise, you'll get hit just like you do for an early IRA distribution (10% penalty plus ordinary income tax). Once per year, the account can be transferred to a different 529 Savings plan without tax hassles. Also, if the beneficiary decides he doesn't need the money, the account can name a second beneficiary without tax problems, as long as the second beneficiary is related to the first.

The plans are state-specific, so some states may actually allow the donors who are residents to deduct their contributions for purposes of state income taxes. Or, maybe if the account owner lives in Maryland but the beneficiary lives in Ohio, Ohio will tax the withdrawals. See, it's tricky. The withdrawals wouldn't be taxed by the federal government, but the tax treatment by the states is always an important factor when recommending these plans. Also note that the MSRB and NASD are actively increasing the regulatory protections for these plans. Believe it or not 529 plans are classified as "municipal securities" and the MSRB and NASD are going to raise the requirements for selling these plans to what they are for selling mutual funds. In other words, lots of disclosure about tax implications, fees, and the fact that folks like you aren't selling them just to be nice.

Prepaid Tuition

If you're pretty sure that junior won't be too good for any of the colleges in your state, you might want to lock him in as a future Boilermaker, Hoosier, or Sycamore through a plan whereby you pay for his tuition credits now for any state school in the fine state of Indiana. I didn't say you were locking him into being accepted at Purdue or IU, but he would get to go to a state school with a certain number of credits already paid for.

What if he decided he wanted to be a Buckeye or Hawkeye, instead?

The financial penalties could be nasty in that case, which is why we need to be reasonably sure that the kid will end up going to school in-state. Also note that these credits cover tuition only—not room and board, or books, lab fees, etc.

VARIABLE ANNUITIES

With a mutual fund the investor gets taxed on dividends and capital gains whenever she receives/takes them. As much as modern Americans love to procrastinate, imagine how much we love to procrastinate when it comes to paying taxes. Not only is it psychologically appealing to just keep putting off the big tax bill, but also there is a major financial advantage to this strategy. See, whether we reinvest our mutual fund dividends or go shopping, we pay tax on that dividend for the tax year it was received. That tax bill reduces the amount we have invested. So, if the account gains 4% next year, it's 4% of a reduced number. This tax burden keeps knocking down our principal, slowing down our ability to earn compounded returns. See, even though a bond might pay 5% fixed, if you're reinvesting those interest payments into more bonds, you will have more money earning interest next year, and even more the year after that. That's called compounded interest. Of course, we can't predict that we'll be able to keep reinvesting at 5%, but there's probably about a 50-50 chance that it will be reinvested at 5% or higher. Reinvestment risk doesn't always work against us, right? Yes, it stinks to reinvest a 5% coupon at 3%, but it is kind of fun to reinvest a 5% coupon payment at 9%. The market price of your bond is down—so what? You aren't thinking about selling, anyway. Just the fact that you're taking your returns and reinvesting them so that you have a bigger principal amount earning some rate of return is a beautiful thing. In fact, since we've stumbled onto one of the few interesting topics related to the Series 7, let's give you a sneak peak at what most of you will see up ahead, whether they've informed you of it or not—the Series 65/66. In the Series 65/66 you'll learn that an investment that grows at 5% for five years in a row is worth a lot more than just 5% more at the end. In fact, if you get 5% for 5 years, your dollar is worth $1.27 at the end of five years. To check my math, just take $1 and multiply it by 1.05. That's one year. Times 1.05 again. That's two years. Keep multiplying by 1.05 until you've done it five times, just as a dollar invested for five years at five percent would do. You end up with $1.27. And, if you're really curious, keep doing it and notice how much faster the principal grows every year. The money would *double* every 14.4 years, as those of you hip to the "rule of 72" already know. If the Series 7 has the audacity to bring up the "rule of 72" concept, what it's saying is that you can take a rate of return and divide it into the number 72. Your answer tells you how many years it takes for the money to double. So, if you get returns of 10%, it takes 7.2 years for your money to double.

That assumes you're not taking any withdrawals and are, instead, reinvesting all the dividends, interest, and capital gains into more securities throwing off more dividends, interest, and capital gains, and so on. So, if you can avoid having to sell a bunch of stock to pay this year's tax bill on your investments, your money will grow faster. That's what tax deferral is all about.

Tax deferral is the main thing that separates a mutual fund from a variable annuity. A mutual fund held in a regular ol' taxable account will subject investors to taxation every year. The dividend and capital gains distributions are taxable, and if the investor redeems some shares for a gain, that's also taxable for the year it occurs. A variable annuity, however, is really a retirement plan where you get to keep all the dividends and capital gains in the account, adding to your principal, and compounding your returns forever and ever and ever.

Whoah, sorry. Not forever. You get to defer taxation until you take the money out, which is usually at retirement. Your money grows much faster when it's not being taxed for 10, 20, maybe 30 years, but every dance reaches the point where you have to pay the fiddler. It's been a fun dance, for sure, but the reality is that you will pay ordinary income tax rates on the earnings you've been shielding from the hungry hands of the IRS all these years.

Ordinary income rates, remember. If you're in the 35% tax bracket, the gains coming out of your variable annuity are taxed at that rate. Which complicates things, since long-term capital gains taken in a regular ol' taxable account are now taxed at no more than 15%.

Oh well. The tax deferral is still a big advantage, and there are other advantages of the variable annuity. I'm looking at a very handy brochure that compares mutual funds and variable annuities. The company, which sells both, is pointing out that no matter how diligently you save for retirement, you could end up outliving your nest egg. Unless you buy an annuity, that is. An annuity comes with a "mortality guarantee," which means that as long as you are alive, you can receive a monthly check. Many readers already know this because they have sold their share of fixed annuities. A fixed annuity is an insurance contract where somebody puts money into the contract, and the insurance company promises to pay a certain rate of return and keep making monthly payments for as long as the annuitant is alive. A variable annuity doesn't promise a particular rate of return, which is where they got the "variable" part, but since investors are investing in little mutual funds of their choosing, maybe they'll end up doing much better than the modest rate that the fixed annuity guarantees. In other words, in a variable annuity, the annuitant bears the investment risk rather than having the insurance company promise a certain rate of return. In exchange for bearing the risks we've looked at in the bond and stock markets, the variable annuitant gets the opportunity to do much better than he would have in a fixed annuity.

Could he do worse?

Sure, but what does he want? If he wants a guarantee, he buys a fixed annuity where the insurance company guarantees a certain rate of return. Now he lives with "purchasing power risk," because if the annuity promises 4%, that's not going to be sufficient with inflation rising at 6%. If he wants to protect his purchasing power by investing in the stock market, he buys a variable annuity, but now he takes on all the investment risks we've discussed.

Life is full of tough choices like that. Just like when I chose "English" as a major when I should have chosen "Finance" or "Anything that could potentially lead to employment." Bottom line is, a variable annuity is really just a mutual fund investment that grows tax deferred. The insurance company has basically crossed a mutual fund with a retirement plan here. Insurance companies then cross-pollinated that concept with an insurance policy, offering a death benefit to folks buying variable annuities. In a regular ol' mutual fund investment, you could put in $80,000 and when you die the investment could be worth $30,000, which is all your family would inherit. In a variable annuity, the death benefit would pay out the $80,000. In fact, if the value of your investments were worth more than the $80,000 you had put in, your family would receive the $90,000 or whatever the account was worth.

Insurance companies sell peace of mind, and that death benefit helps a lot of investors sleep better. Pretty tough to put a price tag on that.

Although, actually, I'm going to be pointing out that price tag in great detail throughout our fascinating discussion of variable annuities, but I don't want to hit you with too much excitement all at once. For now, just know that a variable annuity offers the investment choices that you'd get from a family of mutual funds (growth, value, high-yield bonds, etc.), the tax deferral you'd get from an IRA or 401(k) plan, plus a death benefit similar to what you'd get from a life insurance policy.

PURCHASING ANNUITIES

The two major types of variable annuities are "immediate" and "deferred." Those terms simply define how soon the contract holder wants to begin receiving payments. These are retirement plans, so you do need to be 59½ to avoid penalties, unless you qualify for an exemption. So, some customers might want or need to wait 15 or 20 years before receiving payments. We call that a "deferred annuity," because "deferred" means "I'll do it later," the way some readers may have "deferred" their study process for a while before opening the book and realizing there's, like, a lot to know for this exam.

If the individual is already in her 60's, she may want to start receiving payments immediately. As you can probably guess, we call that an "immediate annuity."

Customers can buy annuities either with one big payment or several smaller payments. The first method is called "single premium" or "single payment." The second method is called "periodic payment." If an investor has a large chunk of money, she can put it in a variable annuity, where it can grow tax-deferred. If she's putting in a big single premium, she can choose either to wait or to begin receiving annuity payments immediately. She has to be 59½ years old to start annuitizing, but if she's old enough, she can begin the pay-out or "annuity phase" immediately. That's called a single payment immediate annuity. Maybe she's only 42, though, and wants to let the money grow another 20 years before taking it out.

That's called a single-payment deferred annuity (SPDA). This way she buys accumulation units with her money and holds them as they—we certainly hope—increase in value, just like mutual fund shares. In fact, the accumulation units will increase in number, too, because all dividend and capital gains distributions from the little mutual funds will be reinvested into more accumulation units—that's the compounding we were discussing a few moments ago.

Many investors put money into the annuity during the accumulation phase (pay-in) gradually, over time. That's called "periodic payment," and if they aren't done paying in yet, you can bet the insurance company isn't going to start paying out. So, if you're talking about a "periodic payment" plan, the only way to do it is periodic deferred. No such thing as a "Periodic Immediate Annuity."

To review, then, there are three methods of purchasing annuities:
- Single-Payment Deferred Annuity
- Periodic-Payment Deferred Annuity
- Single-Payment Immediate Annuity

There is no such thing as a "periodic-payment immediate annuity," which just looks like a test question waiting to be written.

THE SEPARATE ACCOUNT

An insurance company is one of the finest business models ever constructed. See, no one person can take the risk of dying at age 32 and leaving the family with an unpaid mortgage, a bunch of other bills, and a sudden loss of income, not to mention the maybe $15,000 it takes just for a funeral these days. But, an insurance company can take the risk that a certain number of individuals will die prematurely by insuring a huge number of individuals and then using the very precise laws of probability over large numbers that tell them how many individuals will die each year with only a small margin of error. Once they've taken the insurance premiums that individuals pay, they then invest what's left after covering expenses and invest it very wisely in the real estate, fixed-income, and stock markets. They have just as much data on these markets, so they can use the laws of probability again to figure out that if they take this much risk here, they can count on earning this much return over here within only a small margin of error.

And, of course, insurance companies are very conservative investors. That's what allows them to crunch a bunch of numbers and know with reasonable certainty that they will never have to pay so many death benefits in one year that their investments are totally wiped out. This conservative investment account that guarantees the payout on whole life, term life, and fixed annuities is called the "general account." In other words, the general account is for the insurance company's investments.

They then created an account that is separate from the general account and, believe it or not, decided to name it the "separate account." It's really a mutual fund family that offers tax-deferral, but we don't call it a mutual fund, even though it's also covered by the same Investment Company Act of 1940. The Investment Company Act of 1940 defines a separate account like so:

> "Separate account" means an account established and maintained by an insurance company pursuant to the laws of any State or territory of the United States, or of Canada or any province thereof, under which income, gains and losses, whether or not realized, from assets allocated to such account, are, in accordance with the applicable contract, credited to or charged against such account without regard to other income, gains, or losses of the insurance company.

Well, that certainly clears things up, doesn't it?

Anyway, you will get a few questions talking about the "general account" versus the "separate account," so please keep the two separate. When your premium dollars are invested into the general account, you are guaranteed a certain rate of return—whole life, fixed annuity. When your premium dollars are invested into the separate account, welcome to the stock and bond markets, where anything can happen and usually does.

From the perspective of the nice couple sitting across from you at the table, it all looks pretty much the same. You were talking about the Platinum Equity Income Fund a few minutes ago—now that you've switched to your variable annuity pitch, we're still seeing the same darned Platinum Equity Income Fund. What's up with that?

It's the same darned fund, but if you buy it through an annuity purchase, we call it a "subaccount," just to keep everything nice and simple.

FEATURES OF THE VARIABLE ANNUITY CONTRACT

The insurance company makes some promises when you buy the annuity. They promise that if you die during the "accumulation period," your beneficiary will receive the greater of the contract's value or what you put in. That death benefit, of course, comes at a price, but it gives you peace of mind knowing that your wife, for example, won't receive less than you put in should you pass away prematurely. And—if the investments have done well, she'll receive the higher value, too. Most people end up taking the money out as monthly payments for the rest of their life. The insurance company promises to make these monthly annuity payments for as long as the annuitant shall live, even if she ends up living an inconveniently long time. Notice how an annuity gives the insurance company a different kind of "mortality risk." In a life insurance policy, their risk is that somebody will put in $10,000 and die the next month, forcing the company to pay out hundreds of thousands, maybe a million. In an annuity, their mortality risk is that the annuitant will end up living to the ripe old age of 101. The insurance company makes a mortality guarantee, which promises to pay the annuitant each month for the rest of her life. But—as always—they cover their risk with a fee, called a mortality risk fee. An insurance company has the risk that their expenses will rise. They promise to keep expenses level, but they charge you an "expense risk fee" to cover their risk. In fact, usually, the two are combined and referred to as a "mortality and expense risk fee," or "M & E" for those in the real world who love to abbreviate. If the whole thing just doesn't work out, you can surrender the contract for its "surrender value," but watch out here. The first seven or eight years is typically your "surrender period." During that time if you decide to cash in the annuity, you will get hit with a surrender charge, which is often called a "contingent deferred sales charge" just as we saw on the B-shares. These surrender charges start out pretty high—maybe 7 or 8%—which is one reason that deferred annuities are long-term investments. Don't be pitching a deferred annuity to a senior citizen, who might need to access her money for an emergency. You need to be pretty sure the individual can leave the money alone for at least as long as the surrender period.

Most annuities use the contingent deferred sales charge called the "surrender period," but some are still sold with front-end sales charges. Either way, there is a premium tax and administrative fees taken out of the check. The individual then allocates what's left to the various subaccounts, the little mutual funds. Maybe 20% goes into the income subaccount, 20% into the growth subaccount and 60% to the high-yield long-term bond subaccount. From the money invested there are plenty of fees that will be deducted. We have all the operating expenses we saw for mutual funds: management fee, 12b1 fee, other expenses. And, we also have the "mortality & expense risk fee."

The exam might list the expenses deducted from the separate account as:
- mortality risk charges
- expense risk charges
- administrative expenses
- management fees
- 12b-1 fees

What is the maximum that an insurance company can charge for sales charges and expenses? The current regulations just say that the charges and expenses have to be "reasonable."

Seriously.

Bonus Annuities

As if annuities weren't complicated enough already, the exam may expect you to know something about "bonus annuities." With a "bonus annuity" the Annuity Company may offer to enhance the buyer's premium by contributing an additional 1 to 5% of what he/she puts in. Of course, this comes with a price. First, there are fees attached and, second, the surrender period is longer. Third, if the investor surrenders the contract early, the bonus disappears. Remember that an investor will get penalized by the annuity company with a "surrender charge" if they pull all their money out early. For "bonus annuities" that period where the investor could get penalized is longer.

Bonus annuities are not suitable for everyone. Variable annuities in general are not good for short-term investment goals, since the surrender charge will be applied during the first 7 years or so. Should you switch a customer into a bonus annuity? Maybe. But, remember, even though the annuitant can avoid taxes through a 1035 exchange, when she cashes in the annuity, she may get hit with a nasty surrender charge by the current annuity company. Just yesterday I saw that the State of Illinois is coming after an agent who talked somebody into surrendering her annuity in order to buy a very risky investment—the surrender cost the investor over $9,000, a fact the agent apparently forgot to point out. Both the NASD and the state regulators sort of have a real problem with that type of sales practice. And, even if her surrender period had ended, does she have another eight years or so to wait until the surrender period on the new annuity finally goes away? This all goes into determining suitability for an annuity purchase.

Voting Rights

Just like owners of mutual fund shares, owners of variable annuities get to vote their units on important decisions such as:

- Electing the Board of Managers
- Changing the Investment Objectives, Policies
- Ratifying the Independent Auditor/Accounting Firm

PAYING IN, PAYING OUT

Most annuities are non-tax-qualified, which means that they are purchased with after-tax dollars. When you cut the check for, say, $50,000 for the annuity, you get no tax deduction from the IRS. So they won't tax that money again when you take it out. That $50,000 will be your cost basis. You will only pay taxes on the amount of earnings above that and only when you finally take out the money.

When you are allocating your investment among the little subaccounts, you are in the "accumulation phase." Since this is a tax-deferred account, the dividend and capital gains distributions from the equity income or bond subaccount will be automatically reinvested into more accumulation units. Therefore, part of the answer to a likely question is that "both the number and value of accumulation units vary." That's right. You're investing in the unpredictable stock and bond markets, so the value of the "accumulation units" varies right along with the markets. The number varies, too, because you don't take the dividends and capital gains now—they automatically reinvest them into more units.

When you reach the magic age of 59½ you can annuitize the contract. And, you can certainly wait longer than that, too. It's just that, without a qualifying reason, you'd have to pay a 10% penalty tax on the earnings portion of the contract if you're under 59½ years old, and there is always ordinary income tax to pay, plus the possibility of a nasty surrender charge to the annuity company. So, when you reach retirement age, you shift from putting money in to taking money out. When you decide to annuitize, the insurance company converts your accumulation units into a *fixed number of* annuity units. Did you catch the italics? This concept would make a nice, little Roman numeral–type question. Remember—the *number* of annuity units is fixed. It's their *value* that varies. How does the insurance company calculate your first payment? They take the following into consideration:

- Life expectancy
- Age and gender
- AIR
- Settlement option
- Account value

Insurance companies are experts when it comes to knowing when you are going to die. No, they don't hold séances, because I don't mean they know when *you* are going to die, or even the funny-smelling guy in the yellow shirt next to me on the El this morning. I mean, they are really good at knowing what percentage of people are going to die in any given year. They don't know the exact percentage, but they can pick a tight range of outcomes that is so darned dependable that they will win as often as the house wins in Vegas. Yes, a few individuals will always beat the house, but the other 99% will keep the house rolling in dough for years to come. You *might* have a life expectancy of 82 years and still manage to see 100. But only a tiny percentage of folks will end up that far from what's expected. As long as we make enough off the other 99%, we can easily cover the few who end up beating the house.

So, the older you are, the bigger your monthly payment will be. Why? You'll be gone sooner if you're 92 compared to someone who's only 62.

Why would gender matter? Women still manage to live longer, so they'll receive a slightly lower monthly payment. It will all work out the same, though—they're just using the separate mortality tables for men and women. Men, high-strung and risk-taking that we are, still consistently drop several years before women.

We'll explain the funky "AIR," which stands for "assumed interest rate" below, right after we take an exciting look at "settlement options."

SETTLEMENT OPTIONS

When the individual gets ready to annuitize the contract, he tells the insurance company which payout option he's choosing. For the biggest monthly check, he'll choose the "life only" or "straight life" option. That means the company only has to make payments for as long as he lives. As soon as he ceases, so do his payments. If that seems too risky, he can buy a "unit refund life annuity." This way he is guaranteed a certain number of payments. If he dies before receiving them, his beneficiary receives the balance of payments. If he chooses "life with period certain," the company will make payments for the greater of his life or a certain period of time, such as 10 years. If he dies after 2 years, the company makes payments to his beneficiary for the rest of the term. And if he lives longer than 10 years, they just keep on making payments until he finally expires. The "joint and last survivor" option would provide the smallest monthly check because the company is obligated to make payments as long as either one of the parties is still alive. Covering two persons' mortality risks (the risk that they'll live an inconveniently long time) is an expensive proposition to the insurance company, so those monthly checks are going to be the smallest.

AIR AND ANNUITY UNITS

As we said, once the number of annuity units has been determined, we say that the number of annuity units is fixed. So, for example, maybe every month he'll be paid the value of 100 annuity units.

Trouble is, he has no idea how big that monthly check is going to be, since nobody knows what 100 annuity units will be worth month-to-month, just like nobody knows what mutual fund shares will be worth month-to-month. Remember the "fixed share systematic withdrawal plan" from a mutual fund? We said that the fund will redeem a fixed number of shares and pay you whatever they happened to be worth. Again, the units really are mutual fund shares; we just can't call them that. During the pay-in phase, we call the shares "accumulation units." During the pay-out phase, we call them "annuity units," just to keep things nice and simple.

So, how much is an annuity unit worth every month? All depends on the investment performance of the separate account compared to the company's expectations of its performance.

Seriously.

AIR

If the separate account returns are better than anybody expected, the units increase in value. If the account returns are exactly as expected, the unit value stays the same. And if the account returns are lower than expected, the unit value drops from the month before. It's all based on the actuary's best guess, known technically as the "Assumed Interest Rate." If the AIR is 5%, that just means the actuary expects the account to return 5% every year. If the account actually gets a 6% annualized rate of return one month, the individual's check gets bigger. (Remember, during the payout phase, the investor is paid the value of his fixed number of annuity units, so to say that the annuity units have increased in value is the same as saying the individual's check gets bigger). If the account gets the anticipated 5% return next month, that's the same as AIR and the check will stay the same. And if the account gets only a 4% return the following month, the check will go down.

Don't let the exam trick you on this concept. If the AIR is 5%, here is how it would work:

Actual Return:	5%	7%	6%	5%	4%
Check:	$1,020	$1,035	$1,045	$1,045	$1,030

When the account gets a 7% return, the account gets much bigger. So when it gets only a 6% return the following month, that's 6% of a bigger account, and is 1% more than we expected to get. So, just compare the actual return with the AIR. If the actual return is bigger, so is the monthly check. If it's smaller, so is the monthly check. If the actual return is the same as the AIR, the check stays the same.

FIXED VS. VARIABLE ANNUITIES

Notice how the payout varies and, thus, the clever name "variable annuity." If an individual doesn't like the variable part of the annuity she can buy an insurance product called a fixed annuity. In a fixed annuity, the insurance company invests her payments into its general account and guarantees a certain monthly payment. Maybe the payment is $750. That's a guaranteed $750, but that $750 is also just about guaranteed to lose value to inflation. If you keep getting the same flat payment even as prices rise, your payment won't go very far at Wal-Mart, right?

If you want the guaranteed payout, you subject yourself to this "purchasing power" or "constant dollar" risk. If you want to fight inflation, you buy a variable annuity so you can invest at least part of your money in stocks, which are the best protection against inflation. To combat inflation/purchasing power risk, though, you take on investment risk.

Always trade-offs in this business.

But, since Americans simply have to have it all, the industry has also created "combination annuities," which are a hybrid of fixed and variable. Some of the payments the individual makes are put in the general account to guarantee a certain rate of return; some of the payments are allocated to the separate account to try to beat the rate of inflation. So, remember that when the individual is allocating money to the various subaccounts, one of the options is a fixed-return investment into the general account.

Just to keep things nice and simple.

TAXATION OF ANNUITIES

The tax implications of variable annuities are a little tricky.

Accumulation Period

During the accumulation phase, the investment is growing tax-deferred. So, all the dividends and capital gains distributions from the subaccounts are being reinvested into more units, just like most people reinvest their distributions back into a mutual fund. If the individual dies, the death benefit is paid to the beneficiary. The death benefit is included in the annuitant's estate for estate tax purposes, and the beneficiary would have to pay ordinary income tax on anything above the cost basis. If the husband bought the annuity for $50,000, and it's now worth $60,000, she'll receive $60,000 and pay ordinary income rates on the $10,000 or earnings.

Sometimes people just can't stop themselves from cashing in their chips. Not that they haven't been given incentives not to. If they're under 59½ and don't have a qualifying exemption, they will not only pay ordinary income tax on the earnings, but also a 10% penalty tax, too. So, if it's a $60,000 annuity, and a 49-year-old surrenders the contract that he bought for $50,000, he'd pay his ordinary income rate on the $10,000 of earnings and also a 10% penalty of $1,000. You didn't think the IRS would, like, penalize him 10% and then take his ordinary income rate on what's left, did you? It's his ordinary income rate *and* 10% of the excess.

Notice how only the excess over cost basis is taxed and/or penalized. The after-tax cost basis is just the cost basis, which means the IRS taxed that money a long time ago and quickly lost interest in it. The earnings part—that part really intrigues them.

So, if you're not 59½ yet, the IRS is giving you all kinds of reasons not to surrender your contract. And, we already mentioned that the insurance company will keep a percentage on the back end if you surrender during the early years of the contract.

So, you can have your money if you want to, but if you take it out too soon, you'll be taxed on the excess and penalized.

Also, this isn't the same thing as a life insurance contract. With a life insurance policy, people often cash in part of their cash value. If they're only taking out what they put in—or less—the IRS treats it as part of their cost basis. In an annuity, however, if somebody does a random withdrawal for, say, $10,000, the IRS considers that to be part of the taxable earnings. So, if you get a test question where some dude put in $10,000 and with the annuity at $30,000 this dude takes out $10,000, remember that that is *not* treated as his cost basis. The way the IRS sees things, the dude has $20,000 of earnings. So, whatever comes out is treated as part of that $20,000. So, the entire $10,000 random withdrawal is taxed as ordinary income. And, if he's not 59½ yet, the IRS will also penalize him $1,000.

Loans

Some insurance companies allow contract owners to take a loan against the value of the annuity during the accumulation period. Usually, the interest charge is handled by reducing the number of accumulation units owned. If the owner pays back the loan in full, the number of units goes up again. Unlike a loan against a life insurance policy, however, a loan from an annuity is treated as a distribution. In other words, it is not tax-free.

1035 Exchanges

We've mentioned that both annuities and insurance policies allow people to exchange their contract for another without paying taxes. That's fine, just don't forget the surrender period. If somebody still has a 6% surrender fee (contingent deferred sales charge) in effect, and you push them to do a 1035 exchange, the IRS won't have a problem with it, but the NASD almost certainly will. Especially if you get caught.

Annuity Period

When the annuitant begins receiving monthly checks, part of each payment is considered taxable ordinary income, and part is considered to represent the cost basis. This could be referred to as the "exclusion ratio" should the exam decide to hit you with lots of details. Once the annuitant has received all of the cost basis back, each additional annuity payment will be fully taxable.

Also, if the beneficiary is receiving annuity payments through a "life with period certain" or a "joint and last survivor" settlement option, she will pay ordinary income tax on part of each monthly check, too—as always, on the "excess over cost basis."

VARIABLE LIFE INSURANCE

AN INSURANCE PRIMER

I've always felt that it would be awfully rude of me to die unexpectedly and leave family and friends footing the bill for my funeral. That's why I basically "rent" insurance coverage through something called "term life insurance." It's very cheap ($5.50 a month in my case), but it's only good for a certain term—maybe it's a 5-, 10-, or 20-year term. The individual pays premiums in exchange for a guaranteed death benefit payable to a beneficiary if the insured dies during that period. If the insured does not die during that period, the policy expires. If the policyholder wants to renew, he can, but he's older now and more costly to insure. In other words, his premiums will go up, even though the death benefit will stay the same. Plus, he's older and more likely to have some medical condition that raises his rates, too. So, as with all products, there are pluses and minuses.

Also note the language used in insurance:

- Policyholder: the owner of the policy, responsible for paying premiums
- Insured: the person whose life is insured by the policy, usually the policy-holder
- Beneficiary: the party that receives the death benefit upon death of the insured
- Death benefit: the amount payable to the beneficiary upon death of the insured, minus any unpaid premiums or loan balances
- Cash value: a value that can be partially withdrawn or borrowed against

So, let's say that Joe Schmoe buys an insurance policy with a $100,000 death benefit payable to his wife. He's the policyholder and the insured. If he dies, the death benefit of $100,000 is paid to the beneficiary, his wife. As we'll see, most insurance also builds up cash value, which can be withdrawn or borrowed while Joe is still alive. (Note that term does not build up this cash value, which is also why it's relatively cheap insurance.)

Permanent vs. Temporary Insurance

Just as with housing, some prefer to rent for a term, some prefer to buy. Some feel that if you're going to be putting money aside, you might as well end up with something should you have the misfortune of living. Death benefits are only worth something when you die, and, as they say, you can't take it with you. You can leave it behind for your beneficiaries, but many people end up at age 55 realizing that their home is paid off, they've got a $2 million 401(k) that already names their spouse as beneficiary, so why do they need a $1 million death benefit? They're covered for the death part.

With term, they would really have nothing of value at this point to show for all those premiums. With "permanent insurance," however, there would be something called "cash value" that they could tap. They could borrow against it, or maybe withdraw some of it just for fun. The most common type of permanent insurance is called whole life insurance. You pay premiums for your whole life (thus the clever name "whole life"). Some policies have the policyholder stop paying premiums at a certain age, but it's still pretty darned close to his or her "whole life." The premiums are much higher than on the term insurance you sort of "rent," but insurance companies will guarantee a minimum cash value, and you can also pretty well plan for an even better cash value than that. This way it works to protect your beneficiaries if you die unexpectedly and also acts as a savings vehicle where the cash value grows tax-deferred. Maybe at age 55 you decide to borrow $50,000 of the cash value and put in a new kitchen with granite countertops, cherry cabinets, and other shockingly expensive amenities. Plus, remember that to renew a term policy means you pay a higher premium. Premiums are "level" in a whole life policy, meaning they don't go up.

So, term is "cheap," but after a few years you end up with nothing. And to keep it going, you'd have to pay more for the same benefit. Reminds me of how I spent five years paying "cheap" rent to a landlord. It was definitely lower than any mortgage payment would have been, so every month I "saved" at least $300. Only, at the end of this 5-year term, I had forked over 40 g's to the landlord and was left with nothing but the opportunity to renew my lease at a higher rate. I covered myself with a roof over my head for 5 years, and at the end of the 5 years I owned absolutely no part of that roof, not even one cracked, loose shingle.

Whole life is more like buying the house, which is exactly what I did after five foolish years of renting. I had to come up with a down payment, and my monthly mortgage is now $200 more per month than my rent was. But, at the end of 5 years, I'll have some equity in the house that I can tap into for a loan maybe (kind of like cash value). Just like with a whole life policy, I'll be getting at least something back for all those payments I've made over the years.

So, whole life involves premiums that are higher than those for term life insurance, but you end up with something even if you stop paying into the policy. There is a guaranteed cash value, whereas term leaves you with nothing. As with term, the death benefit is guaranteed, too, so this is a very popular product for people who want to protect their families and also use the policy as a savings vehicle, where all that increase in cash value grows tax-deferred. Both term and whole life insurance are purely insurance products, and many readers are not only selling them already, but also could probably tell you infinitely more about insurance products right now.

Don't let them—remind them that they, too, are studying for a very difficult securities exam and have no extra time for holding court at this point.

Well nothing is simple in either the securities or insurance industry. Since some clients crave flexibility, the industry bent over backwards to come up with a flexible form of permanent insurance called "universal life insurance." Think "flexibility" when you see those words "universal life insurance." The death benefit and, therefore, the premiums can be adjusted by the client. They can be increased to buy more coverage or decreased to back off on the coverage and save some money. If the cash value is sufficient, premiums can actually stop being paid by the client and start being covered by the cash value. The cash value grows at a minimum, guaranteed rate, just like on traditional whole life polices, and if the general account does particularly well, the cash value goes up from there. As mentioned, at some point the policyholder may decide to withdraw part of the cash value, or may usually borrow up to 90% of it.

So, whether it's term, traditional whole life, or universal life insurance, we're talking strictly about insurance products. Death benefits and cash values (term has no cash value) are guaranteed by the insurance company, which invests the net premiums (what's left after deducting expenses, taxes, etc.) into its general account. Once you start attaching cash value and death benefits to the ups and downs of the separate account, however, you have created a new product that is both an insurance policy and a security. Opens a whole new market for the company, but it also means that those who sell them need both an insurance and a securities license.

Variable vs. Whole Life

Whole life and term life insurance policies tell clients exactly how much they will pay out upon death. And unlike most securities, when an insurance company says a policy is worth $100,000, it's really worth $100,000. If it's a whole life policy with a death benefit of $100,000, $100,000 is the death benefit paid upon death of the policyholder, as long as the premiums are paid and no loans have been taken out.

So, in term and whole life policies, the investment risk is borne totally by the insurance company through its "general account."

Well, with variable insurance products, the death benefit—as well as the cash value—fluctuates just like it does in a variable annuity. That's what they mean by "variable." It all varies, based on the investment performance of the separate account. The separate account, as we discussed under variable annuities, is made up of subaccounts. The investor chooses from these little quasi-mutual funds trying to meet different investment objectives: growth, long-term bonds, short-term Treasuries, etc.

He can even choose to invest some of the premiums into a fixed account, just to play it safe, and he can switch between the subaccounts as his investment needs change without a tax problem. This stuff all grows tax-deferred, remember.

The cash value is tied to account performance, period. So if the test question says that the separate account grew, it doesn't matter by how much. The cash value increases when the separate account increases. But death benefit is tied to actual performance versus AIR, just like an annuity unit in a variable annuity. So, if the AIR is 6% and the account gets a 4% return, the cash value will increase due to the positive return, but the death benefit will decrease because the account returned less than AIR.

Variable Life Insurance (VLI) policies will pay out the cash value/surrender value whenever the policyholder decides to cash in the policy. But, there's no way to know what the value might be at the time of surrender. If the little subaccounts have performed well, the cash value might be better than expected. But if the market has been brutal, the cash value could go all the way down to zero. Probably not gonna' happen, but it could.

A minimum or fixed death benefit is guaranteed, however. Some refer to it as the "floor." No matter what the market does, the insurance company guarantees a minimum death benefit that could be depleted only by failure to pay premiums or by taking out loans against the policy. Remember that any guaranteed payments are covered by the insurance company's general account. So, the minimum is guaranteed, and the policyholder also has the chance of enjoying an increased death benefit, depending on how well the little subaccounts (inside the separate account) do. As we said, that's tied to AIR, so if the market is kind, the death benefit increases, but if the market is unkind, it could, theoretically, drag the death benefit all the way down to the floor.

Sound familiar? Sounds a lot like investing in...yep, securities.

Again, that's why many insurance agents have to sit for this wonderful exam, called the Series 7. They have strayed far from the safe, guaranteed territory of term and whole life into the less predictable world of variable insurance.

After the money's been allocated to the little subaccounts of the separate account, the insurance company charges regular fees, just like it does in variable annuities:

- mortality risk fee
- expense risk fee
- investment management fees
- administrative charges

The value of the subaccounts and, therefore, the cash value are calculated daily. The death benefit is calculated annually. If the separate account has several below-AIR months, it will take several above-AIR months until the customer's death benefit starts to increase.

Variable Universal Life

Remember that flexibility we discussed that separates traditional whole life from universal life? Well, it probably isn't too surprising that somebody eventually crossed that with variable life to get Variable Universal Life. Now, we have the death benefit and cash value tied to the separate account (variable), plus we have the flexible premium thing (universal) going on. Regular old variable life is called "scheduled premium."

That means the insurance company puts your premium payments on a schedule, and you better stick to it. Variable Universal or Universal Variable Life policies are funded as "flexible premium." That means the client may or may not have to send in a check. With a VUL policy, the customer has to maintain enough cash value and death benefit to keep the policy in force. If the separate account rocks, no money has to roll in from the customer. If the separate account rolls over and dies, look out. Since that's a little scary, some VUL's come with minimum guaranteed death benefits.

Advantages of Variable Insurance

The advantages of variable life insurance include the ability to invest some of the premiums into the stock market, which has historically enjoyed relatively high average returns and done very well at beating inflation. A robust investment market can increase the cash value and death benefit, often faster than the rate of inflation. A traditional whole life policy, on the other hand, that promised to pay $50,000 when it was purchased in 1964 represented a lot of money. But if it pays that $50,000 out in 2008, the $50,000 doesn't go very far, due to inflation. In other words, choosing between whole life and variable life is pretty much the same as choosing between a fixed annuity and a variable annuity. If you worry about purchasing power and trust both your luck and the securities markets, you buy the variable stuff. If you'd rather deal with purchasing power risk in exchange for the comfort of the guarantee, you buy fixed annuities and whole life.

Policy Loans

Variable policies make at least 75% of the cash value available to the customer as a loan after 3 years, and maybe as much as 90%. Never 100%, though. 100% means "game over." Guess what, though—they charge interest on that loan. If the loan is not repaid, that reduces both the cash value and the death benefit of the policy. And if the customer takes out a big loan and then the separate account tanks, he'll have to put some money back in to bring the cash value back to a sufficient level or risk having the policy lapse. Don't worry, though. Some people take out a loan with absolutely no intention of repaying it. They simply don't need as much death benefit, so why not have some fun with the money right now?

Settlement Options

The policyholder can choose from many options concerning the method of payment to the beneficiary. These are called "settlement options." The "lump-sum" method is self-explanatory. "Fixed-period" means that the insurance company will invest the proceeds of the policy into an interest-bearing account and then make equal payments at regular intervals for a fixed period. The payments include principal and interest.

How much are the payments? That depends on the size of the principal, the interest rate earned by the insurance company, and the length of time involved in this fixed period.

The "fixed-amount" settlement option has the insurance company invest the proceeds from the policy and pay the beneficiary a fixed amount of money at regular intervals until both the principal and interest are gone. The amount received is fixed, but the period over which the beneficiary receives payments varies.

So, for "fixed-period" versus "fixed-amount," the decision comes down to this: do you want to receive some money for a fixed period of time, or do you want to receive a fixed amount of money for an uncertain period of time? In other words, do you want to be paid something like $25,000 for exactly three years (fixed-period)? Or, would you prefer being paid exactly $25,000 for about three years (fixed-amount)?

In a "life-income" settlement option, the proceeds are annuitized. That means the insurance company provides the beneficiary with a guaranteed income for the rest of his or her life. Just as with annuities, the beneficiary's age and life expectancy are taken into account to determine the monthly payout, along with the size of the death benefit and the type of payout selected.

There is also an "interest only" settlement option, whereby the insurance company keeps the proceeds from the policy and invests it, promising the beneficiary a guaranteed minimum rate of interest. The beneficiary might get more than the minimum, or not, and may receive the payments annually, semi-annually, quarterly, or monthly. She also has the right to withdraw all the principal, if she gets antsy, or change settlement options.

General Features

Since these variable policies are a little confusing to some, the company has to give the policyholder at least 2 years (24 months) to switch back to traditional whole life without having to provide proof of insurability. The new whole life policy will have the same issue date as the original variable policy.

As with contractual plans, variable policies have a free-look period, which is 45 days from execution of policy application or 10 days after policy delivery. During the first year the customer gets all sales charges in excess of 30%. During the second year the customer gets all sales charges in excess of 10% of the second year's premium.

1035 Contract Exchange

If you buy a variable life policy, you have the opportunity to exchange it for a different policy even if issued by a different company. You don't have to pay taxes since you aren't taking the cash value and, like, going on a fly fishing trip to Alaska. You just cash in one policy and exchange it, tax-free, for another insurance policy. Or, believe it or not, you can even exchange a life policy for an annuity.

You can't turn an annuity into a life policy, though.

Sorry about that.

Regulations

Four federal acts are involved with variable life insurance and variable annuities.

The Securities Act of 1933 covers variable life insurance (and annuities). These products must be registered with the SEC and sold with a prospectus. Even though the company that issues these contracts is an insurance company, the subdivision that sells the securities products has to be a broker-dealer registered under the Securities Exchange Act of 1934. The separate account is defined as an investment company under the Investment Company Act of 1940 and is either registered as a UIT or an Open-End Investment Company as defined under that act. The investment adviser has to register under the Investment Advisers Act of 1940.

And at the state level both securities and insurance regulators are watching these products and those who sell them, too.

The Prospectus

The prospectus is intended to fully inform the client and fully disclose all sales charges and expenses. It must be delivered either before or during the sales presentation to the client (which just sounds like the answer to a test question to me). The sales rep must believe that the product is suitable, and that the client understands and can afford any risks associated with it. The sales charges and expenses must be reasonable, as determined by regulations, as well. Such expenses in a variable life policy are deducted from the net premium after it's been invested by the client in the various subaccounts:

- Investment Management Fee
- Cost of Insurance: based on the policyholder's current age and the amount

that the insurance company has at risk (the difference between the death benefit and the policy's cash value)

- Administrative Charges: compensate insurance company for expenses involved in issuing and servicing policies after they are sold, e.g., record keeping, processing death claims, loans and surrenders, sending required reports to policyholders
- Mortality and Expense Risk Charges: the risk that the insured will die earlier than expected (opposite of mortality risk in an annuity)

Most policies have an "expense guarantee provision," which limits the amount the company may raise the administrative charges, no matter what.

Variable life insurance policyholders get to vote their units pretty much like variable annuitants and mutual fund investors. They get to vote for the folks running the show, and would get to approve any major changes to investment objectives.

Taxation of Life Insurance

When you pay your life insurance premiums, you don't get to take a deduction against income, so they are made after-tax. They usually grow tax-deferred, however, which is nice. When the insured dies, the beneficiary receives the death benefit free and clear of federal income taxes.

Cool!

But the death benefit will be added to the insured's estate to determine estate taxes.

Uncool.

It's that simple when the beneficiary has the lump-sum settlement option, anyway. If we're talking about those periodic settlement options that generate interest, some of those payments could be taxed as interest income.

Rather than take a loan, the policyholder can also do a "partial surrender," whereby the policyholder takes out some of the cash value, not enough to make the policy lapse, of course. Depending on how much has been paid in premiums, taxes may be due on the amount withdrawn. Unlike for variable annuities, the IRS uses FIFO here, assuming that the first thing coming out is the cost basis, not the earnings. Only the part taken out above the premiums paid would be taxed.

If a loan is taken out, there are no immediate tax consequences.

STUDY SHEET

	MUTUAL FUNDS	VARIABLE ANNUITIES
IRS limit on contributions	No	No
Tax-deferred growth	No	Yes
Tax-free transfers among investment options	No	Yes
Tax-free exchange	No	Yes
Taxation	Capital gains, dividends, interest taxable	Gains on withdrawals taxed at ordinary income rates
10% penalty on early withdrawals	No	Yes

	VARIABLE ANNUITY	FIXED ANNUITY
Net premiums invested in the...	Separate Account	General Account
Investment risk belongs to	Annuitant	Insurance Company
Main risk to individual is	Investment Risks	Purchasing Power/ Inflation
Salespersons need	Insurance License plus Series 6 or 7	Insurance License

Number of annuity units is fixed
Value of annuity units varies (separate account vs. AIR)
Number and value of accumulation units varies
Life-only = largest monthly check
Joint and Last Survivor = smallest monthly check

PRACTICE:

68. The AIR for a variable annuity is 3.5%. Last month, your client received a check for $1,000 based on actual performance of 6%. If the actual performance is 5% next month, your client

    A.   will receive slightly less than $1,000

    B.   will receive $1,000

    C.   will receive more than $1,000

    D.   AIR will be increased

69. Annuities may be purchased in all the following ways except

    A.   Single premium immediate

    B.   Single premium deferred

    C.   Periodic deferred

    D.   Periodic immediate

70. The major difference between variable annuities and mutual funds involves

    A.   tax deferral

    B.   investment objectives

    C.   bonds vs. stock

    D.   EPS

71. An annuitant requiring the largest possible monthly check should choose

    A.   life only (straight life)

    B.   periodic immediate

    C.   period certain

    D.   joint and last survivor

72. Your 60-year-old client contributed $10,000 to a non-qualified variable annuity many years ago. Now that the account is worth $40,000, the client takes a lump sum withdrawal of $35,000. If his ordinary income rate is 28%, he will pay

    A.   no taxes until age 65

    B.   no taxes

    C. $8,400 in taxes

    D. $9,800 in taxes

ANSWERS:

68. C – it's hard to see how the check will go up if the return next month is lower than the return this month. Don't do that—don't compare next month's return to this month's return. Only compare the returns to AIR. AIR is 3.5%, so anything higher than that makes the check go up. Seriously.

69. D – "periodic" means the individual has not finished paying in and will continue to pay in periodically. The word "immediate" means the annuity company starts paying out immediately—not if the annuitant hasn't finished paying in, right? If the individual makes a single payment and is old enough, she can immediately go into the annuitization/pay-out phase, but not if she's still making periodic payments into the contract.

70. A – mutual funds give no tax deferral; annuities do. The other three choices don't distinguish the two: either could invest in bonds or stock, and they both have investment objectives. No idea what "EPS" could even mean in this context.

71. A – if the company only has to bear one mortality risk, they'll be more generous with the monthly pay-out. As soon as the annuitant ceases, so do the payments, unlike a "period certain" that locks in payments for a minimum number of years.

72. C – why would there be a penalty? He's over 59½. Also, remember only the earnings are taxed. He only had 30K of earnings, the difference between his 10K contribution and 40K value.

WHAT NOW?

- Review the chapter. *Approximately 1 hour.*
- If you have the Pass the 7 QuizSet, take the Chapter 6 Quiz on Retirement and Variables. *Approximately 45 minutes.*
- If you have the Audio CD set, listen to Disc 4, Tracks 3 and 4. *Approximately 40 minutes.*

CHAPTER 7

Direct Participation Programs

GENERAL PARTNERS, LIMITED PARTNERS

The basic characteristic of a Direct Participation Program (DPP) is that rather than paying taxes at the business level, the partners all take a share of the income and expenses on their own personal income taxes. The partners who provide most of the money to the business are the limited partners (LP's), meaning their liability is limited to their investment. If they put up $100,000, then $100,000 is all they could ever lose as passive investors in the partnership. To maintain their limited liability status (which means they can't be sued for personal assets) they have to stay out of day-to-day management of the business. Day-to-day management is up to the general partner. The general partner either runs the show himself or appoints someone to do it; either way, it's his responsibility to get the thing managed. If he's the manager, he can also be compensated for his efforts through a salary. While the LP's provide most of the capital, the GP (general partner) must have at least a 1% financial interest in the partnership. The GP can enter into legally binding contracts on behalf of the partnership and has the authority to buy and sell property. The general partner has unlimited liability. His fiduciary responsibility to the limited partners means he can never:

- compete with the partnership
- borrow money from the partnership. Could he lend money to the partnership? Sure, but providing capital is really the role of the limited partners, who are supposed to put up and shut up.
- commingle personal assets with partnership assets

Limited partners definitely stay out of day-to-day management decisions, but because of "partnership democracy" they do get to vote on the big issues like: suing the GP, dissolving the partnership, switching GP's. Through partnership democracy, the LP's also get regular financial reports, what the exam could refer to as "the right to copy certain partnership records." So, if you're talking about deciding which assets should be sold, the LP's don't get to decide that. If you're talking about changing the partnership from a baseball team to a soccer team…now the LP's get to vote. Just like common stockholders don't get to decide on every day-to-day issue that pops up at corporate headquarters, but if the corporation wants to change business objectives or buy another company, the stockholders get to vote. If the exam asks if LP's can make loans to the partnership, the answer is yes.

SUITABILITY

These partnerships or DPP's must have economic viability. They can't just be money-losing schemes devised by wealthy folks over several brandy old fashioneds. If the IRS suspects the thing never had a chance to make money, they can deem it an abusive tax shelter and go after folks with the full force of the IRS: audits, penalties, interest, seizure of assets…all falling safely under the "don't go there" category.

So, economic viability is the first consideration for a potential investor. The second would be tax benefits. If folks have a lot of passive income, they can receive passive losses from DPP's and use them to offset that passive income for tax purposes. Public-assisted housing and historic rehab partnerships also offer tax credits to investors.

The third consideration is liquidity because, basically, there isn't any. You buy an interest in a limited partnership, it's yours, baby. Don't think you're going to be calling your broker a few weeks later to sell your position. These things are for the long-term. You buy in as a limited partner and you become a direct participant in the business. A passive participant, but you are directly participating in the gains and losses. That's why they call them Direct Participation Programs in Series Sevenland.

So what do these partnerships do?

For test purposes, they seem to be either in the oil and gas business or real estate. The exam wants you to know which programs are the riskiest and which are the safest.

Well, if you're talking about oil, which is riskier: drilling for oil, or selling oil that's already coming out of the ground?

Obviously, drilling for oil is riskier, since most folks who drill never actually find any oil. Exploratory programs for oil and gas are the riskiest programs and, therefore, carry the highest return potential.

Sometimes folks drill for oil right next to where oil has already been found. It's still risky, but less risky than exploratory programs. They call these developmental programs. They're less risky than exploratory with a lower return potential. The safest program just buys existing production. They call these income programs. They have immediate cash flow and are, therefore, the safest programs with the lowest potential reward.

In real estate, which is riskier, buying raw land or buying into an apartment complex already filled with renters? Raw land is purely speculative and is, therefore, the riskiest type of real estate DPP. You buy a chunk of land betting that an airport will be built nearby in the next five years. If you're right, the land skyrockets in value. If you're not, it doesn't.

New construction programs buy land and put up apartment buildings or office complexes. They're speculative, but once the projects are completed folks can move in and start paying rent. So they're a little safer than raw land and provide a lower reward potential.

Existing properties is sort of like the income program for oil. The business is already flowing; let's buy in. Immediate cash flow. Lower risk, lower reward.

Tax credits are the benefit for government-assisted housing and historic rehab. Remember that a tax credit is always better than a tax deduction. Just to make sure, let's compare a $100,000 tax deduction to a $100,000 tax credit:

$1,000,000	Income		$1,000,000	Income
-$100,000	Deduction		x .30	30% tax rate
$900,000	Net Income		$300,000	Tax
x .30	30% tax rate		-$100,000	CREDIT
$270,000	Tax Owed		$200,000	Tax Owed

Notice how a deduction is subtracted from the top line—revenue. For a credit, you figure the amount of tax you were going to have to pay, and then apply the credit dollar-for-dollar against that amount.

INVESTING IN DPP'S

So if your investor wants to buy into a DPP, he fills out the subscription agreement, signs it, and attaches his check. Only when the General Partner (GP) signs the agreement does he become a limited partner (LP). By signing the agreement, your investor (LP) attests to his net worth and indicates that he understands all the risks involved. When selling the partnership interests, the syndicator can take a "syndication fee" of 10%. So, for a $100,000 partnership interest, a syndication fee of $10,000 could be taken. Most of these interests are sold through private placements. As we saw in the chapter on issuing securities, private placements are generally sold only to accredited investors, so the LP's will disclose their income and net worth on the subscription agreement. Some interests are sold through public offerings, and then, of course, we would need a prospectus. Either way, investors get disclosure of the risks involved, as they do for any new investment that is not specifically excused from the registration requirements of the Securities Act of 1933. If 75% or more of the partnership assets are disclosed, we call it a "specified program." If less than 75% of the assets are disclosed, we call it a "blind pool offering." Maybe the partnership is going to wildcat/speculate on some oil patches—they don't necessarily want anyone else to know where they think the oil is located. Or, if it's raw land, maybe they don't want others to know which area they think is the next hot market. If so—blind pool offering. And it might be kind of fun to know that you just invested a bunch of money in some land that is located, you know, somewhere, probably in the United States.

Sharing arrangements will also be laid out, so the LP knows how he and the GP will share expenses and income. Let's do a quick bullet list here:

- overriding royalty interest: this would give somebody no responsibility for costs, only a share of the royalty stream when oil/gas is sold
- functional allocation: General Partner bears the capitalized costs (oil rig, other equipment) while LP's bear the deductible expenses (intangible drilling costs like labor and geological surveys)
- reversionary working interest: LP's bear all the costs and the GP doesn't get a share of income until all of those costs have been recovered
- disproportionate working interest: the GP receives a disproportionate share of income and bears very little of the costs

The GP has already filed the certificate of limited partnership with the state. This is a public document that provides the following information:

- Name and address of partnership
- Description of the partnership's business
- Life span of the partnership
- Conditions for assignment/transfer of limited partnership interests to others
- Conditions for dissolving the partnership
- Conditions for admitting new partners
- Projected date for return of capital (if one is determined)

The partnership agreement is signed by all partners and is the foundation for the partnership. In this agreement we would find the following information:

- business purpose of the partnership
- terms and conditions
- powers and limitations of the GP's authority

This document binds the partnership and authorizes the GP to run the business. It's a private document, for partners' eyes only. If the partnership is liquidated, either because it went belly-up or because it's time to pull the plug, interested parties would be paid off in the following order:

1. Secured creditors
2. Other creditors
3. Limited partners
4. General partners

Notice that the General Partner has unlimited liability, a fiduciary responsibility to the limited partners, and is also the last one to get paid should the whole thing go belly up?

Oh well. That's the nature of being the GP. Lotta risk, lotta reward.

CASH FLOW AND INCOME

Let's say a limited partner in real estate partnership takes the following share of income and expenses from operations:

> Rental income: $50,000
> Operating expenses: $20,000
> Interest expense: $25,000
> Depreciation: $20,000

So, the Income Statement (P & L) looks like this:

$50,000	Income
-20,000	Expenses
-25,000	Interest
-20,000	Depreciation
-$15,000	Income

The limited partner, assuming he had sufficient passive income to offset, could deduct $15,000 for purposes of tax relief.

But, if we're talking about "cash flow" we add back that non-cash subtraction called "depreciation." Why? Well, depreciation is not an actual outlay of cash. If you buy a printing press for $1 million and it has a useful life of 10 years, you would subtract 1/10 of its value or $100,000 each year on your income statement. Since you're not actually paying out $100,000 in cash each year, you would add that back when figuring "cash flow," just to keep things nice and simple.

So, if we add back the "depreciation" of $20,000, we'd see a positive cash flow of $5,000. In case the exam gets really nasty the day you take it, tell it that we figure cash flow by adding back depreciation.

With that loss of (-$15,000) from his share of the income and expenses, the investor can offset other passive income that he might have from other partnerships or from owning rental properties. Only *passive* income, though—not portfolio or earned income. The test might point out that real estate investment trusts (REITs) do *not* pass through losses. But, remember, real estate limited <u>partnerships</u> do pass through losses to the partners, which is what the partners are often hoping for, especially in the early years. At some point, though, income from the partnership will start to outweigh the fancy little deductions we've been discussing. This is known as the "crossover point," should the exam decide to go there.

Let's make sure you understand depreciation/depletion…these are just accounting entries that allow partnerships to write down the cost of equipment and other assets over time. If a chair costs the business $100 and has a useful life of 10 years, they'll write down $10 of its cost each year for 10 years. If the partnership leases equipment, they'll depreciate the cost of that equipment a little bit every year. If they have to buy an oil rig, same thing. Depletion is for natural resources. As you take oil out of the ground and sell it, you get to take a "depletion allowance" for every barrel of oil sold. It's just a method of cost recovery. You don't really have to understand it. If you can remember that depreciation is for equipment and depletion is only for natural resources, you'll probably be good to go. Also, raw land is not depreciated. Raw land should do the opposite—a-ppreciate, right?

Now, just to make sure the Series is much harder than necessary, the exam might bring up "depreciation recapture." Let's say that the partnership has been using accelerated depreciation. That means they aren't subtracting the value of a fixed asset the nice and neat way I explained. I explained "straight line depreciation," where something with a useful life of 10 years is simply depreciated over 10 equal subtractions. But, many businesses use "accelerated depreciation" whereby they take much larger deductions in the early years. If an LP sells his interest/unit to somebody else, he may have taken larger deductions based on accelerated depreciation. So, the IRS, who as always is here to help, will help themselves to some of that benefit through "depreciation recapture." Basically, they will tax the difference between the cost basis arrived at through accelerated versus straight line depreciation, and I actually can't believe I just wrote a sentence that boring. Sorry—there was no way around it.

RECOURSE DEBT

If a limited partner signs a "recourse note," that means that the creditors/lenders have recourse to go after his personal assets if the partnership defaults. If the LP buys a limited partnership interest for $100,000 and signs a recourse note for which he is responsible for $50,000, his cost basis in the investment is now $150,000, since that is the amount he can lose.

Of course, if it's a non-recourse note, then the creditors have no recourse. So, the recourse debt adds to cost basis, while, of course, the non-recourse debt does not.

Except when it does—real estate programs do allow the LP to add non-recourse debt to his basis, mostly to make sure your Series 7 is that much harder to pass.

CORPORATE CHARACTERISTICS

In order to be considered a "DPP" the business has to "fail the corporate test" or avoid at least two characteristics of corporations. Although DPP's are unable to avoid most characteristics of a traditional corporation, the following can usually be avoided:

- continuity of life
- freely transferable assets

That just means that most partnerships will dissolve after, say, the apartment buildings are sold or the last barrel of oil is depleted. So, there isn't the same "continuity of life" that a 200-year-old corporation would have. And, in general, these interests aren't sold actively on the secondary market, so they aren't "freely transferable" the way common stock is.

WHAT NOW?

- Review this chapter. *Approximately 30 minutes.*
- If you have the Pass the 7 QuizSet, take the Chapter 7 Quiz on DPP's. *Approximately 30 minutes.*

CHAPTER 8

Issuing Securities

Google has made headlines with their famous initial public offering or "IPO," in which they sold stock to investors at $85 and those investors then watched the stock climb to the high 400's. The difference between the initial $85 price and the eventual price of, say, $450, is the difference between the primary and secondary markets. Securities are issued to investors in the primary market. Securities are traded among investors in the secondary market. To do an initial public offering on the primary market, a company simply sells a big ownership stake to investors in exchange for a big infusion of cash that can be used to expand the business. The company takes the money and buys factories, manufacturing equipment, computers, etc., and the investors end up owning a percentage of the company. Now, nothing makes the securities regulators more nervous than to hear that a company wants to raise money from investors. Let's face it, many business owners would say just about anything investors wanted to hear in order to get their hands on a few billion dollars, as anyone who's ever heard Bill Gates or Larry Ellison speak would be sort of hip to. That's why the state and federal securities regulators like to slow down the issuers in much the same way they're slowing you down right now. Just tying you up with a little paperwork, giving you a chance to rethink your whole decision, making sure it's something you really, really want to do.

The SEC wants to see exactly what the issuers will be telling their potential investors in the prospectus. They want the issuers to provide the whole story on the company: history, competitors, products and services, risks of investing in the company, financials, board of directors, officers, etc. And, like a fussy English instructor, they want it written in clear, readable language. Only if investors clearly understand the risks and rewards of an investment do they really have a fair chance of determining a good investment opportunity from something better left alone. If investors consistently get burned on the primary market, pretty soon investors will stop showing up to provide companies with capital, which means companies would have one heck of a time expanding, hiring more workers, and pushing along the local and national economies. So, the government is very much interested in what goes on in the securities markets, which is why Congress passed the Securities Act of 1933. Sometimes referred to as the "Paper Act," the Securities Act of 1933 simply requires issuers of securities to register the securities and provide full disclosure to investors before taking their hard-earned money. The SEC will help the issuer write and rewrite the registration statement, just like a hard-nosed composition instructor might help you do four rewrites of a research paper before finally agreeing to let you graduate. If this section is awkward and this paragraph is unclear, rewrite it. The SEC calls their equivalent of red pen marks "letters of deficiency" and sometimes, when they're feeling especially punchy, "deficiency letters."

Now, an issuer such as Oracle would know all kinds of interesting stuff about multidimensional relational database applications in a non-Unix environment. But, they probably know jack about issuing securities. So, they hire underwriters, also called "investment bankers." An underwriter or investment banker is simply a broker-dealer who helps issuers raise money by issuing securities to investors. All those big-name Wall Street firms have major underwriting or investment banking departments. In fact, I may just go ahead and name names such as Morgan-Stanley, Goldman Sachs, and Merrill Lynch. First, they're all public companies themselves now, and, second, they're so famous that to avoid naming them would be silly. Anyway, once these underwriters help the issuer file registration papers, under the Securities Act of 1933 they go into a "cooling off" period, which will last a minimum of 20 days. This process can drag on and on if the SEC is copping an attitude against the registration statement, but no matter how long it takes, the issuer and underwriters can only do certain things during this "cooling off" period. Number one, they can't sell anything. They can't even advertise. About all they can do is take "indications of interest" from investors, but those aren't sales, just names on a list. And those who indicate their interest have to receive a preliminary prospectus or "red herring." This disclosure document contains almost everything that the final prospectus will contain except for the effective date and the final public offering price or "POP." Remember that the registered representative may NOT send a research report along with the red herring and cannot highlight it or alter it in any way.

It is what it is.

The issuer and the underwriters perform due diligence during the cooling off period, which just means they make sure they provided the SEC and the public with accurate and full disclosure. It's up to them to do this—the SEC is only reviewing the information for clarity. It had better be accurate.

Even though the SEC makes issuers jump through all kinds of hoops, once it's all done, the SEC pretty much washes its hands of the whole affair. They don't approve or disapprove of the security. They don't guarantee accuracy or adequacy of the information provided by the issuer and its underwriters. In other words, if this whole thing goes belly up because of inaccurate disclosure, the liability still rests squarely on the shoulders of the issuers and underwriters, not on the SEC. And there has to be a disclaimer saying basically that on the prospectus. In fact, take a look at the cover of any mutual fund prospectus. The one I'm looking at now says it this way:

> The Securities and Exchange Commission has not approved or disapproved of these securities. Further, it has not determined that this prospectus is accurate or complete. Any representation to the contrary is a criminal offense.

The exam might also throw a question at you about an offering of stock in which the issuing corporation will be offering 10 million shares, and certain large share-holders will be offering 2 million of theirs. Well, as we said, when the proceeds go to the issuer, that's the "primary market." When the proceeds are passed among investors, that's the "secondary market." So, this would be both a "primary and secondary distribution," or a "combined offering." In the real world this happens all the time. You know how storied companies such as Apple and Microsoft had early investors? Well, when those amazing companies did their amazing IPO's, it was time for those early investors to cash in their chips while the company was also taking in vast quantities of capital. So, some of the shares are being offered by the company (primary) and some by certain large investors (secondary).

Just in case you didn't have enough to remember at this point.

EXCUSE, EXCUSES

So, everybody has to register their securities with the SEC, except for everybody who doesn't. The Act of 1933 is a piece of federal legislation, so it's not surprising that the federal government, who came up with the Act, doesn't have to abide by it. That's right, government securities are exempt from this act. They don't have to be registered in this way. Neither do municipal securities.

Why is that? Well, when a corporation tries to take an investor's money, there is always a good chance the investor will lose his money. Companies go out of business all the time, so if their earnings start to evaporate, the bonds go into default, and the shares of common stock are no longer worth the paper they're printed on. That's not the case when the U.S. Treasury sells you a T-note or T-bond. That's just a loan backed by the full faith and credit (the vast taxing powers) of the United States Government.

In other words, you'll get your money back. The U.S. isn't going to pull a Russia on you and suddenly declare, as Russia did back in 1998, "Very sorry—we cannot pay you."

Same for municipal securities. You'll get paid back on a general obligation bond, because it's backed by the full faith and credit of a fiscally responsible state (you hope). Either way, there is such a small chance of default on municipal securities that the issuers (cities, counties, states, school districts, etc.) got an exemption from the arduous registration process laid out under the Securities Act of 1933.

But we're not done handing out excuses; in fact, we're just getting started. Charitable organization securities, such as church bonds, are exempt from the act. So are bank securities, which are already plenty regulated by bank regulators (FDIC, FRB, Comptroller of the Currency). Finally, securities issued by small business investment companies (VC firms) also get a hall pass.

Debt securities that mature in 270 days or less—commercial paper, banker's acceptances, other promissory notes—are also exempt from this arduous registration process. Why would you need a prospectus when loaning GE some money for a few months? Just look at their credit rating and charge them an interest rate commensurate with that rating (commercial paper). What would a prospectus tell you that you couldn't get from Moody's or S&P or your own credit analyst department, right?

So, the state of Oregon is an exempt issuer. Commercial paper is an exempt security. There are also transactions that qualify for exemptions. Believe it or not, we call these exempt transactions. That just means that if you sell the securities in a certain way you can either avoid registration altogether, avoid registration with the SEC, or perhaps just do a "fast-track" method using a scaled-down disclosure document like an "offering memorandum" or an "offering circular" as opposed to the telephone-book-size standard registration statement or "S1."

Still with us?

Boy, you must really want your Series 7. Good for you!

Under Reg A, an issuer can sell up to $5,000,000 worth of securities in a year without having to jump through all the usual hoops. Rather than filing a standard registration statement, the issuer files an offering circular, a much more scaled-down document. This is a small offering, so think of a small Caribbean island where they play lots of Reg-A. But, please save the rest of that fantasy until after passing the test.

The SEC is in charge of interstate commerce, meaning commerce among many states. Therefore, if the issuer wants to sell only to residents of one state, the SEC doesn't have to get involved—there is already a state securities regulator who can deal with this one. So, if the issuer agrees to sell the stock to residents of only one state, they will qualify for a Rule 147 exemption. The issuer's main business is located in this state, and 80% of its assets are located here. Also, the buyers can't sell the security to a non-resident for 9 months. The issuer registers with the state, rather than the SEC, since it's all taking place in that one state. This is also called an "intrastate offering," which recalls the difference between the Internet and an intra-net, right?

The SEC is out to protect the average Joe and JoAnne from fast-talking stock operators pushing worthless paper. But, the SEC doesn't have to provide as much protection to big, sophisticated investors such as mutual funds, pension funds, or high net worth individuals. If anybody tries to scam these multimillion-dollar investors, they'll be in just as much trouble as if they scammed an average investor, but the SEC doesn't have to put up as much protection for the big, institutional investors, who can usually watch out for themselves to a large extent. Therefore, if the issuer wants to avoid the registration process under the Act of 1933, they can limit the sale to these big institutional, sophisticated investors. These investors are often referred to as "accredited investors." They include institutions and the officers and board of directors of the company. Also if an individual has $1,000,000 net worth or makes $200,000 grand a year ($300,000 for married, filing jointly), he/she is accredited. So, an issuer can place their securities under a Reg D transaction with as many of these folks as they want. This "private placement" is, by definition, not being offered to the general public, so the SEC eases up a bit. As much as the SEC ever eases up, anyway. So, a Reg D/private placement transaction is exempt from the Act of 1933 because it is offered to an exclusive group of investors. No more than 35 non-accredited investors can buy these securities, and everybody has to hold the stock for the first year before selling it. The SEC is more relaxed knowing these big rich investors aren't going to make a fast buck on the deal—they have to hold the stock at least one year before selling. After that, a non-affiliated investor would have to comply with volume limits during the second year, and an affiliated investor would have to comply with volume limits all the time because they're, well, affiliated.

See, if you're an insider or affiliate of the company, you always have to file Form 144 with the SEC, announcing that you intend to sell a certain amount of your stock over the next 90 days. We don't want the huge shareholders to dump too much stock at once, which usually drives the price down for everyone else who might want to sell. The volume to be sold over the 90-day period is limited to 1% of the shares outstanding or the average weekly trading volume over the four most recent weeks, whichever is larger. That's surprising, too, because you might think the SEC would stick you with the smaller number.

Go figure.

So you can bet the test will give you at least five weeks—only average the four most recent. And then compare that number to 1% of the outstanding shares. Whichever is larger, that's what an insider/affiliate could sell over the next 90 days.

Oh yeah, and there's also an exemption to the exemption. If the amount being sold is less than or equal to 500 shares AND less than or equal to $10,000, the investor doesn't even have to file form 144.

Aren't you glad you know that?

Rule 144 also covers both "restricted stock" and "control stock." Nothing different about control stock *per se*—it's the people who hold the stock that are different. If you're the CEO of a corporation, or the CFO, or the owner of a major chunk (10%) of the stock, you could control the success of the company and even the share price by buying and selling huge chunks of your stock at strategic times. Therefore, you tell the SEC what you're planning to do with your stock every time you think about selling some of it. You do this by filing a Form 144, which also covers "restricted" stock.

What is restricted stock, you may be wondering. Well, stock sold through a private placement (Reg D) is unregistered and therefore restricted. Restricted means its transfer or sale is restricted—investors have to hold it for a full year before selling it. And, since everything needs at least two names, restricted stock is also called "legend stock" because of the legend printed on the certificate reminding the investor not to transfer the shares until a certain date. In the second year, a non-affiliate of the company has to fill out Form 144 and comply with the volume limits just mentioned. In the third year and beyond, though, he/she can sell the shares freely. Control persons (officers, directors, 10% shareholders, immediate family of insiders) always have to comply with volume limits.

Always.

And, those people can never sell the company's stock short. They can't profit from their company's poor stock performance, in other words. And, if they make a profit on their company's stock held less than 6 months, they'll wish they hadn't. This is called a short-swing profit, and it has to be turned back over to the company with the gain still being taxed by the IRS, who, as always, is here to help.

The final exemption is the 144a exemption. This covers the private resale of securities to institutions. In general, registration requirements are relaxed when the securities are offered privately and to qualified institutional buyers. As always, the SEC provides more protection to the average investor who could get into a general public offering than to the sophisticated buyers who get involved with private offerings of securities.

To review, the Act of 1933 says that non-exempt issuers (corporations) have to register their securities with the SEC. Exempt issuers, exempt securities, and exempt transactions all find a way around the arduous process set forth by the Act of 1933.

UNDERWRITING COMMITMENTS

Issuers receive different levels of commitment from the underwriters. Under a "best efforts" commitment, the underwriters act as agents. In other words, no money at risk. They try to sell, and whatever they can't sell goes back to the issuer. Two types of best efforts underwritings are All or None and Mini-Max. In either case, the underwriters have no money at risk. They just have to sell a minimum amount, or cancel the whole underwriting and return all the money to investors. Only difference is mini-max has both a minimum and a maximum number.

Underwriters only have money/capital at risk when they give firm commitments. Now, they're agreeing to buy the securities outright, then turn around and sell them to the public. The difference between where they buy from the issuer and sell to the public is known as the "spread." The managing underwriter takes a management fee, the underwriters split up the underwriting fee, and whoever makes the sale gets the selling concession. If the total spread is 80 cents, only the managing underwriter can make that amount, and they'd have to make the sale; otherwise, they'd have to concede the selling concession to the party who made the sale. A typical spread might be made up of 10 cents for the management fee, 20 cents for the underwriting fee, and 50 cents for the selling concession. For a total spread of 80 cents per share.

If you see a reference to a "green shoe clause," just remember that this would allow the syndicate to increase the number of shares sold by 15% over the original number of shares in the offering. People must really want the security in that case, right? They're all "green with envy," so this "green shoe" clause would take care of them.

Sorry to resort to such cheesy memory joggers, but many people swear by them.

NASD RULE 2790

If the underwriters have set the public offering price (POP) of a stock at $10, what happens if the stock shoots up to $20 on the secondary market, while they're still selling shares at $10? Wouldn't it be tempting to hold all the shares for their own account and let the price rise even further?

Might be tempting, but it's not allowed by the NASD. These public offerings have to be bona fide (good and true) distributions. That means that if your firm is an underwriter, it has to sell all the shares it is allotted, no matter how tempting it might be to keep most of them for its own account.

RESTRICTED PERSONS

Your firm also has to watch whom they sell the new issue to. A person who may not purchase a new issue of common stock is called a "restricted person." Restricted persons include:
- Member firms
- Broker-Dealer personnel

- Finders and fiduciaries (finders, accountants, consultants, attorneys, etc.)
- Portfolio managers for institutions (banks, S&L's, insurance companies, etc.)

Of course, it would be fun to help your immediate family members profit from a wildly successful IPO such as the one pulled off by Google not so long ago. Unfortunately, NASD Rule 2790 prohibits the offering of new issues to immediate family members, defined as:

- parents
- mother-in-law or father-in-law
- spouse, brother or sister
- brother-in-law or sister-in-law
- son-in-law or daughter-in-law
- children
- any other individual to whom the person provides material support

The last bullet point above mentions "material support," which the NASD is kind enough to define for us:

"Material support" means directly or indirectly providing more than 25% of a person's income in the prior calendar year. Members of the immediate family living in the same household are deemed to be providing each other with material support.

Rule 2790 (which really only applies to offerings of common stock) also requires that before selling a new issue to any account, a member firm must in good faith have obtained, within the twelve months prior to the sale, a representation that the account is eligible to purchase new issues in compliance with this rule.

PRACTICE:

73. What is the maximum number of institutional buyers in a Reg D offering?

A. 35

B. 1% of outstanding shareholders

C. 100

D. none of the above

74. Which of the following may a registered rep do during the cooling off period?

    A.   Highlight the most important points of a red herring for a favored customer

    B.   Attach a research report to the preliminary prospectus

    C.   Use the red herring to gain the SEC's approval of the issue

    D.   Send a red herring to customers who have given indications of interest

75. None of the following has liability for unsold shares except

    A.   member of a selling group in a firm commitment

    B.   member of a syndicate in a firm commitment

    C.   member of a selling group in a best efforts underwriting

    D.   member of a syndicate in a best efforts underwriting

76. All of the following are exempt issuers except

    A.   U.S. government

    B.   XYZ Bank Holding Corporation

    C.   Chicago, Illinois

    D.   Fernwood State Bank

77. All of the following may issue common stock except

    A.   GNMA

    B.   XXR corporation

    C.   FNMA

    D.   FHLMC

78. Which of the following parties takes on liability for unsold shares?

    A.   Member of a syndicate in a best efforts underwriting

    B.   Member of the selling group

    C.   Member of a syndicate in an all or none underwriting

    D.   None of the above

79. Which of the following securities would have to be registered with the SEC prior to an initial public offering?

    A.   ADR's

    B.   XXR Corporation's preferred stock

    C.   XXR Corporation's common stock

    D.   All of the above

80. **Which of the following securities would have to be registered with the SEC prior to an initial public offering?**
    A. Church bonds
    B. ADR
    C. Chicago 7% General Obligation bond
    D. T-notes

81. **The Securities Act of 1934 addressed all the following except**
    A. anti-fraud regulations
    B. registration of new issues
    C. registration of agents
    D. registration of broker-dealers

82. **Which of the following parties has capital at risk in a transaction?**
    A. agent
    B. underwriter
    C. registered representative
    D. broker

83. **Which of the following securities would require that a customer receive a prospectus?**
    A. Variable annuity
    B. Open-end share
    C. Closed-end share during the offering period
    D. All of the above

84. **The Securities Act of 1933 applies to which market?**
    A. First
    B. Secondary
    C. Primary
    D. Third

85. **ARC, Inc. is planning to make an initial public offering of $10,000,000 in only three states, all west of the Mississippi River. Therefore, ARC will**
    A. file an S1
    B. qualify for a Reg A exemption
    C. qualify for a Rule 147 exemption
    D. qualify for a Reg D exemption

86. If a corporate insider sells stock of her company held five months for a profit

    A.   she will be prosecuted for fraud by the SEC

    B.   she will be prosecuted for fraud by the NASD or other DEA

    C.   the profit must be disgorged to the corporation

    D.   she must distribute 1% to the members of the board

87. When must the final prospectus be delivered?

    A.   before accepting payment from the client

    B.   at or before the time payment is accepted

    C.   no later than receipt of confirmation

    D.   no later than settlement

ANSWERS:

73. D

74. D

75. B

76. B

77. A

78. D

79. D

80. B

81 B

82. B

83. D

84. C

85. A

86. C

87. C

WHAT NOW?

- Review the chapter. *Approximately 40 minutes.*
- If you have the Pass the 7 QuizSet, take the Chapter 8 Quiz on Issuing Securities. *Approximately 40 minutes.*
- If you have the Audio CD set, listen to Disc 2, Track 2. *Approximately 12 minutes.*

CHAPTER 9

Trading Securities

In the primary market underwriters help issuers raise money by selling securities to investors. On the secondary market investors trade those securities back and forth. Keeping the difference between the two markets straight is very important, so let me make the point with an analogy. When I was a kid, my friends and I liked to buy and trade baseball cards. Of course, we couldn't buy a baseball card until it was *issued* by the bubble gum company, who'd figured out they could sell a small hard slab of gum for a huge markup if they threw in a few photos of baseball players with statistics on the back. After we'd acquired our newly <u>issued</u> cards on the primary market, we were free to <u>trade</u> the cards on the secondary market among ourselves. We weren't sophisticated enough at age 10 to think of listing standards, hand signals, or regulations, but we managed to do a pretty nice volume without anybody feeling cheated, which is probably more than can be said for most adult-run exchanges. And it was, in fact, a secondary market, where prices were determined purely by supply and demand. After all, what *was* a Nolan Ryan rookie card worth? As much as you could get for it. Maybe as much as a Pete Rose and a Joe Morgan special edition combined. Buying baseball cards of Chicago Cubs players was not so different from buying common stock in the Tribune Company, which owns the Chicago Cubs. The value of my cherished Milt Pappas 1974 card was tied to the number of games Milt and the rest of the team managed to win, just as stock in the Tribune Company is tied to that, as well as to how many newspapers the Tribune manages to sell. Winnings and earnings are really the same thing. If the organization wins, everybody wants to own a little piece of it. Of course, if I'd put my lawn mowing money into Tribune stock rather than all those baseball cards, I'd only be writing this book for something to do about now, but that's another matter.

For the exam, remember the difference between the primary and secondary markets. Securities are issued in the primary market, where the issuer takes money from the investor. Securities are traded on the secondary market among investors.

This chapter is about trading securities on the secondary market.

SELLING SHORT

You've probably heard that every investor should try to buy low and sell high, right? Well, some investors take that same principle and simply try to do it in reverse: they prefer selling high, then buying back low. We call these people "short sellers," because calling them high-risk lunatics wouldn't be polite or good for business.

It works like this. You go to your friend's house and see that she has a new mountain bike that she paid way too much money for. Mind if I borrow your mountain bike, you ask, to which your friend agrees. On the way home you run into another friend, who admires the bike very much. She likes it so much, in fact, that she offers you two thousand bucks for it.

Two thousand bucks? Sold! You take the two thousand bucks and put it in your pocket.

Wait a minute, that wasn't even your mountain bike!

No problem. All you have to do is replace it with an identical machine. A few weeks later you go to the bike store to replace the borrowed bike, and—as predicted—the price has fallen to just $1,000. Perfect! You sold the bike for $2,000 and you can get out of your position by paying just $1,000, keeping the $1,000 difference as your profit. Just buy the bike for $1,000, wheel it over to your friend, and everybody's happy. Notice that you made money when the price went down. The exam might say that you were "bearish" on the price of mountain bikes. When an investor is "bearish," that means he expects and hopes that the price of something will drop.

Short sellers don't sell bikes or search engines short, but they can certainly sell the stock of the companies who make bikes or search engines short. If you think that Google is wildly overpriced and headed for a big drop, borrow the shares from your friendly broker-dealer and sell them at what you think is the top. Sell Google for $100 and, you hope, buy it back later for $30, keeping $70 per share as your profit.

However, many people tried that soon after Google went public (primary market) at $85. When it got to $100 many folks were convinced the stock would only go down from there, so they sold it short at $100. Expecting to buy it back or "cover their short positions" for less than $100, these poor souls must have been really embarrassed to see the stock soon climb up to $400 per share.

Hate it when that happens. Selling something for $100 and buying it back for $400 is not a particularly good business model. That's no different from buying something for $400 and then selling it for $100. It's just more dangerous. When you buy something, you've already lost all you could ever lose. But when you sell stock short, there is no limit to how much you'll have to spend to get out of your position.

I mean, reality would tell us that Google was never going to hit $1,000 a share, but, hypothetically, it could have. Higher even.

So, short sellers are bearish. They profit when the stock goes DOWN. But, they have limited upside and unlimited risk. If you short a stock for $5,000, $5,000 is the maximum you could make, and only if the stock went to zero. Your potential loss is unlimited, since no one can tell you for sure how high the stock could go up against you. When you buy stock, we refer to that as "being long the stock," because we also don't get out much. Long means "buy." Short means "sell."

UPTICK RULE

Short sellers make money when the price of a stock goes down. According to the NYSE uptick rule, however, they can only execute the short sale when the price is moving up. A stock's price has to be at an "uptick" or a "zero-plus tick" for the short sale to be executed. The "+" signs and "0+" sign over the following prices show where short sales could occur:

	-	+	0+	+	-	-	+	+
20.01	19.75	20.00	20.00	20.25	20.03	19.68	19.75	20.05

After "19.75", "20.00" is an uptick. The next "20.00" is a repeat of the last uptick, which we call a "zero-plus tick." 20.25 is another uptick, but after that we see two down ticks in a row (20.03, 19.68). Only when the price moves from 19.68 to 19.75 do we see another plus-tick at which a short sale could occur, followed by another at $20.05. For your test, remember that a one-penny increment is a "tick," so if the stock moves up one penny, that's an uptick. In other words, if you want to sell short, the buyer has to pay a price representing an uptick or a repeat of the last uptick.

If you enter a short sale at the market when the previous trade had been executed at $20, you could not sell short at $19.95. A trade could happen at that price without you, but after that downtick or "minus tick," you would need to execute the short sale at a price higher than $19.95. So, after the trade at $19.95 if somebody would pay $19.96 (plus tick), you could sell your stock short to them. If not, you keep waiting.

DIVISIONS OF SECONDARY MARKET

A big focus of trading securities has to do with four different markets. First of all, you have to remember that "primary" and "secondary" are different terms altogether. The primary market refers to a situation whereby an issuer receives the proceeds of a transaction. In the secondary market, other folks buy and sell securities, at no direct financial benefit to the issuer. The Topps bubble gum company and their underwriters (the retail stores) got our money only one time for each pack of baseball cards. That was the primary market. When we traded our cards among ourselves, we didn't send any money to Topps. That was our secondary market. Similarly, Google's IPO took place on the primary market. The price rose to the stratosphere on the secondary market, where demand outstripped supply.

FIRST MARKET—NYSE AND REGIONAL EXCHANGES

Within the secondary market, there are four separate components. Let's start with the first market or the "exchange market." Imagine a clanging bell and the roar of frantic buyers and sellers in funny-looking jackets all day long until the bell rings again at four o'clock eastern standard time. That's the New York Stock Exchange, the first market. The exam will likely ask you to associate this with the phrase "auction market" or "double auction market." It really is a lot like an auction: confusing hand signals, really fast pace, and people shouting out prices all day long. There are also regional exchanges in Chicago, Philadelphia, Boston, and San Francisco that are based on the NYSE. They tend to focus on regional stocks, but they still fill orders for NYSE-listed securities, such as GE, IBM, or GM. There was also a Cincinnati Stock Exchange and, just to keep things nice and simple, they decided to locate it in Chicago. Seriously. Okay, truth be told, it was renamed the "National Stock Exchange" in 2003, so I should probably stop picking on my chili-loving comrades from Cincinnati. Next edition, I promise. Anyway, the exam will refer to the "first market" as a physical location where buyers and sellers gather at trading posts to bid for and offer securities. Lots of shouting and shoving going on down on the floor, sort of like an NBA playoff game.

The exam wants you to know about four different players who can play down on the floor. The first one is a quick moving point guard called the commission house broker. He works for a brokerage house and fills orders for a commission. Go figure. The more orders he can fill, the more money he can make, which explains why he's always in such a hurry. If he's too busy to fill an order, he can call in somebody off the bench known as a "two-dollar broker." The two-dollar broker is an independent broker who gets a commission to help out when the commission house broker is too busy scoring his own points. Then there are the big power forwards who compete for themselves only. These registered floor traders make a fortune if they can buy low and sell high, in either order, more often than not. The exam is probably most inclined to talk about the fourth player, the big man known as the "specialist." Like a 7-footer on the basketball court, the specialist plays the game with certain inherent advantages.

For example, if I want to buy 10,000 shares for $36, I put in a buy-limit order, and the specialist sees that I'm willing to take a pretty good number of shares off his or her hands for $36. Therefore, if he or she would like to go for an easy slam-dunk, they can pay $36.01 per share and see where it goes. If it goes up, it's a slam-dunk profit when they sell it to a higher bidder. If it goes down, they already know they can pass it off to me for just one penny less than they paid for it.

Nice work if you can get it.

The specialist trades for their own account, carrying an inventory. Specialists are exchange members whose responsibility is to maintain a "fair and orderly market" in a particular listed security. If you want to trade some IBM today, you end up dealing with the specialist in IBM. They aren't exchange employees—they are business people doing business on the floor of the exchange, trying to buy low and sell high, pretty much like everybody else. If no one is trading, the specialist has to step in and start buying to get the stock moving again. They trade in between the highest buy-limit and the lowest sell-limit price among all the fancy limit orders we'll get to in a minute. That's what enabled me to take the cheap shot at them when I talked about their being able to buy stock for one penny above the highest buy-limit order. Sometimes, that's not such a great thing, I guess. But, every job has its price, like having to pass some nightmare of an exam called the Series 7.

Anyway, let's dive into a few testable concepts and then move onto the second or "over-the-counter" market.

Reporting Prices

If I place an electronic order to buy 1,000 shares of, say, GE, my order could be filled in New York, Philadelphia, Boston, San Francisco, or Chicago. In fact, that just happened the other day. As I was purchasing shares in several listed securities through my online broker, I noticed that some stocks were filled in Boston, most in New York, and one in Chicago. That's because they're all part of the "first market."

The Series 7, you see, is not as divorced from the "real world" as some would have you believe. Now, I didn't mean to open a can of worms by talking about electronic orders and the exchange. But, reality is never simple. Although many orders are now placed electronically on the exchange through Super DOT, the exchange is still a place where humans get together and compete. They put on their uniforms, which in this case are just funny colored blazers designed to make an ugly tie and wrinkled shirt look somehow like business attire. They put on their game faces and, when the starting bell sounds, the spit begins to fly and tempers have been known to flare. What are they doing down there? Trying to buy low and sell high, in either order. Just like at an auction, the best price prevails, and you also need to move quickly.

Consolidated Tape

When a listed security is sold, it doesn't matter whether it's sold in the Big Apple, Chi-Town, Beantown, Philly, or San Francisco…the prices are all *consolidated* on the consolidated tape. That means that the seller has to report the price he just sold a certain number of shares at within 90 seconds, whether it was sold in Philly, Boston, et cetera. Which is why you yourself can now waste perfectly good work time staring at prices streaming endlessly at the bottom of a television monitor. Yep, all that "10s GE 35.55" stuff actually means something. It means that somebody sold (and bought) 1,000 shares of GE for $35.55 per share. The number of round lots comes first, then the stock symbol, and then the price that the transaction took place. Let's take a look at some more pretend stock trades on a consolidated tape and then the price at which the transaction took place:

GE	IBM	C	GE
36.55…	10s95.04…	99s75.15…	13,000s36.70

The first thing we see is the stock symbol GE. If there is no number before the symbol, we know that one round lot (100 shares) of GE just traded for $36.55 per share. In the next case "10s" means 10 round lots, or 1,000 shares. So, 1,000 shares of IBM just traded at $95.04 per share. Next, we see that 99 round lots, or 9,900 shares of "C" (for Citigroup) just traded at $75.15 per share. But, when the number of shares gets up to 10,000 or more, they stop talking in round lots and just list the actual number of shares. In other words a trade for 10,000 shares would not be indicated as "100s." Rather, it would be "10,000s" just to keep things nice and simple. Therefore, we read the tape to indicate that 13,000 shares of GE just traded for $36.70 per share.

As usual, things get more complicated. What if you saw the following on your exam and were asked to interpret the report?

MCD12s35 .35

That means 1200 shares of McDonald's traded at $35, followed by a trade for 100 shares at $35. Remember, if there's no number before the price, that means one round lot or 100 shares traded at that price. You also might be fortunate enough to be asked what the following means:

MCD35 .15

That means 100 shares of MickeyDee's traded at $35, followed by another round lot that traded at $35.15. Just to keep things nice and simple. In other words, there is a world of difference between "35.15" and "35 .15." In the first case, 100 shares sold at $35.15. In the second case, 100 shares sold at $35, followed by 100 shares at $35.15.

No wonder these traders are so uptight, huh?

For preferred stock, a round lot is just 10 shares, and they indicate that the only way possible, with an "s/s." Therefore, what does the following report mean?

ABC pr 7s/s.85.05

It means that 70 shares of ABC preferred traded for $85.05 per share.

And, just in case the exam is in an especially foul mood when you sit for it, also memorize the following abbreviations used on the consolidated tape:

- SLD: means that this price is being reported late, long after the actual trade. Oops.
- Halt: sometimes trading in a stock is halted, usually when big news is about to come out on it
- OPD: the first trade that happens after a delayed opening or a trading halt
- Pr: preferred stock (also look for the s/s thingie)
- R/T: somebody's trading rights
- W/S: somebody's trading warrants

Finally, since NYSE stocks can be traded all over the place, the exchange where the transaction in, say, IBM, took place is also indicated with an abbreviation. Rather then delve, I'll just give it to you in a nice little table:

NYSE N	Boston B	INSTINET O
AMEX A	Pacific P	Philadelphia X
NASD T	Chicago M	National C

Quote Screens

In the old days, customers had to call their registered rep to get an idea on the price of a particular stock. Now, of course, stock quotes are all over the Internet. I'm currently logged into my online brokerage account, looking at a quote on Abbott Labs. This is what I see:

ABT   Abbott Labs

Bid – 44.90   Ask – 45.00   B/A size – 300x300

Last – 44.95   Open – 44.85   Close – 44.63

Change - +.32   Change % - .71%

High – 44.99   Low – 44.85

Volume – 925,000

What the heck does all that mean? It means that the last reported trade in Abbott Labs was at $44.95. You could sell ABT at the bid price of $44.90, or you could buy some ABT at the ask price of $45.00. In other words, buyers are trying to take your stock for a little less and sellers are trying to sell you the stock for a little more than the last traded price. The stock previously closed (yesterday) at $44.63, so if the last trade took place at $44.95, that represents a change of + .32, which is less than 1% higher than the previous close. The newscaster would say, "Abbott Labs is up 32 cents," and many people would consider that to be news. The high and low for the day (so far) are self-explanatory, and the number of shares that have changed hands is nearly 1 million, even though trading has only taken place for about an hour at this point. The "size" of the B/A just means that the bid and ask prices are associated with orders to buy or sell 300 shares at those prices. If you saw that the B/A size was 900x200, that would mean that there are a lot more buyers than sellers. You could easily sell 900 shares at the bid price to willing buyers, or buy 200 shares at the ask price from willing sellers.

In case the test wants to pretend that all that information is still abbreviated, memorize the following abbreviations and what they stand for:

- B – Bid
- A – Ask
- O – opening price
- C – closing price
- H – highest price today
- L – lowest price today
- LT – last traded
- NC – net change (how much the last trade is up or down from the previous close)
- V – volume or number of shares traded

Trading Curbs, Halts

Sometimes trading gets a little chaotic, so the NYSE steps in to straighten things out. Many people trade through computer programs. If the stock goes to this price, sell 10,000 shares; if the stock goes to this price, buy 5,000 shares, etc. That's a lot of activity set on "auto-pilot," so if the market gets a little too volatile, the NYSE dictates that trading curbs be turned on. According to NYSE Rule 80A, when the Dow Jones Industrial Average (DJIA) changes by 2% from its previous day's close, trading curbs (restrictions) would be put into effect on program trading and index arbitrage, but not on all trading. The NYSE would also decide when program trading could begin again.

If the market gets extraordinarily volatile, the NYSE will <u>halt</u> trading in all stocks for a certain amount of time, as follows:

- When the DJIA declines by 10% from the previous close, trading halts for one hour
- When the DJIA declines by 20% from the previous close, trading halts for two hours
- When the DJIA declines by 30% from the previous close, everybody goes home

Of course, the Dow is currently in the range of 12,000, so a drop of 10% would be a drop of about 1,200 points, which would make for one screaming headline, not to mention the mileage CNBC could get out of the Dow dropping 3,600 points in a single session. This is known as NYSE Rule 80B, in case the exam absolutely loses its mind the day you take it. Now, please understand that *anything* can happen on the stock market. If the Dow is now at a completely different level as you read these words, that does *not* mean that this book is dated. It just means that the stock market is volatile. When I started this chapter the index was around 10,000. By the time the book went to print, the index was more than 20% higher. Which means I really should have been buying DJX calls rather than writing this book, but hindsight is always 20-20.

The Specialist

Priority, Precedence, Parity

Earlier I mentioned that NYSE stocks can be purchased electronically, and this is done through a system called Super DOT. In fact, most customers like me will end up having our orders filled this way, where we bypass the floor brokers and route our puny little purchases directly to the specialist. The floor brokers typically handle large institutional orders, since a mutual fund or pension fund is not likely to place an order for 1,000,000 shares electronically. Many people believe that for this reason we will continue to have poorly dressed, unkempt human beings screaming and gesticulating madly on the floor of the exchange for a long time to come. In any case, when these electronic orders come in to the specialist, he/she uses priority, precedence, and parity to determine which orders get filled in which order. This means that if more than one order is the same, orders will be filled as follows:

- Priority: the order received first gets filled first
- Precedence: if the time and price are the same, the larger order takes precedence
- Parity: if all conditions are the same, orders are matched in the crowd and the shares are split among the orders

Specialist's Book

It takes a large amount of capital (money) to play the role of the specialist, which is why the "specialist" is generally an employee of a specialist firm. If you're the specialist for IBM, all trades in IBM take place in front of you. Your job is to maintain a "fair and orderly market," which means that if there are no public buy orders, you have to step in and start buying to get the stock moving. If there are no public sell orders, you have to start selling some of your inventory.

Let's say the market for XYZ is:

	Bid	Ask
5 x 5	$20.05	$20.15

That means that 500 shares can be sold at $20.05, and 500 shares can be purchased right now for $20.15. If a public order to buy came in, the specialist could not charge $20.15 or higher for their own account. They would have to improve the price by charging less than $20.15. Similarly, if a public order to sell came in, the specialist cannot buy for his own account at $20.05 or lower. They'd have to pay more than $20.05 to improve the price.

Where did we get that inside market of Bid-20.05, Ask-20.15? From the buy and sell limit orders placed by exchange members. As we'll discuss a little later, traders can name the price they want to pay when they buy or the price they want to receive when they sell. We call these "buy-limit" and "sell-limit" orders. The orders aren't ready to be filled yet, so the specialist puts them on his/her book. The specialist's book for XYZ might look like this:

BUY	XYZ	SELL
2 Bear	20	
3 Morgan 2 Goldman	20.05	
3 Merrill Stp	20.10	
	20.15	2 Prudential 3 Smith Barney
	20.20	2 JP Morgan

What's going on here is that we are looking for the highest price somebody's willing to pay and the lowest price somebody's willing to sell XYZ for, and that becomes the specialist's quote. The "Stp" for "stop" order is ignored here. As we'll see, stop orders are triggered when an actual trade takes place at that price. Limit orders are executed as soon as somebody is willing to meet your limit price. So, ignoring the "Stp" order, we see that the highest price anyone's willing to pay is $20.05, and there are 5 round lots ready to be bought at that price. The lowest price people are willing to sell XYZ for is $20.15, and there are 5 round lots ready to be sold at that price.

So, the specialist's quote becomes Bid-$20.05, Ask-$20.15 with the size at 5x5. Everybody wants to buy low and sell high, so the quote simply represents the lowest price you can buy a stock for (ask) and the highest price you can sell it for (bid).

Finally, if the exam uses the phrase "stopping stock," that just means that the specialist has guaranteed an execution price for a public order and will also seek a better price. If the specialist says "you're stopped at $30" that means the buy order will be filled for no more than $30, or the sell order will be filled for no less than $30. And a better price may actually be obtained.

Listing Standards for NYSE

In order to have your company's stock listed on the NYSE, you'd have to meet the exchange's listing requirements, which include:

- At least 2,000 shareholders owning at least 100 shares each
- At least 1.1 million publicly owned shares
- Certain earnings/valuation requirements

It's actually more complicated than that, but I'm not even sure those numbers will show up on your exam, let alone that the company could meet the requirement with 2,000 shareholders who own 100 shares each *or* 2,200 shareholders as long as the average monthly trading volume is 100,000 shares for the most recent six months. Now it seems we're getting too trivial even for the Series 7, which is a pretty scary thing, actually. The exchange also charges listing fees to these companies since they feel that making money is sort of a good thing.

Nine Bond Rule

Some bonds are listed for trading on the NYSE, and the NYSE is a little bit protective. So, if an order for less than 10 NYSE-listed bonds comes into your broker-dealer, you have to route that order to the NYSE. If you can't get the trade executed at a decent price, *then* you can route it to the OTC (over-the-counter) market.

OVER THE COUNTER

The over-the-counter market is sometimes called the second market. It's not a physical marketplace, but it's definitely a market. Also known as the "interdealer" or "negotiated market." So, the first market is an "auction market," while the second or OTC market is "negotiated," which is a very likely testable point.

Since we don't all gather together on the floor of an exchange, we need big dealers to maintain inventories of over-the-counter stocks. We call these behemoth buyers and sellers "market makers," because they, literally, make a market. What IS a market? It's a two-sided quote, allowing buyers to buy at the ask price and sellers to sell at the bid price. Without these two-sided quotes, what would we do, call up our Great Aunt Lorraine and see if she'd like to go long 1,000 XYZ at $47.72? Uh, no thank you, sweetie, but Aunt Lorraine sure would enjoy a Christmas card this year.

So, market makers put out a bid and ask and stand ready to take either side of the trade, for at least one round lot. For stocks a round lot is 100 shares. So if a dealer or market maker says their quote is 20.00 - 20.11, they stand ready to buy 100 shares at $20.00 or sell 100 shares at $20.11. The difference between where they buy and where they sell is called the "spread," just like the difference between what a car dealer will pay for your trade-in, and what you'll pay for the new car he wants to sell you. Broker-dealers can act as brokers, whereby they charge commissions, or they can deal stock from their own inventory. They get stock for their inventory by negotiating the price with a market maker (thus the "negotiated market" thing). All of these terms (agent, broker, dealer, market maker, bid, ask, etc.) are highly testable, by the way, which is why I'm making this chapter much denser than you or I would probably prefer.

Over-the-counter stocks have more than three letters in their symbols, by the way. So if you see a symbol like "IBM," you know that one's on the first market, whereas if you see "MSFT" or "CSCO," you know that one is considered OTC. People trade these stocks by computer rather than gathering at a big building on Wall Street. The "big guys" of the OTC market are quoted all day long through an electronic quotation system known as NASDAQ, which stands for National Association of Securities Dealers Automated Quotation system.

NASDAQ used to be divided into the "NASDAQ National Market System" and the "NASDAQ SmallCap Market." Now, the NASDAQ National Market is called the "NASDAQ Global Market Companies." This group consists of over 1,450 companies that have applied for listing, having met and continued to meet stringent financial and liquidity requirements and agreed to meet specific corporate governance standards. The former "NASDAQ SmallCap Market" has been renamed the "NASDAQ Capital Market Companies." This group of stocks consists of over 550 companies that have applied for listing, having met and continued to meet financial and liquidity listing requirements and agreed to meet specific corporate governance standards.

NASDAQ Level 1, 2, 3

There are three levels of NASDAQ quoting that the test wants you to know about. The first is called Level 1, which represents the best bid and the best ask. Investors want to pay the lowest ask price when they buy and receive the highest bid price when they sell, which is what Level 1 displays. Among all market makers, Level 1 displays the highest bid and the lowest ask. That makes up a very important concept known as the "inside market" or "inside quote." Everything is based on that. When a dealer sells a security, they have to be close to that inside market, which might look like this:

Bid	Ask
19.75	20.00

Those two prices represent the highest bid and the lowest ask among all market makers currently quoting the stock. If any particular dealer wants to sell to a retail customer higher than 20 or buy lower than 19.75, they have to remain somewhere within 5% in order to conform to the 5% markup rule, which we'll explain in more detail.

Level 2 looks more like the following. Let's say there are three market makers quoting this stock and their quotes look like this:

	Bid	Ask
Dealer 1	19.11	20.00
Dealer 2	19.75	20.50
Dealer 3	19.23	20.25

Among the three market makers, we find the highest bid at 19.75 and the lowest ask at 20.00. That's what makes up the inside quote, shown on Level 1. So, Level 2 identifies each market maker's quote, from which Level 1 pulls the highest bid and lowest ask to provide the "inside market."

Level 3 has input fields that market makers use to enter their quotes. If you're not a market maker, you don't have Level 3. Levels 1 and 2 report quotes. Level 3 lets market makers provide quotes; it's interactive, rather than just a display.

5% Markup Guideline

As it says in the NASD Manual, the 5% "rule" is a guideline that dealers must use to ensure that customers are charged reasonable commissions or markups/markdowns. A firm can act as either a broker or a dealer. When the firm brokers a trade, they add a commission that must be reasonable. When the firm deals stock to the customer, they must charge a markup that is reasonable.

Back to the inside market. The inside market in our example above was Bid-19.75, Ask-20.00. That's the "interdealer market," which means that firms can buy or sell at those prices with market makers. If the firm buys this stock for its inventory, paying $20.00 to the market maker, how much can they tack on when selling it to the customer? It needs to be around 5% above that $20.00. If they charged "$20.35 net," we could judge the fairness of that markup by simply taking the excess of 35 cents compared to/divided by $20.00. That represents a markup of 1.75%, well within the 5% guideline. If they charged $21.00, that would be exactly 5%. But, 5% is not an absolute—even if they're charging 5% or less, they could still be violating the rules. If the stock is extremely liquid—like MSFT or CSCO—maybe they shouldn't be charging anything close to 5%. Or, for some securities, a markup above 5% might be okay. The dealers can take the following into consideration when justifying a higher markup or commission:

- The Type of Security Involved – stocks are riskier than bonds and carry higher charges
- Availability of the Security – inactive securities might take more time and expense to buy or sell
- Price of the Security – low-priced securities usually end up carrying markups that are higher as a percentage of the price. A markup of 10 cents is a big percentage when the stock costs $1.00, while a markup of 50 cents is pretty low on a $100 stock.
- Amount of Money Involved – sorry, kid, if you wanna buy 50 bucks' worth of stock, you ain't gonna' get such a great deal.
- Disclosing the higher markup or commissions before completing the transaction usually takes care of the situation…though not always. If you're truly gouging your clients, prior disclosure isn't going to make it okay.
- Nature of the Services provided – full-service broker-dealers can charge more in commissions and markups because they provide more services. The old "you get what you pay for" thing.

Proceeds Transaction

If a customer sells one stock and uses the proceeds to buy another on the same day, we call this a "proceeds transaction," for obvious reasons. When applying the 5% guideline, the firm has to treat both the sale and the purchase as one transaction. In other words, they can't ding the customer 5% on the sale and on the purchase. The <u>combined</u> commission or markup/markdown must be in the neighborhood of 5%. The NASD Manual says it well when it writes, "the mark-up shall be computed in the same way as if the customer had purchased for cash."

Riskless Principal Transaction

The difference between "broker" and "dealer" is important. When the firm acts as a broker, they are simply finding a buyer or seller for their customer. When the firm acts as a dealer, they are taking the other side of the trade by either buying from the customer or selling to the customer. The firm acts either as a broker or a dealer on a particular transaction, which is why the industry got all clever and named these firms broker-dealers.

So, if you need some stock, maybe the broker-dealer will simply find a seller and get you a decent price. They're acting as a broker/agent, and they would charge you a commission. A-B-C...agents are brokers and they charge commissions. If the firm already had the stock in inventory, they might deal it to you at a markup. They would indicate on your trade confirmation that they acted in a "principal" capacity. To act as a "principal" means that they're taking the other side of the trade, rather than just arranging the trade for a commission (agent/broker).

Well, sometimes a customer will call up and express an interest in buying, say, 1,000 shares of XYZ. The firm puts the customer on hold and then purchases the 1,000 shares for their own inventory. They get the customer back on the line, and they deal the stock to him. There was no risk on this principal transaction, since their holding period is about 3 seconds. Therefore, the industry cleverly named this situation where a principal takes no risk a "riskless principal transaction." As long as the markup conforms to the 5% guideline, everything is hunky dory.

Finally, the 5% markup guideline would not apply to anything sold with a prospectus, since that's a primary market transaction. A variable annuity or mutual fund, therefore, is simply sold at a public offering price, just like an IPO. Also, municipal securities aren't covered by this 5% guideline. The firm just follows the MSRB rule, which says customer transactions must be executed at a fair and reasonable price.

How Firm Is Thy Quote?

When a dealer contacts a market maker, they need to be really clear as to what the market maker actually means with his cryptic little phrases. For example, if the market maker simply responds with a straight answer, that's a firm quote that has to be honored for at least one round lot of 100 shares. If the market maker says, "Bid-20.00, Ask-20.15," that's a firm quote. He doesn't have to say "firm" to make it firm. It's what he *doesn't* say that makes it firm. See, sometimes the market maker is just talking, just giving the dealer a ballpark figure. There are many ways to indicate that the quote is "nominal," which means, "hey, we're just talkin' here." The following phrases indicate that the market maker is only giving a nominal quote:

- It looks like
- It's around
- Subject
- Nominal

- Work it out
- Last I saw

So, if you see any of that weasely language on the exam, call the quote "nominal." If it's just a straight answer, call it a firm quote. Also know that the market maker's quote is only firm for 1 round lot. If the purchasing dealer says, "What's the quote on XYZ?" and the market maker says, "Bid-20, Ask-20.25," the market maker only has to sell 100 shares at $20.25. If the purchasing dealer says, "Great, we'll take 1 million shares at the offer," the market maker would first laugh hard enough to spit water through his nose and then remind the dealer that there was, in fact, this exam called the Series 7 which did, in fact, make it clear that a firm quote is good for 100 shares. Beyond that, we may need to talk.

Now, had the purchasing dealer made it clear how many shares he wanted to buy or sell, then the firm quote would be good for that number of shares.

ACT

For the first market, sellers report to the "consolidated tape" within 90 seconds. The OTC market uses the automated confirmation transaction service (ACT), and, again, sellers report the price to ACT within 90 seconds.

Super Montage

Most NASDAQ trades are executed over a NASDAQ workstation using an automated execution system. This allows trades to happen without using the telephone. Super Montage, which is relatively new, allows for both firm and customer orders as large as 999,999 shares to be entered. The orders have to be either market orders or limit orders that are immediately executable. Orders executed through Super Montage are automatically reported to ACT.

THIRD MARKET

The third market is just a term used when an exchange-listed security gets sold OTC. Maybe an institutional buyer can get a better, negotiated price for an order of 10,000 IBM, a listed security, so they decide to buy it over-the-counter. When an NYSE-listed security trades OTC, we refer to that situation as the "third market."

The Consolidated Quotation Service (CQS) displays quotations on all common stock, preferred stock, warrants, and rights that are registered on the American Stock Exchange or the New York Stock Exchange and trading in the OTC market (third market).

FOURTH MARKET

The "fourth market" is easy to keep separate. It involves direct trading between institutional investors, completely bypassing brokers by using a telecommunications system that the exam might refer to as an "ECN" or "Electronic Communications Network." The exam might even mention INSTINET, a well-known ECN and one that is easy to remember. <u>INSTI</u>tutional investors trade electronically over INSTINET. Institutions are insurance companies, mutual funds, pension funds, big trust departments, etc. They're professionals with millions/billions of dollars flowing in and out of the market. Kind of like an eBay™ for securities, really.

BOND TRADING
Corporate Bonds

Corporate bonds traded over the counter are reported to the NASD's TRACE system, which stands for Trade Reporting and Compliance Engine. Brokerage firms are now required to report price and volume data on all corporate bond transactions to TRACE, within 15 minutes. The NASD publicly disseminates those transaction data immediately on virtually 100 percent of over-the-counter corporate bond activity (approximately 22,000 transactions and $18 billion in volume every day!). Those transaction data are available free of charge at www.nasdbondinfo.com. Recently, the NASD fined a firm $1.4 *million* for failing to report a huge percentage of their bond trades to TRACE. The whole purpose of the TRACE system is to provide transparency (what's going on) in the bond market, so by failing to report the trades, the firm deprived the market of the transparency it needs to remain effective.

Municipal Bonds

As of January 31, 2005, MSRB rules require that transactions in municipal bonds be reported within 15 minutes of trade execution. The MSRB now disseminates trade data about all reported municipal securities transactions almost immediately at www.investinginbonds.com.

TYPES OF ORDERS
Market Order

The exam will ask you to work with market orders, limit orders, stop orders, and even the dreaded stop-limit order. Well, **market orders** are easy. You want to buy 1,000 shares quickly, you place a market order. It will get filled as quickly as possible. We don't know exactly the price it will be filled at, but if we fill it fast enough it will probably be the same price we're looking at right now. *Now* is always the best time to fill a market order, which is also why those players down on the floor are running around like crazy people most of the day. The specialists at the NYSE have the following specialized, nit-picky orders on their "books," which are really computer screens. When somebody wants to name a specific price where a purchase or sale would happen, those orders go on the specialist's book, your exam might say. That's not to imply you can't do the same orders for OTC/NASDAQ stocks. You can. But the test may mention the specialist's "book," so remember that the book has the stop and limit orders on it that we're about to take apart.

Limit Order

Sometimes customers like to name their price. If a stock is at 43, maybe they're starting to get interested in selling it. They'd be a lot more interested if they could sell it for $45, so they enter a **sell limit** order above the current market price. Sell limit @45 means the investor will take 45 or better (*more* is better for a seller). If he can get 45 or 45.15, or even higher, he'll sell his stock.

Another investor is interested in buying a stock currently trading at 30. He'd be a lot more interested in buying it at $25, so he places a **buy limit** order below the current price. That means he'll buy the stock if he can get it for $25 or better (*less* is better for a buyer). If the ticker comes in like this, he'll get filled at $25, his limit price:

30.00, 29.25, 28.75, 27.00, 26.25, 25.25, 25.00

And, if the last two prices had been 25.25, 24.50, he could have been filled at 24.50, which is "or better" than 25.00 when you're a buyer.

Sometimes the stock's price fails to perform like an investor wants it to. If it's entered as a **day** order, the limit order either gets executed that day or it goes away. If the investor is going on vacation for three weeks and doesn't want to look at his stocks while he's gone, he can leave the order open by entering it **GTC**, which stands for **good 'til canceled**. If the order doesn't get filled and the investor doesn't cancel it, the order remains open. Twice a year (April, October) the firm calls the customers with open orders on the books to see if they still want them, a process called "confirming" for obvious reasons.

Stop Order

Stop orders are even more fun. Let's say a technical analyst sees that a particular stock is trading in a narrow range, between 38 and 40. The technical analyst sees no reason to tie up his money in a stock that is stuck in a narrow trading range, known as consolidation. He decides if the stock can break through resistance (40), it will probably continue to rise, which is why he'd like to buy it on the way up. So he places a buy stop above the current market price. Buy stop @41 means that the price first has to reach 41 or higher, at which point the order is triggered. It will be <u>executed</u> at the <u>next available price</u>, whatever that is. Stop orders have a trigger price, at which point they become market orders. So if the ticker came in like this:

40.00, 40.50, 40.75, 41.00…his order would now be triggered or "elected" at 41.00. It would then be filled at the next available price, regardless of what that is. And, if the last two prices had been 40.75, 41.50, the order would have been triggered at 41.50, at which point the price has passed through the stop price of 41. Notice that stop orders don't guarantee a price for execution. The price named as the stop is just the price that triggers or elects the order. The order—now a market order—is filled at the next available price. Again, the stop price is not the exact price, either. A "buy stop at 41" is triggered at 41 or any price higher than that. It's then filled as soon as possible.

A day trader decides to take a large position in a high-risk security, because, well, that's what day traders do. But this particular day trader decides to play it safe and limit his loss. He buys 1,000 shares at $50 a share and immediately enters a sell stop order at 49. This means that as long as the stock stays above $49 he's in. As soon as it slips to 49 or lower, though, he's out. A sell stop at 49 would be triggered as soon as the stock's price hit 49 or lower, at which point it would be sold at the next available price. The exam might tell you that a customer is bullish on a stock but fears a possible downturn in the short-term. What should she do?

Well, if she originally bought in at $20 and the stock is now at $50, you should tell her that selling for more than $50 would be great. At this point, however, she should make sure she doesn't lose too much of the $30 profit she has within her grasp. Many investors end up snatching defeat from the jaws of victory at this point, probably because they don't know how to use sell stops or "stop loss" orders. Not going to happen to us. We'll give up one dollar from here, you tell her, but if it falls to $49 or lower, she's selling and taking her profit. So, if it goes up, great, and if it goes down, she takes a profit, and you immediately put her into another stock…assuming it's suitable, of course.

If somebody wants to get really tricky, they can enter a **stop-limit order**. Now their stop order also names the most they'll pay or the least they'll accept for a particular stock. A buy stop @50, limit 52 would start out as a stop order. The stock has to hit 50 or higher before it's triggered, but the investor also won't pay more than $52 for it. A sell stop @30, limit 29 would be triggered if the stock hit 30 or lower, but the investor will not take less than $29 a share. If the order gets triggered and then the price falls lower than 29, this sell order simply won't get executed, and the investor will end up holding a loser that would have otherwise been sold with a sell-stop (not a stop-limit) order.

Further Specifications

These orders can also be entered as "specialized orders." A **fill or kill** order has to be executed immediately or the whole thing is killed. Fill it or kill it. An **immediate or cancel** order also has to be filled immediately. If the whole thing can't be filled immediately, fill what you can and cancel the rest. So this is the only one that will take a partial execution. An **all or none** order will *not* take a partial execution. Fill <u>all</u> of it <u>or none</u> of it. You don't necessarily have to fill it right away, though. Just don't come back here with half of it filled, okay?

At-the-open and **at-the-close** orders are filled, surprisingly enough, at the open of trading and at the closing price, respectively.

And, just in case the exam feels it has not sufficiently harassed you, remember that the FOK and the AON orders are no longer accepted by the NYSE. They were so infrequently used that the NYSE said fuggedaboudit. NASDAQ trading and bond trading still use the funky orders, though.

Stops and Limits Reviewed

Let's drill down on the stop and limit orders a littler harder, since I suspect you'll be hit with at least three questions on this stuff, and I know from experience just how much most people enjoy working with these concepts. Here goes. Right now, XYZ's last reported price is $25. The BID is $24.90, the ASK is $25.10. Notice how the bidders (buyers willing to let you sell to them) want to buy your stock for 10 cents less, and the offerors/askers would like an extra 10 cents if you want to buy from them. You could certainly enter a market order to buy and pay $25.10, or you could enter a market order to sell and receive $24.90.

Or, you could get fancy. If you want to buy this stock for less, enter a buy-limit order below the inside ASK/offer price. The ASK is $25.10, but you aren't willing to pay one penny more than $24. Fine, enter a buy-limit @24. Nothing will happen unless and until the ASK/offer price drops to $24 or lower.

Three hours later, the ASK price does, in fact, drop to $24, and your order is filled. Congratulations, you just bought a stock whose price is dropping faster than a big league curve ball. But, this time you get lucky, and the stock turns around and starts going up in your favor. Well, heck, you're not greedy or anything, so as soon as this stock could be sold for $30, you'd be okay with a 25% profit, and you enter a sell-limit @30. So, if/when the BID price moves up to $30, you'll sell it to the bidder. You've concluded that this stock isn't likely to move above $30, anyway, so you might as well take your profit at $30. This isn't going to happen in the space of an afternoon, so you mark the order GTC, or "good 'til canceled."

Three weeks later, XYZ begins to move conveniently in your favor. The BID finally rises to $30, and you sell your stock for a $6 profit, minus commissions. Great, that was all the upside there was in the stock, anyway, right?

Wrong. As soon as you sell the stock, it starts to *really* take off, leaving you behind like the sad child nobody ever waits up for. Ouch! This stock is going up without you. But, maybe it's a temporary blip. Maybe there are only a few more points of upside on this stock—let's find out. How? Let's assume that it could easily go to $35 and then drop. But, if it goes above $35, it will keep going. How do we know that?

We don't. Remember, nobody really knows anything when it comes to trading stocks. But, we figure if XYZ breaks through resistance @35 it will continue to go up, which means if the stock goes UP to a certain level, we'll buy it. What kind of weird order is that?

A buy-stop. Let's place a buy-stop @36. That way, if the stock breaks through resistance of $35, we'll buy it just as it's about to make a real break. What if it never makes it to $36?

Then, we never really wanted it.

Now, stop orders aren't based on the BID/ASK the way limit orders are. They're based on actual trades or the "last trade" price. Just means there will have to be an actual transaction at $36 or above before our order gets thrown into the game.

It takes a while, but after a few days, XYZ does break through resistance, and we end up buying shares at $36.15. Remember, stop orders aren't filled at the stop price necessarily. If you're that much of a control freak, you need to add the word "limit" to your buy-stop. But we didn't do that, because we just wanted to make sure we got the stock. You get fussy with a limit price and you might not get the stock at all.

But we did. Turns out, we were exactly right—this stock is a rocket ship headed nowhere but up. But then, in a moment of clarity, we remember that they said the same thing about CSCO, JDSU, and QCOM. Yes, stocks do occasionally reverse directions and go the wrong way on us, so just in case that happens here, let's have a sell-stop in place as a safety net. The stock has gone from our $36.15 purchase price to $45, which is known, technically, as "a real good thing." Let's not let this real good thing slip away, though. If it continues to go up, we want to hold it. But, if it starts to drop, we want to walk away with a profit. So, we enter a sell-stop @44. Remember, we bought at $36.15, and we're sitting on a profit of $8.85 at this point because the stock is trading at $45. With our sell-stop @44, we will only sell if the stock drops. If it goes up, we continue to hold it and enjoy the upside. If it starts to drop, we walk away with a profit.

Turns out, three days later, the stock opens at $43, which triggers our sell-stop (triggered at or below the trigger price of 44). The stock is sold a few ticks later at $42.95, and we walk away with a decent paper profit, while everybody else is in denial, talking about "doubling down," "lowering their average cost," and various other clichés often uttered before disaster finally strikes.

And, disaster does finally strike. Two weeks later, the CEO is indicted for fraud, the company re-states earnings for the past five years, and the whole thing makes the WorldCom debacle look mild by comparison.

Only, it doesn't really affect us. We protected our paper profit and got out with a sell-stop.

PRACTICE:

88. An investor originally purchased 100 shares of INTC at $20 a share. Now the stock is at $60. The investor is still bullish on the stock for the long-term but fears a possible downturn in the short-term. As her registered rep, you would tell her to place a
  A.   Market order to sell
  B.   Sell limit order at $59
  C.   Buy stop order at $61
  D.   Sell stop order at $59

89. A sell stop order would be activated when
  A.   The stock price passes through the trigger price
  B.   The stock price hits or passes through the trigger price
  C.   The stock price hits the trigger price and conforms with the NYSE uptick rule
  D.   None of the above

90. A sell stop at 45 would be triggered at all the following prices except
  A.   44.00
  B.   44.37
  C.   44.87
  D.   46.00

ANSWERS:

88. D

89. B – it doesn't have to pass through the trigger price-if it hits the trigger price OR passes through, the order is elected. Upticks are only for short sales, which this question did not mention.

90. D – at the trigger price or below. Not above the trigger price. That's for buy stops.

WRAP-UP

Well, that sure was fun, wasn't it? Trading Securities is, in many ways, one of the toughest sections on the exam. You'll need to be able to define all the terms (bid, ask, markup, markdown, commission, broker, dealer, agent, principal, limit, stop, etc.). And, you'll need to understand all the concepts.

Perhaps that will become easier if we look at the preceding information from another angle. Let's say that your favorite customer, Michelle Montoya, is interested in buying some stock with some money she recently inherited when her Aunt Marta passed away. You and she, of course, discuss suitability, and you've narrowed it down to three different stocks. The first one is the old dependable General Electric, or GE. Michelle is willing to commit $30,000 to buying GE. How many shares can I get, she asks you. You pull up your quote screen and see that the market for GE is:

Bid	Ask
$29.75	$29.95

Looks like she can get a round lot. She's not interested in naming an exact price or placing a fancy buy-stop order above the inside ask, so you decide to take the simplest route and enter a market order. You quickly fill out the order ticket, indicating that she wants to buy 1000 GE "at the market." You hand the ticket to the wire room, who wires the order to your commission house broker jumping around like a lunatic on the floor of the NYSE. The commission house broker runs to the trading post and buys the 1,000 shares at the best price he can pay right now—$29.95. He sends back an execution report, and you tell Michelle that her order for 1,000 shares was filled at $29.95 per share. Later that day a trade confirmation is printed and delivered to Michelle, showing that she paid $29,950 for 1,000 shares of GE, plus a $50 commission.

Another stock Michelle would like to purchase is an Internet security company trading on NASDAQ. This one is fairly speculative, trading at just $3.67 a share. While not technically a "penny stock," since it is on NASDAQ, it is still trading below $5 a share, which usually gives prudent investors the willies. "Let's see if it goes above $5 a share first, Michelle," you tell her, to which she replies, "but I don't have time to watch the price all day long."

You don't have to, you inform her. And then you explain that if you place a buy-stop order at, say, $5.10, nothing will happen unless and until the stock trades at $5.10 or above. What if it never makes it that high? Then we never wanted it. You mark the order ticket "GTC" and three weeks later the company releases impressive earnings and the stock starts trading above $5.10. Michelle's order is triggered and filled, and, once again, a trade confirmation is created and sent to the customer.

The third stock happens to be one in which your firm makes a market. When Michelle decides she would like 200 shares of QRZ, your firm simply sells some of the stock in their inventory directly to Michelle. Her order confirmation this time would indicate "principal," and the price indicated per share is "$19.75 net." That means that the inside ask was actually a little lower than $19.75 at the time of the trade, but your firm is entitled to a markup/profit, as long as it's reasonable. With the inside ask at $19.50, this represents a 25-cent markup. What is 25 cents divided by (compared to) the inside ask? A markup of 1.28%, well within the fairness guideline.

Now that she has invested a few thousand dollars in common stock, what can she do to protect her investment? She could buy puts, allowing her to sell the stocks for a set price. Or, she could enter sell-stops below the purchase price for each stock. You and she decide on the sell-stops. You decide that if these stocks drop 20% or more, it's time to bail. Rather than staring at the computer all day, you simply place sell-stops about 20% below the price she paid for the stock. This way, if the stock stays where it is or goes up, excellent. You might cancel the sell-stops and place new ones a little higher up. If the stock goes down in a hurry, it will be sold in a hurry, cutting Michelle's losses to a level she can live with.

WHAT NOW?

- Review the chapter. *Approximately 1 hour.*
- If you have the Pass the 7 QuizSet, take the Chapter 9 Quiz on Trading Securities. *Approximately 1.5 hours.*
- If you have the Audio CD set, listen to Disc 2, Track 4. *Approximately 17 minutes.*

CHAPTER 10

Taxation

As you probably know, people like interstate highways, public universities, national parks, a strong national defense, maybe a few lunar landings every decade or so just to show the world we still got it. Unfortunately, the federal government has no money to pay for any of that stuff unless taxpayers are willing to pitch in. Similarly, your state government provides roads, public schools, parks, state troopers, state fairs, etc., and they use the taxes you pay to fund that stuff. So, when you get a paycheck, both the federal and state governments insist on sharing some of it with you. As it turns out, they also insist on sharing the money you earn from investments.

BONDS

We've actually already covered the taxation of bonds in the Debt Securities chapter, but let's do a quick review, anyway, since taxation is of major importance on the Series 7 exam. U.S. Treasury securities (which include T-bills, T-notes, T-bonds, I-bonds, and STRIPS) pay interest that is taxed at ordinary income rates, but only at the federal level. Much to their disappointment, state and local governments can't tax that interest. Not even Maryland. Capital gains are also taxable at the federal level and—unfortunately—the states can tax them, too.

Municipal securities pay interest that is tax-exempt at the federal level. At the state level, it depends on where the bond was issued. If you live in Kentucky and buy a general obligation of Little Rock, Arkansas, Kentucky can tax the interest, and so can your local government. Of course, if you buy the general obligations of Louisville or the State of Kentucky, you'll get a break. Regardless, when you're selling municipal bonds and taking capital gains, those are still taxable as capital gains, either short-term or long-term depending on your holding period.

Corporate bonds and also Ginnie, Fannie, and Freddie pay interest that is taxable at all three levels: federal, state, and local.

And, don't forget the funky zero coupon bonds. These are issued originally at a discount, which is why the creative types named them original issue discount bonds, which immediately became OID's to make sure the industry had enough acronyms. If you buy a zero coupon issued for $500 with a par value that will become $1,000 in 10 years, you basically report the $50 increase each year on a 1099 OID. Yes, the interest income you haven't collected yet is still taxable at this point.

STOCK

Some people are shocked that I own actual shares of stock. That's because mutual funds have been marketed so successfully that many people don't even realize they can, like, buy stock in General Electric, Home Depot, or Starbucks. But, of course, they can do exactly that. If they think those companies will continue to do well over their lifetimes, they can own little pieces of them by purchasing their stock. GE and Home Depot pay dividends. Someday Starbucks will probably do the same.

Dividends

When these companies pay dividends to shareholders, the shareholders are taxed. Currently, the tax on "qualified dividends" is a maximum of 15%. A qualified dividend is what you'd receive from GE or Home Depot. Those companies pay the dividend after they've paid their taxes on the profits they made. So, why should the shareholders get fully taxed on their part of that profit that's already been taxed?

Turns out, Congress and the President say they shouldn't, and the older I get the smarter that sounds. Earn a million dollars in qualified dividends this year and keep $850,000. Not too shabby, from what I understand. But, if the exam wants to play hardball, remember that there are still some dividends that are taxed at ordinary income rates. These are called, surprisingly enough, ordinary dividends. Real Estate Investment Trusts (REITs) pass through 90% of their profits to the shareholders, but the shareholders pay ordinary income tax on those fat dividends. What's the difference? At the time of this writing, ordinary income rates could be as high as 35%. So could mine if people continue to buy Pass the 7™ products with the same enthusiasm they've shown so far. In any case, notice that there are few black-and-white statements that can be made about securities and taxation. If someone says that all dividends are taxed at 15%, he's way off. First, some people only pay 5%, and, secondly, there are ordinary dividends and even royalties that are paid to shareholders, and the taxation is different from the treatment of qualified dividends.

Bottom line is that if you own stock inside a regular old brokerage account, the income those stocks pay to you will be taxable. Companies like GE, Home Depot, and Microsoft pay qualified dividends taxed at 15%. If you own REITs or royalty trusts (oil & gas, for example), the taxation will be a little different. Either way, you'll receive a 1099-DIV to help you and your accountant deal with the tax implications.

Capital Gains

So, the income paid to shareholders is taxable. And, when the shareholders decide to sell their stock to other investors, they could end up selling for more than they paid, and nothing seems to get the IRS's attention faster. See, if you buy $10,000 of GE stock in, say, 1993 and have the audacity to sell that stock for $15,000 in 2007, you have "realized a capital gain" of $5,000. First of all, congratulations on making a profit and, secondly, don't forget your friends and mine at the IRS. At the end of the year when you figure your taxes, you'll have to report the $5,000 capital gain and maybe end up paying taxes on it.

Why just "maybe"? Because, if you're like most investors, you usually have even more stocks that moved in the opposite direction. See, if you bought JDSU, there's about a 99.9% chance that you're sitting on a big, fat "capital loss" at this point. So, if you had purchased, say $15,000 of JDSU in 1999 and sold it for a whopping $1,000 in 2006, you would have realized a $14,000 capital loss, which would more than offset the gain you took on GE. Investors subtract their capital losses from their capital gains taken during the tax year. If they end up with more gains than losses, they have a "net capital gain" for the year. If the stock was held for at least 12 months plus one day, it is treated as a long-term capital gain. Those are taxed at a maximum of 15% currently. If the capital gain had been taken on stock held one year or less, that's a short-term capital gain, taxed at the investor's ordinary income bracket just to keep things nice and simple the way the IRS and the United States Congress like it.

The "long-term" and "short-term" thing has to do with what the exam will call the investor's "holding period." The holding period begins the day after the trade date and stops on the day the stock is sold. So, if you buy stock on February 5th, 2006, you can sell it on February 6th, 2007 for a long-term capital gain. But if you sell it sooner than that, it will be treated as a short-term capital gain.

To determine if the sale triggered a gain or loss, the investor compares the proceeds of the sale with the cost basis on the stock. The fancy phrase "cost basis" means all the money the investor has put into the thing up to this point. If you buy $5,000 of Microsoft common stock and pay a $25 commission, your cost basis is $5,025. The IRS has already taxed that money and won't tax it again. If you sell that stock later for $6,000 and pay another $25 commission, your "proceeds" will be $5,975. So, you would take the proceeds of $5,975 minus the cost basis of $5,025 for a capital gain of $950. If you held it for at least one year plus one day, it's a long-term capital gain taxed at the kinder, gentler rate. If your holding period was less than that, it's a short-term capital gain, which is probably taxed at a higher rate.

Be sure that you are comfortable with the following important words before taking the exam:

- Cost basis
- Proceeds
- Holding period
- Realized capital gain
- Long-term
- Short-term

The exam might try to mess with you by mentioning "unrealized capital gains," so let's take a look at that. If you buy 1000 shares of Starbucks for $10 a share, and the stock is now trading at $55 a share, how much of a capital gains tax do you have to pay at this point?

Not a penny.

This is just a gain on paper, called an "unrealized capital gain." It gives you major bragging rights around the water cooler, but you haven't sold anything yet. It's only when you "realize" your capital gain that the IRS gets concerned. To realize a capital gain means that you've sold the stock. Until you sell it, there are no capital gains taxes to pay.

But don't you have to sell the stock eventually?

Not really. Some people hate the IRS so much that they will *never* sell it. Instead, the stock will pass to their children or grandchildren when they die. Or they'll just give the stock to somebody. Or, maybe they'll donate it to a charity.

Inherited Shares

Let's say that Grandma purchased 1,000 shares of Harley-Davidson back in 1967 for $10 a share. On the day she dies, November 15th, 2006, the fair market value is $50 a share. If you inherit the shares, what is your cost basis?

$50 a share. So, if you sell it a few days later for $55, that's only a capital gain of $5 per share, not $45. It's also treated as a long-term capital gain, even if you sell it right away. The IRS actually explains this quite clearly at www.irs.gov:

> If you inherit investment property, your capital gain or loss on any later disposition of that property is treated as a long-term capital gain or loss. This is true regardless of how long you actually held the property.

See, they do have a heart at the IRS. Imagine if you had to take Grandma's original cost basis. First, that would have made the capital gains tax much, much higher. Secondly, where the heck did Grandma keep her trade confirmations from 1967? Doesn't matter. You just take the "fair market value" as of the date of death. And, again, you can sell it as soon as you want—it's still a long-term capital gain.

Gifts of Stock

Unfortunately, if the stock has appreciated Grandma will have to die in order to get you the nice tax break. See, if Grandma is still toolin' around on her Harley and just, like, *gives* you this stock that has risen about $40 a share, you'd have to take her cost basis of $10. You would also take over her holding period since you are taking over her basis. I'm hoping the exam doesn't hit quite that hard on taxation, but if it does, tell it that you would use Grandma's cost basis, and your holding period would have begun the day Grandma bought the stock.

Charitable Donations of Stock

Maybe Grandma has a more worthy cause than, say, you, and decides to donate the stock to her favorite charity, the National Association of Septuagenarian Hog Enthusiasts. If so, she can deduct the fair market value of the stock on the day of the donation from her ordinary income and reduce her tax bill that year.

You, however, would get squat on that deal, so you may want to talk to her before she goes and gets all philanthropic suddenly.

Capital Losses

As mentioned, investors often end up selling stock for less than they paid, which is not really the point of buying it, but does, unfortunately, happen. Then again, it's not the end of the world. When you sell stock for less than you paid, you get to use that capital loss to reduce the capital gains you may have taken on other sales. And that reduces your capital gains taxes for the year. Some people go overboard. If they take a $10,000 capital gain, they then take a $15,000 capital loss just to make sure they pay no capital gains taxes that year. That extra $5,000 "net capital loss" could be used in future years to offset capital gains. $3,000 of it can also be used to reduce the investor's ordinary income for the current tax year. So, if his adjusted gross income was going to be $50,000, now it's only $47,000. He would only save a percentage of that $3,000, remember. It's not a tax credit; it's a tax deduction. You have to lose a dollar in order to save 25 or 35 cents, in other words. I mean, it's nice, but I wouldn't make it a cornerstone of your long-term investment strategy.

Wash Sales

When the investor realizes the capital loss on his stock, the IRS is cool with that. But, he has to wait a full 30 days and not repurchase that company's stock until the 31st day. Otherwise, he can't use the loss. Also, he could not have purchased that company's stock 30 days before selling it at a loss. So, there is a 60-day window pointing 30 days before and after the sale. Stay out of the stock if you want to use the loss to offset gains for the year.

What if you promise not to buy the stock back for 30 days but simply can't stop yourself? First of all, I can recommend a good therapist, and, secondly, you simply can't use that loss. However, if you took a loss of, say, $5 a share that is now going to be disallowed due to the wash sale, you can add that $5 to your cost basis on the new purchase, meaning you will eventually get the benefit of that loss you tried to take this year.

Just to keep things nice and simple.

The IRS, again, actually explains this all very clearly at www.irs.gov, which is becoming, like, one of my favorite websites lately:

> If your loss was disallowed because of the wash sale rules, add the disallowed loss to the cost of the new stock or securities. The result is your basis in the new stock or securities. This adjustment postpones the loss deduction until the disposition of the new stock or securities.

TAX IMPLICATIONS FOR MUTUAL FUND INVESTORS

When you own shares of a mutual fund, tax treatment will depend on the source of the income you receive.

Stock Funds

If it's a stock fund, the taxation will be a little different from a bond or money market fund. We haven't gotten into the details of mutual funds yet, but they're really just gigantic portfolios of stocks, bonds, etc. You can buy little slices of the gigantic portfolio, which is much easier than picking your own stocks and bonds. Let the mutual fund do that—you'll just own a percentage of whatever they decide to invest in. The mutual fund portfolio will receive dividends from some of the stocks they own, and since they trade their stocks all the time, they'll usually end up with a capital gain for the year. Investors in the mutual fund receive dividends and capital gains distributions from the fund, and these are taxable. The 1099-DIV that the fund sends to investors will show how much they received in qualified versus ordinary dividends, and how much they received in capital gains distributions. Is it a short-term or long-term capital gain? The 1099 will tell you that, too. Remember, the holding period is based on how long the fund held the securities before trading them. It has nothing to do with how long the investor has been in the fund—the investor didn't sell anything. She's just receiving her fair share of the income generated by the mutual fund portfolio. Usually, the fund makes sure the gains distributed are long-term gains, since the 15% maximum tax rate is a lot easier to swallow than the 35% rate some folks pay on short-term gains. Can the fund distribute short-term capital gains? Absolutely. And when they do, they're taxable to the investors as short-term capital gains. The higher a fund's "turnover rate" the more likely it will generate short-term capital gains. But, really, all of the capital gains distributions from mutual funds to investors are long-term, except for the ones that are short-term.

Notice how I separated the dividends from the capital gains. Remember that dividends are what you receive for holding the stock; capital gains are what you make for selling stock at a profit. In a mutual fund, as we'll see, investors get charged for many expenses. The portfolio manager charges a management fee, and investors pay for that. The board of directors likes their six-figure salaries, and shareholders pay for that. There are legal and accounting fees, transfer agent fees, custodial fees, and 12b1 fees that cover all the sales and marketing costs. How does the fund cover these expenses? They use the dividends they receive from the portfolio stocks and the interest payments from the bonds and money market securities that they hold. When the fund takes the dividends and the interest, then deducts all the expenses, they are left with net income. The IRS, who is here to help, generally likes to share profits with companies showing net income, but they will allow the fund to use something funky called the "conduit" or "pipeline theory." If the fund has $1 million in net income, for example, they can distribute 90% or more ($900,000+) to the shareholders and, thereby, avoid being taxed on that money. The shareholders will get taxed on that money, instead. The fund only has to pay taxes on what they did *not* distribute—in this case, $100,000. The fund may also end the year taking more profits than losses trading the portfolio. If so, they realize a net capital gain and also distribute that to the shareholders. They usually only do that once a year, and usually in December.

What can you do with these dividend and capital gains distributions? A, you can tell them where to send the check and go shopping. B, you can automatically reinvest the money into more shares of the fund. So, the IRS would only tax you if you cashed the check, right? No. As it turns out, the IRS could sort of care less what you *do* with the distribution. Whether you cash the check or reinvest into more shares, you get taxed on the distributions. People reinvest these things to avoid paying sales charges to the fund, but it doesn't help them in the least with their pals at the IRS. Remember that whether the dividend or capital gains distribution is paid in cash or reinvested into more shares, the investor is taxed. And that means that when you reinvest a dividend or capital gain, your cost basis rises by that amount. So, if the test question says that Melody has invested $10,000 into the Argood Aggressive Growth Fund and reinvested dividends of $2,000, her cost basis equals $12,000. Cost basis is basically the money you've put into an investment that the IRS has already taxed. The capital gain that may someday materialize is just the amount you manage to sell it for above that amount.

Should you be so fortunate.

Bond Funds

For bond funds, there is really nothing to add to our discussion of bonds held individually. The "dividends" paid are really coming from bond interest received by the portfolio. So, U.S. Treasury funds would pay dividends that are taxable as ordinary income on federal returns but exempt from state or local taxation. Tax-exempt Municipal Bond funds would pay dividends that are tax-exempt for federal returns but may be subject to state and local taxation. This is why some fund companies have rolled out, say, the Maryland Tax-Exempt Fund or the Tax-Exempt Fund of California. That way, residents of those high-tax states can buy mutual funds that pay income exempt from both federal and state taxes. If you're in a state that wants, say, 14% of your income, it might be a good idea to avoid that whenever possible, right? Corporate bond funds, unfortunately, would pay dividends subject to taxation at all three levels.

Capital gains would also be taxable to investors, including capital gains distributions to investors in municipal bond funds. Municipal bonds pay *interest* that is exempt from federal taxation, but nobody said nothin' about no capital gains. Those are still taxable as capital gains.

Money Market Funds

Report amounts you receive from money market funds as dividend income. Money market funds are a type of mutual fund and should not be confused with bank money market accounts that pay interest.

TAX TREATMENT OF VARIABLE ANNUITIES

A variable annuity is basically a cross between a mutual fund, a retirement plan, and an insurance policy. In a non-qualified variable annuity, the investor contributes money that has already been taxed. Therefore, the money she puts into her annuity is her cost basis. The IRS won't tax the money she puts in; they'll only tax the money she takes out above that someday. The money grows tax-deferred, which means all the dividends and bond interest being paid to the investor will not be taxed until money is finally taken out. She put in a total of $10,000. Let's say at retirement, the annuity is worth $50,000. That means that $40,000 of earnings have accumulated. No matter how she takes the money out, she will pay ordinary income tax on that $40,000. The exam will probably call the $40,000 the "earnings" or "the excess over cost basis," just to make you sweat a little. The annuitant can take a lump sum distribution, just like somebody who retires from General Motors. Gimme all my money right now, please. Fine. But, she'll have to pay ordinary income rates on that $40,000, and that money might push her into a higher tax bracket. Since that might push her into a higher bracket, maybe she does a "random withdrawal" of $10,000. Here's where the exam is looking to snare a few insurance agents. Insurance agents might think that since she put in $10,000 and is only taking out $10,000, there will be no tax hassles. Unfortunately, the IRS considers all of the money coming out to be the earnings portion first. The exam might call that LIFO for "last in-first out." The earnings were the last thing into the account, so we consider them to be the first thing coming out. Why?

Because we can.

So, not only will this $10,000 random withdrawal be fully taxable as ordinary income, but also so will the next withdrawals that take us through the $40,000 of earnings.

Many people just "annuitize" the contract, which means they want to receive a monthly check for the rest of their lives. Depending on how long their life expectancy is, each monthly payment will represent part cost basis and part earnings. So, the exam wants you to know that part of each annuity payment is taxable, and part is considered a return of the cost basis.

When people annuitize the contract, they can choose to receive payments for as long as they live, or they can choose to cover a beneficiary. We'll talk about "period certain" and "joint and last survivor" later on. For now, just know that if the wife or the daughter is receiving annuity payments from the annuity purchased by a husband or parent, she is going to pay ordinary income tax on the "excess over cost basis," too. Somebody, in other words, always pays ordinary income tax on the amount above what the annuitant put into the contract. That's the deal you make in exchange for the tax deferral.

What if the annuitant dies while he's still putting money into the contract? This is known as the "accumulation phase," by the way, and if the annuitant has put in $10,000 when he dies, the death benefit will pay his beneficiary the greater of that $10,000 or whatever the contract is currently worth. So, if the annuity is worth $13,000 now, the beneficiary receives $13,000. If the value had dipped to $8,000 due to a tough stock or bond market, the beneficiary would still receive $10,000. And, as always, if the beneficiary receives more than the annuitant has contributed, that excess is taxable to her as ordinary income.

Someday you may meet up with a client who was sold a really lousy annuity from some sketchy company. You might be able to talk her into selling that one and exchanging it for an annuity that you sell. If so, she can do a 1035 tax-free contract exchange. In other words, this is different from selling one mutual fund to buy the proceeds of another fund in the same family—that would still be a taxable event. But annuities are retirement plans, really, so there is a special provision here for tax-free exchanges, just as there is for life insurance.

Since they're retirement vehicles, the individual needs to wait until she's 59½ before taking money out. Otherwise, she'll pay not just her ordinary income rate on the excess over cost basis but also a 10% penalty to the IRS.

72(t) and Substantially Equal Periodic Payments

Speaking of early withdrawal penalties, remember that annuities are by nature retirement plans and are subject to the 10% penalty for withdrawals made before age 59½ or made without a good excuse. One good excuse is to utilize IRS rule "72(t)." As with an IRA, an individual can avoid the 10% penalty if the withdrawal qualifies for an exemption. For example, if the individual has become disabled and can't work, or has certain medical expenses, money can be taken out penalty-free. Notice how I didn't say tax-free.

Basically, a reference to "72t" has to do with an individual taking a series of substantially equal periodic payments. Of course, the industry quickly turned that phrase into the acronym "SEPP." The IRS won't penalize the early withdrawal if the individual sets up a rigid schedule whereby they withdraw the money by any of several IRS-approved methods. Once you start your little SEPP program, stay on it. See, the IRS requires you to continue the SEPP program for 5 years or until you are the age of 59½, whichever comes last. So, if the individual is 45, she'll have to keep taking periodic payments until she's 59½. If the individual is 56 when she starts, she'll still have to continue for 5 years. Either that, or cut the IRS a check for the very penalties she was trying to avoid.

TAXATION OF LIFE INSURANCE

When you pay your life insurance premiums, you don't get to take a deduction against income, so they are made after-tax. They usually grow tax-deferred, however, which is nice. When the insured dies, the beneficiary receives the death benefit free and clear of federal income taxes.

But the death benefit will be added to the insured's estate to determine estate taxes. It's that simple when the beneficiary has the lump-sum settlement option, anyway. If we're talking about those periodic settlement options that generate interest, some of those payments could be taxed as interest income. Rather than take a loan, the policyholder can also do a "partial surrender," whereby the policyholder takes out some of the cash value, not enough to make the policy lapse, of course. Depending on how much has been paid in premiums, taxes may be due on the amount withdrawn. Unlike for variable annuities, the IRS uses FIFO here, assuming that the first thing coming out is the cost basis, not the earnings. Only the part taken out above the premiums paid would be taxed.

If a loan is taken out, there are no immediate tax consequences.

STUDY SHEET

Tax Treatment for INTEREST Payments on Debt Securities

TYPE OF DEBT	FEDERAL	STATE	LOCAL
Corporate/Agency	Taxable	Taxable	Taxable
Gov't/Treasury	Taxable	NOT	NOT
Municipal	NOT	Not if you live there	Not if you live there

Capital gains are fully taxable on *all* debt securities.

Dividends: qualified dividends currently taxed at maximum of 15%. Ordinary dividends (REITs) taxed at investor's ordinary income rate.

Capital gains: long-term capital gains taxed at maximum of 15%. Short-term capital gains (taken within 1 year) taxed at ordinary income rate. For mutual funds, capital gains distributions most likely treated as long-term. For fund shares sold, investor's holding period determines long- or short-term treatment.

Bond interest: taxable as ordinary income to the investor, unless exempt (see chart above).

Capital gains on bonds: fully taxable, even municipal bonds

Inherited securities: recipient steps up cost basis to fair market value on date of death.

Gifted securities: receiver takes giver's original cost basis.

Donated securities: donor deducts fair market value on date of donation from taxable income.

Progressive taxes: the rate rises with the size of the INCOME, GIFT, or, ESTATE.

Regressive taxes: taxed at a flat rate, i.e., SALES, GASOLINE, EXCISE.

PRACTICE:

91. **An investor has contributed $20,000 to a periodic deferred non-quali-
fied variable annuity. The contract is worth $50,000 at retirement. If
the investor takes a random withdrawal of $35,000, what are the tax
consequences?**

A. $50,000 taxed as ordinary income

B. $20,000 taxed as ordinary income

C. $35,000 taxed at long-term capital gains rate

D. $30,000 taxed as ordinary income

92. **An investor in a municipal bond fund receives both income and capital
gains distributions. What is true of the tax treatment of these distributions?**

A. both are taxed at ordinary income rates

B. both are taxed as long-term capital gains

C. the income distribution is most likely tax-exempt at the federal level, while the
capital gains distribution is fully taxable

D. both distributions are tax-exempt at the federal level

93. **If an individual makes qualified contributions to her IRA, her cost basis
is**

A. equal to her contributions

B. equal to her contributions times a cost of living index multiplier

C. zero

D. equal to her average income over the preceding five years

94. **All of the following plans are funded pre-tax except**

A. IRA

B. SEP-IRA

C. 529 Plan

D. Tax-sheltered annuity

95. **All of the following are funded with after-tax contributions except**

    A.   Coverdell plan

    B.   529 Plan

    C.   Roth IRA

    D.   403b/TSA

96. **Interest earned on all of the following is taxable at the state level except**

    A.   GNMA

    B.   FNMA

    C.   T-bill

    D.   Municipal bonds

97. **All of the following are subject to taxation at the federal level except**

    A.   common stock

    B.   preferred stock

    C.   municipal bond

    D.   Treasury note

98. **Which of the following allows an individual to make the largest contribution?**

    A.   Roth

    B.   Traditional IRA

    C.   Keogh

    D.   Variable annuity

99. **Which of the following represents a violation for a securities agent?**

    A.   recommending that an income investor purchase shares of the ABC Equity Income fund simply because it pays regular dividends

    B.   providing a mutual fund prospect with a prospectus before beginning the solicitation

    C.   recommending that an income investor purchase shares of the ABC Equity Income Fund primarily to receive an upcoming dividend distribution

    D.   following up oral recommendations with accompanying statements of risk

100. **All of the following offer tax deferral except**

    A.   insurance policy

    B.   non-qualified annuity

    C.   qualified annuity

    D.   mutual fund

101. **An investor originally invested $10,000 in the XYZ Growth & Income Fund. After reinvesting a $2,000 income distribution and a $1,000 capital gains distribution, her cost basis is**

    A. $10,000

    B. $7,000

    C. $13,000

    D.   not determinable without marginal tax bracket provided

ANSWERS:

91.   D – there is only $30,000 of earnings or "excess over cost basis."
The extra $5,000 is part of her cost basis—she already paid tax on $20,000, remember.

92.   C – the only thing tax-exempt about a municipal bond is the interest/income. Capital gains are fully taxable on all bonds.

93.   C – if the contributions haven't been taxed yet, she has no cost basis. It will all be taxed when it's distributed at retirement.

94.   C – the plans for education (Coverdell, ESA, 529) are all funded with after-tax dollars. The distributions are tax-free as long as everybody plays by the rules.

95.   D – TSA/403b-501c3...all means the same thing. Pre-tax contributions, zero cost basis, all distributions taxed at ordinary income rate.

96.   C – states can't tax the interest on Treasury securities, period.

97.   C – municipal securities offer tax-exempt interest at the federal level. Treasury securities definitely get taxed at the federal level, but only at the federal level.

98.   D – assume there are NO limits to the amount you can put into an annuity. Which is what makes them so much fun to sell.

99. C – choice C represents "selling dividends." Choice A is fine—the agent is selling the fund. In choice C he's trying to sell the dividend—the NAV will drop, and the investor will be taxed. So you don't buy a fund for the upcoming dividend. You buy funds because they make regular dividend payments. See the important difference?

100. D – mutual funds offer no tax advantages per se.

101. C – she gets taxed on reinvested distributions, just as if she'd taken the check and cashed it. If you get taxed, it adds to your cost basis.

WHAT NOW?

- Review the chapter. *Approximately 40 minutes.*
- If you have the Pass the 7 QuizSet, take the Chapter 10 Quiz on Taxation. *Approximately 30 minutes.*
- If you have the Audio CD set, listen to Disc 4, Track 5. *Approximately 15 minutes.*

CHAPTER 11

Economics

MACROECONOMICS

<u>G</u>ross <u>D</u>omestic <u>P</u>roduct (GDP) measures the total output of the American economy. It's the total value of all goods and services being produced, provided and sold. If GDP is increasing, the economy is growing. If GDP is declining, so is the economy. The American economy rides a continuous roller coaster known as the business cycle. All this means is that the economy goes up (expands), hits a peak, contracts, hits bottom (trough), and then comes back up again…just like a roller coaster. Although we refer to the period following the "trough" as a "recovery," it's really just the next expansion, so I would say there are four phases to the business cycle if I got that question on the exam: expansion, peak, contraction, trough.

Also remember that rising prices (known as inflation) are factored into this GDP calculation to arrive at "real GDP." In other words, we don't want to kid ourselves that rising prices is the same thing as rising economic output. We use the CPI (consumer price index) to factor in the effects of inflation, which we'll discuss shortly. Note that the word "real" generally means to subtract the rate of inflation from something. If you got a test question that said Orville Olmeyer has an investment that grows 6% while the CPI rises 3%, Orville's "real rate of return" is 3%—the amount above inflation.

When GDP is rising at a healthy pace, the economy is in a period of expansion. In a period of expansion we would expect to see the following: low unemployment, high industrial production, rising prices (inflation), rising interest rates. When the GDP is stuck in low gear or reverse, we're in a period of contraction or maybe in the trough. Whatever we call it, this period of economic decline can be referred to as either a recession or a depression. A recession is strictly defined as 6 months (2 consecutive quarters) of GDP decline and can last as long as 18 months. After that, we call it a depression. Technically, a recession is when your neighbor loses his job. A depression is when you lose *your* job. Associate the following with recessions and depressions: falling prices, falling interest rates, high unemployment, low industrial production.

INFLATION, DEFLATION

Ever noticed how the "Fed" often seems obsessed with the price of stuff? If the economy grows/expands too fast, prices can go higher and higher until they're out of control. That's called inflation. Inflation is indicated/measured by the CPI, or "consumer price index." The CPI surveys the prices consumers are paying for the basic things consumers buy (movie tickets, milk, blue jeans, gasoline) and tracks the increases in those prices. Sometimes they exclude food and energy from the CPI to measure "core inflation," since food and energy prices are extremely volatile and may give a false appearance that the price of *everything* is rising when it's really just that bad weather has temporarily jacked up the price of food or oil. The exam might say that inflation occurs when the demand for goods and services is growing faster than the supply of these items. Or, it could say something like, "too many dollars chasing too few goods." I like to think of inflation in terms of what would happen if they ran out of beer during the third inning at Wrigley Field and then somebody stood up and said he'd be happy to sell a cold six-pack he somehow managed to smuggle past security. How high would the price of cold beer rise on a hot August afternoon with 40,000 thirsty fans vying for six cold, sweaty cans of beer?

The exam might mention two different types/causes of inflation. Cost-push inflation is when raw material prices rise and producers pass on the cost to consumers. The exam might want you to know that the "PPI" stands for the "producer price index," which measures cost-push inflation. Demand-pull inflation, on the other hand, is when the demand for stuff outstrips the supply of that stuff. Back to Wrigley Field on a hot day. What I described was demand-pull inflation, since the demand for cold beer far outstripped the limited supply and you know some well-moneyed commodities trader wouldn't rest unless he could say he paid "10 g's" for the last cold six-pack in the ball park. Cost-push inflation would result if the cost of hops, barley, and malt used to manufacture the beer, or even the gasoline used to transport the beer, went up. Just like at Frank & Emma's—if the cost of wheat, sugar, flour, cherries, apples, corn syrup, etc., goes up, the company will have to both spend more on ingredients and charge more for their products.

Anyway, that's IN-flation. A beach ball can be inflated or deflated, and so can the economy. If you over-inflate a beach ball it will pop; if you under-inflate it, it's just as useless. Same for the economy. While inflation can make things too expensive for consumers to buy, deflation can make things ever cheaper. Cheaper goods sounds good until you consider that profit margins at businesses will be ever shrinking, as they pay last month's prices for raw materials and then struggle to sell them at next month's cheaper prices. Assuming they can sell anything to anyone—would you rush out to buy something today if you knew it would be cheaper tomorrow? Wouldn't you be tempted to put off your purchases indefinitely, waiting for the price of DVD players, clothing, and automobiles to drop in your favor?

That's an economic slowdown, right? Everybody sitting around waiting to see who'll be the first one to open up his or her wallet. Which is why deflation—while rare—is just as detrimental to the economy as inflation. And that's why the Fed is forever manipulating interest rates in an attempt to find the right economic temperature—not too hot, not too cold. Like Goldilocks, they hope to find the economic porridge just right. Which is another way of saying that demand for stuff and the supply of that stuff are in the right balance. If we have strong demand and tight supply, prices will rise, just as the demand for a Dave Matthews Band concert in a 1,000-seat venue will send the ticket price into the stratosphere. If demand for stuff is weak and the supply of that stuff is high, prices will fall, like the price of a ticket to see the Spin Doctors at a college football stadium.

To review, if the economy grows too fast, we can end up with inflation. And, as we'll soon see, the Federal Reserve Board (or FOMC) will raise interest rates to let some air out of the over-expanding economy. If the economy starts to sputter and stall, we can end up with deflation. And, as we'll soon see, the Fed will have to pump some air back into the economy by lowering interest rates.

ECONOMIC INDICATORS

The Fed monitors many economic indicators to get an *indication* as to whether inflation is trying to rear its ugly head. The exam tends to focus on employment indicators. As you might guess, employment indicators are based on employment. The following indicators tell us how many people are working and how much compensation they're receiving. If people aren't working, that signals an economic slowdown. If employment compensation is rising too fast, that signals inflation, and the Fed might have to step in by raising interest rates.

- Average Weekly New Claims for Unemployment Insurance: if people are showing up for unemployment insurance at a higher rate, that's a bad sign, right? It means their employers don't have enough work for them. If the number of new claims drops, that means economic activity is picking up.
- Unemployment Rate: since everything needs two or three names, this is also called "payroll employment" or "non-farm payroll." It's a figure released by the Bureau of Labor Statistics and includes full-time and part-time workers,

ECONOMIC INDICATORS

Leading – show up before reflected in the economy
- *the average weekly hours worked by manufacturing workers*
- *the average number of initial applications for unemployment insurance*
- *the amount of manufacturers' new orders for consumer goods and materials*
- *the speed of delivery of new merchandise to vendors from suppliers*
- *the amount of new orders for capital goods unrelated to defense*
- *the amount of new building permits for residential buildings*
- *the S&P 500 stock index*
- *the inflation-adjusted monetary supply (M2)*
- *the spread between long and short interest rates*
- *consumer sentiment*

Coincident – show up at about the same time as reflected in the economy
- *the number of employees on non-agricultural payrolls*
- *the Index of Industrial Production*
- *the level of manufacturing and trade sales*
- *the aggregate amount of personal income excluding transfer payments*

Lagging – show up after the fact
- *the value of outstanding commercial and industrial loans*
- *the change in the consumer price index for services from the previous month*
- *the change in labor cost per unit of labor output*
- *the ratio of manufacturing and trade inventories to sales made*
- *the ratio of consumer credit outstanding to personal income*
- *the average prime rate charged by banks*
- *the inverted average length of employment*

whether they're permanent or temporary employees. In other words, if they're on the payroll, we count them as workers, just like they do at City Hall here in Chicago. As the "nonfarm" thing may have tipped you off, we don't count farm workers, since that stuff is very seasonal, and we also don't count employment at tiny businesses or at government agencies. So, this figure tracks how many people are working in the private sector, basically. It is released monthly.

- Employment Cost Index (ECI): this measures the growth of wages and benefits (compensation) because if wages are rising really fast, inflation can't be far behind. It's a quarterly figure, so it's not the most timely of statistics. Still, it tracks trends in compensation. While the monthly employment rate is useful, the ECI gives us more detail, since it tracks the change in benefits paid to workers, rather than just the number of workers.

FISCAL AND MONETARY POLICY

Once we have these indicators, what can we do with them? Depends on whom you talk to. The Keynesians feel that fiscal policy is the best way to control the economy. Fiscal policy is what the President and Congress do: tax and spend. Keynesians recommend that fiscal policy be used to increase aggregate (overall) demand. To stimulate the economy, just cut taxes and increase government spending. Lower taxes leaves more money for Americans to spend and invest, fueling the economy. If the government is spending more on interstate highway construction, that means a lot more folks are going to be hired for construction crews. Or maybe the federal government orders 10 million pies from Frank & Emma's for cafeterias at various Department of Defense, Treasury, Commerce, etc., buildings. Frank & Emma's would suddenly buy more equipment and raw materials and hire more workers, which is how to push the economy forward.

On the other hand, if we need to cool things down, the Keynesians suggest that the federal government increase taxes and cut spending. Higher taxes leave less money for Americans to spend and invest, and decreased spending puts less government money into projects that would otherwise be hiring subcontractors, laborers, etc.

Monetarists feel that controlling the money supply is the key to managing the economy. What is the money supply?

It's the supply of money. Money, like any commodity, has a cost. The cost of money equals its "interest rate." If there's too much demand and too little supply, the cost of money (interest rate) goes up. That slows down the economy and fights inflation. If there's too little demand and too much supply, the cost of money (interest rate) goes down. That helps to stimulate the economy and pump some air back into a deflated economy.

Wait, money has a cost? I thought I paid the cost of things *with* money. Sure, but if I want to start a business, I need money. How much do I have to pay to borrow this money?

That's the interest rate—the cost of borrowing money.

So, how can the money supply be influenced? Through monetary policy, enacted by the Federal Reserve Board. Because of that embarrassing little fiasco known as the 1930's, the Fed likes to make sure that banks don't lend out and invest every last dollar they have on deposit. So, the Fed requires that banks keep a certain percentage of their customer deposits in <u>reserve</u>. This is called, surprisingly enough, the reserve requirement. If the Fed raises the reserve requirement, banks have less money to lend out to folks trying to buy homes and start businesses. So if the economy is overheating, the Fed could raise the reserve requirement in order to cool things down, and if the economy is sluggish, they could lower the requirement in order to make more money available to fuel the economy. However, this is a drastic measure because of the multiplier effect, which means that $1 more or less in reserve has more than just $1's effect on the economy. So it's the least used Fed tool.

The most used tool is open market operations. The Fed can either buy or sell T-bills from/to banks. If they want to cool things down/raise interest rates, they can take money out of banks by selling them T-bills. If they want to fuel a sluggish economy/lower interest rates, they can buy T-bills from banks, thereby pumping money into the system.

Again, interest rates can be thought of as the price of a commodity known as money. Whenever a commodity—corn, sugar, concert tickets—is scarce, its price rises. Whenever something is widely available, its price drops. When money is tight, its cost (interest rate) rises. When money is widely available, its cost (interest rate) falls. So, if the Fed wants to drop rates, they make money more available by buying T-bills from banks. If they want to raise rates, they make money scarce by selling T-bills to banks (who pay for them with…money). Just follow the flow of money.

Then there's the tool that gets talked about the most in the news, the discount rate. When people talk about the Fed raising interest rates by 25 basis points, they're talking about the discount rate. The discount rate is the rate the Fed charges banks that borrow directly from the Fed. If banks have to pay more to borrow, you can imagine that they will in turn charge their customers more to borrow from them. So, if the Fed wants to raise interest rates, they just raise the discount rate and let the banking system take it from there. The Fed doesn't directly set the prime rate or the fed funds rate. They do have influence over the rates through the discount rate, but they don't actually set the other rates. And, of course, they never, ever have anything to do with taxes.

So, think of the Fed as the driver of the economy. If the economy starts going too fast, they let some air out of the tires (raise interest rates) by raising the reserve requirement, raising the discount rate, and selling T-bills. If the economy starts to stall out, the Fed pump some air back in the tires by lowering the reserve requirement, lowering the discount rate, and buying T-bills.

Money Supply

The exam may get more specific about the money supply that the FRB/FOMC can tighten and loosen in order to either fight inflation (tighten) or stimulate the economy (loosen). The money supply can be divided into three separate categories. To save time and to avoid overexciting you, let's just provide you with the cheap bullet points here. Remember that M2 includes M1 plus some more stuff, and M3 includes M2 plus some more stuff:

- M1: cash, coins, checking, NOW accounts. Considered to be the most "narrow" idea of money, the money that's in circulation.
- M2: M1 + savings deposits, and non-institutional money-market funds
- M3: M2 + large time deposits, institutional money-market funds, short-term repurchase agreements, along with other larger liquid assets

INTEREST RATES

As we saw, a tight money supply leads to higher interest rates, which will slow the economy to fight inflation. Loose money leads to lower interest rates, which will pump a little inflation back into a sputtering economy. So, let's take a look at this concept of "interest rates." Interest rates represent the cost of money. If you want $50,000 to start a beauty salon, chances are you have to borrow it. How much you pay for that "capital" is what we call interest rates. When there's a ton of money to be lent out, lenders will drop their rates in order to get you to borrow. When money is tight, however, borrowers have to compete with each other to get a share of the limited capital and pay higher and higher rates. Again, if the concert is a sell-out, fans bid the price of the tickets ever upward; and when the performer is a has-been, the price of the tickets plummets.

Okay, so one way to borrow money is by selling bonds to investors. How much should you pay the buyers of your bonds?

How about zero? Zero percent financing sure sounds tempting to a borrower; unfortunately, the buyers of debt securities demand compensation. They're the lenders of the money, and they demand current interest rates in return for lending their hard-earned cash. So, debt securities pay investors exactly what they have to pay them in order to entice them to lend money through the purchase of these debt securities (bonds, notes, bills, certificates, etc.). If a corporation could get by with paying zero percent in order to borrow money through a bond issuance, you know they would. Since they can't do that, they offer investors only as much as they have to in order to obtain the loan. Sort of like you would do when applying for a mortgage. Would you give anyone even one extra basis point for a mortgage? Probably not. When you borrow money through a mortgage you have to pay the current rate of interest, just as the issuer of a bond must pay.

The exam may ask you to work with the following interest rates. They don't really warrant an in-depth discussion, so here's a quick list that should suffice:

- Discount rate: the rate banks have to pay when borrowing from the FRB
- Fed funds rate: the rate banks charge each other for overnight loans in excess of $1 million. Considered the most volatile rate, subject to daily change
- Call money rate or "broker call loan rate": the rate broker-dealers pay when borrowing on behalf of their margin customers
- Prime rate: the rate that the most credit-worthy corporate customers pay when borrowing

Whether we use fiscal or monetary policy, our efforts will influence interest rates. And interest rates can either make it easier or harder for companies to do business and for consumers to consume.

YIELD CURVES

City, county, and state governments borrow money by issuing municipal bonds. Municipal bonds are usually issued under a "serial maturity," which means that a little bit of the principal will be returned every year, until the whole issue is paid off. Investors who buy bonds maturing in 2025 will generally demand a higher yield than those getting their principal back in 2007. The longer your money is at risk, the more of a reward you demand, right? If a friend wanted to borrow $1,000 for one month, you'd probably do it interest-free. What if they wanted to take three years to pay you back? You could get some interest on a thousand dollars by buying a bank CD, which carries no risk, right? So, if somebody's going to put your money at risk for an extended period of time, you demand a reward in the form of an interest payment.

Same with bonds. If your bond matures in 2025 when mine matures in 2007, isn't your money at risk for 18 more years? That's why your bond would be offered at a higher yield (interest rate) than mine. If I buy a bond yielding 5.35%, yours might be offered at more like 5.89%. The extra 54 basis points is your extra reward for taking on extra risk.

This is how it works under a normal yield curve, where long-term bonds yield more than short-term bonds.

Guess what, sometimes that yield curve gets inverted. Suddenly, the rule flies out the window, and folks are getting higher yields on short-term bonds than on long-term bonds. The cause of this is generally a peak in interest rates. When bond investors feel that interest rates have gone as high as they're going to go, they all clamor to lock in the high interest rates for the longest period of time. In a rush of activity, they sell off their short-term bonds in order to hurry up and buy long-term bonds at the best interest rate they're likely to see for a long time. Well, if everybody's selling off short-term bonds, the price drops [and the yield *increases*]. And if they're all buying up long-term bonds, the price increases [and the yield *drops*]. That causes the yield curve to invert. There are also "humped yield curves," where the intermediate maturities have the highest yield, and a "flat yield curve," which has to be the best example of an oxymoron you're likely to see. A flat curve?

Whatever, dude.

A "flat yield curve" would imply that short-, intermediate-, and long-term bonds are all yielding about the same, meaning that demand and supply for all maturities is similar.

To figure your way out of any yield curve jam, just remember that yields and prices are inverse. So, if the short-term debt has a higher yield (inverted or "negatively sloped yield curve), its price has gone down due to low demand/high supply. In a normal yield curve, short-term debt would have a lower yield/higher price due to a high demand for the short-term debt relative to supply…why are the long-term bonds yielding more on the right side of this yield curve? Long-term commitments scare investors, so their demand for these long-term commitments is lower than the supply, pushing price *down* and *yield* up.

Another yield concept the test might throw at you considers the difference in yields between high-rated and low-rated bonds, known as a yield spread. Remember that coupon rates don't change—they're simply printed on the bond. So, how could the yield of a bond that's already been issued go up? Only if its price starts to fall. If you get 5% a year, that's $50. If you get that $50 by paying $400, your yield is higher than for someone who bought that same bond paying $50 a year for $800. In fact, it's twice as high, right? Then again, why the heck is your $1,000 face value bond worth only $400 in the open market? Because it's a poor credit risk, a junk bond, a high-yield bond—whatever the heck we decide to call it. So, if folks are only willing to pay cheap prices for these higher-risk bonds, that makes the yield spread widen, and that's a negative indicator for the economy. Basically, it means folks are nervous about issuers' ability to repay. If investors don't demand a significantly higher yield on the low-rated bonds (they're willing to pay higher market prices for junk bonds), that means in general they are confident about issuers' ability to repay, which is a positive indicator.

BALANCE OF TRADE, BALANCE OF PAYMENTS

Balance of trade tracks money in and money out of the economy specifically for goods. If we export more than we import, we have a trade <u>surplus</u>. If we import more than we export, we have a trade <u>deficit</u>. Imports and exports are directly affected by the value of the American dollar relative to foreign currencies.

As our <u>dollar strengthens</u>, our <u>exports become less attractive</u> to consumers in other countries, whose weak currency can't buy our expensive stuff. When our <u>dollar weakens</u>, our <u>exports are more attractive</u> because suddenly their strong currencies can buy lots of our relatively cheap stuff. Likewise, a strong dollar makes foreign travel less expensive for Americans, whereas a weak dollar makes foreign travel *more* expensive. It's just a way of asking how much of their stuff does our dollar buy?

Balance of payments tracks all money coming in versus going out of the economy. So, it counts both imports vs. exports and also investments. If more money is coming in than going out, we have a <u>surplus</u>. That could happen if the Japanese are suddenly buying lots of American securities. If more money is going out than coming in, we have a <u>deficit</u>, which could happen if Americans start buying Japanese securities.

So if we had a trade deficit with France, would a strong dollar or a weak dollar help to bring us back to a surplus?

Well, if we were already importing more from France than we're exporting, we would want to make our exports more attractive to the French and our imports from France less attractive to Americans, which would happen as the dollar...weakens.

The value of the dollar compared to another currency also comes into play when an investor buys an ADR, especially when it comes time to paying dividends. If the U.S. Dollar increases in value, when the underlying stock pays a dividend in the foreign currency, the foreign currency received by the bank will need to be converted to U.S. Dollars for distribution to the holder of the ADR. As a result of the rise in the value of the dollar relative to the foreign currency received by the bank, the foreign currency will purchase fewer U.S. Dollars for distribution to the holder of the ADR. As a result of the rise in the value of the U.S. Dollar, the dividend payment received by the holder of the ADR is lower.

Similarly, if the dollar is strong (Yen is weak), the ADR won't be worth as many dollars, since 1,000 Yen would suddenly be worth fewer of the strong American dollars.

TYPES OF INDUSTRIES

That ends the big view of the overall economy. Now let's look at industries within the economy: defensive, cyclical, and growth. Remember the business cycle and GDP? Well defensive industries do okay regardless of where we are in the business cycle. These industries produce products that consumers buy no matter what, like food, cigarettes, and alcohol. You know, the important stuff. Prescription drugs and bandages also represent defensive industries. Certainly utilities also qualify. When you come home at night do you check the current economic figures before turning on the heat or air conditioning? Heck no.

But if we're in a recession, you might put off the purchase of a new car, which is why automobiles represent a cyclical industry. In good times, people load up, but in bad times they hold off. If you think of steel and products made from steel, like cars, heavy equipment, and big industrial machinery, you're thinking of cyclical industries. During expansions, these industries do well. During contractions, they don't. All depends on the business *cycle*. Warren Buffett often likes to buy stocks of companies that make things people buy day after day without much deliberation: soda pop, razor blades, underwear, paint, bricks, etc. If it has a strong brand name (Coca-Cola®, Gillette®, Dairy Queen®), so much the better. So, he favors the defensive, or "non-cyclical" industries, and you sort of have to like his results so far.

Then there are growth industries, like technology, which Mr. Buffett typically avoids like the plague. Growth stocks tend not to pay dividends because they're reinvesting their earnings into *growth*. Remember that, to date, the cash cow known officially as Oracle® has paid exactly zero dividends to the holders of common stock.

Zero. Which means the Oracle dividend plus a couple of dollars might buy you a cup of coffee at Starbucks®, a company also still finding better things to do with their earnings than just sending it out to the shareholders.

So, if the test tells you that one company pays a lot of dividends (high dividend pay-out) and another pays low dividends, the former is a utility or at least a defensive company, while the latter is a growth or maybe a technology company. While Frank & Emma's is in an old, mature boring business—manufacturing—they are a growth *company*. A company whose earnings are growing fast and which appears to have a lot more room to grow…guess what we call stock in that growth company?

Growth stock.

Again with the lack of creativity.

PRACTICE:

102. **If the American dollar weakens relative to the Japanese Yen, which of the following statements is true?**
   A.   American exports to Japan become more competitive with Japanese goods
   B.   American exports to Japan become less competitive with Japanese goods
   C.   Americans' vacation dollars go farther in Japan
   D.   None of the above

103. **Which of the following is a leading indicator?**
   A.   Housing starts
   B.   GDP
   C.   Savings
   D.   Personal income

104. **In order to stimulate a sluggish American economy the Federal Reserve Board might take which of the following actions?**
   A.   Cut taxes
   B.   Raise taxes
   C.   Cut the discount rate
   D.   Raise the reserve requirement

105. **In order to stimulate a sluggish economy, the administrators of fiscal policy have which of the following tools available?**
   A.   reserve requirement
   B.   discount rate
   C.   tax rates
   D.   LIBOR

106. **Which of the following is the least defensive industry?**
   A.   aerospace
   B.   tobacco
   C.   alcohol
   D.   prescription drugs

ANSWERS:

102. A – if our currency weakens, the stuff we make is cheap to the Japanese, making it easier to export our cheap American goods to Japan.

103. A – housing starts/building permits tell us if there is a big wave of construction up ahead or a big slowdown in construction of new homes.

104. C – lower interest rates make it easier to buy houses and other big-ticket items, stimulating the economy. The FRB has nothing to do with setting tax policy.

105. C – tax and spend—that's all there is to fiscal policy.

106. A – when the economy sputters, people travel less and airlines order fewer planes. Surely no one is expected to forego alcohol and tobacco just because the economy is in a slump.

WHAT NOW?

- Review the chapter. *Approximately 30 minutes.*
- If you have the Pass the 7 QuizSet, take the Chapter 11 Quiz on Economics. *Approximately 30 minutes.*
- If you have the Audio CD set, listen to Disc 5, Track 1. *Approximately 19 minutes.*

CHAPTER 12

Portfolio Analysis

FUNDAMENTAL ANALYSIS

There are two main ways to analyze stocks: fundamental analysis and technical analysis. Fundamental analysts, believe it or not, look at the company's fundamentals to see if it is profitable or likely to become more profitable in the future. A fundamental analyst looking at Frank & Emma's fruit pies would not want to hear about the high and low closing price for the year or whether the stock had been trading above or below its 200-day moving average. The fundamental analyst wants to know if it's worth buying a share of this company's bottom line, meaning the company either has a bottom line now or is likely to have a bottom line profit in the near future. Information on the company's revenues and costs would be important, as would the margin of profit. How many units (pies) are they selling each year, and is that number growing impressively? How much is the cost of all the ingredients and equipment rising? Do they have enough cash flow to finance the growth we're hoping for? How much does the stock cost compared to the profits (if any) of the company? If you have heard any of the following terms, you have at least heard some of the vocabulary used by fundamental analysts:

- P/E ratio
- Earnings Per Share (EPS)
- Price-to-book
- Current Ratio
- Gross Margin
- Net Margin
- Cash flow

Two basic financial reports used by fundamental analysts include the balance sheet and the income statement. If you ever check stock quotes online, chances are you can click on "financials" and see a public company's balance sheet and income statement.

BALANCE SHEET

The basic formula for the balance sheet or "statement of financial condition" states that Assets have to equal Liabilities plus Net Worth.

$$Assets = Liabilities + Net\ Worth$$
$$or:$$
$$Assets - Liabilities = Net\ Worth$$

Assets represent what a company owns. Liabilities represent what a company owes. You take what a company owns, subtract what it owes, and that's the net worth of the company. Just like if you took your assets and subtracted all your liabilities, you'd come up with your personal financial "net worth." We also refer to "net worth" as "shareholders' equity," which reminds us that shareholders are the owners, so the difference between what the company owns and what it owes belongs to the shareholders.

Assets

Assets are divided into three types. The first type is current assets. Current assets represent cash and anything that could easily be converted into cash within 12 months: cash & equivalents, accounts receivable, inventory. Cash is cash, and it's a good thing. "Equivalents" are money market instruments—cash earning little tiny rates of interest, which is also a good thing. Commercial paper, banker's acceptances, repurchase agreements, T-bills…those are all "cash equivalents" listed here on the balance sheet. Accounts receivable is what customers owe the company. Frank & Emma's has already sold and shipped pies to supermarkets and big retail outlets, for which they fully anticipate getting paid over the next few months. So, they list that payment as an asset (money coming IN). Inventory is the stuff the company makes and plans to sell (convert to cash) just as soon as possible. Frank & Emma's doesn't let their pies sit in a warehouse very long, but on any given day there could be well over $5 million worth of pies waiting to be shipped out to customers. That stuff has value, and the company fully intends to sell that inventory for cash very soon, making the inventory a current asset.

Fixed assets include machinery, furniture and fixtures. This stuff is being used by the business every day. It could all be converted into cash, but it would take a while, and we wouldn't get anywhere near what we paid for the stuff if we liquidated it. Frank & Emma's would list the value of the land and buildings, as well as the value of the assembly line equipment, as well as the furniture and cheesy artwork hanging on the walls of the visitor lobby. Those are all fixed assets. They get depreciated over time, so the company usually reflects the original cost of the equipment and then shows how much value has been depreciated (written down) at this point. I don't think the 7 is going to turn this into an accounting exam, though. In fact, I'm betting that we're going a little overboard here, although if that's the worst thing we do in preparing for the exam, we're in pretty good shape, just like Frank & Emma's.

Then there are intangible assets. When the Jif peanut butter company purchases Smucker's or Crisco, they pay big money for those brand names. A brand name is an intangible asset whose value would be accounted for on the balance sheet. In other words, it's not a hard, tangible thing like a printing press, but it does have value in that it produces sales and profits for the corporation. If a company acquires trademarks or patents, those intangibles also have value and will be listed on the balance sheet. Goodwill is another intangible asset that might show up on the exam. It works like this—some day Frank & Emma's may discover that as they try to break into the Pacific Northwest, some regional pie maker sort of has the market sewn up. So, FREM could either choose to compete with the smaller competitor or use the Bill Gates method of competition, known technically as "crush them or buy them, whichever is cheaper." Since Jeremy, Jason, and Jennifer like to avoid nasty legal battles, maybe they decide to buy the competitor for $30 million, when all the assets are really worth only $25 million. FREM would carry that $5 million excess as "goodwill" on the balance sheet and periodically re-assess the value of the goodwill. The brand name is so strong and the customer base so loyal that FREM feels the extra $5 million was well worth it. It brings them, literally, goodwill.

Add all three types of assets (what the company owns), and you have Total Assets.

Liabilities

On the other side of the equation we find liabilities, which represent what a company owes. Anything that has to be paid within 12 months is a current liability. Accounts payable, accrued wages, and accrued taxes all represent bills the company has to pay in the short-term, which is why they're called current liabilities. Bond interest, paid twice a year, is also a current liability, since it has to be paid in the current year.

The principal amount of the bond that has to be paid more than a year out is simply a long-term liability. Add the two together and you have Total Liabilities.

Net Worth

Net worth (AKA "shareholders' equity" or "owners' equity") has to do with stock and any earnings that haven't been paid out since the company's inception. We know that the par value of preferred stock is $100. So a company places the total par value of its preferred stock under Net Worth. Common stock is assigned a par value of, say, $1, so if a company has 1,000,000 shares of common, they would list the par value of their common stock as $1,000,000 and place it under Net Worth. If investors bought the IPO at $11, that represents a surplus of $10 above the par value, so the company would list "paid-in surplus" of $10,000,000 under Net Worth as well. Also note that if you get a question about the effects of a stock split or stock dividend on par value, just tell the exam that par value is reduced right along with the market price of the stock. Any earnings that have been retained are listed as—you guessed it—retained earnings. When a company first declares a dividend, they "take it out of" retained earnings. So, if they're about to pay a $1 dividend, they reduce retained earnings by $1, and also add $1 to "current liabilities." I predict the exam will ask a question about either declaring the dividend, or paying it. When the dividend is paid, the company simply takes $1 out of cash to pay down/eliminate the $1 of current liabilities. As if you didn't have enough stuff to worry about at this point.

When looking at a balance sheet, you will find that:

Total Assets = Total Liabilities + Net Worth

Or:

Total Assets − Total Liabilities = Net Worth,
a.k.a. "shareholders' equity"

You can easily find the balance sheets of public companies online—it would be worth spending ½ hour perusing the balance sheet of companies with whom you are familiar. I, for one, enjoyed seeing this morning that Microsoft owns a securities portfolio that was worth about 36 *billion* dollars last time they reported. That's on top of about $2 *billion* of *cash*. All of their liabilities—current and long-term together—add up to $22 billion. They have about $38 billion in cash and securities to offset that.

Now *that* is a strong balance sheet. And probably not a company that anyone in his right mind would want to compete with.

Ratios and Other Measures

Current Assets represent what a company owns. Current Liabilities represent what a company owes. Hopefully, the company owns more than it owes, right? Fundamental analysts take Current Assets and subtract Current Liabilities in order to measure working capital (sometimes called "net working capital"). This is a measure of how able a company is to finance current operations. We're talking about short-term <u>liquidity</u>. Same thing you think about for your home budget. How many bills do we have to pay this month, versus how much income we'll be receiving? When a company's liabilities (bills) exceed its assets (stuff used to pay bills), that company is in great danger of becoming insolvent. Likewise, if a company's assets exceed its liabilities, that company is in a strong position to fund current operations, just as you would be if you had $1,000 in total bills and $4,000 in gross income.

Working Capital = Current Assets − Current Liabilities

If a company has $6 million in Current Assets and $1 million in Current Liabilities, it has $5 million in working capital.

Analysts also express current assets and current liabilities as a ratio, known as the current ratio. If a company has $6,000,000 in current assets and $1,000,000 in current liabilities, that's a current ratio of 6:1.

They could also apply a more stringent test, known as either the AcId Test or QuIck Ratio. The "I" has been accented to remind you that "Inventory" is subtracted from current assets before we compare them to current liabilities. So if $3,000,000 of the company's current assets were made up of inventory, we would subtract that out, leaving us with $3,000,000 in current assets to divide by $1,000,000 in current liabilities for a quick ratio of 3:1.

Working capital, current ratio, and quick/acid tests measure a company's short-term liquidity—how able they are to meet all of their day-to-day expenses and obligations. The company's debt ratio provides a more long-term view of just how much debt the company has taken on. Companies that are too highly leveraged run the risk of defaulting on their bonds, which sends them into a disaster known as "bankruptcy." Similarly, when you apply for a mortgage, the lender is very curious about how much debt you have already taken on. If you owe $25,000 and have just under $25 in your checking account, that might just add a few basis points to the interest rate they'll charge you. To find a company's debt ratio, just take the total debts and divide them by (compare them to) total assets. The higher the number you come up with, the more leveraged the company is. If too much of a company's capitalization comes from borrowing, fundamental analysts could start to worry that future profits will be eroded by future interest payments on the debt. Utility companies are the most highly leveraged, which means they do most of their capitalization through borrowing. So, if interest rates are up, that affects utility companies more than most other companies, since interest rates represent the cost of borrowing.

PRACTICE:

Using the balance sheet below, come up with the following measures:

Working capital
Current ratio
Quick ratio
Debt ratio

CURRENT ASSETS		
Cash & Equiv's	$9,000,000	
Acct's Receivable	$1,000,000	
Inventory	$10,000,000	
Total Current Assets		$20,000,000
Fixed Assets	$6,000,000	
Other Assets		
Intangible, goodwill	$4,000,000	
TOTAL ASSETS		$30,000,000
CURRENT LIABILITIES		
Acct's Payable	$3,000,000	
Accrued Wages	$3,000,000	
Accrued Taxes	$4,000,000	
Total Current Liab's		$10,000,000
Long-Term Liab's		
7% 10-year bonds		$10,000,000
TOTAL LIABILITIES		$20,000,000
NET WORTH		
Preferred Stock @par		$1,000,000
Common stock @par $1		$1,000,000
Paid-In Surplus		$4,000,000
Retained Earnings		$4,000,000
TOTAL NET WORTH		$10,000,000

ANSWERS:

Working capital is $10 million.

Current ratio is 2:1.

Quick ratio is 1:1 (subtract $10 million inventory first!)

Debt ratio = .67 ($20 million total liabilities/$30 total assets)

INCOME OR EARNINGS STATEMENT

The income statement starts with revenue and ends up with earnings available to common, assuming there *are* any earnings, which can sometimes be a dangerous assumption. And, since everything needs at least three names in this business, the income statement is sometimes called the "earnings statement," or the "profit & loss" statement, or the "statement of earnings," or "that hilarious piece of fiction we finally got the auditors to sign off on."

One of the most basic questions you can ask a corporation is, "Are you guys making more than you're spending?" To see the answer for yourself, read the income statement. On the income statement, a company takes sales (revenue) and subtracts the cost of goods sold. If Frank & Emma's sells $50 million of pies and has a cost of goods sold (what they paid to buy flour, sugar, butter, corn syrup, fruit, etc.) of $25 million, we could say they have "gross margins" of 50%. In other words, after subtracting the cost of the stuff they bought to make the pies, the company is left with $25 million out a' $50 million. Remember that in math, "out a'" means *divide*. 25 out a' 50 = 50%.

The company then subtracts all the costs for selling products and running the office: sales commissions, advertising, salaries, etc. The exam might also call them "SG&A" expenses, which stands for "Selling, General, and Administrative" expenses. Some companies list SG&A expenses separately from depreciation and amortization, but it all gets subtracted before figuring "operating earnings." If the company buys a piece of equipment with a useful life of five years, they subtract 1/5 of its value every year to represent the portion they use that year. So, depreciation expense is not a cash outlay that year, but it's a more accurate way to reflect the cost of the equipment than pretending it was purchased and consumed in one year. We depreciate tangible stuff and we "amortize" intangible stuff. An intangible asset—as we saw on the balance sheet—would include the value of patents, copyrights, and goodwill. These days accountants have to estimate the loss of value each year on these intangibles and put it down as a number on the income statement (and balance sheet). So, we were left with $25 million after subtracting the cost of the pie ingredients (cost of goods sold). If the SG&A, depreciation of the assembly line, and amortization all totaled $5 million, we'd be left with $20 million of "operating earnings." To figure the operating profit margin, we would just divide this $20 million out a' $50 million to get a 40% operating profit margin. Another name (because everything needs at least two or three names!) would be EBIT, which stands for "Earnings Before Interest and Taxes."

If EBIT stands for "Earnings *Before* Interest and Taxes," we would then, naturally, subtract the interest the company has to pay *before* figuring their taxable income. Yes, the IRS rewards companies for borrowing money, just like they reward you for the interest you pay on your mortgage. It's all tax deductible.

To review, the company takes their revenue then deducts cost of goods sold, SG&A expenses, depreciation, and amortization. We're at the "operating earnings" point now. Then, they subtract the interest they have to pay to borrow money and arrive at pre-tax income or taxable income. Yes, that's one problem with making a profit—the IRS expects a piece in the form of corporate taxes. So, to answer a question about a company's "pre-tax margins," just divide what they have before (pre-) paying tax by revenues.

The company pays their taxes on their taxable income and subtracts that amount to get "net income <u>after</u> tax." Some folks like to call it "the bottom line," which is exactly what it is—the bottom line of the income statement. The "put your cards on the table" line that shows whether the company made a profit or not. If, after all the above subtractions, we're left with, say, $5 million, we'd have a "net margin" of 10%, right? $5 million out a' $50 million means we're left with 10% of what we started with. A 10% net margin. A profit.

Cool.

Measurements Such as EPS, PE, etc.

But the company has to get all the way down to this line of the income statement before they even think about paying dividends. Who gets dividends first? Preferred stockholders. So, they subtract the preferred dividends from net income after tax and end up with earnings available to common. Then they divide the earnings available to common by the number of outstanding common shares to get Earnings Per Share or EPS. If the company has $5,000,000 in earnings with 1,000,000 shares outstanding, that represents $5 of earnings per share. EPS = $5.

Think of earnings available to common as the big pie the corporation bakes for common stockholders every year. The question stockholders ask is how big is this year's pie, and how many slices do we have to cut it into?

That's earnings per share.

We could apply a more stringent test that assumes all convertibles (bonds, preferred, warrants) are actually turned into common stock. This means that our $5,000,000 in earnings could end up being divided among more shares, sort of like sharing a cherry pie big enough for eight friends among 75 friends. We'd all get a piece, but it probably wouldn't be worth eating. If the above company ended up with 1,250,000 shares outstanding after conversion, their fully diluted EPS would be only $4. Same old earnings pie cut up into more slices.

Now that we have our earnings per share, we can also find out how much gets paid out in dividends. Guess what we call this?

The dividend payout ratio. This just takes the annual dividends paid and divides it by the EPS. Our above company has an EPS of $5. If they paid out $1 in common dividends, they'd have a 1:5 or 20% dividend payout ratio. If they paid $2.50 in dividends, that would be a 50% payout ratio, which means they must be a utility company. Utility companies pay more dividends than most other companies. So, they can do more borrowing than other companies and also pay more dividends…must be a defensive industry, right? An industry that can depend on people using their product regardless of economic figures. Growth companies reinvest their earnings into growing their business, so their dividend payout ratio would be among the lowest. Frank & Emma's, as indicated in their annual report, has no intention of paying dividends at this time or in the near future. For now, this growth company is better off reinvesting profits into expansion. Those radio and TV ads aren't cheap. Neither are the factory and distribution facilities. Maybe some day, when they're more mature and don't have any real need for the next $10 million of profits, they'll start passing it out to shareholders as dividends. Until then, the shareholders will simply have to be satisfied with the growth they receive through an increased share price. If they're an income investor, they'll want to buy some FREM common stock later on, when the company starts paying, you know, *income.*

With EPS figured, we can also express the PE ratio. This just compares the market price of a stock to its earnings per share. Sort of like asking how much do I have to put down in order to get how much in earnings per share? If I pay $30 for a stock with an EPS of $5, I'm paying "six times earnings," or a PE ratio of 6. The exam could get real tricky and tell you that a stock has an EPS of 5 and a PE of 20…what's the price of the stock?

Twenty times five = $100.

PE of 20 means that the stock's price is 20 times greater than its EPS.

Just basic algebra and a basic understanding of the terminology.

PRACTICE:

Use an income or "Profit & Loss" Statement to come up with gross margin, operating margin, pre-tax margin, and net margin.

REVENUE	$100,000,000
Cost of Goods Sold	-$55,000,000
SG&A Expenses	-$6,000,000
Depreciation, Amortization	-$4,000,000
OPERATING INCOME	$35,000,000
(Interest Expense)	-$10,000,000
PRE-TAX INCOME	$25,000,000
Taxes	-$5,000,000
NET INCOME after tax	$20,000,000
Preferred dividend	-$1,000,000
EARNINGS AVAILABLE TO COMMON	$19,000,000

ANSWERS:

Gross margin = 45%

Operating margin = 35%

Pre-tax margin = 25%

Net margin = 20%

And, to figure EPS just take the $19 million of earnings divided by the number of
outstanding shares, which would be found on the company's balance sheet.

FOOTNOTES

In a company's quarterly and annual reports, the financial statements are accompanied by footnotes that help to clarify the numbers. For example, is the inventory valued as LIFO or FIFO? What does the company mean by "equivalents" in its "cash and equivalents" line item—debt securities with 1 year to maturity? Six months? Three months? How/when does a company recognize "revenue"? Is it when the company ships pies to a distributor, or only when somebody has actually paid for the product? They might even list the high and low closing prices of the stock over each quarter in the footnotes.

In general, reading the footnotes is an integral component to analyzing the financial picture of a company and almost as interesting as watching paint dry.

TECHNICAL ANALYSIS

Okay, so that's what a fundamental analyst looks at. Technical analysts don't care about that stuff. They don't care about EPS, PE ratio, current ratio, debt ratio, etc. Technical analysts primarily look at charts of stock prices. They study past trends and price patterns in order to predict future trends and price patterns. If you tried to give a technical analyst a hot stock tip concerning Frank & Emma's, he'd cut you off as soon as he had the stock symbol FREM. See, he couldn't care less if they make pies, computers, cars, or loans. All he wants to see is what the stock has been doing and, based on that, try to figure out what it's going to do next.

CHARTS AND PATTERNS

If a technical analyst sees that a stock has been trading between 20 and 25 for the past three months, he'll call the low number—20—support and the high number—25—resistance, like this:

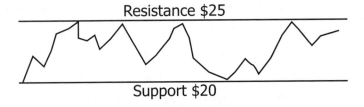

This just means that whenever the stock goes up, it meets resistance at $25, and whenever it falls, it finds support at $20. Resistance is often referred to as the market being "overbought" and support is called an "oversold" market, since everything needs at least two names in this business. So, maybe the technical trader consistently tries to buy close to $20 and sell as soon as it nears $25. Or, maybe he waits until the stock breaks through resistance before buying it, reasoning that if it hits a breakout it will keep running up. He could enter a buy-stop order slightly above the resistance point, based on the idea that if the stock price breaks through resistance it will keep going up a while. Or, maybe he hangs onto a stock until it loses support before selling, known as a breakdown/breakout. The technical trader could place a sell-stop order to sell the stock short below the support line, figuring if the stock lost support it would go into a free fall from there.

A head and shoulders pattern signals the reversal of a trend. So, a head and shoulders "top" indicates the bull trend is about to end—a bearish signal. A head and shoulders bottom indicates the bear trend is about to end—a bullish signal.

A head and shoulders top would look something like this:

So, when you see that right shoulder beginning to form, you're supposed to conclude that the stock price is headed for a big drop. And, if this pattern were flipped upside down, just flip what I said upside down.

But, please, don't try this at home. Especially when you should be studying for a difficult test called the Series 7.

If a stock is trading in a narrow range between support and resistance, it is consolidating. A chart of a stock in consolidation appears to be moving sideways, like this:

The exam might talk about consolidation as the place where sophisticated investors (mutual funds, pension funds, big Wall Street traders, etc.) are getting into or out of the stock. Since these geniuses are so incredibly sharp, when we see them buying, it must mean the stock is going up, and when we see them selling, it must mean the stock is heading down. At this accumulation or distribution point, the price moves "sideways," which is also known as "consolidation."

Technical analysts look to see how many stocks advance versus how many stocks decline. Guess what we call this? The advance/decline line. If advancers outpace decliners by 2:1, that means that twice as many stocks went up that day. And if decliners outpace advancers 2:1, that means that twice as many stocks went down that day. This tells the technical analyst something about buying/selling opportunities, based on pure supply and demand of shares in the marketplace.

Volume is also of interest to the technical analyst. Volume just indicates the total number of shares traded on, say, the NYSE, AMEX, NASDAQ, or the regional exchanges in Chicago, Philadelphia, Boston, etc. Analysts expect stock prices to rise on increasing volume. They would tend to place more significance on the fact that stock prices increased minutely on decreasing volume. Often, that situation is considered a reversal of a bullish trend, which is, of course, a bearish signal.

The exam may bring up the "200-day moving average," which is a very important technical indicator. A moving average smoothes out temporary blips and makes it easier to spot trends. To track a moving average, we continuously kick out the oldest data and replace them with the newest. For example, a batting average tells us the percentage with which a baseball player successfully hits the ball over the entire season. A 30-day moving average would track his batting average just over the previous 30 days. The difference between the two approaches is the difference between, "How is he hitting this year?" and "How has he been hitting lately?" Technical analysts want to know how many and which stocks closed at a price above or below their 200-day moving average. If a stock has been trading below its 200-day moving average, it may be in a clear downtrend, or vice versa for a stock trading above its 200-day moving average. So, a technical analyst may want to buy stocks trading above their moving average and sell short those stocks trading below their moving average. Rather than focusing on what a particular stock did, technical analysts might prefer to predict the direction of the overall market or index based on the number of stocks trading above or below their 200-day moving averages.

The exam might also talk about a market being "oversold" or "overbought." First, let's do the "oversold" thing. If the broad indices such as the S&P 500 are declining, but the number of stocks declining versus those advancing is actually shrinking, the market is considered to be "oversold." Huh? What that means is, yes, the market is still dropping, but it seems to be losing energy in that direction, since the *number* of stocks dropping is, uh, dropping. So, the bear market is losing steam, and that means we're due for a rally. How do you know when it's done being "oversold" as opposed to having maybe seven more days of shock and awe in store for naïve early comers? I have no idea. I'm just telling you about a point that has a chance of showing up on the exam. I wouldn't put my money into a stock based on some crap like this, since every full-time professional trader can see these numbers and work with them faster and 100 times better than I. I just buy stocks based on solid fundamental analysis and who wins the Super Bowl. But, technical analysts are the dominant force these days, so let's get back to their little tricks of the trade. An "oversold" market is basically a bear market that is losing steam and about to reverse in an upward, bullish direction. Maybe the market rises a while, until it is "overbought." An "overbought" market is a situation where the overall indices such as the S&P 500 and the Dow have been advancing, but the <u>number</u> of advancers compared to decliners is shrinking. In other words, the bull market is losing steam. It's about to stall out completely and tumble back downhill at a violent, breakneck pace. Time to sell short, buy puts, sell calls, what have you.

THEORIES

The technical analyst knows how incredibly smart he is. So much smarter than the small time investor, in fact, that all he has to do is track what odd lot investors are doing and bet the other way. If odd-lotters are buying, he sells. If odd-lotters are selling, he buys. Why? Because folks who can only afford an odd lot (<100 shares) of stock at a time always buy too high and sell too low. This is known as the odd-lot theory, and please do not try this at home.

The short interest theory has to do with how many open short sales are out there. Now, we know that short sellers profit when a stock's price drops, but this theory also recognizes that short sellers eventually have to cover or buy back their shorts. So, if there are a lot of uncovered or "open" shorts out there, they might all suddenly be forced to buy the stock in a hurry. That would create buying pressure that would drive up the stock's price, which is why a large number of open short positions is a *bullish* indicator.

Technical analysts also use indexes such as the Dow (30 huge "industrial" stocks), the S&P 500 (the overall market), the NASDAQ 100 (mostly technology), the Russell 2000 (small cap), or the Dow Jones Wilshire 5000 (r-e-a-l-l-y broad) and others to confirm trends. If the Dow is making new highs or new lows, a technical analyst might conclude that we are in either a bull or a bear market. Remember that the number included in the index's name usually refers to how many stocks make up the index. So, the Dow Jones Wilshire 5000 covers many more stocks than the S&P 500. The Dow Jones Industrial Average is comprised of only 30 industrial stocks; the Dow Jones Composite is made up of only 65 stocks. The theory is that however these indexes move is how the overall market will move.

Or not.

The so-called Dow Theory places major importance on the movement in the DJIA and the DJ Transportation Index. Believers of the Dow Theory preach that a major trend is confirmed only when both of the aforementioned indices reach a new high or low.

INVESTMENT STYLES, OBJECTIVES

GROWTH

Perhaps you have heard of "growth funds" and "value funds" before. Both invest in stock, but for different reasons. A growth fund is a mutual fund that invests in companies whose earnings are expected to grow rapidly. Trouble is, those earnings have inconveniently not actually been earned yet, so if we base a stock's price on how much it *should* or *will probably* earn over the next 5–10 years, that stock price is propped up by the shaky crutch of speculation. The company reports earnings every quarter—what if the Wall Street analysts have predicted earnings of one penny per share but the "growth company" actually reports a *loss* of one penny per share?

Usually, the stock drops faster than a big-league curve ball. Growth stocks are expensive, which means they trade at high "P/E ratios" or "high multiples." Starbucks, for example, is trading today for about 48 times earnings. Valero, a company that turns oil into gasoline, trades at just 6 times earnings.

VALUE

A "growth index" would track stocks trading at high P/E ratios. A "value index" would track stocks trading at lower P/E ratios. Simply put, value stocks trade at lower multiples than growth stocks. Why are they trading so cheap? Usually, because the company has hit a snag, or maybe it operates in an industry that is currently taking it on the chin. A value investor sees that an old established company such as, say, Anheuser-Busch, is now trading at a very low price-to-earnings (PE) ratio. Why? Maybe the earnings have been flat or shrinking lately. Maybe the company purchased a big brewery and is having trouble integrating it. Maybe Americans are currently on low-carb diets, what have you. A value investor might decide that the stock in this company is still worth more than people realize. He says its "intrinsic value" is $50 a share while the market is selling it for about $42 per share and, therefore, he loads up his shopping cart with it like my Aunt Barbara at a Big Lots back-to-school sale.

Long-established companies are the ones likely to pay dividends. And, even though a dividend *could* be cut or suspended, that doesn't happen very often. Why not? First, the headlines will make the company look really lame. Second, the board of directors—who declare dividends—are almost always huge shareholders themselves. If you owned 10 million shares of stock, would you vote to cut or suspend the dividend?

Probably not. So, since dividends usually stay the same or increase over time, when these value stocks start trading cheaper and cheaper, their dividend yields are increasing. Therefore, the exam could point out that value stocks offer higher yields.

They are also, generally, not as volatile as growth stocks. See, when a stock pays regular income, that always takes some of the volatility out of holding the stock. Similarly, when you throw a dinner party, your guests might start getting volatile if it's taking too long for the main course to show up. Well, to reduce the volatility of the crowd, you can always feed them some appetizers now. That's pretty much how dividend income works. So, since growth stocks seldom pay any income, investors can get a little testy as they wait for this supposed feast that's supposed to show up any year now.

INCOME

An "income investor" is, surprisingly, an investor seeking income. Where is the best place to seek income? Debt securities. Is that the only place? No—equities also pay income, which explains why there are equity income funds. Check out the current dividend yield on the following stocks:

- Altria (Philip Morris) – 4.4%
- General Electric – 3.0%
- Anheuser-Busch – 2.3%

When you consider that U.S. Treasury notes and bonds—the safest stuff on the planet—often yield about as much as the Altria dividend, that the dividend is taxed at 15% maximum versus ordinary income for the T-note or T-bond interest, and that Altria offers MUCH more growth potential than anything issued by the United States Treasury, you're forced to remember that stock can be a great place to invest.

Except when you lose all your money.

So, an equity income investor would purchase stocks that pay consistent or generous dividends. Most folks would just buy an "equity income fund" and let the portfolio managers decide which stocks pay the best dividends. Either way, the main objective here is the dividend income.

Income investors will also purchase preferred stock, since that dividend has to be paid before any dividends can be paid to common stock. But, generally, the phrase "income investor" describes a gentlemen or lady who prefers bonds. A corporation has to pay bond interest, while a dividend can always be cut or suspended entirely. Plus, if you buy bonds issued by state governments or Uncle Sam, the chance of default is usually quite remote in the case of the states and virtually nonexistent in the case of the United States Treasury.

Just how much income an income investor will end up seeking depends on her risk tolerance, objectives, and time horizon. As we'll soon see, bonds with long maturities usually offer higher yields, but they present more risk in terms of rising interest rates.

Low-rated bonds yield more than high-rated bonds, but they also subject the investor to the risk of further credit downgrades or outright default.

CAPITAL PRESERVATION

I suppose capital preservation could be the only objective of an investor, but any time he seeks capital preservation, he ends up earning some income, too. He would preserve his capital with U.S. Treasury securities, primarily. And, while he knows the principal value of the investment will be paid out at maturity, he will also earn interest on the T-bills, T-notes, and T-bonds. A U.S. Government Securities mutual fund would likely say that its objective is "preservation of capital and income consistent with that goal." How much income can you seek on things that are guaranteed by the U.S. Treasury? Not much—but what do you want? High yield or sleep? You can't have both.

Whether someone chooses T-bills, T-notes, T-bonds, or STRIPS has to do with time horizon and risk tolerance. If an investor is very concerned that rates will rise, stick her in T-bills and call it a day. If she wants to avoid reinvestment risk, stick her into STRIPS, which return all the interest at the very end. If she has a time horizon of 2–10 years, recommend T-notes. A longer time horizon would make T-bonds more suitable.

LIQUIDITY

If an investor plans to buy a house over the next several months or few years, keep their money out of the stock market. While you could put them into a short-term bond fund, I wouldn't recommend that, either. Why not? If rates rise, even short-term bond funds will see their NAV's drop. Put this investor, instead, into the money market. She'll earn relatively low rates of interest compared to long-term corporate and junk bonds, but that's okay. She'll also be able to cut checks against the value of her money market mutual fund investment, where the share price is magically maintained at $1.

The most *illiquid* investment would be a limited partnership (DPP). Thinly traded securities (some municipal bonds, OTC Bulletin Board stocks) also present more liquidity risk simply because there aren't as many buyers creating demand for the securities. So, "How soon might you need to access this money?" is a real good question to ask before deciding whether to put somebody into a money market mutual fund or a long-term bond fund. Note that the NASD rules on suitability say that you can't recommend investments unless the customer has provided financial information to you, unless you're just talking about money market mutual funds.

INVESTMENT RISKS

One of the best ways to understand investment risks is to read through the first pages of several different mutual fund prospectuses. I'm looking at the prospectus for a growth fund right now, which declares that its investment goal is "growth of capital." It then says that "dividend income, if any, will be incidental to this goal." In other words, the fund invests in growth stocks but some companies that are expected to grow will also pay dividends and this fund is not too proud to cash the check. The "principal strategy" tells me that the fund focuses on companies with $5 billion or more of market value (mid- or large cap, depending on whom you talk to) and uses fundamental analysis to determine which companies show strength in terms of EPS, revenue, profit margins, etc. The next section is called "important risks," and this prospectus lists investment risks such as:

> Stock market risk, or the risk that the price of securities held by the Fund will fall due to various conditions or circumstances which may be unpredictable

The exam might refer to the above "stock market risk" as "market risk" or "systematic risk." In any case, market/systematic risk is the risk that an investment will lose its value due to an overall market decline. As the prospectus says, the circumstances may be unpredictable. For example, no one can predict the next war or where the next tsunami or hurricane will hit, but when events like that take place, they can have a devastating effect on the overall stock market. Whether they panic because of war, weather, interest rate hikes, inflation, etc., the fact is that when sellers panic, stock prices plummet. The test might bring up the fact that market risk or "systematic risk" is measured by the beta coefficient. The "beta" shows how volatile a particular stock is compared to the S&P 500, which measures the overall market. A beta of .6 means that when the market goes up or down, this stock only moves 60% as much. A beta of 1.5 means that when the market moves, this stock jumps 1.5 times as much. So, a beta of less than 1 means the stock is less volatile than the market, while a beta of more than 1 means the stock is more volatile than the overall market. And, of course, the overall market is already plenty freaking volatile.

What can an investor do to combat market or "systematic" risk? Bet *against* the market. That's right—buy puts on the NASDAQ 100 or the S&P 500. Or, use the ETF's that track those indices and sell the suckers short. Now, if the market rises, your stocks make money. And, if the market drops, your little side-bet makes money. To bet the other way, remember, is called "hedging." If you own Microsoft common stock, you can buy puts on Microsoft or sell covered calls to hedge your position.

That would protect against "non-systematic risk," or the risk of one stock dropping. If you own a broad spectrum of the overall market, you can buy puts or sell calls on the S&P 500 index, or you can sell Spiders short to profit from the possible market decline in order to protect against market or systematic risk.

Buying stock in any company presents business risk. Business risk would be exemplified by the risk of competition or the risk that the company is getting into VHS right as DVD's are taking off. The risk of poor management (which we Krispy Kreme shareholders are still trying to recover from), of better competitors, or of products/services becoming obsolete are all part of business risk.

My handy prospectus also mentions that "foreign securities carry additional risks including currency, natural event and political risk." Well said. See, the American business climate and financial markets are pretty darned dependable, especially when compared to, say, Libya. Of course, we might occasionally want to raise the bar a little bit, but you get the point. Remember that political risk is part of the package if you want to invest in emerging market funds. An emerging market by definition is in a country where the markets are still, you know, emerging. They're not fully developed, a little awkward, a little bit volatile, basically like teenagers—bright future, but some days you really aren't sure if they're going to make it. You could buy 1 million shares of a networking startup company headquartered in Baghdad. That would certainly be a growth opportunity where everybody's talking about "getting in on the ground floor." Trouble is, the political insurgents in Iraq may turn that ground floor into a pile of rubble, and if the rebels take over the country and nationalize all industry, those 1 million shares might not be worth the paper they're printed on. Also, since most countries use a different currency from the American dollar, foreign exchange risk is also part of the package. The value of the American dollar relative to foreign currencies, in other words, is a risk to international and emerging markets investors. So, even if it's a developed market, such as Japan, if you're investing internationally into Japanese stocks, the value of the yen versus the dollar presents foreign exchange or currency risk. The natural event risk is fairly self-explanatory, as it refers to the fact that a tsunami, earthquake, hurricane, etc., could have a devastating effect on a country's economy, possibly the economy of an entire area such as Europe or Southeast Asia.

Now, you might think that a "growth fund" would invest only in growth stocks, but nothing is ever that simple in the investment world. As my handy prospectus here for a *growth* fund tells me:

> The Fund may also invest in fixed-income securities of
> any maturity such as convertible bonds and convertible
> preferred stocks. The fixed-income securities will be

```
rated at the time of purchase within the four highest
grades assigned by independent ratings agencies or in
non-rated equivalents.
```

Why would a growth fund also invest in fixed-income securities? Lots of reasons. First, when you name your fund, you generally just have to make sure that 80% of your investments fit within the implications of that name. For example, a "tax-exempt bond fund" needs to have at least 80% of its assets in bonds that are actually, you know, tax-exempt. Second, a mutual fund has lots of expenses represented by the investment adviser, board of directors, consulting and legal fees, etc, so they need some fixed-income securities to pay enough consistent income to cover those expenses. Third, as we just saw, the prospectus for this particular growth fund named convertible bonds/preferred specifically. That's because those fixed-income securities have a market value tied to the market value of the company's common stock. So, why not start out just collecting dividends or interest, and if the stock price rises, they'll catch that growth as well?

RISKS TO BONDHOLDERS

Investing in bonds is inherently less frightening than investing in stocks, as mutual fund prospectuses will list as an accepted assumption. For example, this prospectus says that the growth fund might be suitable if you "can accept the risks of investing in a portfolio of common stocks." See? It's like one of Jefferson's self-evident truths—stocks are inherently more volatile than bonds. Of course, there are still many risks involved with bond investing. Since the prospectus for this "growth fund" brings up the fact that the fund also invests in fixed-income securities, naturally it has to disclose the risks that fixed-income securities present. For example:

```
The value of any fixed-income security held by the
Fund is likely to decline when interest rates rise
```

What the prospectus is talking about is called "interest rate risk," which is the risk that rates will suddenly shoot up, sending the market price of your bond down. The longer the term on the bond, the more volatile its price. When rates go up, all bond prices fall, but the long-term bonds suffer the most. And, when rates go down, all bond prices rise, but the long-term bonds go up the most. So, a 30-year government bond has no default risk, but carries more interest rate risk than a 10-year corporate bond. As we'll mention later, "duration" is how we measure a bond's price volatility given a small change in interest rates.

Bet you can't wait. In any case, the reason we see short-term and intermediate-term bond funds is because many investors want to reduce interest rate risk. Maybe they have a shorter time horizon and will need this money in just a few years—they can't risk a huge drop in NAV due to a sudden rise in long-term interest rates. They will probably sacrifice the higher yield offered by a long-term bond fund, but they will sleep better knowing that rising rates won't be quite as devastating to short-term bonds.

The prospectus I'm looking at actually covers several of the family's funds. In the bond fund prospectus, we see that the important risks include:

```
Risk that the value of the securities the Fund holds
will fall as a result of changes in interest rates,
an issuer's actual or perceived creditworthiness or
an issuer's ability to meet its obligations
```

The first part of that statement is the interest rate risk we just discussed. The second part has to do with credit/default risk. What if S&P and Moody's decide to downgrade the bond ratings? Hate it when that happens, and so does this mutual fund. Unfortunately, neither of us has figured out how to prevent it. Notice how they separate the "perceived" from the "actual" creditworthiness—in other words, if the markets perceive the bonds as shaky, their price will plummet whether the company ever misses an interest or principal payment. And, if the issuer actually *does* discover they, like, can't pay you, that would also tend to be a problem. Of course, U.S. Treasury securities have no default risk, but some municipal securities and most corporate bonds carry default/credit risk to a certain degree.

The bond fund prospectus then writes, "call risk, or the risk that a bond might be called during a period of declining interest rates." Most municipal and corporate bonds are callable, meaning that when interest rates drop, the issuer will get tired of paying you the higher fixed rate they started out paying. Just like a homeowner refinancing from a 9% to a 6% mortgage, corporate and municipal bond issuers will borrow new money at the lower rate and use it to pay you off much sooner than you expected. First, your bond price stops rising in the secondary market once everyone knows the *exact* call price that will be received. Second, what do you do with the par value they give you? Reinvest it, right? And, where are interest rates now? Down—so you probably take the proceeds from a 9% bond and turn it into a 6% payment going forward. Hmm—you used to get $90 per year; now you can look forward to $60. Couldn't you protect yourself by buying non-callable bonds? Sure—and they'll offer you lower rates than callable.

Purchasing power risk has to do with inflation. If inflation erodes the value of money, an investor's return simply isn't worth what it used to be. Fixed-income investments carry purchasing power risk, which is why investors often try to beat inflation by investing in common stock. The ride might be a wild one, but the reward is that we should be able to grow faster than the rate of inflation, whereas a fixed-income payment is, well, fixed, even when inflation rises. Note that high inflation does not *help* stocks. It's just that in a period of high inflation, stock will probably perform better than fixed-income securities. So, during an expansion, where inflation tends to rise, you're better off in equities/stock. During a period of decline/contraction, bonds are the place to be, since their price will rise as interest rates fall due to the cooling demand for money/capital.

Remember that bonds paying regular interest checks force investors to reinvest into new bonds every few months or so. What kind of rates/yields will debt securities be offering when they go to reinvest the coupon payments?

Nobody knows, which is why it's a risk. In other words, it's very annoying to take a 9% interest payment and reinvest it at 3%, but it does happen. To avoid reinvestment risk buy a debt security that gives you nothing to reinvest along the way—zero coupons, e.g., Treasury STRIPS.

Notice how bondholders can get hit comin' or goin'. If it's a corporate bond—and even some municipal securities—you could end up getting stiffed (default risk). If rates go up, the price of your bond gets knocked down (interest rate risk). If rates go down, callable bonds are called (call risk), and the party's over, plus you have to reinvest the proceeds at a lower rate than you were getting (reinvestment risk). And, even if none of the above calamities strikes, inflation could inch its way up, making those coupon payments less and less valuable (purchasing power risk).

Oh well. If you want fixed-income, you take on these risks to varying degrees, depending on which bond you buy and when you buy it.

So, nobody ever wins by purchasing bonds?

No.

Except when they do.

Can you think of a situation where buying bonds could turn out extremely profitable? What if you purchased a bunch of 30-year, non-callable bonds right when interest rates were sky high and getting ready to plummet? Wouldn't that make your purchase price extremely cheap (rates high/price low) and, then, suddenly the market price would shoot sky high as interest rates started to fall, the faster the better?

How often is that going to happen, and how are you going to know when rates have peaked?

Beats me. But if you figure it out, please contact me at your earliest convenience.

MORE RISKS

Marketability or liquidity has to do with the ability to sell an investment quickly and at a fair price. Money market securities are easy to buy and sell at a fair price; municipal bonds, DPP's (limited partnerships), and thinly traded stocks are not. How much money could you make on your house if you had to sell it today?

Might have to drop your asking price pretty severely, unless there were, like, 10 buyers pounding on your door for an opportunity to put in a bid, right? So, thinly traded securities have "liquidity risk" compared to securities with more active secondary markets.

Legislative or regulatory risk means that if laws change, certain companies could be greatly affected. Suddenly, Microsoft® has to give away its operating systems for free.

Ouch. That would certainly impact the stock price, right?

Or, what if an investor bought a bunch of dividend-paying stocks in order to reap the rewards of a Republican-inspired lower tax rate on dividends, only to see a Democrat take office and rescind the kinder, gentler tax rate?

Hate it when that happens.

Non-systematic risk means that any particular stock or bond could take a huge hit for all kinds of reasons. Diversifying a portfolio reduces this risk, by spreading it out among more holdings.

Opportunity cost is just the shoulda'/coulda' principle. If you pass up an investment opportunity to make 5%, your opportunity cost is 5%, and you need to do better than 5% with the opportunity you choose instead. If you coulda' made 5% and you end up making 7% with another investment, you made 2% better than your opportunity cost. If you coulda' made 5% on a government bond but your brother-in-law talked you into a stock that helped you lose 80%, stop listening to your brother-in-law, unless you want to sell all of his recommendations short from now on.

PRACTICE:

107. Which of the following would be of least interest to a technical analyst?

A.   Advance/decline line

B.   Historical prices

C.   Daily trading volumes

D.   PE ratio

108. A fundamental analyst would be concerned with all of the following except

A.   Current ratio

B.   Working capital

C.   Income statements

D.   Open short positions

109. XXR common stock has a dividend payout ratio of 40%, EPS of $3.00, and a PE ratio of 12. What is the market price of XXR common stock?

A. $12

B. $20

C. $36

D. $15

110. RRT Corp. had Net Income of $10,000,000 last year. After the company pays $1,000,000 in preferred dividends, an owner of one of the company's 1,000,000 common shares would notice an EPS of

A. $10

B. $9

C. $3.33

D. $5

111. **When a company issues long-term convertible debentures, all of the following are affected except**

A.   current assets

B   accounts payable

C.   total assets

D.   working capital

112. **Where would an investor go to determine if a change in accounting methods has had a material effect on a company's reported earnings?**

A.   Statement of cash flows

B.   Footnotes

C.   Corporate Charter

D.   CNBC

113. **A company's net profit margin is**

A.   higher than its gross margin

B.   always the same as its gross margin

C.   net income divided by revenues

D.   net income divided by interest expense

114. **A company's gross margin would include revenue and**

A.   bond interest

B.   federal taxes

C.   cost of goods sold

D.   paid-in surplus

115. **The theoretical liquidation value of a share of common stock is known as the**

A.   liquidation ratio

B.   book value

C.   par value

D.   market value

ANSWERS:

107.   D – if it has to do with the company in any way, it's not a concern for technical

analysts. They only care about stock prices and what other traders are doing: volume, advance/decline, support/resistance.

108.   D – the fundamental analyst doesn't care whose shorts are open. He/she cares about companies and industries—not traders.

109.   C – P/E just means "price to earnings." If the price is 12 times the earnings, the price of the stock must be 12 x $3, or $36.

110.   B – EPS is simply "earnings available to common" divided by the number of outstanding shares. After paying the preferred dividend, the pie would be worth $9,000,000 cut into 1,000,000 slices. Each slice of equity is worth $9 in earnings.

111.   B – if you issue securities, you sell them for cash, which affects current assets, total assets, and working capital right there. How would that affect "accounts payable"? It wouldn't. Those are the bills the company owes their suppliers.

112.   B – was there a more tempting answer given?

113.   C – like most fancy-sounding terms, net margin is simpler than it sounds. It just means, "how much are you left with on the bottom line compared to what you started with on the top line?"

114.   C – revenue – cost of goods sold = gross "profit." Divide that by the revenue to get "gross profit margin." And, if your company can't make an actual profit, just keep talking about this one long enough to exercise your stock options.

115.   B – sure hope all those assets are listed accurately on the balance sheet.

WHAT NOW?

- Review the chapter. *Approximately 1 hour.*
- If you have the Pass the 7 QuizSet, take the Chapter 12 on Portfolio Analysis. *Approximately 40 minutes.*
- If you have the Audio CD set, listen to Disc 5, Track 2. *Approximately 18 minutes.*

CHAPTER 13

Customers & Brokerage Procedures

OPENING ACCOUNTS

Before your firm executes a customer's order, a new account will be opened. All new accounts require a new account form, and the exam may refer to NYSE Rule 405, which requires that the registered rep and the firm get to know as much about the client as possible.

NEW ACCOUNT CARD

You, the registered rep, will fill out the new account form (card), often over the telephone. You should obtain the following information from the new customer:

- Full name and address
- Home and work phone numbers
- Social security or Tax ID number
- Employer, occupation, employer's address
- Net worth
- Investment objectives (speculation, growth, income, growth & income, preservation)
- Estimated annual income
- Bank/brokerage firm reference
- Whether employed by a bank or broker-dealer
- Third-party trading authorization (if any)
- Citizenship (doesn't have to be an American)
- Legal age
- How account was obtained (referring broker-dealer, investment adviser)
- Whether client is an officer, director, or 10% shareholder of a publicly traded company

Once you pass your Series 7 and 63, maybe you'll be lucky enough to be asked to become a principal at the firm, which means you'll need a Series 24 or 9 and 10. The principal has sign-off power over all kinds of stuff. One thing a principal must always sign off on is a new account. So, the registered rep signs the new account form, and the principal/branch manager signs it.

To make sure they got all the information right, the firm needs to send the customer a copy of the new account form (new account card) within 30 days of opening the account and within 30 days of any major change in the information. Every 36 months the firm must verify the customer's information, too.

ACCOUNT AGREEMENT

Even though no rule says the customer has to sign the new account card, many firms like to make sure that customers are bound by NASD arbitration rather than having the opportunity to sue them in civil court over some bad stock recommendations. The test might refer to this as a "pre-dispute arbitration clause." When the customer signs an agreement to use NASD arbitration in any dispute with the firm, then they can't file suit in civil court. They could join a class action, although that seems a bit much for the exam. A new account agreement might also explain how certain procedures work at the firm, and the customer's signature means they understand that payment for stock purchases is, like, a requirement. The firm might also want a signature card so they have something to check against when verifying a customer's signature on, say, a stock power or a request for a cash distribution out of the account.

Finally, if the test asks whether a customer's educational background is a relevant detail, tell it to get real. Long Term Capital Management was a hedge fund with Ph.D.'s and even a Nobel laureate on board—they managed to lose about half a *billion* dollars with their big-brained bets on markets they thought they understood. Conversely, plenty of high school dropouts understand that the stock market is, in fact, a place to *make* money, a concept many MBA's and Ph.D.'s are still struggling to grasp as they wait for the Dow to hit 36,000.

Anyway, if a customer refuses to supply financial information, your firm can still open an account, as long as they have reason to believe the customer can afford one. Maybe Bill Gates' daughter doesn't want to tell you her net worth and annual income. You could still probably assume that she can cover any margin call you'd ever have to make by selling a spare 100,000 shares of Microsoft. Remember that customer information is confidential, meaning you only provide it to others if the customer gives permission or if a legal action, like a subpoena, requires it.

INSTRUCTIONS FOR SECURITIES, CASH, MAIL

Securities

When a customer buys securities, somebody has to hold them. There are three basic ways this can happen:

- Transfer and ship
- Transfer and hold in safekeeping
- Hold in street name

Maybe Grandma wants to put the cute, colorful Disney stock certificates right over the crib in the spare bedroom. She'll request that you register the certificates in her name and ship them—transfer and ship. I, myself, don't want the responsibility of protecting the certificates from damage or misplacement. I mean, I could get them re-issued by the transfer agent if that happened, but that's a pain in the neck, and there will be fees involved. So, I let my broker-dealer hold the certificates in safekeeping. In fact, I've never seen the stock certificates I allegedly own in my SIMPLE, Roth, and Traditional IRA. I do, of course, keep all the monthly statements they send me. These securities are registered in my name but held in safekeeping at the firm. The firm could charge a reasonable fee for this, but, luckily, mine doesn't. The third method, "street name," means that the securities are registered in the name of the broker-dealer for the benefit of the customer. The exam might say that the firm is the "nominal owner" and the customer is the "beneficial owner."

Cash

Stocks have been known to pay dividends. Bonds and money-market securities pay interest to the account. Also, customers will liquidate securities from time to time. So, the customer needs to indicate what should be done with the cash in the account. It can be "swept" into a money-market account (usually a government/Treasury money market account for ultimate safety and hideous yields). The cash can be sent to the customer, or it can be reinvested into more securities.

"Receipt versus payment" is generally for trusts or other institutional accounts. These multi-million-dollar investors are often so uptight that they refuse to release any money from the account until the securities purchased are delivered. The exam could call this "RVP" or "DVP." And, since even the acronyms need three names, they could call this a "cash on delivery" or "COD" account. RVP stands for "receipt versus payment," and DVP stands for "delivery versus payment." Receipt versus payment means that when we receive the certificates, we'll pay for them. Delivery versus payment means that just as soon as you pay us, we'll deliver the certificates.

And not a moment sooner.

Mail

The firm will be sending the customer monthly or (at least) quarterly account statements confirming the positions in the account and the value of the securities and the cash. Also, any time the customer buys or sells, a trade confirmation will be mailed to the customer's address of record. These days, statements and confirmations are often sent by email, but a customer would have to sign off on this method, which is much faster and cheaper for the firm to use. Confirmations and statements have to be sent to the customer. If the customer wants his investment adviser or attorney to receive the confirmations and statements, you can send a *copy*, but the customer still has to receive the documents, too. Of course, nobody can force him or her to open up the mail, but that ain't the firm's problem. If a customer will be traveling, he/she can send a written request to the firm to hold the customer's mail while he/she is away. If traveling domestically, mail can be held for 2 months; if traveling abroad, 3 months.

Finally, if some local celebrity doesn't want everybody at the firm gossiping about her account, she can actually have an account identified solely by a number. We call these "numbered accounts," believe it or not. As long as the firm has a signed statement from the customer identifying her as the owner of the account, we're good to go.

TYPES OF ACCOUNTS

There are 5 basic types of customer accounts:
- Individual
- Joint
- Corporate
- Partnership
- 3rd party/fiduciary

INDIVIDUAL ACCOUNTS

If an individual opens an account, the firm will only take orders from that individual. Not his wife, or his secretary, or even his bowling buddy Bob…only the individual. Surprisingly enough, we call these individual accounts. The only way you'll take buy or sell orders from somebody other than the individual is if the individual has granted 3rd-party trading authorization or "power of attorney" to someone else and you have that on paper. The first account you opened for Michelle Montoya was an individual account, and you would only take orders from Michelle on that one.

JOINT ACCOUNTS

Two or more adults can open a joint account. If two (or more) individuals want to share an account, they will open it either as JTwROS or JTIC. JTwROS stands for joint tenants with rights of survivorship. Rights of survivorship means that the survivor gets the assets if the other party dies. They go straight to the surviving owner(s), bypassing probate, should the exam try to get all legalistic on you.

A joint tenants in common account is a little different. Here the assets are split according to the customers' instructions. Michelle and her sister Christina recently set up a joint account as "tenants in common." If Christina dies, then her share of the assets goes to her estate rather than directly to Michelle, and vice versa. If the account were set up as Joint Tenants with Rights of Survivorship, the assets would pass directly to Michelle if Christina dies, and to Christina if Michelle passes away.

If it's a joint account, orders will be accepted from any party listed on the account. Mail can be sent to either party. But if you're talking about cutting a check, the check has to be made out to all names on the account. You wouldn't cut a check, for example, to Michelle Montoya and remind her to settle up with Christina next time she sees her. The check would be made out to, "Michelle Montoya and Christina Montoya, Joint Tenants in Common." They would need a bank account titled the same way then in order to cash the check. The securities would be registered in more than one name, so all parties would have to sign certificates if they were transferring ownership.

Easy, testable points.

CORPORATE ACCOUNTS

Businesses also open investment accounts. If it's a corporation, the registered rep needs to look at the corporate resolution to verify which parties have the authority to trade and withdraw assets from the account. If a corporation wants to trade on margin, you need to look at their corporate charter and bylaws to see if that's allowed. The officers of the corporation who have authority to transact business must sign a "certificate of incumbency" within 60 days, and your firm needs to keep that on file.

PARTNERSHIP ACCOUNTS

We talked about partnerships in the exciting "DPP" chapter. If you open an investment account for a partnership, you need to obtain a partnership agreement, which states who may enter orders. If the partnership wants to trade on margin, you'll need to make sure it's not prohibited by the partnership agreement.

3RD PARTY/FIDUCIARY ACCOUNTS

Then there are accounts where somebody manages the assets for the benefit of somebody else. These are known as "fiduciary" accounts, which is a fancy term that means, basically, that somebody manages the assets for the benefit of somebody else. Or, we can call them "third party accounts," since a third party manages the assets on behalf of someone else. You'll have to verify that the fiduciary has the authority to manage the account. They will either have "full power of attorney" or "limited power of attorney." Limited power of attorney allows them to enter buy and sell orders. Full power of attorney allows them to have cash and/or securities withdrawn from the account. The fiduciary always has to act solely for the benefit of the other party. They can charge reasonable expenses to administer the account, as banks obviously didn't set up those giant trust departments purely for philanthropic purposes.

Trust Account

Let's start with the trust account. If you're a movie buff, perhaps you remember that Orson Welles' character in *Citizen Kane* was set up with a fat trust account early on, which largely explained why he later said, "It might be fun to own a newspaper." Of course, not all trust accounts are for budding millionaires, but I sure as heck never had one when I was growing up and didn't know anyone else who did. Later, I started attending Grateful Dead concerts during that foggy period known as "college," which is when I met hundreds of trust fund hippies selling cucumber and granola sandwiches from the back of Mommy and Daddy's spare Beemer.

In any case, in a trust account a trustee is managing the assets for the benefit of a third party. The rep needs to look at a copy of the trust agreement to make sure the trustee actually has the authority to manage the account and what limitations have been placed on the trustee's authority. It will only be set up as a margin account if the trust agreement specifically permits such foolishness.

UGMA/UTMA Accounts

A minor child is not considered a "legal person," as you'll see when preparing for that nasty little exam that comes next: the Series 63 or 66. That means that a minor cannot open up an investment account, so an adult opens an account for the benefit of the child. When the child becomes an adult, the assets will be re-registered to the new adult, but until then we'll have an adult custodian manage the account. If a donor wants to donate money for the benefit of a minor, all she has to do is set the account up as either an UGMA or UTMA (depending on the state) account, which doesn't require any supporting documentation. The rep just opens it as either UGMA or UTMA, making sure there's just one adult custodian and one minor child per account. That's highly testable. If you see "Michelle and Javier Montoya as custodians for…" stop right there. You can't have two adults as custodians. And you can't have more than one minor child per account. A proper title for an UGMA account would look something like this:

Michelle Montoya, Custodian F.B.O. Alicia Rodriquez under California's Uniform Gift to Minors Act

F.B.O. means "for benefit of." If you've ever done a direct rollover from a 401(k) to another plan, the check they cut named the new custodian followed by "F.B.O." and then your name.

The gifts cannot be taken back once given, even if the child turns out to be an underachieving little brat. In other words, the gifts are all "irrevocable and indefeasible." The "indefeasible" part means you cannot treat the gift you make as a loan the child will someday pay back. It's a gift. Here's a quick link to debt securities and municipal bonds in particular—a "covenant of defeasance" means the issuer can do an advance refund of a bond issue, which they usually do when rates drop. To defease means to pay off a loan.

These accounts cannot be opened as margin accounts and states may have lists of allowable investments for UGMA/UTMA accounts. Since your niece won't be needing the money for, say, eight years, surely you can sort of "borrow" from the account from time to time as needed, as long as you repay her, right?

We won't even dignify that with a response.

Of course you can—just don't get caught.

For "UTMA" just remember that the "T" stands for "transfer." Under the Uniform Transfer to Minors Act, the transfer of assets can be pushed back to as late as 25 years of age. Maybe you want the kid to get his master's degree before you re-register the account in his name. Or maybe you just oppose giving 19-year-olds an account worth $1.1 million on general principles. Most states are UGMA, some are UTMA.

Some students get confused when asked if securities could be sold to cover an 11-year-old's attendance at a summer music camp.

Of course—this account is for the benefit of the minor. Just make sure the custodian isn't enriching herself or taking back gifts. The exam may point out that it is the minor's social security number listed on the account, and that after a certain amount, the income is taxable. Use the parents' tax bracket until the kid is 14; after that, use the child's tax bracket. And, if the minor child dies, the assets do not pass to the custodian, the donor, or the parents. They pass to the minor's estate, should the exam be in a morbid mood the day you take it.

Guardian Account

As much as we wish it weren't so, parents do die or become incapable of raising their children. If the parents are unable to care for their children, a court will appoint an adult as guardian. You may open a guardian account, as long as the guardian provides a court appointment no more than 60 days old. If the court appointment is older than that, you'll need a new one before opening the account.

Estate Account

The executor or administrator of an estate may open an investment account. If so, you'll need a copy of the will and the court appointment (letters of office). You'll also need a copy of the death certificate. The court appointment naming the executor/administrator must be no more than 60 days old. Estate accounts are, generally, only open for a few months, maybe two years. T-bills and other money market securities are the usual recommendation for such accounts. Michelle is named as executor in her grandmother's will, so when her grandmother passes away, Michelle may need to open an account in the name of the estate. The account would have its own tax ID number, just like a corporation or other legal entity, and might be registered as:

> **Michelle Montoya Independent Executor for the Estate of Rosalie M. Montoya**

Discretionary Account

The registered rep might be appointed as a third party manager. We call these discretionary accounts because buying and selling decisions will be up to the rep's discretion. That means if the rep wants to buy 1,000 shares of MSFT, he can do so without even bothering to call the client. The client would have to sign a trading authorization form, and the account would be reviewed more frequently, but that's about it. From then on, the rep can choose any of the following three A's:

Action

Asset

Amount

That means the rep can choose whether to buy or sell, what to buy or sell, and how much to buy or sell without contacting the customer. Without discretionary authority a registered rep can never determine any of the three A's. Unless the account is a discretionary account, the only thing a rep can determine is the time or price at which to execute a transaction. So, if a client calls you up and says, "Buy me some computer chip manufacturers today," do you need discretionary authority before you buy 100 shares of Intel?

You bet. If you choose the asset, that constitutes discretion.

If a client calls up and says, "Pick up 1,000 shares of INTC today," do you need discretion? No, your client has chosen the asset (INTC), the action (buy) and the amount (1,000) shares. Only thing left for you to decide is the best time and price to do it, and time/price does not equal discretion.

Each discretionary order ticket would be marked "discretionary," by the way, and a particular principal would be assigned to make sure the securities purchased are appropriate and that the rep isn't churning in order to win the big trip to Hawaii. If a registered representative purchases unsuitable investments for a discretionary account, it's not just a bad idea—it's a violation of NYSE and NASD rules. Just this morning, I read that the NYSE recently imposed a censure and a 6-month bar on a registered representative who misused his discretionary authority over an account.

DEATH OF A CUSTOMER

What should you do if one of your clients dies?
1. Cancel all open orders
2. Mark the account "deceased"
3. Freeze the account
4. Await proper legal papers

The proper legal papers authorizing you to transfer or sell securities are:
- Letters testamentary
- Inheritance tax waivers
- Certified copy of death certificate

If it's a discretionary account, the discretion is immediately revoked/terminated. If it's an UGMA account (sad, but it happens, unfortunately), the exam may expect you to know that the assets are not immediately transferred to the child's parents. Rather, they become part of the child's estate.

There is a relatively new type of account called "Transfer on Death" or "TOD," to make sure it has at least two names before people even get comfortable with it. In a TOD account, the owner specifies a beneficiary who will receive the assets upon death of the account owner. This can be advantageous, as a joint account's assets could be held up due to a lawsuit (divorce, for example), while the assets would not be at risk of legal action in a TOD account.

ACCOUNTS FOR INDUSTRY PERSONNEL, IMMEDIATE FAMILY

The new account card asks if the customer, spouse, or the customer's minor child works for a broker-dealer. If so, the employer will be notified in writing. If the member firm belongs to the NYSE, permission to open the account is required. For MSRB and NASD firms, notification is required before the firm opening the account can proceed. For NYSE and MSRB firms, duplicate trade confirmations will automatically be sent to the employer, but for NASD firms, duplicates are sent only upon request from the employer.

ACCOUNT TRANSFERS

Clients have been known to get huffy and transfer their account to another firm. This is generally done through something called an ACAT, which stands for Automated Client Account Transfer. The ACAT provides instructions to the broker-dealer for transfer and delivery. The firm receiving the request has three business days to validate the instructions or take exception to them. Once the account and positions have been validated, the firm has four additional business days to complete the transfer. The following are the reasons that the firm might "take exception" to the transfer instructions:

- Customer's signature is invalid or missing
- Account title does not match the carrying firm's account number
- Social security number does not match
- Account number is wrong

SIPC

I mentioned that my broker-dealer was holding my cash and securities. What if it turned out that they were on the brink of bankruptcy and started pledging my securities and draining my cash position to keep their creditors off their backs? If the firm went belly-up, the folks who now have my cash and/or securities aren't likely to let go of them.

Luckily, my accounts are covered by SIPC. Perhaps you've seen the little "SIPC" sign in the office of a broker-dealer? It stands for the Securities Investor Protection Corporation, a non-profit, industry-funded insurance company. It provides coverage of each customer account up to a total of $500,000 of which only $100,000 may be cash. So, if the investor has securities worth $300,000 and a cash position of $180,000, SIPC will cover all the securities but only $100,000 of the cash. Remember that commodities are not considered securities and are not covered. Mutual funds are held by the transfer agent, so if your broker-dealer fails, they weren't holding your mutual fund shares, anyway.

If a broker-dealer goes belly-up, a trustee is appointed and on that day we value each account and cover each separate customer up to the full amount. A separate customer means a separate account title. So Michelle Montoya's individual account is covered up to 500K. Her JTIC account with her sister Christina is covered as a "separate customer." Her IRA is treated as a "separate customer." The UGMA she manages for her niece is covered separately. The only accounts that get combined are cash and margin accounts for the same person.

One of the most important points about SIPC is that it is *not* the same thing as the FDIC. In fact, at SIPC's website (www.sipc.org) there is a link under "Who We Are" called "Why We are NOT the FDIC." I could easily picture a test question related to the fact that securities investments are not protected by FDIC. You have probably seen that warning on the first page of most mutual fund prospectuses, too. FDIC insures bank deposits. When a bank also sells securities, they have to use disclaimers such as "No bank guarantee," "not FDIC insured," or "may lose value" so that customers understand just how far they have wandered from the safety and security of a bank deposit, CD, etc., even if they are in the same building.

BROKERAGE OFFICE PROCEDURES

OTHER PEOPLE'S MONEY COUNTS

Apparently, I've not only embraced the cheesy memory joggers; I've actually elevated them to the status of a section heading.

Oh well. Sometimes these things are great. "Other-People's-Money-Counts" is just a cheesy yet effective way to remember the four separate departments of a broker-dealer:

- Order Room
- Purchasing and Sales
- Margin
- Cashiering

Order Room

When you, the registered rep, finally talk your customer into buying 10,000 shares of some hopelessly overvalued stock, you will present the order for execution to the order room. Since everything needs at least two names on this exam, we also call this the "wire room" because the order is then wired to the appropriate exchange. Once the order has been executed, the order room forwards a confirmation or "execution report" back to you and also to the next department—purchasing & sales.

Purchasing and Sales

After the order has been executed the "P&S" department inputs the transaction to the customer's account. The "P&S" department also mails (or e-mails) the trade confirmation to the customer, and that trade confirmation must be delivered no later than the settlement date, which is always T + 3 except when it isn't. Purchasing and sales is also responsible for billing.

Margin Department

Now, you might think that something called the "margin department" would only handle transactions in margin accounts. No, that would make way too much sense. All transactions are sent through the margin department, whether for cash or margin accounts. The margin or "credit" department calculates the amount owed by the customer and the date the money is due. This department also calculates any money due to a customer.

Cashiering

The cashiering department processes all securities and payments delivered to the firm. This department also issues checks to customers. When the margin department issues a request, the cashiering department also forwards certificates (stocks, bonds) to the transfer agent. Basically, the cashiering department handles all receipts and distributions of cash and securities.

CONFIRMATIONS

What would this industry call a document that confirms a trade? Would you believe, a "trade confirmation"? The confirmation below is one of my actual trade confirmations, so it is exactly as it appears in the real world, except for the parts I made up.

ACCOUNT #	TRANSACTION #	CAPACITY	ACCOUNT EXECUTIVE	
26597-5	006530698	Agent	GH	
Activity	Quantity	CUSIP	Price	Principal Amt.
Bought	10,000	3890227	$25.49	254,900.00
Trade Date	Settlement Date	Interest	Commission	Net Amount
04/22/2003	04/25/2003	N/A	$10.99	254,910.99
Symbol	Trade Description			
LGTO	Legato Systems, Inc.			

Trade confirmations must be delivered no later than settlement, which is the completion of the transaction. Confirmations are often delivered by e-mail these days, a much faster and cheaper method.

Execution Errors

The registered rep has to check execution reports with order tickets. If the customer wanted to buy 1,000 shares of Cisco and ended up buying 1,000 shares of Sysco, well that's not what the customer ordered and is not, therefore, the customer's trade. The firm would have to eat that one. Likewise, if the customer had entered a buy-limit @30 but the firm accidentally bought the stock for more than $30 a share, the customer would not have to accept the transaction. Or, if she had ordered 100 shares but the firm bought 10,000 shares, those extra zeroes would not be her problem.

Reporting Errors

But if the rep merely gives the customer a mistaken report when the firm, in fact, did exactly as instructed, that's just a mistaken report. If the customer's order was filled as instructed, it's the customer's trade.

SETTLEMENT

We were yakking away about "regular way" and "T + 3" way back in the Equity Securities chapter. For corporate and municipal securities regular way settlement is T + 3. The Trade Date is the "T," so if you trade on Monday, the transaction settles on Thursday, assuming there are no holidays to mess it up. Watch out for that, by the way. If a trade occurs on, say, Friday, June 30th, the 4th of July is going to be a factor. For the exam, please remember that the 4th of July typically occurs on the fourth day of July. When Treasury securities (bills, notes, bonds, STRIPS) are traded, they settle next business day or "T + 1." That's always "regular way settlement," which means, surprisingly, that this is the regular way.

Of course, you can already see where this is headed—securities transactions always settle "regular way," except when they don't.

Cash Settlement

When you absolutely, positively must settle the trade *today*, some broker-dealers will arrange a "cash settlement" for you. A "cash settlement" settles "same day," meaning the day you buy it is the day that settlement occurs. Of course, you have to have the cashier's check, wire transfer, or suspicious brown bag of cash ready to go, and the seller has to have the securities available for delivery on the day of the trade. If the trade happens before 2:00 PM, it settles by 2:30 PM. If the trade happens after 2:00 PM, it settles within 30 minutes, which sounds like the same thing but really isn't.

Next Day

This one is tricky. For a next day settlement, would you believe the cash and securities have to be available by—get this—the next day?

Seller's Option

In case the exam hasn't met its quota of trivial factoids, it may ask you about a seller's option. This is where the seller likes the price they can get today but—for whatever reason—won't be able to come up with the securities for a while. In this case the seller specifies the date on which they will be able to deliver the securities and may not deliver sooner than the fourth business day following the trade (I guess it would be T + 3 if it were any earlier, right?). If the seller specifies a certain date but ends up wanting to deliver the securities earlier, they have to give the buyer a one-day written notice of their intention.

Buyer's Option

The buyer could also specify the date when payment will be made for securities and accept delivery, which is pretty much the flip-flop of the seller's option.

RVP/DVP/COD

I'm not sure why the exam thinks that RVP/DVP/COD is, like, some BFD. As we mentioned earlier in this chapter, some trusts and other fiduciary accounts won't allow cash to be released until securities are received. Or, if they're selling securities, they won't release them until payment has been received. These settlements can end up taking a while, but no later than 35 calendar days after the trade.

GOOD DELIVERY

Remember that some customers still choose to have their securities "transferred and shipped." So when they sell stock, they have to deliver the certificates. Usually, it's the broker-dealer for the seller delivering the certificates, but, either way, if the stock or bond certificate is registered to Joe B. Kuhl, then it has to be signed exactly as: Joe B. Kuhl. Under no circumstances, can the customer sign the certificate *Joey Kuhl*, no matter how cool he may, in fact, be.

If a client forgets to endorse the certificate, should you put it back in the mail? No, just send her a stock power and have her sign that instead. If it's a bond, guess what you'd send her?

A bond power.

These are also known as "powers of substitution." In any case, it's usually the power of substitution that gets signed, rather than having the customer sign the back of the stock or bond certificate. That way, if the customer messes up the signature, they haven't really destroyed anything of value. The transfer agent has to accept the signature as valid, so, a "signature guarantee" is used. This is a medallion/stamp that NYSE member firms as well as bank officers have. The stamp means that the elite holders of the sacred stamps have verified that this signature is valid.

The transfer agent would reject the following signatures:

- Signature of a minor child
- Signature of an individual now deceased
- Signature of one person in a joint account (gotta have all signatures)

When you study for the Series 63, you'll remember that minors and dead individuals are not "legal persons," but we'll save that excitement for a later date.

When certificates come in, the back office has to be able to separate round lots (100s) from odd lots (<100). So, if the trade is for 540 shares, what we'd like to see is five certificates good for 100 shares each and one certificate for 40 shares. We could also take a certificate for 90 shares and immediately stack it with a certificate for 10 shares—that would make a round lot, right? So, if we received 5 certificates for 90 shares, 5 certificates for 10 shares, and one certificate for 40 shares, that would be good delivery, too. We'd take a 90 and a 10 and make a round lot five times; then we'd have the odd lot of 40 separated all by itself.

What about 6 certificates for 90 shares each? Six times ninety = 540, right?

Yes, but it's not good delivery. If you take a certificate for 90 shares and stack it with another one for 90 shares, you do not have a round lot. It has to be stackable into round lots without exceeding a round lot.

If we had a certificate for 200 shares and one for 300 shares that would be fine. 200 and 300 are immediately "breakable" into round lots of 100, right?

Did we mention this stuff is crazy?

Bond certificates delivered between broker-dealers must be $1,000 or $5,000 par value. If there are coupons (bearer, principal-only) missing, that's a problem. The receiving broker-dealer would actually cop such an attitude that if the missing coupon represented $60 of interest, they would deduct $60 from the money they send to the other firm. So there. If it's a municipal bond, the legal opinion has to be attached. If there was no legal opinion obtained, the certificate needs to be stamped "ex-legal." Ex- means "without," as in "ex-dividend," which means the stock is trading without the dividend.

Delivery can be rejected by the firm representing the buyer if:

- Certificates are mutilated
- Certificates don't comply with the weird round lot thing we just looked at
- All attachments are not present (affidavit of domicile, stock power, etc.)

- Signature is invalid
- Signatures are not guaranteed
- Securities are delivered prior to the settlement date

If you related to the *Citizen Kane* reference, chances are you also caught the movie *Wall Street*. I still remember the older guy at the firm saying something to Bud Fox about a customer who had "Dee-Kayed" him over a trivial amount of money. Since everything must be abbreviated, the phrase "don't know" was long ago abbreviated as "DK," even though it takes just as long to say the abbreviation, which is also two syllables. If a broker-dealer confirms a trade with another broker-dealer, the firm receiving the confirmation has to confirm the trade within four business days. If not, the confirming party can demand a confirmation, or that the other firm "DK" the trade. If the other firm truly "doesn't know" the trade—doesn't know a darned thing about it, in other words—it's as if the whole thing never happened.

If the buying broker-dealer doesn't receive stock certificates from the sell side by the settlement date, they have failed to receive them, which is why the industry very cleverly termed this a "fail to receive." The exam might also come from the other perspective and call it a "fail to deliver," which is pretty much what caused the other firm to "fail to receive." Again, Wall Street and Madison Avenue might be in the same city—same borough even—but the two streets could not be further apart when it comes to the creativity of language. On Madison Avenue we get phrases like "choco-riffic." From Wall Street we get a "DK" for "don't know."

Whatever—the lack of creativity in the language makes it that much easier to figure out what the words mean. The words mean exactly what they seem to mean in the securities industry. What else could we possibly call the day the dividend is payable other than the "payable date"? The regular way for settlement is called "regular way settlement." Whatever works—we aren't trying to win Clio awards.

Think back to our "Equity Securities" chapter. Remember what we said on page 15, paragraph 8, line 1? No? Okay, we were talking about the whole "DERP" thing. If a stock is purchased on or after the ex-dividend date, the seller is entitled to the dividend, and if the stock is purchased before the ex-date, the buyer is entitled to the dividend. Sometimes things get screwed up. The buyer purchases the stock before the ex-date, but the seller still ends up getting the dividend. In this case, the customer's broker-dealer would send a "due bill" for the dividend to the other broker-dealer and would expect them to fork over the cash that is due.

ACCOUNT STATEMENTS

At the least, a broker-dealer has to send account statements to their customers quarterly. It would only be that infrequently if there had been no activity in the account. Since there is usually activity in the account, most account statements are sent monthly. If any of the following had occurred in the account during the month, a monthly statement would be sent:

- Purchases or sales of securities
- Dividend and/or interest received
- Addition or withdrawal of cash or securities
- Margin interest charged to a margin account (don't worry, that chapter's next)

The account statement shows:

- All positions in the account (for example a "1,000" next to "Abbott Labs" and the symbol "ABT" to remind me just how much I have riding on that company)
- All activity since the last statement (there's a shocker)
- All credit and debit balances (don't worry, margin accounts are coming up, as promised)

PROXIES

Back in olden days small shareholders weren't likely to cast votes at the annual meeting, unless they happened to live near corporate headquarters. The Securities Exchange Act of 1934 covered a whole lot of ground, and part of the ground covered had to do with public corporations/issuers letting shareholders vote by proxy. This way, I don't have to travel from Chicago to Redwood Shores, California just to throw in my two cents about Oracle's employee stock incentive plan or Larry Ellison's desire to buy up yet another annoying rival. I can just fill out the little form I get from my broker-dealer and let them vote per my instructions. Usually these proxies go ahead and tell you how management thinks you should vote. I ain't sayin' they'd take me out back if I voted the wrong way, but I ain't takin' no chances, neither. I can either vote the way they want me to, or if I sign the proxy and fail to indicate how I want to cast my votes, then the board of directors/management of the company get to use those votes as they see fit. If the matter is of no major importance, the broker-dealer can cast the votes on behalf of their customer, if the customer has failed to return the proxy at least 10 days prior to the annual meeting. A major issue, such as whether HP and Compaq should merge, would be a different matter. We're talking more like the decision to retain KPMG as the firm's auditor. The Act of '34 also requires public companies to report quarterly and annually. So, the broker-dealer will end up forwarding those reports as well as proxy materials to their customers, but they won't charge the customers. This stuff is all a cost that the issuer has to bear, ever since that embarrassing little fiasco known as the 1920's. Another name for a proxy is an "absentee ballot," just to make sure it also has at least two names.

Oh, and just in case you've been told that what you're learning only matters in the "test world" not the "real world," I attended the Northern Trust annual share-holders meeting in the spring of 2006. The very first item of business was that the Board of Directors planned to switch from cumulative to statutory voting. An angry shareholder stood up and tried to shame the board for taking away the power that minority shareholders have with cumulative voting. How he, himself, first got elected to a corporate board through cumulative voting, which—as the test wants you to know—provides a benefit to small/minority shareholders, who can pool all of their votes for just one candidate.

The board listened patiently to the impassioned plea of the pro–cumulative-voting shareholder, paused three seconds out of respect, and then promptly approved their plan to switch to statutory voting.

Why send in a proxy statement when you can attend such fascinating drama in person? Of course, the Northern Trust headquarters is just a 25-minute El ride for me—I'm not getting on one of those hideous four-hour West Coast flights just to cast a vote or attend the meeting for Oracle, Intuit, etc. With proxy voting, I don't have to.

DIFFERENT TYPES OF BROKER-DEALERS

The exam may want you to know the difference between a "carrying broker-dealer" and an "introducing broker-dealer." And, let's face it, you're dying to know yourself. The fundamental difference between carrying broker-dealers and introducing broker-dealers is that carrying broker-dealers focus more on carrying while introducing broker-dealers focus primarily on introducing.

Okay, maybe I'd better look it up.

Oh, here we go. A carrying broker-dealer actually maintains possession of a customer's cash and securities. Another name for a carrying firm is a "self-clearing member." If I started a broker-dealer firm, I'd probably want somebody a little better at record keeping holding my customers' cash and securities, and, after they saw the registration statement, I'm pretty sure the SEC would sort of insist. So, I'd be getting the customers, and the carrying or "self-clearing" firm would hold and be respon-sible for my customers' cash and securities. Better yet, now the account statements and trade confirmations will be sent by the clearing firm to my customers. Or, just to make your exam a little harder, my firm may decide to clear through an "omnibus account." This way, all trades from my customers would be cleared inside this one giant omnibus account, and the clearing firm wouldn't know who bought which shares of, say, Oracle today—just that the customers of my firm ended up buying 50,000 shares of ORCL.

REG T

How long does a customer have to pay for stock?

Well, the trade settles between broker-dealers at T + 3, but the customer actually has 5 business days before he's required to pay for the stock. Payment is requested at T + 3; it's required at T + 5, or two business days after regular way settlement, whichever is easier for you to remember. On the third business day following the trade date, the buying broker-dealer sends the money to the selling broker-dealer **regardless** of what the customer does. If the customer still hasn't paid for the transaction two business days after that, the broker-dealer can either request a five-day extension from their SRO, or just sell the stock that the other side has delivered on the open market to get whatever they can get for it. If they end up losing money on the deal, they'll hold the customer responsible for the loss. Either way, they'll "freeze" the account for 90 days, which just means the customer won't be able to pull this trick on them anytime soon. For 90 days no purchase orders will be accepted unless the cash is already sitting in the account. And, if we're talking less than $1,000, that's chump change in this business so we don't have to freeze the account.

DELIVERY OF SECURITIES

Customers have a longer time frame when it comes to delivering the securities they have sold through the broker-dealer. If you get a question on this, tell the exam that the customer has 10 business days from the settlement date to deliver the securities. If they fail to do so, the broker-dealer has to perform a "buy-in" of the securities, which means they have to buy the securities and deliver them to the other side. If they have to pay more than the trade was executed for, they're going to be ticked, and they can take the difference from their customer.

PRACTICE:

116. **Which of the following is required on the New Account Form?**

    A.   registered rep's signature

    B.   customer's signature

    C.   neither A nor B

    D.   both A and B

117. **Which of the following would be considered the most important when opening an account?**

    A.   customer is over 30 years old

    B.   customer's wife works for an NASD member firm

    C.   customer prefers bonds

    D.   customer is a registered Democrat

118. **Which of the following is a true statement concerning the opening of a new account?**

    A.   the customer cannot be asked for bank or brokerage references

    B.   the customer cannot be asked to provide net worth and income level

    C.   the customer does not have to sign the new account form

    D.   the customer's spouse is automatically granted trading authorization

119. **When opening a new account, if your customer wants to trade options**

    A.   he must submit to a polygraph administered by an NASD member

    B.   he must submit to a polygraph administered by a licensed law enforcement professional

    C.   he must provide information to help determine suitability

    D.   he may not trade options if his net worth is below $1.5 million

120. **If a customer refuses to provide a tax ID number or social security number:**
   A. the account cannot be opened under NASD rules
   B. the account cannot be opened under SEC rules
   C. withholding will result
   D. she must pre-file electronically

121. **Without contacting the customer, a registered rep managing a discretionary account could purchase all of the following except:**
   A. common stock
   B. preferred stock
   C. speculative options
   D. municipal bonds where a control relationship exists

122. **Your customer tells you to buy 1,000 shares XYZ at a good price today. This order**
   A. cannot be executed under any circumstances
   B. cannot be executed 10 minutes before market close
   C. is discretionary
   D. is not discretionary

123. **Your customer has read an enticing article extolling the many advantages of investing in real estate; therefore, she calls and says, "I want you to buy as many REITs as you think I can afford right now." This is an example of**
   A. painting the tape
   B. frontloading
   C. a discretionary order
   D. a non-discretionary order

124. **When the account is non-discretionary, the registered representative may not determine**
   A. number of shares
   B. time
   C. price
   D. all of the above

125. **All of the following may open discretionary accounts except**

    A.   individuals

    B.   corporations

    C.   partnerships

    D.   fiduciaries

126. **If a corporation wishes to open a trading account as a margin account**

    A.   this cannot occur under any circumstances

    B.   this can only occur if the NYSE and NASD approve the arrangement

    C.   the corporate charter and bylaws must be provided

    D.   only U.S. treasury and agency securities may be purchased

127. **When you discover that one of your customers has died, you must do all of the following except**

    A.   mark the account "deceased"

    B.   freeze the account

    C.   cancel all sell stop and buy limit orders

    D.   liquidate all positions

128. **The husband of a customer calls and tells you his wife wants to sell 1,000 shares of ORCL immediately. What should you do?**

    A.   refuse the order

    B.   mark the order "unsolicited"

    C.   mark the order "joint and several"

    D.   execute the order in a timely fashion

129. **A registered rep learns that two former college roommates now sharing an investment account as joint tenants in common have each moved to opposite coasts and rarely see each other. The representative holds a conference call and discovers that Joann, in Philadelphia, prefers dividends while Barbara, in San Rafael, prefers interest payments. Therefore, the rep decides to start sending checks to Joann for the dividend income and checks to Barbara for the interest income received in the account. This is**

    A.   standard operating procedure

    B.   a violation known as "painting the tape"

    C.   improper procedure for joint accounts

    D.   perfectly acceptable as long as the agreement is duly notarized

130. **As the custodian for her nephew's account, Marilyn Mason would rather not charge a fee for her services. Rather, she would like to receive 10% of the account's appreciation each year so that she receives no benefit in poor performing years. This arrangement is**

   A.   standard operating procedure

   B.   a violation known as "painting the tape"

   C.   improper procedure for UGMA/UTMA accounts

   D.   perfectly acceptable as long as the agreement is duly notarized

131. **Donald Diversey has a cash account with securities valued at $120,000 and a cash position of $380,000. He and his wife have a joint account with $400,000 in securities and $90,000 in cash. What is the SIPC coverage for their accounts?**

   A. $500,000 covered for cash account; $500,000 for joint account

   B. $480,000 covered for cash account; $500,000 for joint account

   C. $220,000 covered for cash account; $490,000 for joint account

   D. $500,000 total for both accounts combined if at same broker-dealership

132. **None of the following statements are true concerning SIPC except**

   A.   covers market risk

   B.   does not cover government securities exempt from Regulation T

   C.   covers losses in commodity futures

   D.   is an industry-funded, non-profit insurance company

ANSWERS:

116.   A – we don't need the customer's signature on the new account form. The rep and his/her supervisor must sign the form. The exam might call the rep's boss the principal, supervisor, or branch manager, because everything needs at least three names on this test.

117.   B – whenever the customer or the customer's spouse works for an NASD member firm, certain special handling of the account must be undertaken. For example, these customers are prohibited from buying new issues under NASD Rule 2790.

118.   C – you definitely ask for financial information, including bank and brokerage

references. The spouse does not automatically have trading authorization. If they want to set that up, they have to fill out the proper form(s).

119. C – doesn't "C" just look like the right answer? Polygraphs? Those things aren't even admissible in court—can you picture registered reps administering these things and how badly the test would be abused in order to get the customer cleared for trading?

120. C – no idea why someone would refuse to give you a tax number or why you'd open an account for somebody so uncooperative, but if they don't give that information, the firm will have to withhold some income every year for your friends and mine at the IRS.

121. D – just another MSRB rule to memorize.

122. D – time/price do NOT equal discretion.

123. C – the rep would have to choose the Asset (which REITs) and the Amount (how many shares), so this is definitely a discretionary order. Without discretion, all the rep can choose is time of day and the price to pay.

124. A – without discretion, all the rep can choose is time of day and the price to pay.

125. D – a fiduciary is responsible for making decisions for a third party. Fiduciaries include trustees in a trust account, or a custodian for an UGMA account. These folks can't pass off their responsibility to a registered rep by granting him/her discretion. They can take advice from the rep, but they can't let the rep choose the Activity, Asset, or Amount.

126. C – memorize it.

127. D – don't liquidate positions yet. Just stop trading the account, which is called "freezing" the account. And don't start passing anything out until the appropriate legal documents have come in: death certificate, trust document, will, etc.

128. A – only accept this order if the husband has been granted trading authorization (power of attorney) and you have that on file.

129. C – all "distributions" have to be made out to all names on the account. The firm doesn't send part to one tenant and part to another. They're joint tenants—it's not your problem how they share things. Just send the proceeds to both names on the account.

130. C – if the custodian for the UGMA is appointed by a donor, then a reasonable

fee can be charged to the account. But no way can the custodian receive gains or appreciation on the account.

131.   C – in the first account, SIPC covers all securities but only 100K cash for a total of $220,000. Plus the other 490K for the joint account. Look for the cash position bigger than 100K for these questions.

132.   D – SIPC doesn't cover commodities, because those aren't securities.

WHAT NOW?

- Review this chapter. *Approximately 1 hour.*
- If you have the Pass the 7 QuizSet, take the Chapter 13 Quiz on Customers & Brokers. *Approximately 33 minutes.*

CHAPTER 14

Margin Accounts

Maybe you've purchased a house before. Chances are you didn't just buy the thing outright. If the house cost $200,000, maybe you put down $20,000 and then borrowed the rest from the mortgage lender. Why was the mortgage lender willing to spot you $180,000 on a house worth $200,000? Two reasons. One, they're going to charge you interest on that loan for many years to come. And, two, if you can't pay them back, they'll just sell the house.

When the collateral we're pledging is real estate, we can easily put down just 10%, or even less, and then borrow the rest by pledging the house to the lender. When we buy stock "on margin," we have to start out by putting down 50% of the purchase price. If you want to buy $200,000 of stock, the broker-dealer can loan you ½ of that, or $100,000, and you can put down just $100,000. Pretty neat, huh? If the stock pays dividends, you get dividends on twice as many shares. If the stock goes up 10%, you make 10% of $200,000 rather than the mere $100,000 you could have afforded in a cash account. Also, whatever upside this stock delivers belongs solely to you—you're just going to pay back the broker-dealer what they lent you and pay interest on the balance until it's paid off. When this stock increases, that increase is all yours.

So, broker-dealers love margin accounts. It opens up a whole new line of business—suddenly they're credit card companies, and they don't even have to issue the little plastic cards. Plus, credit card companies have no collateral from their customers—your VISA account is backed up solely by your tendency to repay. In a margin account, you pledge the assets you're buying on credit to the lender, the broker-dealer. If things turn south on you, they can sell the stock or bond to recover the money they lent you. So, the interest rate they charge is actually lower than what you'd pay on a credit card.

People talk about the "equity" in their houses all the time. That means that maybe they bought the house for $200,000 and borrowed $180,000 to do that. If so, their account starts out like this:

$200,000	MARKET VALUE
-$180,000	MONEY OWED
=$20,000	EQUITY

Just remember that "equity" simply equals the difference between what somebody owns (assets) and owes (liabilities). When we looked at financial statements, we said that the shareholders' equity was the difference between what the company owns (assets) and owes (liabilities) on the balance sheet.

Okay, so house prices have been increasing rapidly the past few years, even though that may have come to a halt right about now. In any case, let's say that this home's value increased 15% for three years running. Believe it or not, when an investment of that size compounds for just three years at 15%, it is suddenly worth $304,175. To check my math, just take $200,000 times 1.15, times 1.15, times 1.15. That's the formula for "future value" that many of you will work with on your Series 66, and there's no law that says it can't show up on your Series 7, either. Anyway, part of each monthly mortgage payment knocks down the principal that was borrowed, and maybe these homeowners diligently overpaid each month by a few hundred dollars. Suddenly, the value of their asset has risen while the amount owed has dropped. Their account now looks like this, maybe:

$304,175	MARKET VALUE
-$170,000	MONEY OWED
=$134,175	EQUITY

What can these happy homeowners do with that equity? They can transfer all the high-interest credit card debt they've accidentally accumulated to a home equity loan and start funding that debt at a lower interest rate. Or, they can borrow money and put on a second-story addition. That's just what comes to mind as an example; frankly, nobody cares what they do with the money. They have some equity, let 'em play with it a little. You only go around once, right?

In a margin account, you aren't buying houses; you're buying stocks and bonds. What if you had bought JDSU at $250 a share on credit, and then the stock dropped to $2.50? You would have had yourself a serious collateral problem. That broker who hasn't returned a phone call in three weeks is suddenly going to be paging you, emailing you, cell-phoning you, text-messaging you, and possibly even sending out a team of Navy SEALS to locate you and get you to put some more money on the table in order to stay in this high-stakes game called margin trading.

This is, of course, where "margin accounts" get their bad name, but they're not all bad. I have one myself. The trick is to party responsibly. My margin account entitles me to a cash advance of exactly $4,822.70 this morning. Or, I could buy $9,645.40 worth of stock completely on *credit*. But, nobody's holding a gun to my head, so I just keep paying 100% in my so-called "margin account." Basically, to be approved for options, you also turn your account into a margin account. Why? If you want to exercise a call, you'll need to come up with a bunch of cash in a hurry, so having the account approved for margin is real handy. Or, if you write puts, you will occasionally have to buy a bunch of stock, and margin accounts let you buy twice as much stock as you would otherwise be able to purchase. Same for the call seller who suddenly has to purchase a really expensive stock to deliver to a really happy call holder. Without trying to blow your mind completely, I will tell you that even though an options account is also approved for margin, options are not actually purchased "on margin." Rather, they are paid in full, probably because they can fluctuate 40–80% in the space of an afternoon. So, a "margin account" is simply a different type of account than a "cash account." In a cash account, you have to pay in full when you purchase securities, and you cannot sell short in a cash account. If your account is approved for margin trading, you can buy securities on credit and sell them short if you really like to party.

REG T

The Securities Exchange Act of 1934 gave the Federal Reserve Board the authority to regulate margin accounts. The "Fed" regulates credit, and one form of credit is the margin account, in which the broker-dealer fronts the customer half the purchase price. In the 1920's, too many customers were holding stock on margin without putting down enough money. When the prices of those stocks collapsed, they ended up owing money with nothing to show for it all. The Fed would sort of like to prevent another 1929-style market crash if at all possible. So, to purchase stock on margin, the broker-dealer follows Regulation T (Reg T), which states that a listed stock can be pledged as collateral by the customer in exchange for a loan from the broker-dealer of half the market value. That sure is a long way to say that the customer has to put down half, isn't it? But Reg T really tells broker-dealers how much credit they can extend to their customers—that percentage has been 50% for quite some time. The industry sometimes refers to the amount that a customer puts down as the "fed call." For a test question, when a customer buys $200,000 of stock, he puts down ½ or $100,000. The other ½ or $100,000 is provided by the broker-dealer, who looks forward to charging interest on that $100,000 for just as long as the customer would like to go on owing them. The amount that the customer puts down is referred to as "the margin." Margin simply means "per cent," but sounds more sophisticated somehow.

RUNNING THE NUMBERS

Say a customer went long 1,000 shares @40 and made the required Reg T deposit of half or $20,000. At that point the customer's account looks like this:

```
LMV    -   Dr    =   Equity    Reg T Deposit
$40,000   $20,000   $20,000    $20,000
```

LMV stands for "long market value." It could just be referred to as "market value" or "current market value," to make sure you have three names for the same darned thing. The "Dr" stands for "debit register." This is simply the amount the customer borrowed and still owes his broker-dealer, like the mortgage balance that the home-owner still owes the lender.

So, the long market value of the stock he bought is $40,000. He made the required Reg T deposit of half—20K—so the broker-dealer fronted him the other half. Do you suppose the broker-dealer wants that money back?

You bet, so it's a debit (Dr) to the client's account until he pays it off.

He "owns" an asset worth 40K and he owes 20K to the lender. That's why his equity is $20,000. Just like if you owed $80,000 on your mortgage when your house was worth $100,000—the difference of $20,000 would be your equity.

Simple, right?

So, the investor has $20,000 of equity. What happens if the stock rises, to, say, $50 a share? The account looks like this:

```
LMV    -   Dr    =   Equity
$50,000   $20,000   $30,000
```

The amount owed to the broker dealer (Dr) didn't change. The long market value of the stock went up, increasing the equity dollar-for-dollar. Now, let's compare the equity of $30,000 to Reg T, which is 50% of the market value or "LMV." Reg T wants to see 50% equity in the account. Does this customer have at least half his "LMV" as equity? More, actually. Half of 50K is $25,000. The customer has $30,000 of equity. That's excess equity of $5,000. Like this:

```
LMV    -   Dr    =   Equity  -  Reg T  =  Excess Equity
$50,000   $20,000   $30,000    $25,000    $5,000
```

You know how a lot of homeowners have recently been borrowing more money long before they've really started to pay off their mortgage? Well, in a margin account you can do the same thing. Since this customer has "excess equity" of $5,000, we certainly wouldn't require him to do something crazy and, like, pay back the lender. Heck no. Instead, the customer has $5,000 credited to a special little line item called "SMA." SMA is just a line of credit that the customer can tap. I mean he can withdraw $5,000 of his cash, like it's in a savings account, right?

Not at all. The $5,000 is just a number—as with Social Security there's actually no money there. But, if the customer wants to borrow that *amount* of money, he can.

See why customers love margin accounts, especially when the markets are moving in the proper direction? The customer can just tell the broker-dealer to cut him a check for $5,000, which will be added to his tab, like this:

LMV   -   Dr   =   Equity
$50,000 $25,000 $25,000

Borrowing the cash didn't affect the long market value of the securities. We added the amount borrowed to the debit balance, which reduced equity and wiped out the SMA. SMA can be used as a cash advance that will be repaid with interest. Or, SMA can be used as an initial margin requirement for the purchase of more stock. So, instead of borrowing the cash, the customer could have used the $5,000 SMA credit to purchase $10,000 of stock. If so, the account would have looked like this:

LMV   Dr   Equity   SMA
$60,000 $30,000 $30,000 $0

If the customer buys more stock, that definitely adds to the market value of securities held long in the account. Why did his Dr go up by $10,000? Because the $5,000 of SMA is not the customer's cash—it's just a line of credit. Funny money, no different from your line of credit on a credit card. You can use the credit, but since it isn't your money, it has to be paid back, with interest. The customer in our example used his line of credit (SMA) as his margin deposit, and the broker-dealer fronted him the other half, or $5,000, which is also added to the Dr along with the $5,000 he borrowed for the deposit from SMA. So, he borrowed $5,000 from his line of credit (SMA), plus $5,000 that the broker-dealer fronted him for the additional stock purchase. In other words, when the stock moves your way, you can end up using borrowed money in order to borrow more money.

Reg T absolutely demands that a customer put up 50% of the long market value initially. After that, it really only sort of requests or prefers that the customer have 50% equity. What happens if the customer's equity dips below 50%?

Not much. Even though the account is called "restricted," there really aren't many restrictions. The customer has to put up ½ in order to buy more stock. If the customer sells stock, he can still withdraw ½ the proceeds. So the test question might show an account with less than 50% equity and ask you how much cash the customer can withdraw if he sells a certain amount of stock.

Half.

The proceeds pay down the Dr; and half that amount is credited to SMA, where it can be promptly withdrawn. But, remember, no cash has been moved to SMA. Just a number. No different from a credit card issuer raising your line of credit.

Maybe we should take a look at the numbers there. The market value of the long position is $20,000, and the Dr is $13,000. That means the customer controls a $20,000 asset with not a lot of skin in the game. His equity or ownership is really only $7,000. Half of his long position would be $10,000, but his equity is below that. Therefore, we call this a "restricted account." Let's say he sells $5,000 of stock. The broker-dealer takes the $5,000 raised by selling the stock and pays down the debit by $5,000, since that debit is the money the customer owes them. So, the LMV becomes $15,000, and the Dr becomes $8,000. How much money can the customer borrow after making this sale? Half of the sale, or $2,500. And, if he did that, he'd end up with LMV of $15,000 and a Dr of $10,500. As we'll see, that's pushing it, since his equity is now just 30% of his long position. The SRO's won't let the firm allow him to drop below 25% equity, so this guy is apparently a real party animal. Oh well. If the firm will allow him to control a position with just 30% equity, everything is just hunky dory.

Also, check this out. When the market value of a securities position drops, that does not affect SMA. It certainly reduces the market value of the stock and, therefore, the equity, but SMA is just a line of credit. It does not get taken away. One of the best cheesy memory joggers I've ever heard comes from an instructor who would tell his students that excess equity is the water in the tub. When the excess equity rises, it makes a ring around the tub called "SMA." When the water drains away, the SMA is still here to stay.

SMA does not go away due to a drop in market value. The customer can always use SMA as long as using it does not take him below the minimum maintenance requirement, which we're about to look at right now.

MINIMUM MAINTENANCE

Reg T tells us what to put down on an initial transaction, and any excess above Reg T gives the customer "SMA," but Reg T isn't our only concern. In fact the customer's larger concern is the SRO 25% minimum maintenance requirement. The NYSE and NASD say that a customer's equity can never go lower than 25% of the long market value. If it does, the customer gets a maintenance call to bring the equity up to the minimum 25%. If the customer can't deliver the cash, the firm sells/liquidates securities equal to four times the amount of the maintenance call. The following numbers should help to clarify the concept of the minimum maintenance requirement:

LMV	Dr	Equity	Minimum Call		Liquidate
40,000	20,000	20,000	10,000	0	0

At this point, the customer has twice as much equity as the minimum (25% of long market value).

If the stock goes from 40K down to 30K, we're still okay:

LMV	Dr	Equity	Min.	Call	Liquidate
30,000	20,000	10,000	7,500	0	0

But, if the long market value falls to 24K, we're in trouble:

LMV	Dr	Equity	Min.	Call	Liquidate
24,000	20,000	4,000	6,000	2,000	8,000

The SRO's demand $6,000 in equity, which is ¼ of $24,000, and the customer has only $4,000. So, the customer gets a maintenance call informing him that he needs to deliver $2,000. If the customer does that, the account looks like this:

LMV	Dr	Equity	NYSE	Call	Liquidate
24,000	18,000	6,000	6,000	0	0

He paid down the debit by $2,000 and now he has $6,000 in equity, the bare minimum of 25% of market value. If he didn't have the cash, the firm would have liquidated $8,000 worth of securities. If so, the account would have looked like this:

LMV	Dr	Equity	Minimum Maintenance
16,000	12,000	4,000	4,000

Whereas it used to look like this:

LMV	Dr	Equity	Minimum Maintenance
24,000	20,000	4,000	6,000

Selling the $8,000 worth of securities reduced the LMV and the Dr by an equal amount, leaving the customer with exactly 25% equity. Remember, all we're doing here is selling $8,000 of stock and using the $8,000 to pay down the debit.

By the way, since the firm might have to sell a customer's stock in a hurry, they hold the customer's securities in "street name." That means the certificates are registered in the name of the firm for the beneficial ownership (FBO) of the customer, who hasn't exactly paid for them yet. Also, the 25% requirement is the *minimum* maintenance. That means the broker-dealer can be only that loose about things. Many broker-dealers require a higher minimum maintenance than just 25% to protect themselves from a bunch of dead-beat speculators.

How low can a customer's long market value go before he gets a maintenance call? The test might refer to this as the "account at maintenance." All you do is take the Dr and divide it by .75. If you want to know why, it's because .75 is the "complement" of 25%. Either way, just take the Dr and divide it by .75. That tells you exactly how low the LMV can go before a customer has to worry about a maintenance call. So, if the account looked like this:

LMV	Dr	Equity
40,000	20,000	20,000

To find the lowest LMV or the account "at maintenance," just take the Dr of 20,000 and divide it by .75 to get $26,667. As long as the LMV doesn't dip below that amount, the customer is properly margined. We can check the numbers, too:

LMV	Dr	Equity
26,667	20,000	6,667

Isn't the equity exactly 25% of the LMV in that case?

Yep. So, the customer would still be okay. If the LMV kept falling, he'd get a maintenance call. If it hangs tough or increases, the pressure starts coming off.

See how it works?

DEPOSITING STOCK

In a margin account, the customer can deposit cash equal to the Reg T requirement ("fed call"), or they can pledge fully paid securities. If the margin purchase is for $50,000, Reg T is 50% of that. Therefore, the customer can deposit $25,000 cash, or pledge fully paid securities with a market value of $50,000. Under Reg T, securities have a loan value of ½ (50%) of their current market value.

MARGINABLE SECURITIES

Not everything can be purchased "on margin," but that doesn't mean it can't be purchased within a margin account. A "margin account" is really just an account that has been approved for margin. I have one, myself. Luckily, I never use it to borrow money, much as I immediately shred all those little pretend checks my credit card companies keep sending me. No thanks. Not interested in paying interest on purchases—I'm looking to make money, thank you. Well, if I really wanted to purchase securities "on margin," these are the securities I could buy by depositing half:

- NYSE, NASDAQ, AMEX stocks
- OTC securities on the FRB's approved list

The following can be purchased inside my margin account, but I'd have to pay for them in full:

- Non-NASDAQ OTC securities
- Options
- IPO's or any new issue for 30 days
- Mutual fund shares

I doubt the test would be this mean, but if it is, remember that those funky, long-term options called LEAPS allow me to purchase them by putting down 75%. If you get that question, please watch out for black cats, spilled salt, ladders, and cracked mirrors, as your luck has apparently run out on this planet.

EXEMPT FROM REG T

Just to keep things nice and simple, they decided to make certain securities exempt from the Reg T requirement of 50%. For government securities, the customer can put down 1–7% of the par value (depends on the broker-dealer). For municipal securities, the customer can deposit the greater of 7% of par or 15% of market value. Agency securities also have much lower requirements.

SHORT POSITIONS

Short accounts work a little different. Remember that when a customer sells short, he is selling borrowed securities in anticipation that he can buy them back to replace them at a lower price. So, if he wants to sell short $10,000 worth of securities, he has to deposit half that value, or $5,000 to meet the Reg T requirement. If he did so, his account would look like this:

Cr	$15,000
SMV	-$10,000
Equity	$5,000

The "Cr" stands for the "credit" and the "SMV" stands for "short market value," or, perhaps, we could just call it the "market value." In any case, when the customer sells short $10,000 worth of securities, that $10,000 is credited to the customer's account. Remember, he sold some stock—somebody paid him $10,000 for that stock. That somebody doesn't know or care that the seller is "short" the stock; to the buyer of the stock the other side is simply a seller.

So, our investor gets the proceeds from the sale and also deposits 50% of that to meet the Reg T requirement, which is added to the $10,000 he took in for selling the stock for a total credit of $15,000. For the exam questions "Cr" will remain unchanged; it's the "SMV" or "short market value" that fluctuates. Think about that for a second—which numbers move in a margin account? The ones with "MV" in their name, which stands for "market value." Market value is what changes in a margin account, whether long (LMV) or short (SMV). And, equity is always a percentage of market value or "MV."

If the "SMV" goes down, as the investor hopes, he'll end up with more equity. For example, if the SMV dropped to just $5,000, the customer's equity would increase by $5,000, like this:

Cr	$15,000
SMV	-$5,000
Equity	$10,000

Remember, the credit didn't change. He started with a credit of $15,000, and that's all the credit he's going to have. It's the market value (SMV) that changed, dropping in the desired direction for our short seller.

And if the market value of the securities sold short were to increase (ouch!), his equity would shrink, like this:

Cr	$15,000
SMV	-$11,000
Equity	$4,000

How high can the SMV go before a customer gets one of those nasty maintenance calls? For short accounts, customers need 30% of their SMV as equity. If the customer's SMV is $11,000, he needs at least $3,300 in equity. You can find the highest SMV at maintenance by taking the "Cr" and dividing it by 1.3. Since the customer has a credit of $15,000, just divide that by 1.3, and you see that the highest SMV without a maintenance call would be $11,538. As long as the securities' value doesn't exceed that number, his account will remain properly margined.

COMBINED EQUITY

Keep this simple. To find combined equity just find the equity for the long positions and add it to the equity for the short positions. You can also remember that the formula for combined equity would be:

LMV + Cr - Dr - SMV

Which is just another way of saying, "Add the two things that go on top and subtract the two things that go on the bottom."

So if a customer had a LMV of $20,000, a Cr of $20,000, a Dr of $10,000, and SMV of $10,000, his combined equity would be $20,000:

LMV   + Cr   -   Dr   -   SMV
20,000 + 20,000 - 10,000 - 10,000

In other words, he has $10,000 equity on the long positions, and $10,000 equity on the short positions. He has to have 25% equity for the long, and 30% for the short. This customer is okay on both fronts.

INITIAL REQUIREMENTS

SHORT POSITIONS

For an initial transaction in a short account, the customer has to put up at least $2,000, end of story. If they sell short $3,000 worth of stock, half of that would be $1,500. Too bad, they still put up $2,000. Otherwise, it's just half of the SMV, which gets added to the proceeds of the short sale to make the Credit. You can also think of the Cr as being 150% of the SMV, or "half again" as much after the customer makes the required Reg T deposit.

LONG POSITIONS

For long positions it's a little trickier. Of course, the customer has to put down ½ the LMV for the Reg T deposit. If the securities are worth $5,000, he deposits half, or $2,500. But, if he wants to buy $3,600 worth of stock, half of that falls short of the SRO minimum $2,000 deposit. In this case, he'd put down $2,000.

And, if the total value of the securities is below $2,000, he has to put down 100% of their value. So, if he buys $1,800 worth of securities, he just pays the full $1,800.

Simple, right?

So, if the first trade is worth more than $4,000, the customer puts up half. If the first trade is between $2,000 and $4,000, the customer puts up the minimum of $2,000. And, if the first trade is less than $2,000, the customer puts down 100% of the securities' value.

Might help to remember the following chart:

INITIAL PURCHASE	CUSTOMER DEPOSITS
> $4,000	50% of purchase price
$2,000 – $4,000	$2,000 SRO minimum
< $2,000	Full purchase price

OPENING A MARGIN ACCOUNT

When a customer opens a margin account, he will be asked to sign the following:
- Credit agreement
- Hypothecation agreement
- Loan consent

The credit agreement states the terms and conditions for the credit extended to the customer. It includes information about how interest is charged and which interest rate it will be tied to (LIBOR, broker call rate, prime rate, etc.). The hypothecation agreement pledges the customer's securities purchased on margin as collateral for the loan. It also allows the broker-dealer to re-hypothecate those securities as collateral for a loan at a bank to obtain the money they're going to front the customer. If you speak Spanish, you probably know the word "hipoteca," which would be on a sign for a business that makes loans. Hypothecate/hipoteca. As usual, Spanish is pretty close to the Latin that many English words are based on. To "hypothecate" securities means to pledge them as collateral for a loan. Finally, the loan consent is not something the customer has to sign, unlike the credit agreement and hypothecation agreement. But, if the customer does sign the loan consent, the broker-dealer can lend out their securities to customers who want to sell short.

DOUBLE OR NOTHING

So, are margin accounts a really good thing, or a really bad thing?

Absolutely.

Like the Southern Comfort sitting on the shelf, it all depends on who opens it.

Basically, a margin account allows you to maximize your gains but also your losses. Let's look at two more scenarios to drive this point home, and then I promise to lay off the numbers for a while. Say that you purchase 1,000 shares @20 ($20,000) using just $10,000 of your own money. Put down $10,000, broker-dealer fronts you the other $10,000. You get lucky, the stock rises to $25 per share (25,000), and you sell it. After paying back the broker-dealer their $10,000, you walk away with $15,000, which is an extra $5,000. How did you do? You put down $10,000 and made a 50% profit. If you had only been able to buy the $10,000 worth, or 500 shares, you would have put down $10,000 and sold for $12,500, which is only a 25% profit.

With margin, your profit was doubled.

Then again, let's say that after putting down $10,000 for 1,000 shares of stock trading at $20, the stock took an inconvenient nosedive. Instead of going up like it's supposed to, the stock drops to $15 per share. You freak out and sell it for $15,000. You give the broker-dealer back their $10,000, and you're left with $5,000.

Wait a minute, you put down $10,000 and are now left with just $5,000? Isn't that a net loss of 50%? Sure is. And, it wouldn't have been so ugly if you had just bought $10,000 of that stock. If you had purchased 500 shares @20 with your $10,000, and then sold the 500 shares at $15 ($7,500), you would have lost $2,500, or just 25%.

So, with margin you can make twice as much but also lose twice as much. The broker-dealer makes their interest charges, either way, and they help you to buy twice as much stock as you otherwise would have. So, it's definitely a win-win situation for the broker-dealer. The customer will also come out ahead.

Unless he loses.

PRACTICE:

133. If the value of securities increases in a long account, all of the following are affected except
    A.   LMV
    B.   Equity
    C.   SMA
    D.   Dr

134. If the value of securities decreases in a long account, which of the following are affected?

I. SMA

II. Dr

III. LMV

IV. Equity

A. I, II only

B. I, II, III, IV

C. III, IV only

D. IV only

135. If a customer sells $2,000 of securities in a restricted account, all of the following are affected except

A. Dr

B. SMA

C. Equity

D. LMV

136. If a customer uses SMA to buy stock, all of the following are affected except

A. LMV

B. SMA

C. Dr

D. Equity

137. If a customer borrows SMA, all of the following are affected except

A. LMV

B. SMA

C. Dr

D. Equity

138. In a new margin account, a customer buys 100 shares ABC @38 and makes the required Reg T deposit. Three months later ABC is @47. What is the equity?

A. $2,900

B. $2,700

C. $900

D. none of the above

139. **A new margin customer purchases 200 ART @48 and meets the Fed call. Seven and one-half months later—with Reg T at 50%—ART rises to $64 per share. What is the customer's buying power?**
   A. $3,200
   B. $6,400
   C. $2,000
   D. $9,600

ANSWERS:

133.   D – the word "value" is a clue. If the "value" goes up, then the Long Market Value (LMV) is affected, right? As LMV increases, so does equity. If an increase in market value creates excess equity, then SMA is also affected. Dr is just the amount the customer owes the broker-dealer.

134.   C – remember that SMA is the ring around the tub. Excess equity can drain away, but SMA is still here to stay. Once it's credited, it can't be taken away by a drop in the securities' value. Customer has to borrow or use it to buy more stock; otherwise, SMA is here to stay. As the securities' value decreases, so does the equity in the account.

135.   C – obviously, when the customer sells securities, the LMV goes down, right? The proceeds pay down the debit, so Dr is affected. Since the full amount pays down the debit, equity remains the same. LMV goes down 2K, so does the Dr, leaving equity unchanged. Half of the amount of the sale is credited to SMA, which is the amount that can be borrowed, even in a restricted account.

136.   D – the question tells us the customer "uses" SMA, so SMA is definitely affected. It's used to buy more stock, so the LMV goes up. Is SMA free? Nope. It's added to the Dr, so the Dr is also affected. If the customer has $4,000 in SMA and uses it to buy $8,000 of stock, both the LMV and the Dr will be increased by $8,000, which is why equity is not affected.

137.   A – borrowing SMA as a cash advance doesn't affect LMV, since we aren't buying any stock. We're just taking the cash advance. That's a line of credit to the customer and when it's used it's added to the debit register. The customer owes that money, which is why Dr is affected. If LMV stays the same and the Dr is increased, that affects the equity by lowering it, dollar-for-dollar, by the amount added to the Dr.

138. A – now that's a tricky question! If the customer buys $3,800 worth of stock, she'll have to put down $2,000, leaving her with a Dr of $1,800. $4700 - $1800 = $2900 equity.

139. A – the customer put down half initially, or $4,800, leaving a Debit balance of $4800 (it's easy when there are 200 shares—just multiply by half of them). So, when the stock is now worth $12,800, the equity is $8,000. Reg T is $6,400 (half of LMV) so the $1,600 above that is excess equity. Multiply that by two to get the buying/purchasing power.

WHAT NOW?

- Review the chapter. *Approximately 30 minutes.*
- If you have the Pass the 7 QuizSet, take the Chapter 14 Quiz on Margin Accounts. *Approximately 27 minutes.*
- If you have the Audio CD set, listen to Disc 5, Track 3. *Approximately 25 minutes.*

CHAPTER 15

Rules & Regulations

THE SEC

The SEC is the ultimate securities regulator. The NYSE, NASD, MSRB, etc., all answer to the big kahuna known as the "SEC," which stands for "Securities and Exchange Commission." This is not a mere "SRO" or "national securities association" that can regulate its own members. This is an arm of the federal government. Created with the passage of the Securities Exchange Act of 1934, the SEC has five commissioners, with no more than two from a particular political party. The President of the United States gets to name the commissioners (with Congress playing the "advise and consent" role) and he gets to appoint the Chairman, which is why it's always stacked 3-to-2 in favor of the party occupying the White House.

Why does the federal government regulate the securities markets? It has to do with interstate commerce. See, when commerce takes place all within one state, that state has authority over the activity. A state highway here in Illinois is the domain of IDOT (<u>Ill</u>inois Dept of Transportation), but there are also many <u>inter</u>state highways running through this state, which are the domain of the federal government's USDOT. That's because when commerce becomes "interstate commerce," the federal government steps in and lets everyone know they're in charge. In other words, if the commerce is not conducted within just one state, it's not just one state's responsibility—it's the federal government's responsibility. The federal government explains why they have the authority to regulate the securities markets in the Securities Exchange Act of 1934:

Transactions in securities as commonly conducted upon securities exchanges and over-the-counter markets are affected with a national public interest which makes it necessary to provide for regulation and control of such transactions and of practices and matters related thereto...in order to protect interstate commerce, the national credit, the Federal taxing power, to protect and make more effective the national banking system and Federal Reserve System, and to insure the maintenance of fair and honest markets in such transactions.

A very important concept is that the federal government views the purpose and implementation of securities regulations as follows:

Whenever pursuant to this title the Commission is engaged in rulemaking and is required to consider or determine whether an action is necessary or appropriate in the public interest, the Commission shall also consider, in addition to the protection of investors, whether the action will promote efficiency, competition, and capital formation. (Securities Act of 1933, Section 2[b])

The SEC is basically an army of attorneys with the authority to crack the whip whenever somebody tries to manipulate the markets or sell securities fraudulently, or provide investment advice without getting registered, or many, many other things that threaten investors and the markets themselves. They can expel firms and agents from national securities exchanges. They can go after CEO's who provide bogus income statements in their quarterly and annual reports. When they kick somebody out of the industry or investigate a renegade company, they are engaged in civil enforcement. That means they take you to federal court and sue the heck out of you. Since they are part of the federal government, they can also refer criminal cases to the U.S. Department of Justice, which means you might be sweating it out with a roomful of FBI agents in dark suits and sidearms if you aren't careful. That's why we've seen so many executives squirming in the court room in recent times. If you lie on your quarterly and annual reports filed with the SEC, you are committing securities fraud, which carries stiff monetary penalties and scary jail time. We're talking 20 years if the fraud is egregious enough. And, how are quarterly and annual reports circulated? By wire and by mail. This is just a suggestion, but I strongly recommend keeping "wire and mail fraud" off your U-4 for as long as possible.

Let's examine the actual verbiage on the criminal penalties, which I've borrowed and abbreviated from the Securities Exchange Act of 1934, Section 32(a):

Any person who willfully violates any provision of this title, or any person who willfully and knowingly makes, or causes to be made, any statement in any application, report, or document required to be filed under this title, which statement was false or misleading with respect to any material fact, shall upon conviction be fined not more than $5,000,000, or imprisoned not more than 20 years, or both.

Wow.

No thanks.

FEDERAL ACTS

When I hear the phrase "Roarin' 20's," I immediately picture shaky film reels of flappers dancing the Charleston and people partying in speakeasies, but then it always turns ugly, with ruined men jumping out of skyscrapers when the stock market crashes in October 1929. Up to this point the stock market had pretty well ruled itself, but then the Great Crash caused people to lose faith in the whole concept of investing. Well, the federal government is definitely interested in helping to foster a strong capital market that provides much-needed cash to corporate issuers, state and local governments, not to mention the biggest issuer of all—the federal government itself. The securities/capital markets are inherently linked with the banking system, employment, tax revenues, political stability, etc. So, in 1933 the federal government decided that most securities would have to register with a new organization that would be called the Securities and Exchange Commission, who would make sure that investors get a lot more and a lot better information from issuers before turning over their hard-earned money for strange pieces of paper called "stocks" and "bonds."

SECURITIES ACT OF 1933

This so-called "Paper Act" is all about registering a security (the paper) with the SEC, which then gives the company the green light to sell or "issue" their paper to the public. As an investor, before you buy a brand new share of stock, you have to be provided with a prospectus that discloses everything you need to know about the company issuing the paper. That prospectus has been registered with the SEC. In it you can read about the company's history, its products and services, its chances for success, and its chances for failure. You can look at the balance sheet and the income statement. You'll still be taking a risk if you buy—because all securities carry risk—but at least you'll be able to make an informed decision because of this full and fair disclosure of material information.

If you had gotten in on that IPO for Frank & Emma's Fruit Pies (FREM), the prospectus you received would have talked about how the company was founded in 1947 by Francis R. Funkmeyer, who used his GI bill to earn a business degree from Ohio State University and started the company from the money he'd saved up working the night shift at a local tool and dye shop. You would have read how the company was now run by third-generation owners, and how the company had bold plans to expand its reach and market share. You could have looked at the financial statements and read all the risks involved with buying stock in a company with many larger competitors who were much better financed and better known on the national stage. Product liability, union slowdowns, fuel costs, penny-pinching customers like Wal-Mart driving down profit margins…any negative thing imaginable was detailed in the risk disclosure section. You could read about the board of directors and the three officers of the company: Jeremy, CEO, Jennifer, CFO, and Jason, COO. You'd see where they went to college, where they got their MBA degrees, how much of the company's stock they own, etc.

You'd get a pretty good picture of the company before deciding if you want to buy a little slice of its profits in the form of common stock. And that's the whole purpose of the Securities Act of 1933—giving investors enough information to give them a fair shot. Sometimes we refer to the Securities Act of 1933 as the "Paper Act," because it governs how "paper" gets issued for the first time. When a corporation wants to raise cash by selling securities, they have to get a group of underwriters together and fill out a bunch of paperwork for the federal government in the form of a registration statement, or "S1." Part of this information will become the prospectus, which is the disclosure brochure that the public will be provided with. An "underwriter" is just a broker-dealer that likes to take companies public, by the way. Another name for an underwriter is "investment banker," but they don't act like a traditional bank. No deposits or checking offered here.

Here is how the Act of '33 defines the terms *issuer* and *underwriter*:

- The term "issuer" means every person who issues or proposes to issue any security
- The term "underwriter" means any person who has purchased from an issuer with a view to, or offers or sells for an issuer in connection with, the distribution of any security, or participates or has a direct or indirect participation in any such undertaking, or participates or has a participation in the direct or indirect underwriting of any such undertaking

Hmm. Thanks for clearing that up, huh?

Oh well, that's partly why I have a job. Anyway, notice how the term "issuer" includes people who have not yet issued a security. Seems goofy, but they have to write it that way so that as soon as you file your paperwork to issue a security, you are now defined as an "issuer" and, therefore, have to follow all the rules on issuers spelled out by the piece of legislation. If you weren't clearly defined as an issuer at that point, the law wouldn't be able to touch you.

The law really does want to touch you at this point. As we saw earlier, as soon as you register your paper, you go into a cooling off period, where only certain things are allowed. That's because you're an issuer now that you have proposed to issue securities. By the way, your Series 63 may ask you to define "issuer," and the definition should look exactly as we just saw.

The definition of "underwriter" is just sad. There are surely better ways to express that idea, such as:

- An "underwriter" means any person who has purchased securities from an issuer with intent to distribute the securities, working either on their own or as part of a group

Anyway, once the underwriters and the issuer file the registration papers, they go into a "cooling off" period, which will last a minimum of 20 days. This process can drag on and on, but no matter how long it takes, the issuing corporation and its underwriters can only do certain things during this "cooling off" period. Number one, they can't sell anything. They can't even advertise. They can announce that a sale is going to take place by publishing a tombstone ad in the financial press. A tombstone ad is just a boring rectangle with some text—looks like a tombstone. You can see them in the *Wall Street Journal* fairly often, or in most any newspaper at least once in a while. It announces that a sale will take place and informs the reader where he/she can obtain a prospectus. But it is neither an offer nor a solicitation. Remember that for the exam—if somebody reads a tombstone and calls up wanting to buy the securities, nothing has been offered for sale yet. Once the prospectus has been delivered/sent to the client, *now* an offer to sell securities has been made. And, if anybody said or did anything deceptive at this point, we could have a case of fraud on our hands, which is the single most important topic on the Series 63.

But, we'll save the excitement of the Series 63 for a later date.

The underwriters can send out a preliminary prospectus/red herring to certain clients to see if anyone wants to give an "indication of interest," but those aren't sales. Just names on a list. The red herring, by the way, contains almost everything that the final prospectus will contain except for the effective date and the final offering price or "POP." The registered rep may NOT send a research report along with the red herring and may not highlight or alter it in any way.

The issuer and the underwriters hold due diligence meetings during the cooling off period, which just means they make sure they provided the SEC and the public with accurate and full disclosure.

Nothing gets sold until the SEC "releases" the security on the release or effective date. But, even though the SEC makes issuers jump through all kinds of hoops, they don't approve or disapprove of the security. They don't guarantee accuracy or adequacy of the information provided by the issuer and its underwriters. In other words, if this whole thing goes belly up because of inaccurate disclosure, the liability still rests squarely on the shoulders of the issuers and underwriters, not on the SEC. And, there has to be a disclaimer on the prospectus that says something scary like this:

> These securities have not been approved or disapproved by the Securities and Exchange Commission nor has the Commission passed upon the accuracy or adequacy of this prospectus. Any representation to the contrary is a criminal offense.

They're a very serious bunch, this SEC. Let's hope you never find out exactly how serious yourself.

THE SECURITIES EXCHANGE ACT OF 1934

The Act of '33 is about new issues only. The Securities Exchange Act of 1934 covers just about everything else. It is often referred to as the "People Act," which is easy to remember, because it dictates how people may act in the securities markets. Before the Act can tell the players what they can and can't do, though, it has to clearly define the players and clearly define the term "security." That's no different than how we'd have to write a set of rules for the game of basketball, right? We couldn't begin to outlaw "goal tending" unless we first clearly define terms such as goal, rim, net, backboard, shot, and who knows what else?

Here is how the Securities Exchange Act of 1934 defines such terms:

- The term "broker" means any person engaged in the business of effecting transactions in securities for the account of others
- The term "dealer" means any person engaged in the business of buying and selling securities for such person's own account.

When you sit for the Series 63 or 66, you'll see why they very cleverly fused those two bullet points together to define the entity known as a "broker-dealer," which is, "Any person engaged in the business of effecting transactions in securities for the account of others or its own account."

Since this is, after all, the <u>Securities</u> Exchange Act of 1934, it only covers securities. That's why it has to carefully define what a security is. Basically, a security is anything that can be exchanged for value where the investor's fortunes are at risk and are bound up with other investors' fortunes in some common enterprise, where the investors will benefit solely through the efforts of others. That could clearly define common stock, where millions of investors are bound together in their investment in, say, Microsoft, and they'll all benefit solely through the efforts of others, since few investors could write a line of Visual Basic or C++ to save their lives.

And, the beauty of this rather loose definition is that it could include a 10% ownership stake in a racehorse. Or a 15% stake in somebody's soybean farming operation. That way, the regulators can regulate a very broad array of investments, should investors end up getting bilked by shady operators.

This rather broad definition comes from a Supreme Court case referred to as the "Howey Decision," by the way. In that decision, the term "investment contract" was clarified as we just discussed, and an investment contract is specifically mentioned as one example of a "security." The definition of "security" even goes so far as to include "anything commonly known as a security." In other words, if it looks like and walks like a security, it's a security. That means it will probably have to register, and the agents and broker-dealers who sell it will also probably have to register.

The Securities Exchange Act of 1934 has a lot to say about broker-dealers and registered reps having to register. As you might already know, "associated persons" such as registered reps and principals have to register with a "member firm" through a U-4 form. So the firm is the member; you, the registered rep, are an associate of the member firm.

If there were troubling bits of news on that U-4, the individual trying to register with a member firm (or the member firm trying to get registered itself) could be disqualified by statute, which, we very cleverly call a "statutory disqualification." Sounds impressive, but it's no more complicated than you and some friends trying to organize a summer soccer league. Who can play and who can't? Maybe any kid over 12 is too old and, therefore disqualified by the statutes/rules that your soccer club lays down. Statutorily disqualified. Maybe if any kid has had a conviction for gun possession or felony amounts of narcotics, he/she can't join the soccer club. That would be another statutory disqualification.

The Act of 1934, basically, says that if the firm trying to associate with an SRO, or the individual trying to associate with a firm, has been convicted of any felony during the past 10 years, or any misdemeanor that involves fraud, theft, embezzlement, perjury—that kind of stuff—he/they will most likely be disqualified. Also, if other regulators have slapped sanctions/penalties on the firm or individual during the past 10 years, they probably aren't going to get registered with the SEC, either. That includes foreign authorities, the commodity futures regulators, and, of course, the NASD and NYSE.

Notice how a felony is a felony. One's just as bad as another. But, the misdemeanors that could keep somebody out are spelled out like so:

- involves the purchase or sale of any security, the taking of a false oath, the making of a false report, bribery, perjury, burglary, any substantially equivalent activity however denominated by the laws of the relevant foreign government, or conspiracy to commit any such offense;

- arises out of the conduct of the business of a broker, dealer, municipal securities dealer, government securities broker, government securities dealer, investment adviser, bank, insurance company, fiduciary, transfer agent, foreign person performing a function substantially equivalent to any of the above, or entity or person required to be registered under the Commodity Exchange Act (7 U.S.C. 1 et seq.) or any substantially equivalent foreign statute or regulation;

- involves the larceny, theft, robbery, extortion, forgery, counterfeiting, fraudulent concealment, embezzlement, fraudulent conversion, or misappropriation of funds, or securities, or substantially equivalent activity however denominated by the laws of the relevant foreign government

So, if the misdemeanor involved deceit or leaving somebody feeling they'd been robbed, cheated, bilked, or otherwise mistreated in a financial sense, things ain't lookin' too good for this candidate. Probably going to be disqualified by statute, "statutorily disqualified."

The Act of 1934 talked about insider trading, warning investors not to pass around or use non-public information. The penalties were raised in 1988 with the so-called "Insider Trading Act of 1988." Because of this legislation, any person who uses inside information can be penalized under the Securities Exchange Act of 1934 up to three times the amount of the profit made or loss avoided. For "controlling persons" overseeing an inside trader, the penalty can go up to $1 million. Plus, the Justice Department might make a criminal case out of it.

How would anybody catch you? The SEC can pay bounties up to 10% of whatever they extract from the people stupid enough to both use inside information and get caught.

Many securities are exempt (excused) from having to register under the Securities Act of 1933. For example, T-bonds and bank securities don't have to register. Neither do church securities. A few Sundays ago I actually picked up an offering circular for some church bonds on a back table. The first page of the offering circular declares:

```
The offer and sale of these securities have not been
registered with the Securities and Exchange Commission
. . . these securities have not been approved or disap-
proved by the Securities and Exchange Commission or
the securities authorities of any state, nor has the
Securities and Exchange Commission or any state secu-
```

rities authority passed upon the accuracy or adequacy
of this offering circular. Any representation to the
contrary is a criminal offense.

So, the fixed-rate and the adjustable-rate debt securities being offered by this religious organization did not have to be registered with the SEC or state regulators. Goody for them. They are still *securities*, which means that if anyone makes any material misstatement of fact or omits to state a necessary fact in connection with the offer, sale, or purchase of these (or *any*) securities, that would be fraudulent and altogether not a good idea. For example, if this offering circular overstates the cash this religious organization has in the bank in order to falsely raise my confidence in their ability to pay me back, that would be securities fraud. This offering circular has been distributed by the U.S. mail, and whether you're wearing a tight black leather jacket or a flowing, off-white satin robe, you can be busted for mail and securities fraud.

So, the exam might point out that while some securities are exempt from registration under the Securities Act of 1933, *all* securities are subject to the Securities Exchange Act of 1934's anti-fraud provisions. State law could also come down on anyone connected to the offer, sale, or purchase of any security, should that person decide to use deceptive, misleading, or fraudulent means.

The Securities Exchange Act of 1934 also gave the Federal Reserve Board the power to regulate margin. Reg T stipulates how much credit a broker-dealer can extend to a margin customer (50%); Reg U stipulates how much credit a bank can extend to a broker-dealer or public customer. Finally, proxies have to be sent to investors at the issuer's expense to enable shareholders to vote without having to attend the annual shareholder meeting in Keokuk, Iowa.

NASD

The NASD was granted the authority to act as the Self-Regulatory Organization for the OTC (over-the-counter) market with the passage of the Maloney Act of 1938, an amendment to the Securities Exchange Act of 1934. An easy way to remember this is that the Maloney Act of 1938 created the NASD as the SRO for the OTC.

The NASD is organized along four major bylaws:
- rules of fair practice
- uniform practice code
- code of procedure
- code of arbitration

The rules of fair practice describe how to deal with customers without getting the regulators all bent out of shape. Commissions, markups, recommendations, advertising, sales literature, etc., are covered here. These are often referred to as "member conduct rules." The uniform practice code is the code that keeps the practice uniform. Go figure. Settlement dates, delivery of securities, the establishment of the ex-date…all that stuff is covered here. The exam might refer to the uniform practice code as "promoting cooperative effort," which it does. Just keeping the broker-dealers in Boston on the same page as the broker-dealers in Austin. As we'll see a few pages later, violations of conduct rules are investigated and handled under Code of Procedure, while disputes among members (usually concerning money) are handled under Code of Arbitration.

NASD MEMBERSHIP

If your firm wants to join the NASD, they must:
- meet net capital requirements (must be solvent)
- have at least two principals to supervise the firm
- have an acceptable business plan detailing its proposed activities
- attend a pre-membership interview (sort of like Rush Week)

If your firm pledges the Nu Alpha Sigma Delta house, they must agree to:
- abide by the rules of the "Association"
- abide by all federal and state laws
- pay dues, fees, and membership assessments

What are these fees the firm must pay?
- Basic membership fee
- Fee for each rep and principal
- Fee based on gross income of the firm
- Fee for all branch offices

1000. Membership, Registration and Qualification Requirements

Since we had so much fun looking at actual MSRB rules in the Municipal Securities chapter, let's look at some actual NASD rules and definitions related to registration and qualification requirements. The "Commission" is shorthand for the SEC. The "Association" is shorthand for the NASD. Notice how the "Association" frequently uses the same phrase used by the MSRB, NYSE, and CBOE: *conduct inconsistent with just and equitable principles of trade.* That means the NASD expects member firms to conduct themselves in a manner that is fair and honest. If they do something inconsistent with that, they've probably broken a rule and will probably hear from the NASD at its earliest convenience. By the way, you can look at a copy of the NASD Manual by visiting www.nasd.com and we highly recommend doing that. You might even go so far as to read the 2000-numbered and 3000-numbered rules related to communications with the public and transactions with customers.

No, seriously.

First off, firms have to register, and they also have to register their representatives and principals. When they do so, the NASD reminds them not to file misleading information. Basically, it doesn't look good when you're lying before we've even let you into the club, so, as the NASD Manual says:

Filing of Misleading Information as to Membership or Registration

The filing with the Association of information with respect to membership or registration as a Registered Representative which is incomplete or inaccurate so as to be misleading, or which could in any way tend to mislead, or the failure to correct such filing after notice thereof, may be deemed to be conduct inconsistent with just and equitable principles of trade and when discovered may be sufficient cause for appropriate disciplinary action.

Comment: don't file misleading or incomplete applications, and if we're nice enough to point out your mistake, fix it.

Failure to Register Personnel

The failure of any member to register an employee, who should be so registered, as a Registered Representative may be deemed to be conduct inconsistent with just and equitable principles of trade and when discovered may be sufficient cause for appropriate disciplinary action.

Comment: register your representatives. That's why they're called "registered representatives."

Who "should be so registered"?

The NASD lays that out, too:

Definition of Representative

Persons associated with a member, including assistant officers other than principals, who are engaged in the investment banking or securities business for the member including the functions of supervision, solicitation or conduct of business in securities or who are engaged in

the training of persons associated with a member for any of these functions are designated as representatives.

There are different categories of "registered representative," too. A General Securities Representative has a Series 7 and can sell individual stocks, bonds, muni's,
options…generally just about anything. A person with a Series 6 is called a Limited
Representative–Investment Company and Variable Contracts Products. This allows
the individual to sell only mutual funds and variable contracts, plus something that
seldom gets mentioned: a Series 6 holder can also be part of an underwriting for a
closed-end fund. Just the underwriting, though, which is done through a prospectus.
Once they start trading in the secondary market between investors, they're just shares
of stock, and a Series 6 holder can't sell individual shares of stock. Everything they
sell has to come with a prospectus.

So, if you fit the definition of "representative," you have to be registered, as the
NASD indicates below:

All Representatives Must Be Registered
All persons engaged or to be engaged in the investment banking or
securities business of a member who are to function as representatives shall be registered as such with NASD in the category of registration appropriate to the function to be performed as specified in Rule
1032. Before their registration can become effective, they shall pass a
Qualification Examination for Representatives appropriate to the category
of registration as specified by the Board of Governors.

As you probably know, you are registered through a U-4 form, which asks a
bunch of personal questions about your educational and professional background. A
principal has to sign the application and certify that he/she has reviewed your information. Which is why it's not a good idea to use a fictional work history—they, like,
check up on that. Lots of representatives try to conceal their criminal records by, like,
forgetting to report them on the U-4. When the NASD finds out, they usually bar the
representative permanently from association with any member firm. If you decide to
leave your firm, a U-5 must be filled out and submitted to the NASD within 30 days.
You can't just transfer your registration from one firm to the next. The firm you're
leaving completes a U-5, and the firm that is hiring you completes a U-4. If the exam
uses the phrase "termination for cause," that means the registered rep gave the firm
a good reason to fire him. Good reasons to fire a registered representative include:
- Violating the firm's policies
- Violating the rules of the NYSE, NASD, SEC, or any other industry regulator

- Violating state or federal securities laws

If the registered representative is the subject of an investigation by any securities industry regulator, the firm cannot terminate the rep until the investigation is completed. Otherwise, a shady supervisor could say, "Oh, you're being investigated by the State of New York? No problem, we'll just terminate you for cause and make the whole thing go away."

Not.

After becoming a registered representative, you will also need to put in some time earning continuing education requirements. Let's see what the NASD has to say about that:

1120. Continuing Education Requirements

This Rule prescribes requirements regarding the continuing education of certain registered persons subsequent to their initial qualification and registration with NASD. The requirements shall consist of a Regulatory Element and a Firm Element as set forth below.

The Regulatory Element is described like so:

Each registered person shall complete the Regulatory Element on the occurrence of their second registration anniversary date and every three years thereafter, or as otherwise prescribed by NASD. On each occasion, the Regulatory Element must be completed within 120 days after the person's registration anniversary date.

What if you don't complete the Regulatory Element in that time frame?

(2) Failure to Complete

Unless otherwise determined by the Association, any registered persons who have not completed the Regulatory Element within the prescribed time frames will have their registrations deemed inactive until such time as the requirements of the program have been satisfied. Any person whose registration has been deemed inactive under this Rule shall cease all activities as a registered person and is prohibited from performing any duties and functioning in any capacity requiring registration.

The Firm Element is described like this by the NASD Manual:

(2) Standards for the Firm Element

(A) Each member must maintain a continuing and current education program for its covered registered persons to enhance their securities knowledge, skill, and professionalism. At a minimum, each member shall at least annually evaluate and prioritize its training needs and develop a written training plan.

Member firms need principals who review correspondence, approve every account, initial order tickets, handle written customer complaints, and make sure there's a procedural manual for the office to use. In other words, somebody at the firm is ultimately responsible for the business of the firm—that person is the principal.

The NASD says:

All Principals Must Be Registered

All persons engaged or to be engaged in the investment banking or securities business of a member who are to function as principals shall be registered as such with NASD in the category of registration appropriate to the function to be performed as specified in Rule 1022. Before their registration can become effective, they shall pass a Qualification Examination for Principals appropriate to the category of registration as specified by the Board of Governors.

Comment: those of you who have been asked to take the Series 24—that would make you one of these principal-type-people.

Here is how the NASD defines a principal:

Definition of Principal

Persons associated with a member who are actively engaged in the management of the member's investment banking or securities business, including supervision, solicitation, conduct of business or the training of persons associated with a member for any of these functions are designated as principals.

Comment: that one's pretty clear as is.

Also note that, in general, each member must have at least two principals taking care of the stuff that principals are supposed to take care of:

- New accounts
- Trades (transactions)
- Advertising
- Sales literature
- Correspondence
- And, making sure there is a written supervisory and procedural manual

Registration of Research Analysts

(a) All persons associated with a member who are to function as research analysts shall be registered with NASD.

Comment: a research analyst prepares and approves the research reports put together by the firm. You know all those "strong buy" or "market outperform" ratings and the accompanying reports that tell people whether to buy or back off a particular stock? Well, those are prepared by a research analyst. To become a research analyst you generally have to get the Series 7 and then pass another license exam specifically for research analysts (Series 86 and 87). Also note that a *supervisory analyst* has to approve all research reports.

Many people in my classes ask, "If I stop selling for a while, can I just park my license at the firm until I'm ready to use it again?"

Here is how the NASD answers that:

No.

Actually, they go into more detail:

> A member shall not maintain a representative registration with NASD for any person (1) who is no longer active in the member's investment banking or securities business, (2) who is no longer functioning as a representative, or (3) where the sole purpose is to avoid the examination requirement prescribed in paragraph (c).

Comment: if you're out for two years or more, you have to take this exam again, so (3) is saying that your firm had better not pretend you're associated just so you can skip the Series 7 requirement.

A broker-dealer also could not sponsor someone for the Series 7 exam just so the person could sit for the test. As the rules say:

> A member shall not make application for the registration of any person as representative where there is no intent to employ such person in the member's investment banking or securities business.

Many of my students remind me during the class, "But, Bob, I'm not actually going to be selling." To which the NASD says, "Close enough." An "assistant representative" will also have to get a license, because of the following:

All Assistant Representatives—Order Processing Must Be Registered

All persons associated with a member who are to function as Assistant Representatives—Order Processing shall be registered with the Association. Before their registrations can become effective, they shall pass a Qualification Examination for Assistant Representatives—Order Processing as specified by the Board of Governors.

(b) Definition of Assistant Representative—Order Processing

Persons associated with a member who accept unsolicited customer orders for submission for execution by the member are designated as Assistant Representatives—Order Processing.

Of course, not everybody has to register. The following have been granted exemptions from the painful process you're undergoing right now:

Persons Exempt from Registration

(a) The following persons associated with a member are not required to be registered with the Association:

(1) persons associated with a member whose functions are solely and exclusively clerical or ministerial;

(2) persons associated with a member who are not actively engaged in the investment banking or securities business;

(3) persons associated with a member whose functions are related solely and exclusively to the member's need for nominal corporate officers or for capital participation; and

(4) persons associated with a member whose functions are related solely and exclusively to:

(A) effecting transactions on the floor of a national securities exchange and who are registered as floor members with such exchange;

(B) transactions in municipal securities;

(C) transactions in commodities; or

(D) transactions in security futures, provided that any such person is registered with a registered futures association.

Comment: if you're just doing filing/temp work, you're not involved with underwriting or trading securities, you're just sitting on the board for a golfin' buddy, or you're a member of a futures or stock exchange filling orders for the firm, you don't have to register as a "registered representative."

Oh well. I guess we didn't find an exemption for you anywhere above, so you can keep on reading this material and keep that appointment at the testing center. By the way, were you thinking of selling securities as sort of a "part-time job"? Maybe so, but your firm still has to know what you're up to outside the firm. As the NASD makes clear:

> No person associated with a member in any registered capacity shall be employed by, or accept compensation from, any other person as a result of any business activity, other than a passive investment, outside the scope of his relationship with his employer firm, unless he has provided prompt written notice to the member. Such notice shall be in the form required by the member.

So, whenever you have a chance to make money outside the firm, remember to notify the firm in writing. A "passive investment" is not the same thing as working, so if the question talks about a registered representative buying a limited partnership interest (DPP), remember that that's different.

The NASD makes sure that principals are actually supervising registered representatives. The member firm has to establish and maintain written procedures to supervise the various types of business it's engaged in and has to supervise the activities of registered representatives. They must also designate a principal responsible for supervising each type of business in which the firm engages, and they must designate an "OSJ" (Office of Supervisory Jurisdiction), which is pretty much an office with, like, supervisory jurisdiction.

The firm has to perform internal inspections, and I'll just let the NASD explain this one:

> Each member shall conduct a review, at least annually, of the businesses in which it engages, which review shall be reasonably designed to assist in detecting and preventing violations of and achieving compliance with applicable securities laws and regulations, and with the Rules of this Association. Each member shall review the activities of each office, which shall include the periodic examination of customer accounts to detect and prevent irregularities or abuses and at least an annual inspection of each office of supervisory jurisdiction. Each branch office of the

member shall be inspected according to a cycle which shall be set forth in the firm's written supervisory and inspection procedures.

Without getting bogged down in the amazing amount of verbiage used by the NASD, this is how they define office of supervisory jurisdiction (OSJ) and branch office:

- Branch office: any location identified by any means to the public or customers as a location at which the member conducts an investment banking or securities business
- OSJ: "Office of Supervisory Jurisdiction" means any office of a member at which any one or more of the following functions take place:

(A) order execution and/or market making;

(B) structuring of public offerings or private placements;

(C) maintaining custody of customers' funds and/or securities;

(D) final acceptance (approval) of new accounts on behalf of the member;

(E) review and endorsement of customer orders;

(F) final approval of advertising or sales literature for use by persons associated with the member;

(G) responsibility for supervising the activities of persons associated with the member at one or more other branch offices of the member.

Some individuals become upset when they discover that my practice questions can only mimic the actual exam—I didn't actually pay a fraternity brother to, like, steal an old exam for me. How serious is the NASD about protecting the surprise element in their exams? Let's see:

NASD considers all of its Qualification Examinations to be highly confidential. The removal from an examination center, reproduction, disclosure, receipt from or passing to any person, or use for study purposes of any portion of such Qualification Examination, whether of a present or past series, or any other use which would compromise the effectiveness of the Examinations and the use in any manner and at any time of the questions or answers to the Examinations are prohibited and are deemed to be a violation of Rule 2110.

Since that's the case, I decided to start a side business whereby I would text message my customers at the testing center for $100 per correct answer (no fee for incorrect answers). Unfortunately, the NASD says:

> An applicant cannot receive assistance while taking the examination. Each applicant shall certify to the Board that no assistance was given to or received by him during the examination.

What I'm doing right now is copying and pasting key sections of the NASD Manual, which you can see for yourself at www.nasd.com. Don't worry, I got their permission first and, not surprisingly, they're glad to have me show you the real thing in preparation for your exam. This manual makes it very clear to member firms and their associated persons that the NASD has plenty of power to enforce the conduct rules. They have the power to make you or your firm produce documents or testify under oath, and they have the power to inspect the firm and make copies of "books, records, and accounts of such member or person with respect to any matter involved in the investigation, complaint, examination, or proceeding." Failure to comply with a request for documents or testimony, or refusing to admit an inspection is a violation all by itself, sort of like refusing to take a breathalyzer.

After the NASD reviews the evidence, they may decide that the firm or the registered rep has violated the conduct rules. What can they do about it?

A lot.

The sanctions include:

> (1) censure a member or person associated with a member;

> (2) impose a fine upon a member or person associated with a member;

> (3) suspend the membership of a member or suspend the registration of a person associated with a member for a definite period or a period contingent on the performance of a particular act;

> (4) expel a member, cancel the membership of a member, or revoke or cancel the registration of a person associated with a member;

> (5) suspend or bar a member or person associated with a member from association with all members;

> (6) impose a temporary or permanent cease and desist order against a member or a person associated with a member; or

> (7) impose any other fitting sanction.

I don't think public caning is considered a "fitting sanction," but I'd still keep my churning in check if I were you.

So, if an agent/registered representative is suspended, what does that actually mean? Luckily, the NASD is happy to explain:

> If the Association (NASD) or the Commission (SEC) issues an order that imposes a suspension, revocation, or cancellation of the registration of a person associated with a member or bars a person from further association with any member, a member shall not allow such person to remain associated with it in any capacity, including a clerical or ministerial capacity.

But, surely, even if you did get suspended from the firm, it would be a paid suspension, right?

Well, let's see how the NASD answers that:

> If the Association or the Commission suspends a person associated with a member, the member also shall not pay or credit any salary, or any commission, profit, or other remuneration that results directly or indirectly from any securities transaction, that the person associated with a member might have earned during the period of suspension.

Hmm. That looks pretty much like a "no."

Do you suppose the NASD would, like, tell on a suspended rep or firm to anyone else?

Absolutely. Willingly. Happily. "In response to a written inquiry, electronic inquiry, or telephonic inquiry via a toll-free telephone listing, the Association shall release certain information contained in the Central Registration Depository regarding a current or former member, an associated person, or a person who was associated with a member within the preceding two years, through the Public Disclosure Program." The type of information released includes your employment history, current licenses held, any proceeding you're currently involved in, any past disciplinary action against you, and even any monetary awards you had to pay through arbitration, which will be discussed later.

Wow. These guys seem to have a lot of power over your career, huh?

But—rest assured—you have to go pretty far out of your way to get in trouble. Just don't lie, cheat, steal, or get excessively lazy, and you'll probably be all right.

Many students in class seem to think that if the NASD slaps a fine on them, they'll just refuse to pay. The NASD says they'll give you written notice that you, like, owe them. After seven days, if you don't pay, they can summarily revoke your license, which would make it that much tougher to pay your fine. For a firm that won't pay, they use the words "summarily suspend or expel." For registered reps, the phrase is "summarily revoke." If I were more curious, I'd look into that, but I'm not, so I haven't.

Oh yeah, and after you go through the painful ordeal of a hearing and a stiff fine, the NASD can even make you pay for some or all of the costs of the ordeal. As the manual says, "A member or person associated with a member disciplined pursuant to Rule 8310 shall bear such costs of the proceeding as the Adjudicator deems fair and appropriate under the circumstances."

The word "Adjudicator" means the person given power by the NASD to preside over a proceeding against a member or associated person. Could be an individual (natural person) or a group (committee, board, etc.). Notice how there's a "jud" in the word "adjudicator," and relate it to the word "judge."

As if you don't have enough on your mind at this point.

So, let's look in detail at all the conduct rules the Series 7 will likely expect you to know for your exam. Don't memorize the rule numbers, but definitely know what the rules allow and don't allow. The NASD Rules numbered in the 2000s are entitled "Business Conduct." When you pledge the Nu Alpha Sigma Delta house, you need to observe high standards. Rule 2110 is the most central to all of the rules for member firms:

2110. Standards of Commercial Honor and Principles of Trade

A member, in the conduct of his business, shall observe high standards of commercial honor and just and equitable principles of trade.

Often other rules will state something like, "doing such and such would be considered conduct inconsistent with high standards of commercial honor and just and equitable principles of trade and a violation of Rule 2110." For example, not paying an arbitration award would be a violation of the basic NASD Rule 2110. So would:

IM-2110-2. Trading Ahead of Customer Limit Order

If you enjoyed those limit orders we examined in "Trading Securities," you'll recall that a customer might want to buy 1,000 shares of Oracle @ $15. When the customer enters that order, maybe the firm is trading for its own account in Oracle, too. So, they have the customer order to buy 1,000 shares of Oracle @15 and when they see that the ASK is $15 and the size is (10) or 10 round lots, they go ahead and buy the stock...for their own trading account.

What about the customer who wanted to buy the stock at that price?

Screw him, the guy's a jerk, right?

Wrong. This NASD rule states:

> . . . will require members to handle their customer limit orders with all due care so that members do not "trade ahead" of those limit orders. Thus, members that handle customer limit orders, whether received from their own customers or from another member, are prohibited from trading at prices equal or superior to that of the limit order without executing the limit order.

Then there is further clarification of that with the following:

> A member firm that accepts and holds an unexecuted limit order from its customer (whether its own customer or a customer of another member) in a Nasdaq or exchange-listed security and that continues to trade the subject security for its own account at prices that would satisfy the customer's limit order, without executing that limit order, shall be deemed to have acted in a manner inconsistent with just and equitable principles of trade, in violation of Rule 2110

When you're about to place some huge freakin' customer order to buy a bazillion shares of Google, you can pretty well guess that the price is about to go up. So, why not buy some Google for yourself, your firm, your wife, heck why not the nice-looking lady down the street with the fire-red Porsche while you're at it?

Not. That's called front-running, or taking advantage of an order you're about to place by buying some of the stock for yourself first. As the NASD states:

IM-2110-3. Front Running Policy

> It shall be considered conduct inconsistent with just and equitable principles of trade for a member or person associated with a member, for an account in which such member or person associated with a member has an interest, for an account with respect to which such member or person associated with a member exercises investment discretion, or for certain customer accounts, to cause to be executed:
>
> (a) an order to buy or sell an option or a security future when such member or person associated with a member causing such order to be executed has material, non-public market information concerning an imminent block transaction in the underlying security, or when a customer

has been provided such material, non-public market information by the member or any person associated with a member; or

(b) an order to buy or sell an underlying security when such member or person associated with a member causing such order to be executed has material, non-public market information concerning an imminent block transaction in an option or a security future overlying that security, or when a customer has been provided such material, non-public market information by the member or any person associated with a member; prior to the time information concerning the block transaction has been made publicly available.

How do we know if the order is a "block transaction"? Luckily, the rule defines that as:

A transaction involving 10,000 shares or more of an underlying security, or options or security futures covering such number of shares is generally deemed to be a block transaction, although a transaction of less than 10,000 shares could be considered a block transaction in appropriate cases.

If you're a big Wall Street broker-dealer the research reports your analysts put out encouraging folks to buy or sell a particular security can have a huge impact on the price of the stock. So, if your research department is about to issue a "strong buy" recommendation and a glowing report on Google tomorrow morning, why not buy a boatload of Google shares today, and then release the report tomorrow? Won't that be fun? Your customers will want to buy the stock tomorrow at higher and higher prices and, heck, you'll be right here to sell it to them, at higher and higher prices.

As the NASD states:

IM-2110-4. Trading Ahead of Research Reports

The Board of Governors, under its statutory obligation to protect investors and enhance market quality, is issuing an interpretation to the Rules regarding a member firm's trading activities that occur in anticipation of a firm's issuance of a research report regarding a security. The Board of Governors is concerned with activities of member firms that purposefully establish or adjust the firm's inventory position in Nasdaq-listed securities, an exchange-listed security traded in the OTC market, or a derivative security based primarily on a specific Nasdaq or exchange-listed security in anticipation of the issuance of a research report in that same security. For example, a firm's research department may prepare a research report recommending the purchase of a particular Nasdaq-listed security. Prior to the publication and dissemination of the report, however, the trading department of the member firm might purposefully accumulate a position in that security to meet anticipated customer demand for that security. After the firm had established its position, the firm would issue the report, and thereafter fill customer orders from the member firm's inventory positions.

The Association believes that such activity is conduct which is inconsistent with just and equitable principles of trade, and not in the best interests of the investors. Thus, this interpretation prohibits a member from purposefully establishing, creating or changing the firm's inventory position in a Nasdaq-listed security, an exchange-listed security traded in the third market, or a derivative security related to the underlying equity security, in anticipation of the issuance of a research report regarding such security by the member firm.

See? These regulators take all the fun out of the business.

We saw that firms can't trade ahead of their customer limit orders, and it's basically the same deal with customer market orders.

2111. Trading Ahead of Customer Market Orders

(a) A member must make every effort to execute a customer market order that it receives fully and promptly.

(b) A member that accepts and holds a market order of its own customer or a customer of another broker-dealer in a Nasdaq or exchange-listed security without immediately executing the order is prohibited from trading that security on the same side of the market for its own account, unless it immediately thereafter executes the customer market order up to the size and at the same price at which it traded for its own account or at a better price.

This next NASD Rule is shocking in its draconian reach:

2120. Use of Manipulative, Deceptive or Other Fraudulent Devices

No member shall effect any transaction in, or induce the purchase or sale of, any security by means of any manipulative, deceptive or other fraudulent device or contrivance.

So, apparently, the NASD is in full agreement with that whole anti-fraud stuff in the Securities Exchange Act of 1934.

2210. Communications with the Public

The first part of this rule defines "sales literature," "advertising," "correspondence," etc., but before we distinguish the various types of communications, let's understand the main points:

- A principal (compliance officer) has to approve the firm's communications and file them.
- The communications had better not be misleading in any way, shape or form.

(1) Standards Applicable to All Communications with the Public

(A) All member communications with the public shall be based on principles of fair dealing and good faith, must be fair and balanced, and must provide a sound basis for evaluating the facts in regard to any particular security or type of security, industry, or service. No member may omit any material fact or qualification if the omission, in the light of the context of the material presented, would cause the communications to be misleading.

(B) No member may make any false, exaggerated, unwarranted or misleading statement or claim in any communication with the public. No member may publish, circulate or distribute any public communication that the member knows or has reason to know contains any untrue statement of a material fact or is otherwise false or misleading.

(C) Information may be placed in a legend or footnote only in the event that such placement would not inhibit an investor's understanding of the communication.

(D) Communications with the public may not predict or project performance, imply that past performance will recur or make any exaggerated or unwarranted claim, opinion or forecast. A hypothetical illustration of mathematical principles is permitted, provided that it does not predict or project the performance of an investment or investment strategy.

(E) If any testimonial in a communication with the public concerns a technical aspect of investing, the person making the testimonial must have the knowledge and experience to form a valid opinion.

Okay. Seems fair enough—don't mislead your clients with a bunch of misleading communications. The exam may also want you to know the different types of communication. Understand that all communications have to be at least monitored by the firm, but that your correspondence with customers would only have to be monitored, while the advertising and sales literature produced at the firm would have to be approved before it went out. Either way, the communications had better not be misleading.

But, let's just let the NASD define their own terms at this point:

(a) Definitions

For purposes of this Rule and any interpretation thereof, "communications with the public" consist of:

(1) "Advertisement." Any material, other than an independently prepared reprint and institutional sales material, that is published, or used in any electronic or other public media, including any Web site, newspaper, magazine or other periodical, radio, television, telephone or tape recording, videotape display, signs or billboards, motion pictures, or telephone directories (other than routine listings).

(2) "Sales Literature." Any written or electronic communication, other than an advertisement, independently prepared reprint, institutional sales material and correspondence, that is generally distributed or made generally available to customers or the public, including circulars, research reports, market letters, performance reports or summaries, form letters, telemarketing scripts, seminar texts, reprints (that are not independently prepared reprints) or excerpts of any other advertisement, sales literature or published article, and press releases concerning a member's products or services.

(3) "Correspondence" consists of any written letter or electronic mail message distributed by a member to:

(A) one or more of its existing retail customers; and

(B) fewer than 25 prospective retail customers within any 30 calendar-day period.

(4) "Institutional Sales Material" consists of any communication that is distributed or made available only to a:

(A) governmental entity or subdivision thereof;

(B) employee benefit plan that meets the requirements of Section 403(b) or Section 457 of the Internal Revenue Code and has at least 100 participants, but does not include any participant of such a plan;

(C) qualified plan, as defined in Section 3(a)(12)(C) of the Act, that has at least 100 participants, but does not include any participant of such a plan;

(D) NASD member or registered associated person of such a member; and

(E) person acting solely on behalf of any such institutional investor.

(5) "Public Appearance." Participation in a seminar, forum (including an interactive electronic forum), radio or television interview, or other public appearance or public speaking activity.

(6) "Independently Prepared Reprint."

(A) Any reprint or excerpt of any article issued by a publisher, provided that:

(i) the publisher is not an affiliate of the member using the reprint or any underwriter or issuer of a security mentioned in the reprint or excerpt and that the member is promoting;

(ii) neither the member using the reprint or excerpt nor any underwriter or issuer of a security mentioned in the reprint or excerpt has commissioned the reprinted or excerpted article; and

(iii) the member using the reprint or excerpt has not materially altered its contents except as necessary to make the reprint or excerpt consistent with applicable regulatory standards or to correct factual errors;

If you read all that exciting text closely, you noted that a letter or email to fewer than 25 prospects is considered "correspondence," what the test might call "group correspondence." But if the number is 25 or more, now it's "sales literature." Why would it matter? Sales literature has to be pre-approved. And, if it concerns investment companies, sales literature and advertising have to be filed with the NASD within 10 days of first use. A new firm would actually pre-file that stuff for the first year, in case the exam has absolutely lost its mind and expects everyone to be the Rain Man coming in.

1) Date of First Use and Approval Information
The member must provide with each filing under this paragraph the ac-

tual or anticipated date of first use, the name and title of the registered principal who approved the advertisement or sales literature, and the date that the approval was given.

This is also self-explanatory:

(7) Spot-Check Procedures

In addition to the foregoing requirements, each member's written and electronic communications with the public may be subject to a spot-check procedure. Upon written request from the Department, each member must submit the material requested in a spot-check procedure within the time frame specified by the Department.

As is this:

(2) Record-keeping

(A) Members must maintain all advertisements, sales literature, and independently prepared reprints in a separate file for a period of three years from the date of last use. The file must include the name of the registered principal who approved each advertisement, item of sales literature, and independently prepared reprint and the date that approval was given.

(B) Members must maintain in a file information concerning the source of any statistical table, chart, graph or other illustration used by the member in communications with the public.

Okay, enough of NASD Rule 2210.

We've seen that corporate stock, corporate bonds and municipal bonds settle "T + 3," and that the broker-dealer has to deliver a trade confirmation by settlement, or what the passage below calls "completion of each transaction." Here it is in the original legalese:

2230. Confirmations

A member at or before the completion of each transaction with a customer shall give or send to such customer written notification disclosing (a) whether such member is acting as a broker for such customer, as a dealer for his own account, as a broker for some other person, or as a broker for both such customer and some other person; and (b) in any case in which such member is acting as a broker for such customer or for both such customer and some other person, either the name of the person from whom the security was purchased or to whom it was sold for such customer and the date and time when such transaction took place or the fact that such information will be furnished upon the request of such customer, and the source and amount of any commission or other remuneration received or to be received by such member in connection with the transaction.

This next one doesn't seem to require much explanation, so let's enjoy it in its original state:

2240. Disclosure of Control Relationship with Issuer

A member controlled by, controlling, or under common control with, the issuer of any security, shall, before entering into any contract with or for a customer for the purchase or sale of such security, disclose to such customer the existence of such control, and if such disclosure is not made in writing, it shall be supplemented by the giving or sending of written disclosure at or before the completion of the transaction.

My online broker holds my securities in "street name," which means in the name of their clearing company. I am the beneficial owner. Therefore, when the companies whose stock I own send out proxy materials and annual reports, my broker has to forward them to me, as we see below:

2260. Forwarding of Proxy and Other Materials

(a) A member has an inherent duty to forward promptly certain information regarding a security to the beneficial owner (or the beneficial owner's designated investment adviser) if the member carries the account in which the security is held for the beneficial owner and the security is registered in a name other than the name of the beneficial owner.

This next rule seems to make perfect sense to me—if the member firm is holding my cash and securities, maybe I'd like to see how their financial condition is looking.

2270. Disclosure of Financial Condition to Customers

(a) A member shall make available to inspection by any bona fide regular customer, upon request, the information relative to such member's financial condition as disclosed in its most recent balance sheet prepared either in accordance with such member's usual practice or as required by any state or federal securities laws, or any rule or regulation thereunder.

(b) As used in paragraph (a) of this Rule, the term "customer" means any person who, in the regular course of such member's business, has cash or securities in the possession of such member.

There is a big difference between an unsolicited order and an investment that your client makes based on one of your recommendations. If you're recommending an investment, you have to make sure that the investment is suitable for the client, based on her time horizon, investment objectives, risk tolerance, etc. This next rule is perfectly clear as is:

2310. Recommendations to Customers (Suitability)

(a) In recommending to a customer the purchase, sale or exchange of any security, a member shall have reasonable grounds for believing that the recommendation is suitable for such customer upon the basis of the facts, if any, disclosed by such customer as to his other security holdings and as to his financial situation and needs.

(b) Prior to the execution of a transaction recommended to a non-institutional customer, other than transactions with customers where investments are limited to money market mutual funds, a member shall make reasonable efforts to obtain information concerning:

(1) the customer's financial status;

(2) the customer's tax status;

(3) the customer's investment objectives; and

(4) such other information used or considered to be reasonable by such member or registered representative in making recommendations to the customer.

Notice a few things above. First, you base your recommendations on "the facts, if any, disclosed by such customer." That means if your client discloses assets of $300,000, then that is the number you're working with, even if everyone at the corner tavern swears she's worth five million easy. Also note that they used the words "non-institutional customer," which would be an individual, not a bank, trust department, mutual fund, insurance company, etc. These are the folks who need your recommendations, and the NASD needs you to know why you're recommending this particular investment to this particular client. Notice also that if the "investments are limited to money market mutual funds," you don't really need the customer's financial picture. The money market funds will just be a safe holding place to generate whatever short-term interest rates happen to be at the time until the investor decides what to do with her cash.

The NASD is, again, very clear in the rule below:

IM-2310-2. Fair Dealing with Customers

(a)(1) Implicit in all member and registered representative relationships with customers and others is the fundamental responsibility for fair dealing. Sales efforts must therefore be undertaken only on a basis that can be judged as being within the ethical standards of the Association's Rules, with particular emphasis on the requirement to deal fairly with the public.

(2) This does not mean that legitimate sales efforts in the securities business are to be discouraged by requirements which do not take into account the variety of circumstances which can enter into the member-customer relationship. It does mean, however, that <u>sales efforts must be judged on the basis of whether they can be reasonably said to represent fair treatment for the persons to whom the sales efforts are directed, rather than on the argument that they result in profits to customers.</u>

The part I underlined often shocks some of my students—hey, they say, as long as the guy makes money, why not? Well, the NASD takes the radical view that your sales efforts be judged on whether they represent fair treatment to your customers, so we'll work with that notion, shall we?

The NASD really gets hot with this next series of examples of how you can end up being unfair to your customer and, therefore, without a license.

(1) Recommending Speculative Low-Priced Securities
Recommending speculative low-priced securities to customers without knowledge of or attempt to obtain information concerning the customers' other securities holdings, their financial situation and other necessary data. The principle here is that this practice, by its very nature, involves a high probability that the recommendation will not be suitable for at least some of the persons solicited. This has particular application to high pressure telephone sales campaigns.

(2) Excessive Trading Activity
Excessive activity in a customer's account, often referred to as "churning" or "overtrading." There are no specific standards to measure excessive-

ness of activity in customer accounts because this must be related to the objectives and financial situation of the customer involved.

(3) Trading in Mutual Fund Shares

Trading in mutual fund shares, particularly on a short-term basis. It is clear that normally these securities are not proper trading vehicles and such activity on its face may raise the question of Rule violation.

(4) Fraudulent Activity

(A) Numerous instances of fraudulent conduct have been acted upon by the Association and have resulted in penalties against members. Among some of these activities are:

(i) Fictitious Accounts

Establishment of fictitious accounts in order to execute transactions which otherwise would be prohibited, such as the purchase of hot issues, or to disguise transactions which are against firm policy.

(ii) Discretionary Accounts

Transactions in discretionary accounts in excess of or without actual authority from customers.

(iii) Unauthorized Transactions

Causing the execution of transactions which are unauthorized by customers or the sending of confirmations in order to cause customers to accept transactions not actually agreed upon.

(iv) Misuse of Customers' Funds or Securities

Unauthorized use or borrowing of customers' funds or securities.

(B) In addition, other fraudulent activities, such as forgery, non-disclosure or misstatement of material facts, manipulations and various deceptions, have been found in violation of Association Rules. These same activities are also subject to the civil and criminal laws and sanctions of federal and state governments.

(5) Recommending Purchases Beyond Customer Capability

Recommending the purchase of securities or the continuing purchase of securities in amounts which are inconsistent with the reasonable expectation that the customer has the financial ability to meet such a commitment.

Believe it or not, the regulators feel that broker-dealers should get their customers the best possible price when they buy and when they sell. As the NASD explains:

2320. Best Execution and Interpositioning

(a) In any transaction for or with a customer, a member and persons associated with a member shall use reasonable diligence to ascertain the best inter-dealer market for the subject security and buy or sell in such market so that the resultant price to the customer is as favorable as possible under prevailing market conditions. Among the factors that will be considered in determining whether a member has used "reasonable diligence" are:

(1) The character of the market for the security, e.g., price, volatility, relative liquidity, and pressure on available communications;

(2) the size and type of transaction;

(3) the number of primary markets checked;

(4) location and accessibility to the customer's broker/dealer of primary markets and quotations sources.

This is why a very likely Series 7 question would have you answer that a customer order to buy should be filled at the lowest ask/offer price possible and a customer order to sell should be filled at the highest bid price possible at the time.

The violation called "interpositioning" has to do with unnecessarily inserting yourself into a transaction. As the NASD explains:

(b) In any transaction for or with a customer, no member or person associated with a member shall interject a third party between the member and the best available market except in cases where the member can demonstrate that to his knowledge at the time of the transaction the total cost or proceeds of the transaction, as confirmed to the member acting for or with the customer, was better than the prevailing inter-dealer market for the security. A member's obligations to his customer are generally not fulfilled when he channels transactions through another broker/dealer or some person in a similar position, unless he can show that by so doing he reduced the costs of the transactions to the customer.

The member firm needs to be careful what they do with the securities they're holding for their customers:

2330. Customers' Securities or Funds

c) Authorization to Lend
No member shall lend, either to himself or to others, securities carried for the account of any customer, which are eligible to be pledged or loaned unless such member shall first have obtained from the customer a written authorization permitting the lending of securities thus carried by such member.

Remember how short sellers borrow securities? That's partly what the above is talking about—get the loan consent form signed before you go loaning your customers' securities, okay?

The firm needs to keep their assets separate from the assets that clearly belong to the customer, as we see in the next item within Rule 2330:

d) Segregation and Identification of Securities
No member shall hold securities carried for the account of any customer which have been fully paid for or which are excess margin securities unless such securities are segregated and identified by a method which clearly indicates the interest of such customer in those securities.

In case the exam wants to play really rough concerning the segregation of customer securities, let's throw the following clarification into the mix:

Rule 2330(d) requires members to segregate and identify by customers both fully paid and "excess margin" securities. With regard to a customer's account which contains only stocks, it is general practice for firms to segregate that portion of the stocks having a market value in excess of 140% of the debit balance therein.

So, if the "Dr" or "debit register" in a margin account is $5,000, 140% of that would be $7,000, and anything above that would be considered "excess margin" securities.

As you already know, you and your firm do not guarantee customers against losses, nor could you afford to.

(e) Prohibition Against Guarantees
No member or person associated with a member shall guarantee a customer against loss in connection with any securities transaction or in any securities account of such customer.

Can you share or "go halvsies" with your clients? Let's see what the NASD thinks about "sharing" with customers:

> (f) Sharing in Accounts; Extent Permissible
>
> (1)(A) Except as provided in paragraph (f)(2) no member or person associated with a member shall share directly or indirectly in the profits or losses in any account of a customer carried by the member or any other member; provided, however, that a member or person associated with a member may share in the profits or losses in such an account if (i) such person associated with a member obtains prior written authorization from the member employing the associated person; (ii) such member or person associated with a member obtains prior written authorization from the customer; and (iii) such member or person associated with a member shares in the profits or losses in any account of such customer only in direct proportion to the financial contributions made to such account by either the member or person associated with a member.

And then, just to keep things nice and simple, the NASD says, "Well, that whole proportionate sharing thing doesn't *always* apply," as we see right after the above otherwise clear passage:

> (B) Exempt from the direct proportionate share limitation of paragraph (f)(1)(A)(iii) are accounts of the immediate family of such member or person associated with a member. For purposes of this Rule, the term "immediate family" shall include parents, mother-in-law or father-in-law, husband or wife, children or any relative to whose support the member or person associated with a member otherwise contributes directly or indirectly.

I would bank on a question about sharing with your mother-in-law who is also your customer.

Rule 2340 "Customer Account Statements" says that the firm must send account statements to clients no less frequently than every quarter. However, it is almost always going to be at least once per month, because if there has been any "account activity," the statement has to go out monthly. As we see from their definition of "account activity," it's pretty tough to imagine an account without any of that over the period of one month:

> (c) Definitions

For purposes of this Rule, the following terms will have the stated
meanings:
(1) "account activity" includes, but is not limited to, purchases, sales,
interest credits or debits, charges or credits, dividend payments, transfer
activity, securities receipts or deliveries, and/or journal entries relating
to securities or funds in the possession or control of the member.

Even if you're not trading every month, chances are you receive an interest
payment or dividend. If you're in a margin account, there will be interest debited to
your account, so account statements will always be sent monthly except when they're
sent quarterly. What, exactly, is an "account statement"? The NASD defines it as:

[an account statement is a document]. . . containing a description of
any securities positions, money balances, or account activity to each
customer whose account had a security position, money balance, or
account activity during the period since the last such statement was
sent to the customer.

As we know, margin trading is just a little high-risk, so lots of disclosure is, naturally, required:

2341. Margin Disclosure Statement

(a) No member shall open a margin account, as specified in Regulation
T of the Board of Governors of the Federal Reserve System, for or on
behalf of a non-institutional customer, unless, prior to or at the time
of opening the account, the member has furnished to the customer,
individually, in writing or electronically, and in a separate document,
the margin disclosure statement specified in this paragraph (a). In addition, any member that permits non-institutional customers either to
open accounts on-line or to engage in transactions in securities on-line
must post such margin disclosure statement on the member's Web site
in a clear and conspicuous manner.

2350. Broker/Dealer Conduct on the Premises of Financial Institutions

Rule 2350 has to do with broker-dealers operating on the premises of a bank,
which is pretty wild, if you think about it. Kind of like going to the local pharmacy
and finding a hash bar operating on Aisle 5, just past the anti-inflammatories. I mean,

sure, it all fits under the heading of "drugs," I guess, but one type is tightly regulated while the other is just, you know, partying.

Anyway, bank deposits are guaranteed by the FDIC. Banks are very safe, which is why we have phrases such as, "it's money in the bank," or, "you can bank on it." Stocks and bonds are associated with the word "broker," and that is probably not just a coincidence. In any case, the NASD is just a little nervous about bank customers not understanding that they have wandered far from the umbilical safety of FDIC-insured deposits when they visit the friendly broker-dealer up on the 11th floor:

(c) Standards for Member Conduct

No member shall conduct broker/dealer services on the premises of a financial institution where retail deposits are taken unless the member complies initially and continuously with the following requirements:

(1) Setting

Wherever practical, the member's broker/dealer services shall be conducted in a physical location distinct from the area in which the financial institution's retail deposits are taken. In all situations, members shall identify the member's broker/dealer services in a manner that is clearly distinguished from the financial institution's retail deposit-taking activities. The member's name shall be clearly displayed in the area in which the member conducts its broker/dealer services.

(2) Networking and Brokerage Affiliate Agreements

Networking and brokerage affiliate arrangements between a member and a financial institution must be governed by a written agreement that sets forth the responsibilities of the parties and the compensation arrangements. The member must ensure that the agreement stipulates that supervisory personnel of the member and representatives of the Securities and Exchange Commission and the Association will be permitted access to the financial institution's premises where the member conducts broker/dealer services in order to inspect the books and records and other relevant information maintained by the member with respect to its broker/dealer services.

(3) Customer Disclosure and Written Acknowledgment

At or prior to the time that a customer account is opened by a member on the premises of a financial institution where retail deposits are taken, the member shall:

(A) disclose, orally and in writing, that the securities products purchased or sold in a transaction with the member:

(i) are not insured by the Federal Deposit Insurance Corporation ("FDIC");

(ii) are not deposits or other obligations of the financial institution and are not guaranteed by the financial institution; and

(iii) are subject to investment risks, including possible loss of the principal invested; and

(B) make reasonable efforts to obtain from each customer during the account opening process a written acknowledgment of receipt of the disclosures required by paragraph (c)(3)(A).

(4) Communications with the Public

(A) All member confirmations and account statements must indicate clearly that the broker/dealer services are provided by the member.

(B) Advertisements and sales literature that announce the location of a financial institution where broker/dealer services are provided by the member or that are distributed by the member on the premises of a financial institution must disclose that securities products: are not insured by the FDIC; are not deposits or other obligations of the financial institution and are not guaranteed by the financial institution; and are subject to investment risks, including possible loss of the principal invested. The shorter, logo format described in paragraph (c)(4)(C) may be used to provide these disclosures.

(C) The following shorter, logo format disclosures may be used by members in advertisements and sales literature, including material published, or designed for use, in radio or television broadcasts, Automated Teller Machine ("ATM") screens, billboards, signs, posters, and brochures, to comply with the requirements of paragraph (c)(4)(B), provided that such disclosures are displayed in a conspicuous manner:
—Not FDIC Insured
—No Bank Guarantee
—May Lose Value

The Series 7 will likely ask a few questions about borrowing from or lending to customers. Those words make the regulators a little nervous—I mean, how, exactly, does that registered representative define "borrowing" from a customer? Is this like an actual loan from a bank that happens to be his customer? Or, is this like a little old lady who seldom monitors her account and, therefore, probably won't even notice that the $50,000 was missing for a few weeks? We're talking, of course, about:

Rule 2370. Borrowing From or Lending to Customers

(a) No person associated with a member in any registered capacity may borrow money from or lend money to any customer of such person unless: (1) the member has written procedures allowing the borrowing and lending of money between such registered persons and customers of the member; and (2) the lending or borrowing arrangement meets one of the following conditions: (A) the customer is a member of such person's immediate family; (B) the customer is a financial institution regularly engaged in the business of providing credit, financing, or loans, or other entity or person that regularly arranges or extends credit in the ordinary course of business; (C) the customer and the registered person are both registered persons of the same member firm; (D) the lending arrangement is based on a personal relationship with the customer, such that the loan would not have been solicited, offered, or given had the customer and the associated person not maintained a relationship outside of the broker/customer relationship; or (E) the lending arrangement is based on a business relationship outside of the broker-customer relationship.

How do they define "immediate family" here? Quite broadly, actually:

(c) The term immediate family shall include parents, grandparents, mother-in-law or father-in-law, husband or wife, brother or sister, brother-in-law or sister-in-law, son-in-law or daughter-in-law, children, grandchildren, cousin, aunt or uncle, or niece or nephew, and shall also include any other person whom the registered person supports, directly or indirectly, to a material extent.

Being a member of the NASD is a big deal. Such a big deal that if somebody is *not* a member, your firm had better not extend any of the membership privileges to this mere civilian, as we see in Rule 2420:

2420. Dealing with Non-Members

(a) No member shall deal with any non-member broker or dealer except at the same prices, for the same commissions or fees, and on the same terms and conditions as are by such member accorded to the general public.

So, if you let me buy a mutual fund below the NAV, I would be forever grateful, but the NASD would be forever on your back.

We already mentioned that registered reps can receive continuing commissions in some cases. Let's see how the NASD explains this rather good piece of news:

IM-2420-2. Continuing Commissions Policy

The Board of Governors has held that the payment of continuing commissions in connection with the sale of securities is not improper so long as the person receiving the commissions remains a registered representative of a member of the Association.

However, payment of compensation to registered representatives after they cease to be employed by a member of the Association — or payment to their widows or other beneficiaries — will not be deemed in violation of Association Rules, provided bona fide contracts call for such payment.

Also, a dealer-member may enter into a bona fide contract with another dealer-member to take over and service his accounts and, after he ceases to be a member, to pay to him or to his widow or other beneficiary continuing commissions generated on such accounts.

An arrangement for the payment of continuing commissions shall not under any circumstances be deemed to permit the solicitation of new business or the opening of new accounts by persons who are not registered. Any arrangement for payment of continuing commissions must, of course, conform with any applicable laws or regulations.

Keep the charges reasonable between you and your customers, and keep the charges fair *among* your customers, as we see here:

2430. Charges for Services Performed

Charges, if any, for services performed, including miscellaneous services such as collection of moneys due for principal, dividends, or interest; exchange or transfer of securities; appraisals, safe-keeping or custody of securities, and other services, shall be reasonable and not unfairly discriminatory between customers.

Rule 2440 tells firms to give customers fair and reasonable prices when taking the other side of the transaction, and we looked at the 5% markup policy, with all the relevant factors, in the chapter on Trading Securities.

Rule 2510 covers discretionary accounts, which we covered when we were talking about—go figure—discretionary accounts. Just means that the firm needs to have the discretionary authorization in writing before executing the first transaction. The transactions need to be suitable and if, God forbid, you and your firm start executing excessive transactions just to enrich yourselves…well, you'd never do a thing like that or be dumb enough to get caught, right?

And, again, time/price are not a big deal. So, if I ask you to "buy 1,000 shares of a software company," that's a discretionary order. If I tell you to "buy 1,000 shares of Oracle today," that requires no special authorization. It's a "market not held" order, as we mentioned, where you or the floor broker down on the NYSE floor can wait until the time and the price are right before executing the transaction.

Rule 2711 is trying to clean up the abuses of the go-go 90's, where firms would issue "strong buy" reports on a particular stock, not because it was a good investment for their retail customers, but because the "strong buy" recommendation would help prop up the stock price long enough to let Bernie Ebbers of MCI WorldCom exercise his stock options for a nice $10 million profit. Then, since Bernie is pleased as punch, perhaps he'll use the firm's investment banking department for his next merger or additional offering of stock. See? Bernie's rich and happy, we're rich and happy, and the retail investors…well, as PT Barnum said, there's a sucker born ever minute.

From now on, investment banking can have no say over the compensation of a research analyst, who had better NOT be promoting a company's stock just to help land investment banking business or to pay some company bank after using the firm's investment bank. We'll actually see the same rule under NYSE rules, so let's save the excitement for a few pages in order to keep this page-turner humming along.

Speaking of the go-go 90's, as it turns out, there were two basic types of IPO's: the ones where people made millions of dollars in an afternoon as easily as shooting fish in a barrel, and those that the public actually got to buy. So, since the big players in the industry decided to pass out hot IPO's to their agents, their agents' wives, husbands, mothers-in-law, etc., the NASD has had to crack the whip. Reminds me of high school, when the whole school would lose weight room privileges because two or three knuckleheads thought it would be a good idea to set off an M-80 directly under the supine bench. In any case, there is almost no way for you or your immediate family to buy an IPO now, as we see from Rule 2790 below:

2790. Restrictions on the Purchase and Sale of Initial Equity Public Offerings

(a) General Prohibitions

(1) A member or a person associated with a member may not sell, or cause to be sold, a new issue to any account in which a restricted person has a beneficial interest, except as otherwise permitted herein.

(2) A member or a person associated with a member may not purchase a new issue in any account in which such member or person associated with a member has a beneficial interest, except as otherwise permitted herein.

b) Preconditions for Sale

Before selling a new issue to any account, a member must in good faith have obtained within the twelve months prior to such sale, a representation from:

(1) Beneficial Owners

the account holder(s), or a person authorized to represent the beneficial owners of the account, that the account is eligible to purchase new issues in compliance with this rule;

Who are these "restricted persons," you might ask?

10) "Restricted person" means:

(A) Members or other broker/dealers

(B) Broker/Dealer Personnel

(i) Any officer, director, general partner, associated person, or employee of a member or any other broker/dealer (other than a limited business broker/dealer);

(ii) Any agent of a member or any other broker/dealer (other than a limited business broker/dealer) that is engaged in the investment banking or securities business; or

(iii) An immediate family member of a person specified in subparagraph (B)(i) or (ii) if the person specified in subparagraph (B)(i) or (ii):

a. materially supports, or receives material support from, the immediate family member;

b. is employed by or associated with the member, or an affiliate of the member, selling the new issue to the immediate family member; or

c. has an ability to control the allocation of the new issue.

(C) Finders and Fiduciaries

(D) Portfolio Managers

(i) Any person who has authority to buy or sell securities for a bank, savings and loan institution, insurance company, investment company, investment advisor, or collective investment account.

(ii) An immediate family member of a person specified in subparagraph (D)(i) that materially supports, or receives material support from, such person.

(E) Persons Owning a Broker/Dealer

(vi) An immediate family member of a person specified in subparagraphs (E)(i)–(v) unless the person owning the broker/dealer:

a. does not materially support, or receive material support from, the immediate family member;

b. is not an owner of the member, or an affiliate of the member, selling the new issue to the immediate family member; and

c. has no ability to control the allocation of the new issue.

And, just how does this rule define "immediate family"? Very broadly:

"Immediate family member" means a person's parents, mother-in-law or father-in-law, spouse, brother or sister, brother-in-law or sister-in-law, son-in-law or daughter-in-law, and children, and any other individual to whom the person provides material support.

"Material support" means directly or indirectly providing more than 25% of a person's income in the prior calendar year. Members of the immediate family living in the same household are deemed to be providing each other with material support.

NASD RULE 2820, VARIABLE CONTRACTS,

This rule tells member firms that when they accept payment from a customer for a variable contract, the price at which the money is invested is the price next computed when the payment is accepted by the insurance company. Just an obvious restatement of the "forward pricing" concept you already know for mutual funds, which are the same thing as variable annuities minus the tax-deferral and death benefit. The member firm has to transmit the application and payment promptly to the insurance company. No member who is a principal underwriter may sell variable contracts through another broker-dealer unless the broker-dealer is a member, and there is a sales agreement in effect between the parties. The agreement must also provide that the sales commission be returned to the insurance company if the purchaser terminates the contract within seven business days. Sorry, that rule doesn't favor you very much, but it is what it is. Also, member firms can only sell variable annuities if the annuity/insurance company promptly pays out when clients surrender their contracts. In other words, if the insurance company is lame, the member firm can't just keep shrugging their shoulders and going, "Hey—what are ya' gonna do—we just sell the darn things."

Associated persons (you) may not accept compensation from anyone other than the member firm. The only exception here is if there is an arrangement between you and the other party that your member firm agrees to, and your firm deals with a bunch of other requirements. Associated persons (you) may not accept securities from somebody else in exchange for selling variable contracts. The only non-cash compensation that can be offered or accepted would be:

- gifts that do not exceed an annual amount per person fixed periodically by the Association and are not preconditioned on achievement of a sales target. The gift limit is still $100, by the way.
- an occasional meal, a ticket to a sporting event or the theater, or comparable entertainment which is neither so frequent nor so extensive as to raise any question of propriety and is not preconditioned on achievement of a sales target.
- payment or reimbursement by offerors in connection with meetings held by an offeror or by a member for the purpose of training or education of associated persons of a member

For that last bullet, remember that the associated person (you) would have to get your firm's permission to attend and that your attendance and reimbursement of expenses cannot be preconditioned on your meeting a sales target. Only you—not your guest—can have your expenses reimbursed, which is a rule just begging to be bent like a freakin' pretzel but let's keep moving. The location of the meeting has to be appropriate, too, meaning if the offeror's office is in Minneapolis, it looks real suspicious when the meeting is held in Montego Bay, mon. And—as always—the record keeping requirements are tougher than we'd like. As the rule states, your "member firm shall maintain records of all compensation received by the member or its associated persons from offerors. The records shall include the names of the offerors, the names of the associated persons, the amount of cash, the nature and, if known, the value of non-cash compensation received."

Your firm can give you non-cash compensation for selling variable contracts, but they can't compensate you more for selling one variable contract than for another. This rule states that the non-cash compensation arrangement requires that the credit received for each variable contract security is equally weighted.

NASD RULE 2830, INVESTMENT COMPANY SECURITIES

Mutual funds and variable annuities are both investment companies covered under the Investment Company Act of 1940. Since they are so similar, it's not surprising that this NASD rule on investment company securities is very similar to the one we just looked at on variable contracts. Like the previous rule, this one tells member firms who act as underwriters/distributors of investment companies that they need to have a written sales agreement between themselves and other dealers. If the other dealer is not an NASD member, they would have to pay the full public offering price, which would make it real tough for them to make a profit. As before, member firms need to transmit payment from customers to the mutual fund companies promptly.

Excessive Charges

This rule also tells member firms not to offer or sell shares of investment companies if the sales charges are excessive. What makes the sales charges excessive? Well, you already know that 8.5% of the public offering price is the maximum sales charge. Also note that if the fund does not offer breakpoints and rights of accumulation that satisfy the NASD, the fund cannot charge 8.5%. As you already know, it would be a violation to describe a mutual fund as being "no load" or as having "no sales charge" if the investment company has a front-end (A-shares) or deferred (B-shares) sales charge, or whose 12b1 fees exceed .25 of 1%.

Withhold Orders

Although I would have thought this truth were self-evident, this NASD rule states that, "No member shall withhold placing customers' orders for any investment company security so as to profit himself as a result of such withholding." Another part of this rule says that member firms can only purchase investment company shares either for their own account or to fill existing customer orders—they can't just pick up a batch of shares and then see if anybody wants them, in other words.

Anti-Reciprocal Rule

This next thing seems highly testable to me. Broker-dealers cannot decide to sell particular investment company shares based on how much trading business the investment company does or would consider doing through the firm. The ol' "pay to play" method is a big no-no, in other words. Be very broad in your understanding of this rule—if it looks at all as if a member firm is tying the promotion of particular funds to the amount of trading commissions they receive when the fund places trades through them, it's not passing the smell test. This would also apply to a member firm offering to compensate their branch managers and reps more for selling the shares of those investment companies who execute transactions through the firm, generating fat commissions.

So, I just told you that a broker-dealer (member firm) cannot sell mutual fund shares if the mutual fund trades through the broker-dealer, generating commissions for the member firm, right?

No. What I'm saying is that the firm can't tie the promotion/sale of the mutual fund to the level of trading the fund does or intends to do through the firm. Similarly, firms definitely compensate their branch managers and representatives for selling mutual fund shares; they simply can't compensate them more for selling the shares of the funds willing to "pay to play."

Interestingly, as I look at the NASD's website this morning, I see that the regulators just fined a firm over $12 million for placing mutual funds on a "preferred list" in exchange for those funds doing lots of lucrative trading business through the firm. The news release calls it a "shelf space program," which is a great name for it. See, in the supermarket, all the products you see are there because the company paid a fee for "shelf space." Well, that's okay for cookies and crackers, but not for mutual funds.

This all boils down to the fact that a broker-dealer should recommend a mutual fund because it's the best investment for a particular client, not because the broker-dealer will make money from the mutual fund when it executes its trades through the firm.

If a transaction involves the purchase of shares of an investment company that imposes a deferred sales charge when the investor redeems the shares some day, the written confirmation must also include the following legend: "On selling your shares, you may pay a sales charge. For the charge and other fees, see the prospectus." The legend must appear on the front of a confirmation and in, at least, 8-point type.

I am not making that up. 8-point type. What's more, I understand that the members of the rowdy 9-point-font faction of the rules committee had to be forcibly restrained several times before finally bowing to the demands of their relentless, 8-point-font-favoring colleagues.

Finally, everything I told you about NASD Rule 2820 concerning receipt of payment from other sources, including non-cash compensation, holds true here, too. So, assuming you haven't fallen asleep or died of boredom yet, you might want to do a quick review of that section.

THE 3000 RULES

And now let's look at a few of the "3000" rules (I'm talking about the numbers used—there are *not* actually 3,000 rules to go through, my stressed-out, overly excitable friends). NASD Rule 3010 takes the radical view that firms must supervise their principals and their representatives. If they don't supervise them, the NASD will kick out the whole bunch. In fact, it's somewhat amusing to me (as one not subject to any NASD action of any type) to see that when a firm gets busted for breaking a rule, they also get busted for not having better written procedures and/or processes that could have prevented the nonsense that happened from happening. It's like a little bonus violation that punishes the crazy reps who were pushing high-risk securities on senior citizens and the principals in charge who should have been smart enough to prevent that crap from happening. As this rule states:

> b) Written Procedures
>
> (1) Each member shall establish, maintain, and enforce written procedures to supervise the types of business in which it engages and to supervise the activities of registered representatives, registered principals, and other associated persons that are reasonably designed to achieve compliance with applicable securities laws and regulations, and with the applicable Rules of NASD.

The very next item below that one informs firms that the NASD may notify them that because certain of their reps come from "disciplined firms," the firm must now tape-record every word that passes between the shady reps and the customers. Sounds like a pain in the neck for the firm, don't it? They'd not only have to tape-record all conversations and keep them on file the usual three years, but also file regular reports with the NASD to assure them that while these two reps did have a brief career with Soprano and Aprile Securities, they're actually keeping the churning in check quite nicely at this point and have only used threats of violence twice in the immediately preceding fiscal quarter.

In other words, if you have a bunch of disciplinary problems in your past, it's time to find a new career.

The federal government sort of insists that broker-dealers do not open up accounts for Osama Bin Laden or anyone who funnels money to the wacky multimillionaire cave dweller. NASD Rule 3011 lays out the rules for preventing money laundering:

> **3011. Anti-Money Laundering Compliance Program**
> On or before April 24, 2002, each member shall develop and implement a written anti-money laundering program reasonably designed to

achieve and monitor the member's compliance with the requirements of the Bank Secrecy Act (31 U.S.C. 5311, et seq.), and the implementing regulations promulgated thereunder by the Department of the Treasury. Each member's anti-money laundering program must be approved, in writing, by a member of senior management.

The Bank Secrecy Act (BSA) authorizes the U.S. Treasury Department to require financial institutions such as banks and broker-dealers to maintain records of personal financial transactions that "have a high degree of usefulness in criminal, tax and regulatory investigations and proceedings." It also authorizes the Treasury Department to require any financial institution to report any "suspicious transaction relevant to a possible violation of law or regulation." These reports, called "Suspicious Activity Reports" are filed with the Treasury Department's Financial Crimes Enforcement Network ("FinCEN").

This is done secretly (thus the law's middle name), without the consent or knowledge of bank customers, any time a financial institution determines that a transaction is suspicious. The reports are made available electronically to every U.S. Attorney's Office and to 59 law enforcement agencies, including the FBI, Secret Service, and Customs Service.

Recently, the U.S. Treasury Department used the Bank Secrecy Act (BSA) to require that for transmittals of funds of $3,000 or more, broker-dealers are required to obtain and keep certain specified information concerning the parties sending and receiving those funds. In addition, broker-dealers must include this information on the actual transmittal order. Also, any cash transactions over $10,000 require the same type of uptight record keeping. For these, broker-dealers must file a Currency Transaction Report with FinCEN.

Why? Because terrorist organizations fund their operations through money laundering. Since broker-dealers are financial institutions, they're lumped in with banks and required to do all kinds of record keeping to help the government prevent these operations.

With the passage of the "USA Patriot Act" broker-dealers and other financial institutions have to help the government monitor suspicious activity that could be tied to money laundering. Broker-dealers now have to report any transaction that involves at least $5,000 if the broker-dealer knows, suspects, or has reason to suspect that it doesn't pass the smell test. The NASD spells out four specific characteristics that would make a broker-dealer file a "suspicious activity report" (SAR). A SAR would be filed if the transaction falls within one of four classes:

- the transaction involves funds derived from illegal activity or is intended or conducted to hide or disguise funds or assets derived from illegal activity;

- the transaction is designed to evade the requirements of the Bank Secrecy Act
- the transaction appears to serve no business or apparent lawful purpose or is not the sort of transaction in which the particular customer would be expected to engage and for which the broker/dealer knows of no reasonable explanation after examining the available facts; or
- the transaction involves the use of the broker/dealer to facilitate criminal activity

Broker-dealers now have to have a "customer identification program" whereby they require more information to open an account. They now have to get the customer's date of birth. If the customer is not a U.S. citizen, the firm will need:

- taxpayer ID number
- passport number and country of issuance
- alien ID card
- other government-issued photo ID card

Even the U.S. citizen may need to show a photo ID, just as you do when you go take your Series 7 exam.

Finally, the federal government now maintains an Office of Foreign Asset Control (OFAC) designed to protect against the threat of terrorism. This office maintains a list of individuals and organizations viewed as a threat to the U.S. Broker-dealers and other financial institutions now need to make sure they aren't setting up accounts for these folks, or—if they are—they need to block/freeze the assets.

This next rule is self-explanatory,.

3020. Fidelity Bonds

(a) Coverage Required

Each member required to join the Securities Investor Protection Corporation who has employees and who is not a member in good standing of the American Stock Exchange, Inc.; the Boston Stock Exchange; the Midwest Stock Exchange, Inc.; the New York Stock Exchange, Inc.; the Pacific Stock Exchange, Inc.; the Philadelphia Stock Exchange, Inc.; or the Chicago Board Options Exchange shall:

(1) Maintain a blanket fidelity bond, in a form substantially similar to the standard form of Brokers Blanket Bond promulgated by the Surety Association of America, covering officers and employees which provides against loss and has agreements covering at least the following:

(A) Fidelity

(B) On Premises

(C) In Transit

(D) Misplacement

(E) Forgery and Alteration (including check forgery)

(F) Securities Loss (including securities forgery)

(G) Fraudulent Trading

3030. Outside Business Activities of an Associated Person

Many students seem shocked when I tell them that they'll need to notify their employing broker-dealer before doing any type of work outside the firm. As this rule stipulates:

> No person associated with a member in any registered capacity shall be employed by, or accept compensation from, any other person as a result of any business activity, other than a passive investment, outside the scope of his relationship with his employer firm, unless he has provided prompt written notice to the member. Such notice shall be in the form required by the member.

3040. Private Securities Transactions of an Associated Person

Some people who attend my live classes seem to imagine that they'll be maintaining their independence and autonomy even after associating with a member firm. They can't believe they'd have to tell the firm about the landscaping business they're planning to open with their brother-in-law Joey next spring. They're appalled that, say, Ameritrade would have the audacity to inform their employer that they just opened an investment account at their firm. They also don't see why they can't join up with a member firm but continue to offer whatever type of investment opportunity comes up to their clients.

Well, the NASD wants all activities of a registered representative to be monitored, so if the registered representative is sitting in his office offering investors a chance to invest in his sister's new diner down the street without telling his firm, there is no way the firm could monitor his wacky sales activities. That could even be the answer to a Series 7 question asking why "selling away" is a violation—because it gives your principal/firm no opportunity to supervise your activities. It also gives them no opportunity to say, "Are you out of your f*#*#in' mind, you little piece of #*#*?" before calmly explaining the spirit and applicability of NASD Rule 3040 to your renegade little attitude. So, a registered representative cannot be offering securities to investors that his firm knows absolutely nothing about. As this rule makes clear:

> No person associated with a member shall participate in any manner in a private securities transaction except in accordance with the requirements of this Rule.

> (b) Written Notice
> Prior to participating in any private securities transaction, an associated person shall provide written notice to the member with which he is associated describing in detail the proposed transaction and the person's proposed role therein and stating whether he has received or may receive selling compensation in connection with the transaction.

Once you've provided written notice to your employer they can either approve or disapprove of your little plan. If they approve your activities, the transaction must be recorded on the books and records of the member, and the member has to supervise the rep's participation in the transaction as if the transaction were executed on behalf of the member. In other words, your boss is going to be enjoying free meals at your sister's diner for perpetuity, on the odd chance that he'll let you offer shares in the company at all. What if the firm says they disapprove of your activity?

Don't do it. And if you do, don't get caught. Otherwise, we'll see you up on the NASD website with words like "selling away," "suspension," and "conduct inconsistent with just and equitable principles of trade."

3050. Transactions for or by Associated Persons

On the new account form, we ask if the customer is associated with a member firm. If your broker-dealer knows that the customer is associated with a member firm, or if an associate of a member firm has discretion over the account, your firm must:

- notify the employer member in writing, prior to the execution of a transaction for such account, of the executing member's intention to open or maintain such an account;
- upon written request by the employer member, transmit duplicate copies of confirmations, statements, or other information with respect to such account; and
- notify the person associated with the employer member of the executing member's intention to provide the notice and information required

You will soon be an associate of a member firm, so when you want to open an investment account with another firm, first of all, what the heck are you thinking? Do you understand *nothing* about office politics? Secondly, this NASD rule states:

> A person associated with a member, prior to opening an account or placing an initial order for the purchase or sale of securities with another member, shall notify both the employer member and the executing member, in writing, of his or her association with the other member; provided, however, that if the account was established prior to the association of the person with the employer member, the associated person shall notify both members in writing promptly after becoming so associated.

As in baseball, disputes in the sport known as investing are settled in arbitration. In other words, member firms can't sue each other in civil court if an underwriting turns sour and one member of the syndicate is convinced they are owed an additional $1 million from another member, who acted as syndicate manager in the IPO. That sort of dispute must be submitted to arbitration. That means you get one shot, no appeals. As we saw earlier, firms get their customers to sign pre-dispute arbitration agreements, but they have to be very upfront what the heck that means in the document they're getting the customer to sign. The rule (3110) stipulates that the warning has to look like this:

> This agreement contains a pre-dispute arbitration clause. By signing an arbitration agreement the parties agree as follows:
>
> (A) All parties to this agreement are giving up the right to sue each other in court, including the right to a trial by jury, except as provided by the rules of the arbitration forum in which a claim is filed.
>
> (B) Arbitration awards are generally final and binding; a party's ability to have a court reverse or modify an arbitration award is very limited.
>
> (C) The ability of the parties to obtain documents, witness statements and other discovery is generally more limited in arbitration than in court proceedings.
>
> (D) The arbitrators do not have to explain the reason(s) for their award.
>
> (E) The panel of arbitrators will typically include a minority of arbitrators who were or are affiliated with the securities industry.
>
> (F) The rules of some arbitration forums may impose time limits for

bringing a claim in arbitration. In some cases, a claim that is ineligible for arbitration may be brought in court.

(G) The rules of the arbitration forum in which the claim is filed, and any amendments thereto, shall be incorporated into this agreement.

Only by getting the customer to sign this agreement would your firm know that when somebody loses a bunch of money selling stock short or trading like a fiend, that somebody will not be able to drag them through civil court, with appeal after appeal. Arbitration is faster and cheaper for all involved.

NASD Rule 3080 makes sure that your firm provides you, the registered rep, with the same written disclosure that you are bound by NASD Arbitration whenever you are asked to sign a U-4 or U-5 form.

CODE OF PROCEDURE

So, the NASD (and the NYSE) has member conduct rules that you really, really do not want to break, especially if you end up getting caught. The NASD investigates violations of the conduct rules through Code of Procedure, which spells "COP." Just like on the street, if somebody breaks the rules, you can call a COP. When we mentioned words such as "suspend, expel, bar, and censure," those are all part of this Code of Procedure. Maybe a staff member of the NASD found out some rather disturbing information during a recent routine examination of a firm, or maybe one of your customers got ticked about losing 90% this year and then found out you were breaking rules along the way. Either way, you'll be notified and asked to respond to the charges in writing. All requests for information must be met within 25 days, so start writing. Remember that you have to cooperate with the investigation, producing documents or testimony as required. And if it's decided that you broke a rule, you could be censured, fined, suspended, expelled, or barred.

Which is bad.

You would get to appeal, assuming you can afford the legal fees. The appeals first go to the National Adjudicatory Council (NAC), then to the SEC, and even into the federal courts.

But it would be easier if you didn't get in trouble in the first place.

What is the maximum fine the NASD can impose?

Trick question—for a major violation, they've never actually set a cap. If it's a "minor rule violation," the maximum fine would usually be no more than $5,000. You would receive an offer from the NASD to use what they call "summary complaint procedure," and if you want to avoid a hearing as much as they apparently do, you need to accept it within 10 business days. Minor rule violations typically involve the failure to pay fees or file reports in a timely fashion. For the exceedingly curious, they are codified in NASD Rule IM-9216.

If you reject their offer to play nice, there will be a hearing, where any of the aforementioned penalties can be assessed:

- Censure
- Fine (any amount)
- Suspension (up to 1 year) from the member firm or all member firms
- Expelled (up to 10 years)
- Barred (game over, history, toast)

I doubt the test would mess with you on this point, but although "acceptance, waiver, and consent" is often used for minor rule violations (MRVs), it is also used for larger fines when the respondent does not want a hearing.

Now, if you'd like to see how this test world stuff works in the real world, simply go to www.nasd.com and www.nyse.com. Look for links to "regulation" or "disciplinary actions" and see the amazing audacity of registered representatives who run afoul of the SRO rules and regulations. You can probably find real-world examples of most of the violations we just examined in a few minutes.

CODE OF ARBITRATION

When broker-dealers are arguing over money, they have to take it to "arbitration." Under the Code of Arbitration members of the NASD must resolve money disputes with an arbitrator or arbitration panel, which cuts to the chase and makes their decision quickly. There are no appeals to arbitration. If they say your firm owes the other side one million dollars, your firm will have to open their checkbook and cut a check for one million dollars. End of story. A customer is free to sue a firm or registered rep in civil court unless the customer signs the arbitration agreement. Once that's signed, the customer is also bound by the Code of Arbitration, which means they can't sue you in civil court. Which is why most firms get their customers to sign arbitration agreements when the new account is opened. Civil court is too costly and time-consuming. Arbitration can be very painful, but at least it's quick. Like a root canal. Or being crushed by a 10-ton truck.

When securities professionals go to arbitration over an amount of $25,000 or less, they often use Simplified Industry Arbitration. Here there is just one arbitrator and no hearing. The claims are submitted in writing, and the arbitrator reaches a decision.

Larger amounts of money are handled by 3 or 5 arbitrators, some from the industry and some from outside the industry. Evidence and testimony is examined and the arbitration panel makes a final determination. Maybe they say the lead underwriter owes your firm $1 million. Maybe they say they owe you nothing. All decisions are final and binding in arbitration, unlike civil court where the appeal process can go on and on. So, if the arbitration panel says you owe somebody $50,000, you have to, like, pay them. Failure to comply with the arbitration decision could lead to a suspension, and now you're really not having a good day.

The bylaw doesn't specifically mention the word "money." The precise wording looks like this:

> any dispute, claim, or controversy arising out of or in connection with the business of any member of the Association, or arising out of the employment or termination of employment of associated person(s) with any member

So, money is the first "dispute, claim or controversy" that pops into my mind. Because, if it isn't money *per se*, there's still probably a 99% chance that the dispute led to somebody losing money or not making what they expected to. Anyway, the exam is likely to refer to it in the dry language "dispute, claim or controversy," while I prefer to call it what it usually is: money.

NYSE RULES

Even before they decided to eventually merge into just one regulatory organization, the NYSE and NASD were pretty much on the same page in most cases. In fact, the Series 7 exam is owned by the NYSE, who protects it with a copyright, and the test is administered by the NASD. So, when we say that churning is bad, both SRO's are in total agreement. In fact, violating the other SRO's rules is a violation of *your* SRO's rules. Remember that—not only will the NASD come after you for breaking an NASD or SEC rule, but also they will nail you for breaking the rules of the NYSE, MSRB, CBOE, and any of the exchanges we talked about in "Trading Securities."

NYSE RULE 405

Just a few years ago people were still talking about the "know thy customer" rule. The word "thy" being a bit archaic, we can probably just refer to NYSE Rule 405 as the "know *your* customer" rule these days. This just means that a registered rep's main job is to help a client determine which investments are suitable, given the client's time horizon, investment goals, financial needs, and risk tolerance. Obviously, you can't do your job if you don't know at least that much about the investor. So, when opening a new account, you and your firm must get this information from your client.

ACCOUNTS FOR NYSE EMPLOYEES

The NYSE, NASD, and MSRB all want their members to know about any accounts their employees are setting up at other firms. All three SRO's require that the member firms be at least notified when an employee sets up an investment account elsewhere, but the NYSE is the most uptight about this. The NYSE members have to give *permission* to the other firm before they can open an account for their employee. Let's lay it all out in tabular format, since—chances are—you've had just about enough excitement by now:

NYSE	MSRB	NASD
Permission	Notification	Notification
Duplicate trade confirmations	Duplicate trade confirmations	Duplicates only upon request

APPRENTICESHIP

Remember that for MSRB firms, the apprenticeship period is 90 days, during which a new rep cannot deal with the public and/or receive commissions. Well, the NYSE is even more uptight—here, the apprenticeship period is 120 days.

RULE 472. COMMUNICATIONS WITH THE PUBLIC

This is the rule that stipulates that "each advertisement, market letter, sales literature or other similar type of communication must be approved in advance by the member firm. Communications must not contain any untrue statement or omission of a material fact. They may not promise specific results or contain exaggerated or unwarranted claims, opinions for which there is no reasonable basis, or projections or forecasts of future events that are not clearly labeled as forecasts." So, if you get a fax today explaining how you can "triple your money in just 7 days" by investing in a mining company you've never heard of, chances are the firm's offices look pretty much they way they looked in the movie *Boiler Room*. If a firm wants to list stock picks, they have to give you data based on at least a 12-month period. They also have to show the effects of commissions and other trading costs and must compare these stock picks to the general market climate. I mean, if your stock picks are up 15% when the overall market is up 20%, you ain't lookin' so good, even if 15 is a positive number. Of course, these past stock picks cannot even imply that future results are somehow indicated or guaranteed.

When an NYSE member firm issues a research report, it must be approved by a supervisory analyst. A supervisory analyst must be registered as such by the NYSE and is required to pass a separate examination (Series 16). Why?

Back in the late 1990's, many so-called "analysts" were merely trying to pump up the price of a stock to make the issuing corporation's management happy enough to use the firm's investment banking services next time they needed to raise money on the primary market. Many of the "buy" or "strong buy" ratings had nothing to do with research—it was just that analysts got staggering bonuses based on the investment banking business they helped bring in with their well-coordinated cheerleading efforts. Which means that if you actually believed one word these talking head analysts said and lost half your retirement savings taking their recommendations, you can sleep better knowing they all made multi-million-dollar salaries and bonuses off your excessively trusting nature.

So, the NYSE has made the linking of research analysts and investment banking a big no-no. From now on, research analysts may not be subject to the supervision, or control, of any employee of the member's investment banking department. And, personnel engaged in investment banking activities may not have any influence or control over the compensation of a research analyst. Also, research reports may not be subject to review or approval by investment banking personnel or by the company whose stock is being "researched." Analysts also are no longer allowed to help solicit investment-banking business by attending IPO road shows or promising to give high ratings to the issuer's stock in exchange for doing business with the firm.

So from here on out, research is supposed to be based on objective inquiry and honest interpretation of the facts, all because a few million small-time investors mistakenly assumed that a "buy" rating meant the stock was, like, a good buy and lost half their retirement nest eggs in the process.

Geeze Louise. The regulators are taking all the fun out of this business.

Research reports nowadays must indicate the following, if applicable:

- The member has managed or co-managed a primary offering of this issuer's securities in the past 12 months
- The member has received any compensation from the issuer for investment banking activities in the past 12 months
- The member expects to receive or intends to seek compensation for investment banking services from the subject company in the next three months
- The member is making a market in the subject company's securities at the time the research report is issued
- The terms "buy" or "strong buy," for example, must be clearly explained. And the following is verbatim from the NYSE rule: "Definitions of ratings terms also must be consistent with their plain meaning. Therefore, for

example, a 'hold' rating should not mean or imply that an investor should sell a security."

You may find this amusing, frightening, or, perhaps, both, but according to research done by a firm here in Chicago (Zacks Investment Research), in late 1999 the percentage of recommendations where analysts told us to SELL stock was a whopping 1%.

One percent.

Yes, 99% of the 6,000 companies being "analyzed" should have been either held or purchased. So, once the drugs had worn off, the industry sort of woke up and realized that maybe more than 1% of all stocks should be sold. Therefore, the NYSE rule says that when a firm is doing the "strong buy," "buy," or "hold" recommendations, they need to indicate which percentage of stocks analyzed are assigned each rating.

Finally, when analysts appear on those mind-numbing talk shows, they have to disclose the fact that they or a household member have an interest in the stock being analyzed. That way we can try to determine if the analyst wants us to buy the stock because it's a good investment or because if enough of us place buy orders tomorrow, his warrants/options/futures, etc., will work out real well for him and his immediate family.

MORE FEDERAL ACTS

Now let's look at some other pieces of federal legislation that are within the scope of the Series 7.

TRUST INDENTURE ACT, 1939

To protect bondholders, Congress passed the Trust Indenture Act of 1939. If a corporation wants to sell $5,000,000 or more worth of bonds that mature outside of a year, they have to do it under a contract or indenture with a trustee, who will enforce the terms of the indenture to the benefit of the bondholders. In other words, if the issuer stiffs the bondholders, the trustee can get a bankruptcy court to sell off the assets of the company so that bondholders can recover some of their hard-earned money. Sometimes corporations secure the bonds with specific assets like airplanes, securities, or real estate. If so, they pledge title of the assets to the trustee, who just might end up selling them off if the issuer gets behind on its interest payments. So just remember that an indenture is a contract with a trustee, who looks out for the bondholders.

THE INVESTMENT COMPANY ACT OF 1940

The Investment Company Act of 1940 classified investment companies as face-amount certificates, UIT's, or management companies. Remember that the "management companies" are the open- and closed-end funds. This is the act that sets rules for registration and operation of mutual funds, separate accounts, etc. It also gives the SEC the authority to continuously revise rules and write new ones to stay on top of an ever-changing marketplace. For example, the SEC has written a rule telling a tax-exempt bond fund that under normal circumstances 80% of its assets are actually, you know, tax-exempt. Or, in order to protect investors perhaps a mutual fund's board of directors has to be a majority, or even 75% "non-interested." This is the Act that gives the SEC the authority to regulate the mutual fund industry, or at least go back and forth like an old married couple with the industry's powerful lobbying group called the "Investment Company Institute."

INVESTMENT ADVISERS ACT OF 1940

If you want to give people your expert advice on their specific investment situation and charge a fee, you have to register under the Investment Advisers Act of 1940. Only registered advisers can charge "wrap fees," too, because those fees contain a component for advice. Investment advisers are the individuals/companies managing mutual funds and separate accounts, as well as managing money for other customers. With your Series 7 you will be paid a commission when executing customer buy and sell orders. If you worked for the investment advisory unit of your firm, you would be paid as a percentage of the assets your client has under the firm's management. In fact, many readers will take the Series 66 after the Series 7 because they will be serving accounts that pay commissions for trading securities as well as accounts that pay a percentage of assets. Charging a percentage of assets is part of the investment advisory business, and most states require that you have the 65/66 (same license) in order to get paid that way. Since you would be representing an investment adviser, you would be considered an "investment adviser representative."

Some people like to compensate you and your firm for a percentage of assets as opposed to paying commissions every time they buy and sell. See, when you convince me to buy a really hot stock, you get a commission when I do. What if the stock tanks after that? Then you can call me again and convince me to sell that dog, and if I do, you get the same commission all over again. Plus, now that I'm sitting on some cash, why not take another one of your hot stock tips so that you can make another commission off me? In other words, no matter how my investments work out, you get a commission when I buy and a commission when I sell. Is it good for me to buy and sell frequently? Probably not—but how else can you get paid as my agent?

You can't, unless your firm is charging a percentage of assets and you have the Series 65/66 license for "IAR's." Now, I'll just let one of your portfolio managers run my portfolio and pay you guys maybe 1% of whatever the assets are worth. Each quarter you would deduct .25% of my account value as a "management fee," and it will be like having my own little private mutual fund. No sales charges or other operating expenses—I just pay my fees to your firm based on the value of the assets you're managing for me. If you do a good job and my account grows, your 1% annual fee gets bigger, too. And, when your stock and bond picks stink, your 1% will be a smaller and smaller number. I'm thinking that might get your attention, so maybe I prefer paying a percentage of assets rather than getting charged every time I buy and sell a security.

So, which billing method should a financial services firm use? Whichever one makes the most sense for the client. If the regulators feel that your firm is sticking people into a fee- or percentage-based billing structure just because it puts more money in the firm's pocket, they will take swift and harsh action. Your firm has to explain the difference to clients and steer them toward the method that would be most economical for them. See, if someone only trades a few times a year, their commissions might represent significantly less than 1% or whatever the management fee is. Then again, someone who trades more frequently or someone who needs a lot more advice/supervision might be better off paying 1–2% of assets.

The reason many readers are getting both their Series 7 and Series 65/66 is so that they can serve the client whether she chooses to pay commissions per transaction or just pay a percentage of assets for portfolio management and related services.

INSIDER TRADING & SECURITIES FRAUD ENFORCEMENT ACT OF 1988 (ITSFEA)

Although the Act of 1934 talked about insider trading, apparently it didn't quite get the message across. So in 1988 Congress passed the Insider Trading & Securities Fraud Enforcement Act of 1988 and raised the penalties for insider trading, making it a criminal offense with stiff civil penalties as well. If your brother-in-law happens to be the Chief Financial Officer of a public company and over a few too many martinis lets it slip that his company is going to miss earnings estimates badly this quarter, just pretend like you didn't hear it. Tell your principal and no one else. If you start passing out that information, or if you—God forbid—buy a bunch of puts on the stock, you could go to federal prison. More likely, the SEC would just sue the heck out of you in federal court and try to extract a civil penalty of three times the amount of the profit made or loss avoided.

How would they ever catch me, though?

Interestingly enough, those words have been carved into many federal prison cell walls since they passed the Insider Trading and Securities Fraud Enforcement Act of 1988. As we mentioned earlier, the SEC offers bounties of up to 10% of the amount they get out of the inside traders. Any material information the public doesn't have, that's inside information. Don't pass it around, don't use it. People who violate the act can be held liable to what they call "contemporaneous traders." That means that if you're dumping your shares based on an inside tip, and that hurts me, we might need to have a little talk with our attorneys.

TELEPHONE CONSUMER PROTECTION ACT

The Telephone Consumer Protection Act of 1991 is not specific to the securities business. This act sets rules on cold calling. When calling a prospect, you must identify yourself and the firm you represent. If the prospect rejects your offer and asks to be taken off your call list (put on the "don't-call" list), your firm may not contact this individual again. You may only call prospects Monday through Friday between 8 AM and 9 PM in the prospect's time zone (unless they've indicated in writing that's it okay to call them at other times). All faxes must contain contact information of the firm sending them so that prospects can call up and ask to be put on the don't-call list if they want. And, the caller must identify who she is, who she works for, and the fact that she is trying to interest the person in securities investments. Non-profits are exempt from these restrictions, as is legitimate debt collection. So if VISA™ calls you about your $20,000 credit card balance, you will not be able to say, "I'm not interested. Please put me on your don't-call list."

Well, I guess you can *say* it. It just won't help you very much.

STUDY SHEET

SECURITIES ACT OF 1933

"Paper Act" nickname   Primary Market   Prospectus

If the issuer/security has no exemption from these registration requirements, the security must be registered with the SEC, and customers must receive full and fair disclosure through a prospectus. An issuer/security with no exemption = "non-exempt"

Exempt from these registration requirements:
- Treasury securities
- Agency securities
- Municipal bonds
- Bank securities (not bank HOLDING companies, though)
- Small Business Investment Companies (VC firms)
- Charitable/church securities
- Debt securities that mature 270 days or less

Red Herring = preliminary prospectus, used to solicit indications of interest
Cooling Off Period = 20 days minimum, no sales or advertising during this period

SECURITIES EXCHANGE ACT OF 1934

- Nicknamed "People Act"—really does tell people/firms how to act
- Created the Securities and Exchange Commission
- Broker-dealers and associated persons (reps) must register
- Reps must fill out U-4
- No fraudulent, unethical sales practices allowed on any security
- Public companies must file quarterly and annual reports with SEC
- Insider Trading is not allowed
- Gave FRB power to regulate margin
- Issuers must solicit proxies and pay the cost of forwarding to customers

TRUST INDENTURE ACT OF 1939

Corporations issuing more than $5,000,000 par value of bonds that mature longer than 1 year must use an indenture, which is a contract between the issuer and a trustee looking out for the bondholders.

INVESTMENT COMPANY ACT OF 1940

Classified Investment Companies as:

Face-amount	UIT	Management Company
	Non-managed	Open or Closed-End

Set rules for registration, operation, and sales of investment companies

INVESTMENT ADVISERS ACT OF 1940

If someone wants to manage money/charge a fee for investment advice, they must register as an "investment adviser."

To charge a "wrap fee" one must register as an investment adviser.

INSIDER TRADING ACT OF 1988

Raised penalties for insider trading. Violating the act could lead to CRIMINAL convictions, like Mr. Waksal, now serving 7 years in a federal prison.

Civil penalties are "treble damages." "Treble" means "triple."

CONSUMER PROTECTION ACT OF 1991

Firms must maintain Don't-Call lists for folks who aren't interested.

Only call prospects Monday through Friday between 8 AM and 9 PM in prospect's time zone.

Faxes must contain contact information.

USA PATRIOT ACT (2001)/ANTI-MONEY LAUNDERING

—purpose is to prevent "clean" money from being used to fund terrorist activities.

Firms must now:

* File SARs (Suspicious Activity Reports) on financial behavior which is commercially illogical
* Report currency transaction deposits of $10,000 or more to the IRS on Form 4789
* Report suspicious transactions of $5,000 or more to IRS

NASD ANTI-MONEY LAUNDERING RULES

—at a minimum, firms must now:

* Provide ongoing training for appropriate personnel
* Establish and implement policies and procedures that can be reasonably expected to detect suspicious transactions
* Establish and implement policies, procedures, and internal controls designed to achieve compliance with anti-money laundering requirements

- Provide for independent testing for compliance to be conducted by member personnel or by a qualified outside party
- Designate an individual or individuals responsible for implementing and monitoring day-to-day operations and internal controls of the program

NASD

Empowered by Maloney Act of 1938, making it the SRO/DEA for the OTC

UNIFORM PRACTICE CODE

Keeps the industry "uniform," using standardized settlement dates, deliver requirements, ex-dividend dates, etc.

CONDUCT RULES

- Must pass exam before offering securities to the public.
- Must re-take exam if out of industry for two years+
- No "parking" of licenses—must be associated with a firm for license to be current
- No splitting commissions except with registered agents at the same firm or a related firm
- Must notify member firm (your employer) if working outside the firm or maintaining investment accounts outside the firm
- All sales literature must contain the name of the member firm who created it and date of first publication
- All advertising must include name of the member firm (except blind recruiting ad)
- All sales literature and advertising must be approved and filed by a principal
- Sales literature and advertising concerning investment companies also filed with NASD within 10 days of first use
- Registered rep may not hold investment seminars not approved by firm, and firm must approve invitations, handouts, slide shows, etc.
- Private securities transactions. Registered rep may not offer/sell securities outside supervision and knowledge of employing broker-dealer. Otherwise, violation called "selling away."
- U-4 is not transferred: U-5 to terminate, U-4 to associate with a member firm
- NASD members and their reps may NOT use "NASD" on a business card if that tends to imply that they are somehow endorsed by the NASD. NASD must not be larger than the firm's or the rep's name.

- Member firms can't promote certain mutual funds based on the trading business they generate from that fund (anti-reciprocal rule)
- Member firms only distribute mutual funds through other member firms, must have written sales agreement, and only fill orders for the firm's own account or an existing customer order

COP

How the NASD handles violations of Member Conduct Rules

Break a rule, somebody could call the COP

Appeals to NAC - SEC - Federal Courts

CODE OF ARBITRATION

Handles money disputes. All parties bound by the decision.

Customer only has to use this method if he's signed arbitration agreement

No appeals to arbitration

PRACTICE:

140. **Which of the following securities would have to be registered with the SEC prior to an initial public offering?**
   A. ADR's
   B. XXR Corporation's preferred stock
   C. XXR Corporation's common stock
   D. All of the above

141. **Which of the following securities would have to be registered with the SEC prior to an initial public offering?**
   A. Church bonds
   B. T-notes
   C. Chicago 7% General Obligation bond
   D. None of the above

142. **The Securities Act of 1934 addressed all the following except**

   A. fraudulent offers, sales of securities

   B. registration of broker-dealers

   C. registration of agents

   D. registration of new issues

143. **Which of the following parties have capital at risk in a transaction?**

   A. principal

   B. dealer

   C. market maker

   D. all of the above

144. **Which of the following parties have capital at risk in a transaction?**

   A. agent

   B. underwriter

   C. registered representative

   D. broker

145. **The NASD**

   A. is an SRO

   B. is a DEA

   C. was created via the Maloney Act of 1938

   D. all of the above

146. **The SEC is**

   A. an SRO

   B. a government body

   C. the Securities Ethical Committee for the NASD

   D. none of the above

147. **The sponsor of a mutual fund is trying to increase sales. She visits 50 broker-dealers and offers to award $400 to the registered representative who sells the most shares of the fund. This is**

   A. a great way to increase sales

   B. permissible so long as prior notice is filed with the NASD

   C. permissible so long as prior notice is filed with the SEC

   D. not acceptable

148. The NASD's Conduct Rules prohibit which of the following?

A. choosing the price paid for a security after a non-discretionary customer has named the action, asset, and amount of shares

B. splitting commissions with other registered representatives

C. choosing the security to be bought/sold in the absence of discretionary authority

D. all of the above

149. The NASD's Conduct Rules prohibit which of the following?

A. borrowing money from a bank customer

B. borrowing money from an S&L customer

C. making projections for mutual fund performance

D. all of the above

150. All of the following securities would need to be registered with the Securities and Exchange Commission except a

A. T-bond

B. Mutual fund

C. Closed-end share during the offering period

D. Variable annuity

ANSWERS:

140. D – all securities have to be registered with the SEC, except for all the securities that don't have to be registered with the SEC. The ones that don't have to register are "excused" or "exempt" from the pain-in-the-neck process of registration. The excused securities are: Treasuries, Muni's, Banks, Charitables, Small Business Investment Companies (VC firms), and short-term promissory notes.

Since we don't see any of that in this question, nobody has an excuse; everybody registers.

141. D – all securities have to be registered with the SEC, except for all the securities that don't. The ones that don't have to register are "excused" or "exempt" from the pain-in-the-neck process of registration. The excused securities are: Treasuries, Muni's, Banks, Charitables, Small Business Investment Companies (VC firms), and short-term promissory notes.

142.   D – registration of securities was covered by the Securities Act of 1933, which is the only thing that Act covers. The Act of 1934 has a much broader scope: anti-fraud regulations, registrations of firms and associates, margin, yada, yada.

143.   D – in the sense of "money at risk" these are basically synonymous terms. Note that agent/representative/broker do NOT have money at risk.

144.   B – only the underwriter has money at risk here. The other three terms are synonymous, and these individuals (like yourself) do not have $ at risk. Only your jobs.

145.   D – a gift of a question--always accept the few gifts the test is giving away for free.

146.   B – it oversees the SRO's, but the SEC is a government body. The President appoints the chairman.

147.   D – maximum gift to a person in the business is $100.

148.   C – choosing time/price does not involve discretion. Discretion involves choosing the security, the number of shares, and whether to buy or sell. You can split commissions with registered agents at your firm or a firm under common control.

149.   C – no projections for mutual funds. Usually, the agent can't borrow from a client—unless the client is a lending institution or an immediate family member. Even there, inform the firm and/or consult their written policy on borrowing/ lending activities with customers.

150.   A – Treasuries are exempt from the Act of 1933.

WHAT NOW?

- Review the chapter. *Approximately 50 minutes.*
- If you have the Pass the 7 QuizSet, take the Chapter 15 Quiz on Rules and Regulations. *Approximately 35 minutes.*
- If you have the Audio CD set, listen to Disc 5, Track 4. *Approximately 18 minutes.*

Not Done Yet: Trusts, Estates, Gifts and Other Taxation Concerns

You have probably noticed how much the IRS enjoys taxing people while they're alive. Did you know they also enjoy taxing people when they die? Conservatives generally call this unfortunate reality the "death tax," while liberal politicians simply refer to it as the "estate tax," but, whatever we call it, the fact is that when someone dies, the IRS and state tax collectors may end up taxing the value of assets (house, farm land, bank account, IBM stock, etc.) that pass to the heirs.

ESTATES

Elvis Presley is a not a person; however, the Estate of Elvis Presley *is* a person. As the exam might expect you to know, the following are not legal persons:

- Dead people
- Minor children
- Individuals declared mentally incompetent by a court

That means they can't open investment accounts or enter into binding legal contracts. So, a dead person, such as the king of rock 'n' roll, is not a legal person. However, the assets of a deceased individual such as Elvis Presley (Graceland, recording royalties, residuals from lame beach movies) go into a legal "person" known as an estate. The estate is an entity, a "legal person." Like a corporation, it has an FEIN (federal employee identification number). Also like a corporation, the assets of the estate are separate from the assets of the beneficiaries of the deceased person's will. So, if Grandma dies and somebody files a claim that she still owes him $800,000, what happens if all of Grandma's assets are only worth $100,000?

Dude should have tried to collect sooner. Maybe he'll get every last dollar of that 100 grand, but the children and grandchildren do not have to make up the difference—the estate is a separate legal entity, just like a corporation. Similarly, you might be able to sue one of Donald Trump's corporations or partnerships, but you aren't getting one dollar out of the Donald personally.

So, an estate (like a corporation, partnership, limited liability company, etc.) is a separate legal entity. When Grandma dies, her checking and savings accounts, CD's, real estate, life insurance, etc., all go into a new legal entity called an estate. If you were named the executor of the estate, it's your job to get several death certificates and do lots of paperwork required to transfer her checking and savings to a new bank account entitled, say, Jason Miller, Executor for the Estate of Maude L. Miller, Deceased. If Grandma owned stocks and bonds, they need to be re-titled in the name of the estate, as well. This will require affidavits, signature guarantees, stock powers, letters of office...the whole nine yards. When you effect these transfers of ownership, make sure you have plenty of original death certificates and that the court appointment/letters of office are no more than 60 days old.

Perhaps you've heard the phrase that the only certainties in life are death and taxes—well, when we talk about estates, we're talking about both. When someone dies, the assets go into his/her estate and taxation is definitely a concern. Are all estates taxed? No, but if you aren't careful, your children and grandchildren can end up getting nailed for a bunch of taxes when they inherit your house, farm land, securities portfolio, etc. We'll look at the strategy of establishing trusts to minimize estate taxes in a few minutes, but, first, let's make sure we understand how an estate is treated for purposes of taxation.

Income of the Estate

An estate is generally open at least six months. That is because all creditors have six months to file a claim on the assets if they feel they are still owed money. An announcement is published in a local newspaper to all potential creditors, and if there is anyone that you know of who might even *think* they're a creditor, you will probably send them notice directly. If no one files a claim in that period, the executor might then distribute the assets to all the beneficiaries according to the instructions left in the will. Since there is actually a two-year window for plaintiffs to file a legal *complaint* against the estate, maybe the estate stays open two years...either way, think of an estate account as a short-term account where safe, short-term debt securities are generally the only appropriate investments.

Whether it's within six months or two years, the assets of the estate will eventually be distributed to the heirs/beneficiaries. What happens if the stocks, bonds, CD's, etc., earn interest/dividends in the meantime? That income is taxable to the estate.

Of course, the legal fees charged by the estate attorney will often cancel that income out, but if the estate earns, say, $5,000 in dividend income when the legal bills are just $2,000, there is $3,000 of taxable income there.

Is the Estate Going to Pay Estate Taxes?

More important, when the assets of the estate are transferred to the beneficiaries, the IRS (who, as always, is here to help) may want to help the estate out of some of those assets. Will the estate be taxed? First, we start with the gross estate—the value of the assets before we start taking deductions. The following are included in the value of the gross estate:

- house, farm land, bank account, checking account, investment accounts, clothing, oil paintings, etc.
  - includes value of insurance and annuity contracts!
- assets placed in revocable trusts
- does not include assets placed in irrevocable trusts (except certain property transferred within three years of death!)

So, we add up all of those values and then we start subtracting things to knock down the value of this estate enough to avoid estate taxes. The following will reduce the value of the gross estate:

- Funeral and administrative expenses
- Debts owed at the time of death
- Any charitable gifts made after death
- The marital deduction

The "marital deduction" means that husbands and wives pass their property to one another without paying estate taxes—it's when the assets then go from the "second to die" to the heirs that things get dicey. So, after we've added the value of all the assets (gross estate) and subtracted the first three bullet points above, maybe what's left is $1 million. Will we have to pay estate taxes?

No. Currently, there is a lifetime credit of $2 million for estates. Since the taxable estate is below that number, we avoid paying estate taxes. The assets distributed to the heirs are taxable to them on their individual income tax returns, but we won't pay the estate tax.

How are the heirs taxed? Remember that when Grandma died, we took the fair market value of her securities as our cost basis—when we sell the stocks and bonds for more than that fair market value, that excess is a *long-term capital gain*.

Also note that, generally, the state only goes after estate taxes when the estate is large enough to be taxed at the federal level.

GIFTS

What if several months ago Grandma had gone in for her regular check-up and found out from her doctor that she had maybe two months to live? To avoid forcing her heirs to pay estate taxes, couldn't she just start handing out big, fat envelopes of cash to all the kids and grandkids?

Sure. In fact, the IRS is totally cool with that, to the extent that "IRS" and "totally cool" could ever go together. See, the gifts that Grandma gives while she is alive are also taxable if they are over a certain amount. That number is forever changing—used to be $10,000 per person per year, then $11,000, and now it's $12,000. Whatever the amount is, there is an "annual gift tax exclusion," which means that if Grandma gives anyone other than her husband (who died years ago) a gift worth more than $12,000, she either has to pay gift taxes or start chipping away at her lifetime gift tax credit. That credit is currently $1 million. The amount of the credit that was used up over her lifetime will reduce the amount of the credit you and the other beneficiaries can use when trying to reduce the size of the estate in order to avoid paying estate taxes.

Just to keep the tax code nice and simple, the way Congress and the IRS like it.

So, what is a gift?

The IRS defines a gift as "transferring property to someone else and expecting nothing in return." The IRS also points out that the following can be considered gifts:

- selling something at less than its value
- making an interest-free or reduced-interest loan

Wait, so when Grandma sold Uncle Bill the back forty for $70,000 below market value, that could have been considered a "gift" to Uncle Bill?

You betcha'.

So, when Grandma goes around giving people things worth more than the current annual exclusion, she either files a return and pays gift taxes, or she files a return and tells the IRS that she's using part of her lifetime credit to avoid cutting a check at this time. What if the gift is worth no more than the current exclusion of $12,000?

Nobody cares.

In the following cases, no gift taxes would be due and no returns would have to be filed:

- Gifts made to a spouse
- Gifts that do not exceed current exclusion amount

- Paying tuition costs for someone else—payable directly to educational institution
- Paying medical costs for someone else—payable directly to the care provider
- Political, charitable donations

Gift Splitting

The IRS, believe it or not, is actually very clear on the topic of gift splitting, so let's copy and paste from Publication 950 from www.irs.gov, which states:

> Harold and his wife, Helen, agree to split the gifts that they made during 2006. Harold gives his nephew, George, $21,000, and Helen gives her niece, Gina, $18,000. Although each gift is more than the annual exclusion ($12,000), by gift splitting they can make these gifts without making a taxable gift.

All that means is that half of $21,000 ($10,500) and half of $18,000 ($9,000) would be less than the annual exclusion of $12,000, so they can treat each gift as half from Harold and half from Helen. No gift taxes are due and none of the lifetime credits have to be used up, but the IRS still requires that they file a return since they're getting pretty darned fancy with their little gift-splitting maneuver.

TRUSTS

During our fascinating look at estates we mentioned the phrases "revocable trust" and "irrevocable trust." First, what the heck is a trust? Like an estate or a corporation, a trust is also a separate legal entity. The trust holds assets, just as a corporation or estate holds assets. The person who administers the trust is the trustee. The one who grants the assets to the trust is called the grantor. And the ones who benefit from the trust are cleverly called the "beneficiaries."

You may recall that when an adult sets up an UGMA account, the minor owns all the assets as soon as he/she becomes an adult. For an UTMA account, the transfer can be pushed back as late as age 25. But, if you set up a trust, you can specify all types of things in the trust agreement and, thereby, assure that your kids will be rich enough so that they can do anything, but not rich enough so that they can do nothing with the rest of their lives. You extreme movie fans probably recall that Citizen Kane was taken from his parents at a young age but set up with a trust that allowed him to say one day, "It might be fun to run a newspaper."

Sure—especially when you don't need to make any money at it.

And, if you're a well-read fan of literature, perhaps you've read a novel called

The Ginger Man. In that rather entertaining book, the main character is an absolute screw-up who keeps screwing up because he knows his rich father will die someday, making work, career, etc., completely unnecessary. Unfortunately, when the old man dies, the main character discovers that he will have full access to all the assets placed in trust...in just 20 more years.

Yikes!

Well, clearly, the father knew the son was a hard-drinking screw-up who would do absolutely nothing with his life if he could get by with it. The trust agreement allowed the old man to specify how the trust could be used by his son after he himself had passed away.

So, a trust can allow you to take care of your kids after you're gone without turning them into Paris Hilton wannabes. The exam might point out other advantages of establishing trusts:

- Faster and less costly way to transfer property upon death compared to a will
  - Avoid probate court process (time, expense), especially if property owned in several different states
- Eliminate challenges to estate—specifically disinherit anyone who posts a challenge to your wishes upon your death
- Keep transfer of property private—probate can expose assets to public
- Reduce amount of estate taxable to heirs

Revocable, Irrevocable

As we said, reducing the amount of the taxable estate will come down to the difference between revocable and irrevocable trusts. In general, assets placed in an irrevocable trust do not count as part of the estate, while the assets placed in a revocable trust do count. What's the difference? As always, let the words talk to you—if the trust is revocable, the person who set it up (grantor) can always take back (revoke) the assets. Therefore, not only are those assets still taxable to the grantor while he/she is alive, but when he/she dies, those assets do count towards the value of the estate. If a grantor sets up an irrevocable trust, the assets, obviously, can not be revoked. Therefore, the assets are no longer taxable to the grantor while he/she is alive, and when he/she dies, the assets do not count towards the value of the estate that the heirs are hoping to keep below the amount that triggers estate taxes.

Except when they do. Even in an IR-revocable trust, certain property transferred within three years of death DOES count as part of the taxable estate. And, if the irrevocable trust states that income is to be used or held for the benefit of the grantor or the grantor's spouse, the grantor will be subject to taxation while he/she is alive.

Tax Liability

The irrevocable trust will either distribute income to the beneficiaries, or it won't. Either way, the interest, dividends, and capital gains generated are taxable. If the income is distributed to the beneficiaries, they include it on their own income tax forms. If the income is not distributed, it is taxable to the trust.

In a revocable trust, or even in an irrevocable trust where the grantor or grantor's spouse benefits from the income, the grantor is subject to taxation while he/she is still alive.

So, to sum up on estates and trusts, when the estate earns income, that income is taxable to the estate. And, when the estate distributes property to the beneficiaries, that might—or might not—trigger estate taxes. Either way, the beneficiaries will pay capital gains taxes on stocks and bonds sold above cost basis, and will report their distribution from estate assets on their own income taxes. Some folks establish a trust to simplify the process and maybe avoid the estate tax. If it's an irrevocable trust, generally, those assets don't get counted toward the estate for tax purposes. Of course, now there is a trust to think about—the interest, dividends, and capital gains earned by this trust will either be taxable to the trust if it all remains in the trust, or taxable to the beneficiaries when distributed to them.

AMT

AMT stinks, no matter how you look at it. From our standpoint, it stinks because it's boring and it violates many basic things we thought we knew about taxation. From the standpoint of those who get hit with it, it stinks because they have to, you know, pay it.

See, if you're in a certain income bracket, you will be subject to an "Alternative Minimum Tax," or "AMT." That means that even though people say that municipal bonds pay tax-free interest, you will actually report *some* municipal bond interest on your AMT form as a "tax preference item." Generally, municipal bonds that are considered "private purpose" by the tax code subject investors to reporting income on their AMT forms. That's why many tax-exempt mutual funds also buy bonds that are not subject to AMT taxes.

When the IRS gets hot, they really get hot, so let's just let them explain the AMT for us. The following comes from their page-turning thriller entitled *Publication 556 – Alternative Minimum Tax*:

> The tax laws give preferential treatment to certain kinds of income and allow special deductions and credits for certain kinds of expenses. The alternative minimum tax attempts to ensure that anyone who benefits from these tax advantages pays at least a minimum amount of tax.

> The alternative minimum tax is a separately figured tax that eliminates many deductions and credits, thus increasing tax liability for an individual who would otherwise pay less tax. The tentative minimum tax rates on ordinary income are percentages set by law. For capital gains, the capital gains rates for the regular tax are used. You may have to pay the alternative minimum tax if your taxable income for regular tax purposes plus any adjustments and preference items that apply to you are more than the exemption amount.

I don't see how or why this exam would get extremely detailed on this topic, since investment advisers are not inherently CPA's. I would expect to see mention of the fact that certain municipal bonds subject investors to AMT. If it's considered a "private purpose bond" under the tax code, the investor will actually end up paying some tax on that municipal bond interest that is usually thought of as "tax-free."

Just to keep things nice and simple.

A test question might also bring up the fact that the owner of a limited partnership interest will need to consult the instructions to his little K-1 and may have to add certain tax preference items such as "accelerated depreciation" to his AMT form. The test question might say that "straight line depreciation" would not be a tax preference item, just in case it hasn't already killed you with boredom.

WASH SALES

As you know, investors will sometimes end up selling stocks or bonds for more than they paid for them. More often, they will sell even more securities for *less* than they paid for them, an activity I myself have not yet developed a taste for. But, as you know, if an investor takes $10,000 in capital gains, he can also take capital losses that offset some or all of that, maybe with even some more left over for future years. Why would he want to do that? One, he can avoid paying capital gains taxes. Two, he can use $3,000 to reduce his taxable income for the year.

Let's say he sells $10,000 at a capital gain but $15,000 at a capital loss. That's a net loss of $5,000. So, there are no capital gains taxes to pay, and he can use $3,000 of that $5,000 to offset ordinary income for the year, reducing his tax bill. The remainder is carried forward for future years.

That's the benefit of selling securities at a loss—you can offset your ordinary income. Of course, you do actually have to lose money, and this is not a tax *credit* for crying out loud, just a deduction to income. If you're in the 25% bracket, you can lose a dollar in order to save twenty-five cents, basically.

And, the IRS is just fine with that. But, in order to use that loss, stay out of that stock for at least 30 days. If you sell MSFT at a loss, don't buy any Microsoft stock for

30 days—and, you could not have purchased any 30 days before you made the sale. Also, don't get clever and buy bonds or preferred stock that converts to Microsoft common stock, and don't buy calls or sell deep-in-the-money puts on Microsoft. In short, don't get cute. Just take your little capital loss and stay out of Microsoft for 30 days both before and after the sale.

What if you promise not to buy any Microsoft common stock over the next 30 days but simply can't stop yourself? First, I can recommend a good therapist and, second, you simply can't use the loss now because of wash sale rules. Never fear, though, because if you took a $7-per-share loss on Microsoft, you would simply add $7-per-share to your cost basis on the new purchase. In other words, you'll eventually get the benefit of that loss you took, but not now.

When you sell a bond at a loss, there is a similar rule. Either wait 30 days to buy a replacement, or, if you want to sell a GE bond at a loss and buy another GE bond, you'll need to substantially alter some features of the bond: interest rate, maturity, call feature, or some combination. Or, just buy a bond from a different issuer.

PRACTICE:

1. **Which of the following items would be included in the gross estate for purposes of federal estate tax liability?**
   I.   life insurance policy
   II. value of the decedent's primary residence
   III. a house transferred to an irrevocable trust 24 months prior to death
   IV. a house transferred to a revocable trust

   A. I
   B. II, III
   C. I, IV
   D. I, II, III, IV

WHY: that's the nature of a trick question. Assets placed in an irrevocable trust are not included, except when they are. A house transferred within 3 years of death would be included in the taxable estate.

ANSWER: D

2. **Which of the following items would reduce the amount of the gross estate for purposes of figuring the taxable estate?**

    I.   funeral and administrative expenses
    II. market value of municipal bonds
    III. charitable gifts made after death
    IV. marital deduction

    A. I, III
    B. I, II, IV
    C. III, IV
    D. I, III, IV

WHY: don't read too fast—yes, interest on municipal bonds is tax-free, but that has nothing to do with this question.

ANSWER: D

3. **Mr. Jeffries sets up a trust for the benefit of his adult daughter, Amber, from which his wife may withdraw only if necessary. Therefore, income on the trust will be taxed to**

    A. Mrs. Jeffries as the contingent beneficiary
    B. Mr. Jeffries as the donor
    C. Amber as the primary beneficiary
    D. the trust because it is a separate legal entity

WHY: a husband and wife are an economic unit, so if the wife can withdraw from this trust, that's the same thing as Mr. Jeffries being able to draw from it. Therefore, the income is taxable to him.

ANSWER: B

4. **Darlene has made the following gifts for Tax Year 2006: a $14,500 check to her brother, Virgil, for tuition at a state college, $8,000 to her husband, Cletus, for a second-hand four-wheel-drive pickup truck, $17,000 to her girlfriend, Becky Sue, and a $15,000 check to her mother's primary physician. Which of the following statements best describes the tax implications of these gifts?**

    A. the amount subject to gift taxes is $5,000
    B. no gift taxes are due
    C. the amount subject to gift taxes is $7,500
    D. the amount subject to gift taxes is $19,500

WHY: since the IRS realizes how easy it would be for all the Darlenes and Virgils out there to say that a check was for "tuition," Darlene really needed to cut the check directly to the educational institution. Same thing for paying someone's medical expenses—to make sure it's a tax-free gift, cut the check directly to the provider. So, the $14,500 to Virgil is $2,500 over the annual exclusion, and the $17,000 to Becky Sue exceeds the current annual exclusion by $5,000, for a total of $7,500.

ANSWER: C

5. **One of your clients, Rachel, has inherited securities through her Aunt Jessica's will. Aunt Jessica purchased 1,000 shares of Harley-Davidson for $5,200 twenty years earlier. On the day Aunt Jessica died, the fair market value of Harley-Davidson common stock was $30 per share. If Rachel sells all shares four months later for $40 per share, the tax implications will be**
   A. $34,800 taxed at long-term capital gains rates
   B. short-term gain of $10,000
   C. $40,000 taxed at long-term capital gains rates
   D. long-term gain of $10,000

WHY: keep it simple. For an inheritance of appreciated securities, the cost basis is the fair market value on the date of death. Any gain is long-term.

ANSWER: D

6. **Jarod Stevens had the following results on four stock sales this year:**
   $15,000 in long-term gains
   $5,000 in long-term losses
   $5,000 in short-term gains
   $13,000 in short-term losses
   Therefore, the tax implications are:
   A. short-term capital gain of $8,000
   B. long-term capital gain of $2,000
   C. short-term capital gain of $2,000
   D. long-term capital gain of $15,000

WHY: step one, line up the long-term gains and the long-term losses, then line up the short-term gains with the short-term losses. Jarod ends up with $10,000 in long-term capital gains, but has $8,000 in short-term losses. That's a net gain of $2,000 and it's treated as a long-term capital gain. Why a long-term capital gain? Because it's the long-term net capital gain of $10,000 that triggered the capital gains tax.

ANSWER: B

7. **Jarod Stevens had the following results on four stock sales this year:**

    $15,000 in long-term gains

    $23,000 in long-term losses

    $15,000 in short-term gains

    $5,000 in short-term losses

    Therefore, the tax implications are:

    A. short-term capital gain taxed at a maximum of 15%

    B. no net gains or losses

    C. short-term capital gain of $2,000 taxed at ordinary income rates

    D. long-term capital loss of $8,000, short-term capital gain of $8,000

WHY: line up the long-term with long-term, and the short-term with short-term. You end up with a net long-term loss of $8,000 and a net short-term gain of $10,000. The $8,000 in losses brings the total capital gain down to $2,000, which will be taxed as a short-term capital gain. Why a short-term capital gain? Because it was the short-term net gain that triggered the tax.

ANSWER: C

8. **Jarod Stevens had the following results on four stock sales this year:**

    $15,000 in long-term gains

    $5,000 in long-term losses

    $5,000 in short-term gains

    $17,000 in short-term losses

    Therefore, the tax implications are:

    A. short-term capital gain of $2,000

    B. long-term capital gain of $2,000

    C. short-term capital gain of $5,000

    D. short-term capital loss of $2,000, which offsets ordinary income

WHY: match up long-term with long-term and short-term with short-term, then net out your results. There is a net long-term gain of $10,000 and a net short-term loss of $12,000. That makes it a net loss of $2,000, which can be used to offset ordinary income.

Too bad Jarod couldn't have lost another $1,000 on our lousy stock picks to take full advantage of our services, huh?

ANSWER: D

9. **Within her IRA, Marla Mathers purchased 1,000 shares of ABC @14 on January 12th, 2004. The next day, she also purchased 1,000 shares of XYZ @15. On January 11th, 2006, she sells all her ABC stock for $19 per share and all her XYZ stock for $7 per share. Therefore, which of the following accurately describes the tax implications?**

   A. Marla may reduce her ordinary income by $3,000
   B. There will be no effect on taxation of this account
   C. The purchase of XYZ within 30 days of the ABC purchase triggers wash sale rules
   D. The amount of the capital loss depends on Marla's marginal tax rate

WHY: believe it or not, I don't actually enjoy being a mean jerk at your expense. Please know that I wouldn't do it if I didn't care so much. Seriously.

Anyway, as soon as I wrote "IRA," all notions of capital gains, losses, wash sales, etc., flew right out the window. Unfortunately, most of you kept right on a' readin' and a' figurin'. Watch out for the tricks. They're not just on the exam—there are tricks in the real world. What if you told an investor something about a Traditional IRA that was only true of a Roth IRA—just how upset might a customer be if your confusion cost them some money and led to IRS hassles? Remember that in a retirement plan, gains, interest, and dividends just stay in the account growing tax-deferred. Some day the money will come out, and you will either pay ordinary income rates (never cap gains), or—in some cases—no tax at all (Roth, 529, Coverdell).

ANSWER: B

10. **Which of the following represents an accurate statement concerning gifts?**

   A. If a wife gives her husband $15,000 in Tax Year 2006, no gift taxes are due, but the amount above the annual exclusion must be reported to the IRS.
   B. If an individual pays the tuition of another individual, the individuals must be related; otherwise, the payment is considered a taxable gift.
   C. When "gift splitting" is utilized, no taxes are due and no forms must be filed.
   D. A gift of $24,000 can be considered half from the husband and half from the wife in order to avoid paying gift taxes for 2006.

WHY: the IRS doesn't care about gifts between husband and wife—I mean, they're invasive, but they're not Geraldo. If you pay tuition for someone else, it makes no difference if the two of you are related or not. Just make sure you pay the educational institution directly. That way it's a non-taxable gift, and you don't even need to file a return. For 2006, the wife could give somebody $24,000 and consider that as 1/2 from her, 1/2 from her husband, even if her husband never talks to the loud, pushy sorority sister who drops in for unannounced seven-day visits with alarming regularity. When you use gift splitting, no taxes are due, and you don't have to use up the lifetime credit. But, since you're getting fancy, you do need to file a return to let the IRS know what's up.

ANSWER: D

11. Which of the following statement(s) is/are accurate concerning wash sale rules?

I.   It is illegal to sell common stock at a loss and then repurchase it within 30 days.

II. If a loss is disallowed due to wash sale rules, the investor adds the loss to the cost basis on the re-purchase.

III. An investor may sell MSFT common stock at a loss and purchase MSFT preferred stock within 30 days and still claim the loss on the common stock.

IV. Wash sale rules do not apply to a Traditional IRA or Roth IRA.

A.   I

B.   II, IV

C.   II, III, IV

D.   I, IV

WHY: kind of a nasty question, since a "wash sale" has another meaning in terms of manipulating stock prices on the secondary market. But, if you see the phrase "wash sale" on an exam, there is about a 99.9% chance that they're talking about taxation issues.

Nothing illegal about repurchasing the security within 30 days, but—as another answer choice points out—you don't get to use that loss. Instead, you add it to the cost basis on the re-purchase in order to keep the tax code nice and simple. Preferred stock is a whole different animal from common stock, and so are bonds. Unless they are CONVERTIBLE bonds or CONVERTIBLE preferred—that stuff can be converted to common stock immediately in most cases. Finally, once you throw in the retirement account angle all of this capital gain/capital loss stuff flies out the window.

ANSWER: C

Dealing with Test Questions

There is no substitute for knowing the material. Unfortunately, that will only take you so far on the Series 7. In order to pass your exam, you need to sharpen your test-taking skills as much as possible. See, the test is very tricky. It likes to lead you down a false path and then ditch you, just to see if you can get yourself out of the forest. Many test-takers panic when they encounter unexpected forks in the trail, or unforeseen obstacles in their path. That's why we've provided this section on test-taking strategies. The following strategies will provide a sort of compass that can help guide you through all the nasty twists and turns you'll encounter on your exam.

Lesson One: Weeding out the unnecessary information.

The exam loves to give test-takers more information than they need to answer a question. If a test-taker needs three numbers, the exam will be sure to provide more like five or six.

Like this:

> **On August 12 August Augustus bought an XYZ Aug 50 put @ 3 when XYZ Corporation's common stock was trading at $52. On August 15, when the underlying stock is trading at $45, August buys the stock on the open market and exercises his Aug 50 put. What is August's gain or loss on the Aug 50 put that he purchased on August 12?**
> A. $300 gain
> B. $300 loss
> C. $200 gain
> D.   none of the above

Do you really need all that information given in the question? Of course not. That's why they gave it to you. So let's get rid of what we don't need. First of all, you could remove the word "August" and all the abbreviations thereof from the question.

So now it looks like this:

An investor bought a 50 put @ 3 when XYZ Corporation's common stock was trading at $52. When the underlying stock is trading at $45, the investor buys the stock on the open market and exercises his put. What is the investor's gain or loss?

Much easier to read now, right?

But there are still more weeds to pull. Do you need to know what XYZ Corporation's common stock was trading at when the investor bought the put?

Nope.

So now we're down to this:

An investor bought a 50 put @ 3. When the underlying stock is trading at $45, the investor buys the stock on the open market and exercises his put. What is the investor's gain or loss?

That's all the information we need to answer what used to look like a hard question. By weeding out the inessential noise from the essential information, we just reduced a 64-word question down to a 36-word question, a reduction of 44%.

So, are you ready to attack the question now that we've got the upper hand?

Good. Break out Mr. T-chart and let's knock this thing out. The investor bought the put for "3". That's money-out, so let's place $3 in the money-out column. He buys the stock at the market price of $45, so let's place $45 in the money-out column as well. He exercises his put, which gives him the right to sell the stock at the strike price of $50. So, let's place $50 in the money-in column. Then total it up. $48 went out, and $50 came in. Sounds like a gain of $200, doesn't it? So, the answer is C.

Lesson Two: Beware of trap doors.

Sometimes the exam can get downright nasty. You will encounter questions that intentionally mislead you. In fact, that's one of the main techniques used to test Series 7 candidates. The idea is to see if candidates can hang onto what they've learned, in spite of various tricks and traps that might spring up along the way. Sort of an intellectual obstacle course, if you will.

So, all we need to do is get in shape. Let's start with this one:

XYZ Corporation issued 1,000,000 shares of non-cumulative 6% preferred stock in June of 2004. In 2005 preferred stockholders received $2 in annual dividends. In 2006 XYZ's board of directors declared no dividends. Now in 2007, the board has declared the full 6% dividend. How much does the company have to pay in dividends on the 1,000,000 shares of preferred stock before dividends can be paid to common shareholders?

A. $6

B. $16

C. $20

D. $26, plus interest and back taxes

Careful! The question is misleading you. They've presented a scenario where dividends have been missed in the past. Well, holders of cumulative preferred stock would have to receive missed dividends plus current dividends before anybody else received a dime. But this question is talking about NON-cumulative preferred stock, which is why the correct answer is "A, $6." Non-cumulative preferred stockholders either receive the stated 6%, or they don't. In the year 2007, they do. The two previous years, they didn't. See how the whole question turned on the prefix "non"?

Careful. The Series 7 can get really tricky if you let it.

Lesson Three: Turn Roman numerals into an advantage.

Roman numeral questions intimidate some test takers, but they're really the easiest type to answer. If you can use the process of elimination effectively, you'll end up with an edge over these seemingly tough questions.

The following are considered to have an equity position in a corporation.

I.   common stockholders

II. preferred stockholders

III. convertible bondholders

IV. mortgage bondholders

A. I and II

B. I, II, and III

C. II and III

D. I, II, III, and IV

The question asks for "equity positions," right? Equity equals "ownership."

Bondholders aren't owners, they're creditors. So all you need to do is read the word "bondholders," and eliminate any choice that contains "III" or "IV." That gets rid of choices B, C, and D in one fell swoop.

With those choices gone, you're left with only:

A. I and II

Why? Because every other choice contained choice "III."

See how quickly you can annihilate the Roman numeral questions? Find something you know is false and eliminate all choices that contain that one. Like this:

Which of the following are true concerning bonds that are both callable and convertible?

I. If called, the owners have the option of retaining the bonds and will continue to receive interest.
II. After the date it is called, interest will cease.
III. Upon conversion, there will be dilution.
IV. The coupon rate would be less than the rate for a nonconvertible bond.

A. I and III
B. I, III, and IV
C. II, III, and IV
D. II and IV

When you read, "If called, the owners have the option of retaining the bonds and will continue to receive interest," a red flag should go up. You know that when a corporation calls a bond, that's it. Turn in your bonds, everybody, take the premium above par, and that's that. So choice "I" is completely false. Knowing that, we can eliminate any choice that contains Roman numeral "I."

So, now we're down to just:

C. II, III, and IV
D. II and IV

At this point, we just went from a 25% chance to a 50% chance, doubling our odds of success very quickly. So now what's different about choices "C" and "D?"

Right, both contain "II and IV," so all we have to do is read choice "III," which says, "Upon conversion, there will be dilution."

That's true of convertible bonds, right? If bondholders convert to common stock, there will be more shares of common stock. The corporation's earnings/profits don't change, but there are more shares to cut the earnings pie into. That's dilution. That's why "III" is in and choice "C" is correct.

Although I prefer the "negative approach," whereby I find something that's false and eliminate any answer choice that contains that one, you can also use the "positive approach." Here, you find something you're pretty sure is true and eliminate anything that does not contain that one.

Let's look at the same question from this angle:

Which of the following are true concerning bonds that are both callable and convertible?

I.   If called, the owners have the option of retaining the bonds and will continue to receive interest.

II. After the date it is called, interest will cease.

III. Upon conversion, there will be dilution.

IV. The coupon rate would be less than the rate for a nonconvertible bond.

A.   I and III

B.   I, III, and IV

C.   II, III, and IV

D.   II and IV

Which one of the four Roman numeral choices looks like it's true? Choices "III" and "IV" are kind of tough, right? What about choice "II"? You're pretty sure that once the bond is called, interest payments cease, right?

Okay, so if the answer choice does not contain a "II," let's eliminate it.

Choice A is gone. Choice B is gone.

And now we're right where we were before, trying to decide if choice "III" is correct. Why choice "III"? Because, once we eliminate A and B, our final answer will contain "II" and "IV." Does it also contain a "III"?

If you know that converting a bond into shares of stock will increase the number of slices the earnings pie must be cut into, you know the answer does contain a "III," which is why the answer is, again, "C."

See how easy that is? Just do it step-by-step. If you aren't sure about the choices, find one you are sure about and use it to eliminate other choices.

Lesson Four: Try reading the last sentence first.

Long test questions are not always harder than short test questions. Usually, a long question is designed to confuse test-takers. Reading from left to right, we take in all the irrelevant information provided in the question only to discover that the last sentence is leading us in a completely different direction. So, we get frustrated and have to read the whole paragraph over, conscious that the clock is still ticking.

Try reading the last sentence first, since that's usually where the question is located. For example:

In early October, an active options investor named Shirley went long 10 XXR Oct 60 calls @ 4.75 when the underlying stock was trading @61. After little movement in the stock's market price, Shirley continues to hold the calls, which she eventually expects to exercise close to expiration. How many shares of stock would change hands if Shirley exercised her calls?

See how the question appears to be about gains/losses but actually ends up asking about something else? All the question wants you to know is that 100 shares are covered in each equity option contract. So, if 10 options are exercised, we're talking about 1,000 shares changing hands. If we had read the last sentence first, we would have seen that right off and not been distracted by all the irrelevant verbiage in the first two sentences.

Another technique is to read the choices before you even look at the question. The four choices usually tell you what the question is about, whether it's about numbers, definitions, rules and regulations, taxes, etc. If you have a sense of where the question is going before you read it, you'll probably go in with a major advantage.

Lesson Five: Don't make the question harder than it is.

Many of the exam questions are very difficult. Some are moderately challenging. Some are downright easy. Like a skilled big-league pitcher, the Series 7 throws a devastating mix of fast balls, curve balls, and change-ups. Just when you get used to doing tricky questions on muni rules and regs, the exam will throw an easy question on variable annuities. Swing too fast, and you'll strike out every time.

So, if you encounter an easy question, don't assume you need to turn it into a hard question.

For example, you could see something like:

A standardized equity options contract covers 100 shares of the underlying instrument. If Carol Calloway holds 10 QRS Nov 50 puts, how many options does she own?
A. 100
B. 1,000
C. 10
D. 10,000

Maybe you caught the trap right away, but many test-takers would use the information provided in the first sentence and read it into the second sentence, which is a trap. If you do that, you end up thinking about how many *shares* of stock are covered in Carol Calloway's 10 QRS puts. Her 10 contracts cover 1,000 shares, but the question asks how many options does she own?

Ten.

The correct answer is "C, 10."

See? It's an easy question. It's just being asked in a tricky way.

Glossary

1035 contract exchange: a tax-free exchange of one annuity contract for another, one life insurance policy for another, or one life insurance policy for an annuity. The contracts do not have to be issued by the same company.

10Q: a public corporation's quarterly report filed with the SEC and made available to shareholders. Required by the Securities Exchange Act of 1934.

10K: a public corporation's audited annual report filed with the SEC and sent to shareholders. Required by the Securities Exchange Act of 1934.

12b-1 fee: an operating expense to mutual fund investors covering distribution expenses (selling, advertising). For no-load funds the maximum 12b-1 fee is .25%.

401(k) plan: qualified defined contribution plan usually offering employer-matched contributions.

403b, 501c3: tax-exempt, non-profit organization retirement plans funded with pre-tax dollars.

75-5-10 rule: diversification formula for a fund advertising itself as "diversified." 75% of the portfolio must have no more than 5% of assets invested in any one security, and no more than 10% of a company's outstanding shares may be owned.

A

A-Shares: mutual fund shares sold with a front-end sales load/charge. Lower annual expenses than B- and C-shares.

Acceptance, Waiver, and Consent (AWC): a method used to settle relatively minor violations of the conduct rules with the NASD. The hearing is waived and the person who violated rules accepts the findings of the disciplinary committee and consents to stop screwing up.

Account executive (AE): a fancy name for a registered representative or securities salesperson. The "AE" on a trade confirmation is identified by his or her initials to aid the client in his or her attempts to blame somebody when the stock goes down.

Accredited investor: a high-net-worth investor who can do things the Average Joe and JoAnne can not. An accredited investor can invest in hedge funds, which are unregistered investments that do not allow investors to sell for the first two years and do not even disclose what the money is being invested in. Accredited investors can also buy unregistered shares of stock on the primary market through private placements. An individual is accredited if she has over $1 million net worth or earns over $200,000 a year, $300,000 a year for married couples.

Accrued interest: what the buyer pays the seller on most bond transactions. This is the seller's rightful portion of the next interest check that the buyer will receive.

Accumulation Units: what the purchaser of an annuity buys during the pay-in phase, representing a proportional share of the separate account.

Ad valorem tax: basically a property tax. Latin for "as to value." As the value of your house goes up, so do your property taxes. Perhaps you've noticed.

Adjustable Rate Preferred Stock: preferred stock whose dividend is tied to another rate, often the rate paid on T-bills.

ADR/ADS: American Depository Receipt/Share. A foreign stock on a domestic market. Denominated in dollars, leaving the investor subject to foreign exchange risk. Sponsored ADR's typically give voting rights to the holder, while unsponsored ADR's typically do not. Toyota Motors Corporation trades on the NYSE as an ADR with the symbol "TM."

AIR: Assumed Interest Rate. Determined by an actuary, representing his best estimate of the monthly annualized rate of return from the separate account. Used to determine value of annuity units for annuities and death benefit for variable life contracts.

All or None: a type of underwriting whereby the syndicate will cancel the offering if a sufficient dollar amount is not raised.

Annuity Units: what the annuitant holds during the pay-out phase. Value tied to AIR.

Arbitrage: a strategy of trying to profit from an inefficiency or disparity of prices between two securities. If a convertible bond is trading for less than the underlying shares of stock, an "arbitrage opportunity" is available for anyone aggressive enough to short the stock and cover it by purchasing the bonds. Or, if a larger company looks likely to buy a smaller company, an arbitrageur could buy calls on the smaller company's stock and buy puts on/sell calls against the larger company's stock, betting that the announcement will send the smaller company's stock up and the acquiring company's stock down, at least temporarily.

Ask, Asked: the higher price in a quote representing what the customer would have to pay/what the dealer is asking the customer to pay. Customers buy at the ASK because dealers sell to customers at the ASK price.

Assets: pluses to a company's or individual's account: cash, investments, accounts receivable, inventory, etc.

Asset Allocation: maintaining a percentage mix of equity, debt, and money market investments, based either on the investor's age (strategic) or market expectations (tactical).

Associated Person: a registered representative or principal of a broker-dealer. The folks who need to take license exams such as the Series 7 (registered rep, principal) and Series 24 (principal). The folks required to file a U-4 in order to associate with a member firm.

Authorized: number of shares a company is authorized to issue by its corporate charter.

B

B-Shares: mutual fund shares charging a load on the back end. B – back end. When the investor sells/redeems the shares, a percentage is retained for the distributors. The percentage declines over time and after 6–8 years, the shares typically convert to A-shares, which charge lower annual operating expenses.

Backing Away: failure to honor a firm quote on the OTC market, a violation.

Balance of Payments: all money flowing into versus out of a country. Includes trade with foreign nations as well as investments.

Balance of Trade: exports from a country versus imports into the country. More exports = a trade surplus. More imports = trade deficit.

Balance Sheet: a statement of financial condition in which the assets are compared to the liabilities of an individual or a company.

Balanced Fund: a fund that maintains a mix of stocks and bonds at all times.

Balloon Maturity: a loan in which some of the principal is paid off early, with most of it coming due at the very end. Some bonds and some mortgages are structured this way.

Basis Points: a way of measuring bond yields or other percentages in the financial industry. Each basis point is 1% of 1%. Example: 2% = .0200 = 200 basis points.

Bearer Bond: an unregistered bond that pays principal to the bearer at maturity. Bonds have not been issued in this way for over two decades, but they still exist on the secondary market.

Best Efforts: a type of underwriting leaving the syndicate at no risk for unsold shares, and allowing them to keep the proceeds on the shares that were sold/subscribed to.

Beta: a measure of a stock's or a portfolio's volatility compared to the overall market. A beta of more than 1 means the investment is more volatile than the overall market, while a beta of less than 1 means the opposite.

Bid: what a dealer is willing to pay to a customer who wants to sell. Customers sell at the bid, buy at the ask.

Block Trade: a stock transaction of at least 10,000 shares.

Blotter: a daily record of all transactions effected through a broker-dealer.

Blue Chip: stock in a well-established company. Ideal for growth investors with limited risk tolerance.

Blue Sky: a reference to state securities law and state registration requirements for securities, agents, broker-dealers, and investment advisers.

Board of Directors: the group in charge of directing a company by establishing policies, hiring and firing officers, reporting the financials, etc. Elected by the shareholders.

Bond: a debt security issued by a corporation or governmental entity that promises to repay principal and pay interest either regularly or at maturity.

Bond Anticipation Note (BAN): a short-term note that a municipality uses to borrow money that will be paid back from the proceeds of an upcoming bond sale.

Bond Counsel: the law firm that renders a legal opinion concerning an issue of municipal securities.

Bond Point: 1% of a bond's par value. 1 bond point = $10.

Book Entry: a security maintained as a computer record rather than a physical certificate. All U.S. Treasuries and many mutual funds are issued in this manner.

Book Value: the hypothetical liquidating value of a share of common stock. Buying a stock close to its book value gives an investor a "margin of safety," a term used by Benjamin Graham, Warren Buffett's professor at Columbia and the father of "value investing."

Branch Office: any location identified by any means to the public or customers as a location at which the member conducts an investment banking or securities business.

Breakpoint: a discounted sales charge or "volume discount" offered on A-shares at various levels of investment.

Breakpoint Selling: preventing an investor from achieving a breakpoint. A violation.

Broker Call Loan Rate: interest rate that broker-dealers pay when borrowing on behalf of margin customers.

Broker-Dealer: any person in the business of effecting transactions in securities for the account of others (broker) or for its own account (dealer). Morgan-Stanley, for example, or Bear Stearns, Goldman Sachs, Charles Schwab, etc.

Bulletin Board: OTC stocks too volatile and low-priced for NASDAQ. A sort of purgatory for former Internet high-flyers.

Business Cycle: a progression of expansions, peaks, contractions, troughs, and recoveries for the overall (macro) economy.

C

C-Shares: often called "level load." Mutual fund shares bought with a 1% 12b-1 fee (high annual expenses) and usually no front-end load. suitable only for shorter-term investors.

Call: noun – a derivative that gives the holder the right to buy something at a stated exercise price. Verb – "to buy."

Call Protection: the period during which a security may not be called or bought by the issuer, usually lasting five years or more.

Call Risk: the risk that interest rates will fall and bonds will be called/forcibly redeemed early.

Call Spread: simultaneously buying a call and selling a call on the same underlying instrument.

Callable: a security that may be purchased/called by the issuer as of a certain date, e.g., callable preferred, callable bonds. Generally pays a higher rate of return than non-callable securities, as it gives the issuer flexibility in financing.

Capital Gain: selling a security for more than you bought it.

Capital Gains Distribution: distribution from fund to investor based on net capital gains realized by the fund portfolio.

Capital Loss: selling a security for less than you bought it.

Capital Risk: the risk that an investor will lose some or all of his investment.

Capping: a form of market manipulation in which shady characters sell a stock in order to depress its price.

Cash Account: a securities account requiring the customer to pay for all transactions in full, no later than five business days after the trade or "two days after regular way settlement," which is the same darned thing. As opposed to a margin account in which an investor can purchase stocks and bonds by putting down no more than half the purchase price.

Cash Equivalents: money market instruments, the top line of a company's balance sheet.

Cash Settlement: same-day settlement of a trade requiring prior broker-dealer approval. Not the "regular way" of doing things.

Cash Value: the value of an insurance policy that may be "tapped" by the policyholder through a loan or a partial surrender.

Clearing Firm: a broker-dealer that carries its customers' cash and securities and/or provides this service to introducing broker-dealers.

Closed-End Fund: an investment company that offers a fixed number of shares that are not redeemable. Shares are traded on the secondary market.

CMO: Collaterized Mortgage Obligation. An incredibly esoteric debt security that few people understand. Based on a pool of mortgages or a pool of mortgage-backed securities. Pays interest monthly but returns principal to one tranche at a time.

Code of Arbitration: NASD method of resolving money disputes in the securities business. All decisions are final and binding on all parties.

Code of Procedure: NASD system for enforcing member conduct rules.

Collateral Trust Certificate: a bond secured by a pledge of securities as collateral.

Combination Privilege: allows investors to combine purchases of many mutual funds within the family to reach a breakpoint/reduced sales charge.

Commercial Paper: a short-term corporate promissory note usually maturing in 270 days or less to claim an exemption to registration under the "Act of 1933."

Commingling: a violation in which the firm or agent mixes their assets with those of their customers.

Commissions: why you're still reading this book. A fee charged for executing a securities transaction on behalf of an investor.

Common Stock: the most "junior security," because it ranks last in line at liquidation. An equity or ownership position that usually allows the owner to vote on major corporate issues such as stock splits, mergers, acquisitions, authorizing more shares, etc.

Conduit Tax Treatment: a favorable tax treatment achieved if a company (REIT, mutual fund) distributes 90%+ of net income to the shareholders.

Contractual Plan: a plan allowing the participant to gradually accumulate mutual fund shares by paying regular installments to a "plan company." Not legal in all states due to complexity of rules and high sales loads.

Conversion/Exchange Privilege: a feature offered by many mutual funds whereby the investor may sell shares of one fund in the family and use the proceeds to buy another fund in the family at the NAV (avoiding the sales load). All gains/losses are recognized on the date of sale/conversion for tax purposes.

Convertible: a preferred stock or corporate bond allowing the investor to use the par value to "buy" shares of the company's common stock at a set price.

Cooling Off Period: the period after the registration statement for an issue of securities has been filed. Lasting a minimum of 20 days and often longer depending on SEC deficiency letters. No sales or advertising allowed during this period, which lasts until the effective or release date.

Coupon Rate: a.k.a. "nominal yield." The interest rate stated on a bond representing the percentage of the par value received by the investor each year.

Covered Call: selling a call against the stock you already own. Eliminates the unlimited risk presented by naked call writing.

CPI: Consumer Price Index, a measure of inflation/rising prices for basic consumer goods and services. Represents the greatest risk to most fixed-income investors.

Credit Risk: a.k.a. "default" or "financial" risk. The risk that the issuer will default on a debt security.

Cumulative Preferred: preferred stock where missed dividends go into arrears and must be paid before the issuer may pay dividends to other preferred stock and/or common stock.

Cumulative Voting: method of voting whereby the shareholder may take the total votes and split them up any way he chooses. Said to benefit minority over majority shareholders. Total votes are found by multiplying the number of shares owned by the number of seats up for election to the Board of Directors.

Current Yield: annual interest divided by market price of the bond. For example, an 8% bond purchased at $800 has a CY of 10%. $80/$800 = 10%.

CUSIP: Committee on Uniform Securities Identification Procedures. A CUSIP number is assigned to a security for purposes of tracking.

Custodian: maintains custody of a mutual fund's securities and cash. Performs payable/receivable functions for portfolio purchases and sales. In an UGMA, the custodian is the adult named on the account who is responsible for the investment decisions and tax reporting.

D

Dated Date: date when interest begins to accrue for a new issue of bonds.

Death Benefit: the amount payable to the beneficiary of a life insurance (or annuity) contract, minus any outstanding loans and/or unpaid premiums.

Debenture: fancy name for an unsecured corporate bond. Backed by the issuer's ability (or inability) to pay. No collateral.

Debt Limit: maximum amount of general obligation debt that an issuer can have outstanding at any one time.

Debt Security: a security representing a loan from an investor to an issuer. Offers a particular interest rate in return for the loan, not an ownership position.

Debt Service: the schedule of interest and principal payments that must be made to retire a loan by the maturity date.

Declaration Date: the date the Board declares a dividend.

Defensive Industry: an industry that can easily survive an economic downturn as its products and services tend to be purchased regardless of economic climate. Includes food, basic clothing, healthcare, pharmaceuticals, alcohol, tobacco and other essentials.

Deferred Annuity: an annuity that will begin to pay out in the future, as opposed to an immediate annuity that begins to pay out, believe it or not, immediately.

Deferred Compensation: a non-qualified business plan that defers some of the employee's compensation until retirement.

Defined Benefit: a qualified corporate pension plan that, literally, defines the benefit payable to the retiree.

Defined Contribution: a qualified corporate plan that defines the contribution made on behalf of the employee, e.g., profit sharing, 401(k).

Department of Enforcement: NASD enforcers of the member conduct rules, a group you never want to hear from, especially by certified mail.

Depletion: an accounting/tax deduction taken by a partnership when natural resources (gold, oil) are sold.

Depreciation: an accounting/tax deduction taken to reflect the gradual loss of value on a capital asset such as a printing press, or an apartment building.

Depression: what you'll feel if you score a 69 or lower on the exam. In economic terms, a depression is six quarters (18 months) of economic decline.

Discount Bond: any bond traded below the par value, e.g., @97.

Discount Rate: interest rate charged by FRB to member banks who borrow from the FRB.

Discretion: when a registered representative chooses any of the three A's—activity, asset, amount.

Disintermediation: the flow of money away from lower-yielding bank deposits to higher-yielding debt securities. Usually occurs when the Fed is tightening the money supply and raising interest rates.

Distribution Expenses: the cost of distributing/marketing a fund, including selling, printing prospectuses and sales literature, advertising, and mailing prospectuses to new/potential clients. Covered by sales charges/12b-1 fees.

Distributor/Underwriter/Sponsor: an NASD member firm that bears distribution costs of a fund upfront, profiting from the sales charges paid by the investors.

Diversified: a portfolio in which many different companies, industries are represented. The "don't-put-all-your-eggs-in-one-basket" method of investing. Fights non-systematic risk. A "diversified" mutual fund must follow the 75-5-10 rule.

Dividend: money paid to holders of common and preferred stock whenever the Board is feeling especially generous.

Dividend Payout Ratio: annual dividends divided by the earnings per share. A measure of how liberally a corporation pays out its profits to the shareholders.

Dividend Yield: annual dividends divided by market price of the stock. Equivalent to current yield for a debt security.

Dividend/Income Distributions: distributions from a fund to the investors made from net investment income. Typically, may be reinvested at the NAV to avoid sales charge.

Do Not Reduce (DNR): a little box on an order ticket that when checked indicates that a buy-limit or sell-stop order should not be reduced when a cash dividend is paid on the stock.

Dollar Cost Averaging: investing fixed dollar amounts regularly, regardless of share price. Usually results in a lower average cost compared to average of share prices, as investors' dollars buy majority of shares at lower prices.

Don't Know: a frightfully common response to Series 7 questions. Also, a broker-dealer's response to a request for a confirmation of a trade they, literally, don't know anything about. The firm abbreviates their confusion with the letters "DK," for "don't know."

Due Diligence: meeting between issuer and underwriters with the purpose of verifying all information contained in a registration statement/prospectus.

E

Earnings Per Share (EPS): the earnings of the company divided by the shares of common stock. This measures the amount of profits that are tied to each share of common stock.

Eastern Account: a bond underwriting in which each firm is responsible for a percentage of any unsold bonds the group has at the end, regardless of the firm's production. Often called an "undivided account."

Effective Date: date established by SEC as to when the underwriters may sell new securities to investors. a.k.a. "release date."

Efficient Market Theory: the theory stating that markets immediately and efficiently process all information into an accurate market price and, therefore, actively selecting stocks is pointless.

Eligibility: a section of ERISA that outlines who is/is not eligible to participate in a qualified plan. 1,000 hours worked over one year, 21 years old, etc.

Equipment Trust Certificate: a corporate bond secured by a pledge of equipment, e.g., airplanes, railroad cars.

ERISA: the Employee Retirement Income Security Act, governs pension plans in the private sector. A true qualified plan must conform to all the many requirements of ERISA, for example 401(k), defined benefit pension plans, and Keoghs have strict funding, participation, and vesting requirements.

Exchange Privilege: a feature offered by a mutual fund family allowing investors to sell shares of one fund and buy shares of another fund in the family without a sales charge.

Exchanges: auction markets where people don funny-colored jackets and scream like maniacs, complete with arcane hand gestures, wide eyes, and flying spittle.

Ex-Date: two days before the Record Date for OTC and exchange-listed securities. The date upon which the buyer is not entitled to the upcoming dividend. Note that for mutual funds, this date is established by the Board of Directors, usually the day after the Record Date.

Executor: the party in charge of a deceased individual's estate.

Exempt Security: a security not required to be registered, i.e., a US Treasury Bond.

Exercise: to use an option to buy or sell something at a stated price. An option can be traded, or it can be exercised at the strike price of the contract.

Expense Ratio: a mutual fund's operating expenses compared to/divided by its average net assets. Shows how efficiently a fund company invests your money versus how much they spend on management fees, board of director salaries, 12b-1 fees, etc.

F

Face-Amount Certificate: a debt security bought at a lower price than the face-amount. An investment company.

FDIC: what you aren't getting from your securities investments. Bank deposits are insured up to $100,000 per account in case the bank fails. Securities investments are not insured by the FDIC, as any mutual fund prospectus will shout out in bold letters.

Fed Funds Rate: interest rate charged on bank-to-bank loans. Subject to daily fluctuation.

FHLMC: a.k.a. "Freddie Mac." Like big sister Fannie Mae, a quasi-agency, public company that purchases mortgages from lenders and sells mortgage-backed securities to investors. Stock is listed on NYSE.

Fidelity Bond: insurance that protects investors from employees and broker-dealer firms that might accidentally steal their securities or, you know, lose them.

Fiduciary: someone responsible for the financial affairs of someone else, e.g., custodian, trustee, or registered rep in a discretionary account.

Fill or Kill: an order that must be filled in its entirety and immediately when the price conforms. If not, kill it.

Firm Commitment: an underwriting in which the underwriters agree to purchase all securities from an issuer, even the ones they failed to sell to investors. Involves acting in a "principal" capacity, unlike in "best efforts," "all or none," and "mini-max" offerings.

Fiscal Policy: Congress and President. Tax and Spend.

Flexible Premium: a premium that is flexible. Characteristic of "universal" insurance.

Flow of Funds: a statement for a revenue bond showing how revenues will be allocated and how the debt service will be prioritized, being paid either out of gross or net revenue.

FNMA: a.k.a. "Fannie Mae." Like little brother Freddie Mac, Fannie buys mortgages from lenders and sells mortgage-backed securities to investors. A quasi-agency, a public company listed for trading on the NYSE.

FOMC: the FRB's Federal Open Market Committee. Sets short-term interest rates by setting discount rate, reserve requirement and buying/selling T-bills to/from primary dealers.

Forward Pricing: means that mutual fund shares are bought and sold at the next computed price, not yesterday's stale prices.

Fourth Market, INSTINET: an ECN (electronic communications network) used by institutional investors, bypassing the services of a traditional broker. Institutionals = INSTINET.

Fraud: the use of deception or manipulation to gain an unfair advantage over someone in connection with the offer, sale, or purchase of any security.

Free-Look: period during which a contract or policyholder may cancel and receive all sales charges paid. Not a popular phrase among seasoned insurance agents.

Front-end Load: a mutual fund class A-share that charges a sales load on the front-end, when the shares are purchased. As opposed to a back-end load or B-share that charges a load when the shares are sold/redeemed.

Frozen Account: an account that is in the naughty chair for 90 days because the owner failed to make payment within the time frame established by Reg T. While the account is frozen, the customer has to have cash in the account to cover any purchase order.

Fully Registered Bonds: bonds that are fully registered. A physical certificate with the owner's name, and interest payable automatically by the paying agent (no coupons).

Fundamental Analysis: studying a corporation's sales, profits, and other financial measures in order to determine a good investment from a poor one.

Fungible: items that can be easily exchanged since one is just as good as any other. For example, $20 bills are fungible—if 100 people each put a $20 bill into a box, shook up the box, and then pulled out one bill each, no one would have lost anything, except perhaps precious time proving a painfully obvious point. Puts and calls are fungible, which is why the call that I exercise can be assigned to any member firm, who can in turn assign it to *any* customer who wrote that series of options. A MSFT Jun 50 call is a MSFT Jun 50 call, just like 100 shares of MSFT is 100 shares of MSFT.

Functional Allocation: a sharing arrangement for a DPP in which the GP takes the tangible costs and the IDC's (intangible drilling costs) such as labor and geological surveys go to the LP's.

G

GDP: Gross Domestic Product, the sum total of all goods and services being produced by the economy. A positive GDP number is evidence of economic expansion.

General Account: where an insurance company invests net premiums in order to fund guaranteed, fixed payouts.

General Obligation bond (GO): a municipal bond backed by the issuer's full taxing authority. A school bond, for example.

General Partner (GP): the party that manages a limited partnership and is liable for the debts of the company.

Generic Advertising: an advertisement that promotes a firm or a family of mutual funds without recommending any specific securities.

GNMA: a.k.a. "Ginnie Mae," nickname for Government National Mortgage Association. A government agency (not a public company) that buys insured VA and FHA mortgages from lenders, selling pass-through certificates to investors. Monthly payments to investors pay interest and also pass through principal from a pool of mortgages. Recall that bonds pay interest and return principal only at maturity, while "pass throughs" pass through principal monthly. Thus, the clever name "pass through."

Good 'Til Cancel (GTC): a limit or stop order that remains open until it is either executed or canceled.

Growth: investment objective that seeks "capital appreciation." Achieved through common stock. Requirement for people saving up for retirement. Growth funds buy stocks in companies whose earnings are expected to grow faster than other companies'. Dividends are of secondary or even no importance to this investor.

Growth & Income: a mutual fund that purchases stocks offering both growth and income, believe it or not. A company such as GE, for example, pays consistent dividends but might also offer some growth over the long-term.

Guardian Account: an account opened on behalf of a minor by a court-appointed guardian.

H

Head and Shoulders: a price pattern that signals the reversal of a trend to a technical analyst.

Hedge: an offsetting position designed to reduce the risk taken by another position. For example, after buying stock, the investor can hedge by purchasing a put on or selling a covered call against that stock.

Holding Period: the period during which an investor held a security. The holding period determines whether a capital gain/loss is long-term or short-term.

Hypothecate: to pledge a security as collateral for a loan (margin accounts).

I

Immediate or Cancel (IOC): a limit or stop order in which the investor will accept whatever part of the order becomes immediately available at the specified price, with any remainder canceled. For example, a buy-limit for 1,000 shares of MSFT @25 marked "immediate or cancel" would allow the floor broker to purchase just 600 shares if they became available at $25 or lower, canceling the remaining 400 shares if they were not immediately available. On the other hand, a "fill or kill" order for 1,000 shares would have been killed if the price had dropped to $25 or lower with only 600 shares available.

Immediate Annuity: an annuity that begins to pay out—get this—immediately.

Income: investment objective that seeks current income, found by investing in fixed income, e.g., bonds, money market, preferred stock.

Income Bond: a bond that only pays interest if the issuer has enough income to do so.

Income Statement: a corporation's statement of profit or lack thereof. The income statement shows the company's revenue over the quarter or fiscal year, then subtracts all the related costs (cost of goods sold, salaries, paper, toner, interest expenses, and taxes) to show whether there is any money left in the form of a profit.

Indication of Interest: an investor's expression of interest in buying a new issue of securities. Not a binding agreement.

Industrial Development Bond (IDR/IDB): a municipal bond issued to build a facility that will be leased to a corporation.

Inflation: rising prices, as measured by the Consumer Price Index (CPI).

Inside Market: the highest bid and lowest offer price for a security.

Interest Rates: the cost of a commodity called money.

Interpositioning: a violation in which another party is placed between a customer and the best market for a security.

Intrinsic Value: the amount that an option is in-the-money. A MSFT Nov 50 call has $3 of intrinsic value if MSFT trades at $53, for example.

Inverse Relationship: when one goes up, the other goes down, and vice versa. Interest Rates and Yields are inversely related to Bond Prices.

Inverted Yield Curve: a situation in which short-term interest rates are higher than intermediate- or long-term interest rates.

Investment Adviser: a business that is compensated for advising others as to the value of or advisability of investing in securities. The entity that manages mutual funds/separate accounts for an asset-based fee.

Investment Banking: the business of helping companies with mergers and acquisitions, performing IPO's and additional offerings. Buying securities from an issuer and re-offering them at a higher price to investors, keeping the "spread" for your trouble.

Investment Company Act of 1940: classified Investment Companies and set rules for registration and operation.

IRA: Individual Retirement Account. If the word "Roth" does not precede it, assume it's a "Traditional IRA" offering tax-deductible (pre-tax) contributions and fully taxable distributions.

Issued Shares: the number of shares that have been issued by a corporation.

Issuer: a person who issues or proposes to issue securities.

Issuing Securities: raising capital by offering securities to investors on the primary market.

J

JTIC: Joint Tenants In Common account where the assets of the deceased party pass to the deceased's estate, not the other account owner(s).

JTWROS: Joint Tenants With Rights Of Survivorship account where the assets of the deceased party pass to the other account owner(s).

Junk Bond: a bond backed up by a shaky issuer. Often called a "high-yield" or "high-income" bond.

K

Keogh: qualified retirement plan available to sole proprietorships.

Keynesian Economics: a belief that fiscal policy is the best way to manage the economy, that the government can increase "aggregate demand" for goods and services by implementing the proper taxing and spending policies.

L

Large Cap: a stock where the total value of the outstanding shares is large, generally greater than $10 billion. For example, GE, MSFT, IBM.

LEAPS: long-term options contracts that allow people to speculate on prices that are up to 39 months into the future. As opposed to an ordinary option, which expires in 9 months maximum and is usually only traded a few months in advance.

Legislative Risk: the risk that legislation will be passed that has a negative impact on a securities investment. For example, if automobile manufacturers were suddenly required to produce vehicles that get 90 mpg by the end of 2008, stock in Ford and GM might take a slight hit that day.

Letter of Intent: LOI, a feature of many mutual funds whereby an investor may submit a letter or form expressing the intent to invest enough money to achieve a breakpoint.

Level Load: a class of mutual fund share that charges a high 12b-1 fee. C-shares are often called "level load" due to the 1% 12b-1 fee.

Leverage: the use of borrowed money, i.e., raising capital by issuing bonds.

Liabilities: minuses to the account of an individual or business, e.g., credit card debt, bonds, accounts payable.

Life Only: a payout option whereby the insurance/annuity company promises to make payments only for the rest of the annuitant's life.

Life with Joint and Last Survivor: a payout option whereby the insurance/annuity company promises to make payments to the annuitant for the rest of his life, then to the survivor for the rest of her life.

Life with Period Certain: a payout option whereby the insurance/annuity company promises to make payments to the annuitant for the rest of his life or a certain period of time, whichever is greater.

Life with Unit Refund: a payout option whereby the insurance/annuity company promises to make at least a certain number of payments to the annuitant.

Limit Order: a buy or sell order in which the price for execution is stipulated.

Liquidity: the ease with which a security can be sold for a decent price.

Liquidity Risk: the risk that when you want to sell, nobody cares.

Long: to buy or own.

Long-term Gain: selling a security held for more than 12 months for more than you bought it.

Long-term Loss: selling a security held for more than 12 months for less than you bought it. Congratulations. Long-term losses are used to offset any long-term gains.

Lump Sum Payment: a settlement/payout option for annuities or insurance where the annuitant or beneficiary receives a lump sum payment.

M

Maintenance Call: a friendly phone call from your broker to inform you that while everything in your margin account is doing just fine, you will need to deposit more money just the same. For long positions, when the equity drops below 25% of market value a maintenance call will occur. For short accounts, as soon as equity drops below 30% a maintenance call will occur.

Maintenance Covenant: a pledge that the issuer will keep the facility financed by a revenue bond properly maintained so that people will actually pay to use the thing in order to generate the revenues needed to pay the bondholders.

Maloney Act of 1938: an amendment to the Securities Exchange Act of 1934 giving the NASD the authority to act as the SRO for the OTC (over-the-counter market).

Management Company: one of the three types of Investment Companies, including both open-end and closed-end funds.

Management Fee: what an investment adviser charges to manage a portfolio, usually expressed as a percentage of assets. Mutual funds charge investors management fees that are paid to the portfolio manager, which is usually and quite coincidentally a subsidiary of the mutual fund company.

Manager's Fee: typically the smallest piece of the spread, paid to the managing underwriter for every share sold by the syndicate.

Mark Down: the profit a dealer receives by purchasing a security for less than the seller would probably like.

Mark to the Market: calculating the current value of securities positions to determine if a customer has excess equity or if perhaps a maintenance call is required.

Mark Up: the profit a dealer makes by selling a security for more than the buyer would probably like.

Market Maker: a dealer in the OTC market maintaining an inventory of a particular security and a Bid and Ask price good for a minimum of 100 shares.

Market Out Clause: a clause giving the underwriters the ability to bail on a securities offering if there is a material problem with the issuer. For example, if the CEO and CFO are hauled off in handcuffs today, tomorrow's IPO is so not happening.

Material Information: any information likely to affect an investment decision. For example, the sales and profits of a company are material when deciding to buy or sell their stock or bonds. The color that they paint their visitor lobby at head-quarters is probably immaterial to an investor.

Maturity: the date that a bond pays out the principal, a.k.a. "redemption."

MBIA: Municipal Bond Investors Assurance Corporation, insures municipal bonds against default.

Mini-Max: a type of best efforts underwriting where the syndicate must sell a minimum amount and may sell up to a higher, maximum amount.

Modern Portfolio Theory: a theory that looks at the portfolio as a whole in terms of risk/reward as opposed to considering each security within the portfolio on its own.

Monetary Policy: what the FRB implements through the discount rate, reserve requirement, and FOMC open market operations.

Money Market Mutual Fund: a highly liquid holding place for cash. Sometimes called "stable value" funds, as the share price is generally maintained at $1.

Moral Obligation Bond: a revenue bond in which legislatures can vote to possibly raise enough money to make up for shortfalls in revenue.

Mortality Guarantee: a promise from an insurance company to pay an annuitant no matter how long he lives, or to pay an insurance policyholder no matter how soon he dies.

Mortgage Bond: a corporate bond secured by a pledge of real estate as collateral.

Mutual Fund: a gigantic investment pie that sells slices to investors and uses the money paid for the shares to buy ingredients for the pie.

N

Narrow-Based Index: an index focusing on just one market sector or some narrowly defined geographic region, perhaps. A pharmaceutical index would group stocks of pharmaceutical companies, and a telecommunications index would focus, believe it or not, on telecommunications companies.

NASDAQ: National Association of Securities Dealers Automated Quotation system. The main component of the OTC market. Stocks that meet certain criteria are quoted throughout the day on NASDAQ, e.g., MSFT, ORCL, and INTC.

National Adjudicatory Council: NAC, the first level of appeal for a party sanctioned by the Department of Enforcement under the NASD's Code of Procedure.

National Securities Clearing Corporation: the clearing intermediary through which member firms reconcile all their buy and sell transactions.

NAV: the net asset value of a mutual fund share. Assets – Liabilities/Outstanding Shares.

Net Worth: the difference between assets and liabilities. Add up the value of your house, bank accounts, IRA, etc. Subtract everything you owe—credit card debt, mortgage balance, student loans. The difference is your personal "net worth" and with any luck it starts with a plus sign.

Net Investment Income: what a mutual fund pays dividend distributions from. Dividends plus interest minus expenses = net investment income. 90%+ is often distributed to investors under the "conduit tax theory."

Net Revenue Pledge: a flow of funds statement revealing that debt service on the bonds will be paid out of net revenue, after operating expenses are met.

NIC (net interest cost): the calculation of an issuer's total cost of borrowing money through a bond issue. Used to determine the winning syndicate in a competitive-bid underwriting of municipal securities.

No-Load Fund: a fund with no load. There is no sales charge to buy or sell shares of a no-load fund, but the fund may still charge a 12b-1 fee up to .25%. If the company calls itself "100% no-load," that means there is no sales charge and also no 12b-1 fee.

Nominal Yield: the interest rate that a bond pays to investors as stated right there on the bond certificate.

Non-diversified: a fund that doesn't care to meet the 75-5-10 rule, preferring to concentrate more heavily in certain issues.

Not Held Order: an order in which the customer names everything except the price/
time for execution.

O

Odd Lot: an annoying order for fewer than 100 shares of stock.

Odd Lot Theory: the theory that people who can only afford to buy under 100 shares
of stock consistently buy too high and sell too low, so just do the opposite of what
these geniuses are doing, and you'll do fine.

Offering Circular: a document given to investors when a prospectus is not required. For
example, an offer of church bonds would not have a prospectus registered with the
SEC but would still come with a document detailing what is being offered and why
an investor might want to buy it or maybe leave it the heck alone. Since this offering
document is being circulated, they decided to call it an "offering circular."

Official Notice of Sale: the document that an issuer publishes in order to attract
underwriters interested in taking an issue of bonds to investors on the primary
market.

Official Statement: the offering or financial disclosure document that an investor
receives when purchasing an issuer's municipal securities.

Open-End Fund: a.k.a. "mutual fund," an investment company that sells an unlimited
number of shares to an unlimited number of investors on a continuous basis. Shares
are redeemed by the company rather than traded OTC or on the exchanges.

Open-End Issue/Covenant: a bond that allows the issuer to sell future bonds backed
by the same collateral and having equal claims as the original bonds.

Options Clearing Corporation (OCC): the party that issues and guarantees performance of listed options contracts.

Options Disclosure Document: the prospectus given to people considering the trading
of options. Must be delivered at or before the time that the ROP approves the
account for trading. Explains how options work and how they often don't.

Order Ticket: the ticket that the registered representative fills out when placing an
order. The order ticket or "order memorandum" names the security to be purchased,
the number of shares, whether it's a market/limit/stop order, whether discretion
is being used, which exchange the security trades on, etc.

Original Issue Discount (OID): a bond issued originally at a discount. Unless it's
a municipal OID, the amount that the par value increases/accretes each year is
taxable to the investor as if she had actually, like, received the money.

OTC/Over-the-Counter: called a "negotiated market." Includes NASDAQ and also Bulletin Board and Pink Sheet stocks, plus government, corporate, and municipal bonds.

Out-of-the-Money: an option whose strike price would give no one an advantage since it isn't even close to the market price. If MSFT trades at $33, a MSFT Aug 50 call would be *way* out-of-the-money, and so would a MSFT Aug 20 put.

Outstanding Shares: the number of shares a corporation has outstanding. Found by taking Issued shares minus Treasury stock.

Overriding Royalty Interest: a type of sharing arrangement that gives somebody a share of revenue without having to share any risk. For example, if oil were found on your land, the oil drilling partnership might offer you an overriding royalty interest for the right to drill on your property.

P

Par, Principal: the face amount of a bond payable at maturity. Also, the face amount of a preferred stock. Preferred = $100, Bond = $1,000.

Parity: when the underlying common stock trades for exactly the market value of the convertible preferred stock or convertible bond. For example, if the bond is convertible into 50 shares of stock and the stock trades for $24, the bond would trade at parity if its market price were exactly $1,200.

Partial Call: a provision by which the issuer calls only part of a bond issue, usually by a lottery.

Partial Surrender: life insurance policyholder cashes in part of the cash value. Excess over premiums is taxable.

Participating Preferred Stock: preferred stock whose dividend is often raised above the stated rate.

Pass-Through Certificate: a mortgage-backed security (usually GNMA) that takes a pool of mortgages and passes through interest and principal monthly to an investor.

Payable Date: the date that the dividend check is paid to investors.

Payroll Deduction: non-qualified retirement plan offered by some businesses.

Pension Plan: a contractual retirement plan in which the employer promises to pay a benefit to the employee in retirement.

Performance Figures: total return for a mutual fund over 1, 5, and 10 years, or "life of fund" for newly established funds. Only past performance may be indicated, and there must be a caveat that past performance does not guarantee future results.

Periodic Deferred Annuity: method of purchasing an annuity whereby the contract holder makes periodic payments into the contract. The pay-out phase must be deferred for all periodic payment plans.

Permanent Insurance: insurance that remains in place permanently, as opposed to term insurance, which keeps expiring and has to be renewed at higher rates. Whole life and variable life insurance are forms of permanent insurance, while term insurance is temporary.

Pink Sheets: a virtually unregulated part of the OTC market where thinly traded, volatile stocks change hands.

Placement Ratio: the dollar amount of bonds sold out of the dollar amount of bonds offered on the primary market last week, published in the daily Bond Buyer.

Plus Tick Rule: the rule that allows short sales to only be executed at a plus tick or the repeat of a plus tick (zero-plus tick). In other words, a short sale can not be executed at a price that is lower than the previous price reported to the tape.

POP: public offering price. For an IPO, this includes the spread to the underwriters. For a mutual fund, this includes any sales loads that go to the underwriter/ distributor.

Power of Substitution: a document that when signed by the security owner authorizes transfer of the certificate to another party.

Preemptive Right: the right of a common stockholder to maintain her percentage of ownership. If the corporation offers additional shares, she has the right to buy enough to maintain the same percentage she owns today.

Preferred Stock: a fixed-income equity security whose stated dividends must be paid before common stock can receive any dividend payment. Also gets preference ahead of common stock in a liquidation (but behind all bonds and general creditors).

Preliminary Prospectus: a prospectus that lacks the POP and the effective date. a.k.a. "red herring." Used to solicit indications of interest.

Price-to-Earnings ratio: comparison of a stock's market price to the earnings associated with that share of stock. A stock with an EPS (earnings per share) of $2 would have a price-to-earnings (PE) ratio of 20 if it were trading for $40. If the PE ratio were 30, the stock would trade for $60.

Price Spread: buying and selling two options where the only difference is in the strike prices. If an investor buys the XYZ Jun 50 call and sells the XYZ Jun 60 call, he has established a price spread.

Primary Market: where securities are issued to raise capital for the issuer.

Prime Rate: interest rate charged to corporations with high credit ratings for unsecured loans.

Principal Transaction: a transaction in which the firm takes the other side as opposed to merely arranging a transaction. Rather than charging a "commission," a principal transaction involves a markup or markdown.

Private Placement: a private offering of securities to a limited number of sophisticated investors that thereby escapes registration requirements.

Private Securities Transaction: an offering of an investment opportunity not sponsored by the firm. Requires permission from the firm and any disclosure demanded; otherwise, a violation called "selling away."

Profit Sharing: a defined contribution plan whereby the company shares any profits with employees in the form of contributions to a retirement account.

Prospectus: a disclosure document that details a company's plans, history, officers, and risks of investment. It's the red herring plus the POP and the effective date.

Proxy: method of voting for shareholders who will not be attending the annual shareholder meeting.

Put: noun – a derivative giving the owner the right to sell something at a stated exercise price. Verb – "to sell."

Q

Qualified Legal Opinion: exactly what the issuer does *not* want from the bond counsel, as this opinion expresses some doubts/uncertainties concerning the legality and tax status of the municipal bonds about to be issued.

Qualified Plan: a retirement plan that qualifies for deductible contributions on behalf of employers and/or employees if it meets IRS approval, and is covered by ERISA. For example, 401(k), defined benefit, Keogh.

Quick Ratio: Current Assets minus Inventory divided by Current Liabilities. A more stringent measure of a corporation's solvency.

Quote: the prices at which a security can be purchased (offer) and sold (bid) as well as the number of shares available to buyers and sellers at those quoted prices.

R

Random Withdrawals: a settlement option in an annuity whereby the investor takes the value of the subaccounts in two or more withdrawals, rather than one lump sum.

Rate Covenant: a promise by the issuer to raise rates if necessary to generate sufficient revenues to pay the debt service to the holders of revenue bonds.

Real Estate Investment Trust (REIT): a trust that owns real estate and sells units/shares to investors. Typically pays high dividend yields because they pass through at least 90% of net income to investors. Most REITs trade on the exchanges alongside MSFT, GE, ORCL, etc.

Real Estate Limited Partnership: as opposed to a REIT, this investment is not traded among investors and does pass through a share of the losses to investors.

Recapture: e.g., in a limited partnership an apartment building may be sold for more than its depreciated cost basis. If so, that is recaptured by the IRS, who, as always, is here to help.

Recession: from two quarters (6 months) to six quarters (18 months) of economic decline.

Record Date: the date determined by the Board of Directors upon which the investor must be the holder "of record" in order to receive the upcoming dividend. Settlement of a trade must occur by the record date for the buyer to receive the dividend.

Recourse Loan: a loan that gives the creditors the recourse to come after the limited partners for a certain amount of debt if the partnership can't pay them.

Red Herring: a.k.a. "preliminary prospectus." Contains essentially the same information that the final prospectus will contain, minus the POP and effective date.

Redeemable security: a security that is sold back to the issuer rather than traded among investors. An open-end mutual fund is a redeemable security, while a closed-end fund is traded among investors.

Redemption: for mutual funds, redemption involves the sale of mutual fund shares back to the fund at the NAV (less any redemption fees, back-end loads). For bonds, the date that principal is returned to the investor, along with the final interest payment.

Reg T: established by the FRB as the amount of credit a broker-dealer may extend to a customer pledging a security as collateral for a margin loan. Currently 50% of market value.

Reg U: established by the FRB as the amount of credit a bank may extend to a broker-dealer or public customer pledging a security as collateral.

Registered as to Principal Only: a bond with only the principal registered. Interest coupons must be presented for payment.

Registrar: audits the transfer agent to make sure number of authorized shares is never exceeded.

Regular Way Settlement: the normal time frame for settling/clearing a transaction between the buy and the sell side. Regular way settlement is T + 3 for corporate stock, corporate bonds, and municipal bonds, T + 1 for listed options and Treasury securities trading on the secondary market.

Reinvestment Risk: the risk that a fixed-income investor will not be able to reinvest interest payments or the par value at attractive interest rates.

Release Date: date established by the SEC as to when the underwriters may sell new securities to the buyers, a.k.a. "effective date."

Repurchase Agreement: a short-term loan that is fully secured. One party sells securities today for, say, $1 million and agrees to repurchase them in 30 days for $1.05 million. The extra amount paid is the seller's interest for the loan. Part of the money market.

Reserve Requirement: the percentage of customer deposits that banks have to lock up in reserve, established by the Federal Reserve Board of all people.

Resistance: the point at which a stock's price rises but then attracts enough sellers to knock the price back down a while.

Retained Earnings: earnings that have been retained. Seriously. It's the profits that the company has made but simply refuses to pay out in the form of dividends. Rather, the earnings are retained by the company and reinvested into the business.

Revenue Anticipation Note (RAN): a short-term loan to a municipality backed up with some revenues they have not actually collected yet.

Reverse Split: artificially raising the market price for a share of stock by creating fewer shares. A 1:10 reverse split means that your 100 really cheap-looking shares will become just 10 expensive-looking shares after the split. If you owned 100 shares @1, you will soon own 10 big shares worth $10 each.

Rights: short-term equity securities that allow the holder to buy new shares below CMV.

Rights of Accumulation: feature of many mutual funds whereby a rise in account value is counted the same as new money for purposes of achieving a breakpoint.

Riskless Simultaneous Transaction: a transaction in which the firm already has a customer order, then buys the security for inventory just long enough to sell it on a principal basis, at a markup, as opposed to executing the order as an agent for a commission.

Roth IRA: individual retirement account funded with non-deductible (after-tax) contributions. All distributions are tax-free provided the individual is 59½ and has had the account at least five years.

S

Sales Charge, Sales Load: amount of the POP that goes to the distributors. POP – NAV.

Sales Literature: written materials distributed by a member firm to a controlled audience and designed to increase business. Research reports, market letters, flyers, circulars, and other written materials sent to a selected audience are considered "sales literature." Other examples of sales literature include computer slide shows and a form letter sent to 25 or more prospects in a 30-day period.

Scheduled Premium: life insurance with established, scheduled premium payments, i.e., whole life, variable life. As opposed to "universal" insurance, which is "flexible premium."

Secondary Market: where investors trade securities among themselves and proceeds do not go to the issuer.

Secondary Offering: a transaction in which certain large shareholders receive the proceeds of a stock sale. When companies perform their IPO, a certain percentage of the shares are usually being offered by the founders; whenever the proceeds go to someone other than the issuer, the word "secondary" is used. When the issuer receives the proceeds, the word "primary" is used.

Sector Fund: a.k.a. "specialized." A fund that concentrates heavily in a particular industry or geographic area, e.g., "The Japan Fund," or the "Technology Fund." Higher risk/reward than funds invested in many industries.

Secured Bond: a corporate bond secured by collateral, e.g., mortgage bond, collateral trust certificate, equipment trust certificate.

Securities Act of 1933: a.k.a. "Paper Act," regulates the new-issue or primary market, requiring non-exempt issuers to register securities and provide full disclosure.

Securities Exchange Act of 1934: a.k.a. "People Act." Very broad scope covering short-sales, corporate reporting, anti-fraud rules, insider trading ban, solicitation of proxies, gave FRB power to regulate margin, etc.

Securities and Exchange Commission: SEC, empowered by passage of Securities Exchange Act of 1934. A government body, the ultimate securities regulator.

Security: an investment of money subject to fluctuation in value and negotiable/marketable to other investors.

Self-Regulatory Organization: SRO, e.g., NASD. An organization given the power to regulate its members with passage of the Maloney Act.

Selling Away: a violation that occurs when a registered representative offers investment opportunities not sponsored by the firm.

Selling Concession: typically, the largest piece of the underwriting spread going to the firm credited with making the sale.

Selling Dividends: the deceptive practice of enticing an investor to purchase a stock or mutual fund primarily for the upcoming dividend. The investor will pay the full purchase price, then immediately receive part of it back and pay tax on the difference.

Selling Group: a group of selling broker-dealers willing to help a syndicate place a new issue of securities with some of their customers. The selling group has no liability and profits by purchasing securities "at the concession" from the syndicate and selling them to investors at the higher public offering price (POP).

Separate Account: an account maintained by an insurance/annuity company that is separate from the company's general account. Used to invest clients' money for variable annuities and variable insurance contracts. Registered as an investment company.

SEP-IRA: retirement plan available to small businesses, similar to Keogh. Favors high-earning employees.

Settlement: final completion of a securities transaction, when the new owner is recognized officially by the transfer agent.

Settlement Options: payout options on annuities and life insurance.

Short Sale: method of attempting to profit from a security whose price is expected to fall. Trader borrows certificates through a broker-dealer and sells them, with the obligation to replace them at a later date, hopefully at a lower price. Bearish position.

SIMPLE IRA: retirement plan for small business with no more than 100 employees and no other retirement plan. Favors lower-earning employees (as compared to SEP-IRA).

Single Payment Deferred Annuity: annuity purchased with a single payment wherein the individual defers the payout or "annuity" phase of the contract.

Single Payment Immediate Annuity: annuity purchased with a single payment wherein the individual goes immediately into the payout or "annuity" phase of the contract.

Sinking Fund: an account that an issuer deposits money into for the sole purpose of returning the principal due on a bond issue.

SIPC: Securities Investor Protection Corporation, a non-profit, non-government, industry-funded insurance corporation protecting investors against broker-dealer failure.

Small Cap: a stock where the total value of all outstanding shares is considered "small," typically between $50 million and $2 billion.

Special Tax Bond: a revenue bond backed by special taxes on items such as alcohol, tobacco, hotel & motel, and gasoline. For example, to back the debt service on the bonds issued to build Soldier Field here in Chicago, the city was smart enough to use hotel & motel taxes. I mean, who better to tax than a bunch of out-of-towners with fat expense accounts?

Specialist: a member of the NYSE charged with "maintaining a fair and orderly market" in a particular security. Trades for own account, not an exchange employee.

Spread: generally, the difference between a dealer's purchase price and selling price, both for new offerings (underwriting spread) and secondary market quotes. For underwritings the spread is the difference between the proceeds to the issuer and the POP.

Stabilizing: perhaps the only time that market manipulation is allowed—the syndicate may place bids for the stock on the secondary market designed to prop up the price immediately after a primary offering/IPO. The bid can be no higher than the POP, but placing big orders to buy the stock at or near the POP can have a stabilizing effect on the market price for that stock.

Standby Underwriting: a firm commitment for a rights offering in which an underwriter "stands by" willing to subscribe to any of the shares that existing shareholders don't want.

Statutory Disqualification: registration rule by an SRO, the SEC, or a state regulator preventing persons with regulatory or criminal pasts from being accepted for registration in the securities business. Typically, any felony, securities-related misdemeanor, or regulatory action over the past 10 years will disqualify an applicant for registration.

Statutory Voting: method of voting whereby the shareholder may cast no more than the number of shares owned per candidate/item.

Stock Ahead: a frustrating condition in which a customer's limit order could be filled based on the market price but isn't yet because there are other orders ahead getting filled at the moment.

Stop Order: an order to buy or sell a security that is activated when the security hits or passes through the stop price, then becomes a market order.

Stop-Limit Order: a stop order that once activated becomes a limit order executed at the customer's limit price or better.

Stopping Stock: a courtesy in which the specialist guarantees a price but seeks a better price for execution of a public order.

Straddle: buying a call and a put with the same strike price and expiration month or selling a call and a put with the same strike price and expiration month.

Straight Preferred Stock: a preferred stock whose missed dividends do not go into arrears, a.k.a. "non-cumulative preferred."

STRIPS: Separate Trading of Registered Interest and Principal of Securities. A zero coupon bond issued by the U.S. Treasury.

Subaccount: investment options available within the separate account for variable contract holders.

Subordinated Debenture: corporate bond with a claim that is subordinated or "junior" to a debenture and/or general creditor.

Surrender: to cash out an annuity or life insurance policy for its surrender value.

Syndicate: a group of underwriters bringing an issuer of securities to the primary market.

Systematic Risk: the risk that the overall market can decline at any point. To offset, investors buy puts on broad-based indices or sell ETF's short. Seriously.

T

T + 3: regular way settlement, trade date plus three business days.

TAN (Tax Anticipation Note): a short-term loan to a municipality backed up by some taxes they haven't actually collected yet.

Tax-Deferred: an account where all earnings remain untaxed until "constructive receipt."

Tax-Equivalent Yield: what a taxable bond would have to pay in order to be equivalent to the municipal (tax-free) bond that an investor is considering. For example, if an investor in the 30% bracket is eyeing a tax-free municipal bond that yields 7%, the tax-equivalent yield would be found on a taxable corporate bond offering 10%. To calculate, take the tax-free yield of 7% and divide by 70% (100% minus tax bracket).

Tax Preference Item: an item receiving favorable tax treatment that has to be added to income for purposes of AMT. Accelerated depreciation, for example, or interest paid by private purpose municipal bonds.

T-bills: direct obligation of U.S. Government. Sold at discount, mature at face amount. Maximum maturity is 1 year.

T-bonds: direct obligation of U.S. Government. Pay semi-annual interest. Quoted as % of par value plus 32nds. 10–30-year maturities.

Term Bond/Maturity: a bond issue in which all the principal is paid on the same date.

Technical Analysis: studying past price patterns in order to predict future price patterns.

Tender Offer: when an issuer offers to buy their securities from investors either for cash or other securities.

Term Life Insurance: form of temporary insurance that builds no cash value and must be renewed at a higher premium at the end of the term.

Third Market: NYSE-listed stock traded over-the-counter.

Third-Party Account: account managed on behalf of a third party, e.g., trust or UGMA.

TIC (true interest cost): a calculation of the total cost of borrowing through a bond issue including the time value of money. Either TIC or NIC is used to determine the winning bid for a competitive underwriting of municipal bonds.

Time Value: the amount of the option's premium that exceeds the intrinsic value. For example, with MSFT trading at $46, a MSFT Oct 45 call @2 has $1 of "time value."

T-notes: direct obligation of U.S. Government. 2–10-year maturities. Pay semi-annual interest. Quoted as % of par value plus 32nds.

Tombstone: a bland announcement allowed during the cooling off period listing the issuer, the type of security, the underwriters, and directions for obtaining a prospectus.

Total Return: measuring growth in share price plus any income distributions. For example, a stock purchased at $10 that rises to $12 and pays a $1 dividend gives the investor a total return of 30% ($3 outa' $10 = 30%).

Trade Confirmation: the written notification of a completed securities transaction, sent no later than settlement of the trade.

Trading Authorization: a form granting another individual the authority to trade on behalf of the account owner. Either "limited" (buy/sell orders only) or "full" (buy/sell orders plus requests for checks/securities) authorization may be granted. Sometimes referred to as "power of attorney."

TRAN (Tax & Revenue Anticipation Note): a short-term loan to a municipality backed up by some taxes and some revenues they haven't actually collected yet.

Transfer Agent: issues and redeems certificates. Handles name changes, validates mutilated certificates. Distributes dividends, gains, and shareholder reports to mutual fund investors.

Transfer on Death: individual account with a named beneficiary—assets transferred directly to the named beneficiary upon death of the account holder.

Treasury Receipts: zero coupon bonds created by broker-dealers backed by Treasury securities held in escrow. Not a direct obligation of U.S. Government.

Treasury Securities: securities guaranteed by U.S. Treasury, including T-bills, T-notes, T-bonds, and STRIPS.

Treasury Stock: shares that have been issued and repurchased by the corporation. Nothing to do with US Treasury.

Trust Indenture Act of 1939: corporate bond issues in excess of $5 million with maturities greater than 1 year must be issued with an indenture.

TSA: Tax-Sheltered Annuity. A qualified retirement plan for non-profit organizations such as schools, hospitals, and religious institutions funded with pre-tax dollars.

Two-Dollar Broker: an independent exchange member who executes orders for commission house brokers and the public for a fee.

U

UGMA: Uniform Gifts to Minors Act. An account set up for the benefit of a minor, managed by a custodian.

UIT: Unit Investment Trust. A type of investment company where investments are selected, not traded/managed. The ETF's such as "Spiders" are created as Unit Investment Trusts that passively hold the underlying index securities.

Underlying Security: the security that an options contract is based on. Microsoft common stock is the underlying security of a MSFT May 50 call.

Unqualified Legal Opinion: exactly what the issuer wants from the bond counsel, this opinion is issued without any qualifications or reservations.

Underwriter: a broker-dealer that distributes shares on the primary market.

Underwriting Spread: the profit to the syndicate. The difference between the proceeds to the issuer and the POP.

Uniform Practice Code: how the NASD promotes "cooperative effort," standardizing settlement dates, Ex-dates, accrued interest calculations, etc.

Universal Life Insurance: a form of permanent insurance that offers flexibility in death benefit and both the amount of, and method of paying, premiums.

UTMA: just like UGMA, only the kid has to wait as late as 25 years of age to have the assets re-registered solely in his/her name. The "T" stands for "transfer."

V

Variable Annuity: a tax-deferred investment without maximum contributions in which the individual invests in the separate account and subaccounts of his own choosing. The individual bears investment risk in exchange for the opportunity to protect purchasing power.

Variable Life Insurance: form of insurance where death benefit and cash value fluctuate according to fluctuations of the separate account.

Variable Universal Life Insurance: flexible-premium insurance with cash value and death benefit tied to the performance of the separate account.

Vertical Spread: a multiple option in which an investor purchases one option and sells another where the only difference between the contracts is the strike price. For example, a MSFT Jun 60 put and a MSFT Jun 65 put would make a vertical spread, also called a "price spread" to make sure it has at least two names.

Vesting: a schedule for determining at what point the employer's contributions become the property of the employee in a qualified retirement plan.

Visible Supply: a figure published in the daily Bond Buyer showing the total par value of municipal bonds to be issued over the next thirty days.

Voluntary Accumulation Plan: a plan in which the investor elects to have a certain amount of money deducted regularly and automatically invested into a mutual fund.

W

Warrants: long-term equity securities giving the owner the right to purchase stock at a set price. Often attached as a "sweetener" that makes the other security more attractive.

Wash Sale: after selling a security for a loss, repurchasing that security within 30 days. This disallows the loss for the current tax year, but the investor adds the amount of the loss to his cost basis on the new purchase, in order to keep tax reporting nice and simple.

Western Account: a syndicate account in which each member is responsible for their allotment of bonds only. Also called a "divided account" to make sure it has two names.

When Issued: a security that has been sold prior to the creation/availability of the certificates.

Whole Life Insurance: form of permanent insurance with a guaranteed death benefit and minimum guaranteed cash value.

Wildcatting: drilling for oil.

Wire Room: also called the "order room," this is the department that wires transactions to the appropriate exchange.

Withdrawal Plan: a systematic method of withdrawing money from a mutual fund in which the fund liquidates a certain number of shares, or sells enough shares to raise a certain amount of money on, say, a monthly or quarterly basis.

Workable Indication: prices at which a municipal securities dealer may be willing to trade, not a firm quote.

Working Capital: a measure of a corporation's liquidity in which current liabilities are subtracted from current assets to produce, we hope, a positive number.

Y

Yield: the income that a security provides to the owner. As opposed to the capital appreciation a security could provide by rising in market value.

Yield to Maturity: calculation of all interest payments plus/minus gain/loss on a bond if held to maturity.

Yield to Call: calculation of all interest payments plus/minus gain/loss on a bond if called before maturity.

Z

Zero Coupon: a debt security that does not pay current interest but, rather, returns a higher par value at maturity.

Zero-minus Tick: the repeat of a minus tick that would not allow a short sale to be executed.

Zero-plus Tick: the repeat of a plus tick that would allow a short sale to be executed.

Index

C

D

First Books®
Order Form
RELOCATION AND BUSINESS RESOURCES

	# COPIES	TOTAL
Pass the 6™ by Robert Walker	_____ x $49.95	$_____
Pass the 63™ by Robert Walker	_____ x $37.95	$_____
Pass the 65™ by Robert Walker	_____ x $89.95	$_____
Pass the 66™ by Robert Walker	_____ x $69.95	$_____
Pass the 7™ by Robert Walker	_____ x $89.95	$_____
The Art of On-the-Job Writing by Philip Vassallo	_____ x $21.95	$_____
The Art of E-mail Writing by Philip Vassallo	_____ x $15.95	$_____
Recruiting and Retaining a Diverse Workforce by Natalie Holder-Winfield	_____ x $21.95	$_____

Relocation Books—Invaluable guides for people moving to a new city

	# COPIES	TOTAL
Newcomer's Handbook® for Atlanta	_____ x $24.95	$_____
Newcomer's Handbook® for Boston	_____ x $26.95	$_____
Newcomer's Handbook® for Chicago	_____ x $24.95	$_____
Newcomer's Handbook® for London	_____ x $20.95	$_____
Newcomer's Handbook® for Los Angeles	_____ x $23.95	$_____
Newcomer's Handbook® for Minneapolis-St. Paul	_____ x $25.95	$_____
Newcomer's Handbook® for New York City	_____ x $24.95	$_____
Newcomer's Handbook® for Portland, Oregon	_____ x $25.95	$_____
Newcomer's Handbook® for San Francisco Bay Area	_____ x $24.95	$_____
Newcomer's Handbook® for Seattle	_____ x $24.95	$_____
Newcomer's Handbook® for the USA	_____ x $23.95	$_____
Newcomer's Handbook® for Washington D.C.	_____ x $24.95	$_____
Neighborhood Guide for Texas (Dallas-Ft. Worth, Houston, Austin)	_____ x $17.95	$_____
The Moving Book: A Kids' Survival Guide	_____ x $20.95	$_____
Max's Moving Adventure	_____ x $ 8.95	$_____
The Pet-Moving Handbook	_____ x $ 9.95	$_____
Furniture Placement and Room Planning Guide…Moving Made Easy	_____ x $12.95	$_____

SUBTOTAL $_____

POSTAGE & HANDLING ($8.00 first book, $1.50 each add'l.) $_____

TOTAL $_____

SHIP TO:

Name _____

Title _____

Company _____

Address _____

City _____ State _____ Zip _____

Phone Number ( ) _____

E-mail _____

Send this order form and a check or money order payable to:
First Books®
6750 SW Franklin St., Suite A
Portland, OR 97223-2542
P: 503.968.6777   F: 503.968.6779
Allow 1-2 weeks for delivery
www.firstbooks.com